Phil Edmonston

LEMON-AID

2005|06

USED CARS and MINIVANS

Phil Edmonston

LEMON-AID

2005 | 06

USED CARS and MINIVANS

Published in Canada by Fitzhenry & Whiteside, 195 Allstate Parkway, Markham, Ontario L3R 4T8

www.fitzhenry.ca   godwit@fitzhenry.ca

1   3   5   7   9   10   8   6   4   2

Library and Archives Canada has catalogued this publication as follows:

Edmonston, Louis-Philippe, 1944-
Lemon-aid used cars and minivans / Phil Edmonston.

Annual.
2003-
Imprint varies.
Continues: Edmonston, Louis-Philippe, 1944- Lemon-aid used cars, ISSN 1485-1121.
ISSN 1701-6908
ISBN 1-55041-967-6 (2005-2006 edition)

1. Used cars-Purchasing-Periodicals. 2. Vans-Purchasing--Periodicals.
I. Title.

TL162.E3398   629.222'2'05   C2002-900797-6

Fitzhenry & Whiteside acknowledges with thanks the Canada Council for the Arts,
the Government of Canada through the Book Publishing Industry Development Program (BPIDP),
and the Ontario Arts Council for their support of our publishing program.

Printed in Canada by Webcom Limited
Packaged by Colborne Communications, Toronto
Publications manager: Greg Ioannou
Project co-ordinator: Paula Krulicki
Lead editor: Jennie Worden
Layout and production: Paula Krulicki, Rachel Rosen, Ingrid Paulson,
Adam Antoszek-Rallo, Shannon McDunnough, Sharon Bailey
Editing: Jennie Worden, Rachel Rosen, Andrea Battiston, Greg Ioannou,
Monika Grigo, Barbara Czarnecki
Design: Ingrid Paulson

CONTENTS

Key Documents..................................... xi

Introduction   THE GOOD, THE BAD, AND THE DEADLY 1

Part One   CHEAP WHEELS 8

Why Canadians Buy Used 13
Be Wary of Quality Rankings 19
Choosing a Safe, Reliable, and "Green" Vehicle .. 21
When and Where to Buy 23
Buying Without Fear and Loathing 27
Paying the Right Price 30
Financing Choices 31
Dealer Scams 32
Private Scams................................... 36
Summary: Buying the Best for Less 37

Part Two   WARRANTIES, WEASELS, AND WINNING! 39

How Long Should a Part or Repair Last? 42
Warranty Rights 49
Three Steps to a Settlement 66
Using the Courts 75
Key Court Decisions............................. 79
Product Liability................................ 79
Implied Warranty............................... 80
Repairs 85
Secret Warranties............................... 86
False Advertising 87

Part Three   1970–2004 RATINGS 89

Definitions of Terms............................. 92

SMALL CARS 102
Daewoo 103
DaimlerChrysler 104
 Neon, SX2.0, SRT-4 104
Ford 109
 Escort, ZX2 109
 Focus 112
General Motors 118
 Cavalier, Sunfire 118
 Saturn S-series, L-series, Ion 124
Honda 132
 Civic, del Sol 132
Hyundai 140
 Accent 140
 Elantra 143
Kia 147
 Rio 147
Mazda 150
 Protegé, Mazda3 150
Nissan 154
 Sentra 154
Subaru 158
 Impreza, Forester, WRX 158
 Legacy, Outback 163
Suzuki 167
 Aerio, Esteem 167
Toyota/General Motors 170
 Corolla, Matrix/Vibe 170
Toyota 177
 Echo 177
Volkswagen 180
 Cabrio, Golf, Jetta 180

MEDIUM CARS 186
Acura 188
 1.6, 1.7L EL 188
 CL-Series 189
 Integra 193

DaimlerChrysler 196
 Breeze, Cirrus, Stratus 196
Ford 200
 Sable, Taurus 200
General Motors 211
 Achieva, Alero, Grand Am, Skylark 211
 Bonneville, Cutlass, Cutlass Supreme,
  Delta 88, Grand Prix, Impala, Intrigue,
  LeSabre, Lumina, Malibu, Monte
  Carlo, Regal 218
 Century, Ciera 235
Honda 239
 Accord 239
Hyundai 247
 Sonata 247
Mazda 250
 626, MX-6, Mazda6 250
Nissan 255
 Altima 255
Toyota 261
 Camry, Solara 261
Volkswagen 271
 New Beetle 271
 Passat 275

LARGE CARS 280
DaimlerChrysler 281
 300M, Concorde, Intrepid, LHS, New
  Yorker, Vision 281

Ford 289
   Cougar, Thunderbird 289
   Crown Victoria, Grand Marquis 295

LUXURY CARS 302
Acura 307
   RL 307
   TL 309
Audi 313
   90, A4, A6 (100), A8, S6, TT Coupe 313
BMW 319
   3 Series, 5 Series, M Series, Z3 319
Ford/Lincoln 327
   Continental, LS, Mark VII, Mark VIII,
      Town Car 327
General Motors 335
   98 Regency, Park Avenue 335
   Aurora, Riviera 338
   Cadillac Catera, Eldorado, Seville 342
   Cadillac Concours, DeVille 346
Infiniti 349
   G20, I30/I35, J30, Q45 349
Kia 356
   Magentis 356
Lexus 357
   ES 300, GS 300, 430, LS 400/430
   SC400/430 357
Mercedes-Benz 363
   300 series, 400 series, 500 series,
      E-Class 363
   C-Class 366
Nissan 369
   Maxima 369
Toyota 375
   Avalon 375

Volvo 378
   850, C70, S40, S70, V40, V70 378
   900 series, S80, S90, V90 384

SPORTS CARS 389
DaimlerChrysler 391
   Avenger, Sebring 391
Ford 396
   Mustang, Cobra 396
General Motors 400
   Camaro, Firebird, Trans Am 400
   Corvette 405
Mazda 411
   Miata 411
Toyota 413
   Celica 413

MINIVANS 417
DaimlerChrysler 420
   Caravan, Voyager, Grand Caravan,
      Grand Voyager, Town & Country 420
   PT Cruiser 429
Ford 433
   Windstar/Freestar 433
Ford/Nissan 444
   Villager, Quest 444
General Motors 448
   Astro, Safari 448
   Lumina, Lumina APV, Montana, Silhouette,
      Trans Sport, Venture 453
Honda 460
   Odyssey 460
Kia 467
   Sedona 467

Mazda 469
   MPV 469
Toyota 473
   Sienna, Previa 473

APPENDIX I   INTERNET FACT-FINDING 480

APPENDIX II   OTHER USED CHOICES 486

Depreciation Quirks 487
Ten Used Car "Golden Rules" 487

ALTERNATIVE USED CHOICES **488**
   Acura Vigor, Legend 488
   BMW Mini Cooper 489
   Chrysler Dart, Valiant, Duster, Scamp,
      Diplomat, Caravelle, Newport,
      New Yorker Fifth Avenue,
      Gran Fury, 2000GTX, Stealth,
      Crossfire, Laser, Talon, Prowler 490
   Ford Maverick, Comet, Fairmont,
      Zephyr, Tracer, Mustang, Capri,
      Cougar, Thunderbird V6, Torino,
      Marquis, Grand Marquis, LTD,
      LTD Crown Victoria, Festiva, Probe 493
   GM Chevette, Acadian, Nova,
      Ventura, Skylark, Phoenix, Spectrum,
      Camaro, Firebird, Malibu, LeMans,
      Century, Regal, Cutlass, Monte Carlo,
      Grand Prix, Bel Air, Impala, Caprice,
      Roadmaster, Laurentian, Catalina,
      Parisienne, LeSabre, Bonneville,
      Delta 88 493

GM Geo Storm 494
GM Cadillac Brougham, Fleetwood 494
GM Sunbird 495
GM/Suzuki Chevrolet, Geo Metro,
   Pontiac Firefly, Suzuki Sprint,
   Suzuki Swift 496
Honda CRX, Prelude 497
Hyundai Tiburon 498
Jaguar S-Type 498
Kia Sephia, Spectra, Magentis, Rio 499
Mazda MX-3, MX-6, 929, RX-7 499
Mercedes-Benz 190E 500
Merkur XR4Ti 500
Nissan Micra, Pulsar, NX, Stanza, 300ZX . 500
Porsche 911, Boxster 502
Subaru Justy, Loyale 502
Toyota early models, LE Van, Celica,
   MR2, Cressida, Supra, Tercel, Paseo . . . 503
Volvo 240 Series, 700 Series 504
"Beaters" You Will Hate 504

APPENDIX III   LEMON-PROOFING 510

Safety Check 510
Exterior Check 511
Interior Check 513
Road Test 514
Cutting Driving Costs 516

KEY DOCUMENTS

Lemon-Aid is a feisty owner's manual that has no equal anywhere. We don't want you stuck with a lemon, or to wind up paying for repairs that are the automaker's fault and are covered by secret "goodwill" warranties. That's why we are the only book that includes many hard-to-find, confidential, and little-known documents that automakers don't want you to see.

In short, we know you can't win what you can't prove.

The following photos, charts, documents, memos, court filings and decisions, and service bulletins are included in this index so that you can stand your ground and be treated fairly. Photocopy and circulate whichever document will prove helpful in your dealings with automakers, dealers, service managers, insurance companies, or government agencies. Remember, most of the hundreds of summarized service bulletins outline repairs or replacements that should be done for free.

Introduction The Good, the Bad, and the Deadly

Rusty Mercedes photo 2
2001–04 Chrysler AC water leaks TSB 3
1995–2004 GM intake manifold gasket TSB 4
1999–2004 GM poor transmission performance TSB 4
1999–2004 GM inaccurate fuel gauge TSB 5
2001–04 Honda Civic doesn't move in drive TSB 5
2002–04 Toyota Camry sulfur odour TSB 5
2003–04 Honda Accord sulfur odour TSB 6

Part One   Cheap Wheels

Saturn lemon photo 8
J.D. Power quality surveys 9–10
1996–98 Ford coolant loss/engine oil contamination TSB .. 13
NHTSA 1995–98 Ford Windstar defect report 15
VIN sticker photo 28

Part Two   Warranties, Weasels, and Winning!

Pontiac lemon photo 40
Used car expressed warranty clauses 41

Reasonable part durability chart 43–44
Used vehicle complaint letter 46
Secret warranty claim letter 47
2002–05 Ford inaccurate fuel gauge TSB 52
2004 RAV4 sulfur dioxide odours TSB 56
Chrysler AC memo 58
NHTSA recall guidelines 62
EDR photo 64
Bad paint photo 72
Three good paint defect judgments 73–74
Dufour complaint letter and judgment 81

Part Three Ratings

Ford 10-year brake refund program memo 90
Ford free coil spring program memo 93
Value of options by model year chart 100
Honda Civic crash test photo 101

Small Cars

1995–99 Chrysler head gaskets TSB 107
1995–99 Chrysler oil seepage TSB 107
2003 Neon water leaks TSB 108
2000 Ford Focus 10-year coil spring TSB 116
2000–03 Ford Focus trunk leaks TSB 117
Cavalier crash test photo 119
1995–2003 GM tranny flares TSB 121
2002–03 GM engine overheating TSB 122
2003 GM transmission shudder 123
2003–04 Saturn coolant loss TSB 129
2002–04 Saturn extended warranty coverage TSB 130
1996–2004 Hyundai poor shifts TSB 142
1998–2003 Mazda mildew odour TSB 153
2003–04 Toyota sulfur odours TSB 171

Medium Cars

1995–2000 Chrysler rough idle TSB 198
2000–01 Ford fuel smell/manifold gasket TSB 210
2000–03 Ford Taurus no-starts/hard starts TSB 210
1997–2004 GM faulty tail lights TSB 216
1997–2002 GM brake pulsation TSB 217
1996–2003 GM engine oil/coolant leaks TSB 229
2000–03 GM loss of coolant recall 230
2000–03 GM loss of coolant TSB 231
1995–2004 GM intake manifold and gasket redesign TSB . 231

1997–2001 GM oil leaks TSB 232
1997–2001 GM shift lever TSB 238
1998–2003 Honda oil leaks TSB 245
2003 Honda no reverse TSB 245
2002–03 Nissan Altima engine crank TSB 258
2002–03 Nissan Maxima and Altima hesitation TSB 259
2002–03 Nissan Altima engine buzz TSB 259
2002–03 Nissan Altima fuel sloshing TSB.................. 259
2002–03 Nissan Altima suspension clunk TSB............. 260
1997–2001 Toyota trunk leaks TSB 267
2002–03 Toyota shift shudder TSB.......................... 267
2002–03 Toyota brake vibration TSB 268
2002–03 Toyota AC blower TSB.............................. 268
2004 Toyota vehicle pulling to left TSB..................... 268
2002–04 Toyota Camry intake manifold rattle TSB 269

Large Cars/Wagons

1993–2001 Chrysler loose steering TSB..................... 286
1998–2002 Chrysler erratic AC TSB 287
2000–04 Chrysler slow fillup TSB 287
2003–04 Chrysler automatic transmission delay TSB 288
1994–2001 Ford no forward gear TSB........................ 293
1999–2001 Ford brake noise TSB 293
Ford Cougar 10-year warranty 294
Ford intake manifold photo 298
1996–2001 Ford intake manifold TSB........................ 299
1999–2002 Ford engine head gasket leakage TSB.......... 299
2000–03 Ford engine grinding noise TSB................... 300
2001–04 Ford engine ticking noise TSB 300

Luxury Cars

Audi engine sludge memo..................................... 302
2000–02 Cadillac poor shifting TSB 303
Customer satisfaction chart.................................. 304
1996–2002 Acura security/electrical system TSB.......... 309
2001–03 Audi engine misfires TSB 318
1999–2002 Lincoln Continental engine hesitation TSB... 332
Infiniti headlight work order................................. 350
2000–04 Infiniti abnormal shifting TSB 354
2004 Lexus pulls to left TSB 362
Maxima quality issues list 371–372

Sports Cars

1999–2004 Mustang exhaust leak TSB....................... 399

2001–02 Ford drivebelt slipping TSB 399
1997–2004 GM Corvette fluid leak TSB 409
1999–2001 GM Corvette high oil consumption TSB 410

Minivans
1996–2003 Ford intake manifold oil/coolant leak TSB 418
1996–2000 Chrysler strut tower rusting TSB 426
1996–2005 Chrysler rear brake rusting TSB 427
1997–2001 Chrysler brake noise TSB 427
1996–98 Ford coolant loss, etc., TSB 441
1999–2003 Ford parking assist false activation TSB 442
Nissan low quality scores 445
1996–2003 GM engine rattle TSB 452
1997–2001 GM paint bubbling TSB 458
1999–2002 GM transmission noise TSB 459
2002–03 Honda timing belt recall 465
2002–04 Honda rear brake clunk TSB 466
1998–2003 Toyota rear break squeal TSB 478

Appendix I   Internet Fact-Finding

2004 Toyota NHTSA owner complaint 483

Appendix II   Other Used Choices

Bargain beaters chart 488

Appendix III   Lemon-Proofing and Cutting Driving Costs

Van rust photo 511

Introduction

THE GOOD, THE BAD, AND THE DEADLY

How to Be a Millionaire

Thirty-seven percent of millionaires buy used cars, which is one reason why they're so well off.

GETTING RICH IN AMERICA
DWIGHT R. LEE AND RICHARD B. MCKENZIE

Acura Airbag Danger

On Mar 29, 2000 a Canadian woman was killed by her airbag in a minor fender bender accident in Toronto. A car hit her from behind at low speed and she was nudged into the car in front of her. Her airbag deployed and the coroner stated that she was killed by a "blunt force blow which shattered her aorta". She was 5 ft tall and was in a 2000 Acura, which one would assume had the latest 2nd generation airbag. The Coroner stated that no one of such short stature should have an airbag since it is virtually impossible to get far enough away from the wheel. She was a close friend of mine....

"ELLEN"
www.plescia.org/oldair/00000185.htm

So you're looking for a used car. Smart move. But now you have a choice: You can read through this book, and save thousands of dollars and possibly your life, or you can rush in, find a "bargain," and put it at risk.

Lemon-Aid Used Cars and Minivans 2005–06 starts with the premise that the auto industry is fundamentally crooked and will sacrifice quality to maximize profits— even if it puts your life or pocketbook in peril (think Ford/Firestone rollover/tire cover-up and $5,000–$9,000 Audi, Chrysler, Saab, Mercedes, and Toyota engine sludge cleanouts).

Now, If You Can't Trust Mercedes...

After helping resolve tens of thousands of auto complaints over the past 35 years, I am convinced that you *don't* get what you pay for. There is no relation between

Mercedes-Benz: A luxury lemon? What do you call $32 million in engine sludge refunds paid to owners of its 1998–2002 models, under a little-known 10-year warranty?

how much you pay and the reliability and safety of the vehicle that you get—ask any Cadillac, Jaguar, or Land Rover owner.

That's why *Lemon-Aid* is such a popular annual guide. It exposes the lies, obfuscations, and deception to even out the playing field. Sure, it's long, but we need that much space to publish the actual confidential service bulletins that give you free "goodwill" repairs, keep the service bay bullcrap to a minimum, and keep us out of jail for what we write. *Lemon-Aid* is a uniquely Canadian owner's action manual that pulls no punches in disclosing what's a fair price, which cars and minivans are lemons, which repairs are the automakers' responsibility, and which scams you should avoid.

Paying a fair price is crucial now that low-percentage new-car financing, rebates, and subsidized 3- and 5-year leases have driven used prices to new lows. Since last year, fully loaded off-lease vehicles and used rentals have potentially been veritable bargains (Budget is a good source)—if you know what to buy and how to use depreciation timing to your advantage (Ford Crown Vic, yes; Cadillac Catera, no; Hyundai, yes; Saturn, no; Honda Odyssey, yes; Nissan Quest and Toyota Sienna, no).

Sudden Acceleration Returns

Sudden, unintended acceleration has not gone away since Audi paid off claimants and adopted the shift/brake interlock in the mid-'80s. GM lost an $80 million unintended-acceleration case in 2003. And Ford settled two large lawsuits for undisclosed amounts in 2004. Now Toyota is under the gun. Toyota's image as a builder of quality vehicles has been legendary. It has taken a battering since 1997, when angry owners refused to pay $6,000–$9,000 to repair sludged-up engines on most of Toyota's lineup through 2003. The company relented, and extended the engine warranty up to eight years on an estimated 3.3 million Toyota and Lexus models (Audi, Saab, and VW have just announced a similar "goodwill" program).

More recently, Toyota has been accused by owners of using dangerously defective automatic transmissions on its 1999–2004 Lexus ES 300 series and Camry models. One owner wrote to me:

Difficulty shifting my 2004 Camry from Park to Reverse, then upon shifting into Drive the car accelerated uncontrollably, would not stop, collided with a mobile home, air bags did not deploy, resulting in the death of one passenger and injury of driver.

A look at the NHTSA safety complaint database shows almost 600 diverse complaints registered on the 2002 Camry alone (100 complaints would be about normal for a 3-year-old vehicle). As of February 2005, the 2004 Camry had generated 141 complaints. In the past, Toyota has reacted positively when faced with product deficiencies. *Lemon-Aid* trusts that it will get itself "in gear," and resolve these customer complaints as well.

Secret Warranties

Car buyers are fed up with cars that suddenly accelerate, airbags that don't go off when they should or deploy when they shouldn't, and ABS brakes that don't brake. Car owners often find out, after shelling out thousands of dollars on repairs, that secret "goodwill" warranties could have paid for their engine, transmission, and other repairs. Who gets these free repairs? It's mainly owners who get a copy of the relevant internal service bulletins from *Lemon-Aid*, or owners who scream the loudest. Take a look at the following confidential service bulletins from Chrysler, General Motors, Honda, and Toyota, giving millions of car owners rights to significant repair refunds following major mechanical and body failures. Peruse carefully all the other bulletins concerning free repairs found throughout this book—does one apply to your car? Your neighbours' cars? Take copies of these bulletins to the dealer, but don't be shocked if the service manager and automaker lie through their teeth, denying these bulletins exist—until you threaten to file your copy in small claims court (ouch!).

> **CHRYSLER A/C WATER LEAKS**
> BULLETIN NO: 23-010-04   DATE: APRIL 29, 2004
>
> **SUBJECT:** Passenger Compartment Floor Water Leak.
> **OVERVIEW:** This bulletin involves sealing the opening for the evaporator hose/drain tube with RTV sealer.
>
> 2001–2004 Caravan, Voyager, Town & Country and Dakota; 2001–2003 Durango
>
> **SYMPTOM/CONDITION:** Water may enter the passenger compartment between the HEVAC housing and the bulkhead. A foam seal is used to seal the heater housing to the bulkhead. Condensation from the A/C evaporator can run along the evaporator drain tube and enter the passenger compartment if the seal between the HEVAC housing and the bulkhead is not sealed properly. This will result in wet passenger compartment carpet when the air conditioning is operating.

Intake Manifold Gaskets

Afflicting Ford's and GM's entire lineup for almost a decade, intake manifold gasket failures cause engine oil or coolant leaks, and can cost from $1,000 to $5,000 to repair (if you "cook" the engine). Here is the most recent admission from GM that they screwed up the gasket's original design at the factory.

GM'S REDESIGNED ENGINE INTAKE MANIFOLD AND GASKETS

BULLETIN NO: 04-06-01-017   DATE: MAY 26, 2004

NEW UPPER INTAKE MANIFOLD AND GASKET KITS

1995–1997 Buick Riviera; 1995–2004 Buick Park Avenue; 1996–2004 Buick Regal; 1997–2004 Buick LeSabre; 1998–1999 Chevrolet Lumina; 1998–2004 Chevrolet Monte Carlo; 2000–2004 Chevrolet Impala; 1995–1996 Oldsmobile Ninety-Eight; 1995–1999 Oldsmobile Eighty-Eight; 1998–1999 Oldsmobile Intrigue; 1995–2004 Pontiac Bonneville; and 1997–2003 Pontiac Grand Prix. All with 3.8L V6 engines.

OVERVIEW: New upper intake manifold and gasket kits have been released. These new kits will provide the dealer with the ability to get exactly what is necessary for a correct repair. **In addition some of the gaskets have been updated to a more robust design**. Please reference the part numbers when ordering from GMSPO.

GM Fuel Gauges and Transmissions

Faulty fuel gauges have been a constant problem with GM's entire lineup since 1996, and there are many bulletins addressing the issue. This is the latest internal bulletin updating the model years affected. Note that nowhere does GM deny liability due to "bad gas" or poor maintenance.

GM POOR TRANSMISSION PERFORMANCE

BULLETIN NO: 01-07-30-038B   DATE: JAN. 26, 2004

POOR PERFORMANCE OF TRANSMISSION, SLIPPING (CLEAN TRANSMISSION VALVE BODY AND CASE OIL PASSAGES OF DEBRIS)

1999–2004 Passenger Cars and Light Duty Trucks; 2003–2004 HUMMER H2 with 4L60-E/4L65-E Automatic Transmission

SYMPTOMS: Some customers may comment on any of the following conditions:
- The SES lamp is illuminated.
- No 3rd and 4th gear.
- The transmission does not shift correctly.
- The transmission feels like it shifts to Neutral or a loss of drive occurs.

The vehicle free wheels above 48 km/h (30 mph). High RPM needed to overcome the free wheeling. The most likely cause is chips or debris plugging the bleed orifice of the 2–3 shift solenoid (367). This will cause the transmission to stay in 2nd gear when 3rd gear is commanded and return to 1st gear when 4th gear is commanded.
- Inspect/Clean the 2–3 shift valve (368), the 2–3 shuttle valve (369) and the valve bore of debris / metal chips.
- Inspect/Clean the 2–3 shift solenoid (367) opening of debris / metal chips. While inspecting the 2–3 shift solenoid (367), look for a screen over the solenoid opening. If the solenoid DOES NOT have a screen, replace the solenoid with P/N 10478131 that does have a screen over the solenoid opening.

GM INACCURATE FUEL GAUGES

BULLETIN NO: 04-08-49-018A   **DATE: JUNE 2004**

Cranks But No Start, Stall, Inaccurate/Incorrect Fuel Gauge Reading, No Fuel, Vehicle is Out of Fuel and Fuel Gauge Reads Above Empty (Replace Fuel Level Sensor)

2001–2004 Cadillac Trucks; 1999–2004 Chevrolet and GMC Trucks with Gasoline Engine

CONDITION: Some customers may comment on the vehicle stalling and will not restart, vehicle ran out of fuel, vehicle appears to be out of fuel but the fuel gauge reads above empty. The fuel gauge may read 1/4 tank.

Honda Transmissions

Even Honda's venerable Civic has serious automatic transmission failures. To its credit, Honda usually repairs the problem for free under a "goodwill" policy, no questions asked.

2001–04 HONDA CIVIC DOESN'T MOVE IN DRIVE

BULLETIN NO: 04-036   **DATE: JULY 13, 2004**

SYMPTOM: The vehicle cannot move when you select Drive. The MIL comes on ('01–03 models) or the D indicator blinks ('04 models) with A/T DTC P0730 (shift control system) set.

PROBABLE CAUSE: Excessive wear in the 2nd clutch.

VEHICLES AFFECTED: 2001–04 Civic 2-door and 4-door with A/T. **CORRECTIVE ACTION:** Replace the A/T. Use the Honda Interface Module (HIM) to update the PCM software ('01–03 models only).

"Rotten-Egg" Exhaust Smells

Stinky cars and trucks are commonplace with all automakers. Usually, dealers advise owners to change fuel, or drive six months to "clean out" the system. This is just a delaying tactic. Replacing the converter is often the only solution, a fact confirmed by the following Honda and Toyota bulletins listing specific models but applicable to most other automaker models as well.

Whew, enough service bulletins! For a full listing of bulletins and copies of bulletins that may be helpful to you, look in each car model's rating, or check the Key Documents list.

TOYOTA CAMRY EXCESSIVE SULFUR DIOXIDE ODOR

BULLETIN NO: EG011-04   **DATE: MAY 13, 2004**

2002–04 Camry

Some customers may complain of excessive sulfur dioxide odor on 2002–2004 model year Camry vehicles equipped with 1MZ-FE engines under the following conditions:

- Stop and go driving.
- Heavy acceleration.

In order to reduce the odor, a new catalytic converter has been developed.

6

**HONDA ACCORD EXHAUST/
INTERIOR SULFUR SMELL**

BULLETIN NO: 03-091   DATE: APRIL 2, 2004

2003–04 Accord L4 (except vehicles
equipped with mass air flow sensor);
2003–04 Accord V6

SYMPTOM: Sulfur smell in the interior
(smells like rotten eggs).

PROBABLE CAUSE: Unsealed body seams
are allowing a sulfur smell to enter the
interior.

CORRECTIVE ACTION: Replace the catalytic
converter, seal the body seams, and install
flap seals.

Using a manufacturer's own bulletins to prove you're right won't win you friends in Detroit, Stuttgart, or Tokyo. I'll never forget the time, three decades ago, when Ford goons threw me out of the Toronto Auto Show after I demanded that Ford extend its secret American rust repair warranty to Canadians. Three years later, the company relented, and paid out almost $3 million in refunds to members of the Rusty Ford Association, a group organized by the Automobile Protection Association—I founded both groups.

Lemon-Aid isn't just about fallen American and Japanese car quality. European automakers let their owners down, too. Their products aren't half as good as their hype; they do well only because they spend millions of dollars on a fawning North American motoring press corps and market their vehicles to insecure social climbers with more money than brains. Want the truth about European cars? Go to Part Three, or surf the websites recommended by *Lemon-Aid*.

Who Can You Trust?

Lemon-Aid's goal for over 33 years has been to keep auto ownership costs low, to promote safe and reliable vehicles, and to make automakers and dealers more honest and accountable—even as they hire lawyers and PR flacks to plead that wrong is right and that safety is relative (kinda like their own integrity). This guide continues a tradition of publicizing abusive auto industry practices and providing hard-to-get information that may save your life, or at least protect your wallet.

Lemon-Aid's information is biased in favour of its Canadian sources—particularly reports from owners who buy and drive these vehicles—not travel-junket-junkie, free-car-mongering car columnists. We have over two dozen provincial correspondents scattered throughout Canada. Our database also includes U.S. sources, and is refined throughout the year with input from owner complaints, automaker whistle-blowers, lawsuits, judgments, confidential technical service bulletins (TSBs), and independent garages.

We combine test results with owner feedback from sources like the above website to provide a critical comparison of the many cars and minivans sold during the past three decades. If improvements and additional safety features don't justify the higher costs of newer models (most don't), we say so. Safer, more reliable, and often cheaper alternatives are given for each vehicle, and reliability and crashworthiness ratings are shown for each model year.

The Ontario lessor of a 2003 Grand Caravan with water leak/corrosion problems put this website up only after Chrysler Canada mishandled his claim (*www.donotbuydodge.ca*).

Finally, for frugal readers, this year's guide includes a helpful appendix that rates the best vehicles available starting at $1,000, and offers tips on reaching the 10-year/250,000 km mark without spending a fortune.

2005–06 New Car Guide Improvements

No, your eyes aren't playing tricks on you, this year's *Lemon-Aid* is larger and has a revised layout to make it easier to read and to find important documents.

We have also added more content. *Lemon-Aid*'s 500+ pages now give you more current information, along with exact duplicates of memos and service bulletins. This way, you won't pay for factory mistakes, and defects will be diagnosed quickly and correctly.

We have also increased our reliance on field reports relative to scams, prices, and court decisions sent in by drivers throughout Canada. Nevertheless, if you have a question not covered in this book, or would like to register your own comments, simply send me an email at *lemonaid@earthlink.net*.

Lemon-Aid makes you an empowered shopper and driver. By knowing what to buy, how much to pay, and when you shouldn't pay, your dollar will go much further and servicing disputes will be kept to a minimum.

Phil Edmonston
April 2005

Part One

CHEAP WHEELS

Why Saturn's a Pain in Uranus

Tell your readers to stay away from the 1996 Saturn. You can't get parts, and it is a piece of junk. Only 2 cylinders firing, my mechanic can't find the problem, the ignition module was replaced to see if it was the source, and it still won't run properly. The check engine light used to come on all the time, the car had no power in the rain. The wires were replaced 3 times, the plugs replaced many times. Carbon buildup was cleaned up twice before. I bought it in 2000 for $6,500 with 89,000 km (thankfully it is paid for, I am ready to walk away). My nearest Saturn dealer is 100 km away, and it is not worth my while to fix it up. Other than the fact the car won't rust, it is a piece of junk. I will never buy another domestic car. We have a 1992 Civic with 330,000 km on it, that is more reliable than the Saturn.

M. B.
OTTAWA, SEPTEMBER 2004

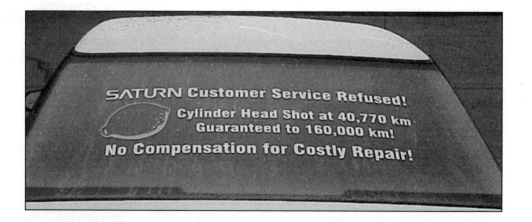

A Buyer's Market

Saturn's lemon orchard aside, there are a lot of cheap, reliable used cars and mini-vans available this year. They are mostly rear-drive American cars, most of which are no longer manufactured, or small Japanese and South Korean models that are a bit harder to find but well worth the effort.

Canadians aren't large-car lovers. We are small-minded when choosing what we drive. The Honda Civic is our favourite small car; in the States, it's the larger Toyota Camry. Small SUVs, like the Subaru Forester, the Honda CR-V, and the Toyota RAV4, make up almost half of our market, but only a quarter of the sales south of the border. As far as minivans go, we believe that less is more and favour small imports over Detroit's truck-based rear-drives.

Within these parameters, there are plenty of good buys available. To get the best deal, buy a 3- to 5-year-old vehicle listed in Part Three as a Recommended or Above Average buy. Keep it for at least another five to seven years. Sure, you'll lose a few thousand dollars in depreciation each following year, but that'll be more than offset by the low price you paid initially, lower insurance costs, cheaper servicing from independent garages, and a reasonable residual value.

There are lots of other reasons why now is a great time to buy a used car or mini-van. Over the past decade, new-car prices have moderated, creating a large reservoir of affordable used cars. And as we enter 2006, used prices continue to decline, principally in response to high fuel and insurance costs, generous new-car rebates, and low-percentage financing programs.

But prices are only one factor to consider. Vehicle quality and dependability are equally important. Sure, you can prance around telling your friends how you "stole" that used GM Saturn or Ford Windstar—until you have to spend $3,500 for engine or transmission work (and sometimes both). Granted, some of the junk is fairly well known, and vehicles are safer now; however, they are also loaded with high-cost optional convenience and performance features that you can probably do without.

But let's not just pick on Ford, GM, and Chrysler. European automakers make their share of lemons as well. J.D. Power and Associates rank Mercedes' quality as much worse than average. If, however, you were a steady reader of *Lemon-Aid* over the past 33 years, you would have been wary of Mercedes' poor quality almost a decade ago, and you would probably have saved money

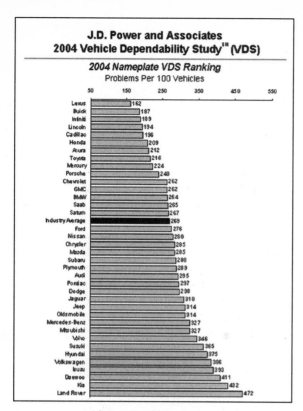

**J.D. Power and Associates
2004 Vehicle Dependability Study℠ (VDS)**

2004 Nameplate VDS Ranking
Problems Per 100 Vehicles

Nameplate	Problems Per 100 Vehicles
Lexus	162
Buick	187
Infiniti	189
Lincoln	194
Cadillac	196
Honda	209
Acura	212
Toyota	216
Mercury	224
Porsche	240
Chevrolet	262
GMC	262
BMW	264
Saab	265
Saturn	267
Industry Average	269
Ford	276
Nissan	280
Chrysler	285
Mazda	285
Subaru	288
Plymouth	289
Audi	295
Pontiac	297
Dodge	298
Jaguar	310
Jeep	314
Oldsmobile	314
Mercedes-Benz	327
Mitsubishi	327
Volvo	346
Suzuki	365
Hyundai	375
Volkswagen	396
Isuzu	393
Daewoo	411
Kia	432
Land Rover	472

buying a Lincoln Town Car or Toyota Avalon instead.

There's absolutely no correlation between safe and dependable transportation and the amount of money a vehicle costs. In fact, almost the opposite conclusion can be reached: Cheap, simple vehicles, originally retailing for $10,000 to $20,000, that have been on the market for a few years are far better buys than most cars costing two or three times as much. Again, J.D. Power confirms this fact.

Lemon-Aid Best and Worst Buys

Smart buys

Acura Integra
Chrysler Colt, Sebring, and Avenger
Ford Crown Victoria, Escort, Grand Marquis, Mustang, and Probe
GM Camaro, Firebird, Astro, and Safari
Honda Accord, Civic, CR-V, and Odyssey
Hyundai Accent, Elantra, and Tiburon
Lincoln Town Car
Mazda 323, 626, Mazda3, Mazda6, Miata, MPV, MX-6, and Protegé
Nissan Sentra
Toyota Avalon, Camry, Corolla, Cressida, Echo, Sienna, and Tercel

Dumb buys

Cadillac Catera and Cimarron
Chrysler Concorde, Horizon, Intrepid, LHS, minivans, New Yorker, Neon, and Omni
Ford Focus, Sable, Taurus, and Windstar
GM Corvette, Fiero, Vega/Astre
Hyundai Excel, Pony, early Sonatas, and Stellar
Infiniti G20
Jaguar (all models)
Kia (all models)
Lexus ES series

Lincoln Continental (front-drive)
Mercedes-Benz 190, C-Class, and M series
Merkur (all models)
Nissan 240Z, 250Z, 260Z, B210
Saab (all models)
Saturn Ion, L-series, S-series, and Vue
Suzuki Samurai and X-90
VW Eurovan and Passat

 Note in the list above how frequently so-called "premium" luxury brands have fallen out of favour, are orphaned by shoppers, and are then abandoned by the automakers themselves, leaving early purchasers with pseudo-luxo junk.

Also, keep in mind that many Honda, Toyota, and Nissan vehicles have had a resurgence of engine and transmission problems in addition to an apparent overall decline in reliability. For example, Nissan engineers are presently falling over themselves trying to correct Altima and Quest glitches. As they capture the market share, it seems the Asian automakers are skating on their earlier reputations and cutting quality, thereby committing the same mistake Detroit did years ago. Nevertheless, they are still far ahead of the American automakers in terms of quality control.

A Short History of Dangerous Junk

I've spent almost 35 years battling automakers and dealers who lie through their teeth as they try to convince customers that their vehicles are well made and that defects are caused mainly by the proverbial "nut behind the wheel," poor maintenance, or abusive driving. That's why the auto industry has such a lousy reputation—car owners know better. The average Canadian has personally experienced the lying, cheating, and stealing that's so rampant at all levels of the automotive manufacturing and marketing process, or knows someone else who has.

Firestone wasn't an aberration; it was a microcosm of what goes on throughout the industry. When the tires started shredding in other countries and injuries and deaths started to mount, Ford used a secret warranty program to pay off Explorer owners in South America and the Middle East. When the media discovered the cover-up, Ford lied to both customers and officials, saying either that it wasn't aware of the tire failures or that it was all Firestone's fault. Both excuses were shot down in subsequent probes carried out by Saudi Arabia and Venezuela.

The Venezuela federal Consumer Defense and Protection Agency (Indecu) recommended in September 2000 that both Firestone and Ford face criminal charges for their role in tire defects that led to at least 47 deaths in that country since 1998.

Indecu blamed both companies for the tire problems, stating that the accidents were the result of "a macabre combination between a suspension that is set too soft, and tires that are not appropriate for the Explorer." It also claimed that the companies "concealed vital information from Venezuelan citizens" and held a secret meeting where it was decided that there was a problem with the tire design. It was decided that a "nylon cap" layer would be added to the tire to help prevent tread separation. Firestone began producing tires labelled as having the extra layer, many of which in fact did not. It later recalled the "mislabelled" tires.

(See *www.wsws.org/articles/2000/sep2000/tire-s05.shtml* and *www.citizen.org/auto-safety/suvsafety/ford_frstone/articles.cfm?ID=12306.*)

This dishonesty and poor quality control has always been a part of the automobile industry. When I founded the Automobile Protection Association in Montreal in the fall of 1969, American Motors was giving out free television sets with its new cars; the television sets lasted longer than the Eagle (Ford now gives free Dell computers to 2005 Focus buyers). Volkswagen had a monopoly on hazardous and poorly heated Beetles and later, self-starting Rabbits; Ford was churning out bio-degradable cars and trucks (and denying that it had a secret "J-67" warranty to cover rust repairs). Firestone was dragged, kicking and screaming, into announcing the recall of 11 million tires for catastrophic tread separation in the late '70s, and Chrysler's entire product line was "rain-challenged"—stalling and leaking in wet weather because of faulty ballast resistors, distributor caps, rotors, and misaligned body panels.

Japanese and European cars imported into Canada during the '70s were unreliable rustbuckets. Yet they got a toehold in the North American car market because the Big Three's products were worse—and they still are. Seizing the opportunity, foreign automakers smartened up within a remarkably short period of time. They quickly built reliable and durable cars and trucks and offered them fully loaded and reasonably priced.

Meanwhile, American automakers continued pumping out dangerous and unreliable junk throughout the '90s—including GM's Chevy Vega, Firenza, and Fiero, as well as early Saturns, Cavaliers, Sunbirds, and the Lumina/Trans Sport minivan; Chrysler's Omni, Horizon, Dynasty, Imperial, Concorde, Neon, and post-'90 minivans; and Ford's Pinto, Bobcat, Tempo, Topaz, Taurus, Sable, Contour, Mystique (mistake?), Merkur, Bronco, Explorer, and Windstar. Not surprisingly, sales continued to nosedive.

Then, in the early '90s, Detroit got a second chance to prove itself. The minivan carved out a new, popular marketing niche and American SUVs like the Ford Explorer were piling up profits. But, as Micheline Maynard makes crystal clear in *The End of Detroit* (Doubleday), the American auto industry's arrogance disconnected its products from reality, and by focusing mainly on high-profit trucks and

SUVs, Detroit abandoned average car buyers to the Japanese and the South Koreans.

> Foreign companies like Toyota and Honda solidified their dominance in family and economy cars, gained market share in high-margin luxury cars, and, in an ironic twist, soon stormed in with their own sophisticatedly engineered and marketed SUVs, pickups, and minivans. Detroit, suffering from a "good enough" syndrome and wedded to ineffective marketing gimmicks like rebates and zero-percent financing, failed to give consumers what they really wanted: reliability, the latest technology, and good design at a reasonable cost.

Today, Detroit's Big Three quality control is still way below average when compared with Japanese and South Korean automakers. Where the gap is particularly noticeable is in engine, automatic transmission, airbag, and anti-lock brake reliability, as well as fit and finish.

Want proof that not even your dealer's service manager can deny? Take a look at this Ford internal service bulletin depicting serious engine failures and Ford's half-hearted attempt to indemnify owners. Note how the same defect has been replicated over a number of model years.

Why Canadians Buy Used

There are over 18 million cars on Canada's roads, and they're all used—the transformation from new to used occurs as soon as you drive off the dealer's lot. But we don't mind; we love used cars. Canadian car buyers are thrifty, unpretentious, and open-minded. We don't care where a car is made, as long as it's cheap and reliable. We are reluctant to trade in a vehicle that suits our needs just because it's old. In fact, almost 51 percent of Canadians keep cars and trucks nine years or more, says Toronto-based auto consultant Dennis DesRosiers. We are also more conservative than Americans in our vehicle choices, with 86 percent of respondents to the 2000 annual survey by the Canadian Automobile Association (CAA) stating they would buy the same brand of vehicle again.

COOLANT LOSS/ENGINE OIL CONTAMINATION, 3.8L, 4.2L

BULLETIN NO: 99-20-7   DATE: OCT. 04, 1999

SUBJECT:
^ COOLING SYSTEM - 3.8L - UNDETERMINED LOSS OF COOLANT
^ COOLING SYSTEM - 4.2L - UNDETERMINED LOSS OF COOLANT
^ ENGINE - 3.8L - ENGINE OIL CONTAMINATED WITH COOLANT
^ ENGINE - 4.2L - ENGINE OIL CONTAMINATED WITH COOLANT

OVERVIEW: This TSB article is being republished in its entirety to correct the front cover/water pump bolt torque values and the Front Cover Gasket Part Number.

Ford: 1996–97 Thunderbird; 1996–98 Mustang, Windstar; 1997–98 E-150, E-250, F-150; Mercury: 1996–97 Cougar

ISSUE: Engine coolant may be leaking into the engine oil on some vehicles. The internal coolant leak may be difficult to identify. This may be caused by the lower intake manifold side gaskets and/or front cover gaskets allowing coolant to pass into the cylinders and/or the crankcase.

ACTION: Revised lower intake manifold side and front cover gaskets have been released for service.

WARRANTY STATUS: Eligible under the provisions of bumper to bumper warranty coverage and emissions warranty coverage.

Through the '90s, the popularity of used vehicles went up substantially in Canada. Why? According to the Royal Bank, the average Canadian's take-home pay didn't keep pace with the rising cost of purchasing and owning a new vehicle. Canadians are also wary of dealers selling used cars. Of the almost 20 percent of the vehicles on our roads that change hands each year, 70 percent are estimated to be sold privately. Here are some of the main reasons why Canadians prefer buying used vehicles from one another.

1. Less Initial Cash Outlay, Slower Vehicle Depreciation, "Secret" Warranty Repair Refunds, and Better and Cheaper Parts Availability

New-vehicle prices have moderated somewhat over the past few years, but they're still quite high—Dennis DesRosiers pegs the cost of an average new vehicle at over $30,200. Insurance is another wallet buster, costing about $2,500 a year for young drivers. And once you add financing costs, maintenance, taxes, and a host of other expenses, CAA calculates the yearly outlay for a medium-sized car at over $8,252, or 36.7 cents/km; trucks or SUVs may run you about 10 cents/km more. For a comprehensive, though depressing, comparative analysis (cars versus trucks, minivans, SUVs, etc.) of all the costs involved over a one- to 10-year period, access Alberta's consumer information website at *www.agric.gov.ab.ca/app24/costcalculators/vehicle/ getvechimpls.jsp.*

Used vehicles aren't sold with $700–$1,400 transport fees or $495 "administration" charges, either. And you can legally avoid paying sales tax when you buy privately. That's right: You'll pay at least 10 percent less than the dealer's price and you may avoid the 7 percent federal Goods and Services Tax (GST) that applies in some provinces to dealer sales only.

Be practical. When buying a used car or minivan, keep in mind you're simply buying transportation and function. You want no-surprise handling, a comfortable ride, reliable performance, and interior, cargo, and passenger capacity. Because you only need about one-half the cash or credit required for a new vehicle, it's easy to see that you won't have to invest as much money in a depreciating investment. You may even be fortunate enough to forgo a loan.

Depreciation savings

If someone were to ask you to invest in stocks or bonds guaranteed to be worth less than half their initial purchase value after three to four years, you'd probably head for the door.

But this is exactly the trap you're falling into when you buy a new vehicle that will likely lose 60 percent of its value after three years of use (minivans and other specialty vehicles, like sport-utilities and trucks, depreciate more slowly). Here's how that would work out in Ontario:

Cost (new)

Purchase (1999 Honda Accord EX)	$28,000
Federal GST (7 percent)	$1,960
Provincial tax (8 percent)	$2,240
Total price	$32,200

When you buy used, the situation is altogether different. That same vehicle can be purchased four years later, in good condition, and with much of the manufacturer's warranty remaining, for less than one-half its original cost. Look at what happens to the price:

Cost (used)

Purchase price (four years old, 80,000 km)	$14,000
No GST (if sold privately)	—
Provincial tax (8 percent)	$1,120
Total price	$15,120

In this example, the Accord buyer saves $14,000 on the selling price, $1,960 in federal taxes, and $1,120 in provincial taxes, and gets a reliable, guaranteed set of wheels. Furthermore, the depreciation "hit" will be negligible in the ensuing years.

Secret warranty refunds

Almost all automakers use secret "goodwill" warranties to cover factory-related defects, long after the original warranty has expired. This creates a huge fleet of used vehicles eligible for free repairs.

We're not talking about a few months' extension. In fact, some free repairs—like those related to Mercedes engine sludge and GM diesel engines—are authorized up to 10 years or more as part of "goodwill" programs. Still, most secret warranty extensions hover around the 5- to 7-year mark and seldom cover vehicles exceeding 160,000 km or 100,000 miles. This benchmark includes engine and transmission defects affecting Detroit's Big Three,

> **NHTSA CAMPAIGN ID NUMBER: 011007000**
>
> **DEFECT SUMMARY:** This is not a safety defect in accordance with the safety act. However, it is deemed a safety improvement campaign by the agency. Vehicle description: 1995–1998 Ford Windstar Minivans. The front coil springs could potentially fracture due to corrosion.
>
> **CONSEQUENCE SUMMARY:** Some tires have deflated due to contact with a broken spring.
>
> **CORRECTIVE SUMMARY:** Ford is extending the warranty for front coil spring replacement to a total of 10 years of service from the warranty start date, with unlimited mileage. This coverage is automatically transferred to subsequent owners at no charge. If either front coil spring fractures during the coverage period noted above, the dealer will replace both springs at no charge to the owner.

All, not just some, of these springs should have been recalled. Don't want to put your family's lives in danger? Take a copy of the NHTSA's defect report (above) and demand that the springs be changed before they fail, or you'll sue for their replacement in small claims court while holding the dealer and automaker responsible for any fatalities or injuries occurring in the interim.

Honda, Hyundai, Lexus, and Toyota. Ford's 1995–98 Windstars carry a little-known 10-year warranty extension covering front coil spring breakage, and free tire replacement if a tire is punctured.

Knowing which free repairs apply to your car will cut maintenance costs dramatically.

Incidentally, automakers and dealers claim that there are no secret warranties, since they are all published in service bulletins. Although this is technically correct, have you ever tried to get a copy of a service bulletin? Or—if you did manage to get a copy—had the dealer or automaker say the benefits are applicable only in the States? Oh yeah!

Parts

Used parts can have a surprisingly long lifespan. Generally, a new gasoline-powered car or minivan can be expected to run with few problems for at least 200,000–300,000 km (125,000–150,000 mi.) in its lifetime; a diesel-powered vehicle can easily double those figures. Some repairs will crop up at regular intervals, and, along with preventive maintenance, your yearly running costs should average about $800. Buttressing the argument that vehicles get cheaper to operate the longer you keep them, the U.S. Department of Transportation points out that the average vehicle requires one or more major repairs after every five years of use. Once these repairs are done, however, the vehicle can be run relatively trouble-free for another five years or more, as long as the environment isn't too hostile. In fact, the farther west you go in Canada, the longer owners keep their vehicles—an average of 10 years or more in some provinces.

Time is on your side in other ways, too. Three years after a model's launching, the replacement-parts market usually catches up to consumer demand. Dealers stock larger inventories, and parts wholesalers and independent parts manufacturers expand their output.

Used replacement parts are unquestionably easier to come by after this point through bargaining with local garages, carefully searching auto wreckers' yards, or looking on the Internet. And a reconditioned or used part usually costs one-third to one-half the price of a new part. There's generally no difference in the quality of reconditioned mechanical components, and they're often guaranteed for as long as, or longer than, new ones. In fact, some savvy shoppers use the ratings in Part Three of this guide to see which parts have a short life, and then buy those parts from retailers who give lifetime warranties on their brakes, exhaust systems, tires, batteries, etc.

Buying from discount outlets or independent garages, or ordering through mail order houses, can save you big bucks (30–35 percent) on the cost of new parts and another 15 percent on labour when compared with dealer charges. Costco is another good source of savings realized through independent retailers. The retailer sells competitively priced replacement tires and offers free rotation, balancing, and other inspections during the life of the tire.

Body parts are a different story. Although car company repair parts cost 60 percent more than certified generic aftermarket parts, buyers would be wise to buy only original equipment manufacturer (OEM) parts supplied by automakers in order to get body panels that fit well, protect better in collisions, and have maximum rust resistance, says *Consumer Reports* in its February 1999 study. Insurance appraisers often substitute cheaper, lower-quality aftermarket body parts in collision repairs, but *Consumer Reports* found that 71 percent of those policyholders who requested OEM parts got them with little or no hassle. It suggests that consumers complain to their provincial Superintendent of Insurance if OEM parts aren't provided. Ontario car owners have filed a class action lawsuit against that province's major insurers, alleging that making repairs with non-OEM parts is an unsafe practice and that it violates insureds' rights.

With some European models, you can count on a lot of aggravation and expense caused by the unacceptably slow distribution of parts and the high markup. Because these companies have a quasi-monopoly on replacement parts, there are few independent suppliers you can turn to for help. And junkyards, the last-chance repository for inexpensive car parts, are unlikely to carry foreign parts for vehicles that are more than three years old or are manufactured in small numbers.

Finding parts for Japanese and domestic cars and vans is no problem, because of the large number of vehicles produced, the presence of hundreds of independent suppliers, the ease with which relatively simple parts can be interchanged from one model to another, and the large reservoir of used parts stocked by junkyards.

2. Lower Insurance Rates

The price you pay for insurance can vary significantly, not only between insurance companies but also within the same company over time. But one thing does remain constant: The insurance for used vehicles is a lot cheaper than new-car coverage, and through careful comparison shopping, insurance premium payouts can be substantially reduced.

One effective agency that tracks the lowest premiums is The Consumers Guide to Insurance at *www.insurancehotline.com*. It has created a watchdog service to alert drivers to the changes in their insurance rates. For $20 per year, the agency will automatically rerun members' profiles to ensure that they always know which insurer has the lowest rate from its database of 30 insurance companies (representing over 80 percent of the written premiums in Canada).

Those auto owners looking for premium comparisons throughout Canada or insider tips on dealing with insurers should access *www.insurance-canada.ca/cons-quotes/onlineauto.php* or *www.autoinsurancetips.com*.

Some cars sustain lower collision costs than others. To know which ones, you should visit the Insurance Bureau of Canada's Vehicle Insurance Information Centre (Website: *www.ibc.ca/vehinfo.asp*; Tel: 1-800-761-6703 or 416-445-5912). It provides a comprehensive look at the insurance claims experience of the most popular Canadian models of private passenger vehicles. It includes collision, comprehensive, personal injury, and theft results for vehicles three or more years old.

One would expect the best-rated vehicles to cost less to insure, but this isn't necessarily the case. Instead, use the figures as a guide to parts costs and the crashworthiness of different models.

3. Fewer "Hidden" Defects

You can easily avoid any nasty surprises by having your choice checked out by an independent mechanic (for $85–$100) before paying for a used vehicle. This examination before purchase protects you against any hidden defects the vehicle may have. It's also a tremendous negotiating tool, since you can use the cost of any needed repairs to bargain down the purchase price.

It's easier to get permission to have the vehicle inspected if you promise to give the seller a copy of the inspection report should you decide not to buy it. If you still can't get permission to have the vehicle inspected elsewhere, walk away from the deal, no matter how tempting the selling price. The seller is obviously trying to put something over on you. Ignore the standard excuses that the vehicle isn't insured, that the licence plates have expired, or that the vehicle has a dead battery.

4. You Know the Vehicle's History

Smart customers will want answers to the following questions before signing a contract: What did it first sell for, and what is its present insured value? Who serviced it? Has it had accident repairs? Are parts easily available? How much of the original warranty or repair warranties is left? Does the vehicle have a history of costly performance-related defects? What free repairs are available through "goodwill" warranty extensions? (See "Secret Warranties/Internal Bulletins/Service Tips" in Part Three.)

5. Litigation is Quick, Easy, and Relatively Inexpensive

Lawyers win, regardless of whether you win or lose. And you're likely to lose more than you'll ever get back using the traditional court system in a used-car dispute.

But, if you're just a bit creative, you'll discover there are many federal and provincial consumer protection laws that go far beyond whatever protection may be offered by the standard new-vehicle warranty. Furthermore, buyers of used vehicles don't usually have to conform to any arbitrary rules or service guidelines to get this protection.

Let's say you do get stuck with a vehicle that's unreliable, has undisclosed accident damage, or doesn't perform as promised. Most small claims courts have a jurisdiction limit of $3,000–$10,000 (Alberta sets it at $25,000), which should cover the cost of repairs or compensate you if the vehicle is taken back. That way, any dispute between buyer and seller can be settled within a few months, without lawyers or excessive court costs. Furthermore, you're not likely to face a battery of lawyers standing in for the automaker and dealer in front of a stern-faced judge. You may not even have to face a judge at all, since many cases are settled through court-imposed mediators at a pretrial meeting usually scheduled a month or two after filing.

Be Wary of Quality Rankings

There are two major surveyors of automobile quality: J.D. Power and Associates, a private American automobile consulting organization, and Consumers Union, an American non-profit consumer organization that publishes *Consumer Reports*.

J.D. Power

Each year, J.D. Power and Associates publishes the results of two important surveys measuring vehicle quality and owners' customer service satisfaction. Interestingly, these two polls often contradict each other. For example, its Dependability Index places Saturn near the bottom of the list; however, Saturn is placed sixth from the top in the Power Service Index. This leads one to conclude that the car isn't very reliable, but customers get service with a smile!

Power's criticism of Nissan's 2004 Quest minivan has company engineers working overtime. They have already authorized a number of recalls to fix sliding doors, replace the driver's power window switch, repair faulty interior reading lights, replace second-row seat levers, and correct airbag sensors that don't work. Engineers were tipped off to the Quest's glitches in the 2004 J.D. Power and Associates Initial Quality Study, which rated the Quest last among minivans in consumer perceptions of quality during the first 100 days of ownership. Nissan's Titan full-sized pickup and Armada full-sized SUV also placed last in their segments for other problems.

Consumer Reports and CAA's *Autopinion* (*Carguide*)

Consumer groups and non-profit auto associations are your best bets for the most unbiased auto ratings. They're not perfect, though, so it's a good idea to consult several and look for ratings that match from publication to publication. My favourites are *Consumer Reports* and CAA's *Autopinion*. Both publications list only the manufacturer's suggested retail price (MSRP), not the invoice price.

Consumer Reports (*CR*) is an American publication that once had a tenuous affiliation with the Consumers' Association of Canada, until the CAC became practically insolvent and got mired in a sex scandal (its "hot tub diaries" court admission is a must-read). *CR*'s ratings, extrapolated from Consumers Union's annual U.S. member survey, fairly accurately mirror the Canadian experience, except for three drawbacks. Defect trends are spotted late (cross-referencing service bulletins would cure this); components that are particularly vulnerable to our harsh climate usually don't perform as well as the *CR* reliability ratings indicate; and poor servicing caused by a weak dealer body can make some service-dependent vehicles a nightmare to own in Canada, while the American experience may be more benign.

Based on 800,000-plus American and Canadian member responses, *CR* lists used vehicles that, according to owner reports, are significantly better or worse than the industry average. Statisticians agree that *CR*'s sampling method leaves some room for error, but, with a few notable exceptions, the ratings are fair, conservative, and consistent guidelines for buying a reliable new vehicle. My only criticisms of the used ratings are that many makes, like Toyota and Honda, can do no wrong, yet service bulletins and extended warranties show they have serious engine, transmission, door, and electrical problems. What's more, older vehicles are excluded from *CR*'s ratings, and many of the ratings about the frequency of repair of certain components aren't specific enough. For example, don't just tell me there are problems with the fuel or electrical system. Let me know about specific components—is it the fuel pumps that are failure-prone, or the injectors that clog up, or the battery that suddenly dies?

There's also the CAA's annual "Vehicle Ownership Survey," found in the February issue of *Carguide* magazine. It's available from CAA and on newsstands for $5.95 and is kept on display through June. A one-year subscription costs $17.99 in Canada (GST included) and $25.99 elsewhere (Website: *www.carguidemagazine. com*; Tel: 905-842-6591).

Carguide is published six times a year. It contains reams of automaker advertising and publishes mostly general-interest articles as well as summaries of new cars and trucks. Its most useful feature is its used-vehicle ratings, based on CAA's annual sampling of 20,000 owners. That's far less than the number of drivers surveyed by *Consumer Reports*, but at least they're all Canadian. The *Autopinion* supplement gives you a good general idea of those vehicles that have generated the most problems for CAA members (Chrysler Neon, Ford Windstar, and Ford F-Series trucks), but compare its conclusions with *Consumer Reports'* or *Lemon-Aid's* recommendations before you make a definite decision.

Lemon-Aid *and* Consumer Reports' *ratings*

CR and *Lemon-Aid* ratings often agree. Where they differ is in *Lemon-Aid's* greater reliance upon National Highway Traffic Safety Administration (NHTSA) safety complaints, service bulletin admissions of defects, and owner complaints received through the Internet (rather than from a subscriber base, which may simply attract owners singing from the same hymnal).

 In *CR's* best new- and used-vehicle picks for 2004, as published in its December 2004 edition, there are a number of recommendations that defy all logic.

The most puzzling choice is the Ford Windstar, followed by the Saturn Vue and the Jeep Liberty. It is inconceivable that *CR* isn't aware of the multiplicity of power-train, body, and suspension failures affecting these vehicles. Then there's the assorted Chrysler lineup. You'd have to live on another planet not to know that Chryslers are afflicted by chronic automatic transmission, ball joint, body, brake, and AC defects. In fact, *Consumer Reports'* "Frequency of Repair" tables in the same edition give out plenty of black marks to the aforementioned models and components. Yet sloppy research and editing failed to pick up on these contradictions.

Choosing a Safe, Reliable, and "Green" Vehicle

Looking through Part Three and reading through the above-noted websites and magazines can help you find good, reliable used car buys. Finding a safe car is a bit more difficult, though, since few used-car guides want to get into that kind of discussion.

The best indicator of a car's overall safety is NHTSA's front, side, and rollover crashworthiness ratings, applicable to most vehicles made over the past several decades and sold in North America. You will then want to compare NHTSA scores with ratings from the Insurance Institute for Highway Safety (IIHS), which crashes vehicles at a higher speed and at an offset angle, which is more common in collisions than the head-on scenario. Results from these two bodies are posted for each model rated in Part Three. However, there are many other national and international testing agencies that you may consult, and they can be found at *www.crashtest.com/netindex.htm*.

Of course no one expects to be in a collision, but NHTSA estimates that every vehicle, during its lifetime, will be in two accidents of varying severity. So why not put the averages on your side?

Most Environmentally Friendly Vehicles

Consider these important points when making your used-car choice:

- The 18 million cars and light-duty trucks on Canada's roads today are responsible for 12 percent of the nation's greenhouse gas emissions.
- 5,000 deaths a year nationwide are attributed to smog pollutants, which cost the Ontario economy alone $9.9 billion in health care costs and business losses according to the Ontario Medical Association.
- In buying a used vehicle, you are already doing a lot for the environment by not adding to the vehicle population. Nevertheless, in choosing a fuel-efficient, safe, small car, you are also protecting your life and wallet.

Here are *Lemon-Aid*'s picks of the top 10 most environmentally friendly, reliable, and cheap used cars and minivans.

Honda Civic—Not the cheapest, but likely the most reliable
Honda Odyssey—Better-engineered than the Toyota Sienna; price haggling discouraged, though
Hyundai Accent—Rapid depreciation and not so rapid acceleration
Hyundai Elantra/Tiburon—Reliable and carries an excellent warranty; horsepower may be a lie
Mazda MPV—Recent models are better performers and more reliable
Nissan Sentra—Reasonably priced, reliable, and stylish
Suzuki Aerio and Swift—Cheap, cheap, and cheap; an urban dweller
Toyota Corolla—A more spacious and comfortable, though not as reliable, Echo
Toyota Echo—Economical, bland, and reliable
Toyota Tercel—The best of the Toyota triad; a motoring Energizer bunny

Note: We don't recommend electric and gasoline engine hybrids, such as the Toyota Prius and Honda's Insight and Civic Hybrid, because their fuel economy can be 40 percent worse than the automakers report, their long-term reliability is unknown, battery replacement cost is $8,000 (U.S.), their retail prices are almost double what an Echo would cost, and the resale value for a 2001 Prius that originally sold for $29,990 is a disappointing $14,000.

In March 2003, Environmental Defence Canada announced its annual list of the Top 10 "greenest," or least polluting, vehicles. I agree with most of their choices.

1. Toyota Prius
2. Honda Insight
3. Honda Civic Hybrid
4. Toyota Echo
5. Nissan Sentra
6. Mazda3
7. Toyota Corolla
8. Hyundai Elantra
9. Honda Civic
10. Ford Focus

* Except for the Prius, Insight, Hybrid, and Focus, the above-listed cars also have a fairly good reliability record.

When and Where to Buy

When to Buy

In the fall, dealer stocks of good-quality trade-ins and off-lease returns are at their highest level, and private sellers are moderately active. Prices are higher, but there is a greater choice of vehicles available. In winter, prices decline substantially and dealers and private sellers are generally easier to bargain with because buyers are scarce and weather conditions don't present their wares in the best light. In spring and summer, prices go up a bit, as private sellers become more active and increased new-car rebates bring in more trade-ins.

Private Sellers

Private sellers are your best source for a cheap and reliable used vehicle, because you're on an equal bargaining level with a vendor who isn't trying to profit from your inexperience. A good private sale price would be about 5 percent *more* than the rock-bottom wholesale price, or approximately 20 percent *less* than the retail price advertised by local dealers. You can find estimated wholesale and retail prices in Part Three.

Your *Lemon-Aid* guide has levelled the playing field for the consumer when it comes to shopping for new or used vehicles. *Lemon-Aid* has also helped us consumers get the inside edge on how to protect ourselves from car manufacturers, secret warranties, goodwill service, etc.

I recently used your publication to help me in my decision to purchase a 1999 Toyota Tercel. Your *Lemon-Aid* guide also helped me avoid paying an "administration fee." I just walked out of the dealer's showroom. They must have thought I was crazy.

I didn't even have time to take my shoes off when my wife called me and said the Toyota dealership was on the telephone. She had no idea what had happened.

Suffice it to say, this wise consumer didn't pay an "administration fee" so someone could have dinner on me. If there is value in something I will pay it. If not, this customer walks. Here's to many years of carefree driving with my Toyota.

Just an off note. After 17 years of working for General Motors I thought I knew it all about vehicles, making deals, problems, defects, warranties, etc.

Was I wrong. You can never know it all. Keep publishing *Lemon-Aid* and I will keep reading it.

I'm a long-time GM employee who bought his first foreign-made vehicle with the help of Phil Edmonston. Patriotism is one thing, but blowing your hard-earned money for junk is another, just so you can wave the flag.

SINCERELY,
L.C.

Remember, no seller, be it a dealer or private party, expects to get his or her asking price. As with price reductions on home listings, a 10–20 percent reduction on the advertised price is common with private sellers. Dealers usually won't cut more than 10 percent off their advertised price.

Price Guides

The best way to determine the price range for a particular model is to read the *Red Book* and *Black Book* price guides found in most libraries, banks, and credit unions. Some Internet sites list the *Black Book* trade-in value of most used cars. These sites can be accessed free of charge through three links located at *www.canadianblackbook.com/html/consumer.html*. This will give you a reasonably good idea of what the dealer pays between wholesale and retail.

For the wholesale or retail price, those clever *Black Book* people ask that you subscribe to their *Wholesale/Retail Guide* for $144.45 (including GST) and they add the following warning:

> *Notice:* If you are not a licensed automotive dealer, wholesaler, financial institution or insurance company, you may be restricted in which publications and software applications you may purchase.

Now, if you want to use the *Red Book*, which seems more attuned to Quebec and Ontario sales, you can order single copies of their used car and light truck wholesale and retail price guide for $11.95 at *www.canadianredbook.com/default2.asp* (an annual subscription costs $90, plus PST). There are no restrictions as to who may subscribe.

Don't be surprised to find that many national price guides have an Eastern Ontario–Quebec price bias. They often list unrealistically low prices compared with what you'll actually see in the eastern and western provinces and in rural areas, where good used cars are often sold for outrageously high prices or simply passed down through the family. Other price guides may list prices that are much higher than those found in your region. Consequently, use whichever price guide lists the highest value when selling your trade-in or negotiating a write-off value with an insurer. When buying, use the guide with the lowest values as your bargaining tool.

Promises and Precautions

As a buyer, you should get a printed sales agreement, even if it's just handwritten, that includes a clause stating that there are no outstanding traffic violations or liens against the vehicle. It doesn't make a great deal of difference whether the car will be purchased "as is" or as certified under provincial regulation. A vehicle sold as safety "certified" can still turn into a lemon or be dangerous to drive. The certification process can be sabotaged if a minimal number of components are checked, the mechanic is incompetent, or the instruments are poorly calibrated. "Certified" is not the same as having a warranty to protect you from engine seizure or transmission failure. It means only that the vehicle has met minimum safety standards on the day tested.

Make sure the vehicle is lien-free and has not been damaged in a flood or written off after an accident. Flood damage can be hard to see, but it impairs ABS, power steering, and airbag functioning (making deployment 10 times slower).

Canada has become a haven for rebuilt U.S. wrecks. Write-offs are also shipped from provinces where there are stringent disclosure regulations to provinces where there are lax rules or no rules at all.

If you suspect your vehicle is a rebuilt wreck from the States or was once a taxi, use Carfax (Website: *www.carfax.com*; Tel:1-888-422-7329) to carry out a background check to see if the vehicle has been part of a fleet, has been wrecked, has flood damage, is stolen, or shows incorrect mileage on the odometer. The $20 (U.S.) fee by telephone is cut to $14.95 (U.S.) if the order is placed via the Internet. A typical search takes only a few minutes, and most Canadian provinces are included in the database. The search will also turn up vehicles that were trucked across the border as "parts" and then sold to resellers. An initial, free search on the Internet will confirm whether your vehicle is listed in the database.

In most provinces, you can do a lien and registration search yourself. If a lien does exist, you should contact the creditor(s) listed to find out whether any debts have been paid. If a debt is outstanding, you should arrange with the vendor to pay the creditor the outstanding balance. If the debt is larger than the purchase price of the car, it's up to you to decide whether you wish to complete the deal. If the seller agrees to clear the title personally, make sure that you receive a written relinquishment of title from the creditor before paying any money to the vendor. Make sure the title doesn't show an "R" for "restored," since this indicates that the vehicle was written off as a total loss and may not have been properly repaired.

Even if all documents are in order, ask the seller to show you the vehicle's original sales contract and a few repair bills in order to ascertain how well it was maintained. The bills will show you if the odometer was turned back, and will also indicate which repairs are still guaranteed. If none of these can be found, run (don't walk!) away. If the contract shows that the car was financed, verify that the loan was paid. If you're still not sure that the vehicle is free of liens, ask your bank or credit union manager to check for you. If no clear answer is forthcoming, look for something else.

Repossessed Vehicles

Repossessed vehicles are usually bad buys. They are often found at auctions, but they're sometimes sold by finance companies and banks as well. Fortunately, courts have held that these institutions are legally responsible for defects found in what they sell. Also, their deep pockets and abhorrence of bad publicity means you'll likely get your money back if you make a bad buy from a lending institution. The biggest problem with repossessions is that they were likely abused or neglected by their financially troubled owners, and these problems may not come to light until you've had the vehicle too long to make a successful claim. Although you rarely get to test-drive or closely examine these vehicles, a local dealer may be able to produce a vehicle maintenance history by running the Vehicle Identification Number (VIN) through its manufacturer's database.

 ## Rental and Leased Vehicles

The second-best choice for getting a good used vehicle is a rental company or leasing agency. Budget, Hertz, Avis, and National rental car agencies have a large supply of used cars and minivans to sell at cut-rate prices. These vehicles usually have one to two years of service and have gone approximately 80,000–100,000 km. Rental companies will gladly provide a vehicle's complete history and allow an independent inspection by a qualified mechanic of the buyer's choice, as well as arrange competitive financing. Rental car companies also usually settle customer complaints without much hassle so as not to tarnish their image with rental customers.

Rental vehicles are generally well maintained, sell for a few thousand dollars more than privately sold vehicles, and come with strong guarantees, like Budget's 30-day money-back guarantee.

Vehicles that have just come off a 3- or 5-year lease are much more competitively priced, generally have less mileage, and are usually as well maintained as rental vehicles. You're also likely to get a better price if you buy directly from the lessee rather than going through the dealership or an independent agency, but remember that you won't have the dealer's leverage to extract post-warranty "goodwill" repairs from the automaker.

Buying Without Fear and Loathing

No matter from whom you're buying a used vehicle, there are a few rules you should follow to get the best deal.

First, have a good idea of what you want and the price you're willing to pay. If you have a pre-approved line of credit, that will keep the number-crunching and extra fees to a minimum. Finally, be resolute and polite, but make it obvious that you are a serious buyer and won't participate in any "showroom shakedown."

Here's a successful real-world technique used by Kurt Binnie, a frequent *Lemon-Aid* tipster:

1) Wireless Handheld VIN searches

Imagine the surprise of the used-car salesman when I pulled out my BlackBerry [a hand-held wireless device] and did a VIN search right in front of him using Carfax. Threw him right off balance. Carfax results for Ontario vehicles give a good indication, but not the complete MTO [Ministry of Transport of Ontario] history. I bought the UVIP [Used Vehicle Information Package] package before closing the deal. For the car I ended up buying I didn't even tell the sales staff that I was running the VIN while I was there. I was able to see it wasn't an auction vehicle or a write-off. This technique should work with pretty much any WAP [Wireless Application Protocol] enabled phone.

2) Buying a problem used car without the problems

A previous car I owned was a 1994 Mazda 626 4cyl manual tranny... There are a myriad of complaints at the NHTSA as well as in Mazda discussion forums about this. Same thing goes for the 2.5 V6. Resale values on that car were really low,

Mazda's 626 is a particularly good buy, but watch for automatic transmission flaring or gear hunting.

so armed with the proper knowledge of what components to avoid, a consumer can get a low cost, relatively reliable vehicle that has taken a resale value hit. I never had any major issues with the 4-cylinder manual and have never found any major issues except for the distributors on '93, '94 models.

Kurt's letter goes on to describe how he avoids negotiations with sales staff and managers. He figures out the price he's willing to pay beforehand, using a combination of book values and the prices listed at *www.trader.ca*. He then test-drives the vehicle, runs the VIN through his BlackBerry, and makes a point-blank, one-time offer to the dealer. He has also found that used-car staff often have no knowledge about the vehicles on their lots beyond the asking price, making no distinction between a car manufactured early or late in the model year. An alert buyer could get a car built in August 2002 for the same price as a September 2001, since they're both used 2002 cars.

VIN stickers tell you more than the dealer may want you to know.

Kurt runs a car blog dedicated to preventing people from buying the wrong car, and also tells them how to fix common failures (like Subaru's clutch shudder) on most vehicles. He answers most questions via email. Although Kurt's not a mechanic, he's quite resourceful. If he doesn't have the answer, he knows where to get it. His website address is *www.onthehoist.com*.

New-Car Dealers

I bought my used 1995 fully loaded GMC Vandura full-sized van from a new-car dealer. It was a trade-in that had always been serviced by the selling dealer—who showed me the vehicle's complete repair history. Selling for $30,000 originally, it sold for $10,000 when I bought it four years later. The dealer probably made a couple thousand on the deal.

Most used-car buyers prefer to deal with private sellers. In fact, the Federation of Automobile Dealer Associations of Canada states that 20 years ago, 86 percent of used cars were sold by new-car dealers but today that number is less than 25 percent, mainly because of the GST, which has driven buyers into the arms of private sellers.

Nevertheless, I feel that new-car dealers aren't a bad place to pick up a good used car or minivan. Yes, prices can be up to 20 percent higher than those for vehicles sold privately, but zero percent financing plans are trimming used values dramatically. Moreover, dealers are insured against selling stolen vehicles or vehicles with finance owing or other liens. They also usually allow prospective buyers to have the vehicle inspected by an independent garage, offer a much wider choice of models, and have their own repair facilities to do warranty work. Additionally, if there's a possibility of getting post-warranty "goodwill" compensation from the manufacturer, your dealer can provide additional leverage, particularly if he or she is a franchisee for the model you have purchased. Finally, if things do go terribly wrong, dealers have deeper pockets than do private sellers, so there's a better chance of getting paid if you win a court judgment against the firm.

"Certified" Vehicles

Almost all automakers provide "certified" used vehicles that have been refurbished by the dealer according to the manufacturer's guidelines. Sometimes, an auto association will certify a vehicle that has been inspected and had the designated defects corrected. In Alberta, the Alberta Motor Association (AMA) will perform a vehicle inspection at a dealer's request. On each occasion, the AMA gives a written report to the dealer that identifies potential and actual problems, required repairs, and serious defects.

Automaker-certified vehicles are guaranteed for mechanical fitness, and carry a warranty according to the age of the vehicle. But these vehicles don't come cheap, mainly because manufacturers force their dealers to bring them up to better-than-average condition before certifying them. The higher price can be reduced by choosing an older certified model, or amortized by keeping the vehicle longer.

Used-Car Leasing

Leasing is not a good idea for new or used vehicles. It has been touted as a method of making the high cost of vehicle ownership more affordable: Don't you believe it. Leasing is generally costlier than an outright purchase, and for most people, the pitfalls far outweigh any advantages. If you must lease, do so for the shortest time possible and make sure the lease is close-ended (meaning that you walk away from the vehicle when the lease period ends). Also, make sure there's a maximum mileage allowance of at least 25,000 km a year and that the charge per excess kilometre is no higher than 8–10 cents.

Used-Car Dealers

Used-car dealers usually sell their vehicles for a bit less than what new-car dealers charge. However, their vehicles may be worth a lot less, because they don't get the first pick of top-quality trade-ins. Many independent urban dealerships are marginal operations that can't invest much money in reconditioning their vehicles, which are often collected from auctions and new-car dealers reluctant to sell the vehicles to their own customers. And used-car dealers don't always have repair facilities to honour the warranties they do provide. Often, their credit terms are easier (but more expensive) than those offered by franchised new-car dealers.

That said, used-car dealers operating in small towns are an entirely different breed. These small, often family-run businesses recondition and resell cars and trucks that usually come from within their community. Routine servicing is usually done in-house, and more complicated repairs are subcontracted out to specialized garages nearby. On one hand, these small outlets survive by word-of-mouth advertising, and wouldn't last long if they didn't deal fairly with local townsfolk. On the other hand, their prices will likely be higher than elsewhere, due to the better quality of their used vehicles and the cost of reconditioning and repairing what they sell under warranty.

Auctions

First of all, make sure it's a legitimate auction. Many are fronts for used-car lots where sleazy dealers put fake ads in complicit newspapers pretending to hold auctions that are no more than weekend selling sprees.

Furthermore, you'll need lots of patience, smarts, and luck to pick up anything worthwhile. Government auctions—places where the mythical $50 Jeeps are sold—are fun to attend but highly overrated as places to find bargains. Look at the odds against you: It's impossible to determine the condition of the vehicles put up for bid, prices can go way out of control, and auction employees, professional sellers, their relatives, and their friends usually pick over the good stuff long before you ever see it.

To attend commercial auctions is to swim with the piranhas. They are frequented by "ringers" who bid up the prices, and by professional dealers who pick up cheap, worn-out vehicles unloaded by new-car dealers and independents. There are no guarantees, cash is required, and quality is apt to be as low as the price. Remember, too, that auction purchases are subject to provincial and federal sales taxes, the auction's sales commission (3–5 percent), and in some cases, an administrative fee of $25–$50.

If you are interested in shopping at an auto auction, remember that certain days are reserved for dealers only, so call ahead. You'll find the vehicles locked in a compound, but you should have ample opportunity to inspect them and, in some cases, take a short drive around the property before the auction begins.

Paying the Right Price

Even though prices have become considerably more moderate, get ready for sticker shock when pricing minivans, medium-sized SUVs, and pickups. These vehicles depreciate very little, and it's easy to get stuck with a cheap one that's been abused through hard off-roading or lack of care. Even those vehicles with worse-than-average reliability ratings, like the Ford Focus and Chrysler minivans, still command higher-than-average resale prices for the simple reason that they're popular, though not as popular as they once were.

 If you don't want to pay too much when buying used, you've got the following four alternatives.

- Buy an older vehicle. Choose one that's five years old or more and has a good reliability and durability record. Buy extra protection with an extended warranty. The money you save from the extra years' depreciation and lower insurance premiums will more than make up for the extra warranty cost.
- Look for off-lease vehicles sold privately by owners who want more than what their dealer is offering. If you can't find what you're looking for in the local classified ads, put in your own ad asking for lessees to contact you if they're not satisfied with their dealer's offer.
- Buy a vehicle that's depreciated more than average simply because of its bland styling, wrong colour (dark blue, white, and champagne are out; silver is in), lack of high-performance features, or discontinuation. For example, many of the Japanese entry-level compacts like the Toyota Echo cost less to own than their flashier American-made counterparts, yet they're more reliable and equally functional for most driving chores.
- Buy a cheaper twin or re-badged model like a fully loaded Camry instead of a Lexus ES, a Camaro instead of a Firebird, or a Plymouth Voyager instead of a Dodge Caravan.

Financing Choices

You shouldn't spend more than 30 percent of your annual gross income on the purchase of a new or used vehicle. By keeping the initial cost low, there is less risk to you, and you may be able to pay mostly in cash. This can be an effective bargaining tool to use with private sellers, but dealers are less impressed by cash sales because they lose their kickback from the finance companies.

Credit Unions

A credit union is the best place to borrow money at low interest rates and with easy repayment terms. You'll have to join the credit union or have an account with it before the loan is approved. You'll also probably have to come up with a larger down payment relative to what other lending institutions require.

In addition to giving you reasonable loan rates, credit unions help car buyers in other ways. Toronto's Metro Credit Union (Website: *www.metrocu.com*), for example, has a CarFacts Centre, which provides free, objective advice on car shopping, purchasing, financing, and leasing. CarFacts advisors provide free consultations in person or by phone.

Banks

Banks are less leery of financing used cars than they once were, and generally charge rates that are competitive with what dealers offer. As of November 2004, the Royal Bank of Canada prime interest rate on loans varied between 4.2 and 5 percent (see *www.rbcroyalbank.com/buyingacar*). The Royal Bank's rate is a reasonable benchmark for comparing rates offered by other financial institutions.

In your quest for a bank loan, keep in mind that the loan officer will be impressed by a prepared budget and sound references, particularly if you seek out a loan before choosing a vehicle. If you haven't gotten a loan, it wouldn't hurt to buy from the local dealer, since banks like to encourage businesses in their area.

The Internet also offers help for people who need an auto loan and want quick approval but don't want to face a banker. Used-car buyers can post a loan application on a bank's website, such as TD Canada Trust's Payment Advantage Auto Loan (*www.tdcanadatrust.com/lending/paal.jsp*), even if they don't have an account.

Dealers

Dealer financing isn't the rip-off it once was, but still be watchful for all the expensive little "extras" the dealer may try to pencil into the contract, because, believe it or not, dealers make far more profit on used-car sales than on new-car deals. Don't write them off for financing, though; they can finance your purchase at rates that compete with those of banks and finance companies. This is because they agree to take back the vehicle if the creditor defaults on the loan (Mitsubishi is adrift in red ink because of its "sub-prime" bad loans to buyers). Some dealers mislead their customers into thinking they can get financing at rates far below the prime rate. Actually, the dealer jacks up the base price of the vehicle to compensate for the lower interest charges.

Dealer Scams

Most dealer sales scams are so obvious, they're laughable. But like the Nigerian email "lost fortune" scam, there are enough stupid people to make these dealer deceptions profitable.

One of the more common tricks is to not identify the previous owner because the vehicle either was used commercially, was problem-prone, or had been written off as a total loss after an accident. It's also not uncommon to discover that the mileage has been turned back, particularly if the vehicle was part of a company's fleet. Your best defence? Demand the name of the vehicle's previous owner and run a VIN check through Carfax as a prerequisite to purchasing the vehicle.

It would be impossible to list all the dishonest tricks employed in used-vehicle sales. As soon as the public is alerted to one scheme, crooked sellers use other, more elaborate frauds. Nevertheless, under industry-financed provincial compensation funds, buyers can get substantial refunds if defrauded by a dealer.

Here are some of the more common fraudulent practices you're likely to encounter.

⚿ Failing to Declare Full Purchase Price

Here's where your own greed will do you in. In a tactic used almost exclusively by small, independent dealers and some private sellers, the buyer is told that he or she can pay less sales tax by listing a lower selling price on the contract. But what if the vehicle turns out to be a lemon, or the sales agent has falsified the model year or mileage? The hapless buyer is offered a refund on the fictitious purchase price indicated on the contract. If the buyer wanted to take the dealer to court, it's quite unlikely that he or she would get any more than the contract price. Moreover, both the buyer and dealer could be prosecuted for making a false declaration to avoid paying sales tax.

Phony Private Sales ("Curbsiders")

Individual transactions account for about three times as many used vehicle sales as dealer sales, and crooked dealers get in on the action by posing as private sellers. Called "curbsiders," these scammers lure unsuspecting buyers through lower prices, cheat the federal government out of the GST, and routinely violate provincial registration and consumer protection regulations. Bob Beattie, executive director of the Ontario Used Car Dealers Association, *www.ucda.org*, says his organization has found that about 20 percent of so-called private sellers in Ontario are actually curbsiders. Dealers in large cities like Toronto, Calgary, and Vancouver believe curbsiders sell half of the cars advertised in the local papers. This scam is easy to detect if the seller can't produce the original sales contract or show repair bills made out over a long period of time in his or her own name. You can usually identify a car dealer in the want ads section of the newspaper—just check to see if the same telephone number is repeated in many different ads. Sometimes you can trip up a curbsider by requesting information on the phone, without identifying the specific vehicle. If the seller asks you which car you are considering, you know you're dealing with a dealer.

Legitimate car dealers claim to deplore the dishonesty of curbsider crooks, yet they are their chief suppliers. Dealership sales managers, auto auction employees, and newspaper classified ad sellers all know the names, addresses, and phone numbers of these thieves but don't act on the information. Newspapers want the ad dollars, auctions want the action, and dealers want someplace they can unload their wrecked, rust-cankered, and odometer-tricked junkers with impunity. Talk about hypocrisy, eh?

Curbsiders are particularly active in Western Canada, importing vehicles from other provinces where they were sold by dealers, wreckers, insurance companies, and junkyards (after having been written off as total losses). They then place private classified ads in B.C. and Alberta papers, sell their stock, and import more. Writes one Vancouver *Lemon-Aid* reader frustrated by the complicity of the provincial government and local papers in this rip-off:

> The story is the lack of sensitivity by the newspapers who turn a blind eye and let consumers get ripped off.... The newspapers are making money, ICBC [Insurance Corporation of British Columbia] is making money, the cops acknowledge wide-scale dumping on the West Coast.... Governments have no willpower to take on organized fraud.

Buyers taken in by these scam artists should sue in small claims court both the seller and the newspaper that carried the original classified ad. When just a few cases are won in court and the paper's competitors play up the story, the practice will cease.

"Free-Exchange" Privilege

Dealers get a lot of sales mileage out of this deceptive offer. The dealer offers to exchange any defective vehicle for any other vehicle in stock. What really happens, though, is that the dealer won't have anything else selling for the same price and so will demand a cash bonus for the exchange—or you may get that dubious privilege of exchanging one lemon for another.

"Money-Back" Guarantee

Once again, the purchaser feels safe in buying a used car with this kind of guarantee. After all, what could be more honest than a money-back guarantee? Dealers using this technique often charge exorbitant handling charges, rental fees, or mechanical repair costs to the customer who's bought one of these vehicles and then returned it.

"50/50" Guarantee

This means that the dealer will pay half of the repair costs over a limited period of time. It's a fair offer if an independent garage does the repairs. If not, the dealer can always inflate the repair costs to double their actual worth and write up a bill for that amount (a scam sometimes used in "goodwill" settlements). The buyer winds up paying the full price of repairs that would probably have been much cheaper at an independent garage. The best kind of used-vehicle warranty is 100 percent with full coverage for a fixed term, even if that term is relatively short.

"As Is" Sales

Buying a vehicle "as is" usually means that you're aware of mechanical defects, you're prepared to accept the responsibility for any damage or injuries caused by the vehicle, and that you will pay all repair costs. However, the courts have held that the "as is" clause is not a blank cheque to cheat buyers, and must be interpreted in light of the seller's true intent. Was there an attempt to deceive the buyer by including this clause? Did the buyer really know what the "as is" clause could do to his or her future legal rights? It's also been held that the courts may consider oral representations ("parole evidence") as an "expressed" warranty, even though they were never written into the formal contract. So, if a seller makes claims as to the fine quality of the used vehicle, these claims can be used as evidence. Courts generally ignore "as is" clauses when the vehicle has been intentionally misrepresented, the dealer is the seller, or the defects are so serious that the seller is presumed to have known of their existence. Private sellers are usually given more latitude than dealers or their agents.

Odometer Fraud

When was the last time you heard of a dealership being charged with odometer fraud? Probably a long time ago, if at all.

The RCMP hate odometer complaints because rolling back a vehicle's odometer is a common crime that's hard to prove. In theory, sellers face hefty fines and even imprisonment if they're caught altering the mileage of any vehicle they sell, but in practice, few odometer tampering cases make it to court because intent to defraud is so difficult to prove. Usually, independent outfits are hired to pick up the vehicle or visit the dealership and "fix" the odometer, a practice allowed under Canadian federal and provincial laws.

Misrepresentation

Used vehicles can be misrepresented in a variety of ways. A used airport commuter minivan may be represented as having been used by a Sunday school class. A mechanically defective pickup that's been rebuilt after several major accidents may have plastic filler in the body panels to muffle the rattles or hide rust damage, heavy oil in the motor to stifle the clanks, and cheap retread tires to eliminate the thumps. Your best protection against these dirty tricks is to have the vehicle's quality completely verified by an independent mechanic before completing the sale. Of course, you can still cancel the sale if you learn of the misrepresentation only after taking the vehicle home, but your chances of doing so successfully dwindle as time passes.

I'm finding it difficult finding a reasonably priced used car in the Toronto area. Many of the ads for private sales here turn out to be dealers or mechanics selling cars pretending to be private persons. Also, the prices are ridiculously inflated. Your books are a great read and have made me at least slow down and ask questions. For example, I almost got caught in a lease the other day and pulled out at the last minute. All this advertising had me believe there would be zero down, zero delivery, etc. until I found out there would be a $350 lease acquisition fee and a $250 admin. fee and all kinds of other charges, some legitimate such as licensing. However, my zero down turned into a whopping $1,200! I'm just now getting into your leasing section....

Private Scams

A lot of space in this guide has been used to describe how used-car dealers and scam artists cheat uninformed buyers. Of course, private individuals can be dishonest, too. In either case, protect yourself at the outset by keeping your deposit small and by getting as much information as possible about the vehicle you're considering. Then, after a test drive, you may sign a written agreement to purchase the vehicle and give a deposit of sufficient value to cover the seller's advertising costs, subject to cancellation if the automobile fails its inspection. After you've taken these precautions, watch out for the following private sellers' tricks.

Used Vehicles That Are Stolen or Have Finance Owing

Many used vehicles are sold privately without free title because the original auto loan was never repaid. You can avoid being cheated by asking for proof of purchase and payment from a private seller. Be especially wary of any individual who offers to sell a used vehicle for an incredibly low price. Check the sales contract to determine who granted the original loan, and call the lender to see if it's been repaid. Place a call to the provincial Ministry of Transportation to ascertain whether the car is registered in the seller's name. Find out if a finance company is named as beneficiary on the auto insurance policy. Finally, call up the original dealer to determine whether there are any outstanding claims.

In Ontario, all private sellers must purchase a Used Vehicle Information Package at one of 300 provincial Driver and Vehicle Licence Issuing Offices, or online at *www.mto.gov.on.ca/english/dandv/vehicle/used.htm*. This package, which costs $20, contains the vehicle's registration history in Ontario; vehicle lien information (i.e., if there are any liens registered on the vehicle); the fair market value on which the minimum tax payable will apply; and other information such as consumer tips, vehicle safety standards inspection, retail sales tax information, and forms for bills of sale.

In other provinces, buyers don't have easy access to this information. Generally, you have to contact the provincial office that registers property and pay a small fee for a computer printout that may or may not be accurate. You'll be asked for the current owner's name and the car's VIN, which is usually found on the driver's side of the dashboard.

There are two high-tech ways to get the goods on a dishonest seller. First, have a dealer of that particular model run a "vehicle history" check through the automaker's online network. This will tell you who the previous owners and dealers were, what warranty and recall repairs were carried out, and what other free repair programs may still apply. Second, you could use Carfax (Website: *www.carfax.com*; Tel: 1-888-422-7329) to carry out a background check.

Wrong Registration

Make sure the seller's vehicle has been properly registered with provincial transport authorities; if it isn't, it may be stolen or you could be dealing with a curbsider.

If you are selling a vehicle, protect yourself from legal liability by ensuring the registration has been transferred to the buyer. Normally, once you take the tags and give the buyer a bill of sale, you're no longer the registered owner. Nonetheless, go down to the registry office yourself to make sure the title has changed. As long as you're still listed as the owner of record, you could be sued for damages arising from an accident.

Summary: Buying the Best for Less

You can get a reliable used vehicle at a reasonable price—it just takes some patience and homework. Avoid potential headaches by becoming thoroughly familiar with your legal rights as outlined in Part Two and buying a vehicle recommended in Part Three. The following is a summary of the steps to take to keep your risk to a minimum:

1. Keep your present car at least 8 to 10 years; don't panic because of high fuel costs.
2. Sell to a dealer if the reduction in GST and PST is more than the potential profit of selling privately.
3. Sell privately, if you can get at least 15 percent more than what the dealer offered.
4. Buy from a private party, rental car outlet, or dealer (in that order).
5. Use an auto broker to save time and money.
6. Buy a *Lemon-Aid*-recommended vehicle for savings on depreciation, parts, and service.
7. Buy a 3- or 5-year-old vehicle with lots of original warranty that can be transferred.
8. Choose a vehicle that's crashworthy, cheap to insure, and easy to fix.

9. Carefully inspect front-drive vehicles that have reached their fifth year. Pay particular attention to the engine intake manifold and head gasket, CV joints, steering box, and brakes.

10. Buy a full-sized, rear-drive delivery van and add the convenience features that you would like (seats, sound system, etc.), instead of opting for a more expensive, smaller, less powerful minivan.

Full-sized vans usually come fully loaded and heavily depreciated—giving you the kitchen sink for free. They are also easily converted for physically challenged drivers and passengers.

11. Don't buy an extended warranty for a particular model year unless it's recommended in *Lemon-Aid*.

12. Have repairs done by independent garages offering lifetime warranties.

13. Install used or reconditioned parts; demand that original parts be used for accident repairs.

14. Keep all the previous owners' repair bills to facilitate warranty claims and to let mechanics know what's already been replaced or repaired.

15. Upon delivery, adjust mirrors to reduce blind spots and adjust head restraints to prevent your head from snapping back in the event of a collision. On airbag-equipped vehicles, move the seat backward more than half its travel distance and sit at least a foot away from the airbag housing. Ensure that the airbag, spare tire, and tire jack haven't been removed.

16. Make sure the dealer and automaker have your name in their computers as the new owner of record. Ask for a copy of your vehicle's history, which is stored in the same computer.

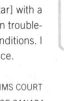

Part Two
WARRANTIES, WEASELS, AND WINNING!

Ford's Engine Woes

A Technical Service Bulletin dated June 28, 1999, was circulated to Ford dealers. It dealt specifically with "undetermined loss of coolant" and "engine oil contaminated with coolant" in the 1996–98 Windstar and five other models of Ford vehicles. I conclude that Ford owed a duty of care to the Plaintiff to equip this vehicle [a 1996 Windstar] with a cylinder head gasket of sufficient sturdiness and durability that would function trouble-free for at least seven years, given normal driving and proper maintenance conditions. I find that Ford is answerable in damages for the consequences of its negligence.

JUSTICE TIERNAY, SUPERIOR COURT OF JUSTICE, OTTAWA SMALL CLAIMS COURT
JOHN R. REID AND LAURIE M. MCCALL V. FORD MOTOR COMPANY OF CANADA
JULY 11, 2003

Windstar "Mental Distress" Worth $7,500!

The plaintiff and his family have had three years of aggravation, inconvenience, worry, and concern about their safety and that of their children. Generally speaking, our contract law did not allow for compensation for what may be mental distress, but that may be changing.... In my view, a defect in manufacture (a faulty 2000 Windstar sliding door) which goes to the safety of the vehicle deserves a modest increase. I would assess the plaintiff's damage for mental distress resulting from the breach of the implied warranty of fitness at $7,500.

JUSTICE SHEPARD, ONTARIO SUPERIOR COURT OF JUSTICE
SHARMAN V. FORD
OCTOBER 7, 2003

Two Roads to a Refund

Used cars turn out to be bad buys for two reasons: either they were misrepresented, or they are afflicted by defects that make them unreliable or dangerous to drive. Misrepresentation is relatively easy to prove; you simply have to show the vehicle doesn't conform to the oral or written sales representations made before or during the time of purchase. These include sales brochures and newspaper, radio, and television ads.

Private sales can easily be cancelled if the mileage has been turned back, if accident damage hasn't been disclosed, or if the seller is really a dealer in disguise. Even descriptive phrases like "well-maintained," "driven by a woman" (is this a positive or negative feature?), or "excellent condition" can get the seller in trouble if misrepresentation is alleged.

Defects are usually confirmed by an independent garage examination that shows the deficiencies are premature, factory-related, or not maintenance-related, or were hidden at the time of purchase. It doesn't matter if the vehicle was sold new or used. In fact, most of the small claims court victories against Ford relating to defective engines and transmissions were won by owners of used Windstars, Tauruses, and Sables who sued both the seller and the automaker.

Nipping That Lemon in the Bud

Here is 35 years' worth of information on strategy, tactics, negotiation tools, and jurisprudence you may cite to hang tough and get an out-of-court settlement or win your case without spending a fortune on lawyers and research. Used-car and minivan defects are covered by two warranties: the *expressed* warranty, which has a fixed time limit, and the *implied*, or *legal*, warranty, which is entirely up to a judge's discretion.

Expressed warranties

The expressed warranty, given by the seller, is often full of empty promises, and allows the dealer and manufacturer to act as judge and jury when deciding whether a vehicle was misrepresented or is afflicted by defects they'll pay to correct. Rarely does it provide a money-back guarantee.

Some of the more familiar lame excuses used in denying expressed warranty claims are "You abused the car," "It was poorly maintained," "It's normal wear and tear," "It's rusting from the outside, not the inside," and "It passed the safety inspection." Ironically, the expressed warranty sometimes says there is no warranty at all, or that the vehicle is sold "as is." Fortunately, courts often throw out these exclusions by upholding two legal concepts:

- The vehicle must be fit for the purpose for which it was purchased.
- The vehicle must be of merchantable quality when sold.

These typical expressed warranty clauses would put Don Corleone to shame.

Not surprisingly, sellers use the expressed warranty to reject claims, while smart plaintiffs ignore the expressed warranty and argue for a refund under the implied warranty instead.

Implied warranties

The implied warranty ("of fitness") is your ace in the hole. As clearly stated in the unreported Saskatchewan decision *Maureen Frank v. General Motors of Canada Limited* (see page 73), in which the judge declared that paint discoloration and peeling shouldn't occur within 11 years of the purchase of the vehicle, the implied warranty is an important legal principle. It is solidly supported by a large body of federal and provincial laws, regulations, and jurisprudence and protects you primarily from hidden defects that may be either dealer- or factory-related. But the concept also includes misrepresentation and a host of other scams.

This warranty also holds dealers to a higher standard of conduct than private sellers since, unlike private sellers, they are presumed to be aware of the defects present in the vehicles they sell. That way, they can't just pass the ball to the automaker or previous owner and walk away from the dispute.

Dealers are also expected to disclose defects that have been repaired. For instance, in British Columbia, provincial law (the *Motor Dealer Act*) says that a dealer must disclose damages that cost more than $2,000 to fix. This is a good law to cite in other jurisdictions.

In spite of all your precautions, there's still a 10 percent chance you'll buy a lemon, says Runzheimer International. It confirms that one out of every 10 vehicles produced by the Detroit Big Three is likely to be a lemon (a figure also used by GM VP Bob Lutz). This number would have likely been much higher if Ford Focus and Windstar, Chrysler Caravan, and GM Saturn owners had also been polled.

Why the implied warranty is so effective

- It establishes the concept of reasonable durability (see "How Long Should a Part or Repair Last," below), meaning that parts are expected to last for a reasonable period of time, as stated in jurisprudence, judged by independent mechanics, or expressed in extended warranties given by the automaker in the past (7 to 10 years/160,000 km for engines and transmissions).
- It covers the entire vehicle, and can be applied for whatever period of time the judge decides.
- It can order that the vehicle be taken back, or a major repair cost be refunded.

> I wanted to let you and your readers know that the information you publish about Ford's paint failure problem is invaluable. Having read through your "how-to guide" on addressing this issue, I filed suit against Ford for the "latent" paint defect. The day prior to our court date, I received a settlement offer by phone for 75 percent of what I was initially asking for.

Plaintiffs may also be given compensation for supplementary transportation, inconvenience, mental distress, missed work, screwed-up vacations, insurance paid while the vehicle was in the repair shop, repairs done by other repairers, and exemplary, or punitive, damages in cases where the seller was a real weasel.

- It is frequently used by small claims court judges to give refunds to plaintiffs "in equity" (out of fairness), rather than through a strict interpretation of contract law.

How Long Should a Part or Repair Last?

How do you know when a part or service hasn't lasted as long as it should, and whether you should seek a full or partial refund? Sure, you have a gut feeling based on the use of the vehicle, how you maintained it, and the extent of work that was carried out. But you'll need more than emotion to win compensation from garages and automakers.

You can definitely get a refund if a repair or part lasts beyond its guarantee but not as long as is generally expected. But you'll have to show what the auto industry considers to be reasonable durability.

Automakers, mechanics, and the courts each have their own benchmarks as to what's a reasonable period of time or amount of mileage that one should expect a part or adjustment to last. I've prepared the following table to show what most automakers consider reasonable durability, as expressed by their original and "goodwill" warranties. An example is Chrysler's 10 year/160,000 km ball joint "goodwill" refunds.

ACCESSORIES

Air conditioner	7 years
Cruise control	5 years/ 100,000 km
Power doors, windows	5 years
Radio	5 years

BODY

Paint (peeling)	7–11 years
Rust (perforations)	7–11 years
Rust (surface)	5 years
Water/wind/air leaks	5 years

BRAKE SYSTEM

Brake drum	120,000 km
Brake drum linings	35,000 km
Brake rotor	60,000 km
Brake calipers/pads	30,000 km
Master cylinder	100,000 km
Wheel cylinder	80,000 km

ENGINE AND DRIVETRAIN

CV joint	6 years/ 160,000 km
Differential	7 years/ 160,000 km
Engine (diesel)	15 years/ 350,000 km

Engine (gas)	7 years/ 160,000 km
Radiator	4 years/ 80,000 km
Transfer case	7 years/ 160,000 km
Transmission (auto.)	7 years/ 160,000 km
Transmission (man.)	10 years/ 250,000 km
Transmission oil cooler	5 years/ 100,000 km

EXHAUST SYSTEM

Catalytic converter	5 years/ 100,000 km or more
Muffler	2 years/ 40,000 km
Tailpipe	3 years/ 60,000 km

IGNITION SYSTEM

Cable set	60,000 km
Electronic module	5 years/ 80,000 km
Retiming	20,000 km
Spark plugs	20,000 km
Tune-up	20,000 km

SAFETY COMPONENTS		Shock absorber	2 years/
Airbags	life of vehicle		40,000 km
ABS brakes	7 years/	Struts	5 years/
	160,000 km		80,000 km
ABS computer	10 years/	Tires (radial)	5 years/
	160,000 km		80,000 km
Seatbelts	life of vehicle	Wheel bearing	3 years/
			60,000 km
STEERING AND SUSPENSION			
Alignment	1 year/	**VISIBILITY**	
	20,000 km	Halogen/fog lights	3 years
Ball joints	100,000 km	Sealed beam	2 years
Power steering	5 years/	Windshield wiper	5 years
	80,000 km		

Much of the table was extrapolated from Chrysler and Ford payouts to thousands of dissatisfied customers over the past decade, in addition to Chrysler's original 7-year powertrain warranty, applicable from 1991 to 1995 and reapplied since 2001. Other sources for this table were the Ford and GM transmission warranties outlined in their secret warranties; Ford, GM, and Toyota engine "goodwill" programs laid out in their internal service bulletins; and court judgments where judges have given their own guidelines as to what constitutes reasonable durability.

Safety features—with the exception of ABS—generally have a lifetime warranty. Chrysler's 10-year "free-service" program, part of its 1993–99 ABS recall, can serve as a handy benchmark as to how long one can expect these components to last on more recent models.

Airbags are a different matter. Those that are deployed in an accident—and the personal injury and interior damage their deployment will likely have caused—are covered by your accident insurance policy. However, if there is a sudden deployment for no apparent reason, the automaker and the dealer should be held jointly responsible for all injuries and damages caused by the airbag.

You can prove their liability by downloading the data from your vehicle's data recorder. This will likely lead to a more generous settlement from the two parties and prevent your insurance premiums from being jacked up. Inadvertent deployment may occur after passing over a bump in the road, slamming the car door, or, in some Chrysler minivans, simply putting the key in the ignition. This happens more often than you might imagine, judging by the hundreds of recalls and thousands of complaints recorded on NHTSA's website.

Use the manufacturer's emissions warranty as your primary guideline for the expected durability of high-tech electronic and mechanical pollution control components, such as powertrain control modules (PCMs) and catalytic converters. Look first at your owner's manual for an indication of which parts on your vehicle are covered. If you come up with few specifics, ask the auto manufacturer for a list of specific components covered by the emissions warranty. If you're stonewalled, ask your local MP to get the info from Transport Canada or Environment Canada, and invest $25 (U.S.) in an ALLDATA service bulletin subscription.

Getting Action

Before we go any further, let's get one thing straight: A telephone call usually won't get you much action from a corporation. Automakers and their dealers want to make money, not give it back. You must send a registered letter or an email to create a paper trail and get attention. What's more, that letter must contain the threat that you will use the implied warranty against the defendant and cite powerful jurisprudence to win your small claims court action in the same region where that business operates.

On the following next two pages are two sample complaint letters that give you much of what you'll need to invoke the implied warranty to get a refund for a bad car or ineffective repairs.

 ## Legal "Secrets" that Work for You

Send a claim letter to both the seller and the automaker and let them work out together how much they will give you back. Make sure your letter is sent to the automaker's legal affairs department (usually in Ontario), where policy is made, and not to where it's simply carried out.

Unfair sales contracts can be cancelled although they aren't supposed to be fair. Lawyers spend countless hours making sure their corporate clients are well protected with ironclad standard-form contracts. Judges look upon these agreements, called "contracts of adhesion," with a great deal of skepticism. They know these loan documents, insurance contracts, and automobile leases grant consumers little or no bargaining power. So when a dispute arises over terms or language, provincial consumer protection statutes require that judges interpret these contracts in the way most favourable to the consumer. Simply put, ignorance can be a good defence.

Hearsay can be admitted if you introduce it the right way. It's essential that printed evidence and/or witnesses (relatives are not excluded) be available to confirm that a false representation actually occurred, that a part is failure-prone, or that its replacement is covered by a secret warranty or internal service bulletin alert. If you can't find an independent expert, introduce this evidence through the automaker reps and dealership service personnel who have to be at the trial anyhow.

They know all about the service bulletins and extended warranty programs cited in *Lemon-Aid*, and will probably contradict each other, particularly if they are excluded from the courtroom prior to testifying. Incidentally, you may wish to have the court clerk send a subpoena requiring the deposition of the documents you intend to cite, all warranty extensions relevant to your problem, and other lawsuits filed against the company for similar failures. This will make the fur fly in Oshawa, Oakville, and Windsor, and will likely lead to an out-of-court settlement. Sometimes, the service manager or company representative will make key admissions if questioned closely by you, a court mediator, or the trial judge. Some questions to ask: Is this a common problem? Do you recognize this service bulletin? Is there a case-by-case "goodwill" plan covering this repair?

USED VEHICLE COMPLAINT LETTER/FAX/EMAIL

WITHOUT PREJUDICE

Date: _____

Name: _____

Please be advised that I am dissatisfied with my used vehicle, a (state model), for the following reasons:

1. _____
2. _____
3. _____
4. _____
5. _____

In compliance with the provincial consumer protection laws and the "implied warranty" set down by the Supreme Court of Canada in *Donoghue v. Stevenson, Wharton v. GM*, and *Sharman v. Ford Canada*, I hereby request that these defects be repaired without charge. This vehicle has not been reasonably durable and is, therefore, not as represented to me.

Should you fail to repair these defects in a satisfactory manner and within a reasonable period of time, I shall get an estimate of the repairs from an independent source and claim them in court, without further delay. I also reserve my right to claim up to $1 million for punitive damages, pursuant to the Supreme Court of Canada's February 22, 2002, ruling in *Whiten v. Pilot*.

I have dealt with your company because of its honesty, competence, and sincere regard for its clients. I am sure that my case is the exception and not the rule.

A positive response within the next five (5) days would be appreciated.

(signed with telephone number, fax number, or email address)

SECRET WARRANTY CLAIM LETTER/FAX/EMAIL

WITHOUT PREJUDICE

Date: _____

Name: _____

Please be advised that I am dissatisfied with my vehicle, a _____, bought from you on _____.

It has had the following recurring problems that I believe are factory-related defects, as confirmed by internal service bulletins sent to dealers, and are covered by your "goodwill" policies:

1. _____
2. _____
3. _____

If your "goodwill" program has ended, I ask that my claim be accepted nevertheless, inasmuch as I was never informed of your policy while it was in effect and should not be penalized for not knowing it existed.

I hereby formally put you on notice under federal and provincial consumer protection statutes that your refusal to apply this extended warranty coverage in my case would be an unfair warranty practice within the purview of the above-cited laws.

Your actions also violate the "implied warranty" set down by the Supreme Court of Canada (*Donoghue v. Stevenson* and *Longpre v. St. Jacques Automobile*) and repeatedly reaffirmed by provincial consumer protection laws (*Lowe v. Chrysler, Dufour v. Ford du Canada*, and *Frank v. GM*).

I have enclosed several estimates (my bill) showing that this problem is factory related and will (has) cost $_____ to correct. I would appreciate your refunding me the estimated (paid) amount, failing which, I reserve the right to have the repair done elsewhere and claim reimbursement in court without further delay. I also reserve the right to claim up to $1 million for punitive damages, pursuant to the Supreme Court of Canada's February 22, 2002, ruling in *Whiten v. Pilot.*

A positive response within the next five (5) days would be appreciated.

(signed with telephone number, fax number, or email address)

Automakers often blame owners for having pushed their vehicle beyond its limits. Therefore, when you seek to set aside the contract or get repair work reimbursed, it's essential that you get an independent mechanic or co-workers to prove the vehicle was well maintained and driven prudently.

When asking for a refund, keep in mind the "reasonable diligence" rule that requires that a suit be filed within a reasonable time after the purchase, which usually means less than a year. Because many factory-related deficiencies take years to appear, the courts have ruled that the reasonable diligence clock starts clicking only after the defect is confirmed to be manufacturer- or dealer-related (powertrain, paint, etc.). This allows you to make a claim up to seven years after the vehicle was originally put into service, regardless of whether it was bought new or used. If there have been negotiations with the dealer or the automaker, or if either the dealer or the automaker has been promising to correct the defects for some time or has carried out repeated unsuccessful repairs, the deadline for filing the lawsuit can be extended.

Yes, you can claim for hotel and travel costs, or compensation for general inconvenience. Fortunately, when legal action is threatened—usually through small claims court—automakers quickly up their out-of-court offer to include most of the owner's expenses because they know the courts will be far more generous. For example, a British Columbia court decision gave $2,257 for hotel and travel costs, and then capped it off with a $5,000 award for "inconvenience and loss of enjoyment of their luxury vehicle," to a motorist fed up with his lemon Cadillac (see *Wharton v. Tom Harris Chevrolet Oldsmobile Cadillac Ltd. and General Motors of Canada Limited*, B.C. Supreme Court, Date: 1999 1202, Docket: C982104, Registry: Vancouver). In the *Sharman v. Ford* case (see the Windstar section), the judge gave the plaintiff $7,500 for "mental distress" caused by the fear that his children would fall out of his 2000 Windstar equipped with a faulty sliding door.

You can ask for punitive, or exemplary, damages when the seller's or the automaker's conduct has been so outrageously bad that you think the court should protect society by awarding you a sum of money large enough to dissuade others from engaging in similar immoral, unethical conduct. I call this the "weasel-whacker" law. In *Prebushewski v. Dodge City Auto (1985) Ltd. and Chrysler Canada Ltd.* (2001 SKQB 537; Q.B. No. 1215), the plaintiff got $25,000 in a judgment handed down December 6, 2001, in Saskatoon. The award followed testimony from Chrysler's expert witness that the company was aware of many cases where daytime running lights shorted and caused 1996 Ram pickups to catch fire. The plaintiff's truck had burned to the ground and Chrysler refused the owner's claim, saying it had fulfilled its expressed warranty obligations, in spite of its knowledge that fires were commonplace. The plaintiff sued on the grounds that there was an implied warranty that the vehicle would be safe. Justice Rothery gave this stinging rebuke in his judgment against Chrysler and its dealer:

> Not only did Chrysler know about the problems of the defective daytime running light modules, it did not advise the plaintiff of this. It simply chose to ignore the plaintiff's requests for compensation and told her to seek recovery from her insurance company. Chrysler had replaced thousands of these modules since 1988. But it had also made a business decision to neither advise its customers of the problem nor to recall the vehicles

to replace the modules. While the cost would have been about $250 to replace each module, there were at least one million customers. Chrysler was not prepared to spend $250 million, even though it knew what the defective module might do.

Counsel for the defendants argues that this matter had to be resolved by litigation because the plaintiff and the defendants simply had a difference of opinion on whether the plaintiff should be compensated by the defendants. Had the defendants some dispute as to the cause of the fire, that may have been sufficient to prove that they had not willfully violated this part of the Act. They did not. They knew about the defective daytime running light module. They did nothing to replace the burned truck for the plaintiff. They offered the plaintiff no compensation for her loss. Counsel's position that the definition of the return of the purchase price is an arguable point is not sufficient to negate the defendants' violation of this part of the Act. I find the violation of the defendants to be willful. Thus, I find that exemplary damages are appropriate on the facts of this case.

In this case, the quantum ought to be sufficiently high as to correct the defendants' behaviour. In particular, Chrysler's corporate policy to place profits ahead of the potential danger to its customers' safety and personal property must be punished. And when such corporate policy includes a refusal to comply with the provisions of the Act and a refusal to provide any relief to the plaintiff, I find an award of $25,000 for exemplary damages to be appropriate. I therefore order Chrysler and Dodge City to pay: Damages in the sum of $41,969.83; Exemplary damages in the sum of $25,000; Party and party costs.

Warranty Rights

The manufacturer's or dealer's warranty is a written legal promise that a vehicle will be reasonably reliable, subject to certain conditions. Regardless of the number of subsequent owners, this promise remains in force as long as the warranty's original time/kilometre limits haven't expired. Tires aren't usually covered by car manufacturers' warranties, and are warranted instead by the tiremaker on a pro-rated basis. This isn't such a good deal, because the manufacturer is making a profit by charging you the full list price. If you were to buy the same replacement tire from a discount store, you'd likely pay less, without the pro-rated rebate.

But consumers have gained additional rights following Bridgestone/Firestone's massive recall in 2001 of its defective ATX II and Wilderness tires. Because of the confusion and chaos surrounding Firestone's handling of the recall, Ford's 575 Canadian dealers stepped into the breach and replaced the tires with any equivalent tires dealers had in stock, no questions asked. This is an important precedent that tears down the traditional wall separating tire manufacturers from automakers in product liability claims. In essence, whoever sells the product can now be held liable for damages. In the future, Canadian consumers will have an easier time holding the dealer, the automaker, and the tire manufacturer liable, not just for recalled products but for any defect that affects the safety or reasonable durability of that product.

This is particularly true now that the Supreme Court of Canada (*Winnipeg Condominium v. Bird Construction* [1995] 1 S.C.R. 85) has ruled that defendants are liable in negligence for any designs that result in a risk to the public safety or health. The Supreme Court reversed a long-standing policy and provided the public with a new cause of action that had not existed before in Canada.

Other Warranties

In the U.S., safety restraints such as airbags and safety belts have warranty coverage extended for the lifetime of the vehicle, following an informal agreement made between automakers and the National Highway Traffic Safety Administration. In Canada, however, many automakers try to dodge this responsibility, alleging that they are separate entities, their vehicles are different, and no U.S. agreement or service bulletin binds them. That distinction is both disingenuous and dishonest, and wouldn't likely hold up in small claims court—probably the reason why most automakers relent when threatened with legal action.

Aftermarket products and services—such as gas-saving gadgets, rustproofing, and paint protectors—can render the manufacturer's warranty invalid, so make sure you're in the clear before purchasing any optional equipment or services from an independent supplier.

How fairly a warranty is applied is more important than how long it remains in effect. Once you know the normal wear rate for a mechanical component or body part, you can demand proportional compensation when you get less than normal durability—no matter what the original warranty said. Some dealers tell customers that they need to have original equipment parts installed in order to maintain their warranty. A variation on this theme requires that routine servicing—including tune-ups and oil changes (with a certain brand of oil)—be done by the selling dealer, or the warranty is invalidated. Nothing could be further from the truth. Canadian law stipulates that whoever issues a warranty cannot make that warranty conditional on the use of any specific brand of motor oil, oil filter, or any other component, unless it's provided to the customer free of charge.

Sometimes dealers will do all sorts of minor repairs that don't correct the problem, and then after the warranty runs out they'll tell you that major repairs are needed. You can avoid this nasty surprise by repeatedly bringing your vehicle to the dealership before the warranty ends. During each visit, insist that a written work order include the specific nature of the problem as you see it and that this is the second, third, or fourth time the same problem has been brought to the dealer's attention. Write it down yourself, if need be. This allows you to show a pattern of non-performance by the dealer during the warranty period and establishes that the problem is both serious and chronic. When the warranty expires, you have the legal right to demand that it be extended on those items consistently reappearing on your handful of work orders. *Lowe v. Fairview Chrysler* (see pages 86–87) is an excellent judgment that reinforces this important principle. In another lawsuit, *François Chong v. Marine Drive Imported Cars Ltd. and Honda Canada Inc.* (see page 86), a Honda owner forced Honda to fix his engine seven times—until they got it right.

A retired GM service manager gave me another effective tactic to use when you're not sure a dealer's warranty "repairs" will actually correct the problem for a reasonable period of time after the warranty expires. Here's what he says you should do:

> When you pick up the vehicle after the warranty repair has been done, hand the service manager a note to be put in your file that says you appreciate the warranty repair, however, you intend to return and ask for further warranty coverage if the problem reappears before a reasonable amount of time has elapsed—even if the original warranty has expired. A copy of the same note should be sent to the automaker.... Keep your copy of the note in the glove compartment as cheap insurance against paying for a repair that wasn't fixed correctly the first time.

Extra-Cost Warranties

Supplementary warranties providing extended coverage may be sold by the manufacturer, the dealer, or an independent third party, and are automatically transferred when the vehicle is sold. They cost between $1,000 and $1,500 and should be purchased only if the vehicle you're buying is off its original warranty, if it has a reputation for being unreliable or expensive to service (see Part Three), or if you're reluctant to use the small claims courts when factory-related trouble arises. Don't let the dealer pressure you into deciding right away.

Generally, you can purchase an extended warranty any time during the period in which the manufacturer's warranty is in effect or, in some cases, shortly after buying the vehicle from a used-car dealer. An automaker's supplementary warranty is the best choice, but will likely cost about a third more than warranties sold by independents. And in some parts of the country, notably British Columbia, dealers have a quasi-monopoly on selling warranties with little competition from the independents.

Dealers love to sell extended warranties, whether you need them or not, because dealer markup represents up to 60 percent of the warranty's cost. Out of the remaining 40 percent comes the sponsor's administration costs and profit margin, calculated at another 15 percent. What's left to pay for repairs is a paltry 25 percent of the original amount. The only reason that automakers and independent warranty companies haven't been busted for this Ponzi scheme is that only half of the car buyers who purchase extended service contracts actually use them.

It's often difficult to collect on supplementary warranties, because independent companies frequently go out of business or limit the warranty's coverage through

**FUEL GAUGE DOES NOT READ
FULL AFTER FILLING TANK**
BULLETIN NO: 04-14-14

2002–05 Ford Taurus, Sable

ISSUE: Some 2002–05 Taurus/Sable vehicles may exhibit a fuel gauge which indicates the tank is only 7/8 full after filling the fuel tank. This may be due to the the calibration of the fuel level indication unit.

ACTION: To service, remove the fuel delivery module and replace the fuel level indication unit. DO NOT REPLACE THE ENTIRE FUEL DELIVERY MODULE FOR THIS CONDITION.

WARRANTY STATUS: Eligible under provisions of new vehicle limited warranty coverage and emissions warranty coverage.

OPERATION: 041414A

DESCRIPTION: Replace Fuel Gauge tank unit

TIME: 1.3hrs (includes time to remove tank, drain and refill)

Unfortunately, few owners will ever see bulletins like the one shown above, and most will end up paying for repairs that are really Ford's responsibility.

subsequent mailings. Both situations are covered by provincial laws. If the bankrupt warranty company's insurance policy won't cover your claim, take the dealer to small claims court and ask for the repair cost and the refund of the original warranty payment. Your argument for holding the dealer responsible is a simple one: By accepting a commission to act as an agent of the defunct company, the dealer took on the obligations of the company as well. As for limiting the coverage after you have bought the warranty policy, this is illegal, and it allows you to sue both the dealer and the warranty company for a refund of both the warranty and repair costs.

Emissions Control Warranties

These little-publicized warranties can save you big bucks if major engine or exhaust components fail prematurely. They come with all new vehicles and cover major components of the emissions control system for up to 8 years/130,000 km, no matter how many times the vehicle is sold. Unfortunately, although owner's manuals vaguely mention the emissions warranty, most don't specify which parts are covered. The U.S. Environmental Protection Agency has intervened on several occasions with hefty fines against Chrysler and Ford, and ruled that all major motor and fuel-system components are covered. These include fuel metering, ignition spark advance, restart, evaporative emissions, positive crankcase ventilation, engine electronics (computer modules), and catalytic converters, as well as hoses, clamps, brackets, pipes, gaskets, belts, seals, and connectors. Canada, however, has no government-defined list, and it's up to each manufacturer and the small claims courts to decide which components are covered.

Many of the confidential technical service bulletins listed in Part Three show parts failures that are covered under the emissions warranty, even though motorists are routinely charged for their replacement. The following example, applicable to Ford's 2002–05 Taurus and Sable, shows that the automaker will pay for fuel gauge repairs under the emissions warranty. Applying the same principles to other automakers' fuel gauges should be a breeze.

Make sure you get your emissions system checked out thoroughly by a dealer or an independent garage before the emissions warranty expires and before having the vehicle inspected by provincial emissions inspectors. In addition to ensuring you pass provincial tests, this precaution could save you up to $1,000 if both your catalytic converter and other emissions components are faulty.

The World of Secret Warranties

Few vehicle owners know that secret warranties exist. Automakers are reluctant to make these free repair programs public, because they feel that doing so would weaken confidence in their product and increase their legal liability. The closest they come to an admission is sending a "goodwill policy," "product improvement program," or "special policy" technical service bulletin (TSB) to dealers or first owners of record. Consequently, the only motorists who find out about these policies are the original owners who haven't changed their addresses or leased their vehicles. The other motorists who get compensated for repairs are the ones who read *Lemon-Aid* each year, staple TSBs to their work orders, and yell the loudest.

Remember, second owners and repairs done by independent garages are included in these secret warranty programs. Large, costly repairs, such as blown engines, burned transmissions, and peeling paint, are often covered. Even mundane little repairs, which can still cost you a hundred bucks or more, are frequently included in these programs.

If you have a TSB, but you're still refused compensation, keep in mind that secret warranties are an admission of manufacturing negligence. Try to compromise with a pro rata adjustment from the manufacturer. If polite negotiations fail, challenge the refusal in court on the grounds that you should not be penalized for failing to make a reimbursement claim under a secret warranty you never knew existed!

Here are a few examples of secret warranties that may save you thousands of dollars. More extensive listings are found in Part Three's model ratings.

Acura/Honda

1999–2003 Acura CL and TL; Honda Accord, Prelude, and Odyssey models

Problem: Defective automatic transmission and torque converter. **Warranty coverage:** This "goodwill" warranty extension was confirmed in the August 4, 2003, edition of Automotive News. Honda will fix or replace the transmission free of charge up to 7 years/160,000 km (100,000 mi.) whether owners bought their vehicle new or used. The company will also reimburse owners who already paid for the repair.

Audi, Chrysler, Mercedes-Benz, Saab, Toyota, and VW

1997–2004 Audi A4; 1999–2002 Chrysler models equipped with a 2.7L V6; 1998–2002 Mercedes-Benz; 1998–2003 Saab 9-3 and 9-5 models; 1997 through 2002 Toyota and Lexus vehicles with 2.2L 4-cylinder or 3.0L V6 engines; and 1997-2004 VW Passat

Problem: Engine sludge. **Warranty coverage:** Varies; usually 7–10 years/160,000 km. Automakers can't automatically deny this free repair because you don't have proof of all of your oil changes, unless they can show that the sludge was caused by a missed oil change (which, according to independent mechanics, is impossible to do). Remember, the warranty has been extended to fix a factory-related problem that occurs despite regular oil changes. That's why it's the automaker's responsibility.

Service bulletins, press releases, and dealer memos are all admissions of responsibility. From there, the legal doctrine of "the balance of probabilities" applies. To wit: Defect definitely causes engine sludge; a missed oil change may cause engine sludge. Therefore, it is more probable that the defect caused the sludge.

Once the sludge condition is diagnosed, the dealer and automobile manufacturer are jointly liable for all corrective repairs, plus additional damages for your inconvenience, loss of use or the cost of a "loaner" vehicle, and the cost to replace the oil. The automaker's owner notification letter may not have gone out to Canadian owners, since it is not required by any Canadian recall or by statute. If a letter goes out, it is usually sent only to first owners of record.

Some automakers say owners must use a more expensive special oil to prevent sludge. This after-sale stipulation is illegal, and can also provide owners with a reason to ask for damages, or even a refund, since it wasn't disclosed at the time of sale. All of the letter restrictions and decisions made by the dealer and the manufacturer can be easily appealed to the small claims court, where the sludge letter is powerful proof of the automaker's negligence.

Audi and VW

2001–03 cars equipped with 1.8L engines, including the Audi TT and A4; and the VW Golf/GTI, Jetta, New Beetle, and Passat. The companies also included the Passat W8 engine, all VWs equipped with the 2.8L VR6; as well as the Audi 3.0L V6 engine. In total, approximately 530,000 cars are affected by this action.

Problem: Defective ignition coils. When these coils fail, the vehicle suddenly stalls and won't start. **Warranty coverage:** VW will fix every single car by replacing the coils whether they are broken or not. There is no mileage or time limit on this warranty extension.

Chrysler

1995–99 models equipped with 4-cylinder engines

Problem: Faulty engine head gaskets will cause the engine to overheat, lose power, burn extra fuel, and possibly self-destruct. **Warranty coverage:** Without a court threat, Chrysler usually denies any problem or refund program exists. If you have the assistance of your dealer's service manager, expect an offer of 50 percent (about $1,500). File the case in small claims court and Chrysler will sweeten the offer by up to 75 percent.

Your small claims court filing likely won't go beyond the pretrial mediation stage; Chrysler reps are loath to defend engine head gasket cases in front of independent garage testimony. However, if you must go to court, arm yourself with the following consumer's court story.

> Phil, I sued DaimlerChrysler for $2,000 (the cost of repairs for the head gasket, and the resulting ruined cylinder head), and won…. Chrysler sent a letter refusing to reimburse me, after I sent the first request for goodwill warranty coverage (my car had 90,000 miles [144,000 km] when the head gasket blew). I filed the court case just against DaimlerChrysler (not including the used-car dealership where I bought the car—this was unintended, I just forgot to put them on the case too), and they let it go to court without contacting me and trying to offer a deal. The Chrysler district manager for my area, and the service manager from the dealership where I had the car serviced (not where I bought it) showed up to fight for Chrysler, and the only evidence they brought was a copy of my car's original warranty. Their argument was that there had been no recall on the part, my car was out of warranty, and thus they were not responsible for the costs.
>
> The district manager even said, "Yeah, some of the gaskets in these Neons have failed, but not all of them!"
>
> My argument was that this was a faulty product (evidenced by multiple websites discussing the matter); it had been redesigned because it was faulty (I included a copy of the TSB for the new head gasket); it failed in my car; ruined my head; and they were responsible for the cost of repairs. I discussed the secret warranty at length, and in my evidence included a copy of an invoice I printed off of *www.geocities.com/norman_neon*, which states "goodwill warranty assistance" covered the cost of repairs.
>
> I mentioned this part of my submitted evidence right after the Chrysler guy said, "There is no goodwill warranty on this part." It was all just great! Thanks for all your help….
>
> SINCERELY,
> T.W.

Chrysler, Ford, General Motors, and Asian Automakers

All years, all models

Problem: Faulty automatic transmissions that self-destruct, shift erratically, gear down to "limp mode," are slow to shift in or out of Reverse, or are noisy. **Warranty coverage:** If you have the assistance of your dealer's service manager, expect an offer of 50–75 percent (about $2,500). File the case in small claims court and a full refund will be offered up to 7 years/160,000 km. Acura, Honda, Hyundai, Lexus, and Toyota coverage varies between seven and eight years.

> I've just been told that I need my fourth transmission on my '96 Town & Country minivan, with 132,000 miles [212,000 km] on it. I've driven many cars well past that mileage with only *one* transmission. The dealer asked Chrysler, who said they would not help me. My appeals to Chrysler's customer service department yielded me the same result.... Chrysler split some of the costs with me on the previous rebuilt replacements.

All years, all models

Problem: Premature wearout of brake pads, calipers, and rotors. Produces excessive vibration, noise, and pulling to one side when braking. **Warranty coverage: Calipers and pads:** Goodwill settlements confirm that brake calipers and pads that fail to last 2 years/ 40,000 km will be replaced for 50 percent of the repair cost; components not lasting 1 year/20,000 km will be replaced for free. **Rotors:** If they last less than 3 years/ 60,000 km, they will be replaced at half price; replacement is free up to 2 years/ 40,000 km.

EXCESSIVE SULFUR DIOXIDE ODORS

BULLETIN NO: EG010-04   DATE: MAY 7, 2004

2004 RAV4

SYMPTOM/CONDITION: Some customers may complain of excessive sulfur dioxide odour under the following conditions:
^ Stop and go driving.
^ Heavy acceleration.
CORRECTIVE ACTION: In order to reduce the sulfur dioxide odor, a new catalytic converter has been developed.

All years, all models

Problem: A nauseating rotten-egg smell permeates the interior. **Warranty coverage:** At first owners are told they need a tune-up. Then they are told to change fuel and to wait a few months for the problem to correct itself. When this fails, the catalytic converter will likely be replaced and the power control module recalibrated. Toyota has been particularly hard hit by this stink (see bulletin left).

Chrysler, Ford, General Motors, and Honda

All years, all models

Problem: Faulty paint jobs that cause paint to turn white and peel off horizontal panels. **Warranty coverage:** Automakers will offer a free paint job or partial compensation up to 6 years/no mileage limitation. Thereafter, most manufacturers offer 50–75 percent refunds on the small claims court-house steps.

In *Maureen Frank v. General Motors of Canada Limited*, the Saskatchewan small claims court set a 15-year benchmark for paint finishes, and three other Canadian small claims judgments have extended the benchmark to seven years, to second owners, and to pickups.

In *Del Guidice v. Honda Canada Inc.*, Quebec Superior Court, August 2004, a class action petition is pending against Honda Canada for paint peeling on 1998–99 Hondas.

Chrysler, Ford, General Motors, and Hyundai

1994–2003 almost all Detroit models; 1998–99 Hyundai Accent

Problem: A serious engine defect from 1994 to 2003 caused by irrational price-cutting. These automakers have serious problems with poor-quality engine head gaskets and plastic intake manifolds failing at 60,000–100,000 km. The engine may overheat, lose power, burn extra fuel, and possibly self-destruct. Under the best of circumstances, the repair will take a day and cost about $800–$1,500. **Warranty coverage:** Without a court threat or a copy of a warranty extension or service bulletin, these companies usually deny any problem or refund program exists. If you have the assistance of your dealer's service manager, expect a 50 percent offer up to 5 years/100,000 km (about $1,000, if other parts are damaged). Later model Windstars will be covered up to 7 years/160,000 km if you threaten to cite the Dufour or Reid Windstar judgments (see pages 80–81).

No matter which automaker you are dealing with, filing your claim in small claims court always sweetens the company's settlement offer. Furthermore, you won't likely have to step inside a courtroom to get your refund, since most small claims court filings are settled at the pretrial mediation stage.

Eventually, the original free engine repair may have to be corrected again. Car owners are told they had one kick at the can and that's it, but once again, small claims court judges don't always see it that way. Courts have held that the company's first repair was an admission that the product was faulty; its correction must last a reasonable period of time or be redone.

Chrysler/Jeep

1989–93 Cherokee and Wagoneer; 1990–93 Dynasty, New Yorker, Fifth Avenue, and Imperial; 1991–92 Eagle Premier; 1991–93 minivans

Problem: ABS brakes that fail or malfunction. **Warranty coverage:** Piggybacking a service campaign onto a recall, Chrysler extended the warranty to 10 years/160,000 km on a number of costly ABS components. Owners will also be reimbursed for previous ABS repairs—not applicable to calipers, pads/shoe linings, or other maintenance items. Two other ABS components, piston seals (excessive wear) and the pump motor (deterioration), will be repaired free of charge at any time during the life of the vehicle.

Don't worry about the '93 cut-off date. This warranty extension is useful mainly as a benchmark under the implied warranty as to how long these components should last and how much you should pay on a pro-rated basis. Let's say you have a 1999 model with an ABS braking system that had a major failure of the above components in 2003. Since the system only lasted five years, instead of 10, you should ask for 50 percent off your bill.

> Hi Phil. I thought I should let you know that Chrysler sent me a cheque to cover the full cost of the repair of my ABS brakes. I appreciate your book providing the copy of Safety Recall 685 as it sure makes things a whole lot easier when you have a document like that to refer to.
>
> FRED K.

1993–99 Concorde, Intrepid, New Yorker, LHS, Vision, and Grand Cherokee

Problem: AC evaporator failure or malfunction. **Warranty coverage:** 7 years/115,000 km. Although this "goodwill" extension has expired, it sets a benchmark for what Chrysler considers the normal durability of its ACs.

ADDENDUM TO BASIC WARRANTY

The following applies to 1993 through 1997 New Yorker, LHS, Concorde, Intrepid, Vision and Grand Cherokee vehicles equipped with factory-installed air conditioning:

> *The Basic Warranty coverage for the air conditioner evaporator has been extended to 7 years or 115,000 kilometres, whichever occurs first, from the vehicle's warranty start date.*
>
> *This extended coverage applies to all owners of the vehicle. All of the other warranty terms apply to this extension.*

Sure, this warranty extension expired in the '90s, but the principle is the same for all model years: Chrysler said then that the benchmark for durability is at least seven years. Why would it be any less now?

Ford

1992–2004 Aerostar, Focus, Sable, Taurus, and Windstar

Problem: Defective front coil springs may suddenly break, puncturing the front tire and leading to loss of steering control; this is particularly troublesome with Focus (2000 model), Taurus, Sable, Aerostar, and Windstar. **Warranty coverage:** Under a "Safety Improvement Campaign" negotiated with NHTSA, Ford will replace *broken* coil springs at no charge up to 10 years/unlimited mileage. The company initially said that it wouldn't replace the springs until they have broken—if you were alive to submit a claim—but it relented when threatened with a lawsuit. 1997–98 models that are registered in rust-belt states and Canada have been recalled for the installation of a protective shield (called a spring catcher bracket in the Canadian recall) to prevent a broken spring from shredding the front tire.

1996–99 Taurus SHO

Problem: Frequent failures of engine cam sprockets, resulting in ruined engines. Because engines are so expensive and in short supply, this repair can cost you $8,000–$20,000. As more of these cars move into the 60,000 km+ mileage range, more will experience this failure. Estimates are that 5–10 percent of V8-equipped vehicles will be affected. Reasons for this defect, its cause, correction, internal bulletins, claims procedures, and class action filing are found on *www.v8sho.com/ SHO/96shohome.html*. **Warranty coverage:** Insiders tell me Ford will cover repairs when threatened with small claims suits on cars that haven't passed 7 years/160,000 km. Without the court threat, owners are offered 50 percent up to 100,000 km.

2000–01 Focus

Problem: Premature corrosion of the rear wheel bearings may cause the wheel to wobble. **Warranty coverage:** Under ONP #01B85, Ford said it would replace the rear wheel bearings at no charge until December 31, 2002, as long as you live right—that is, as long as you live in the right part of the country. This regional extended warranty is clearly illogical and Ford's cut-off date is arbitrary and unfair. Focus owners may ask for a pro rata refund from Ford or simply claim a complete refund in small claims court.

Ford/Lincoln

1996–2001 Crown Victoria and Lincoln Town Car fleet vehicles

Problem: Intake manifolds may crack at the coolant crossover, resulting in engine coolant leakage. **Warranty coverage:** ONP #01M02 will pay for the intake manifold's replacement up to seven years, regardless of mileage. Ford has refunded repair costs to non-fleet vehicles when threatened with small claims court action.

1998–2000 Crown Victoria and Lincoln Town Car fleet vehicles

Problem: Rear suspension upper control arm brackets may crack and allow the bracket to separate from the frame. This will cause a clunking noise and cause the rear suspension to feel loose. **Warranty coverage:** ONP #00B60 will pay for the crack repair and the installation of a reinforcement bracket. Affected owners who drive non-fleet cars should demand a refund, using small claims court action for leverage.

GM

1997–2003 Venture, Trans Sport/Montana, and Silhouette

Problem: Roof paint delamination and peeling; rust perforation. **Warranty coverage:** GM will replace, repair, or repaint the roof for free up to 6 years/100,000 km.

1998 Cavalier/Sunfire

Problem: Excessive oil consumption. **Warranty coverage:** Customer Satisfaction Campaign will cover the cost of eliminating the problem. Service bulletin number: 98017; Date of bulletin: 08/98; NHTSA Item Number: SB615103.

1999 Cavalier/Sunfire

Problem: Defective throttle valve cable produces erratic engine performance. **Warranty coverage:** Customer Satisfaction Campaign will cover the cost of replacing the throttle valve cable. Service bulletin number: 99039; Date of bulletin: 07/99; NHTSA Item Number: SB606219.

2001 Alero

Problem: Transmission bearing failure. **Warranty coverage:** Customer Satisfaction Campaign for 4T40-E transaxle converter bearing failure inspection/replacement. Service bulletin number: 01031; Date of bulletin: 04/01; NHTSA Item Number: SB619400.

2001 DeVille

Problem: Engine crankshaft pulley failure. **Warranty coverage:** Customer Satisfaction Campaign allows for a rebuilt crankshaft or engine replacement.

Service bulletin number: 01012; Date of bulletin: 02/01; NHTSA Item Number: SB619207.

Honda

1996–2000 Honda Civic and 1997–99 CR-V

Problem: Harsh-shifting automatic transmission and torque converter. **Warranty coverage:** Honda will fix or replace the transmission free of charge up to 7 years/160,000 km (100,000 mi.) under a "goodwill" program, whether owners bought their vehicle new or used.

1998–2003 Honda Accord, Odyssey, and Pilot models equipped with 6-cylinder engines

Problem: Defective aluminum engine block. **Warranty coverage:** Repair or replace engine under a "goodwill" program.

VW

1998–2002 New Beetles and 1999–2002 Golfs, GTIs, and Jettas. 850,000 vehicles are affected

Problem: If window clamp malfunctions, it prevents the window from being raised or lowered. **Warranty coverage:** The new clamp and the work to install it will be free of charge under this special warranty.

Recall Repairs

Vehicles are recalled for one of two reasons: They are either potentially unsafe, or they don't conform to federal pollution control regulations. Whatever the reason, recalls are a great way to get free repairs—if you know which ones apply to you, and you have the patience of Job.

Almost a half-billion unsafe vehicles have been recalled by automakers for the free correction of safety-related defects since American recall legislation was passed in 1966 (a weaker Canadian law was enacted in 1971). During that time, about one-third of the recalled vehicles never made it back to the dealership for repairs; owners were never informed, they just didn't consider the defect that hazardous, or they gave up waiting for corrective parts.

Subsequent American legislation targets automakers who drag their feet in making recall repairs. Owners on both sides of the border may wish to cite the following NHTSA guidelines for support:

Dealer Recall Responsibility (U.S. States, Territories, and Possessions)

The U.S. National Traffic and Motor Vehicle Safety Act provides that each vehicle that is subject to a recall must be adequately repaired within a reasonable time after the customer has tendered it for repair. A failure to repair within 60 days after tender of a vehicle is *prima facie* evidence of failure to repair within a reasonable time.

If the condition is not adequately repaired within a reasonable time, the customer may be entitled to an identical or reasonably equivalent vehicle at no charge or to a refund of the purchase price less a reasonable allowance for depreciation. To avoid having to provide these burdensome remedies, every effort must be made to promptly schedule an appointment with each customer and to repair their vehicle as soon as possible. In the recall notification letters, customers are told how to contact the U.S. National Highway Traffic Safety Administration if the recall is not completed within a reasonable time (....)

Incidentally, the above NHTSA guidelines were part of a service bulletin sent by GM to its dealers, outlining an 11-year special warranty and recall on its 1994–2000 trucks with faulty 6.5L fuel injection pumps (Bulletin #00064C; September 2002).

If you've changed your address or bought a used vehicle, it's smart to pay a visit to your local dealer, give him your address, and get a "report card" on which recalls, free-service campaigns, and warranties apply to your vehicle. Simply give the service advisor your Vehicle Identification Number (VIN)—found on the dash just below the windshield on the driver's side, or on your insurance card—and have the number run through the automaker's computer system. Ask for a computer printout of the vehicle's history (or have one faxed to you), and make sure you're listed in the automaker's computer as the new owner. This ensures that you'll receive notices of warranty extensions and emissions and safety recalls.

Still, don't expect to be welcomed with open arms when your vehicle develops a safety- or emissions-related problem that's not yet part of a recall campaign. Automakers and dealers generally take a restrictive view of what constitutes a safety or emissions defect, and frequently charge for repairs that should be free under federal safety or emissions legislation. To counter this tendency, look at the following list of typical defects that are clearly safety-related. If you experience any of these, insist that the automaker fix the problem at no expense to you, and that it cover the cost of a car rental:

- airbag malfunctions
- corrosion affecting safe operation
- disconnected or stuck accelerators
- electrical shorts
- faulty windshield wipers
- fuel leaks

- problems with original axles, drive shafts, seats, seat recliners, or defrosters
- seatbelt problems
- stalling or sudden acceleration
- sudden steering or brake loss
- suspension failures
- trailer coupling failures

In the U.S., recall campaigns force automakers to pay the entire cost of fixing a vehicle's safety-related defect for any vehicle purchased up to eight years before the recall's announcement. Getting automakers to cover the costs within a reasonable period beyond that time is usually a slam dunk in small claims court. Recalls may be voluntary or ordered by the U.S. Department of Transportation, and can be nationwide or regional. In Canada, all recalls are considered voluntary. Transport Canada can order automakers only to notify owners that their vehicles may be unsafe; it can't force them to correct the problem. Fortunately, most U.S.-ordered recalls are carried out in Canada as well, and when Transport Canada makes a defect determination on its own, automakers generally respond with an owner notification letter and a recall campaign.

Safety Defect Information

If you wish to report a safety defect or want recall info, you may access Transport Canada's website at *www.tc.gc.ca/roadsafety/recalls/search_e.asp*, but it's not very effective.

Unlike the U.S. government's NHTSA website, owner complaints aren't listed, defect investigations aren't disclosed, voluntary warranty extensions (secret warranties) aren't shown, and service bulletin summaries aren't provided. If you aren't Internet-proficient, call Transport Canada at 1-800-333-0510 (toll-free within Canada) or 613-993-9851 (within the Ottawa region or outside Canada) to get additional information.

NHTSA's website is much more comprehensive and easier to use. You can search the database for your vehicle or tires at *www.nhtsa.dot.gov/cars/problems*. It accesses four important database categories applicable to your vehicle and model year: the latest recalls, current and closed safety investigations, defects reported by other owners, and a brief summary of manufacturers' service bulletins. NHTSA's fax-back service provides the same info through a local line that can be accessed from Canada, although long-distance charges will apply (most calls take five to 10 minutes to complete). The following local numbers get you into the automatic response service quickly, and can be reached 24 hours a day: 202-366-0123; 202-366-7800 for the hearing impaired.

If your car has an airbag, it's probably spying on you.

Event data recorders (EDRs) are the size of a VCR tape and, since the early 1990s, have been hidden under the seat or in the centre consoles of about 25 million airbag-equipped Ford and GM vehicles sold in North America. Presently, about 20 percent of all domestic and imported cars carry them.

The data recorders operate in a similar fashion to flight data recorders used in airplanes: They record data during the last five seconds before impact, including the force of the collision, the airbag's performance, when the brakes were applied, engine and vehicle speed, gas pedal position, and whether the driver was wearing a seat belt.

Along with invading the privacy of customers by secretly hiding recorders in their vehicles, Ford and GM have systematically hidden their collected data from U.S. and Canadian vehicle safety researchers, who are investigating thousands of complaints relating to airbags that don't deploy when they should (or deploy when they shouldn't), and anti-lock brakes that don't brake.

This refusal to voluntarily share data with customers and researchers is unfortunate, because the recorders are collecting critical information that could lead to better-functioning safety devices. Experts say that highway safety could be vastly improved if black boxes that record information about car crashes were installed in all cars, just as similar devices are placed in all airplanes. To find out if your car or truck carries an EDR, go to: *www.cbc.ca/consumers/market/files/cars/blackboxes*.

Fortunately, it has become impossible for automakers to hide recorder data now that Vitronix Corporation sells a $2,500 (U.S.) portable download device that

accesses the data and stores it on any PC. It's presently marketed to accident reconstructionists, safety researchers, law enforcement agencies, and insurance companies. Furthermore, litigants can subpoena the info through an automaker's dealer if the data is needed in court. Car owners who wish to dispute criminal charges, oppose their insurer's decision, or hold an automaker responsible for a safety device's failure (airbags, seat belts, or brakes) will find this data invaluable.

Safety benefits

Enthusiastically promoted by government and law enforcement agencies around the world, these data recorders have actually had a positive effect in accident prevention: A 1992 study by the European Union cited by the Canada Safety Council found that EDRs reduced the collision rate by 28 percent and costs by 40 percent in police fleets where drivers knew that they were being monitored.

The recorders are also sending dangerous drivers to jail, helping accident victims reap huge court awards, and prompting automaker recalls of unsafe vehicles. In January 2004, South Dakota Congressman Bill Janklow was convicted of manslaughter for speeding through a stop sign—his EDR readout proved he was driving faster than the speed limit, but slower than police estimated. In October 2003, Montreal police won their first dangerous driving conviction using EDR data (*R. v. Gauthier*, (2003-05-27) QCCQ 500-01-013375-016, *www.canlii.org/qc/jug/qccq/2003/2003qccq17860.html*). In June 2003, Edwin Matos of Pembroke Pines, Florida, was sentenced to 30 years in prison for killing two teenage girls after crashing into their car at more than 160 km/h (100 mph). He was convicted on the strength of the recorder's speed data. Two months earlier, an Illinois police officer received a $10 million (U.S.) settlement after data showed that the driver of a hearse, who was supposedly unconscious from a diabetes attack, actually accelerated and braked in the moments before slamming into the officer's patrol car. In July 2002, New Brunswick prosecutors sent a dangerous driver to jail for two years based on his car's EDR data. (*R. v. Daley*, 2003 NBQB 20 Docket(s): S/CR/7/02, *www.canlii.org/nb/cas/nbqb/2002/2003nbqb20.html*). GM was forced to recall more than 850,000 Cavaliers and Sunfires when its own data recorders showed that the cars' airbags often deployed inadvertently. Incidentally, California is the only jurisdiction where EDR data cannot be downloaded unless the car owner agrees or a court order is issued.

As reported by the National Motorists Association at *www.motorists.org/issues/edrs/mainegovernor.html*, the reliability of EDT data is also increasingly under fire. In a recent high profile case, Maine Governor John Baldacci disputed the data that said that his state-owned and state-trooper-driven Suburban was exceeding the speed limit prior to going out of control and injuring two occupants.

EDR data showed that the SUV was traveling at 114.3 km/h (71 mph) about five seconds before its airbags deployed. The driver of a passing car told investigators that his speedometer showed 88.5 km/h (55 mph). A state police accident reconstruction expert estimated the SUV's speed at somewhere between 88.5 and 104.6 km/h (55 and 65 mph). Additionally, the EDR data showed seatbelts were not buckled, an allegation denied by the Suburban's occupants. Maine police have declined to press charges based on what they now call "conflicting evidence."

Traffic accident reconstructionists Harris Technical Services have prepared a chronological list of dozens of Canadian and American prosecutions related to automotive EDRs, which is available at *www.harristechnical.com*.

Three Steps to a Settlement

Step 1: Informal Negotiations

You can phone the seller or automaker, but don't expect to get much out of the call. Private sellers won't want to talk with you, and dealer customer service agents will tell you the vehicle was sold "as is." They simply apply the dealership's policy, knowing that 90 percent of complainers will drop their claims after venting their anger.

Still, try to work things out by contacting someone higher up who can change the policy to satisfy your request. In your attempt to reach a settlement, ask only for what is fair, and don't try to make anyone look bad.

Speak in a calm, polite manner, and try to avoid polarizing the issue. Talk about cooperating to solve the problem. Let a compromise emerge—don't come in with a hardline set of demands. Don't insist on getting the settlement offer in writing, but make sure that you're accompanied by a friend or relative who can confirm the offer in court if it isn't honoured. Be prepared to act upon the offer without delay so your hesitancy won't be blamed if the seller or automaker withdraws it.

Service manager help

Service managers have more power than you may realize. They make the first determination of what work is covered under warranty or through post-warranty "goodwill" programs, and they are directly responsible to the dealer and manufacturer for that decision (dealers hate manufacturer audits that force them to pay back questionable warranty decisions). Service managers are paid both to save the dealer and automaker money, and to mollify irate clients—almost an impossible balancing act. Nevertheless, when a service manager agrees to extend warranty coverage, it's because you've raised solid issues that neither the dealer nor the automaker can ignore. All the more reason to present your argument in a confident, forthright manner, with your vehicle's service history and Lemon-Aid's "How Long Should a Part or Repair Last?" table on hand. Also bring as many technical service bulletins and owner complaint printouts as you can find from NHTSA's website and similar sources. It's not important that they apply directly to your problem; they establish parameters for giving out after-warranty assistance or "goodwill."

Don't use your salesperson as a runner, since the sales staff are generally quite distant from the service staff and usually have less pull than you do. If the service manager can't or won't set things right, your next step is to convene a mini-summit with the service manager, the dealership principal, and the automaker's rep. By getting the automaker involved, you run less risk of having the dealer fob you off on the manufacturer, and you can often get an agreement where the seller and the automaker pay two-thirds of the repair cost.

Independent dealers and dealers who sell a brand of vehicle used that they don't sell new will give you less latitude. You have to make the case that the vehicle's defects were present at the time of purchase, or should have been apparent to the seller, or that the vehicle doesn't conform to the representations made when it was purchased. Emphasize that you intend to use the courts if necessary to obtain a refund—most independent sellers would rather settle than risk a lawsuit with all the attendant publicity. An independent estimate of the vehicle's defects and cost of repairs is essential if you want to convince the seller that you're serious in your claim and that you stand a good chance of winning your case in court. Come prepared with an estimated cost of repairs to challenge the dealer who agrees to pay half the repair costs and then jacks up the price 100 percent so that you wind up paying the whole shot.

Step 2: Sending a Registered Letter, Fax, or Email

The pen is mightier...

If you haven't sent a written claim letter, fax, or email, you really haven't complained—or at least, that's the auto industry's mindset. If your vehicle was misrepresented, has major defects, or wasn't properly repaired under warranty, the first thing you should do is give the seller a written summary of the outstanding problems, and stipulate a time period within which the seller can fix the vehicle or refund your money. Follow the format of the sample complaint letters prepared for you in this section.

Remember, you can ask for compensation for repairs that have been done or need to be done, insurance costs while the vehicle is being repaired, towing charges, supplementary transportation costs like taxis and rented cars, and damages for inconvenience. If no satisfactory offer is made, ask for mediation, arbitration, or a formal hearing in your provincial small claims court. Make the manufacturer a party to the lawsuit, especially if the emissions warranty, a secret warranty extension, a safety-recall campaign, or extensive chassis rusting is involved.

Step 3: Mediation and Arbitration

If the formality of a courtroom puts you off, or you're not sure that your claim is all that solid and don't want to pay legal costs to find out, consider using mediation or arbitration. These services are sponsored by the Better Business Bureau, Automobile Protection Association, the Canadian Automobile Association, and by many small claims courts where compulsory mediation is a prerequisite to going to trial.

Getting Outside Help

Don't lose your case because of poor preparation. Ask government or independent consumer protection agencies to evaluate how well you've prepared before going to your first hearing. Also, use the Internet to ferret out additional facts and gather support (*www.lemonaidcars.com* is a good place to start).

Invest in Protest

You can put additional pressure on a seller or garage, and have fun at the same time, by putting a lemon sign on your car and parking it in front of the dealer or garage, by creating a "lemon" website, or by forming a self-help group.

Use your website to gather data from others who may have experienced a problem similar to your own. As with placing a newspaper ad, this can help you set the foundation for a meeting with the automaker, or even a class action, and it pressures the dealer or manufacturer to settle. Websites are often the subjects of news stories, so yours may be picked up by the media.

Some more advice from this consumer advocate with hundreds of pickets and mass demonstrations under his belt over the past 33 years: Keep a sense of humour, and never break off negotiations.

Finally, don't be scared off by threats that it's illegal to criticize a product or company. Unions, environmentalists, and consumer groups do it regularly (it's called informational picketing), and the Supreme Court of Canada in *R. v. Guinard* reaffirmed this right in February 2002. In that judgment, an insured posted a sign on his barn claiming the Commerce Insurance Company was unfairly refusing his claim. The municipality of Ste-Hyacinthe told him to take the sign down. He refused, maintaining that he had the right to state his opinion. The Supreme Court agreed.

This judgment means that consumer protests, signs, and websites that criticize the actions of corporations or government cannot be shut up or taken down simply because they say unpleasant things. However, what you say must be true, and your intent must be to inform, without malice.

Sample Claim Strategies

Sudden acceleration, chronic stalling, and ABS and airbag failures

Incidents of sudden acceleration or chronic stalling are quite common. However, they are very difficult to diagnose and individual cases can be treated very differently by federal safety agencies. Sudden acceleration is considered to be a safety-related problem—stalling isn't. Never mind that a vehicle's sudden loss of power on a busy highway puts everyone's lives at risk (as is the case with 2001–03 VW and Audi ignition coil failures). The same problem exists with engine and transmission powertrain failures, which are only occasionally considered to be safety-related. ABS and airbag failures are universally considered to be life-threatening defects. If your vehicle manifests any of these conditions, here's what you need to do:

1. Get independent witnesses to confirm that the problem exists. This includes verification by an independent mechanic, passenger accounts, downloaded data from your vehicle's data recorder, and lots of Internet browsing using *www.lemonaidcars.com* and Google's search engine as your primary tools. Notify the dealer or manufacturer by fax, email, or registered letter that you consider the problem to be a factory-induced, safety-related defect. Make sure you address your correspondence to the manufacturer's product liability or legal affairs department. At the dealership's service bay, make sure that every work order clearly states the problem, as well as the number of previous attempts to fix it. (You should end up with a few complaint letters and a handful of work orders confirming that this is an ongoing deficiency.) If the dealer won't give you a copy of the work order because the work is a warranty claim, ask for a copy of the order number "in case your estate wishes to file a claim, pursuant to an accident." (This will get the service manager's attention.) Leaving a paper trail is crucial for any claim you may have later on, because it shows your concern and persistence, and clearly indicates that the dealer and manufacturer had ample time to correct the defect.

2. Note on the work order that you expect the problem to be diagnosed and corrected under the emissions warranty or a "goodwill" program. It also wouldn't hurt to add the phrase on the work order or in your claim letters that any deaths, injuries, or damage caused by the defect will be the dealer's and manufacturer's responsibility since this work order (or letter, fax, or email) constitutes you putting them on "formal notice."

3. If the dealer does the necessary repairs at little or no cost to you, send a follow-up confirmation that you appreciate the assistance. Also, emphasize that you'll be back if the problem reappears, even if the warranty has expired, because the repair renews your warranty rights applicable to that defect. In other words, the warranty clock is set back to its original position. You won't likely get a copy of the repair bill, because dealers don't like to admit that there was a serious defect present. Keep in mind, however, that you can get your complete vehicle file from the dealer and manufacturer by issuing a subpoena, which costs about $50, if the case goes to small claims or a higher court. This request has produced many out-of-court settlements when the internal documents show extensive work was carried out to correct the problem.

4. If the problem persists, send a letter, fax, or email to the dealer and manufacturer saying so, look for ALLDATA service bulletins to confirm that your vehicle's defects are factory related, and call Transport Canada or NHTSA, or log onto NHTSA's website to report the failure. Also, call the Nader-founded Center for Auto Safety in Washington, D.C. (Tel: 202-328-7700) for

a lawyer referral and an information sheet covering the problem. For tire complaints, also notify researchers at the Strategic Safety website at *www. strategicsafety.com*.

5. Now come two crucial questions: Should you repair the defect now or later, and should you use the dealer or an independent? Generally, it's smart to use an independent garage if you know the dealer isn't pushing for free corrective repairs from the manufacturer, if weeks or months have passed without any resolution of your claim, if the dealer keeps claiming that it's a maintenance item, or if you know an independent mechanic who will give you a detailed work order showing the defect is factory related and not a result of poor maintenance. Don't mention that a court case may ensue, since this will scare the dickens out of your only independent witness. A bonus of using an independent garage is that the repair charges will be about half of what a dealer would demand. Incidentally, if the automaker later denies warranty "goodwill" because you used an independent repairer, use the argument that the defect's safety implications required emergency repairs, to be carried out by whoever could see you first.

6. Dashboard-mounted warning lights usually come on prior to airbags suddenly deploying, ABS brakes failing, or engine glitches causing the vehicle to stall out. (Sudden acceleration usually occurs without warning.) Automakers consider these lights to be critical safety warnings and generally advise drivers to immediately have the vehicle serviced to correct the problem (advice that can be found in the owner's manual) when any of the above lights come on. This bolsters the argument that your life was threatened, emergency repairs were required, and your request for another vehicle or a complete refund isn't out of line.

7. Sudden acceleration can have multiple causes, isn't easy to duplicate, and is often blamed on the driver mistaking the accelerator for the brakes or failing to perform proper maintenance. Yet NHTSA data shows that factory-related defects are often the culprit. For example, 1997–2004 Lexus ES 300/330 and Toyota Camrys may have a faulty transmission that may cause engine surging. So how do you satisfy the burden of proof showing that the problem exists and is the automaker's responsibility? Use the legal doctrine called "the balance of probabilities" by eliminating all of the possible dodges the dealer or manufacturer may employ. Show that proper maintenance has been carried out, that you're a safe driver, and that the incident occurs frequently and without warning.

8. If any of the above defects causes an accident, the airbag fails to deploy, or you're injured by its deployment, ask your insurance company to have the vehicle towed to a neutral location and clearly state that neither the dealer nor the automaker should touch the vehicle until your insurance company and Transport Canada have completed their investigation. Also, get as many witnesses as possible and immediately go to the hospital for a check-up, even if you're feeling okay. You may be injured and not know it because the adrenalin coursing through your veins is masking your injuries. A hospital exam

will easily confirm that your injuries are accident related, which is essential in court or for future settlement negotiations.

9. Peruse NHTSA's online accident database to find reports of other accidents caused by the same failure.

10. Don't let your insurance company settle the case if you're sure the accident was caused by a mechanical failure. Even if an engineering analysis fails to directly implicate the manufacturer or dealer, you can always plead the aforementioned balance of probabilities. If the insurance company settles, your insurance premiums will probably be increased.

Paint and Body Defects

The following settlement advice applies mainly to paint defects, but you can use these tips for any other vehicle defect that you believe is the automaker's or dealer's responsibility. If you're not sure whether the problem is a factory-related deficiency or a maintenance item, have it checked out by an independent garage or get a technical service bulletin summary for your vehicle. The summary may include specific bulletins relating to the diagnosis, correction, and ordering of upgraded parts needed to fix your problem.

1. If you know that your vehicle's paint problem is factory related, take your vehicle to the dealer and ask for a written, signed estimate. When you're handed the estimate, ask if the paint job can be covered by some "goodwill" assistance. (Ford's euphemism for this secret warranty is "Owner Notification Program" or "Owner Dialogue Program," GM's term is "Special Policy," and Chrysler simply calls it an "Owner Satisfaction Notice." Don't use the term "secret warranty" yet; you'll just make everyone angry and evasive.)

2. Your request will probably be met with a refusal, an offer to repaint the vehicle for half the cost, or (if you're lucky) an agreement to repaint the vehicle free of charge. If you accept half-cost, make sure that it's based on the original estimate you have in hand, since some dealers jack up their estimates so that your 50 percent is really 100 percent of the true cost.

3. If the dealer or automaker has already refused your claim and the repair hasn't been done yet, get an additional estimate from an independent garage that shows the problem is factory related.

4. If the repair has yet to be done, mail or fax a registered claim to the automaker (and send a copy to the dealer), claiming the average of both estimates. If the repair has been done at your expense, mail or fax a registered claim with a copy of your bill.

5. If you don't receive a satisfactory response within a week, deposit a copy of the estimate or paid bill and claim letter/fax before the small claims court and await a trial date. This means that the automaker/dealer will have to appear, no lawyer is required, and costs should be minimal (under $100). Usually, an informal pretrial mediation hearing with the two parties and a court clerk will be scheduled in a few months, followed by a trial a few weeks later (the time varies among different regions). Most cases are settled at the mediation stage.

You can help your case by collecting photographs, maintenance work orders, previous work orders dealing with your problem, and technical service bulletins, and by speaking to an independent expert (the garage or body shop that did the estimate or repair is best, but you can also use a local teacher who teaches automotive repair). Remember, service bulletins can be helpful, but they aren't critical to a successful claim.

Other Situations

- If the vehicle has just been repainted but the dealer says that "goodwill" coverage was denied by the automaker, pay for the repair with a certified cheque and write "under protest" on the cheque. Remember, though, if the dealer does the repair, you won't have an independent expert who can affirm that the problem was factory related or that it was a result of premature wearout. Plus, the dealer can say that you or the environment caused the paint problem. In these cases, technical service bulletins can make or break your case.
- If the dealer or automaker offers a partial repair or refund, take it. Then sue for the rest. Remember, if a partial repair has been done under warranty, it counts as an admission of responsibility, no matter what "goodwill" euphemism is used. Also, the repaired component or body panel should be just as durable as if it were new. Hence, the clock starts ticking from the time of the repair until you reach the original warranty parameter—again, no matter what the dealer's repair warranty limit says.

Very seldom do automakers contest these paint claims before small claims court, instead opting to settle once the court claim is bounced from their customer relations people to their legal affairs department. At that time, you'll probably be offered an out-of-court settlement for 50 to 75 percent of your claim.

Stand fast and make reference to the service bulletins you intend to subpoena in order to publicly contest in court the unfair nature of this "secret warranty" program. (Automaker lawyers cringe at the idea of trying to explain why consumers aren't made aware of these bulletins.) One hundred percent restitution will probably follow.

Three good examples of favourable paint judgments are *Shields v. General Motors of Canada, Bentley v. Dave Wheaton Pontiac Buick GMC Ltd. and General Motors of Canada,* and the most recent, *Maureen Frank v. General Motors of Canada Limited.*

Shields v. General Motors of Canada, No. 1398/96, Ontario Court (General Division), Oshawa Small Claims Court, 33 King Street West, Oshawa, Ontario L1H 1A1, July 24, 1997, Robert Zochodne, Deputy Judge. The owner of a 1991 Pontiac Grand Prix purchased the vehicle used with over 100,000 km on its odometer. Beginning in 1995, the paint began to bubble and flake, and eventually peeled off. Deputy Judge Robert Zochodne awarded the plaintiff $1,205.72 and struck down every one of GM's environmental/acid rain/UV rays arguments. Other important aspects of this 12-page judgment that GM did not appeal:

1. The judge admitted many of the technical service bulletins referred to in *Lemon-Aid* as proof of GM's negligence.
2. Although the vehicle had 156,000 km when the case went to court, GM still offered to pay 50 percent of the paint repairs if the plaintiff dropped his suit.
3. Deputy Judge Zochodne ruled that the failure to protect the paint from the damaging effects of UV rays is akin to engineering a car that won't start in cold weather. In essence, vehicles must be built to withstand the rigours of the environment.
4. Here's an interesting twist: The original warranty covered defects that were present at the time it was in effect. The judge, taking statements found in the GM technical service bulletins, ruled that the UV problem was factory related, existed during the warranty period, and represented a latent defect that appeared once the warranty expired.
5. The subsequent purchaser was not prevented from making the warranty claim, even though the warranty had long since expired from a time and mileage standpoint and he was the second owner.

Bentley v. Dave Wheaton Pontiac Buick GMC Ltd. and General Motors of Canada, Victoria Registry No. 24779, British Columbia Small Claims Court, December 1, 1998, Judge Higinbotham. This small claims judgment builds upon the *Ontario Shields v. General Motors of Canada* decision and cites other jurisprudence as to how long paint should last on a car. If you're wondering why Ford and Chrysler haven't been hit by similar judgments, remember that they usually settle out of court.

Maureen Frank v. General Motors of Canada Limited, No. SC#12 (2001), Saskatchewan Provincial Court, Saskatoon, Saskatchewan, October 17, 2001, Provincial Court Judge H.G. Dirauf.

> On June 23, 1997, the Plaintiff bought a 1996 Chevrolet Corsica from a General Motors dealership. At the time the odometer showed 33,172 km. The vehicle still had some factory warranty. The car had been a lease car and had no previous accidents.
>
> During June of 2000, the Plaintiff noticed that some of the paint was peeling off from the car and she took it to a General Motors dealership in Saskatoon and to the General Motors dealership in North Battleford where she purchased the car. While there were

some discussions with the GM dealership about the peeling paint, nothing came of it and the Plaintiff now brings this action claiming the cost of a new paint job.

During 1999, the Plaintiff was involved in a minor collision causing damage to the left rear door. This damage was repaired. During this repair some scratches to the left front door previously done by vandals were also repaired.

The Plaintiff's witness, Frank Nemeth, is a qualified auto body repairman with some 26 years of experience. He testified that the peeling paint was a factory defect and that it was necessary to completely strip the car and repaint it. He diagnosed the cause of the peeling paint as a separation of the primer surface or colour coat from the electrocoat primer. In his opinion no primer surfacer was applied at all. He testified that once the peeling starts, it will continue. He has seen this problem on General Motors vehicles. The defect is called delamination.

Mr. Nemeth stated that a paint job should last at least 10 years. In my opinion most people in Saskatchewan grow up with cars and are familiar with cars. I think it is common knowledge that the original paint on cars normally lasts in excess of 15 years and that rust becomes a problem before the paint fails. In any event, paint peeling off, as it did on the Plaintiff's vehicle, is not common. I find that the paint on a new car put on by the factory should last at least 15 years.

It is clear from the evidence of Frank Nemeth (independent body shop manager) that the delamination is a factory defect. His evidence was not seriously challenged. I find that the factory paint should not suffer a delamination defect for at least 15 years and that this factory defect breached the warranty that the paint was of acceptable quality and was durable for a reasonable period of time.

There will be judgment for the Plaintiff in the amount of $3,412.38 plus costs of $81.29.

Some of the important aspects of the *Frank* judgment are:

1. The judge accepted that the automaker was responsible, even though the car had been bought used. The subsequent purchaser was not prevented from making the warranty claim, even though the warranty had long since expired from a time and mileage standpoint and she was the second owner.
2. The judge stressed that the provincial warranty can kick in any time the automaker's warranty has expired or isn't applied.
3. By awarding full compensation to the plaintiff, the judge didn't feel that there was a significant "betterment" or improvement added to the car that would warrant reducing the amount of the award.
4. The judge decided that the paint delamination was a factory defect.
5. The judge also concluded that without this factory defect, a paint job should last up to 15 years.

6. GM offered to pay $700 of the paint repairs if the plaintiff dropped the suit; the judge awarded five times that amount.
7. Maureen Frank won this case despite having to confront GM lawyer Ken Ready, who had argued other paint cases for GM and Chrysler.

Other paint/rust cases

Martin v. Honda Canada Inc., March 17, 1986, Ontario Small Claims Court (Scarborough), Judge Sigurdson. The original owner of a 1981 Honda Civic sought compensation for the premature "bubbling, pitting, cracking of the paint and rusting of the Civic after five years of ownership." Judge Sigurdson agreed and ordered Honda to pay the owner $1,163.95.

Thauberger v. Simon Fraser Sales and Mazda Motors, 3 B.C.L.R., 193. This Mazda owner sued for damages caused by the premature rusting of his 1977 Mazda GLC. The court awarded him $1,000. Thauberger had previously sued General Motors for a prematurely rusted Blazer truck and was also awarded $1,000 in the same court. Both judges ruled that the defects could not be excluded from the automaker's expressed warranty or from the implied warranty granted by ss. 20 and 20(b) of the B.C. Sale of Goods Act.

Whittaker v. Ford Motor Company (1979), 24 O.R. (2d), 344. A new Ford developed serious corrosion problems in spite of having been rustproofed by the dealer. The court ruled that the dealer, not Ford, was liable for the damage for having sold the rustproofing product at the time of purchase. This is an important judgment to use when a rustproofer or paint protector goes out of business or refuses to pay a claim, since the decision holds the dealer jointly responsible.

See also:

- *Danson v. Chateau Ford (1976) C.P.*, Quebec Small Claims Court, No. 32-00001898-757, Judge Lande
- *Doyle v. Vital Automotive Systems*, May 16, 1977, Ontario Small Claims Court (Toronto), Judge Turner
- *Lacroix v. Ford*, April 1980, Ontario Small Claims Court (Toronto), Judge Tierney
- *Marinovich v. Riverside Chrysler*, April 1, 1987, District Court of Ontario, No. 1030/85, Judge Stortini

Using the Courts

Sue as a Last Resort

If the seller you've been negotiating with agrees to make things right, give him or her a deadline and then have an independent garage check the repairs. If no offer is made within 10 working days, file suit in court. Make the manufacturer a party to the lawsuit only if the original, unexpired warranty was transferred to you; your claim falls under the emissions warranty, a TSB, a secret warranty extension, or a safety recall campaign; or there is extensive chassis rusting due to poor engineering.

Choosing the Right Court

You must decide what remedy to pursue; that is, whether you want a partial refund or a cancellation of the sale. To determine the refund amount, add the estimated cost of repairing existing mechanical defects to the cost of prior repairs. Don't exaggerate your losses or claim for repairs that are considered routine maintenance. A suit for cancellation of sale involves practical problems. The court requires that the vehicle be "tendered," or taken back to the seller at the time the lawsuit is filed. This means that you are without transportation for as long as the case continues, unless you purchase another vehicle in the interim. If you lose the case, you must then take back the old vehicle and pay storage fees. You could go from having no vehicle to having two, one of which is a clunker.

Generally, if the cost of repairs or the sales contract amount falls within the small claims court limit (discussed later), file the case there to keep costs to a minimum and to get a speedy hearing. Small claims court judgments aren't easily appealed, lawyers aren't necessary, filing fees are minimal (about $125), and cases are usually heard within a few months.

Watch what you ask for. If you claim more than the small claims court limit, you'll have to go to a higher court—where costs quickly add up and delays of a few years or more are commonplace.

Small Claims Courts

Crooked automakers scurry away from small claims courts like cockroaches from bug spray, not because the courts can issue million-dollar judgments or force litigants to spend millions in legal fees (they can't), but because they can award sizeable sums to small plaintiffs and make jurisprudence that other judges on the same bench are likely to follow.

For example, in *Dawe v. Courtesy Chrysler* (Dartmouth Nova Scotia Small Claims Court SCCH #206825, July 30, 2004) Judge Patrick L Casey, Q.C., rendered an impressive 21-page decision citing key automobile product liability cases over the past 80 years. He awarded $5,037 to the owner of a new 2001 Cummins-equipped Ram pickup that wandered all over the road; lost power, or jerked and bucked; shifted erratically; lost braking ability; bottomed out when passing over bumps; allowed water to leak into the cab; produced a burnt-wire and oil smell in the interior as the lights would dim; and produced a rear-end whine and wind noise around the doors and under the dash. Dawe had sold the vehicle and reduced his claim to meet the small claims threshold.

Interestingly, small claims court is quickly becoming a misnomer now that Alberta allows claims of up to $25,000 and most other provinces permit $10,000 claims.

There are small claims courts in most counties of every province, and you can either make a claim in the county where the problem happened, or in the county where the defendant lives and conducts business. Simply go to the small claims court office and ask for a claim form. Instructions on how to fill it out accompany the form. Remember, you must identify the defendant correctly, and this may require some help from the court clerk (look for other recent lawsuits naming the same party). Crooks often change their company's name to escape liability; for example, it would be impossible to sue Joe's Garage (1999) if your contract is with Joe's Garage Inc. (1984).

At this point, it wouldn't hurt to hire a lawyer or a paralegal for a brief walk-through of small claims procedures to ensure that you've prepared your case properly and that you know what objections will likely be raised by the other side. If you'd like a lawyer to do all the work for you, there are a number of law firms around the country that specialize in small claims litigation. Small claims doesn't means small legal fees, however. In Toronto, some law offices charge a flat fee of $1,000 for the basic small claims lawsuit and trial.

Remember that you're entitled to bring to court any evidence relevant to your case, including written documents, such as a bill of sale or receipt, contract, or letter. If your car has developed severe rust problems, bring a photograph (signed and dated by the photographer) to court. You may also have witnesses testify, but it's important to discuss a witness's testimony prior to the court date. If a witness can't attend the court date, he or she can write a report and sign it for representation in court. This situation usually applies to an expert witness, such as an independent mechanic who has evaluated your car's problems.

If you lose your case in spite of all your preparation and research, some small claims court statutes allow cases to be retried, at a nominal cost, in exceptional circumstances. If a new witness has come forward, additional evidence has been discovered, or key documents (that were previously not available) have become accessible, apply for a retrial. In Ontario, this little-known provision is Rule 18.4 (1).B.

Alan MacDonald, a *Lemon-Aid* reader who won his case in small claims court, gives the following tips on beating Ford:

> I want to thank you for the advice you provided in my dealings with the Ford Motor Company of Canada, Limited and Highbury Ford Sales Limited regarding my 1994 Ford

Taurus wagon and the problems with the automatic transmission (Taurus and Windstar transmissions are identical). I also wish to apologize for not sending you a copy of this judgment earlier that may be beneficial to your readers. (*MacDonald v. Highbury Ford Sales Limited*, Ontario Superior Court of Justice in the Small Claims Court London, June 6, 2000, Court File #0001/00, Judge J. D. Searle).

In 1999 after only 105,000 km the automatic transmission went. I took the car to Highbury Ford to have it repaired. We paid $2,070 to have the transmission fixed, but protested and felt the transmission failed prematurely. We contacted Ford, but to no avail: their reply was we were out of warranty period. The transmission was so poorly repaired (and we went back to Highbury Ford several times) that we had to go to Mr. Transmission to have the transmission fixed again nine months later at a further $1,906.02.

It is at that point that I contacted you, and I was surprised, and somewhat speechless (which you noticed) when you personally called me to provide advice and encouragement. I am very grateful for your call. My observations with going through small claims court involved the following: I filed in January of 2000, the trial took place on June 1 and the judgment was issued June 6.

At pretrial, a representative of Ford (Ann Sroda) and a representative from Highbury Ford were present. I came with one binder for each of the defendants, the court and one for myself (each binder was about 3 inches thick—containing your reports on Ford Taurus automatic transmissions, ALLDATA Service Bulletins, Taurus Transmissions Victims (Bradley website), Center for Auto Safety (website), Read This Before Buying a Taurus (website), and the Ford Vent Page (website).

The representative from Ford asked a lot of questions (I think she was trying to find out if I had read the contents of the information I was relying on). The Ford representative then offered a 50 percent settlement based on the initial transmission work done at Highbury Ford. The release allowed me to still sue Highbury Ford with regards to the necessity of going to Mr. Transmission because of the faulty repair done by the dealer. Highbury Ford displayed no interest in settling the case, and so I had to go to court.

For court, I prepared by issuing a summons to the manager at Mr. Transmission, who did the second transmission repair, as an expert witness. I was advised that unless you produce an expert witness you won't win in a car repair case in small claims court. Next, I went to the law school library in London and received a great deal of assistance in researching cases pertinent to car repairs. I was told that judgments in your home province (in my case Ontario) were binding on the court; that cases outside of the home province could be considered, but not binding, on the judge.

The cases I used for trial involved *Pelleray v. Heritage Ford Sales Ltd.*, Ontario Small Claims Court (Scarborough) SC7688/91 March 22, 1993; *Phillips et al. v. Ford Motor Co. of Canada Ltd. et al*, Ontario Reports 1970, 15th January 1970; *Gregorio v. Intrans-Corp.*, Ontario Court of Appeal, May 19, 1994; *Collier v. MacMaster's Auto Sales*, New Brunswick Court of Queen's Bench, April 26, 1991; *Sigurdson v. Hillcrest Service & Acklands* (1977), Saskatchewan Queen's Bench; *White v. Sweetland*, Newfoundland

District Court, Judicial Centre of Gander, November 8, 1978; *Raiches Steel Works v. J. Clark & Son*, New Brunswick Supreme Court, March 7, 1977; *Mudge v. Corner Brook Garage Ltd.*, Newfoundland Supreme Court, July 17, 1975; *Sylvain v. Carroseries d'Automobiles Guy Inc.* (1981), C.P. 333, Judge Page; *Gagnon v. Ford Motor Company of Canada, Limited et Marineau Automobile Co. Ltée.* (1974), C.S. 422–423.

In court, I had prepared the case, as indicated above, had my expert witness and two other witnesses who had driven the vehicle (my wife and my 18-year-old son). As you can see by the judgment, we won our case and I was awarded $1,756.52, including prejudgment interest and costs.

Key Court Decisions

The following Canadian and U.S. lawsuits and judgments cover typical problems that are likely to arise. Use them as leverage when negotiating a settlement, or as a reference should your claim go to trial. Legal principles applying to Canadian and American law are similar; Quebec court decisions, however, may be based on legal principles that don't apply outside that province. Nevertheless, you can find a comprehensive listing of Canadian decisions from small claims courts all the way to the Supreme Court of Canada at *legalresearch.org/docs/internet3.html* or *www.canlii.org*.

You can find additional court judgments in the legal reference section of your city's main public library or at a nearby university law library. Ask the librarian for help in choosing the legal phrases that best describe your claim. LexisNexis (*www.lexis-nexis.com*) and Findlaw (*www.findlaw.com*) are two useful Internet sites for legal research. Their main drawback, though, is you may need to subscribe or use a lawyer's subscription to access jurisprudence and other areas of the sites.

 An excellent reference book that will give you plenty of tips on filing, pleading, and collecting your judgment is Judge Marvin Zuker's *Ontario Small Claims Court Practice 2002–2003* (Carswell, 2002). Judge Zuker's book is easily understood by non-lawyers and uses court decisions from across Canada to help you plead your case successfully in almost any Canadian court.

Product Liability

Almost three decades ago, in *Kravitz v. GM*, the Supreme Court of Canada clearly affirmed that automakers and their dealers are jointly liable for the replacement or repair of a vehicle if independent testimony shows that it is afflicted by factory-related defects that compromise its safety or performance. The existence of a secret warranty extension or technical service bulletins also helps prove that the vehicle's problems are the automaker's responsibility. For example, in *Lowe v. Fairview Chrysler* (see pages 86–87), technical service bulletins were instrumental in showing an Ontario small claims court judge that Chrysler's history of automatic transmission failures went back to 1989.

In addition to replacing or repairing the vehicle, an automaker can also be held responsible for any damages arising from the defect. This means that loss of wages, supplementary transportation costs, and damages for personal inconvenience can be awarded. However, in the States, product liability damage awards often exceed millions of dollars, while Canadian courts are far less generous.

Implied Warranty

Reasonable Durability

This is that powerful "other" warranty that they never tell you about. It applies during and after the expiration of the manufacturer's or dealer's expressed or written warranty, and requires that a part or repair will last a "reasonable" period of time. What is reasonable depends in large part on benchmarks used in the industry, the price of the vehicle, and how it was driven and maintained. Look at the reasonable durability table on page 43 for some guidelines as to what you should expect.

Judges usually apply the implied or legal warranty when the manufacturer's expressed warranty has expired and the vehicle's manufacturing defects remain uncorrected. In the following decisions, the implied warranty forced Ford to pay for Ford's Windstar chronic engine failures.

Dufour v. Ford Canada Ltd., April 10, 2001, Quebec Small Claims Court (Hull), No. 550-32-008335-009, Justice P. Chevalier. Ford was forced to reimburse the cost of engine head gasket repairs carried out on a 1996 Windstar 3.8L engine—a vehicle not covered by the automaker's Owner Notification Program, which cut off assistance after the '95 model year.

Schaffler v. Ford Motor Company Limited and Embrun Ford Sales Ltd., Ontario Superior Court of Justice, L'Orignal Small Claims Court, Court File No. 59-2003, July 22, 2003, Justice Gerald Langlois. The plaintiff bought a used 1995 Windstar in 1998. Its engine head gasket was repaired for free three years later, under Ford's 7-year extended warranty. In 2002, at 109,600 km, the head gasket failed again, seriously damaging the engine. Ford refused a second repair. Justice Langlois ruled that Ford's warranty extension bulletin listed signs and symptoms of the covered defect that were identical to the problems written on the second work order ("persistent and/or chronic engine overheating; heavy white smoke evident from the exhaust tailpipe; flashing 'low coolant' instrument panel light even after coolant refill; and constant loss of engine coolant"). Judge Langlois concluded that "the problem was brought to the attention of the dealer well within the warranty

COUR DU QUÉBEC
Division petites créances

QUÉBEC
DISTRICT DE HULL

NO: 550-32-008335-009

Hull, le 10 avril 2001

SOUS LA PRESIDENCE DE:
L'HONORABLE PIERRE
CHEVALIER
Juge de la Cour du Québec

BASTIEN DUFOUR

Partie requérante,

-c.-

FORD DU CANADA LTÉE, 7800,
route Transcanadienne à Pointe-
Claire (Québec) H9H 1C6

Partie intimée

JUGEMENT

Les parties essentielles de la requête se lisent comme suit :

I am hereby claiming from Ford Canada expenses and collateral expenses incurred for the repair of the 3.8 litter engine of a Ford Windstar GL 1996, VIN 2FMDA5147TBA95586.

The said engine had to have the head gasket and thermostat replaced on 02 June 2000, after a total of 118,892 kms indicated on the vehicle odometer. This repair was deemed necessary by my hometown Ford dealership (Mont-Bleu Ford in Gatineau, Que.) after I observed inadequate performance of the interior heating system and abnormal engine coolant temperature indications, and after a leak down test performed by the Mont-Bleu Ford dealership.

I consider such a defect to be abnormal as components such as an engine should have a life expectancy of at least 160,000 kms of 7 years without major repairs such as head gasket repair or replacement.

I have enclosed a copy of my bill showing that this problem is factory related and has cost $1364.35 to correct; this amount includes the cost for the engine head gasket repair and appropriate provincial and federal sales taxes.

L'ensemble de la preuve satisfait le Tribunal par prépondérance de preuve que la détérioration impliquée est survenue prématurément par rapport à un bien identique et que cette détérioration n'est pas due à un défaut d'entretien.

L'article 1729 C.c.Q. stipule qu'en cas de vente par un vendeur professionnel, l'existence d'un vice au moment de la vente est présumée, lorsque la détérioration du bien survient prématurément par rapport à des biens identiques. De plus, les intimés n'ont pas repoussé la présomption en établissant que le défaut serait dû à une mauvaise utilisation du bien par l'acheteur. Selon l'art. 1730, le fabricant est soumis à cette même garantie.

Vu les articles 1729 et 1730 du Code civile du Québec, le Tribunal fait droit à la réclamation et condamne la partie intimée à payer à la partie requérante la somme de 1 364,35 $ avec intérêts au taux légal de 5% depuis la requête, soit le 19 septembre 2000 et les frais de 72 $.

PIERRE CHEVALIER
Juge de la Cour du Québec

period; the dealer was negligent." The plaintiff was awarded $4,941, plus 5 percent interest. This included $1,070 for two months' car rental.

John R. Reid and Laurie M. McCall v. Ford Motor Company of Canada, Superior Court of Justice, Ottawa Small Claims Court, Claim No: #02-SC-077344, July 11, 2003, Justice Tiernay. A 1996 Windstar, bought used in 1997, experienced engine head gasket failure in October 2001 at 159,000 km. Judge Tiernay awarded the plaintiffs $4,145 for the following reason: "A Technical Service Bulletin dated June 28, 1999, was circulated to Ford dealers. It dealt specifically with 'undetermined loss of coolant' and 'engine oil contaminated with coolant' in the 1996–98 Windstar and five other models of Ford vehicles. I conclude that Ford owed a duty of care to the Plaintiff to equip this vehicle with a cylinder head gasket of sufficient sturdiness and durability that would function trouble-free for at least seven years, given normal driving and proper maintenance conditions. I find that Ford is answerable in damages for the consequences of its negligence."

Dawe v. Courtesy Chrysler, Dartmouth Nova Scotia Small Claims Court SCCH #206825, July 30, 2004, Judge Patrick L Casey, Q.C. Small claims doesn't mean small judgments. This recent, 21-page, unreported Nova Scotia small claims court decision is impressive in its clarity and thoroughness. It applies *Donoghue, Kravitz, Davis, et al.* in awarding a 2001 Dodge Ram owner over $5,000 in damages. Anyone with engine, transmission, and suspension problems, or water leaking into the interior, will find this judgment particularly useful.

Fissel v. Ideal Auto Sales Ltd. (1991), 91 Sask. R. 266. Shortly after the vehicle was purchased, the car's motor seized and the dealer refused to replace it, even though the car was returned on several occasions. The court ruled that the dealer had breached the statutory warranties in s. 11 (4) and (7) of the *Consumer Products Warranties Act*. The purchasers were entitled to cancel the sale and recover the full purchase price.

Friskin v. Chevrolet Oldsmobile, 72 D.L.R. (3d), 289. A Manitoba used-car buyer asked that his contract be cancelled because of a chronic stalling problem. The garage owner did his best to correct it. Despite the seller's good intentions, the *Manitoba Consumer Protection Act* allowed for cancellation.

Graves v. C&R Motors Ltd., April 8, 1980, British Columbia County Court, Judge Skipp. The plaintiff bought a used car on the condition that certain deficiencies be remedied. They never were, and he was promised a refund, but it never arrived. The plaintiff brought suit, claiming that the dealer's deceptive activities violated the provincial *Trade Practices Act*. The court agreed, concluding that a deceptive act that occurs before, during, or after the transaction can lead to the cancellation of the contract.

Hachey v. Galbraith Equipment Company (1991), 33 M.V.R. (2d) 242. The plaintiff bought a used truck from the dealer to haul gravel. Shortly thereafter, the steering failed. The plaintiff's suit was successful because expert testimony showed that the truck wasn't roadworthy. The dealer was found liable for damages for being in breach of the implied condition of fitness for the purpose for which the truck was purchased, as set out in s. 15 (a) of the New Brunswick *Sale of Goods Act*.

Henzel v. Brussels Motors (1973), 1 O.R., 339 (C.C.). The dealer sold this used car, brandishing a copy of the mechanical fitness certificate as proof that the car was in good shape. The plaintiff was awarded his money back because the court held the certificate to be a warranty that was breached by the car's subsequent defects.

Johnston v. Bodasing Corporation Limited, February 23, 1983, Ontario County Court (Bruce), No. 15/11/83, Judge McKay. The plaintiff bought a used 1979 Buick Riviera, that was represented as being "reliable," for $8,500. Two weeks after purchase, the motor self-destructed. Judge McKay awarded the plaintiff $2,318 as compensation to fix the Riviera's defects. One feature of this particular decision is that the trial judge found that the *Sale of Goods Act* applied, notwithstanding the fact that the vendor used a standard contract that said there were no warranties or representations. The judge also accepted the decision in *Kendal v. Lillico* (1969), 2 Appeal Cases, 31, which indicates that the *Sale of Goods Act* covers not only defects that the seller ought to have detected, but also latent defects that even his or her utmost skill and judgment could not have detected. This places a very heavy onus on the vendor, and it should prove useful in actions of this type in other common-law provinces with laws similar to Ontario's *Sale of Goods Act*.

Kelly v. Mack Canada, 53 D.L.R. (4th), 476. Kelly bought two trucks from Mack Sales. The first, a used White Freightliner tractor and trailer, was purchased for $29,742. It cost him over $12,000 in repairs during the first five months, and another $9,000 was estimated for future engine repairs. Mack Sales convinced Kelly to trade in the old truck for a new Mack truck. Kelly did this, but shortly thereafter, the new truck had similar problems. Kelly sued for the return of all his money, arguing that the two transactions were really one. The Ontario Court of Appeal agreed and awarded Kelly a complete refund. It stated: "There was such a congeries of defects that there had been a breach of the implied conditions set out in the *Sale of Goods Act*."

Although Mack Sales argued that the contract contained a clause excluding any implied warranties, the court determined that the breach was of such magnitude that the dealer could not rely upon that clause. The dealer then argued that since the client used the trucks, the depreciation of both should be taken into account in reducing the award. This was refused on the grounds that the plaintiff never had the product he bargained for, and in no way did he profit from the transaction. The court also awarded Kelly compensation for loss of income while the trucks were being repaired, as well as the interest on all of the money tied up in both transactions from the time of purchase until final judgment.

Morrison v. Hillside Motors (1973) Ltd. (1981), 35 Nfld. & P.E.I.R. 361. A used car advertised to be in A-1 condition and carrying a 50/50 warranty developed a number of problems. The court decided that the purchaser should be partially compensated because of the ad's claim. In deciding how much compensation to award, the presiding judge considered the warranty's wording, the amount paid for the vehicle, the year of the vehicle, its average life, the type of defect that occurred, and how long the purchaser had use of the vehicle before its defects became evident. Although this judgment was rendered in Newfoundland, judges throughout Canada have used a similar approach for more than a decade.

Neilson v. Maclin Motors, 71 D.L.R. (3d), 744. The plaintiff bought a used truck on the strength of the seller's allegations that the motor had been rebuilt and that it had 210 hp. The engine failed. The judge awarded damages and cancelled the contract because the motor had not been rebuilt, it did not have 210 hp, and the transmission was defective.

Parent v. Le Grand Trianon and Ford Credit (1982), C.P., 194, Judge Bertrand Gagnon. Nineteen months after paying $3,300 for a used 1974 LTD, the plaintiff sued the Ford dealer for his money back because the car was prematurely rusted out. The dealer replied that rust was normal, there was no warranty, and the claim was too late. The court held that the garage was still responsible. The plaintiff was awarded $1,500 for the cost of rust repairs.

"As Is" Clauses

Since 1907, Canadian courts have ruled that a seller can't exclude the implied warranty as to fitness by including such phrases as "there are no other warranties or guarantees, promises, or agreements than those contained herein." See *Sawyer-Massey Co. v. Thibault* (1907), 5 W.L.R. 241.

Adams v. J&D's Used Cars Ltd. (1983), 26 Sask. R. 40 (Q.B.). Shortly after purchase, the car's engine and transmission failed. The court ruled that the inclusion of "as is" in the sales contract had no legal effect. The implied warranty set out in Saskatchewan's Consumer Products Warranties Act was breached by the dealer. The sale was cancelled and all monies were refunded.

Leasing

Ford Motor Credit v. Bothwell, December 3, 1979, Ontario County Court (Middlesex), No. 9226-T, Judge Macnab. The defendant leased a 1977 Ford truck that had frequent engine problems, characterized by stalling and hard starting. After complaining for one year and driving 35,000 km (22,000 mi.), the defendant cancelled the lease. Ford Credit sued for the money owing on the lease. Judge Macnab cancelled the lease and ordered Ford Credit to repay 70 percent of the amount paid during the leasing period. Ford Credit was also ordered to refund repair costs, even though the corporation claimed that it should not be held responsible for Ford's failure to honour its warranty.

Salvador v. Setay Motors/Queenstown Chev-Olds, Hamilton Small Claims Court, Case No.1621/95. The plaintiff was awarded $2,000, plus costs, from Queenstown Leasing. The court found that the company should have tried harder to sell the leased vehicle, and at a higher price, when the "open lease" expired.

Incidentally, in 2004, about 3,700 dealers in 39 American states paid between $3,500 and $8,000 each to settle an investigation of allegations that they and Ford Motor Credit Co. had overcharged customers who had terminated leases early.

Schryvers v. Richport Ford Sales, May 18, 1993, B.C.S.C., No. C917060, Justice Tysoe. The court awarded $17,578.47, plus costs, to a couple who paid thousands of dollars more in unfair and hidden leasing charges than if they had simply purchased their Ford Explorer and Escort. The court found that this price difference constituted a deceptive, unconscionable act or practice, in contravention of the *Trade Practices Act*, R.S.B.C. 1979, c. 406.

Judge Tysoe concluded that the total of the general damages awarded to the Schryvers for both vehicles would be $11,578.47. He then proceeded to give the following reasons for awarding an additional $6,000 in punitive damages:

> Little wonder Richport Ford had a contest for the salesperson who could persuade the most customers to acquire their vehicles by way of a lease transaction. I consider the actions of Richport Ford to be sufficiently flagrant and high handed to warrant an award of punitive damages.
>
> There must be a disincentive to suppliers in respect of intentionally deceptive trade practices. If no punitive damages are awarded for intentional violations of the legislation, suppliers will continue to conduct their businesses in a manner that involves deceptive trade practices because they will have nothing to lose. In this case I believe that the appropriate amount of punitive damages is the extra profit Richport Ford endeavoured to make as a result of its deceptive acts. I therefore award punitive damages against Richport Ford in the amount of $6,000.

See also:

- *Barber v. Inland Truck Sales*, 11 D.L.R. (3rd), No. 469
- *Canadian-Dominion Leasing v. Suburban Super Drug Ltd.* (1966), 56 D.L.R. (2nd), No. 43
- *Neilson v. Atlantic Rentals Ltd.* (1974), 8 N.B.R. (2d), No. 594
- *Volvo Canada v. Fox*, December 13, 1979, New Brunswick Court of Queen's Bench, No. 1698/77/C, Judge Stevenson
- *Western Tractor v. Dyck*, 7 D.L.R. (3rd), No. 535

Repairs

Faulty Diagnosis

Davies v. Alberta Motor Association, August 13, 1991, Alberta Provincial Court, Civil Division, No. P9090106097, Judge Moore. The plaintiff had the AMA's Vehicle Inspection Service check out a used 1985 Nissan Pulsar NX prior to buying it. The car passed with flying colours. A month later, the clutch was replaced and numerous electrical problems ensued. At that time, another garage discovered that the car had been involved in a major accident, had a bent frame and a leaking radiator, and was unsafe to drive. The court awarded the plaintiff $1,578.40 plus three years' interest. The judge held that the AMA set itself out as an expert and should have spotted the car's defects. The AMA's defence—that it was not responsible for errors—was thrown out. The court held that a disclaimer clause could not protect the association from a fundamental breach of contract.

Secret Warranties

It's common practice for manufacturers to secretly extend their warranties to cover components with a high failure rate. Customers who complain vigorously get extended warranty compensation in the form of "goodwill" adjustments.

François Chong v. Marine Drive Imported Cars Ltd. and Honda Canada Inc., May 17, 1994, British Columbia Provincial Small Claims Court, No. 92-06760, Judge C.L. Bagnall. Mr. Chong was the first owner of a 1983 Honda Accord with 134,000 km on the odometer. He had six engine camshafts replaced—four under Honda "goodwill" programs, one where he paid part of the repairs, and one via this small claims court judgment.

In his ruling, Judge Bagnall agreed with Chong and ordered Honda and the dealer to each pay half of the $835.81 repair bill, for the following reasons:

> The defendants assert that the warranty, which was part of the contract for purchase of the car, encompassed the entirety of their obligation to the claimant, and that it expired in February 1985. The replacements of the camshaft after that date were paid for wholly or in part by Honda as a "goodwill gesture." The time has come for these gestures to cease, according to the witness for Honda. As well, he pointed out to me that the most recent replacement of the camshaft was paid for by Honda and that, therefore, the work would not be covered by Honda's usual warranty of 12 months from date of repair. Mr. Wall, who testified for Honda, told me there was no question that this situation with Mr. Chong's engine was an unusual state of affairs. He said that a camshaft properly maintained can last anywhere from 24,000 to 500,000 km. He could not offer any suggestion as to why the car keeps having this problem.

> The claimant has convinced me that the problems he is having with rapid breakdown of camshafts in his car is due to a defect, which was present in the engine at the time that he purchased the car. The problem first arose during the warranty period and in my view has never been properly identified nor repaired.

Automatic Transmission Failures (Chrysler)

Lowe v. Fairview Chrysler-Dodge Limited and Chrysler Canada Limited, May 14, 1996, Ontario Court (General Division), Burlington Small Claims Court, No. 1224/95. This judgment, in the plaintiff's favour, raises important legal principles relative to Chrysler:

- Technical dealer service bulletins are admissible in court to prove that a problem exists and that certain parts should be checked out.
- If a problem is reported prior to a warranty's expiration, warranty coverage for

the problematic component(s) is automatically carried over after the warranty ends.
- It's not up to the car owner to tell the dealer/automaker what the specific problem is.
- Repairs carried out by an independent garage can be refunded if the dealer/automaker unfairly refuses to apply the warranty.
- The dealer/automaker cannot dispute the cost of the independent repair if they fail to cross-examine the independent repairer.
- Auto owners can ask for and win compensation for their inconvenience, which in this judgment amounted to $150.

Court awards quickly add up. Although the plaintiff was given $1,985.94, with the addition of court costs and prejudgment interest, plus costs of inconvenience fixed at $150, the final award amounted to $2,266.04.

False Advertising

Truck Misrepresentation

Goldie v. Golden Ears Motors (1980) Ltd, Port Coquitlam, June 27, 2000, British Columbia Small Claims Court, Case No. CO8287, Justice Warren. In a well-written eight-page judgment, the court awarded plaintiff Goldie $5,000 for engine repairs on a 1990 Ford F-150 pickup in addition to $236 court costs. The dealer was found to have misrepresented the mileage and sold a used vehicle that didn't meet Section 8.01 of the provincial motor vehicle regulations due to its unsafe tires and defective exhaust and headlights.

In rejecting the seller's defence that he disclosed all information "to the best of his knowledge and belief" as stipulated in the sales contract, Justice Warren stated:

> The words "to the best of your knowledge and belief" do not allow someone to be willfully blind to defects or to provide incorrect information. I find as a fact that the business made no effort to fulfill its duty to comply with the requirements of this form…. The defendant has been reckless in its actions. More likely, it has actively deceived the claimant into entering into this contract. I find the conduct of the defendant has been reprehensible throughout the dealings with the claimant.

This judgment closes a loophole that sellers have used to justify their misrepresentation, and it allows for cancellation of the sale and damages if the vehicle doesn't meet highway safety regulations.

MacDonald v. Equilease Co. Ltd., January 18, 1979, Ontario Supreme Court, Judge O'Driscoll. The plaintiff leased a truck that was misrepresented as having an axle stronger than it really was. The court awarded the plaintiff damages for repairs, and set aside the lease.

Seich v. Festival Ford Sales Ltd. (1978), 6 Alta. L.R. (2nd), No. 262. The plaintiff bought a used truck from the defendant after being assured that it had a new motor and transmission. It didn't, and the court awarded the plaintiff $6,400.

Used Car Sold as New (Demonstrator)

Bilodeau v. Sud Auto, Quebec Court of Appeal, No. 09-000751-73, Judge Tremblay. This appeals court cancelled the contract and held that a car can't be sold as new or as a demonstrator if it has ever been rented, leased, sold, or titled to anyone other than the dealer.

Rourke v. Gilmore, January 16, 1928, (Ontario Weekly Notes, vol. XXXIII, p. 292). Before discovering that his new car was really used, the plaintiff drove it for over a year. For this reason the contract couldn't be cancelled. However, the appeals court instead awarded damages for $500, which was quite a sum in 1928!

Vehicle Not as Ordered

Whether you're buying a new or used vehicle, the seller can't misrepresent the vehicle. Anything that varies from what one would commonly expect or from the seller's representation must be disclosed prior to signing the contract. Typical mis-reprenation scenarios include odometer turnbacks, accident damage, used or leased cars sold as new, new vehicles that are the wrong colour and the wrong model year, or vehicles that lack promised options or standard features.

Chenel v. Bel Automobile (1981) Inc., August 27, 1976, Quebec Superior Court (Quebec), Judge Desmeules. The plaintiff didn't receive his new Ford truck with the Jacob brakes essential to transporting sand in hilly regions. The court awarded the plaintiff $27,000, representing the purchase price of the vehicle less the money he earned while using the truck.

Lasky v. Royal City Chrysler Plymouth, February 18, 1987, Ontario High Court of Justice, 59 O.R. (2nd), No. 323. The plaintiff bought a 4-cylinder 1983 Dodge 600 that was represented by the salesman as being a 6-cylinder model. After putting 40,000 km on the vehicle over a 22-month period, the buyer was given her money back, without interest, under the provincial Business Practices Act.

Part Three

1970–2004 RATINGS:
THE BEST AND THE WORST

Media Manipulation

As a motoring journalist, you spend much of your life on exotic car launches, feeding from the bottomless pit of automotive corporate hospitality. And then you come home to tailor a story that perfectly meets the needs of the public relations department that funded it. For sure, you dislike the new "xyz" but what the hell. Say it's fabulous and you're sure to be invited on the next exotic press launch. And so what if some poor sucker reads what you say and buys this hateful car? You're never going to meet him because by then you'll be on another press launch, in Africa maybe, trying out the "zxy"...

I learned...that the single most important feature of motoring journalism—or any kind of journalism for that matter—is speaking your mind. You mustn't become [a ventriloquist's dummy] with a PR man's hand up your bottom...

JEREMY CLARKSON
BORN TO BE RILED

Wise Words From Kitchener

Friends don't let friends drive junk...

A USED CAR DEALER'S SIGN
KITCHENER, ONTARIO

Pay Less, Get More

The primary reasons for buying used are to save money and to have reliable transportation for at least ten years. A good used car or minivan should cost you no more than a third to half of its original selling price ($5,000 to $10,000), and should be between three and five years old. A "new" used car must meet your everyday driving needs and have high crashworthiness and reliability scores. Annual maintenance should cost no more than the CAA-surveyed average of $800, and the depreciation rate should have leveled off. Parts should also be reasonably priced and easily available, customizing should be easy and inexpensive, and servicing shouldn't be given with a shrug or a snarl (sorry, Mercedes and VW).

Frank M. Ligon
Director
Service Engineering Operations
Ford Customer Service Division

Ford Motor Company
P. O. Box 1904
Dearborn, Michigan 48121

October 2004

TO: All U.S. Ford and Lincoln Mercury Dealers

SUBJECT: Customer Satisfaction Program 04N03:
Certain 2003 and 2004 Model Year E-Series Vehicles
Additional Warranty Coverage for Anti-Lock Brake System Module

REF: **DEMONSTRATION / DELIVERY HOLD:** Safety Recall 04S22 Dated October 2004 –
Anti-Lock Brake System (ABS) Module Service

Note: All vehicles affected by Customer Satisfaction Program 04N03 - Additional Coverage for Anti-Lock Brake System (ABS) Module are included in Safety Recall 04S22. All customers with affected vehicles will receive one notification for both 04S22 and 04N03.

PROGRAM TERMS

This program extends the coverage of the Anti-Lock Brake System (ABS) Module to 10 years of service or 150,000 miles from the warranty start date of the vehicle, whichever occurs first. If a vehicle has already accumulated more than 150,000 miles, this coverage will last until September 30, 2005. This program provides one-time replacement coverage, and is automatically transferred to subsequent owners.

VEHICLES COVERED BY THIS PROGRAM

Certain 2003 model year E-Series vehicles built at the Lorain Assembly Plant from April 23, 2002 through September 19, 2003 and certain 2004 model year E-Series vehicles built at the Lorain Assembly Plant from May 06, 2003 through November 19, 2003. Affected vehicles are identified in OASIS.

REASON FOR PROVIDING ADDITIONAL COVERAGE

In a very small percentage of the affected vehicles, a diode in the Anti-Lock Brake System (ABS) Module may experience an electrical short. An electrical short may cause an ABS malfunction that would illuminate the ABS warning light, and in some cases, the module may overheat resulting in burning odor, smoke, and/or fire. Since battery power is always present at the module, this condition may occur when the vehicle ignition switch is in the off position, creating the potential for unattended vehicle fires.

Safety Recall 04S22 dated October 2004 – Anti-Lock Brake System (ABS) Module Service was issued to address the above concern. This program provides additional warranty coverage should the ABS Module need replacement.

SERVICE ACTION

If an affected vehicle experiences a short in the ABS Module, dealers are to replace (one time) the ABS Module. This repair will be performed at no charge to the vehicle owner.

Car columnists almost never disclose secret warranty programs like Ford's 10-year brake refund program, above; *Lemon-Aid* always does.

 ## Depreciation Bargains

When buying new, you want a reliable model that depreciates slowly; when buying used, you want a car that has lost much of its value, but that is still dependable and inexpensive to maintain.

During the past decade, rebates, cut-rate financing, subsidized leases, and a reputation for poor quality have depressed the residual values of Detroit Big Three cars and trucks. According to the *Automotive Lease Guide* (*ALG*), *www.alg.com*, 3-year-old Detroit-made vehicles that come off lease keep between 37 and 48 percent of their sticker value after three years.

ALG also rates automakers for the predicted retained value of their vehicles. Here are their ratings in descending order of their approximate 3-year retained value:

AUTOMAKER RETAINED VALUE RANKINGS (NON-LUXURY)

ABOVE AVERAGE	BELOW AVERAGE
Honda (53%)	*Chevrolet (42%)
Toyota (52%)	Dodge (41%)
Nissan (51%)	Saturn (40%)
Volkswagen (50%)	*Hyundai (40%)
Jeep (48%)	Mitsubishi (39%)
Subaru (46%)	*Pontiac (38%)
Mazda (44%)	Kia (37%)
GMC (43%)	Mercury (37%)
Chrysler (43%)	Buick (37%)
Ford (43%)	Isuzu (35%)
	*Suzuki (35%)

AUTOMAKER RETAINED VALUE RANKINGS (LUXURY)

ABOVE AVERAGE	BELOW AVERAGE
BMW (53%)	Audi (49%)
Lexus (52%)	Land Rover (49%)
Acura (51%)	Cadillac (48%)
Mercedes-Benz (51%)	Jaguar (44%)
Infiniti (50%)	Saab (41%)
Volvo (50%)	*Lincoln (40%)

Manufacturers listed with an asterix have a number of used models that are fairly reliable and cheap, like Chevrolet's Cavalier, Pontiac's Sunfire, Hyundai's Elantra and Santa Fe, and the Lincoln Town Car.

It's interesting to note that Kia's products retain their value almost as well as vehicles sold by Pontiac, Buick, and Mercury.

Dueling Quality Ratings

There are so many groups giving out car ratings each year that it's difficult to know who to believe. *Lemon-Aid* has been a leader in ranking the best and worst used cars and minivans for the past 33 years by following these simple rules:

- Owner reports are the backbone of our rating system. By using as large a pool of owners as possible (including 800,000 responses from *Consumer Reports* subscribers and 22,000 responses from CAA members), we get a reflection of real-world vehicle performance and dependability.
- All anecdotal owner reports are cross-referenced, updated, and given depth and specificity through NHTSA's safety complaint prism.
- Responses are further cross-referenced through automaker internal service bulletins to determine to what extent automakers and dealers may be covering up a serious safety or performance flaw, or asking that owners pay for factory mistakes (particularly engines and transmissions); how many model years are affected; what correction and new part numbers are required; and which secret "goodwill" warranties may apply.
- Finally, our model ratings reflect a wide range of independent sources of information that we access throughout the year to use primarily as a comparative quality benchmark.

Definitions of Terms

We rate vehicles on a scale of one to five stars, with five stars being our top ranking. Half stars indicate a midpoint between two rating levels. Models are designated as Recommended or Not Recommended, with the most recent year's rating reflected by the number of stars beside the vehicle's name.

Recommended

Recommended vehicles are those that will give their owners relatively trouble-free service. This doesn't mean that only luxury Japanese models get a good rating. In fact, Chrysler's Sebring and PT Cruiser, GM's Camaro and Firebird, and Hyundai's Elantra and Tiburon get positive ratings because they are easy to find, fairly reliable, and reasonably priced—that's not the case with many overpriced Hondas and Toyotas.

Recommended vehicles don't need optional, extra-cost ($1,000–2,000) extended warranties.

Usually, but not always, an extended warranty is advised for those model years that aren't rated Recommended. But don't buy too much warranty. For example, if the vehicle has a history of powertrain problems, only buy the cheaper powertrain warranty—not the bumper-to-bumper product. Also, only invest in enough extra warranty to get you through the critical fifth year of ownership. When shopping for an extended warranty, don't be surprised to discover that dealers have the market practically sewn up. You can bargain the price down by getting competing dealers to bid against each other, contacting them by fax or through their websites. Be wary of extended-warranty companies that aren't backed by the major automakers.

Frank M. Ligon
Director
Service Engineering Operations
Ford Customer Service Division

Ford Motor Company
P. O. Box 1904
Dearborn, Michigan 48121

November 2004

TO: All U.S. Ford and Lincoln Mercury Dealers

SUBJECT: **Update: Supplement Announcement**
Customer Satisfaction Program 03M02 – Supplement #2:
New! *Certain 2000 - 2003 Model Year Focus Vehicles*
Additional Coverage for Front Coil Springs

REF: Customer Satisfaction Program 03M02 – Claims Update: Related Damage
Prior Approval dated June 11, 2003.

REF: Customer Satisfaction Program 03M02 – Supplement #1: Adjusted Labor Time
dated May 16, 2003.

REF: Customer Satisfaction Program 03M02: Certain 2000 Model Year Focus
Vehicles - Additional Coverage for Front Coil Springs, dated May 2003.

New!
PROGRAM TERMS
This program extends the coverage on the front coil springs to 10 years of service or 150,000
miles from the vehicle's warranty start date, whichever occurs first. This coverage will
automatically transfer to subsequent owners. *If a vehicle already has more than 150,000 miles,
this coverage will last until May 31, 2005.*

New!
VEHICLES COVERED BY THIS PROGRAM
*Certain 2000 through 2003 model year Focus vehicles built at Wayne Assembly Plant from
March 5, 1999 through January 13, 2003 and Hermosillo Assembly Plant from May 21, 1999
through April 27, 2003.*

New!
REASON FOR THIS SUPPLEMENT
*This bulletin is being re-issued to expand the model year coverage of Customer Satisfaction
Program 03M02. Coverage within 03M02 is extended to certain 2000 through 2003 model year
vehicles.*

REASON FOR PROVIDING ADDITIONAL COVERAGE
In some of the affected vehicles, portions of the front coil springs may not have received
adequate corrosion protection during the manufacturing process. Inadequate corrosion
protection eventually may lead to a fracture of the spring. A spring fracture may result in
suspension noise, possibly accompanied by sagging of one side of the vehicle. This is most
likely to occur on vehicles operated for extended periods of time in high-corrosion areas of
North America. Only a small percentage of the affected vehicles are expected to experience
this concern.

Car magazines and buying guides don't tell you about secret warranties. By using *Lemon-Aid*'s annual collection of
automaker internal memos and service bulletins, you can save hundreds or thousands of dollars on repairs that are
covered by little-known "goodwill" programs, like Ford's November 2004 free coil spring program, shown here.

Above Average/Average

Vehicles that are given an Above Average or Average rating are good second choices if a Recommended vehicle isn't your first choice, isn't available, or is too expensive.

 ## Below Average/Not Recommended

A Below Average vehicle will likely be troublesome; however, a low price and reasonably priced nearby servicing may make it an acceptable buy. Vehicles given a Not Recommended rating are best avoided altogether, no matter how low the price. They may be attractively styled and loaded with convenience features (like early Ford Windstar and Chrysler minivans, for example), but they're likely to suffer from so many durability and performance problems that you will never stop paying for them. Sometimes, however, a Not Recommended model will improve over several model years and garner a better rating (as the Chrysler Neon and GM Astro and Safari minivans have done).

Incidentally, for those owners who wonder how I can stop recommending model years I once recommended, let me be clear: As vehicles age, their ratings change to reflect new information from owners and service bulletins relating to durability and the automaker's warranty performance. For example, Nissan's Quest, Toyota's Sienna, and Ford's Escort have been downgraded because new service bulletins and additional owner complaints show some disturbing trends in dependability and servicing performance. Unlike Enron and Nortel stock analysts, I warn shoppers of changes in subsequent editions of *Lemon-Aid* or in updates to my website, *www.lemonaidcars.com*.

I do more than simply write about failure-prone cars: Throughout the year, I try to get refunds for buyers who have made the wrong choice. I lobby automakers to compensate out-of-warranty owners through formal warranty extension programs or on a case-by-case basis. I also publish little-known court judgments in *Lemon-Aid* to help car owners win their cases or get a fair settlement without my personal assistance.

Some enterprising readers of *Lemon-Aid* use the Not Recommended rating as a buying opportunity. Dave Ingram, a friend and well-known B.C. broadcaster and tax/immigration specialist for CENTA Inc., uses my Not Recommended list as a shopping guide for cheap vehicles: He buys them at depressed prices and refurbishes them, using garages that offer lifetime warranties on major components that I rate as weak. He's done that with several used Cadillacs and Jeep Wagoneers and seems happy with his system. Personally, I don't think he would have done so well without the complicity of his independent garage contacts in North Vancouver, like the mechanics at Fountain Tire.

Reliability data is compiled from a number of sources, including confidential technical service bulletins; owner complaints sent to the author each year by *Lemon-Aid* readers; vehicle owners' comments posted on the Internet; and survey reports and tests done by auto associations, consumer groups, and government organizations. Some auto columnists feel this isn't a scientific sampling, and they're quite right. Nevertheless, it has been mostly on the mark over the past three decades.

Not all vehicles sold since the '70s are profiled; those that are new to the market or relatively rare may receive only an abbreviated mention until sufficient owner or service bulletin information becomes available. Best and worst buys for each model category (e.g., "Small Cars" or "Medium Cars") are listed in a summary at the beginning of each rating section. Also, don't forget to look up the cheap alternatives profiled in Appendix II.

Strengths and Weaknesses

Every automaker has quality shortcomings and many vehicles have serious electrical system glitches that require a trip to Radio Shack, rather than to a dealer's service bay. This isn't so surprising if you consider that today's automobile has more computer power than the Apollo 11 spacecraft that took man to the moon in 1969.

With the Detroit Big Three, engine head gasket and automatic transmissions failures are omnipresent; South Korean vehicles have weak transmissions; and Japanese makes are mostly noted for their electrical system, brake, door, and window glitches, though engine and transmission failures have been appearing more frequently. Finally, the European automakers are in a high-tech bind: Electronic demons constantly bedevil their products, making them unreliable and costly to service; plus, their vehicles are so complicated to understand, diagnose, and service that many mechanics simply throw up their hands in dismay.

Unlike other auto guides, *Lemon-Aid* knows where automotive skeletons are buried and pinpoints potential parts failures, explains why those parts fail, and advises you as to your chances of getting a repair refund. We also give parts numbers for upgraded parts (why replace poor-quality brake pads with the same brand, for example?) and offer troubleshooting tips direct from the automakers' bulletins, so that your mechanic won't replace parts unrelated to your troubles before coming upon the defective component that is actually responsible.

Parts supply can be a real problem. It's a myth that automakers have to keep a supply of parts sufficient to service what they sell, as any buyer of a Cadillac Catera, a Lincoln Continental, or a Ford Contour/Mystique or Tempo/Topaz will quickly tell you. Additionally, apart from *Lemon-Aid*, there's no consumer database that warns prospective purchasers as to which models are "parts-challenged."

The "Secret Warranties/Internal Bulletins/Service Tips" sections and vehicle profile tables show a vehicle's overall reliability and safety, providing details as to which specific model years pose the most risk and why. This helps an independent mechanic check out the likely trouble spots before you make your purchase.

Vehicle History

This section outlines a vehicle's differences between model years, including major redesigns and other modifications.

 ## Safety Summary

Ongoing safety investigations, safety-related complaints, and safety probes make up this section. National Highway Traffic Safety Administration (NHTSA) complaints are summarized by model year, even though they aren't all safety related. The summary will help you spot a defect trend (like cracked Ford and GM engine intake manifolds and faulty fuel gauges) before a recall or bulletin is issued. Another use is that you can prove a part failure is widespread and factory related, and use that information for free "goodwill" repairs or in litigation involving accident damage, injuries, or death. NHTSA records indicate that ABS and airbag failures represent the most frequent complaints from car and van owners. Other common safety-related failures concern sudden acceleration, the vehicle rolling away with the transmission in Park, and minivan sliding doors not opening when they should or opening when they shouldn't.

If *Lemon-Aid* doesn't list a problem you have experienced, go to the NHTSA website's database at *www.nhtsa.dot.gov/cars/problems* for an update. Your vehicle may be currently under investigation or may have been recalled since this year's guide was published.

Automotive News says an estimated 28 percent of the 25 million vehicles recalled this year will probably not be fixed, which is an improvement over the 65-percent fix rate of just a few years ago. *Lemon-Aid* doesn't list most recalls because there are so many, and the info can be easily obtained from either NHTSA or Transport Canada, by telephone or on websites listed in Appendix I. Furthermore, most dealers willingly give out recall info when they run a "vehicle history" search through their computer, since they hope to snag the extra repair dollars. Just make sure you ask the dealer to also check for a "customer satisfaction program," a "service policy," a "goodwill" warranty extension, or a free emissions warranty service.

Secret Warranties/Internal Bulletins/Service Tips

It's not enough to know which parts on your vehicle are likely to fail. You should also know which repairs will be done for free by the dealer and automaker, even though you aren't the original owner and the manufacturer's warranty has long since expired.

Welcome to the hidden world of secret warranties, found in confidential technical service bulletins or gleaned from owner feedback.

Over the years, I've grown tired of having service managers deny that service bulletins exist to correct factory-related defects free of charge. That's why I pore over thousands of bulletins each year and summarize or reproduce in *Lemon-Aid* the important ones for each model year, along with improved parts numbers. These bulletins target defects related to safety, emissions, and performance that service managers would have you believe either don't exist or are your responsibility. If you photocopy the applicable service bulletin included in *Lemon-Aid*, you'll have a better chance of getting the dealer or automaker to cover all or part of the repair cost. Bulletins taken from *Lemon-Aid* have also been instrumental in helping claimants win in small claims court mediation and trials (remember to have the bulletins validated by an independent mechanic or the dealer/automaker witness).

Service bulletins listed in *Lemon-Aid* cover repairs that may be eligible for expressed or implied warranty coverage in one or more of the following five categories (although the description of the repairs is not always specific):

- Emissions expressed warranty (5–8 years/80,000–130,000 km)
- Safety component expressed warranty (this covers seat belts, ABS, and airbags, and usually lasts from 8 years to the lifetime of the vehicle)
- Body expressed warranty (paint: 6 years; rust perforations: 7 years)
- Secret implied warranty (coverage varies from 5–10 years)
- Factory defect/implied legal warranty (depends on mileage, use, and repair cost; may be as high as 11 years according to GM paint delamination jurisprudence)

Use these bulletins to get free repairs—even if the vehicle has changed hands several times—and to alert an independent mechanic about defects to look for. They're also great tools for getting compensation from automakers and dealer service managers after the warranty has expired, since they prove that a failure is factory related and therefore not part of routine maintenance or caused by a caustic environmental substance like bird droppings or acid rain. In small claims court, the argument that bird droppings caused the problem usually loses credibility when only certain models or certain years are shown to be affected, pointing the finger at the paint process and quality. The implied warranty requires that all automakers use the same durability standard, or disclose at the time of sale that their vehicles aren't "bird-proofed."

Their diagnostic shortcuts and lists of upgraded parts make these bulletins invaluable in helping mechanics and do-it-yourselfers troubleshoot problems inexpensively and replace the right part the first time. Auto owners can also use the TSBs listed here to verify that a repair was diagnosed correctly, that the right upgraded replacement part was used, and that the labour costs were fair.

Getting your own bulletins

Summaries of service bulletins relating to 1982–2004 vehicles can be obtained for free from the ALLDATA or NHTSA websites (listed in Appendix I, "Internet Fact-Finding"), but they are worded so cryptically that you really need the bulletins themselves. If you have a vehicle that's off warranty, you should get copies of the hundreds of pages of bulletins applicable to your model year listing factory-related defects and diagnostic short-cuts. These bulletins can be ordered and downloaded from the Internet through ALLDATA for $25 (U.S.). BMW, Acura, and Honda owners are excluded.

Vehicle Profile Tables

These tables cover the various aspects of vehicle ownership at a glance. Included for each model year are the vehicle's original selling price (the manufacturer's suggested retail price, or MSRP), the wholesale and retail price you can expect to pay, reliability ratings (specific defective parts are listed in the "Strengths and Weaknesses" section), and details on crashworthiness.

Prices

Dealer profit margins on used cars vary considerably—giving lots of room to negotiate a fair price if you take the time to find out what the vehicle is really worth. Three prices are given for each model year: the vehicle's selling price when new as suggested by the manufacturer; its maximum used price (▲), which is often the starting price with dealers, and its lowest used price (▼), more commonly found with private sellers.

The original selling price (MSRP) is also given as a reality check for greedy sellers who inflate prices on some vehicles (mostly Japanese imports, minivans, and sport-utilities) in order to get back some of the money *they* overpaid in the first place. This happens particularly often in the Prairie provinces and British Columbia.

Used prices are based on sales recorded as of February 2005. Prices are for the lowest-priced standard model that is in good condition with a maximum of 20,000 km for each calendar year. Watch for price differences reflecting each model's equipment upgrades, designated by a numerical or alphabetical abbreviation. For example, L, LX, and LXT usually mean more standard features are included. Numerical progression usually relates to engine size.

Prices reflect the auto markets in Quebec and Ontario, where the majority of used-vehicle transactions take place. Residents in Eastern Canada should add 10 percent, and Western Canadians should add at least 15–20 percent to the listed price. Why the higher cost? Less competition and inflated new-vehicle prices in these regions. Don't be too disheartened, though; you'll recoup some of what you overpaid when you sell the vehicle down the road.

Why are *Lemon-Aid*'s prices sometimes lower than the prices found in dealer guides like the *Red Book*? The answer is simple: Dealer guides, much like homeowners conducting real estate transactions, inflate their prices so that you can bargain the price down and wind up convinced that you made a great deal.

I use newspaper classified ads from Quebec, Ontario, and B.C., as well as auction reports, to calculate my used values. I then check these figures with the *Red Book* and *Black Book*. I don't start with the *Red Book*'s retail or wholesale figures (prices are inflated about 10 percent for wholesale-private sales and almost 20 percent for retail-dealer sales—compare the two and you'll see what I mean). I then project what the value will be by mid-model year, and that lowers my prices further. I'll almost always fall way under the *Red Book*'s value, but not far under the *Black Book*'s prices.

I print a top and bottom price to give the buyer some margin for negotiation, as well as to account for regional differences in prices, the sudden popularity of certain models or vehicle classes, and the generally depreciated value of used vehicles.

Most new cars depreciate 50–60 percent during the first three years of ownership, despite the fact that good-quality used cars are in high demand. On the other hand, some minivans and most vans, pickups, and sport-utilities lose barely 40 percent of their value, even after four years of ownership.

Since no evaluation method is foolproof, check dealer prices with local private classified ads and add the option values listed below to come up with a fairly representative offer. Don't forget to bargain down the price further if the odometer shows a cumulative reading of more than 20,000 km per calendar year. Interestingly, the value of anti-lock brakes in trade-ins has plummeted in the last few years as they became a standard feature on many entry-level vehicles.

It will be easier for you to match the lower used prices if you buy privately. Dealers rarely sell much below the maximum prices; they claim that they need the full price to cover the costs of reconditioning and paying future warranty claims. If you can come within 5 to 10 percent of this guide's price, you'll have done well.

Value of Options by Model Year

Option	1996	1997	1998	1999	2000	2001	2002	2003	2004
Air conditioning	$200	$300	$300	$400	$500	$600	$700	$800	$950
AM/FM radio & CD player	100	100	100	150	175	200	300	500	600
Anti-lock brakes	0	50	100	125	150	175	300	300	400
Automatic transmission	150	200	250	275	300	400	500	700	800
Cruise control	0	50	50	75	100	125	225	300	350
Electric six-way seat	0	50	100	125	150	175	200	400	450
Leather upholstery	50	100	200	225	325	400	500	800	900
Level control (suspension)	0	50	75	100	125	150	250	350	450
Paint protector	50	50	50	50	50	50	50	50	50
Power antenna	0	0	0	0	0	75	75	75	75
Power door locks	0	50	100	125	150	175	200	250	250
Power windows	0	50	100	125	150	175	225	250	250
Rustproofing	0	0	0	0	25	25	50	50	50
Sunroof	0	50	50	75	125	150	300	500	500
T-top roof	150	200	300	400	500	700	800	1,000	1,000
Tilt steering	0	50	50	75	75	100	175	250	200
Tinted windows	0	0	0	0	25	50	50	50	50
Tires (Firestone)	-100	-100	-100	-100	-100	-150	-150	-150	-150
Traction control	50	100	125	150	175	275	400	500	500
Wire wheels/locks	50	75	100	125	150	175	275	300	350

In the previous table, take note that some options—like paint protector, rust-proofing, and tinted windows—have little worth on the resale market, though they may make your vehicle easier to sell.

Reliability

The older a vehicle, the greater the chance that major components like the engine and transmission will fail as a result of high mileage, and environmental wear and tear. Surprisingly, a host of other expensive-to-repair failures are just as likely to occur in a new vehicle as in an older one. Air conditioning, electronic computer modules, electrical systems, and brakes are the most troublesome components, manifesting problems early in a vehicle's life. Other deficiencies that will appear early, due to sloppy manufacturing and a harsh environment, include failure-prone body hardware (trim, finish, locks, doors, and windows), water leaks, wind noise, and paint peeling/discoloration. The following legend is used to show a vehicle's relative degree of overall reliability; the numbers lighten as the rating becomes more positive.

❶	❷	❸	❹	❺
Unacceptable	Below Average	Average	Above Average	Excellent

Crashworthiness

Some of the main features weighed in the safety ratings are a model's crashworthiness and claims experience (as assessed by NHTSA and various insurers' groups, including the Highway Loss Data Institute and the Insurance Institute for Highway Safety), the availability of standard safety features, and front and back visibility. Also listed here are a summary of safety-related complaints to astound and worry you.

As with most four-door cars tested, four-door Honda Civics give better side-impact occupant protection than two door models (four stars versus two). 1997–2000 model year Civics, though, posed a higher risk of occupant injuries in front and side collisions.

Front and side crash protection figures are taken from NHTSA's New Car Assessment Program (*www.nhtsa.dot.gov/NCAP*). Vehicles are crashed into a fixed barrier, head-on, at 56 km/h (35 mph). NHTSA uses star rankings to express the likelihood of the belted occupants being seriously injured. The higher the number of stars, the greater the protection. NHTSA's side crash test represents an intersection-type collision with a 1,368 kg (3,015 lb.) barrier moving at 62 km/h (38.5 mph) into a standing vehicle. To replicate the front of a car, the moving barrier is covered with material that has "give."

IIHS rates head restraint, frontal offset, and side crash protection as "good," "acceptable," "marginal," or "poor." In the Institute's 64 km/h (40 mph) offset test, 40 percent of the total width of each vehicle strikes a barrier on the driver side. The barrier's deformable face is made of aluminum honeycomb, which makes the forces in the test similar to those involved in a frontal offset crash between two vehicles of the same weight, each going just less than 64 km/h.

The 50 km/h (31 mph) side impact test performed by IIHS is carried out at a slower speed than the NHTSA test, but uses a barrier with a front end shaped to simulate the typical front end of a pickup or SUV. The Institute also includes the degree of head injury in its ratings.

NHTSA Collision Ratings

CHANCE OF SERIOUS INJURY

FRONT	SIDE
⑤ 10% or less	5% or less
④ 11% to 20%	6% to 10%
③ 21% to 35%	11% to 20%
② 36% to 45%	21% to 25%
① 46% or greater	26% or greater

NHTSA Rollover Ratings

ROLLOVER RISK

⑤ Less than 10%
④ Between 10% and 20%
③ Between 20% and 30%
② Between 30% and 40%
① Greater than 40%

SMALL CAR RATINGS

The proverbial "econobox," this size of car is for city dwellers who want economy at any price. Small cars offer excellent gas economy, easy manoeuvrability in urban areas, and a low retail price.

One of the more alarming characteristics of a small car's highway performance is its extreme vulnerability to strong lateral winds, which may make the car difficult to keep on course. Most of these cars can carry only two passengers in comfort—rear seating is limited—and have insufficient luggage capacity. As well, engine and road noise are fairly excessive.

Chevrolet's Cavalier (pictured above) and Sunfire are two soon-to-be 'orphans' that will be replaced by the 2005 Cobalt, a European Opel variant. They can be picked up at "fire sale" prices.

The small size and light weight of some older small vehicles may compromise their crash safety, but not necessarily. Many newer small cars incorporate a body structure that deflects crash forces away from occupants, making these cars more crashworthy than some larger vehicles.

Recommended

Honda Civic, del Sol (1992–2004)
Hyundai Elantra (2001–04)
Mazda Protegé (1999–2003)
Nissan Sentra (2000–04)
Subaru Forester (2001–04)

Suzuki Aerio (2003-04)
Suzuki Esteem (1996–2002)
Toyota Echo (2000–04)
Toyota Tercel (1993–99)

Above Average

Honda Civic, del Sol (1972–91)
Hyundai Accent (2001–04)
Hyundai Elantra (1996–2000)
Mazda3 (All years)
Mazda 323, Protegé (1991–98)

Nissan Sentra (1995–99)
Subaru Impreza (1997–2004)
Subaru Legacy, Outback (1997–2004)
Toyota Paseo (1992–99)
Toyota Tercel (1991–92)

Average

DaimlerChrysler Neon,
   SX 2.0, SRT-4 (2003-04)
General Motors Cavalier,
   Sunfire (2003–2004)
Hyundai Accent (1995–2000)
Hyundai Elantra (1991–95)
Mazda 323, Protegé (1985–90)
Nissan Sentra (1988–94)

Subaru Forester (1998–2000)
Subaru Impreza, Loyale
   (1997–2004)
Subaru Legacy, Outback (1997–2004)
Toyota Corolla (1985–2004)
Toyota Matrix/Vibe (2003–04)
Toyota Tercel (1987–90)
Volkswagen Cabrio, Golf, Jetta (1999–2004)

Below Average

DaimlerChrysler Neon (2000–02)
Ford Escort, ZX2 (1997–2000)
Ford Focus (2004)
General Motors Cavalier,
   Sunfire (1999–2002)
Saturn Ion (2003–04)

Saturn L-series (2000–04)
Saturn S-series (1998–2002)
Subaru Impreza, Loyale (1994–96)
Subaru Legacy, Outback (1989–96)
Volkswagen Cabrio, Golf, Jetta (1993–98)

Not Recommended

Daewoo (2000–02)
DaimlerChrysler Neon (1995–99)
Ford Escort (1981–96)
Ford Focus (2000–03)
General Motors Cavalier,
   Sunfire (Sunbird) (1984–98)

Kia Rio (2001–04)
Nissan Sentra (1983–87)
Saturn S-series (1992–97)
Subaru WRX (2002–04)
Volkswagen Cabrio, Golf, Jetta
   (1985–92)

Daewoo

 ## Not Recommended

South Korean automaker Daewoo marketed three cars in Canada from 2000 to 2002: the Lanos subcompact, the Nubira compact sedan and wagon, and the Leganza luxury sedan. All of these cars are Not Recommended because Daewoo sold its car division to GM, and neither company will service these models, let alone respect the original warranties. By the way, Daewoo depreciation is mind-boggling: A 2002 Leganza that originally sold for $25,495 is now worth about $9,000—if you can find a buyer!

DaimlerChrysler

NEON, SX 2.0, SRT-4 ★★★

RATING: Average (2003–04); Below Average (2000–02); Not Recommended (1995–99). A low-quality, fuel-thirsty small car that has improved a bit during the last three years. 1995–99 models that eat engine head gaskets for breakfast and wallets for lunch are covered by a secret "goodwill" warranty. **Maintenance/ Repair costs:** Higher than average. **Parts:** Easily found and relatively inexpensive. However, Chrysler is particularly slow in distributing parts needed for safety recall campaigns; waits of several months are commonplace. **Extended warranty:** A good idea for the powertrain if the base warranty has expired. **Best alternatives:** Other cars worth considering are the GM Firefly, Metro; Cavalier, or Sunfire (2000 or later); Honda Civic; Hyundai Accent; Mazda Protegé; Suzuki Esteem; and Toyota Echo, Tercel, or Corolla. **Online help:** *www.neons.org, www.carsurvey. org/model_Dodge_Neon.html, www.geocities.com/norman_neon/, www.allpar.com/fix/ secret-warranties.html,* and *www.autosafety.org/autodefects.html.*

 ## Strengths and Weaknesses

A small, noisy car with big quality problems on its first-generation models, the Neon does offer a spacious interior and responsive steering and handling. Nevertheless, it's seriously handicapped by an antiquated, feeble and fuel-thirsty 3-speed automatic gearbox, a DOHC 4-cylinder 150-hp power plant that has to be pushed hard to do as well as the SOHC 132-hp engine, and a mushy base suspension.

The 2003 Neon was renamed the SX 2.0 in Canada. It's roomy and reasonably powered for urban use, and recent refinements have given it a softer, quieter ride while enhancing the car's handling and powertrain performance.

Chrysler has tried to make these low-end cars more appealing by loading up on features that are usually seen only with higher-priced vehicles. One of those higher-priced entries is the $26,950 2004 SRT-4 high-performance version, equipped with a turbocharged 215-hp 2.4L 4-cylinder engine hooked to a manual 4-speed transmission, a hood scoop, 17-inch wheels, a revised suspension, and four-wheel disc brakes.

Reliability has never been the Neon's strong suit, primarily because of major powertrain defects affecting mostly the 1995–99 model years. The most common problem is a biodegradable 2.0L 4-cylinder engine head gasket that's covered by a 7-year/160,000 km secret warranty. The warranty's efficacy has been confirmed by anecdotal feedback from successful claimants.

Many other owners have complained of an abruptly shifting, unreliable automatic transmission, an air conditioning system that often requires expensive servicing following condenser and compressor failures (covered by a secret 7-year warranty), a multitude of electrical glitches, lots of interior noise and water leaks, uneven fit and finish, and poor-quality trim items that break or fall off easily. The finish is not as good as that of most other subcompacts; the thickness of the coat varies considerably, and the paint can chip or fade easily (another defect eligible for a "goodwill" fix).

Year 2003–04 models continue to have engine and transmission glitches, but they are less serious than the failures reported on previous models. Recent problems are mostly caused by poorly calibrated computer modules (an 8-year/130,000 km emissions warranty item).

Some 2002 and later performance defects add new wrinkles. For example, when the car is passing through puddles, water is ingested into the engine though the air intake port (Chrysler will replace the engine when threatened with court action); the AC fails to cool the vehicle adequately; no-start because of early starter rust-out; the rear brake squeaks; the engine noticeably loses power when windows are lowered, the sunroof is opened, or the AC is engaged; and overall poor fuel economy (18–19 L/100 km [15–16 mpg]).

VEHICLE HISTORY: The Neon remained basically unchanged until the '99 models got de-powered airbags. **2000**—A second-generation redesign improved powertrain quality a bit, and added interior room and trunk space. The manual transmission and stereo were also upgraded, traction control was offered, and redesigned doors reduced wind noise and water leaks. **2002**—An upgraded automatic transmission (some reliability problems remain, though). **2003**—Neons were renamed SX 2.0 and given new front and rear fascias, steering wheels, and engine mounts to smooth out engine roughness, and a taller Fifth gear for the manual transmission. **2004**—High-performance version got a small 15-hp power boost and a limited-slip differential. An optional 4-speed automatic transmission is available.

 Safety Summary

All models/years—Fires. • "Inappropriate" airbag deployment or failure to deploy. • Sudden acceleration. • Chronic stalling. • No-start because of rusted-out starter. • Throttle system failures. • Faulty cruise control. • Steering loss. • Steering locks up when it rains. • Chronic transmission failures and slippage. • Transmission suddenly downshifts to First gear when accelerating at 90 km/h. • ABS brake failures. • Defective brake master cylinder. • Premature front brake pad/rotor wearout. • Excessive vibration. • Small horn buttons are hard to find in an emergency. • Trunk lid or hood may fall. • Headlight switch is a "hide and go seek" affair. • Axle shafts may suddenly collapse. **1995–99**—Chronic engine head gasket failures. • Engine camshaft seal leaks oil • Engine motor mount and exhaust doughnut head gasket failures. **1995–2000**—NHTSA probe of seat belt latch. **1998**—Driver-side window exploded in warm weather. • Front right wheel bolt fell out, causing wheel to bend. • Engine surging and stalling. • Engine loses speed rapidly when going uphill. • Excessive engine carbon buildup. • Timing belt broke, causing extensive engine damage. • There is a partial steering hang-up when making a right turn. **1999**—Vehicle suddenly "jumps" out of gear. • In rainy weather, vehicle makes loud noise, sometimes stalls, or loses steering power. • Defective ignition switch fuse causes sudden shutdown. **2000**—Almost 400 safety complaints indicate that the 2000 refinements haven't improved overall reliability or safety. Main problem areas: airbag, automatic transmission, power steering, tires, and brake failures; engine fires; premature brake rotor and pad wear signalled by excessive vibrations and squealing when brakes are applied; steering lock ups; stalling and stumbling; interior/exterior light dimming; seat belts failing to retract; and an inoperative horn. • Snapping noises from the front suspension may be caused by loose front crossmember mounting bolts. • An upgraded right-side motor mount may reduce steering wheel or chassis shaking. **2000–01**—Poor engine idle. **2001**—Engine stalling and stumbling, and airbags failing to deploy are the most frequent problems reported. Other incidents include electrical shorts (lights and gauges), Eagle low-profile tire blowouts, engine damage caused by water ingested through the air intake system, loss of steering, weak trunk lid springs, and an annoying reflection in the front windshield. **2002**—Stalling because of water ingestion into engine when it rains. • Transmission slips between First and Second gear. • Vehicle pulls when cruising or upon acceleration, and tends to wobble side to side at low speed. • Excessive steering wheel vibration makes it hard to maintain control. • Brakes fail to "catch" when first applied. • Airbag light stays lit. • Tailpipe melted part of the rear bumper. **2003**—Engine manifold failure. • Burnt spark plug wires (especially with #4 plug). • Poor braking. • Power-steering failure. • Tire blew because rim peeled off. • Suspension bottoms out when passing over a dip in the road. **2004**—Fractured wheel bearing. • Premature failure of the strut insulator and steering assembly. • Rusted brake rotors. • Sudden headlight failure. • Doors lock and unlock inadvertently.

Secret Warranties/Internal Bulletins/Service Tips

All models/years: Paint delamination, peeling, or fading (see Part Two for info on making a claim). **1995–99**—A new multi-layer steel engine head gasket provided superior sealing characteristics for the above-noted models, which constitutes an admission that the previous head gaskets were poorly designed (the following Chrysler bulletin can be quite useful in getting a head gasket repair refund on any Chrysler engine with a faulty head gasket). • Oil leakage at the cam position sensor is often mistaken for an engine head gasket failure. Chrysler says the cam seal should always be replaced when the head gasket is changed. • Smooth road steering wheel vibration is likely caused by a faulty bushing that should be replaced by Chrysler on a pro rata basis. It's a three-hour repair. **1995–2000**—Eliminating a steering column clunk or rattle. **1996–99**—Troubleshooting a sunroof that

CYLINDER HEAD GASKET

BULLETIN NO: 09-09-98   DATE: NOV. 6, 1998

SUBJECT: Multi-Layer Steel (MLS) Head Gasket installation Procedures

1995–99 (JA) Cirrus/Stratus/Breeze; 1996–99 (JX) Sebring Convertible; 1996–99 (NS) Town & Country/Caravan/ Voyager; 1995–99 (PL) Neon; 1997–99 (GS) Chrysler Voyager (International Market)

NOTE: THIS INFORMATION APPLIES TO MODELS WITH A 2.0L SOHC/DOHC OR 2.4L ENGINE

DISCUSSION: A new Multi-Layer Steel (MLS) head gasket has been developed and is being implemented into production vehicles. Additionally, it has been approved for service applications. This new gasket will provide superior sealing characteristics, but will require extra care in its installation where a composite gasket was previously in place.

OIL SEEPAGE AT CAM POSITION SENSOR

BULLETIN NO: 90-07-98   DATE: DEC. 11, 1998

1995–99 (JA) Cirrus/Stratus/Breeze;
1996–99 (JX) Sebring Convertible (Export Market); 1995–99 (PL) Neon; 1997–99 (GS) Caravan/Voyager (Export Market); 1996–99 (NS) Town & Country/Caravan/Voyager

NOTE: THIS INFORMATION APPLIES TO MODELS WITH A 2.0L SOHC/DOHC OR A 2.4L ENGINE.

DISCUSSION: Whenever performing oil leak diagnosis on one of these models, carefully inspect the cam sensor area to determine if the leak originates from the seal of from other sources. A leak in this area can be misinterpreted as a leaking head gasket.

makes a ratcheting noise when engaged. **1998**—AC compressor lock-up at low mileage. • Sag, hesitation, harsh AC operation, and flickering headlights. • Steering wheel/column rattles and clunks. • Cold-start power-steering noise. • Front brake squeal, creep, or groan. • Paint fogging. • Warning that premium fuel may cause stalling, long cold-start times, hesitation, and warm-up sags. • Popping noise when passing over bumps or making turns. • Sunroof shade rattles in open position. • Vehicle overheats or radiator fan runs continuously. **1998–99**—How to fix a water leak in the left side of the trunk. **1999–2000**—Low mileage AC lock-up. **2000**—Erratic engine performance may be fixed by recalibrating the PCM (powertrain control module). • Delayed automatic transmission engagement likely caused by a faulty front pump. • Harsh AC engagement and clunk noise. • Front suspension creaking. • Front door water leaks. • Power steering moan. • Shake in steering wheel and/or seat at idle. • Poorly seated instrument panel top cover. • Instrument panel creaks. • Rear door glass won't roll down all the way. • High window cranking effort or slow power window operation. • Blower motor noise or vibration. • Front suspension snapping noise. • Deck-lid rattle and water/dust intrusion past the deck-lid seal. • Difficulty moving front seats forward. • Discoloured B-pillar appliqué. • Water enters the horn assembly. **2000–01**—Poor performance of AC and engine. • Power steering moan. • Remedy for AC honking. • Rattling wheel covers. **2000–04**—TSB #19-002-04 admits that a clicking noise heard when turning may be because of a misaligned or defective steering assembly. **2001**—AC expansion valve noise. • Engine hesitation. • Delamination may require the replacement of the accessory drive belt for the power steering pump and AC compressor. • Excessive AC compressor or expansion valve noise. • Front seat rattling. • No-start problem in cold weather. • Rear window may not go all the way down. **2002**—Poor engine and AC performance caused by miscalibrated or faulty computer modules. • Low-speed power steering moan. • Wheel cover rattling when passing over bumps. • If the odometer reading is inaccurate, dealer will reprogram instrument cluster module free of charge under Customer Satisfaction Program #93. • AM radio station static. • Defective fuel filler cap. **2003**—Water leaks onto the right front seat floor (see bulletin at left). **2003–04**—TSB #09-007-04 says an engine snapping sound is Chrysler's fault and can be remedied by chamfering the bore radius on cam bearing caps through L5 and R2 through R5. • Misaligned exhaust tips. **2004**—Hard starts, acceleration stumble. • Intermittent loss of audio.

BODY – WATER LEAKS TO PASSENGER FRONT FLOOR

BULLETIN NO: 23-008-03   DATE: APR. 11, 2003

SUBJECT: Right Side Cowl Water Leak
OVERVIEW: This bulletin involves sealing a right side cowl seam.

2003 Neon/SX 2.0

SYMPTOM: Water on the right front passenger floor.

NEON, SX 2.0, SRT-4 PROFILE

	1996	1997	1998	1999	2000	2001	2002	2003	2004
Cost Price ($)									
Base	12,835	14,750	15,350	15,215	17,995	18,375	18,505	—	—
Sport/SX 2.0	15,515	16,900	17,500	—	—	—	—	14,995	15,195
SRT-4	—	—	—	—	—	—	—	—	26,950
Used Values ($)									
Base ▲	2,000	2,500	3,500	4,500	5,000	6,500	8,000	—	—
Base ▼	1,500	2,000	3,000	4,000	4,500	5,500	7,000	—	—
Sport/SX 2.0 ▲	2,500	3,500	4,000	—	—	—	—	9,000	10,000
Sport/SX 2.0 ▼	2,000	2,500	3,000	—	—	—	—	7,500	9,000
SRT-4 ▲	—	—	—	—	—	—	—	—	19,000
SRT-4 ▼	—	—	—	—	—	—	—	—	17,000
Reliability	❶	❶	❶	❶	❶	❷	❸	❸	❸
Crash Safety (F)	❹	❹	❸	❸	—	❹	❹	❹	❹
Side	—	—	❷	❷	—	❸	❸	❸	❸
Offset	❶	❶	❶	❶	❷	❷	❷	❷	❷

All ratings on a numbered scale where ❸ is good and ❶ is bad. See pages 100–101 for a more detailed description.

Rollover Resistance	—	—	—	—	—	❹	❹	❹	❹
Head Restraints (F)	—	❶	—	❷	❶	❶	❶	❶	❶
Rear	—	—	—	—	—	❶	❶	❶	❶

Ford

ESCORT, ZX2 ★

RATING: Below Average (1997–2000); Not Recommended (1981–96) The Escort has been down-rated because of its many powertrain deficiencies and Ford's lack of parts, servicing, and warranty support. **Maintenance/Repair costs:** Higher than average. Repairs can be done by independents or by Ford or Mazda dealers. **Parts:** Expensive, and getting harder to find. **Extended warranty:** You will need a bumper-to-bumper extended warranty. **Best alternatives:** The GM Firefly or Metro; Honda Civic; Hyundai Accent; Mazda Protegé; Suzuki Esteem; and Toyota Tercel, Echo, or Corolla. **Online help:** *www.tgrigsby.com/views/ford.html* (The Anti-Ford Page) and *www.autosafety.org/autodefects.html.*

 Strengths and Weaknesses

These front-drive small cars are usually reasonably priced and economical to operate, and they provide a comfortable though jittery ride and adequate front seating for two adults. However, they have a Dr. Jekyll and Mr. Hyde disposition, depending on which model year you buy. From 1982 through 1990, these subcompacts were dull performers with uninspiring interiors. Worse, they had a nasty reputation for being totally unreliable and expensive to repair.

VEHICLE HISTORY: 1991—The 1991 model's changeover to more reliable Mazda components gave it a longer wheelbase, making for a more comfortable ride and a slightly roomier interior. **1994**—ABS added to the GT, and all models got a driver-side airbag; motorized seat belts harassed front passengers. **1995**—Dual airbags were installed and motorized seat belts remained (ugh). **1997**—Highlights are fresh styling, a new 110-hp 2.0L 4-cylinder engine, a standard 5-speed manual transmission and optional 4-speed automatic, dual airbags and optional ABS with rear discs. **1998**—Debut of a sporty Escort ZX2 coupe in the States, a year later in Canada. **2000**—Wagons axed and the ZX2 coupe got a firmer suspension and a 130-hp engine.

Owner complaints relating to the 1991–96 model years primarily concern seat belts and airbags, fuel tanks, coil spring and tie-rod failures; automatic transmission and engine (premature timing belt replacement around 90,000 km) breakdowns; and cooling system, brakes, electrical, air conditioning, fuel pump, and ignition system failures. Quality control and reliability improved a bit with the 1997 and 1998 models, but many of the earlier powertrain deficiencies remained.

The 1999 and 2000 models continue to have lots of engine and transmission failures, plus steering vibration, and electrical, fuel, and brake system problems (excessive wear of front brake pads and rotors around 10,000 km).

> My car has had 4 transmissions before 40,000 miles and now at 102,000 miles I'm having to put a new motor in. This car has had excellent care and maintenance and [there is] no reason for this.

 **Safety Summary**

1995–2000—An incredibly high number of safety-related complaints were recorded for these years. The following problems return continually: No airbag deployment; inadvertent airbag deployment; airbag-induced injuries; electrical and engine wiring fires; brake failures, and premature rotor and pad replacement; snapped front and rear coil springs damage tire; sudden tie-rod failure leading to steering loss; automatic transmission that slips, jumps out of gear, leaks, or fails early; unanticipated acceleration; seat belt malfunctions; horn that blows inadvertently, won't blow, or is hard to access; faulty door locks; and speedometer failures (a $400 repair). **1998**—Faulty fuel pump/pressure regulator, CV joints, and wheel bearings. • Delayed shifts. • Steering lock-up. • Defective engine mounts cause excessive vibration. **1999**—Chronic surging and stalling. • Headlight socket melts. • Hood flies open. • Faulty motor mounts cause excessive vibration. • Poor structural integrity (broken welds, distorted sheet metal, and extensive flexing throughout vehicle). • Suspension and alignment problems. • Poor defrosting. **2000**—Chronic stalling. • Vehicle suddenly jumps forward or rearward when the accelerator is only slightly depressed. • Excessive vibration. • Slips in and out of gear when coming to a stop. • Transmission coolant line clamp comes apart. • Delayed transmission engagement, or slippage. • Power-steering loss caused by snapped serpentine belt:

> While driving about 30 mph [50 km/h] power steering went out. Dealer found serpentine belt had snapped, causing bracket to water pump housing to break. Tension rod and water pump housing were replaced at consumer's cost.

• Brake pedal slowly creeps to the floor when applied. • Shock absorber rubbed against tire, causing a blowout. • Sunroof shattered while vehicle was parked. • Windshield suddenly shattered. • Seat belts jam in the retracted position. • Intermittent failure of the power door locks and windows.

Secret Warranties/Internal Bulletins/Service Tips

All models/years: Radio whining or buzzing noise can be eliminated by following the service tips found in TSB #01-7-3. • Repeated heater core failures have also been a frequent problem, covered in TSB #01-15-6. **1993–2000**—Paint delamination, peeling, or fading (see Part Two "Paint and Body Defects," pages 71–75). **1994–98**—Tips on eliminating wind noise around doors are given in TSB #97-15-1. **1997–99**—Positive crankcase ventilation (PCV) system may freeze, resulting in a serious oil leak through the dipstick tube. • A front brake grinding noise, pulling or drag, and uneven brake pad wear are all signs of corrosion affecting the caliper slide pins. • Excessive vibration at idle may be corrected by replacing the engine support crossmember bushings. This repair cost should be covered by Ford up to 7 years/160,000 km. • Tips on silencing a variety of squeaks and rattles. • No restart in cold weather, the cooling fan not shutting off, or the battery going dead all signal the need to change the integrated relay control module. **1997–2000**—Reduced engine power and stalling. **1997–2003**—Excessive vibration countermeasures. **1998**—An erratic transaxle shift may simply be caused by a pinched wire. • Erratic fuel gauge operation or slow fill-ups may be corrected by installing a slosh module fuel gauge kit. **1999**—Tips on reducing noise, vibration, and harshness. **2000**—Delayed transmission engagement; MIL light comes on. • Troubleshooting intake manifold air leaks. • Exhaust system buzzing or rattling (a problem for over a decade). • Fuel fill nozzle clicks off too soon when fuelling up. • PCV freezes up. • Inoperative CD player. • Tips on properly adjusting the transmission range sensor. • Remedy for a burning oil smell. • Troubleshooting poor engine performance at idle and excessive gas consumption. • Remedies for an engine that won't start or shut down properly. • Engine oil leak at the oil pan, front cover, or the front and rear crankshaft oil seal. • Engine oil pan gasket and oil filter leaks. • Vehicle may not start in freezing weather, because of moisture freezing in the fuel pump relay. • Fuel delivery malfunctions. • Eliminating a high idle condition when starting or decelerating. • Improved parking brake cables and rear brake linings are available to reduce rear brake drag. • Light to moderate rear axle whine. • Squeak, creak from driver's area. • Possible causes of a thump or clunk coming from the suspension. • Front seat cushion sagging. • Cause and correction of vinyl dash abrasions and premature wear. • Diagnostic tips to eliminate wind noise around doors. • Revise hood seal to reduce wind whistle. • AC goes into defrost mode when vehicle goes uphill. • Repeated heater core failures.

	1994	1995	1996	1997	1998	1999	2000
Cost Price ($)							
Escort Base/LX	12,195	12,995	13,595	14,595	14,895	14,895	—
GT	13,995	14,295	15,295	—	—	—	—
ZX2	—	—	—	—	—	15,895	17,995
Used Values ($)							
Base/LX ▲	1,000	1,500	2,500	3,000	3,500	4,500	—
Base/LX ▼	800	1,000	2,000	2,500	3,000	3,500	—
GT ▲	2,000	2,500	3,500	—	—	—	—
GT ▼	1,500	2,000	3,000	—	—	—	—
ZX2 ▲	—	—	—	—	—	5,000	6,500
ZX2 ▼	—	—	—	—	—	4,000	5,000
Reliability	❷	❷	❷	❷	❷	❸	❸
Crash Safety (F)	❺	❹	❹	❹	❸	❸	❸
Side	—	—	—	—	❸	❸	❸
Offset	—	—	—	❸	❸	❸	❸

Note: Ratings and prices are also applicable to the Mercury Tracer.

RATING: Below Average (2004); Not Recommended (2000–03). How stupid can Ford be? Consider this: Some Focus models can't be driven through puddles because the low-mounted air intake hose ingests water into the engine ($5,000 repair). Chronic stalling is also a major problem, but Ford's secret warranty doesn't cover afflicted 2002 and 2003 models. **Maintenance/Repair costs:** Predicted to

All ratings on a numbered scale where ❺ is good and ❶ is bad. See pages 100–101 for a more detailed description.

be higher than average once warranty expires. **Parts:** Expensive and sometimes hard to find. **Extended warranty:** A bumper-to-bumper warranty or a rich uncle is a prerequisite to owning a Focus. **Best alternatives:** GM Firefly, Metro, Cavalier, or Sunfire; Honda Civic (it's softer riding, quieter, and has a smoother-running engine); Hyundai Accent; Mazda Protegé; Suzuki Esteem and Swift; and Toyota Corolla, Echo, or Tercel. **Online help:** *www.autosafety.org/article. php?scid=&did=309.*

 ## Strengths and Weaknesses

Hailed as Europe's 1999 Car of the Year (yikes; that should be your first warning sign), Ford's sleek 2000 Focus came to North America shortly thereafter as an uplevel, premium small car. The Escort's base engine, a 110-hp 2.0L 4-cylinder, was carried over to the Focus LX and SE, while the 130-hp twin-cam 2.0L (also used on the Escort ZX2 coupe) became the standard power plant on the ZTS and ZX3 and optional on the SE.

VEHICLE HISTORY: 2002—Debut of a high-performance, 170-hp SVT Focus with sport suspension and 17-inch wheels; and the ZX5, a four-door hatchback that looks like a shortened version of the Focus wagon. **2003**—A standard 5-year warranty came on the scene (should be at least seven years). **2004**—No more anti-skid system and a 145-hp 2.3 L 4-cylinder is added.

The 130-hp 2.0L engine is barely sufficient for highway cruising, where passing and merging require a bit more power. The Focus isn't a quiet car, either. Any decent speed is accompanied by constant engine buzz and some hard shifting with the automatic gearbox. Brakes add to the Focus' symphony of sound by emitting a grinding sound when applied, and the front suspension creaks when the car is put through its paces. There is some vibration felt when driving over smooth highways, and uneven terrain causes the car to bounce about.

The Focus does handle well in city traffic, thanks to its tight turning radius and nimble steering. The small back corner windows are also handy for keeping the rear visibility unobstructed. The car's unusually tall roofline gives ample headroom and allows for a higher, more upright riding position than you'll see with traditional small cars. Front and rear legroom is impressive as well, as long as the front passengers don't push their seats too far back.

This is one of the most unreliable and dangerously defective cars that Ford has built in recent memory. Powertrain, fuel, electrical, and brake system failures are commonplace. Service bulletins are replete with special instructions telling dealers how to practically rebuild the car to make it tolerably driveable. Powertrain problems include chronic stalling (covered up to 10 years by a secret warranty); excessive vibration; poor engine and transmission performance; and 2003 SVT flywheel, pressure plate, and clutch assembly failures. Other problems: failure-prone ignition switch; seatback bar digs into driver's back; power window failure; excessive engine, brake, steering column, suspension, and wheel noise; trunk latch sticks or suddenly opens; trunk leaks water; AC leaks coolant; driver's door won't open from the inside; fuel door lid broke in half; hood latch broke off when closing hood; right rear door moulding fell off; and poor-fitting interior panels.

A threat to your wallet is annoying, but a threat to your genitalia is really scary:

> The 2004 Focus cigarette lighter after being pushed in and getting hot popped out of the holder and landed either on the occupant's lap or on the carpeting. When this was shown to the rental company, and a demonstration was done, the lighter burned the representative's legs. This was a Budget rental vehicle.

 Safety Summary

2000—NHTSA is probing rear door latch failures on wagons. **2000–01**—Ford admits to chronic stalling and extends engine computer warranty to 10 years (see Secret Warranties below). **2000–02**—NHTSA continues to investigate complaints of chronic stalling (see *www.autosafety.org/EA02-022-OpeningMemo.pdf*), while Ford attempts different fixes outlined in confidential service bulletins. • Chronic stalling, with loss of brakes and steering, believed to be caused by faulty fuel pump. • Airbag deploys for no apparent reason or after vehicle hits a pothole. • Sudden brake loss. • Differential fluid leaks on brake components (right side), causing brake loss. • Defective speed control causes sudden acceleration in spite of corrective recall. • Other sudden acceleration incidents ascribed to faulty power control module (PCM) and driver's shoe being caught under the plastic console. • Sudden acceleration in Reverse. • Collapse of tie-rod and axle, leading to loss of control. • Defective axle wheel bearing. • Sudden pull to the left when turning left. • Clutch pedal spring pops out, injuring driver. • Pedal fell on floorboard. • Transmission slippage and failure. • Inaccurate fuel gauge (sender and fuel pump replaced). • Windshield cracks for no reason. • AC condensation drips on accelerator pedal. • Exhaust fumes enter passenger compartment. • Smoking electrical wiring in dash. • Under-hood fire ignited after AC engaged. • Driver-side seat belt won't deploy. • Emergency brake often fails to engage because button on handle stays depressed. • Vehicle was cruising at 110 km/h when gas pedal fell off its mounting. • Frayed accelerator throttle cable snapped; cable also kinks, causing hesitation, acceleration, and surging. • Stabilizer bar suddenly broke. • Car left in Park rolled downhill. • Rear end is very unstable in snow, feels "wobbly" under normal conditions, and throws rear passengers about. • Sudden, unintended acceleration, then engine cuts out. • Engine shuts down while cruising on the highway. • New engine needed after roadway rainwater ingested into engine because of low air intake valve. • Transmission hard to shift into Second and Reverse in cold weather. • Fuel tank leak because of cracked filler pipe. • No brakes. • No steering. • Steering wheel locks while driving. • Broken rack and pinion. • Airbags didn't deploy. • Tie-rod suddenly broke off. • Front and rear wheels buckle. • Collapsed front wheel.

My father owns this vehicle, but he bought it for me for safety reasons. I am a 16-year-old female. Travelling at normal highway speed on a dry, two-lane highway with no traffic at night, my 2002 Ford Focus lost control due to the front control arm fracturing. My right front tire ended up totally unattached to the control arm and only staying attached to the vehicle by the hold of the tie-rod. My vehicle swerved into the median and into the oncoming traffic (thankfully no traffic was around).

• Rear hatch opens on its own. • Faulty rear wheel bearings cause wheel to wobble and wander. • Original Firestone tires wear out prematurely. • Child restraint bracket puts dents in the rear seat. • Inaccurate fuel gauge sender and fuel pump replaced. • Windshield cracks or shatters for no reason. • AC condensation drips on accelerator pedal. • Exhaust fumes enter passenger compartment. • Dash lights flicker, then quit. **2003**—Chronic stalling. • Airbags failed to deploy. • Reports of severe back trauma from seatback failure in rear-enders. • Transmission and axle failures. • Sudden brake loss. • Excessive vibration. • Trunk latch suddenly releases. • Sunlight washes out speedometer reading. • Windshield cracks for no reason. **2004**—Sudden acceleration. • Chronic stalling and surging continues to be a problem. • Automatic transmission self-destructed.

Vehicle has stalled/sputtered while driving or idling. I took the vehicle to the dealer on 3 separate occasions and each time they said something different was wrong. The dealer replaced the idle air control valve, cleaned out the entire fuel tank, replaced the fuel pump and filter and have now replaced the transmission.

• Wheel bearing failure. • No-start because ignition cylinder seized. • Tire feathering.

Secret Warranties/Internal Bulletins/Service Tips

All models: 2000—Ford Campaign No. 03M02 allows for the free replacement of fractured front coil springs up to 10 years or 240,000 km (150,000 mi.). • Under Special Service Instruction 00204, Ford will reprogram the powertrain computer module to correct poor engine performance on vehicles equipped with a manual transmission. • ONP 99B21 will replace the fuel pulse damper free of charge and ONP 99B22 will pay the costs associated with replacing the side engine mount. • Vehicles equipped with a manual transmission will have their clutch master cylinder and pedal return spring replaced, free of charge, under ONP 00B59. • Ford also announced in Special Field Action 0012 that it will henceforth guarantee all original equipment tires for 3 years/58,000 km (36,000 mi.). • Defective Sony subwoofer speakers will be replaced for free under ONP 01B73. **2000–01**—Chronic stalling fix. Reuters News Service reported on November 20, 2003, that a faulty fuel delivery module linked to chronic engine stalling would be replaced free of charge by Ford up to 10 years, without any mileage limitation (Campaign No. 03N01). Ford spokesman Glenn Ray told Reuters, "It's a product improvement program. There is nothing fundamentally wrong with the quality of the fuel

Director
Service Engineering Operations
Ford Customer Service Division

Ford Motor Company
P.O. Box 1904
Dearborn, MI 48121-1904

May 2003

TO: All U.S. Ford and Lincoln Mercury Dealers

SUBJECT: Customer Satisfaction Program 03M02: Certain 2000 Model Year Focus Vehicles – Additional Coverage for Front Coil Springs

OASIS:

- Yes

OWNER LIST:

- No

PROGRAM TERMS:

This program extends the coverage on the front coil springs to 10 years of service or 150,000 miles from the vehicle's warranty start date, whichever occurs first. This coverage will automatically transfer to subsequent owners. If a vehicle already has more than 150,000 miles, this coverage will last until December 31, 2003.

VEHICLES COVERED BY THIS PROGRAM

Certain 2000 model year Focus vehicles built at Wayne Assembly Plant from March 5, 1999 through December 23, 1999 and at Hermosillo Assembly Plant from May 21, 1999 through December 30, 1999.

REASON FOR PROVIDING ADDITIONAL COVERAGE

In some of the affected vehicles, portions of the front coil springs may not have received adequate corrosion protection during the manufacturing process. Inadequate corrosion protection eventually may lead to a fracture of the spring. A spring fracture may result in suspension noise, possibly accompanied by sagging of one side of the vehicle. This is most likely to occur on vehicles operated for extended periods of time in high-corrosion areas of North America. Only a small percentage of the affected vehicles are expected to experience this concern.

SERVICE ACTION

If a front coil spring should fracture, the dealer technician will replace both front coil springs, check front wheel alignment and, if necessary, adjust toe angle at no charge to the owner of the vehicle.

delivery module. It doesn't fail instantaneously or suddenly." • Replace rear wheel bearings through December 31, 2003, regardless of mileage, under Ford Campaign No. 01B85. **2000–02**—Low power and stalling (see 1997–2000 Escort section on page 111). • AC evaporator case/cowl leaks water into the interior. • AC fluttering noise. • Whistling from the heater plenum. • Repeated heater core failure. • Turn signal lamps won't self-cancel. **2000–03**—Troubleshooting rear-end water leaks (see bulletin on next page). **2000–04**—Remedy for front suspension creak, crunch, grinding, or rattle. **2001**—Difficult to shift out of Park. • 2.0L Zetec engines may hesitate, surge, or idle roughly in cold weather. • Intermittent stalling, hesitation, or lack of power. • Engine may produce higher-than-normal idle speed, or run roughly at idle. • Slight engine vibration at idle. • Troubleshooting the Check

All ratings on a numbered scale where ⑤ is good and ❶ is bad. See pages 100–101 for a more detailed description.

Engine light. • Eliminating a burning oil smell. • Rear brake squeal may be caused by the composition of the lining material. • Power steering pump pulley may squeak or chirp upon start-up. • Ignition key may be difficult to turn in cylinder. • Seat seams may split. 2002–03—Hard starts and poor driveability may be caused by an incorrect PCM calibration. 2002–05—TSB #04-15-2 says erratic windshield wiper operation is a Ford defect caused by a faulty wiper relay. 2004—Loss of power, hesitation, or misfire after a cold start. • Runs rough in wet weather. • Harsh transmission engagement. • Premature clutch wear. • Transmission clunking or rattling. • Grinding when shifting into Third gear. • Gear rattle from the transaxle at idle. • Inoperative speed control system. • Intermittent no-starts; odometer may show all dashes. • Customer Satisfaction Program #04B16 will pay for the correction of front seat heater element pads that may shift. • Diagonal wear or cupping of the rear tires. • Engine belt squeal.

FOCUS PROFILE

	2000	2001	2002	2003	2004
Cost Price ($)					
LX	14,995	16,015	15,970	16,275	16,475
ZX3	16,697	16,690	17,390	17,550	17,775
Wagon SE	17,695	17,271	18,995	19,165	19,375
Used Values ($)					
LX ▲	5,000	6,000	7,000	9,000	11,500
LX ▼	4,000	5,000	6,500	8,000	10,000
ZX3 ▲	5,500	6,500	8,000	9,500	12,000
ZX3 ▼	5,000	5,500	7,000	8,500	10,500
Wagon SE ▲	6,000	7,000	9,000	10,500	13,000
Wagon SE ▼	5,000	6,000	8,000	9,500	11,500
Reliability	❶	❷	❷	❷	❷
Crash Safety (F)					
2d	⑤	⑤	④	④	④
4d	④	④	⑤	⑤	⑤
Wagon	—	—	⑤	⑤	⑤
Side					
2d	④	④	④	④	④
4d	❸	❸	—	❸	❸
Offset	④	④	④	④	④
Head Restraints	—	❷	❷	❷	❷
Rollover Resistance	④	④	④	④	④

General Motors

RATING: Average (2003–04); Below Average (1999–2002); Not Recommended (1984–98). GM's best small cars, which isn't saying much; engine, transmission, and brake repair bills will run you bankrupt if you get a pre-1999 model. Try to get a 2003 or later model with a 4-speed automatic transmission; it will be a bit more reliable, reduce engine noise, and make for more responsive performance. The base Sunbird changed its name to the Sunfire in 1995; it shares the Cavalier's basic design. The Cavalier Z24 convertible was replaced by the LS in 1995. **Maintenance/Repair costs:** Average. Repairs aren't dealer dependent; however, ABS troubleshooting is a real head-scratcher. **Parts:** Reasonably priced; often available for much less from independent suppliers. **Extended warranty:** Not essential. You should balance the cost of an engine head gasket ($800–$1,000) with that of an extended warranty that will likely cost twice as much. **Best alternatives:** Honda Civic; Hyundai Accent or Elantra; Mazda Protegé; Mazda3, Nissan Sentra; Suzuki Esteem and Swift; and Toyota Corolla, Echo, or Tercel. Also take a look at the slightly more upscale Hyundai Tiburon. **Online help:** *www.autosafety.org/article.php?did=41&scid=46* and *www.autooninfo.info/RelPerChevroletCharts.htm*.

 ## Strengths and Weaknesses

These twins are two of the lowest-priced cars to come equipped with standard ABS and dual airbags (1995–2003). In fact, GM claims it lost $1,000 on every one it sold. These small cars are attractively styled (especially the Pontiac Sunfire), come with lots of interior room, and offer a nicely tuned suspension. The ride and handling have also improved markedly since 1999, with power rack-and-pinion steering, a longer wheelbase, and a wider track. The Sunfire is identical to the Cavalier, except for its more rakish look. The Cavalier Z24 and Sunfire are performance versions, equipped with a more refined version of the less-than-reliable Quad 4 2.4L DOHC 16-valve 4-cylinder power plant.

VEHICLE HISTORY: 1995—Wider and taller than previous models; standard dual airbags and ABS; a stiffer structure; and an improved suspension. **1996**—LS sedan and convertible got standard traction control, and the Z24 picked up a new dual-camshaft 2.2L engine. **1998**—The base engine lost five horses. **1999**—2.4L twin-cam engine and front brake lining upgrades. **2000**—A slightly restyled front and rear end; an improved storage area; standard AC and PASSLOCK security system; upgraded standard ABS; and a smoother-shifting 5-speed manual transmission. **2003**—Restyled and lengthened; a new 140-hp 2.2L engine; a stiffer suspension; larger wheels and rear brakes; three-point centre seat belts; optional front side airbags; and ABS. **2004**—ABS is no longer standard on base models; CD player reads MP3-formatted discs.

Snappy road performance (with the correct engine and transmission hookup) has been marred by abysmally poor powertrain reliability. The early 2.0L versions are lacklustre performers—overwhelmed by the demands of passing and merging. On top of that, major reliability weaknesses afflict many mechanical and body components through the 1998 model year, where engine, transmission, electronic module, and brake failures are particularly common. Specifically, owners report that engine blocks crack, cylinder heads leak, and the turbocharged version frequently needs expensive repairs.

For 1990–94 versions, the Cavalier's base 2.2L 4-cylinder and optional 3.1L engines replaced the failure-prone 2.0L and 2.8L power plants. Unfortunately, the newer engines also have a chequered reputation, highlighted by reports of chronic head gasket failures afflicting the 4-cylinder power plant. Air conditioning and hood latch failures, seat belt defects, and a plethora of body deficiencies are also commonplace. Door bottoms and wheel housings are particularly vulnerable to rust perforation. Premature paint peeling and cracking, discoloration, and surface rust have been constant problems.

Since 1999, these vehicles have become a bit more reliable and durable. Nevertheless, owners are still plagued by troublesome engines, faulty brakes, airbags that continue to malfunction and injure occupants, chronic stalling, and transmission and fuel pump failures. The Getrag manual gearbox isn't very reliable, nor is it easily repaired, and faulty computer modules, fuel injection, and cooling systems cause stalling and a shaky idle. The power steering may lead or pull, and the steering rack tends to deteriorate quickly, usually requiring replacement some time shortly after 80,000 km. The front MacPherson struts also wear out rapidly, as do the rear shock absorbers. Many owners complain of rapid front brake wear and warped brake discs after a year or so. One owner reported the following brake repairs to NHTSA:

> Front brake rotors are warping and had to be turned at 1,600 miles [2,560 km] and 1,800 miles [2,880 km]. They then were replaced at 2,800 miles [4,480 km]. They would cause the vehicle to jump when braking.

Owner-reported problems for the past four model years: Front vacuum leak causes vehicle to lose power; lots of electrical system glitches; hard starts; chronic stalling; slipping transmission; grinding noise when shifting gear; rattling noise when shifting from First to Second gear; frequent steering failures and noisy steering; excessive pulsation when braking; airbag warning lamp coming on continuously; a symphony of interior noises; and windows that may fall off their tracks and slide between the door panels. Fit

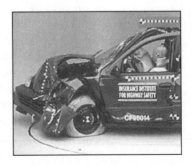

and finish quality is still quite variable, often leading to poor paint application, inside and outside body panel gaps, and lots of exposed screw heads. Most body hardware is fragile (for example, the bumper can come apart).

 **Safety Summary**

Although safety-related complaints have been separated according to model and year, there is considerable overlap since these two vehicles are practically identical. **All years:** Engine head gasket and intake manifold failures. • Transmission slippage or breakdown. • Owners report complete brake failure and lock-up, extended stopping distances, ABS that self-activates, premature rotor warpage and pad wear, and a grinding and knocking noise when braking. • Airbags fail to deploy or deploy accidentally. • Sudden acceleration, stalling. • Weak door hinges. • Inoperative horn. **1998**—Fire in the trunk area. • Airbag-induced burns and fractures are common. • Loose or broken engine mounts. • Chronic engine overheating. • Steering wheel locks up after a cold start. • Steering shaft sheared off when turning. • Inaccurate fuel gauge. • One Saskatchewan *Lemon-Aid* reader reports that the rear bumper will crack extensively in cold weather if hit only slightly. • Windshield glare from the dash. • Driver seat lever interferes with entry/exit. **1999–2001**—Engine fires. • Leaking fuel tank. • Plastic fuel tank is easily punctured. • Right wheel axle twisted off vehicle. • Chronic hesitation, stalling, and surging. • Clutch will not disengage, causing sudden acceleration. • Brake failure caused by leaking master cylinder fluid. • ABS locked up, causing vehicle to go into a skid. • Seat belt failed to retract. • Transmission wouldn't go into Reverse, transmission failed to engage upon start-up, automatic transmission locks up in Second gear, and vehicle rolled away even though parked with parking brake engaged. • When vehicle is in Drive with foot on the brake, it lurches forward, stalls, and produces a crashing sound. • During highway driving, the vehicle suddenly accelerated without steering control. • Rear leaf spring U-bolts broke, causing entire rear end to drop. • Front right side of the vehicle collapsed because of wheel bolts shearing off, causing the wheel to detach completely. • Springs are too weak, causing poor stability and control. • Floor mat impedes clutch pedal travel. • Sudden brake cable breakage while driving, brake grinding noise, and early warping of the front and rear brakes. • When driving with door locked, door came ajar. • Hood flew up while driving. • Misaligned driver's door. • Windshield water leaks. **2002**—Reverse tail light bulb exploded, causing light assembly to catch on fire. • Considerable fuel spillage when refuelling. • Left rear axle fell off. • Plastic bumper fell off while driving. • Headlights often go out. **2003**—Tire jack collapsed. • Transmission allows vehicle to roll backward when parked. • Inoperative fuel gauge. • Stalling caused by defective fuel pump. • Burnt electrical wires and light sockets. • Excessive driver-side mirror vibration. **2004**—Fire ignited in engine compartment. • Strong fuel odour in the interior. • Stuck accelerator pedal. Engine surging, sudden acceleration, and hard starts because of defective computer module. • Frequent transmission clutch assembly and flywheel failures. • Windshield wiper malfunctions. • Rear window water leak because of faulty weatherstripping. • Trunk lid bolts sheared off.

Secret Warranties/Internal Bulletins/Service Tips

All models/years: GM has a new kit that it says will eliminate AC odours. • A rotten-egg odour coming from the exhaust isn't as easily eradicated. Usually caused by a malfunctioning catalytic converter; this repair is routinely covered by GM's emissions warranty. • Paint delamination, peeling, or fading (see Part Two "Paint and Body Defects," pages 71–75). • Plastic wheel nut covers tend to fall off. GM will replace them for free on a case-by-case basis, says TSB #01-03-10-009. **All models: 1985–2000**—Snow may intrude into the rear brake drum assembly and interfere with braking, says TSB #00-05-24-001, April 2000. Don't pay the full shot for what is basically GM's poor design. **1995–98**—A bulge in the front bucket seatback requires additional bracing to correct. • Install a drain path in convertibles to prevent water from collecting in the rear footwell area. **1995–99**—A faulty rear lid (trunk) latch may need only a new cable. **1995–2000**—Instrument panel squeak or rattle, scratched right front door trim panel, or right-side end of instrument panel contacting door trim panel can be fixed by removing the instrument panel assembly and realigning the tie bar. • GM will install upgraded rear brake backing plates to prevent snow intrusion freezing the brake shoes to the drums. Bargain down the installation cost since it is GM's fault in the first place. **1995–2003**—Engine head gasket failures that include overheating, loss of coolant, coolant odour, coolant leaks around the cylinder head, and white smoke from the exhaust. Sometimes the heater won't work, or a film (from the coolant) will be deposited on the inside glass surfaces. If the coolant leaks inside the engine, it can cause severe engine damage from overheating. GM "goodwill" covers head gasket problems for 7 years/160,000 km (100,000 mi.), whichever comes first. Remember, if you have an engine head gasket failure on a GM vehicle or engine not included in the above-noted programs, don't despair. Simply use the same benchmarks for your own vehicle and threaten small claims action on those grounds. Make sure you cite TSB #98054A, "Campaign: Cylinder Head Gasket Failure, Coolant Leakage," published September 1998. Incidentally, some *Lemon-Aid* readers say minor head

---

BULLETIN NO: 03-07-30-021   DATE: MAY 2003

A/T – SHIFT FLARE/SES LAMP ON/DTC'S SET

SUBJECT: Neutral flare and/or rpm flare while in Drive, no 1–2 upshift, Service Engine Soon (SES) light illuminated, diagnostic trouble codes (DTCs) P1810, DTC P1815 set (replace transmission fluid pressure (TFP) manual valve position switch)

1995–2003 Chevrolet Cavalier; 1997–2003 Chevrolet Malibu; 1999–2003 Oldsmobile Alero; 1995–2003 Pontiac Sunfire; 1998–2003 Pontiac Grand Am with 4T40E Transmission (RPO MN4) or 4T45E Transmission (RPO MN5)

SYMPTOMS: Some customers may comment on a neutral flare and/or rpm increase while in Drive or no 1–2 upshift and/or the Service Engine Soon (SES) telltale may be illuminated. On 1995–2002 model vehicles, the Powertrain Control Module (PCM) may set a DTC P1810 while on 2003 model vehicles, the PCM may set a DTC P1815. The cause may be the transmission fluid pressure (TFP) switch (also known as the pressure switch manifold [PSM]). It will be referred to as the TFP switch in this bulletin.

gasket leaks can be plugged by inexpensive sealers. • Automatic transmission delay and surging (flare); see the bulletin on previous page. **1996–2002**—Coolant leakage from the water pump weep hole will be plugged by installing a free coolant collector, says TSB #01-06-02-012. **1997–2002**—A clunk noise from the front of the vehicle when turning may be fixed by simply lubricating the intermediate shaft, says TSB #01-02-032-001A. **1998**—A delayed, slow, or non-existant 2–3 upshift may require a new transmission case cover or assembly. • A 2.2L cold engine hesitation, sag, or stall may be corrected by recalibrating the power control module (PCM). **1998–2004**—TSB #03-08-67-009A says a binding sunroof likely needs a new sunroof motor. **1999–2000**—No Third and Fourth gear may require a new direct clutch piston assembly. **1999–2002**—Problems opening the fuel-filler door can be fixed by installing a free fuel-filler pocket, says TSB #01-08-65-001. **2000**—Premature connecting rod failure if engine is run at high rpm with low mileage. • Rough engine idle, misfire, or Check Engine light coming on are all

---

ENGINE – OVERHEATING/ COOLANT CONSUMPTION/SMOKE

BULLETIN NO: 03-06-01-022   DATE: JULY 29, 2003

SUBJECT: Guidelines for Cylinder Bore Liner Replacement on the L4 Ecotec Engine

2002–03 Chevrolet Cavalier, Oldsmoblie Alero, Pontiac Grand Am, Pontiac Sunfire with 2.2L Engine (VIN F - RPO L61)

SYMPTOM/CONDITION: Replacement of the cylinder bore liner is now a validated service repair process and an alternative to engine block or engine assembly replacement. Conditions for engine cylinder bore liner replacement are somewhat difficult to determine and may initially appear as other common customer concerns. Customer may comment on conditions such as:

^Engine overheating

^Engine coolant consumption

^White smoke from vehicle exhaust

^Poor heater performance

^Excessive engine oil consumption

^Unusual engine knocking noises

---

because of a poorly calibrated computer module. • Possibility of engine coolant leaks caused by the upper radiator hose rubbing against the battery tray. • Automatic transmission may not go into Third or Fourth gear. • Mismachined sealing surface on forward clutch housing (4T40-E transmission). • Grinding or growling from transmission when in Park on an incline. • Vehicles equipped with a 2.2L engine may produce an annoying engine or transmission whine. • Door rattles. • Driver-side manual mirror doesn't adjust when the adjusting lever is moved. **2000–02**—Harsh transmission shifts accompanied by the Service Engine Soon lamp warning is caused by a short in the input speed sensor wiring, says TSB #00-06-04037A. • A wet road "sizzle" noise coming from the rear of the vehicle requires the installation of free wheelhouse liners, says TSB #01-08-58-005. • Inaccurate fuel gauge readings can be corrected for free by installing a new fuel tank sender sensor kit under Customer Satisfaction Campaign #00101 (see "Inaccurate fuel gauge readings" TSB, page XXX <catch>). **2000–03**—Troubleshooting engine problems (see bulletin at left). **2001–02**—If the vehicle fails to crank or start, the battery cable connection may be at fault. • Inoperative cigarette lighter will be replaced for free, says TSB #01-08-49-016. **2001–05**—TSB #01-07-30-030A says there are four likely causes for harsh 1–2 upshifts. None of them are the owner's fault. **2002**—ABS light comes on when transmission is placed in Second or Fourth gear. • 4-speed automatic transmission fluid leakage. • Faulty automatic transmission converter pump. • Customer Satisfaction Campaign inspection for transaxle converter bearing failure is detailed in TSB #01031. • Inaccurate fuel gauge readings. **2002–04**—A slipping automatic transmission may need a new driven sprocket support assembly, says TSB #03-07-30-012A. • Stuck in Second or slipping in Fourth gear: Owner should repair conduit splice/reposition conduit or inspect/reinstall evap. emission vent solenoid or replace, if necessary, per TSB #03-07-30-036. Power steering may cut out in cold weather. • Tips on silencing squeaky wheels. **2003**—Troubleshooting erratic shifting (see following bulletin).

SES LAMP ON/FIRM SHIFTS/NO DOWNSHIFTS/SHUDDER

BULLETIN NO: 02-07-30-039C   DATE: JUNE 12, 2003

SUBJECT: Firm transmission shifts, shudder/chuggle, transmission won't downshift on deceleration, Service Engine Soon light illuminated, DTC P0742 set (perform diagnostics and replace TCC PWM solenoid)

2003 Buick Century, LeSabre, Park Avenue, Regal, Rendezvous; 2003 Cadillac DeVille, Seville; 2003 Chevrolet Cavalier, Impala, Malibu, Monte Carlo, Venture; 2003 Oldsmobile Alero, Aurora, Silhouette; 2003 Pontiac Aztek, Bonneville, Grand Prix, Grand Am, Montana, Sunfire

---

• Correcting transmissions that won't shift, or shift erratically (replace driven sprocket support assembly). **2003–04**—TSB #03-01-38-012A recommends that the AC system components be repositioned to cure an underhood rattle or growl. Troubleshooting AC problems, per TSB #03-01-38-005A. **2004**—Automatic transmission fluid leak caused by faulty reverse servo cover and seal.

CAVALIER, SUNFIRE PROFILE

	1996	1997	1998	1999	2000	2001	2002	2003	2004
Cost Price ($)									
Cavalier	13,030	14,390	14,765	15,365	15,765	14,260	14,500	15,785	16,125
Z24	17,643	19,000	19,295	20,035	20,515	21,165	22,475	21,550	22,125
Z24 Conv./LS	22,925	24,285	25,880	26,450	27,200	—	—	—	—
Sunfire GT	13,380	15,340	15,960	16,135	16,165	14,755	14,790	15,485	16,125
Used Values ($)									
Cavalier ▲	2,500	3,000	4,000	4,500	5,000	6,000	7,000	8,000	10,500
Cavalier ▼	2,000	2,500	3,500	4,000	4,500	5,000	6,000	7,000	9,500
Z24 ▲	4,000	4,500	5,500	6,500	8,000	9,000	11,000	13,000	15,500
Z24 ▼	3,000	4,000	4,500	5,000	7,000	8,000	10,000	11,500	14,000
Z24 Conv. /LS ▲	6,000	6,500	7,500	8,500	9,500	—	—	—	—
Z24 Conv. /LS ▼	5,000	5,500	6,500	7,500	8,500	—	—	—	—

Sunfire GT ▲	3,000	3,500	4,500	5,000	5,500	6,500	7,500	8,500	11,000
Sunfire GT ▼	2,500	3,000	4,000	4,500	5,000	5,500	6,500	7,500	10,000
Reliability	①	②	②	③	③	③	③	③	③
Crash Safety (F)									
Cavalier 2d	—	—	③	③	③	③	③	④	④
Cavalier 4d	③	③	④	④	④	④	④	④	④
Side									
Cavalier 2d	—	—	①	①	①	①	①	①	①
Cavalier 4d	—	—	①	①	①	①	①	①	①
Offset	②	②	②	②	②	②	①	①	①
Head Restraints	—	②	—	②	—	②	①	①	①
Rollover Resistance	—	—	—	—	—	④	④	④	④

Note: NHTSA says the Sunfire safety ratings should be identical to the Cavalier's score.

SATURN S-SERIES, L-SERIES, ION   ★★

RATING: *S-series coupe:* Below Average (1998–2002); Not Recommended (1992–97). *L-series:* Below Average (2000–04). *Ion:* Below Average (2003–04). Saturn is a microcosm of all that is wrong with GM. It has lost billions of dollars; Saturn models are late to market, bland, and inappropriate; and quality control is the pits, especially as it relates to powertrain dependability. Japanese and South Korean competitors have been proven to offer far better quality at a competitive cost. Even GM's less pretentious models, like the Cavalier and Sunfire or the minuscule Metro and Firefly, offer better quality and value for your money. As bizarre as it may appear, the Saturn division has a better reputation than the car it sells. **Maintenance/Repair costs:** Average; repairs aren't dealer dependent, unless you're seeking some Saturn "goodwill" refunds, or have CVT transmission glitches. **Parts:** Higher-than-average cost. CVT parts are often back-ordered and are hellacious to troubleshoot. **Extended warranty:** Don't go anywhere near a used Saturn unless you're armed to the teeth with a comprehensive extended warranty. **Best alternatives:** Honda Civic LX, Hyundai Elantra, and Toyota Corolla perform much better and are more reliable. **Online help:** *www.geocities.com/saturn_hate/index. html, fixmysaturn.netfirms.com, www.geocities.com/lafire000/,* and *koenigland.com/ saturn.*

Strengths and Weaknesses

The entry-level S-series is far from high-tech and remained virtually unchanged until it was replaced by the 2003 Ion. The base model provides a comfortable driving position, adequate instrumentation and controls, unobstructed visibility, good braking, dent-resistant body panels, and better-than-average crashworthiness

All ratings on a numbered scale where ⑤ is good and ❶ is bad. See pages 100–101 for a more detailed description.

scores. But, balancing these advantages, buyers have to contend with excessive engine noise, limited rear seat room, glitch-prone anti-lock brakes and traction control, the coupe's third-door window that doesn't roll down, and serious factory-related deficiencies. *L-series*: In an attempt to save money by adapting a European car to the American market, Saturn brought out the LS sedan and LW wagon, derivatives of GM's Opel Vectra. Some major differences, however, include a lengthened body, a standard ignition theft-deterrent system, a re-engineered chassis to give a more comfortable ride, and the use of a homegrown 137-hp 2.2L 4-banger constructed with aluminum components (remember the Vega?). Other components lifted directly from the European parts bin are the Opel's 3.0L V6 engine, a manual transmission from Saab, and German-made braking systems.

The more expensive L-series models provide a more comfortable driving position and a roomy interior with a full range of convenience features, instruments, and controls. The 2002 L-series got standard head curtain airbags, ABS brakes, four-wheel disc brakes on all but the base model, and traction control. The V6 powertrain matchup, firm ride, impressive high-speed stability, and impressive braking all point to the L-series' European heritage. Additionally, there's better soundproofing and lots of storage areas, including a large, accessible trunk.

Ion: A larger, more comfortable, and more powerful vehicle than its S-series predecessor, the Ion is powered by a 140-hp 2.2L 4-cylinder engine, and gives buyers the choice of either a four-door coupe or sedan. Other features include power steering, a CVT automatic transmission, speed-sensitive windshield wipers, split folding rear seatbacks, and plastic body side panels.

The Ion's deficiencies mirror those of the S-series coupe it replaced and its L-Series big brother. The only added wrinkle is the CVT transmission, which, despite an extended warranty following widespread quality complaints, is destined for the trash heap. In the meantime, Ion and VUE SUV owners are likely to face long servicing waits and mind-boggling depreciation.

VEHICLE HISTORY: *Coupe*: **1992**—Returns with upgrades to reduce engine noise and vibration. **1993**—A standard driver-side airbag. **1994**—A recalibrated transmission. **1995**—A standard passenger-side airbag, 15 more horses for the base engine, and minor styling changes. **1996**—An upgraded 4-speed automatic. **1999**—An innovative third half-door on the driver's side. **2000**—Front seats were given more travel. **2003**—Ion replaced the coupe. *Ion*: **2003**—Ion arrives with a fuel-efficient continuously variable transmission (CVT), used since the late 1800s in milling machines and lathes, and in widespread use overseas by Japanese and European automakers. After first extending the warranty in 2003, Saturn dropped the CVT in its 2005 models because of quality problems. **2004**—Upgraded interior materials and a high-performance Red Line model sporting a 205-hp 4-cylinder engine and sundry other performance features. *Saturn L-series*: **2002**—Standard curtain side airbags. **2003**—A restyled front end and four-wheel disc brakes. **2004**—Standard ABS and traction control; the 5-speed manual transmission is no more.

Saturns have exhibited a plethora of serious body and mechanical problems, which GM has masked by generously applying its base warranty to vehicles owned by original buyers. Owners of used Saturns are treated like they're from another planet, however, and frequently complain that they had to pay dearly for GM's powertrain and body mistakes. Servicing quality has been spotty, too, and will likely become more problematic as GM takes the division off life-support in an effort to make it profitable—which to most observers is a lost cause.

The loud, coarse, standard single-cam engine gives barely adequate acceleration times with the manual transmission. This time is increased with the 4-speed automatic gearbox, which robs the engine of what little power it produces. Other generic problems affecting all model years are rough running, stalling, hard starting, and very poor gas mileage.

GM has been upfront in admitting its vehicles' failures; for example, it extended its "goodwill warranty" to six years on 1994–96 Saturns that overheat and blow their engine head gaskets. Nevertheless, in some cases the engine repair only lasts for a little while, as other powertrain problems soon appear:

> My '96 SW1 suffered a cracked cylinder head, which was repaired under a "goodwill" policy. Subsequently, four weeks later my engine seized and had to be replaced.
>
> I have gone all the way up the line with Saturn and their "experts" are claiming there is no relation to the two incidents, but are refusing to explain why. I will be taking them to court to get the $3,000 back for the repairs.
>
> The irony of this all is as I was trying to sell the vehicle (I will never buy a Saturn again), my transmission failed, as did the clutch disc. This is another $3,000 worth of repairs. I bought the car for $13,000 in June of 2000 with only 67,000 km on it. Since January 27, 2002, when it had 144,000 km on it, I have had $9,000 in repairs to it. Please, please tell your readers, public, and whoever you can to stay away from Saturn! They make terrible vehicles and are even worse in customer service.

How ironic that a company ranked number one in dealer service according to the J.D. Power and Associates 2002 Customer Service Index Study can't assume its responsibilities when the original warranty expires.

Technical service bulletins and other owner complaints indicate that a variety of major quality problems are likely to crop up throughout all model years. These include self-destructing engines; chronically malfunctioning automatic transmissions; failure-prone brake, ignition, fuel, and electrical systems (are flickering, dimming lights your cup of tea?); alternator and AC compressor failures; a host of body defects, led by paint delamination, rattles, wind and water leaks; poorly welded exhaust systems; and failure-prone Firestone tires (mostly the Affinity brand).

 ## Safety Summary

All models/years: Reports of stuck accelerators. • Airbag failed to deploy. • Seat belt failed to restrain driver in collision. • Gear lever slips out of gear and is hard to put into Reverse. • Manual transmission jumps out of Third and Fifth gear. • Frequent brake failures. • Brake rotor warpage and frequent pad replacement. • Sudden head gasket failure causes other engine components to self-destruct. • Chronic stalling. • Loss of steering control. • Poor horn performance. *SC1:* **2000–01**—Fuel sloshing sound when fuel tank is half full. • Brake pedal makes a loud popping noise or drops to the floor, without warning. **2002**—Stabilizer bar actually causes excessive vibration. *SC2:* **2000–01**—Seat belt tightens on any sudden movement, however slight. • The small, recessed horn buttons make it hard to find and activate the horn without looking down. *SC2:* **2002**—Ineffective, noisy brakes. *SL:* **2000–01**—Steering wheel came apart while driving. • Total loss of steering when the retaining clip was omitted during assembly. *SL1:* **2000–01**—Windshield wipers fail to adequately clean the windshield. • Defrosting system doesn't work properly, causing moisture damage and poor visibility. **2002**—Seat belt suddenly unlatched when vehicle was rear-ended. Engine makes a ticking noise and then suddenly stalls in traffic. • In a rear-ender, seat lever released, causing seatback to suddenly recline. • Unable to shift to a lower gear when going downhill. • Inaccurate fuel gauge. *SL2:* **2000–01**—Sudden acceleration. • Seat belts are hard to engage. • When driving at night, one sees multiple lights when looking through the rear view mirror at the vehicle in back, as well as the reflection of the defroster lights. • During rainy weather, rear windshield view is distorted or wavy. **2002**—Faulty throttle position sensor (TPS) causes vehicle to maintain speed when braking. *SW2:* **2000–01**—Automatic transmission slippage caused collision. • Film collects on interior of windshield. *Ion:* **2003**—Airbag failed to deploy. • Chronic stalling. • Cracked cylinder head. • Transmission gear slippage creates a highway hazard.

> My 2003 Saturn Ion Quad 3's transmission slips constantly. A tech from Spring Hill says this is normal. Trying to turn left in front of oncoming traffic is a nightmare. The rear quarter panel is cracked and being replaced. The rear bumper is being painted because of scratches from the trunk rubbing. The front bumper is being painted because of runs in the paint. None of the body panels seem to match up. They're attempting to fix a popping noise in the front end. They're replacing the [driver-side glass] because it is severely scratched. It sometimes runs rough at first crank.

• Steering knuckle sheared off. • Steering lockup. • Chronic turn signal failures; turn signal won't work if cigarette lighter is being used. • Key sticks in ignition. • Knee hits ignition, shutting off engine. • Seatbelt anchor bolt broke. • Seatbelt retractor fell apart. • Premature tire failures. • **2004**—Frontal airbags failed to deploy. • Accelerator pedal fell off. • CVT transmission causes sudden deceleration. • Multiple transmission replacements. • Engine replacement. • Doors don't close fully. • Water leaking into the trunk caused serious electrical shorts (lights, etc.). • Electronic assisted steering almost caused fatalities. • Fuel-filler pipe spits back fuel when refueling. • Saturn cell phone charger can short circuit lights, etc. until more robust resistors and capacitators are installed. • Firestone tire tread separation. *L-series:* **2000–01**—Transmission can't be shifted into a forward gear. • Location of power seat button allows it to be accidentally activated, causing seat to suddenly recline. • Power door locks short out. **2000–02**—Inoperative rear door glass confirmed by TSB #02-T27. • Electrical short causes all lights and gauges to suddenly come on. • Seat belt won't lock up at sudden stops. **2002**—Headlights and interior lights go out, flicker, or dim intermittently when foot is taken off accelerator, or clutch or cooling fan is engaged. • Tire rims broke off. • Door handles don't go back into place after being used. **2003**—Prematurely worn brake pads and rotors. • Headlight dimming and flickering:

> A tractor trailer was passing me on the interstate. Just as his trailer was approximately 2/3 past me, my lights dimmed out on my car by themselves. The driver of the tractor trailer thought I had flashed my headlights at him, to let him know he had cleared my car and was safe to come into my lane, which was not the case. This made the drivers behind me and the tractor trailer in all 3 lanes slam on their brakes. The truck driver almost lost control of his rig trying to keep from hitting me when he realized that he did not have clearance as my lights "suggested" to him that he had.

2004—Engine surging. • Headlights create a shadow on the road and flicker or go out. • Headlight glazing. • Constant dashlight dimming. • Poorly performing Firestone tires.

Secret Warranties/Internal Bulletins/Service Tips

All models/years: Reprogramming of the power control module (PCM) and engine control module (ECM) now have equal coverage under the emission warranty (8 years/130,000 km [80,000 mi.]), per TSB #04-1-08, published June 2004. **1991–2001**—GM admits in TSB #01-T-07 that a cracked engine coolant temperature sensor may be the culprit behind hard starts, poor engine performance, engine overheating, and leaking or low coolant. **1996–2001**—Water leaks into headliner are likely caused by a faulty sunroof or plugged drain hole grommets. **1996–2004**—A rotten-egg odour coming from the exhaust is likely the result of a malfunctioning catalytic converter, which you can have replaced free of charge under GM's emissions warranty. **1998**—Dozens of bulletins target a plethora of rattles, whistles, pops, clicks, and knocking and grinding noises. • Sunroof, footwell, and trunk water leaks are also common problems addressed in a variety of service bulletins. • Excessive vehicle vibration. • Loss of AC vent airflow. • Reducing AC odours. • Power steering pump drive shaft seal leak. • Intermittent no-start. • Transaxle whine in Second gear. • Rear brake noise and pulsation countermeasures. **1999**—Harsh shifting. • Steering column popping. • Rattle, pop, or clicking noise from front of vehicle. • AC noise (hissing). • Clunking noise in front side door when windows are operated. • Troubleshooting chronic short circuits. • Water leak onto headliner and/or left footwell area and rear luggage compartment. • Excessive vibration at cruising speed. **1999–2002**—GM says in TSB #01-T-35 that it may replace the windshield washer pump seal and affected nozzle if the spray pattern is unacceptable. **2000**—In a March 2000 Customer Satisfaction Campaign letter (No. 00-C-09) sent to dealers, GM admits that the Saturn 2.2L 4-cylinder engines "were produced with internal engine components that may fail prematurely. The most likely symptom you may experience is an engine miss accompanied by an engine noise." GM says it will replace the engine at no charge with no mileage or time limitations, in addition to providing a loaner vehicle or paying rental costs. **2000–01**—Delayed, harsh engagement into Reverse or Drive, erratic shifting between First and Second gear, or no Second or Third gears. • AC odours upon start-up. • Steering wheel shake or vibration at highway speeds. • Inoperative power windows and sunroof. **2000–02**—If the engine produces a whistling noise, GM suggests you replace the engine intake manifold gasket in TSB #02-T-22. Of course, this should be a free repair, under #J025-1. • GM has a quick fix for headliner sagging at rear of sunroof opening. • Water leaks into the interior will be fixed under warranty, says TSB #00-T-41A. **2002**—Transmission fluid leakage is likely from a faulty transaxle temperature sensor. *Ion:* **2003–04**— Engine coolant leakage into oil:

LOSS OF COOLANT/NO EXTERNAL LEAKS EVIDENT

BULLETIN NO: 03-06-123-001   DATE: NOV. 2003

Slight Loss of Coolant or Low Coolant Light Coming On with No Signs of External Leaks (Perform Service Procedure in this Bulletin)

2003–2004 Saturn VUE and ION; 2004 L300 Vehicles with 2.2L Engine (VINs D, F–RPO L61)

Some customers may comment that the low coolant light is coming on and/or the coolant level is low with no external leaks visible. Low coolant may be accompanied by one of the following when the engine is cold:
• Engine difficult to start; misfiring; or white smoke, or coolant odour from the tailpipe.

This condition may be caused by porosity in the aluminum of the cylinder head casting and require a new cylinder head or cylinder block.

• Intermittent no-starts may be caused by solidified grease in the ignition switch; a new switch must be installed at Saturn's expense (after all, it's their grease). • All Saturn Ion and VUE vehicles produced since the summer of 2002, equipped with a continuously variable transmission (CVT), have extended warranty coverage on the transmission to 5 years/120,000 km (75,000 mi.) (see next page). • Low-speed

VTI A/T EXTENDED WARRANTY COVERAGE

BULLETIN NO: 04020

SPECIAL POLICY ADJUSTMENT—EXTENDED TRANSMISSION WARRANTY COVERAGE FOR VARIABLE TRANSMISSION WITH INTELLIGENCE (VTI) TRANSMISSION

2002–2004 VUE Vehicles; 2004 ION Quad Coupe Vehicles

Saturn has determined that 2002, 2003 and 2004 VUE and 2003 and 2004 ION Quad Coupe vehicles equipped with the VTi transmission may experience certain transmission concerns that might affect customer satisfaction, and may require repair or replacement.

SPECIAL POLICY ADJUSTMENT: This special policy bulletin has been issued to extend the warranty on the VTi transmission assembly for a period of 5 years or 75,000 miles (120,000 km), whichever occurs first, from the date the vehicle was originally placed in service, regardless of ownership. The repairs will be made at no charge to the customer. A vehicle rental allocation of $35 U.S./day will be given for three days, for more days, dealers are to call the Customer Assistance Centre.

grinding noise or hesitation requires the installation of a new transaxle control module (TCM) or its recalibration, says TSB #03-07-30-051. • Automatic transmission delay, surging requires the replacement of the control valve body and recalibration of the ECM (TSB #03-07-30-052). • Clutch chatters and won't release. • No movement in Drive may require a new VT25E transaxle assembly, per TSB #04-07-30-024. • If you're lucky, the TCM may only need to be reprogrammed to cure upshift delays, harsh downshifts, or erratic gear engagement. • Coolant leak from water pump plug; upgraded water pump. • Fuel system buzzing or growling from rear of vehicle. • A squeak, rattle, pop, or clunk from the front of vehicle can be silenced by replacing the front stabilizer shaft insulators, says TSB #04-03-08-003A. • Water leaks into the interior. • Rear door cracking. • Noisy sunroof. • Faulty blower motor. *L-series:* **2000–01**—No Third and Fourth gear (replace direct clutch piston assembly). • Steering wheel shake or vibration at highway speeds. • Front doors re-lock after being unlocked with key. • Rattle from behind the right-hand side of the instrument panel. • Wind whistle from the front door glass area and from the outside rear-view mirror. • Inoperative rear door glass. **2000–02**—A free revised intake manifold gasket will cure engine whistle. • Troubleshooting the most common water leaks into the interior. • Headliner sagging. • Misaligned rear bumper. **2000–03**—Poor AC automatic temperature control performance. **2000–04**—Blue smoke at a V6 engine's startup can mean you need to replace the engine valve guides or cylinder head, per TSB #04-06-01-010. Obviously, this bulletin and implied warranty statutes mean GM has to assume the cost of this repair up to 7 years/160,000 km. • A defective or contaminated fuel sender is the likely cause of inaccurate fuel readings. GM will adjust or replace the sender under a secret "goodwill" warranty (see TSB #03-08-49-022). **2002**—Inadequate horn performance. **2004**—Loss of engine coolant (see Ion TSB, earlier).

All ratings on a numbered scale where ⑨ is good and ❶ is bad. See pages 100–101 for a more detailed description.

SATURN S-SERIES, L-SERIES, ION PROFILE

	1996	1997	1998	1999	2000	2001	2002	2003	2004
Cost Price ($)									
SL	12,998	13,948	14,188	13,488	13,588	14,358	14,245	—	—
SC	15,348	16,028	16,418	16,618	16,743	16,763	16,765	—	—
LS/L100	—	—	—	—	19,255	20,065	21,125	—	—
LW/LW200	—	—	—	—	24,400	25,235	23,325	25,355	—
L300	—	—	—	—	—	—	—	—	23,030
Ion	—	—	—	—	—	—	—	15,495	14,775
Used Values ($)									
SL ▲	2,500	3,000	3,500	4,500	5,500	6,000	7,500	—	—
SL ▼	2,000	2,500	3,000	3,500	5,000	5,000	6,500	—	—
SC ▲	3,500	4,000	4,500	5,500	6,500	7,000	8,500	—	—
SC ▼	3,000	3,500	4,000	4,500	5,500	6,000	7,500	—	—
LS/L100 ▲	—	—	—	—	6,500	7,500	9,500	—	—
LS/L100 ▼	—	—	—	—	5,500	6,500	8,500	—	—
LW/LW200 ▲	—	—	—	—	8,500	9,500	11,500	13,500	—
LW/LW200 ▼	—	—	—	—	7,500	8,000	10,500	12,500	—
L300 ▲	—	—	—	—	—	—	—	—	16,500
L300 ▼	—	—	—	—	—	—	—	—	15,000
Ion ▲	—	—	—	—	—	—	—	9,000	10,000
Ion ▼	—	—	—	—	—	—	—	8,000	9,000
Reliability	❶	❶	❶	❶	❶	❷	❷	❷	❷
Crash Safety (F)	④	④	⑤	⑤	—	—	—	—	—
L-series	—	—	—	—	—	④	⑤	④	④
Ion	—	—	—	—	—	—	—	⑤	⑤
Side	—	③	③	③	—	—	—	—	—
L-series	—	—	—	—	—	❷	③	③	③
Ion	—	—	—	—	—	—	—	③	③
Offset	③	③	③	③	③	③	③	—	—
L-series	—	—	—	—	③	③	③	③	③
Ion	—	—	—	—	—	—	—	—	③
Head Restraints	❶	❶	❶	❶	❶	❶	❶	—	—
Ion	—	—	—	—	—	—	—	❶	❶
L-series	—	—	—	—	—	❶	❶	❶	❶
Rollover Resistance	—	—	—	—	—	④	④	④	④

Honda

CIVIC, DEL SOL ★★★★★

best buy

RATING: Recommended (1992–2004); Above Average (1972–91). If you want to get a reliable, fuel-frugal buy at a cheap price, the 1992–96 models are your best bet for their lighter weight and tighter handling. Any CRX represents a good buy, as well. Earlier Civics have been downgraded because of the increasing number of safety- and performance-related defects reported by owners as these vehicles put on the years. Defects include airbags that fail to deploy or deploy with such force that they cause severe injuries, ABS brake failures and constant rotor and pad maintenance, sudden acceleration, original equipment tire failures, and considerable instability on wet roads. **Maintenance/Repair costs:** Average. Repairs can be carried out by independent garages, but the 16-valve engine's complexity means that more expensive dealer servicing may be unavoidable. Owners should check the engine timing belt every 3 years/60,000 km and replace it every 100,000 km ($300). **Parts:** Parts are a bit more expensive than most other cars in this class; airbag control modules and body panels may be back-ordered for weeks. **Extended warranty:** A waste of money. These cars are so reliable, the only way dealers make service bucks is to gouge on scheduled servicing. **Best alternatives:** GM Firefly or Metro, Hyundai Accent or Elantra, Mazda Protegé, Nissan Sentra, Suzuki Esteem or Swift, and Toyota Echo or Corolla. The CRX's '93 del Sol replacement was a cheapened spin-off that carried over the CRX's faults, without its high-performance thrills. Si models are Honda's factory hot rods (the Acura 1.6 EL is an Si clone), which provide lots of high-performance thrills, without the bills. Despite four-wheel disc brakes, the Si's mediocre braking and its lack of low-end torque are the car's main performance flaws. **Online help:** *www.cartrackers.com/Forums/live/Honda, www.carsurvey.org/model_Honda_Civic.html,* and *www.epinions.com/auto_Make-Honda.*

Strengths and Weaknesses

Civics have distinguished themselves by providing sports-car acceleration and handling with excellent fuel economy and quality control that is far better than what American, European, and most other Asian automakers can deliver. Other advantages: a roomy, practical trunk; smooth-shifting automatic transmission; a comfortable ride; good front and rear visibility; high-quality construction; bullet-proof reliability; and simple, inexpensive maintenance. Also, these cars can be easily and inexpensively customized for better driving performance or to gain a racier allure.

Some Civic disadvantages: The Si's suspension may be too firm for some, and its spoiler may block rear visibility. It's hard to modulate the throttle without having the car surge or lurch. The base engine loses its pep when the Overdrive gear on the automatic transmission engages in city driving, and the VTEC variant is noisy. Seats lack sufficient padding, rear access is difficult, rear seat room is limited to two adults, there's lots of engine and road noise, and an unusually large number of safety-related complaints include airbag malfunctions, sudden acceleration, and complete brake failure.

The 1984–95 Civics suffered from failing camshafts, crankshafts, and head gaskets, as well as prematurely worn piston rings.

What are minor body faults with recent models turn into major rust problems with older Civics, where simple surface rust rapidly turns into perforations. The underbody is also prone to corrosion, which leads to severe structural damage that compromises safety. The fuel tank, front suspension, and steering components, along with body attachment points, should be examined carefully in any Civic more than a decade old.

The 1996 redesign improved overall reliability and handling and increased interior room, but engine head gasket failures on non-VTEC engines continued to be a problem through the 2000 model year.

Year 2001 and later models are marginally better performers, yet quality control still needs improvement. Heading the list of owner complaints are engine crankshaft failures; transmission malfunctions; weak front springs and shocks; frequent brake repairs (rotor warpage and pad replacement); AC failures; suspension knocks and squeaks; a subpar stereo system; erratic fuel gauge readings; delaminated paint; and chronic water leaks.

Owners also complain of a constantly lit Check Engine light; faulty engine computer module and oxygen sensor; early replacement of the crankshaft pulley and timing belt; and fuel and electrical system failures. Other common problems: windshield air leaks and noise; warped windshield mouldings (see service bulletin below); hard-to-access horn buttons; windows that fall off their tracks; side mirrors that vibrate excessively; headlights that can't be focused properly and are prone to water leaks; gas-tank fumes that leak into the interior; and premature rusting, uneven paint application, chalky spots, and paint delamination. Here's what this owner of a 2001 Civic discovered:

> Paint is developing crow's feet in four separate places...body shop said it was due to bird droppings or sap. I believe this to be impossible and believe it to be a defect in the paint. Blemishes and loss of gloss continue to develop in the paint.

Insight and Civic Hybrid

Stay away from used hybrid vehicles regardless of whether they're made by Ford, GM, Honda, or Toyota. Build quality is inconsistent, the electrical and braking systems can be quite hazardous, maintenance is highly dealer-dependent, depreciation is a bit faster than with comparable makes, and fuel economy is illusory. Says this owner of a 2003 Honda Hybrid:

> The Hybrid is supposed to get 48 mpg/city and 47 mpg/highway. Even the fine print states that the actual mileage should range between 40–56 in the city and 39-55 on the highway.

> I have been tracking/documenting my actual mpg. My mpg has never exceeded 35. Since fuel economy is the primary reason for purchasing the Hybrid, potential customers should be extremely skeptical of the claims.

Honda was the first automaker to introduce gas-electric hybrid technology to North American consumers when it launched the Honda Insight in the States in December 1999, followed by the Civic Hybrid in March 2002. Neither vehicle has sold as well as the Toyota Prius.

Insight, a two-passenger hatchback coupe, uses a small electric motor to assist the three-cylinder gasoline engine during hard acceleration. The engine recharges the battery pack when coasting or braking, and returns to battery power when the car is stopped. The car has very little interior room and poor rear visibility, is slow to accelerate, has a harsh ride and little soundproofing, and is tossed about by moderate crosswinds. Toyota's Prius seats four and uses a more versatile hybrid system, wherein the electric motor is dominant and gasoline and electric power vary, depending upon driving conditions.

The Hybrid looks and feels just like a Civic, both inside and out. It carries a 3-year/60,000 km base warranty, a 5-year/100,000 km powertrain warranty, an 8-year/160,000 km battery pack warranty, and emissions-related equipment that's covered by a more extensive warranty. The Civic Hybrid comes in second to the Toyota Prius, a much more refined hybrid. A good alternative is a Honda Civic HX or base Toyota Echo—two cars that sell for about half the price, get great gas mileage, and don't depreciate as much. Some of the car's advantages are that it does offer some fuel savings, it's smooth-shifting, it gives a comfortable ride, and it provides good front and rear visibility.

On the other hand, the Hybrid's fuel economy may fall short by 25 to 45 percent, says *Consumer Reports*; cold weather performance isn't as fuel-efficient as advertised; and the AC increases gas consumption and shuts off at stoplights, encouraging drivers to sneak up on lights. *Car and Driver* magazine concluded in its September 2004 issue that one would have to drive a Toyota or Honda hybrid 165,000 miles to amortize its higher costs. Furthermore, the car's unique dual power plants can make for risky driving, as this Hybrid owner warns:

> [With a] 2003 Honda Civic Hybrid on a snowy road, coming over a small rise while going around a moderate curve under 40 mph [64 km/h], the battery charging function, activated by driver taking foot off the gas before cresting the hill, produced progressively stronger engine braking effect on the front wheels, equivalent to an unwanted downshift and causing fishtailing and poor response to corrective steering, so that the car slid across the road and into a snow bank and concrete abutment, causing $6,000 (US) in damage. If there had been oncoming traffic, there could have been serious injuries or fatalities.

Repairs and servicing are very complicated to perform; highway rescuers are wary of cutting through the 500-volt electrical system to save occupants; and there's no long-term reliability data. Honda Hybrid performance and overall quality issues include rough shifting; a rotten-egg smell that intrudes into the cabin; premature brake and rear strut wear, a constantly lit airbag light, poor quality radio speakers, a rear bumper cover that may fall off, be mis-aligned, or come loose, and chipped paint.

VEHICLE HISTORY: 1992—A driver-side airbag, a base 102-horsepower, 1.5L 4-cylinder, plus a frugal CX and VX with 70- and 92-hp 4-cylinder engines, and a sporty Si with ABS. **1994**—A standard passenger-side airbag. **1996**—ABS for EX sedans, upgraded engines, a longer and better soundproofed body, and split folding rear seatbacks. **1999**—The Si is upgraded; new front and rear styling. **2001**—More interior room, additional horsepower, and fresh styling; no more hatchback; Insight hybrid is launched in Canada a year after its American debut. **2002**—Arrival of the 160-hp SiR sporty hatchback, improved fit and finish, a firmer suspension, and a rear stabilizer bar (except on the base model). Front suspension uses MacPherson struts, which increases interior space while watering down the car's sporty performance. Insight given a continuously variable transmission

(CVT). **2003**—New gauges, a CD player for the HX and the arrival of the Civic Hybrid. **2004**—Revised styling and upgraded features, like larger tires.

 ## Safety Summary

All models: 1995–2004—Spoiler and head restraint restricts rear visibility, and large rear-view mirror restricts forward visibility for tall drivers. • Numerous safety defects, including sudden acceleration, engine and transmission malfunctions, and airbags that fail to deploy, deploy inadvertently, or deploy with such force they cause severe injuries:

> My '98 Civic was totalled by another driver's negligence; I was told by a lawyer that because my son and I were not killed in the accident we could not file a claim against the manufacturer for the airbags not deploying even though it was a head-on collision.

• Ball joints on these vehicles don't have a castellated nut to secure the ball in position; the nut can back off, and the ball pulls out of the steering arm. • Other safety-related complaints: dangerous instability on wet roads, sudden acceleration or stalling, faulty cruise control, ABS brake failures and constant rotor and pad replacement, defective automatic transmission, transmission that suddenly jumps into Reverse, original equipment tire failures, hood and trunk lids that come crashing down, inoperative door locks, cracked windshields, and headlights and interior lights that suddenly go out. **2000**—Accelerator pedal sticks; cables mounted too tight. • Accelerator cable got hung up in the cruise control, causing the vehicle to suddenly accelerate. • While driving, vehicle suddenly accelerated because of the throttle sticking open, and brakes couldn't stop the car. • Car suddenly accelerated when passing another vehicle. • Gas pedal keeps sticking while driving at a low speed. • Transmission popped out of gear and brake pedal went right to the floor, without any braking effect. • Brakes locked up and vehicle pulled to the left when coming to an emergency stop. • Sudden steering loss while driving. • Excessive vibration because of engine main bearing failure. • Transmission sometimes fails to change gear. • Vehicle suddenly went into Reverse although shift lever was put into Drive. • While stopped at a light on a hill, vehicle suddenly shifted into Reverse. • Another driver had the same thing happen, except this time the transmission shifted into Neutral. • Transmission was stuck in Reverse. • Faulty power door lock makes it impossible to open door from the inside or outside. • Dome light won't work when doors are open. • Tail lights don't work when the headlights and dash lights are on. • Rear-view mirror is poorly located and is non-adjustable, creating a large forward blind spot for tall drivers. • Sheet metal fatigue on both front fenders. • Faulty hood support rod causes the hood to come crashing down. • Exterior rear-view mirror becomes loose, despite dealer efforts to tighten it. **2001**—Car caught on fire near where the oxygen sensor wires are located. • Child became entangled in rear-seat shoulder belt and had to be cut free. • Car hesitates or stalls when decelerating. • Vehicle surged forward when put into Reverse and engaged Reverse when put into Drive:

While shifting the gear in Reverse the car went forward, and when I shifted it to Drive, the car went backward. When I stepped on the gas pedal lightly, it accelerated really fast and when I lightly step on the brake, it abruptly stops.

The Honda service department is trying to fix this car. The first problem reported was the "power switch," secondly they reported that it's a "transmission problem," but still couldn't figure out what else is the problem. Lastly, they notified me that the problem is the "transmission solenoid."

• Transmission may suddenly pop out of Second gear while underway, or refuse to shift into Third or Fourth gear. • Transmission leaks. • Vehicle rolls back when stopped on an incline. • Sudden brake failure (master cylinder replaced). • When brakes are applied first thing in the morning, they don't "grab," resulting in extended stopping distance. • Leaking front strut causes poor handling and front-end noise. • Incorrect fuel gauge and speedometer readings. • Airbag warning light is constantly lit (heating coil or core is suspected). • Loose door latches. • Interior lights dim when AC is engaged. • Water leaks into trunk through tail lights, onto driver's side carpet through door or firewall, or wets front passenger-side carpet (AC condensate suspected). 2002—Airbags fail to deploy:

My 2002 Honda Civic EX hit another vehicle squarely in the rear end while travelling approximately 15 mph [24 km/h]. Neither of the front airbags deployed! The collision repair centre could find nothing wrong with my airbags. The tow truck operator and the collision repair centre told me that there was some sort of alert out for 2001 and 2002 Honda Civics where the airbags didn't deploy after a front-end collision.

• Cellular phone (Nokia) electromagnetic signals may cause sudden acceleration. • Vehicle continues to accelerate when brakes are applied. • Cracked engine block causes oil leakage. • Car rolls backward on an incline with an automatic transmission. • Car was in Park on an incline and rolled away. • Vehicle downshifts on its own. • Sudden failure of the front tie-rod. • Complete loss of steering. • Seat belt doesn't fully retract. • Windshield cracked for no apparent reason. 2003—Braking can cause the car to accelerate. • Vehicle suddenly accelerated with complete brake loss. • Sudden steering lock-up. • Transmission jumps into Neutral, multiple transmission failures. • Power window failure. • Faulty Firestone tires. • Loose driver's seat. • Seatbelts ratchet up uncomfortably. • Poor radio speaker quality. • The head-high interior support handle may injure the driver in a collision. 2004—Stuck accelerator pedal. • Sudden, unintended acceleration, loss of brakes, hit a brick wall head-on, and front airbags didn't go off. • Problems with the main rear crankshaft seal. • Excessive steering wheel vibration/shimmy and vehicle pulling to one side blamed on tires and bad brake rotors. • Drivetrain bucks and jolts when descending a hill. • Loose tie-rod bolts. • Premature leakage, failure of the front struts. • Weak trunk springs allowed lid to drop on owner's fingers. • Dunlop original equipment tires' (SP20FE P185/70R14) side wall blew; these tires are also frequently blamed for causing excessive vibration/shimmy. • Weak seatbacks collapse when the vehicle is rear-ended at moderate speeds. • Rear seat belt unlatched on its own. • Driver-side quarter window shatters from freezing temperatures. • An opaque film is deposited on the interior glass caused by polymer vapours "outgassing" from the plastics used in the vehicle's interior. • Head restraints restrict driver's rearward visibility. *Insight*: **2001**—Random events of power loss cause significant reduction of engine power when it is most needed. • CVT transmission failure. • Steering becomes abnormally unstable when vehicle is driven above 50 km/h over uneven, or grooved roadways. • Vehicle is prone to hydroplaning on wet roads. • Tire tread separation. *Civic Hybrid*: **2003**—Vehicle lost all forward power while cruising on the highway. • Chronic stalling. • Excessive brake vibration. Vigorous brake pumping needed to get adequate braking. • Hazardous braking system. • Seatbelt locks up. • In cold weather, power windows won't roll back up until vehicle warms up. • Prematurely worn shock absorbers. • Driver seat design can cause serious back pain. • Electromagnetic field may be a health hazard:

> With the use of a gaussmeter, an instrument used to measure electro magnetic fields, the consumer found that vehicle had a high electromagnetic field. The highest level occurred when the engine draws power from the battery via the integrated motor assist or when the battery was charging.

2004—Trunk caught fire while vehicle was parked. • Sudden, unintended acceleration when foot was taken off of the accelerator pedal. • Front wheels locked up when brakes were tapped lightly. • Excessive vibration caused by prematurely worn brakes.

Secret Warranties/Internal Bulletins/Service Tips

All models/years: Most Honda TSBs allow for special warranty consideration on a "goodwill" basis even after the warranty has expired or the car has changed hands. Referring to the "goodwill" euphemism will increase your chances of getting some kind of refund for repairs that are obviously related to a factory defect. • Seat belts that are slow to retract will be replaced for free under Honda's seat belt lifetime warranty, says TSB #03-062, issued September 16, 2003. **1988–2000**—A rear suspension clunk can be silenced by replacing the rear trailing arm bushing. **1996–98**—A poorly performing AC may need a new condenser fan motor and shroud. **1996–2000**—Poor AC performance. • Harsh shifts. **1996–2001**—Oil pressure switch Product Update Campaign (secret warranty); another free fix if the dealer is on your side. **1998–2004**—Deformed windshield moulding. **2000**—Steering pull or drifting. • Whistling or howling noise coming from the top middle of the windshield at highway speeds. • Moon roof seal sticks up or leaks. • Key is difficult to remove from the ignition switch; rear door lock tab is hard to open. **2001**—Product Update Campaign for the inspection or replacement of the engine control module/PCM. • Delayed upshift after a cold start. • Stiff manual transmission shifter; pops out of gear. • Rear main seal leak troubleshooting tips. •

Separation of the lower control arm ball joints. • Noisy or stiff steering. • Fluid leakage. • Troubleshooting tips for front-brake groan or squeal. • Engine vibration and under-hood rattling; rattling when passing over rough roads; headliner may rattle from hitting the frame. • Creaking sound heard coming from the right side of the dash when passing over rough terrain. • Front suspension noise. • Clutch pedal squeaks or clicks when pressed. • Erratic fuel gauge readings, especially when parked on an incline; fuel gauge won't read full. • Sticking speedometer and tachometer needles. • Windshield cracking at the lower corners. • Damaged or cracked foglight lens. • Audio Update Campaign (secret warranty). • AC condensate drips onto passenger-side carpet. • Water leaks into trunk. • Driver's seat rocks back and forth. • Seat belt slow to retract. **2001–02**—Engine hesitation when accelerating is often caused by low oil pressure. • A growling noise from the engine area is likely caused by a worn alternator bearing. • Troubleshooting front brake groan or squeal. • Rear suspension squeak (replace the rear knuckle bushing under a "goodwill" warranty). **2001–03**—Driver's seat rocks back and forth (TSB #01-057). • Dashboard creaking. • Clicking noise when turning (manual transmission). • Water leaks into the trunk. **2001–04**—If vehicle won't move in Drive, it's likely caused by excessive Second clutch wear, says TSB #04-036. • Hard to close trunk lid. • A-pillar rattles. **2002**—Automatic transmission slippage. • Shift lever may be difficult to move. • Troubleshooting a noisy clutch. • Creaking or ticking from the dash or front strut; clean and install shims. • Hard-to-turn seatback lock. • Front windows won't fully roll down. **2003–04**—Sticking door lock cylinder. *Hybrid*: **2003**—A CVT transmission update. • Sticking door lock cylinder. • Notchy-feeling clutch. • Deformed windshield molding. **2004**—Hard to close trunk lid. • A-pillar rattles. • Sticking door lock cylinder. • Deformed windshield molding. *Insight*: **2000–01**—Free replacement of the Park brake lever, battery condition monitor, and motor control module. **2001–02**—Water leaks into the trunk.

CIVIC PROFILE

	1996	1997	1998	1999	2000	2001	2002	2003	2004
Cost Price ($)									
Base Civic	12,995	13,495	14,000	14,200	14,200	15,800	15,900	16,000	16,150
Si	17,495	17,895	17,995	18,800	18,800	19,800	19,902	20,700	20,800
SiR	—	—	—	—	—	—	25,500	25,500	25,500
del Sol	20,495	20,995	—	—	—	—	—	—	—
Insight	—	—	—	—	—	26,000	26,000	26,000	26,000
Hybrid	—	—	—	—	—	—	—	28,500	28,500
Used Values ($)									
Civic ▲	4,000	4,500	5,500	6,500	7,500	8,500	10,000	11,000	13,000
Civic ▼	3,500	4,000	5,000	5,500	6,500	7,500	9,000	10,000	12,000
Si ▲	5,500	6,500	7,500	8,500	10,000	11,500	13,000	15,000	17,000
Si ▼	5,000	6,000	6,500	7,500	9,000	10,500	11,500	14,000	15,500

SiR ▲	—	—	—	—	—	—	16,000	18,500	21,000
SiR ▼	—	—	—	—	—	—	15,000	17,500	19,500
del Sol ▲	5,000	6,500	—	—	—	—	—	—	—
del Sol ▼	4,500	5,000	—	—	—	—	—	—	—
Insight ▲	—	—	—	—	—	13,500	16,000	18,000	21,000
Insight ▼	—	—	—	—	—	12,500	14,500	16,500	19,000
Hybrid ▲	—	—	—	—	—	—	—	20,500	22,500
Hybrid ▼	—	—	—	—	—	—	—	19,000	21,000
Reliability	❸	❸	❸	❹	❹	❹	❹	❹	❹
Crash Safety (F)	—	❹	❹	❹	❹	❺	❺	❺	❺
4d	❹	❹	❹	❹	❹	❺	❺	❺	❺
Insight	—	—	—	—	❹	❹	❹	❹	❹
Side	—	—	❸	❷	❷	❺	❸	❸	❸

Hyundai

ACCENT ★★★★

RATING: Above Average (2001–04); Average (1995–2000). Having afflicted Canadians with its Pony, Stellar, and Excel misadventures, it's about time Hyundai got a product right. Just as Honda and Nissan have improved since bringing out their '70s rustbuckets, Hyundai has learned from its mistakes and brought out more reliable, better-warranteed cars—at bargain prices. Think of the Accent as a refined Metro/Sprint from South Korea, with more standard features. The absence of ABS is no big loss and should lead to cheaper maintenance costs as the car ages. However, the skinny tires and small engine relegate the car to an urban environment. **Maintenance/Repair costs:** Average. **Parts:** Reasonably priced and easily found. **Extended warranty:** Consider getting an optional powertrain warranty as protection from occasional engine head gasket and tranny failures. **Best alternatives:** GM Firefly or Metro, Honda Civic (an old Honda CRX in good condition would be a master stroke), Hyundai Elantra, Mazda Protegé, Nissan Sentra, Suzuki Esteem, and Toyota Echo or Corolla. **Online help:** *www.carsurvey.org/model_Hyundai_Accent.html.*

 Strengths and Weaknesses

Launched as a '95 model, the early Accent was basically an Excel that had been substantially upgraded to provide decent performance and reliability at a phenom-

All ratings on a numbered scale where ❺ is good and ❶ is bad. See pages 100–101 for a more detailed description.

enally low price. Of course, with its small 4-cylinder engine, the Accent is no tire-burner, but it will do nicely for urban commuting and grocery shopping. Invest in larger wheels and tires that equip the GT for safer highway handling.

VEHICLE HISTORY: Until the redesigned 2000 models arrived, the Accent hadn't changed much over the years. **1996**—Height-adjustable seat belts and a 105-hp GT hatchback. **1997**—Models saw the debut of a GS hatchback and a GL sedan. **1998**—New engine mounts to cut down vibration, in addition to restyled front and rear ends. **1999**—Power steering and longer warranties. **2000**—A smoother-shifting automatic transmission; a stiffer, better-performing suspension; a stronger and quieter-running engine; and a more comfortable driving position with good visibility. **2001**—Engine got 16 additional horses. **2003**—A slightly larger engine and restyled front and rear end.

Problem areas include the engine cooling system and cylinder head gaskets (engine overheating), engine sputtering, a Check Engine light that constantly comes on, and chronic automatic transmission failures (an extended transmission warranty is suggested for models no longer under warranty). Owners also frequently complain of excessive front-end vibration; wheel bearings, fuel system, and electrical component failures; premature front brake wear; and excessive noise when braking.

Safety Summary

All models/years: Horn controls may be hard to find in an emergency. • Rear head restraints appear to be too low to protect occupants. • Rear seat belt configuration complicates the installation of a child safety seat (pre-2001 models). **All models: 1998–99**—Airbags failed to deploy, or deploy inadvertently. • Complete brake failure. • Sudden transmission failure. • Headlights flicker when turning and high beam is inadequate. • Engine control monitor melted. • Fuel gauge failures. **2000**—Fire erupted in the dashboard area. • Accelerator sticks. • Hood flew up and smashed through the windshield. • Left and right axles broke while vehicle was underway. • Transmission sticks between First and Second gear and pops out of Fifth gear. • No shifting because of a failure of the control shaft assembly. • Premature transmission clutch replacement. • In snowy, icy, or wet road conditions, there's an unpredictable loss of rpm and powertrain response, making for difficult handling and control. • Headlight failures caused by defective relay switch. • Windshield wipers fail because of the wiper linkage disconnecting from the wiper motor. • Seat belts tighten uncomfortably. **2001**—Gas pooled underneath the rear seat. • Airbags fail to deploy. • Steering shook so badly that driver lost control of vehicle. • Transmission jumps from Drive to Neutral. • Gearshift jumps out of Reverse. • Seat belts unlatch during impact; passenger seat belt tightens uncomfortably. • Windshield and rear window suddenly shattered. • Early ignition coil replacement. **2002**—Airbags failed to deploy. • Throttle body sensor failure causes car to accelerate on its own; intermittent high engine revs. • Chronic stalling. • Automatic transmission failures characterized by slippage, free-wheeling, jerky shifts, and a clunking noise. • Rear brake drums may be out of round. • When stopped, brake pedal sinks slowly to the floor and car rolls away (possibly faulty brake master cylinder). • Manual windows fall down. **2003**—Under-hood fire. • Airbags failed to deploy. **2004**—Airbag failed to deploy. • Airbag deployed when passing over railroad tracks. • Small original equipment wheels and tires make the car unstable at high speeds. • Automatic transmission downshifts abruptly.

Secret Warranties/Internal Bulletins/Service Tips

All models/years: Tips on troubleshooting excessive brake noise. • Apparent slow acceleration upon cold starts is dismissed as normal. • A new AC "refresher" will control AC odours. • Accents produced through November 11, 1996 are eligible for the free installation of coil spring guides. **1995–98**—Harsh shifting may be fixed by installing an upgraded transaxle control module (TCM). • Clutch drag may be caused by a restriction in the hydraulic line from grease used during the assembly of the clutch master assembly. **1995–2001**—TSB #03-40-018 says a defective kickdown servo switch could cause automatic transmission malfunctions. **1996–2004**—A defective pulse generator may cause harsh, delayed, and erratic shifting, says TSB #03-40-022. The following TSB, published in March 2004, says many automatic transmission breakdowns can be traced to faulty transaxle solenoids. **1998–99**—Defective exhaust manifolds will be replaced for free on a case-by-case basis under Hyundai Campaign #03-01-004. **2000–01**—Hyundai has a free kit that will free up stiff manual transmission shifting. **2000–02**—Free bracket reinforcement. **2002**—Harsh or delayed automatic transmission shifting. **2003**—Troubleshooting a clicking noise from the speakers.

A/T—ERRATIC/SLIPPING SHIFTS/MIL ON

BULLETIN NO: 03-40-007-1   DATE: MARCH 2004

Incorrect operation of the transaxle solenoids for the 1996–2000 Elantra, 1997–2001 Tiburon and 1996–2004 Accent may result in the following symptoms:

- Erratic shift or slipping
- Transaxle held in 3rd gear Fail-safe
- Diagnostic Trouble Codes–P0740, P0741, P0742, P0743, P0745, P0747, P0748, P0750, P0752, P0753, P0755, P0757, P0758, P0760, P0765 (see DTC Information shown in this bulletin)
- MIL illuminated

ACCENT PROFILE

	1996	1997	1998	1999	2000	2001	2002	2003	2004
Cost Price ($)									
L/GS	10,495	10,995	11,295	11,565	11,565	11,995	12,395	12,395	12,895
GL 4d	12,695	12,995	12,995	13,245	13,595	13,595	13,795	13,795	14,195
Used Values ($)									
L/GS ▲	2,500	3,000	4,000	4,500	5,500	6,500	7,000	8,000	9,000
L/GS ▼	2,000	2,500	3,500	4,000	4,500	6,000	6,000	7,000	8,000

All ratings on a numbered scale where ⑨ is good and ❶ is bad. See pages 100–101 for a more detailed description.

GL 4d ▲	3,500	4,000	4,500	5,000	6,000	7,000	7,500	8,500	9,500
GL 4d ▼	3,000	3,500	4,000	4,500	5,500	6,500	7,000	7,500	9,000
Reliability	③	③	④	④	⑤	⑤	⑤	⑤	⑤
Crash Safety (F)	③	③	③	—	—	—	—	—	⑤
4d	③	③	③	③	—	—	④	④	④
Side	—	—	—	—	—	—	③	—	④
4d	—	—	—	—	—	③	③	③	⑤
Head Restraints	—	❶	—	❶	—	③	③	③	—
Rollover Resistance	—	—	—	—	—	④	④	④	④

ELANTRA ★★★★★

RATING: Recommended (2001–04); Above Average (1996–2000); Average (1991–95). Shhhhh! This is the car auto columnists laugh at and then buy for their families. Hyundai's quality is the best of the South Korean automakers' and generally much better than what Detroit offers. Another advantage is that the Accent, Elantra, and Tiburon fly under most buyers' radar, making them more available and much more reasonably priced than better-known brands. There's only a $1,000–$3,500 difference between the high-end and entry-level models. Try to find a 2001–04 model with an unexpired comprehensive 5-year/100,000 km base warranty, or buy any post-1996, pre-2001 version, but give up some of your savings to buy an extended powertrain warranty to protect your wallet from the occasional transmission failure. **Maintenance/Repair costs:** Average. Dealer servicing has improved considerably and independent garages find the Elantra's simple mechanical layout quite easy to diagnose and service. **Parts:** Reasonably priced and easily found. **Extended warranty:** Not necessary on post-2001 models. Base warranty is sufficient, though insensitive warranty administrators could use an attitude adjustment. **Best alternatives:** GM Firefly or Metro; Honda Civic; Hyundai Accent;

Mazda Protegé; Nissan Sentra; Suzuki Esteem or Swift; and Toyota Echo, Tercel, or Corolla. **Online help:** *www.autosafety.org* and *www.carsurvey.org.*

 Strengths and Weaknesses

This conservatively styled "high-end" front-drive sedan was launched as a 1992 model, carrying a 113-hp 1.6L 4-cylinder engine. It's only marginally larger than the failure-prone Hyundai Excel, but its overall reliability is much better, making it a credible alternative to the Mazda Protegé, Nissan Sentra, Saturn, and Toyota Corolla. The redesigned 1996 and later versions actually narrow the handling and performance gap with the segment leader, Honda's Civic.

Elantra's 1993 4-cylinder gained 11 more horses and is fairly smooth and efficient when mated with the 5-speed manual transmission. On all model years, though, the 4-speed automatic transmission cuts power by at least 10 horses and is a bit noisy. Adding to the horsepower gap, Hyundai admits it has fudged horsepower numbers by about four percent on its entire model lineup for the last decade. The lesser power isn't easily discernible in city driving, but can be worrisome when merging with high-speed traffic.

There is some excessive body lean when cornering, but overall handling is fairly good, mainly because of a relatively long wheelbase and sophisticated suspension. Brakes are adequate, though sometimes difficult to modulate. Conservative styling makes the Elantra look a bit like an underfed Accord, but there's plenty of room for four average-sized occupants. Tall drivers might find the driver's seat rearward travel insufficient, which makes headroom a bit too tight.

VEHICLE HISTORY: 1996—Totally redesigned with additional interior room, improved performance and handling, and a quieter-running engine; a wagon and 130-hp 1.8L engine were added, along with dual airbags and upgraded seat belts. **1999**—Mildly revised styling. **2001**—Another revision saw the wagon disappear, increased interior and engine size (now a 140-hp 2.0L 4-cylinder), and added four-wheel disc brakes and ABS. **2002**—Debut of a GT hatchback, which is a bargain when one totes up the cost of its standard features. **2003**—The GT adds a four-door sedan. **2004**—Minor interior and exterior revisions.

Owners of 1996–2000 model Elantras report few serious defects; however, as with most Hyundai products, transmission failures are commonplace and have been the object of numerous service bulletins (see the Accent "Secret Warranties/ Internal Bulletins/Service Tips") and recalls. Airbag failures are another frequent complaint. Other problem areas: body deficiencies (fit, finish, and assembly), a leaking sunroof, paint cracking, engine misfire and oil leaks (some oil burning), hard starting, and warped brake rotors. Post-'96 models' passing power with the automatic gearbox is perpetually unimpressive, and the trunk's narrow opening makes for a relatively small trunk. The power problem is attenuated with the revamped 2001 versions.

This having been said, the above-noted problems are in no way as severe or as frequent as what you would find with the Detroit Big Three competition.

The 2001–03 models are noted for chronic stalling; excessive brake noise and chassis vibration (see "Service Tips" below); a passenger-side scraping noise when underway; wind howling in the interior when encountering a crosswind; a humming noise emanating from the corners of the windshield; tire thumping; delayed window defrosting; and rainwater seeping in under the door.

Safety Summary

All models/years: Airbags failed to deploy. • Chronic stalling. • Erratic transmission shifting and excessive noise. • Sudden brake loss. • Warped front brake rotors and master cylinder failure. • Passenger seat belt retracts and locks so that passengers are unable to move. **1998–99**—Faulty speed sensor. • Cracked transmission case. • Low beam headlights give poor illumination. • Poorly designed jack. **1999**—AC makes a grinding noise. • Defective heater fan and motor assembly. • Trunk lid doesn't close properly. • Loose driver's seat. • Defective door handle. • Paint/clearcoat cracking. **2000**—Vehicle rolled forward even though emergency brake was applied. • Clutch slave cylinder failure. • Vehicle pulls left continuously. • Sudden steering failure; loose steering. • Low beam doesn't light up driver's view; instead, the light reflects outward to the left or right. • AC circulates bad air. • Tire jack is too small and weak. • Defective side moulding. **2001**—Driver-side airbag deployed for no reason. • Sudden, unintended acceleration. • Check Engine light remains lit. • Child had to be cut free from jammed rear centre seat belt. • Seat belt failed to lock up in a collision. • Brakes randomly engage by themselves and overheat/pulsate. • Rear doors freeze shut in cold weather. **2002**—Seatback failure when car was rear-ended. • Brake and gas pedals are set too close together. • While driving in rainstorm, all interior and exterior lights shut off. **2003**—Engine surging while on the highway. • Vehicle suddenly lost all power. • Complete loss of brakes. • Headlights will read "dim" but will actually be on high. • Distracting windshield glare. • Seat belts fail to lock. **2004**—Airbag fails to deploy or deploys for no reason. • Almost 100 complaints that the passenger-side front airbag is disabled when a normal-sized adult is seated; recall doesn't correct the problem for all claimants.

> Repeated intermittent illumination of "passenger airbag off" beginning within days of purchase. Failures occur when anyone sits in passenger seat. Adults weighing 190, 170, and 140 have turned airbags off. Poodle weighing 9 lbs turned airbags on!

Back cover on passenger seat pops out. • Faulty crankshaft position sensor causes the engine to stall. • Engine surging. • Stabilizer bar snapped, causing vehicle to fishtail. • Warped brake rotors. • Defective batteries corrode cables and leak acid. • Passenger seat collapsed in a frontal collision at moderate speed.

🔍 Secret Warranties/Internal Bulletins/Service Tips

All models/years: Hyundai has a new brake pad kit (#58101-28A00) that the company says will eliminate squeaks and squeals during light brake application. Hyundai also suggests that you replace the oil pump assembly if the engine rpm increases as the automatic transmission engages abruptly during a cold start. • A harsh downshift when decelerating may require a free transmission replacement, says bulletin #98-40-001. • Poor shifting may be caused by an inhibitor switch short circuit. TSB #98-50-001 provides information regarding some brake noises and appropriate services for each condition. • Intermittent slippage in Fourth gear. • Troubleshooting vibration and ride harshness. **All models: 1996–98—**DOHC engine timing chain noise repair. **1996–99—**Transmission oil leakage likely caused by a defective oil pump housing seal. **1996–2000—**Erratic automatic transmission operation can be traced to faulty transaxle solenoids. **1999–2002—**Harsh or delayed Park–Reverse or Park–Drive engagement. **2001–02—**Troubleshooting 2–3 shift flaring usually requires a simple updating of the transaxle control module (TCM), says TSB #02-40-001. **2002—**Troubleshooting engine rpm fluctuation. **2002–03—**Excessive chassis vibration when cruising. According to one Hyundai staffer, the problem is presently being resolved through a secret warranty campaign that pays for a wheel exchange. **2003—**Automatic transmission sticks in Second gear. • Harsh shifts into Drive or Reverse. • Rough running engine may require an upgraded fuel pump. • Corrosion in the front door wiring connector.

ELANTRA PROFILE

	1996	1997	1998	1999	2000	2001	2002	2003	2004
Cost Price ($)									
GL	13,495	13,995	14,295	14,595	14,875	14,875	15,295	15,295	15,630
GLS/VE	16,745	17,245	17,545	17,695	17,475	17,075	16,995	16,995	17,525
GT	—	—	—	—	—	—	18,495	18,495	19,015
Used Values ($)									
GL ▲	3,500	4,500	5,000	6,000	6,500	7,500	8,500	10,000	11,500
GL ▼	3,000	4,000	4,500	5,000	6,000	6,500	7,500	9,000	10,500
GLS/VE ▲	4,000	5,500	6,000	6,500	7,500	8,500	9,000	11,000	12,500
GLS/VE ▼	3,500	5,000	5,500	6,000	6,500	7,500	8,000	10,000	11,500
GT ▲	—	—	—	—	—	—	10,500	12,500	14,500
GT ▼	—	—	—	—	—	—	9,000	11,500	13,000

All ratings on a numbered scale where ⑤ is good and ❶ is bad. See pages 100–101 for a more detailed description.

Reliability	3	4	4	4	4	5	5	5	5
Crash Safety (F)	4	3	3	3	—	4	4	4	5
Side	—	—	3	—	—	5	5	5	5
Offset	3	3	3	3	3	—	1	5	5
Head Restraints	—	1	—	3	—	1	1	1	1
Rollover Resistance	—	—	—	—	—	—	—	4	4

Kia

After going bankrupt in 1998, Kia was bought by Hyundai (it's also partly owned by Ford through Ford's Mazda affiliation) and now sells two small cars, a mid-sized sedan, a minivan, and a sport-utility. Unlike on-the-ropes Daewoo, Kia has the money and backing to build a solid, stable dealer organization in Canada, but it'll take a great deal of time. Unfortunately, Hyundai doesn't want to invest in Kia, so the company continues to struggle.

Despite Kia's impressive sales over the past few years, thanks to low prices and a comprehensive base warranty, all of the consumer and government feedback I've seen paints a very poor picture of Kia's quality control and crashworthiness, particularly when it comes to automatic transmission performance and durability (a Daewoo bugaboo, too). Kia is continually beset by labour unrest, few dealers can be found outside of large urban areas, and, if Hyundai finds that warranty costs for Kia defects threaten its overall profits, customers will be abandoned in a heartbeat (remember the Pony and Stellar?).

RIO ★

RATING: Not Recommended (2001–04). Why am I so hard on the Rio? Simple; it doesn't offer a modicum of the performance or reliability that other cars deliver for the same price or less. Try a Hyundai Accent or a Toyota Echo instead. **Maintenance/Repair costs:** Average. **Parts:** Average cost, and parts are easily found, despite the small dealer network. **Extended warranty:** A bumper-to-bumper warranty is a must-buy, which wipes out your low sales price savings. **Best alternatives:** GM Firefly or Metro; Honda Civic; Hyundai Accent or Elantra; Mazda Protegé; Nissan Sentra; and Toyota Echo, Tercel, or Corolla. **Online help:** *www.autosafety.org* and *www.carsurvey.org*.

Strengths and Weaknesses

A bit smaller than the Sephia and Spectra, the Rio hails from South Korea and is a spin-off of the Aspire, marketed from 1995 to 1997 under the Ford nameplate. It's one of the cheapest cars on the market and offers both a sedan and wagon version. Functional styling, limited safety and performance features, and cheap interior and exterior materials reflect the fact that Kia puts fuel economy and a low base price before safety, performance, convenience, and simple good taste.

Base Rios are equipped with a puny 104-hp 1.6L 4-cylinder engine teamed with a 5-speed manual transmission. Options available include a 4-speed automatic trans-axle; ABS; air conditioning; power steering, door locks, and windows; and foglights. Side airbags aren't offered. Fuel economy: 6.8–8.6L/100 km.

Highly manoeuvrable in city traffic and quite fuel efficient, this small car is, nevertheless, poorly suited for highway cruising or driving situations that require quick merging with traffic. Kia's horsepower ratings may be just as suspect as Hyundai's, and reports of chronic stalling sap owner confidence even more.

VEHICLE HISTORY: You may be wondering how such a low-quality car ever saw the light of day, so I will digress a bit. Vehicles like the Rio are built and propped up through import tariffs to prevent foreign automakers from capturing the home country's market and jobs. Quality isn't a consideration when you're one of the few players in the game. To keep the factories humming, these cars are exported to Third World countries where a low purchase price gives them a huge advantage. When they arrive in Europe and North America, price takes a backseat to quality, reliability, and safety, and auto shoppers look elsewhere for their "bargains." This has been the story with Daewoo, Kia, Fiat, Lada, Dacia, and Yugo.

Kia's products, unlike Daewoo's, do have a track record—and it's not good. In fact, *Consumer Reports* says in its April 1999 New Car edition, "You'd have to search far and wide to find a car that's worse than this small Korean model." CR's early conclusion is confirmed by the proportionally large number of safety-related complaints recorded by NHTSA below.

2003—Subtle styling changes, a slightly larger engine, and extra standard and optional features. Kia claims engineering updates reduce noise and vibration, suspension alterations improve ride comfort, and larger front brakes increase stopping power. None of these pretensions are supported by driver feedback. **2004**—Wagon gets standard alloy wheels (okay, that's undisputable).

Owners report problems with the automatic transmission, seat belts, and electrical and fuel systems; frequent front-end alignments; unreliable tires; and weak, prematurely worn, and noisy brakes. Writes this owner of a 2002 Rio:

I had the front brakes replaced due to a clip that fell off and got between the brake pad and drum, and the rear brakes replaced due to brake dust and glazing of drums. Now less than two weeks later, I'm starting to have the same grinding noise in the rear brakes again.

Other areas of complaint: weak and noisy engine performance; busy, harsh ride; slow and imprecise highway handling; limited passenger room and problematic entry and exit; tire thumping; small audio controls and missing remote trunk release; low-budget interior materials; small door openings and limited rear headroom and legroom; trunk's small opening doesn't take bulky items and doesn't offer a pass-through for large objects; optional tilt steering wheel doesn't tilt much; poor body construction; and a small dealer network that may complicate servicing and warranty performance.

 **Safety Summary**

All models: 2001—NHTSA probes airbag non-deployment. **2001–02**—Defective fuel line ignited an under-hood fire. • Hood flew up and broke front windshield. • Side airbag failed to deploy. • Vehicle disengages from Overdrive because of a missing transmission control modulator. • Transmission jumps out of gear when brakes are applied. • Brakes stick and pedal goes to the floor without vehicle stopping. • Brakes are noisy. • Excessive shaking and vibration; vehicle swerves all over the road. • Chronic stalling. • Rear seat belt shreds or jams. • Steering binds and grinds when turned; on other occasions it's too loose. • Premature tire wear. • Vehicle assembled without a horn. • Various electrical problems, including clock spring failure, cause the Check Engine light and airbag warning lamp to remain lit. • Fuel light constantly stays lit. • Bent wheel rims.

My 2002 Rio has been towed repeatedly due to the car shutting down. They said first it was the alternator and fuel pump, now they say it is the battery cable. Today is the 15th of September, and I still do not have the new car I bought.

Please help before it shuts down in highway traffic and I get killed.

2003—Sudden steering loss. • No starts and constant stalling, particularly, in cold weather, because of faulty engine computer module. • Premature failure of the engine and transmission. • Engine runs hot. • In damp weather, brakes grab abruptly and won't release or they don't "catch" at all.

The brake fell off the pad. In most normal cars the brakes are held on with a pop rivet. Not this car. They are held on with thin pieces of aluminum. Everyone knows how easy aluminum bends and twists and that's exactly how mine were. And the brake is held onto the pad with glue!!!

The car was involved in an accident due to a driver side rear wheel freezing up without touching the brakes, causing vehicle to veer off the road.

Power steering fluid leaks. • Steering column bolt snapped. • Seatbelt cuts across the driver's and passenger's throat. • Burning rubber or plastic smell in the cabin. • Wheel lug nuts sheared off. • Windshield wiper nuts often come off. **2004—** Frequent mass air flow sensor failures cause chronic stalling.

Secret Warranties/Internal Bulletins/Service Tips

All models: 2001—Revised transmission shift lever and bushing spacer. • Reinforced fuse box cover latch. • Troubleshooting automatic transmission concerns. **2001–02—**Special Service Campaign addresses premature transmission failures. **2003–04—**TSB #013 addresses different remedies for curing hard starts in cold weather (reprogramming software is one field fix).

RIO PROFILE

	2001	2002	2003	2004
Cost Price($)				
S	11,995	12,095	12,351	12,650
RS	12,995	13,095	13,251	13,550
Used Values ($)				
S ▲	4,000	5,000	6,500	8,500
S ▼	3,000	4,500	6,000	7,500
RS ▲	4,500	5,500	7,000	9,000
RS ▼	4,000	5,000	6,500	8,000
Reliability	❶	❷	❷	❸
Crash Safety (F)	—	❹	❹	❹
Side	❸	❸	❷	❷
Head Restraints	❶	❶	❶	❶
Rollover Resistance	—	❹	❹	❹

Mazda

PROTEGÉ, MAZDA3 ★★★★★

RATING: *Protegé*: Recommended (1999–2003); Above Average (1991–98); Average (1985–90). *Mazda3*: Above Average (All years). The cars are plentiful at bargain prices; the best buys of all, though, are the totally revamped 1999 and later models. **Maintenance/Repair costs:** Higher than average. Repairs are dealer dependent.

All ratings on a numbered scale where ❺ is good and ❶ is bad. See pages 100–101 for a more detailed description.

Parts: Expensive, but easily found. **Extended warranty:** Not necessary. **Best alternatives:** GM Firefly or Metro, Honda Civic, Hyundai Accent or Elantra, Nissan Sentra, Suzuki Esteem or Swift, and Toyota Echo or Corolla. **Online help:** *www.autosafety.org* and *www.carsurvey.org*.

 Strengths and Weaknesses

Protegés are peppy performers with a manual transmission hooked to the base engine. The automatic gearbox, however, produces lethargic acceleration that makes highway passing a bit chancy on pre-1995 models. Engine performance, handling, and fuel economy are much better on more recent designs. Overall durability started improving with the 1991 and later Mazda 323 and Protegé, both of which were also sold as Ford Escorts. Nevertheless, pollution-control components and the electrical system have been troublesome. Watch out also for automatic transmission malfunctions, air conditioner breakdowns, and engine oil leaks.

VEHICLE HISTORY: 1991–95—Reasonably reliable and inexpensive. **1995–98**—Redesigned versions are better buys for cheapskate shoppers looking for more reliability with a dash of additional performance at an affordable price. Powered by a standard, fuel-efficient, 1.5L engine mated with a manual 5-speed transmission, these econoboxes are among the most responsive and roomiest small cars around. **1999**—A restyled interior and exterior and a more powerful engine lineup. **2000**—Premium models received front-seat side airbags and an improved ABS system. **2002**—The introduction of the Protegé5 four-door hatchback sport wagon and the MP3, a higher-performing sedan variant. **2003**—A turbocharged 170-hp MazdaSpeed Protegé debuted and sold in small quantities. **2004**— Protegé replaced by the Mazda3.

Although 1996–2003 Protegés are far more reliable than most American-made small cars, their automatic transmissions continue to be the car's weakest link (a problem also seen with Ford's Escort and Hyundai's lineup), with erratic shifting and locking up in Fifth gear. Owners also report fuel system glitches, electrical problems, and front brake vibration, rotor warping, and premature pad wear. Other generic deficiencies: weak rear defrosting; chronic engine stalling (a secret warranty applies up to seven years); AC failures; and body defects, including wind and water leaks into the interior.

Mazda3

An econobox with flair, the front-drive 2004 Mazda3 is a totally new entry-level small car that replaces the Protegé. With considerable engineering help from Ford and Volvo, these cars use a platform that will also serve future iterations of the Ford Focus and Volvo S40. Powered by 150-hp 2.0L and 160-hp 2.3L 4-cylinder engines coupled with either a 5-speed manual or a 4-speed Sport mode automatic transmission, the car offers spirited acceleration and smooth, sporty shifting. Handling is enhanced with a highly rigid body structure, front and rear stabilizer bars, multi-link rear suspension, and four-wheel disc brakes. Interior room is also quite ample with the car's relatively long 263.9-cm (103.9-in.) wheelbase, extra width, and straight sides, which maximize headroom, legroom, and shoulder room.

Some minuses: The car could use a bit more passing power with the standard engine; prematurely worn out brake rotor and pads continue to be reported; some minor fit and finish deficiencies; a high deck cuts rear visibility; there's limited rear footroom; and some Mazda dealers have been accused of overcharging for scheduled maintenance. Other reported problems for the Mazda3 include excessive fuel consumption, which is about 15 percent more than advertised; the gas and brake pedal are too close together; drivers easily catch the side of their shoe against the brake when accelerating (consider customized racing pedals); the driver's right knee rubs the console; a front-end clunk is felt upon hard acceleration; a popping/creaking/rattling noise emanates from the rear end (hatch struts may be the culprit); driver door and dash rattles; Goodyear tires perform poorly in rain and slush (Michelin Pilots, and Hakkapeliittas winter tires are better performers); door ajar light comes on for no reason; paint is unusually thin; CD changer is failure-prone; and the passenger side wiper may not clean the windshield sufficiently (top three inches of arch not touched).

 ## Safety Summary

All models/years: Airbags failed to deploy. • Transmission failures and malfunctions. • Poor headlight illumination. **1995–99**—Cracked fuel line caused fire. • Sudden tire tread separation (Firestone). • Chronic stalling. • Excessive brake fade. • Metal rods in driver's seat could cause severe back injuries in a rear-end collision. • Driver's seat belt buckle wouldn't unlatch. • Brake pedal pad is too narrow and should be coated with non-skid material. • Severe static electricity shock when exiting vehicle. **1999–2002**—Delayed braking. • Check Engine light activation is your first warning sign that automatic transmission is faulty. • Car rolled backward and hit a tree, despite being parked with brakes applied. • Vehicle constantly pulls to the right. • Passenger unable to disengage seat belt. • Bucket seat seatbacks contain metal support bars that are extremely uncomfortable. **2001**—Loss of brakes. • Gear shift lever jumped from Drive to Neutral while vehicle was underway. • Defective steering column coupling. • Broken rear axle causes severe pulling to one side. • Windows take a long time to defrost. • **2002**—Continual stalling. • Brake line split, leading to rear-ender. **2003**—Nauseating fumes entered the vehicle. • Brake pedal pushed almost to the floor before brakes work, and they produce excessive noise. • Passenger seat belt won't disengage. • Passenger seat belt broke; seat belt case and release button broke while trying to release belt. *Mazda3:* **2004**—Premature wearout of brake pads and rotors. • The transmission can be hard to shift, especially from Third to Fourth gear. • Huge accumulation of brake dust on the rear wheels. • Brake rotors are prematurely grooved. • Hard starts because of a faulty fuel pump. • AC doesn't cool the car and prevents the car from accelerating.

Secret Warranties/Internal Bulletins/Service Tips

All models: 1995–98—Poor engine performance may require a new intake valve. • Excessive vibration in gear or at idle may mean the engine mount material has hardened or cracked. • Erratic shifting may signal that the valve body harness is defective. • If the gear selector lever is hard to operate, it's likely that the lower manual shaft in the transfer case has excessive rust. • An inoperative AC may have a corroded pressure switch terminal assembly. **1996–98**—A noisy driveshaft can be silenced by installing a countermeasure dynamic damper. **1997–98**—A 1–2 upshift shock at light throttle may require the replacement of the large and small accumulator spring with a single spring. • If the brake warning light is constantly lit, even though the brakes check out okay, it's likely that the speedometer assembly transistor has been damaged. **1998–2003**—Dealing with musty, mildew-type AC odours. **1999**—No shift from Second to Third gear. • Manual transmission jerking or hesitation. • Inoperative wiper motor. • Weather stripping comes off rear doors. • Door key may jam in locks. • Excessive exhaust resonance noise. • Engine rattling. • Clutch squealing. • Off-centre steering wheel. **1999–2000**—Mazda will replace the mass airflow sensor free of charge up to 7 years/112,000 km (70,000 mi.). Problems with this component include a lack of power, hesitation, or a poor idle. Don't argue, simply tell the dealer you are aware of the replacement campaign, and anyway, it's a part covered by the

AC – MUSTY/MILDEW ODOURS
BULLETIN NO: 07-001/03

1998–2002 626; 1998–2003 Protegé; 2000–03 Protegé5; 2000–03 MPV; 1998 MPV; 1998–2002 Millenia; and 1999–2003 Miata.

SUBJECT: This odour is the result of mould growth in the AC evaporator/cooling unit, which is caused by condensation, dust, and pollen within the cooling unit. This condition is usually worse during high humidity conditions. "Mazda Air Cooling Coil Coating" is available to encapsulate the mould to reduce odours. If the product is properly applied, it can effectively reduce the musty/mildew odour for up to three years.

more comprehensive emissions warranty. **2000**—Excessive exhaust resonance noise. **2000–01**—Clutch squealing. • Inoperative wiper motor. • Off-centre steering wheel. **2002**—Tips on eliminating AC odour. **2003**—Cold engine rattling. • Wind noise around doors. • Eliminating a rotten-egg exhaust smell. *Mazda3*: **2004**—Whine in the steering system. • Front wipers don't wipe well. • Loose door trim screw cap. • Paint stains on the roof, hood, and trunk. • Squeaking rear brakes.

PROTEGÉ, MAZDA3 PROFILE

	1996	1997	1998	1999	2000	2001	2002	2003	2004
Cost Price ($)									
Protegé	13,895	14,685	14,675	14,970	15,095	15,795	15,795	15,795	—
Mazda3	—	—	—	—	—	—	—	—	16,195
Used Values ($)									
Protegé ▲	2,000	3,500	4,500	5,000	6,000	8,000	9,000	11,000	—
Protegé ▼	1,500	2,500	4,000	4,500	5,000	7,000	8,000	10,000	—
Mazda3 ▲	—	—	—	—	—	—	—	—	13,500
Mazda3 ▼	—	—	—	—	—	—	—	—	12,500
Reliability	④	④	④	④	④	⑤	⑤	⑤	④
Crash Safety (F)	—	③	③	—	④	⑤	⑤	⑤	④
Side	—	—	—	—	③	③	③	③	③
Offset	③	③	③	③	③	③	③	③	⑤
Head Restraints	—	①	—	②	②	③	③	③	②
Rear	—	—	—	—	—	②	②	②	②
Rollover Resistance	—	—	—	—	—	—	—	④	④

Nissan

 SENTRA ★★★★★

RATING: Recommended (2000–04); Above Average (1995–99); Average (1988–94); Not Recommended (1983–87). **Maintenance/Repair costs:** Higher than average on early models, but anybody can repair these cars. **Parts:** Reasonably priced and easily obtainable. **Extended warranty:** Not required. **Best alternatives:** A GM Firefly or Metro, Honda Civic, Hyundai Elantra, Mazda Protegé, Suzuki Esteem or Swift, and Toyota Echo or Corolla. **Online help:** *www.autosafety.org* and *www.carsurvey.org*.

⟨!⟩ Strengths and Weaknesses

Until the 1991 models arrived, early Sentras were a crapshoot; more recent models are cheap, generally reliable, inexpensive to repair; and give good fuel economy. So what's not to like? Rudimentary ride and handling, and subpar build quality. Quality improved considerably with the 1991 version, yet the vehicle's base price rose only marginally, making these later model years bargain buys for consumers looking for a reliable "beater."

The 1991–94s handle better, although some quality problems remain. These include faulty fuel tanks, leaking manual and automatic transmissions, and noisy engine timing chains and front brakes; problems that have all afflicted these cars over the past decade. Fortunately, with the exception of computer failures and ABS malfunctions, repairs are still relatively simple to perform. The redesigned 1995–97 models introduced fresh styling, a longer wheelbase, a peppier power plant, standard dual airbags, and side door beams.

VEHICLE HISTORY: 1995—Larger, and better performing. 1998—New front and rear ends and a new 140-hp SE sedan. 2000—Underwent a major redesign, offering more powerful engines, a better ride, and enhanced handling. It's well worth the $1,000–$2,000 increase from the '99 version and is basically identical to the costlier 2001 version. 2002—The 145-hp SE model was replaced at the top of the line by the SE-R and SE-R Spec V; the latter offering a 180-hp engine, a limited-slip differential, and a sport-tuned suspension, to compete against the Honda Civic SiR and Mazda's high-performance spin-offs. Four-wheel disc brakes also become a standard feature. 2003—Arrival of the GXE, equipped with a 165-hp 2.5-litre engine, ABS, and front side airbags.

The 1995–2002 owner complaints concern stalling and hard starting; engine rattles; electrical glitches; premature brake wear and excessive brake noise; automatic transmission whine; AC solenoid failures and AC that blows hot air or freezes up;

and accessories that malfunction. Owners have also had to contend with a recurrent steering clunk noise, clutch, clutch switch, suspension strut, wheel bearing, and catalytic converter failures. Crank position sensor malfunction may prevent vehicle from being started. Body assembly is also targeted with some complaints of loose windshield mouldings, poor body fit, paint defects, and air and water leaks into the interior through the trunk and doors.

The 2003–04 models are slightly improved, but owners are still plagued by automatic transmission, fuel system, and electrical problems. Front brake pads and rotors wear out quickly; there's excessive bouncing and vibration caused by prematurely worn struts; doors vibrate noisily; passenger-side windows leak; rear bumpers may fall off; and some incidents of excessive wind noise around the windshield moulding.

 **Safety Summary**

All models/years: Brake and accelerator pedals set too close together. • Airbags fail to deploy, or deploy inadvertently. • Steering lock-up. • Chronic stalling. • Sudden acceleration. • Premature tire wear. • Horn blows on its own. **1998–99**—ABS failures. • Defective brake master cylinder. • Excessive stopping distance. • Sticking throttle. • Ignition key breaks off in the ignition. • Faulty power door locks. • Vehicle leaks when it rains. • Windshield wiper washer leaks, and washer produces acrid fumes that enter the cabin. • Front seats jam when moved back. **1999**—Loss of braking; extended braking distance. • Fuel filler flap fell into fuel filler tube. **2000**—Suspension attachment bolts broke off. **2001**—Brakes easily lock up at all speeds. • Warped brake rotors. **2002**—Fire ignited in the headlight assembly:

> I am a professional fire investigator. This vehicle fire originated with the headlight assembly. The burn patterns clearly indicate this to be the area of origin and the supporting burn patterns indicate the fire originated in the headlight assembly. Even though this recall does not specifically address a possible fire hazard, I believe the fire is related to the recall problem.

• Fire erupted in the engine compartment. • Sudden acceleration and frequent stalling. **2003**—ABS brake failure; brakes lock up at low speed, particularly on wet roads. • Windshield wipers, turn signals, headlights, horn, and hazard lights may suddenly fail. • Continental tire tread separation. • The gas and brake pedals may be set too far apart for some. **2004**—Airbag failed to deploy. • Sudden, unintended acceleration. • Stalling; repeatedly loses all engine power and high-speed bucking (surging). • Erratic, rough idling. • Early automatic transmission replacement. • ABS brake failure. • Brakes lock up at low speed, particularly on wet roads. • Keyless remote doesn't work and back door doesn't open from the inside, apparently because of a short in the electrical system. • Continental and Firestone tire tread peeling off. • While driving, windshield wipers, turn signals, headlights, horn, and hazard lights failed.

Secret Warranties/Internal Bulletins/Service Tips

All models/years: TSB predicts the lifetime of the vehicle's timing belt. • Flashing lights when signal lights are engaged. • Faulty master cylinder causes brake pedal to slowly drop to the floor. • Engine pinging on light acceleration. **1995–99**—Harsh shifts and low power with the automatic transmission may be because of reduced movement of the A/T throttle wire cable inside the cable housing. • A self-activating horn can be fixed by replacing the horn springs and spring insulators. **1997–99**—Harsh shifts and low power with the automatic transmission. • Horn self-activates. • More tips on silencing squeaks and rattles. • Diagnosing causes of brake judder and steering wheel shimmy. • Extended-life pads for the front brakes. • Curing sulfur odour. • Slow retraction of the front seat belt. **1999–2001**—Hard starting in cold weather or at high altitude. • Engine pings with light-to-moderate acceleration. • Exhaust manifold heat shield rattle. • Automatic transmission won't upshift. • Tips to improve downshifting (modified downshift spring). • Brake pedal slowly drops to floor (master cylinder check). • Vehicle wanders or pulls to one side. • Horn activates randomly. • Noisy, vibrating speedometer. • Water condensation from AC. • Rotten-egg exhaust odour. • Anti-theft system prevents starting. **2000**—Vehicle lacks power; transmission sticks in Third gear. • Slow fuel fill; pump nozzle clicks off continually. • Erratic AC vent flow. • Front suspension squeak, rattling. • Windshield hum or whistle. **2000–04**—TSB #AT04-002, published March 10, 2004, says abnormal shifting of the automatic transmission is likely because of a defective control valve assembly. **2001–02**—Low power or poor running. • Water leak in trunk area. • Rear brake caliper knock, clunk, or rattle. **2003**—Anti-theft system may make for hard starts or no-starts. • Troubleshooting tips for a lit MIL light. • Turn signals may be too fast. • AC may operate erratically and have a sticking case door.

SENTRA PROFILE

	1996	1997	1998	1999	2000	2001	2002	2003	2004
Cost Price ($)									
Sentra	13,448	13,698	14,498	15,398	15,398	15,298	15,598	15,598	15,798
Used Values ($)									
Sentra ▲	2,500	3,500	4,500	5,500	7,000	8,000	9,500	11,000	12,500
Sentra ▼	2,000	3,000	4,000	5,000	6,500	7,500	8,500	10,000	11,500
Reliability	4	4	4	4	4	5	5	5	5
Crash Safety (F)	—	4	3	—	—	4	4	4	4
Side	—	—	3	—	—	—	—	2	2
Offset	—	—	1	1	1	1	1	1	1
Head Restraints	—	2	2	2	2	2	1	1	1
Rollover Resistance	—	—	—	—	—	—	4	4	4

Subaru

RATING: *Impreza*: Above Average (1997–2004); Below Average (1994–96). *Forester*: Recommended (2001–04); Average (1998–2000). *WRX*: Not Recommended (2002–04). **Maintenance/Repair costs:** Higher than average. Mediocre, expensive servicing is hard to overcome because independent garages can't service key AWD components. Only buy a Subaru if you must have AWD and you're confident you can get dependable service from your local Subaru dealer. **Parts:** Expensive and hard to find. Emissions components are often back ordered for months, but cheap aftermarket components can be found outside the dealer network. **Extended warranty:** Budget about $1,000 for an extended powertrain warranty. **Best alternatives:** If you don't need the AWD capability, you're wasting your money. Here are some front-drives worth considering: the Honda Civic, Hyundai Elantra, Mazda Protegé, Nissan Sentra, Suzuki Esteem or Swift, and Toyota Echo or Corolla. Some recommended small vehicles with 4×4 capability that are set on a car, not a truck, frame (providing more carlike handling), include the GM Vibe, Honda CR-V, and the Toyota Matrix or RAV4. **Online help:** *techinfo.subaru.com/ html/shoppingHome.jsp; www.autosafety.org; www.carsurvey.org;* and *www.i-club.com.*

 ## Strengths and Weaknesses

These well-equipped small cars have one of the most refined AWD drivetrains you'll find (prior to 1996, they were mostly front-drive economy cars). With their four-wheel traction, Subarus provide good handling without any torque steer, lots of storage space with the wagons, and good fuel economy. On the other hand, Subaru makes you pay dearly for the AWD capability, overall mechanical reliability is so-so, body workmanship is barely average, and braking can get downright scary. Furthermore, small doors and entryways restrict rear access, the coupe's narrow rear window and large rear pillars hinder rear visibility, heat and air distribution is often inadequate, and front and rear seat legroom may be insufficient for tall drivers. Without their AWD capability, these cars would be "back-of-the-pack" used car picks.

Impreza

The full-time 4×4 Impreza is essentially a shorter Legacy with additional convenience features. It comes as a four-door sedan, a wagon, and an Outback Sport wagon, all powered by a 135-hp 2.2L or a 165-hp 2.5L 4-cylinder engine. The 2.5L performs much better with the Impreza and Forester than with the Legacy Outback. It is smooth and powerful, with lots of low-end torque for serious off-road use. The automatic transmission shifts smoothly. The manual transmission's "hill holder" clutch prevents the car from rolling backward when starting out. These Subarus hurtle through corners effortlessly with a flat, solid stance and plenty of grip. Tight cornering at highway speeds is done with minimal body lean and no loss of control, and steering is precise and predictable.

VEHICLE HISTORY: *Impreza:* **1995**—A coupe and an Outback model were sold with optional AWD. **1996**—A mix of front-drives and all-wheel drives, along with a new sport model, a new Outback wagon (for light off-roading), and larger engines. **1997**—Additional power and torque, a restyled front end, and a new Outback Sport wagon. **1998**—A revised dash and door panels, the Brighton was dropped, and the high-end 2.5 RS was added. **1999**—Stronger engines, more torque, and upgraded transmissions. **2002**—The 2.2L 4-cylinder was dropped, along with Subaru's pretensions for making affordable entry-level cars. Totally redesigned models include the 2.5 TS Sport Wagon, 2.5 RS Sedan, Outback Sport Wagon, the sporty WRX Sedan, and Sport Wagon. There is no longer a two-door version available. **2004**—Larger headlights and a slightly restyled front end. The WRX STi sedan arrived with a 300-hp turbo 2.5 and upgraded suspension, brakes, and steering. *Forester:* **1998**—Launched as a cross between a wagon and a sport-utility. Based on the shorter Impreza, the Forester uses the Legacy Outback's 2.5L 165-hp engine coupled with a 5-speed manual transmission or an optional 4-speed automatic. Its road manners are more subdued, and its engine provides more power and torque for off-roading. **1999**—A quieter, torquier engine, a smoother-shifting transmission, and a more solid body. **2000**—Standard cruise control (L) and a limited-slip differential (S). **2003**—Improved interior materials, upgraded suspension, enhanced handling and ride quality, larger tires and fenders, and revised head restraints and side-impact airbags. **2004**—A new turbocharged 2.5 XT.

Post-'95 Subarus are noted for improved, though only average quality control, spotty servicing, and serious automatic transmission and brake deficiencies. There's also a history of premature clutch failures and shuddering, particularly after a cold start-up. Owners report poor engine idling; frequent cold-weather stalling; manual transmission malfunctions; rear wheel bearing failures; excessive vibration caused by the alloy wheels; premature exhaust system rust-out and early brake caliper and rotor scoring and wear; minor electrical short circuits; catalytic converter failures; doors that don't latch properly; body panel and trim fit and finish deficiencies characterized by water leaks and condensation problems from the top of the windshield or sunroof; the windshield cracking and scratching too easily; and paint peeling. In addition to the paint peeling from delamination, owners report that Subaru paint chips much too easily. Says the Alberta owner of a 2001 Impreza:

> I have a chipping 2001 Subaru Impreza Outback Sport and have been trying to get the dealership to deal with it. The car is now one year old and has over 50 rock chips on the hood alone. I barely touched the car when putting in the gas and the paint fell off. I spent the extra money on paint protection when I got the car and I am afraid of what

might be left after I pay this car off. We use the car for skiing so it does see a little gravel (it's Alberta!) and I bought it because it was backed by the Ski Association.

Safety Summary

All models: 1994–2004—A history of subpar engine performance (hesitating, then suddenly accelerating, unintended acceleration, poor engine idling, cooling, and frequent cold weather stalling), premature clutch failures, and frequent brake failures and costly servicing. Numerous reports of airbags failing to deploy or injuring passengers after deployment. Airbags are a serious problem with all Subarus: They can fail to deploy in an accident, deploy inadvertently while parked, turning, or if the underside of the car scrapes the road; if the car drives over a dip in the road, hits a pothole, is stuck in a ditch, or is being washed; they can even deploy if the key is put into the ignition. • Sudden acceleration. • Brake malfunctions and ABS brake failures. • The premature replacement of brake sensors, pads, and rotors, and hubcaps that constantly fall off because of their poor design. • Front shoulder belts are uncomfortable and rear seat belts are hard to buckle up. **1998**—Oil leak from oil filter seam caused fire. • Front strut assembly failure. • Cruise control failed to disengage when brakes were applied. • Excessive shaking at highway speeds. • Seatback collapsed when vehicle was rear-ended. • Subaru told car owner that tendency to pull to the right was a design feature. • Sudden brake loss after linings, calipers, and master cylinder had been replaced. **1999**—Engine failure caused by cracked #2 piston. • When accelerating or decelerating, vehicle will begin to jerk because of excessive play in the front axle. • Wheel bearing failures. • Transmission plug fell out. • Front bumper skirt catches on parking blocks, resulting in bumper twisting and being ripped off. • The centre rear seat belt's poor design prohibits the installation of many child safety seats. **2000**—Driver burned from airbag deployment. **2001**—Wheel bearing failures. ABS overreacts. **2000–03**—Soft pedal and late brake engagement—pedal goes almost to the floor. *WRX:* **2002**—Erratic transmission performance:

> First gear is a major issue in my vehicle. I can only engage First gear if I'm at a complete stop. So if I've slowed down to 5–10 mph [8–16 km/h] I'm forced to go into Second gear, which not only wears out my clutch prematurely, but could also cause an accident if I needed to build speed quickly. The transmission overall seems to be a big issue with WRX owners. Please go to *www.i-club.com* and under forums. Do a search for tranny and also First gear. You will see a slew of issues.

• Poor ABS braking performance, resulting in extended stopping distance, related to bad design and premature component wearout. Owners of 2002 and 2003 WRXs are particularly affected by poor braking that runs counter to the high-performance hype found in Subaru's ads:

> While attempting to slow my 2003 WRX for a corner on a well groomed, dry, gravel road the ABS system of the car initiated a mode that would not allow the car's brakes to function at all. During the episode (which has been and can be recreated) pedal pressure and pedal height was maintained as during normal braking operations. The brakes would not work despite the fact that I was standing with both feet on the brake pedal. I am in the process of disconnecting my ABS. Subaru North America claims that I'm nuts.

• Exhaust shows heat damage after only 6,400 km (4,000 mi.). **2004**—Sudden STI engine failure. • Engine overheating and excessive turbo lag. • Check Engine light is always lit. • Catalytic converters are often burned out. • Trunk latch defective and headlights fog up. • Speedometer is off by about ten percent. • The deep cowling makes it hard to read the instrument panel. Constant first gear grind. *Forester*: **2000**—The following comments apply to the Forester but may be relevant to Impreza owners, too. • Driver burned from airbag deployment. • Sudden loss of transmission fluid. • Driver's seatback may suddenly recline because seat belt gets tangled up in the recliner lever. • Frequent wheel bearing failures. • Fuel filler cap design is too complicated for gas station attendants to put on properly. **2001**—Airbags failed to deploy. • Breakage of rear-wheel bearings. • Brake and accelerator pedals are too close together. • In a collision, airbags failed to deploy and seat belt didn't restrain occupant. • In a similar incident, shoulder belt allowed driver's head to hit the windshield. • Water leaks through moon roof and top of windshield. • Headlights don't illuminate the edge of the road and are either too bright on High or too dim on Low. • Alarm system self-activated, trapping baby inside of car until fire rescue arrived. • Drivetrain rattles and grinds when shifted into Second or Third gear. • Brakes can fail when braking over bumps at moderate speeds. • Dangerous delay, then surging when accelerating in forward or Reverse. • Surging at highway speeds and stalling at lower rpm. • Transmission failure; gears lock in Park intermittently. • Open wheel design allows snow and debris to pack in the area and throw wheel out of balance, creating dangerous vibration. • High hood allows water into the engine. **2002**—Engine overheating. • Automatic transmission locks in Park. • Vehicle surges forward when brakes are applied. • Hood is too high, allows water to run onto engine. • Brake and gas pedal are too close together. • Snow packs into wheel grooves causing them to be seriously out of balance.

> To clean the wheels entails getting down on hands and knees with a screwdriver and scraping the deposits from the outside groove, behind the wheel "spokes" and around the inside groove. The only access to this is thru the small openings in the "spokes". It always takes at least three such cleaning of all [affected] wheels before one can get all the deposits removed and the wheels back in balance. When you are on the way to church during the middle of winter this situation becomes [intolerable].

• Doors fail to latch or unlatch. • Mirrors are almost always covered with condensation. **2003**—When backing into a parking space the Hill Holder feature activates, forcing the driver to use excessive throttle in Reverse. • Clutch replaced because of excessive chatter; a common complaint. • Sudden, complete brake failure. • Emergency brake seized. • Brake rotors replaced at 20,000 km. • Wheel bearing failure. • Heater, defroster inoperative. • Front seats move fore and aft. • Vehicle has five doors, but only one key hole, plus, the power locks failed. • Remote keyless entry often doesn't work. • Windshield cracked in exactly the same place after twice being hit by a rock. • Another owner reports windshield was replaced three times because of cracks. • When rear hatch window shattered it produced shards, rather than small pellets. • When passenger seat reclines it pinches an airbag cable that shuts off the device. 2004—Engine compartment fire. • Excessive transmission high-pitch whine is distracting. • Inoperative fuel release door button. • Speedometer, odometer, and power windows sometimes don't work. WRX: 2003—Windshield cracking. • Chronic ABS brake failures.

Secret Warranties/Internal Bulletins/Service Tips

All models/years: Troubleshooting tips on a sticking anti-lock brake relay are offered. This problem is characterized by a lit ABS warning light or the ABS motor continuing to run/buzz when the ignition is turned off. • Diagnostic and repair tips are offered on transfer clutch binding and/or bucking on turns. • A rotten-egg smell could be caused by a defective catalytic converter. It will be replaced free of charge, after a bit of arguing, up to five years under the emissions warranty. **All models: 1997–99**—Excessive driveline vibration is covered in TSB #05-33-98R. Subaru's fix requires modifying the differential. **2000–01**—Front oxygen air/fuel sensor cracking. • Likely reasons why the automatic transmission light comes on. • Clutch pedal sticking. • Harsh transmission shifting. • Concerns with brake rotor scoring. • Subpar catalytic converter performance. **2001–03**—Troubleshooting unevenly or prematurely worn brake pads (TSB #06-33-04).

FORESTER, IMPREZA, WRX PROFILE

	1996	1997	1998	1999	2000	2001	2002	2003	2004
Cost Price ($)									
Forester	—	—	26,695	26,695	26,895	28,395	28,395	28,395	27,995
Base/Brighton	17,995	16,991	16,240	17,795	—	—	—	—	—
Sedan 4×4	19,495	21,395	21,395	21,995	21,995	22,196	21,995	22,995	22,995
WRX	—	—	—	—	—	—	34,995	34,995	35,495
Used Values ($)									
Forester ▲	—	—	8,500	10,500	13,500	16,000	18,000	21,500	24,000
Forester ▼	—	—	7,000	9,000	12,000	15,000	17,000	20,000	22,000
Base/Brighton ▲	3,500	4,500	5,500	7,000	—	—	—	—	—
Base/Brighton ▼	3,000	4,000	4,500	6,000	—	—	—	—	—

All ratings on a numbered scale where ⑤ is good and ❶ is bad. See pages 100–101 for a more detailed description.

Sedan 4×4 ▲	4,500	5,500	6,500	8,000	10,000	12,500	14,500	16,000	18,500
Sedan 4×4 ▼	3,500	5,000	6,000	7,000	9,000	11,000	13,500	15,000	17,000
WRX ▲	—	—	—	—	—	—	21,000	25,000	29,000
WRX ▼	—	—	—	—	—	—	19,000	23,500	27,500
Reliability	②	③	③	③	③	③	③	③	③
Crash Safety (F)	④	④	—	—	—	—	④	④	—
Forester	—	—	—	④	④	④	④	⑤	⑤
Side	—	—	③	③	—	—	④	④	—
Forester	—	—	③	③	—	⑤	⑤	⑤	⑤
Offset	—	—	—	—	—	—	⑤	⑤	⑤
Forester	—	—	—	⑤	⑤	⑤	⑤	⑤	⑤
Head restraints	—	②	—	—	—	②	③	③	—
Forester	—	—	—	②	—	③	③	—	—
WRX	—	—	—	—	—	—	—	—	②
Rollover Resistance	—	—	—	—	—	—	—	④	—
Forester	—	—	—	—	—	③	③	③	④

LEGACY, OUTBACK

RATING: Above Average (1997–2004); Below Average (1989–96). A competent, full-time 4×4 performer for drivers who want to move up in size, comfort, and features. Available as a four-door sedan or five-door wagon, the Legacy is cleanly and conventionally styled, with a hint of the Acura Legend in the rear end. The AWD is what this car is all about. It handles difficult terrain without the fuel penalty or clumsiness of many truck-based SUVs. **Maintenance/Repair costs:** Higher than average. Repairs are dealer dependent. **Parts:** Parts aren't easily found and can be costly. **Extended warranty:** You should invest in an extended warranty to cover likely powertrain deficiencies after the base warranty has expired. **Best alternatives:** The Honda CR-V, Hyundai Santa Fe, Suzuki Grand Vitara, and Toyota RAV4. **Online help:** *www.autosafety.org* and *www.carsurvey.org*.

Strengths and Weaknesses

Costing a bit more than the smaller Impreza, these Subaru models are well-appointed, provide a comfortable ride and acceptable handling with the right options, and have lots of cargo room. On the downside, owners report problematic automatic transmission performance when it's hooked to the base engine; the 2.5L is a sluggish performer, undoubtedly because of the car's heft; excessive engine noise; mediocre handling on base models; excessive 4-cylinder engine noise; power window and lock switches aren't easily accessible; cramped back seat with a tight fit for the middle rear-seat passenger; limited rear headroom for tall passengers; trunk hinges can damage cargo and cut into storage space; seat belts may be too short for large occupants; and servicing is very dealer-dependent.

The Outback is a marketing coup that stretches the definition of sport-utility by simply customizing the all-wheel-drive Legacy to give it more of an outdoorsy flair. American Motors tried the same marketing approach with the Eagle in the '70s and failed miserably because of poor quality control, lousy marketing, and a passive public whose concept of off-road thrills was watching James Dean at the drive-in.

First launched in 1989 as front-drives, these compacts are a bit slow off the mark. The 5-speed is a bit notchy, and the automatic gearbox is slow to downshift, has difficulty staying in Overdrive, and is failure-prone. Early Legacy models are noisy, fuel-thirsty cars with bland styling that masks their solid, dependable AWD performance. Actually, the availability of a proven 4×4 powertrain in a compact family sedan and wagon makes these cars appealing for special use. In spite of their reputation for acceptable dependability, though, Subarus are not trouble-free—engine, clutch, turbo, and driveline defects are common on the early models through to the 1998 versions.

VEHICLE HISTORY: 1995–98—These redesigned models have sleeker styling, additional interior room (though legroom is still at a premium), a bit more horsepower with the base engine, and a new 2.5L 4-cylinder driving the 1996 AWD GT and LSi. The Outback, a Legacy/Madison Avenue spin-off, was transformed into a sport-utility wagon with a taller roof. Even with the improvements noted above, acceleration is still only passable (if you don't mind the loud engine), but highway handling and ride are remarkably good. The 1997 models marked a return to the company's 4×4 roots, with the repackaging of its Legacy and Impreza 4×4 lineup as Outbacks. A Legacy 2.5L GT all-wheel-drive sporting sedan, or wagon variant, also joined the group that year. In addition to these re-designated models—and the squeezing out of a bit more horsepower from its limited range of engines—Subaru continued to tap the sport-utility craze by offering a greater variety of AWD vehicles. **1999**—Debut of an upgraded 2.2L engine. **2000**—Longer and carrying a new 2.5L engine. **2001**—Two new Outback wagons, featuring a more powerful 3.0L engine, joined the lineup. **2002**—The addition to the lineup of the H6-3.0 VDC Outback sedan, equipped with a standard 3.0L engine. **2003**—New front end styling, GT gets an upgraded engine and a semi-manual Sport Shift; Outback suspension is upgraded to improve cornering and reduce front-end plow. **2004**—35th Anniversary Editions of Legacy and Outback add standard features.

The 2.5L engine is a competent performer only with a manual gearbox. The 4-cylinder engine is noisy and rough-running. It's tuned more for low-end torque than for speedy acceleration. The 6-cylinder is adequate, but doesn't feel like it has much in reserve. The automatic transmission shifts into too high a gear to adequately exploit the engine's power and is reluctant to downshift into the proper gear. The manual transmission's shift linkage isn't suitable for rapid gear changes.

Base models don't handle well. They bounce around on uneven pavement, the rear end tends to swing out during high-speed cornering, and there's too much body lean in turns at lesser speeds. Higher-end models handle well, though there's some excessive lean when cornering. The GT's firmer suspension exhibits above-average handling.

The Legacy and the Outback have had more than their share of reliability problems over the years. Powertrain defects can sideline the car for days. Engine and transmission problems keep showing up. One owner of a '98 Legacy Outback has replaced his engine twice, at 800 km and 4,000 km. There are several reports of the transmission jumping out of gear when using First gear to slow down or to descend a steep grade. From 1999 through 2003, servicing can be awkward because of the crowded engine compartment, particularly on turbocharged versions.

Other problems: automatic transmission front seals and clutch breakdowns are most common, the transmission sometimes downshifts abruptly while descending a long grade or travelling on snow-packed highways, and the front brakes require frequent attention. Check Engine and ABS warning lights come on constantly for no reason. Shock absorbers, constant velocity joints, and catalytic converters also often wear out prematurely. Other problems that appear over most model years include chronic electrical and fuel system malfunctions; hard starting, surging and stalling in cold weather; starter and ignition relay failures; and snow packed inside the wheelwells, binding steering. Misadjusted door strikers make for hard closing/opening.

 Safety Summary

All models/years: Many reports of ABS brake failure and premature wearout of brake components. • Small horn buttons may be hard to find in an emergency. **All models: 1998**—Oil leak from oil filter seam caused fire. • Sudden brake loss after linings, calipers, and master cylinder had been replaced. • Cruise control failed to disengage when brakes were applied. • Excessive shaking at highway speeds. • Seatback collapsed when vehicle was rear-ended. • Subaru told car owner that tendency to pull to the right was a design feature. **1999**—Sudden acceleration. • Chronic cold engine hesitation, stalling. • Engine failure because of cracked #2 piston. • When accelerating or decelerating, vehicle will begin to jerk because of excessive play in the front axle. • Tire blowout; air slowly escapes. • Front bumper skirt catches on parking blocks, resulting in bumper twisting and being ripped off. • The centre-rear seat belt's poor design prohibits the installation of many child safety seats. **2000–01**—Igniter failure allowed unburned gasoline to flow into catalytic converter and resulted in chronic stalling. • Sudden, unintended acceleration in forward gear and in Reverse. • Vehicle suddenly veers to the right when accelerating or braking. • Cruise control failed to disengage when brake pedal was depressed. • Fuel sloshes in fuel tank because of the absence of baffles. • During a collision, airbags deployed but failed to inflate. • The suspension's design causes severe pulling to one side. • Excessive steering and vehicle vibration when passing over uneven pavement. • Steering lock-up while driving. • Knocking and clunking noise heard when turning. • Vehicle's rear end bounces about when passing over bumps. • Engine failure because of a cracked #2 piston. • Frequent surging from a stop. • Hard to shift from Park to Reverse. • Cracked seat belt buckle. • Seat belts are too short for large occupants. • Rear centre seat belt prevents the secure attachment of child safety seats. • Misadjusted door strikers make for hard closing/opening. • Snowstorm ice builds up in the wheelwell, making turning difficult. • Sudden tire blowout. **2002**—Sudden acceleration. • While idling in Park, vehicle suddenly jumped into Drive. **2003**—Chronic stalling in forward gear and in Reverse, particularly with 6-cylinder-equipped models; evidence that Subaru is buying back these problem cars:

> On multiple occasions, and with multiple drivers, I have had two 2003 Outbacks with frequent stalling when moving from Neutral to First, or to Reverse. This is potentially dangerous when moving out into traffic. Subaru denies receiving prior complaints (despite the material on your site) and in general denies that there is any problem. They also compelled me to sign a "gag" clause as part of a deal whereby they exchanged car #1 for car #2.

2004—Believe it or not, owners still complain of engine hesitation when accelerating from a coastdown or a stop, then suddenly surging, as the transmission hunts for a lower gear. This has been a generic problem with many Subarus for almost a decade. • Automatic transmission failure. • Seatbelt came undone during a collision.

Secret Warranties/Internal Bulletins/Service Tips

All models/years: Troubleshooting tips on a sticking anti-lock brake relay are offered. This problem is characterized by a lit ABS warning light or the ABS motor continuing to run/buzz when the ignition is turned off. • Diagnostic and repair tips are offered on transfer clutch binding and/or bucking on turns. • A rotten-egg smell could be caused by a defective catalytic converter. It will be replaced, after a bit of arguing, free of charge, up to five years under the emissions warranty. **1997–99**—Excessive driveline vibration is covered in TSB #05-33-98R. Subaru's fix requires modifying the differential. **2000–01**—Loose bolts on the front seat belt retractor. • Inlet heater hose leaks engine coolant. • Probable causes for the automatic transmission temperature light flashing. • Measures that will eliminate brake squeal. **2000–04**—Door mirror makes wind noise. **2002**—Excessive blower motor noise. • Countermeasures to reduce brake squeal. **2003**—Defective engine water pump. • Improved Sport Shift cold weather operation. • Defective transmission parking pawl rod. • Roof rack wind noise. • Premature suspension corrosion (see bulletin excerpt on next page):

Certain rear suspension subframe components were produced with poor paint quality which, after continued exposure to corrosive road salts for a period of several years, could result in rust-out of the component and possible breakage of the subframe. If such breakage occurs while the vehicle is being operated, control of the vehicle could be affected, increasing the risk of a crash.

Remedy: Dealers will clean and rustproof the rear suspension subframe.

LEGACY, OUTBACK PROFILE

	1996	1997	1998	1999	2000	2001	2002	2003	2004
Cost Price ($)									
Legacy	23,195	—	—	—	—	—	—	—	—
Legacy 4×4	25,195	19,995	19,995	20,495	23,595	24,295	27,395	27,295	27,295
Used Values ($)									
Legacy ▲	4,000	—	—	—	—	—	—	—	—
Legacy ▼	3,000	—	—	—	—	—	—	—	—
Legacy 4×4 ▲	5,000	6,500	8,500	10,500	13,000	15,000	18,000	21,000	23,000
Legacy 4×4 ▼	4,000	5,500	7,000	9,000	11,500	13,500	17,500	19,000	21,000
Reliability	②	③	③	③	③	③	③	③	③
Crash Safety (F)									
Legacy 4d	④	④	④	④	—	④	④	④	④
Side	—	—	③	③	—	④	④	③	④
Wagon	—	—	—	—	—	—	—	④	④
Offset	③	③	③	③	⑤	⑤	⑤	⑤	⑤
Head Restraints	②	②	②	②	②	③	③	③	④

Suzuki

AERIO, ESTEEM ★★★★★

RATING: *Aerio:* Recommended (2003–04). *Esteem:* Recommended (1996–2002). Suzuki's Aerio entry-level front-drive sedan and wagon replace the Esteem and offer optional all-wheel drive, making them among the lowest-priced AWD vehicles available in Canada. Both models come with a 145-hp 4-cylinder engine that's among the most-powerful standard engines in this class. Every Aerio comes with AC, power windows and mirrors, tilt steering wheel, CD player, and split folding rear seats. The GS sedan and SX use 15-inch alloy wheels, the S uses 14-inch steel rims. With the Esteem, getting the most horsepower bang for your buck means shopping for an Esteem sport model or looking over the upgraded year 2000 versions. Wagons are especially versatile and reasonably priced for the equipment provided. Both the base GL and upscale GLX come loaded with standard features that cost extra on other models. The GL, for example, comes with power steering, rear window defroster, remote trunk and fuel-filler door releases, tinted glass, and a fold-down rear seat (great for getting extra cargo space). GLX shoppers can look forward to standard ABS, power windows and power door locks, and a host of other interior refinements. **Maintenance/Repair costs:** Average. **Parts:** Average cost, and parts are easily found. **Extended warranty:** A toss-up. Some long-term powertrain protection would be helpful. **Best alternatives:** GM Firefly or Metro; Honda Civic; Hyundai Accent or Elantra; Mazda Protegé; Nissan Sentra; and Toyota Echo, Tercel, or Corolla. **Online help:** *www.autosafety.org* and *www.car-survey.org*.

Strengths and Weaknesses

The Esteem is a small four-door sedan that is a step up from the Swift (see General Motors/Suzuki). Smaller than the Honda Civic and Chrysler Neon, it has a fairly spacious interior, offering rear accommodation (for two adults) that is comparable to or better than most cars in its class. It stands out with its European-styled body and large array of such standard features as AC, a fold-down back seat, and remote trunk and fuel-door releases. The roomy cabin has lots of front and rear headroom and legroom for four adults. Cargo space is fairly good with the sedan; exceptional with the wagon's rear seats folded.

The small 95-hp engine delivers respectable acceleration and overall performance is acceptable, thanks to the Esteem's four-wheel independent suspension, which gives just the right balance between a comfortable ride and no-surprise handling. For a bit more power, look for a '96 or later sport variant that carries a 125-hp power plant.

VEHICLE HISTORY: 1998—A wagon version joined the lineup. **1999**—New front-end styling, 14-inch wheels, and an upgraded sound system. **2000**—More power provided by a 122-hp 1.8L engine. **2003**—Esteem was replaced by the Aerio. **2004**—The 145-hp 2.0-litre is replaced by a 155-hp 2.3-litre engine.

Some of the drawbacks to owning one of these econoboxes: Small tires compromise handling, and power steering doesn't transmit much road feedback. The Esteem's automatic transmission also may shift harshly and vibrate excessively between gear changes. Braking is mediocre for a car this light.

During the relatively short time the Esteem has been on the market, it has proven to be a high-quality, reliable small car. In this respect, it competes well with its Detroit-built rivals like the Chevrolet Cavalier, Dodge Neon, and Ford Escort, while being outclassed by the Honda Civic, Mazda Protegé, and Toyota Corolla. Problems reported by owners: premature front brake wear, noisy front brakes, occasional electrical short circuits, wind and water intrusion into the passenger compartment, and fragile body panels and trim items. Many owners complain of paint peeling.

 Safety Summary

All models: 1998—Airbag failed to deploy. • Seat belt failed to lock up in a collision. • Vehicle is unstable at high speed. • Door handle failures. **1999**—Engine oil leak sprays oil throughout the engine compartment. • Loss of power when accelerating. • Stuck accelerator pedal. • Chronic stalling. • Transmission and brake failures. • Brakes continue to squeal even after installing new rotors and pads. **2000**—No airbag deployment. • Sudden acceleration from a stop. • Automatic transmission bangs into gear. • Gear shift lever fell from Drive to Neutral and is hard to move. • Excessive steering wheel vibration and noise. • Windshield seal vibrates and cracks in cold weather. **2001**—Automatic transmission stuck in lower gear. • Brake failure. • Complete electrical failure fixed temporarily by lifting the hood and jiggling the master control fuse. **2002**—Inaccurate gas gauge. **2003**—Airbags failed to deploy. • Cracked or bent aluminum wheel rim. • Frequent wheel bearing failures.

Secret Warranties/Internal Bulletins/Service Tips

All models: 1998–99—Remote-entry battery failure because of defective fob diode. **1999–2002**—Voluntary emissions recall to replace the vapour control valve. **2000–04**—Battery discharge can be avoided by installing an upgraded alternator, says TSB #TS-03-06304.

AERIO, ESTEEM PROFILE

	1996	1997	1998	1999	2000	2001	2002	2003	2004
Cost Price ($)									
Aerio	—	—	—	—	—	—	—	15,785	15,995
Aerio SX (AWD)	—	—	—	—	—	—	—	19,785	20,395
GL	13,495	13,495	13,895	13,995	15,495	15,695	16,195	—	—
GLX	14,495	15,495	16,895	17,195	18,491	18,795	19,795	—	—
Used Values ($)									
Aerio ▲	—	—	—	—	—	—	—	10,000	11,000
Aerio ▼	—	—	—	—	—	—	—	9,000	10,000
Aerio SX (AWD) ▲	—	—	—	—	—	—	—	13,000	14,500
Aerio SX (AWD) ▼	—	—	—	—	—	—	—	11,500	13,500
GL ▲	2,000	2,500	3,500	5,000	6,500	8,000	9,500	—	—
GL ▼	1,500	2,000	3,000	4,000	5,500	6,500	8,500	—	—
GLX ▲	3,000	3,500	4,500	6,500	7,500	9,000	11,500	—	—
GLX ▼	2,500	3,000	4,000	6,000	6,500	8,000	10,000	—	—

Reliability	4	4	4	4	4	5	5	—	4
Crash Safety (F)	—	—	—	—	—	—	—	—	4
Side	—	—	—	—	—	—	—	—	3
Offset	—	—	—	—	—	—	5	5	5
Head Restraints	—	—	—	—	—	—	2	2	2
Esteem	—	—	—	—	—	2	—	2	—

Toyota/General Motors

COROLLA, MATRIX/VIBE ★★★

RATING: *Corolla*: Average (1985–2004). Be wary of serious safety deficiencies that include airbag malfunctions, airbag-induced injuries, sudden acceleration, brake failures, seat belt failures, windshield reflections, dash gauge "wash out," and poorly designed headlights that misdirect the light beam. Since the 1997 model was "de-contented" through the use of lower-quality materials, less soundproofing, and fewer standard features, there has been a noticeable reduction in quality control. The 1995–96 models combine the best array of standard features, quality control, and reasonable (for a Toyota) used prices. 1998–2001 models are good second choices with their horsepower-enhanced engine. But don't take any used Toyota equipped with Firestone tires. *Matrix/Vibe*: Average (2003-04) Aimed at the youth market, these versatile spin-offs don't provide enough horsepower to justify their sporty pretensions and they aren't suitable for anyplace more rugged than Vancouver's Stanley Park. Higher Vibe prices quickly fall near the Matrix level after a few years and the Vibe also generates more owner complaints than the Matrix does. **Maintenance/Repair costs:** *Corolla*: Lower than average, and repairs can be done anywhere; *Matrix/Vibe*: Powertrain and body part supply is a bit problematic. **Parts:** Corolla parts are reasonably priced and easily found; Vibe parts aren't easily found and are frequently back-ordered several weeks in Western Canada. **Extended warranty:** Not needed. **Best alternatives:** GM Firefly or Metro, Hyundai Accent or Elantra, Mazda Protegé, Nissan Sentra, and Suzuki Esteem or Aerio. For the cabin storage space and all-wheel drive, check out the Subaru Forester. **Online help:** *www.matrixowners.com*, *www.autosafety.org*, and *www.carsurvey.org*.

All ratings on a numbered scale where is good and **1** is bad. See pages 100–101 for a more detailed description.

Strengths and Weaknesses

A step up from the Tercel/Echo, the Corolla has long been Toyota's standard-bearer in the compact sedan class. Over the years, however, the car has grown in size, price, and refinement to the point where it can now be considered a small family sedan. All Corollas ride on a front-drive platform with independent suspension on all wheels.

Post-1987 models are much improved over earlier versions, and many are still on our roads after 15 years. The two-door models provide sporty performance and good fuel economy, especially when equipped with the 16-valve engine. The base engine, however, lacks power and is agonizingly slow merging and passing on the highway. Owners report problems with premature front suspension strut and brake wear; brake vibration; faulty defrosting that allows the windows to fog up in winter; and rusting of body seams, especially door bottoms, side mirror mounts, trunk and hatchback lids, and wheel openings.

The 1990–94 Corolla's problems are limited to harsh automatic shifting, early front brake pad and strut/shock wearout, AC high-pressure tube leaks, electrical glitches, ignition problems, windshield wiper linkage failures, and some interior squeaks and rattles. They do, however, still require regular valve adjustments to prevent serious engine problems. Less of a problem with these later models, rusting is usually confined to the undercarriage and other areas where the mouldings attach to sheet metal.

The 1995–99 models have chronic seat belt retractor glitches and airbag malfunctions. Additionally, owners report powertrain, brake, and electrical problems; poor rear windshield defrosting; vibrations, squeaks, and rattles afflicting the brakes, steering, and suspension; and body trim imperfections that include water leaking through the doors.

The 2000–02 models continue to have relatively serious quality problems that include engine oil leaks, stalling out after a refuel, Firestone tire failures, transmissions that pop out of Drive into Neutral, or refuse to shift at all, a suspension that easily bottoms out, the vehicle wandering all over the road, faulty strut assemblies, warped brake rotors, fenders that are easily dented, a windshield that's easily cracked, and seat belt shoulder straps mounted too high, cutting across the driver's neck.

EXCESSIVE SULFUR DIOXIDE ODOUR

BULLETIN NO: EG016-04   DATE: MAY 28, 2004

'03–'04 Corolla

SYMPTOMS: Some customers may complain of excessive sulfur dioxide odor on 2003–2004 model year Corolla vehicles under the following conditions:

- Stop and go driving.
- Heavy acceleration.

ACTION: In order to reduce the sulfur dioxide odor, the Electronic Control Module (ECM) (SAE term: Powertrain Control Module/PCM) fuel cut control logic has been modified and a new catalyst is provided. Follow the repair procedure to reflash the ECM and replace the catalytic converter assembly. Matrix and Vibe models are receiving similar attention.

How do you have your eggs? Rotten, if you own a Corolla, Matrix, or Vibe

Year 2003-04 Corolla, Matrix, and Vibe owners report many more mechanical and body problems, with the Vibe leading the way in incidents listed. Problems include engine surging; excessive steering wander; transmission clutch failures; with transmission in Park, the vehicle rolling away; defective crankshafts; power-steering pump failures; and a rotten-egg smell coming from the exhaust or through the vents.

VEHICLE HISTORY: 1993—Redesigned model is larger and equipped with a driver-side airbag and optional ABS. **1994**—A passenger-side airbag and improved seat belt retractors. **1995**—A torquier 1.8L engine added with 10 fewer horses (105) than the '94. **1996**—Five fewer horses (100), new front and rear ends, and an upgraded manual transmission. **1997**—An upscale CE version debuts, while the wagon is axed. 1998—Another redesign produced a slightly more powerful engine (120 horses), two inches more in length, and optional front passenger side-impact airbags. **1999**—Addition of a front stabilizer bar to improve handling. **2000**—Five additional horses and tilt steering on the CE and LE. **2001**—A slight face-lift and the addition of a new sport-oriented variant called the Corolla S. The VE was dropped and the formerly mid-level CE replaced it, carrying fewer standard features. The LE dropped to the CE's former level and was also "de-contented," losing its standard AC and power windows, locks, and mirrors. **2003**—Redesigned to be taller, wider, and longer; adds a new 4-speed automatic transmission; gets five more horses; and the launch of the Matrix/Vibe. **2004**—Arrival of the high-performance Corolla XRS.

Matrix/Vibe

These small front-drive or all-wheel-drive sporty wagons are a cross between a mini SUV and a station wagon, and are packaged like a small minivan. Vibe is built in Fremont, California, at GM's NUMMI factory. The nearly identical Toyota Matrix is manufactured in Toyota's Cambridge, Ontario plant, alongside the Corolla, whose platform it shares though it provides a larger interior volume.

The front-drive Matrix/Vibe is equipped with a 130-hp engine, 5-speed manual overdrive transmission, and lots of standard features; however, the weak, buzzy base engine can be felt throughout the car; 4×4 models are about 10 percent heavier and get seven fewer horses (123) than the already power-challenged 130-hp front-drive. Says Forbes magazine:

> [B]oth all-wheel-drive cars are saddled with a really wretched 4-speed automatic that almost has to be shifted manually to get the car moving. To put it bluntly, the AWD Vibe and Matrix are so pokey, they feel like they're towing Winnebagos. To boot, the 1.8L engine doesn't hit its paltry torque peak…until a screaming 4200 rpm, at which point the vibration—did somebody say Vibe?—in the cabin is worse than a little off-putting.

The Matrix XRS and Vibe GT are the top-of-the-line performance leaders, with a 180-hp 4-cylinder engine and a high-performance 6-speed manual gearbox, plus

ABS, premium six-speaker stereo, anti-theft system, 17-inch alloy wheels, and unique exterior cladding.

These vehicles hail from factories that have garnered high quality ratings and also come with similar warranties. If you really need additional horsepower, get either the XRS or GT. But keep in mind that there are better quality high-performance choices out there, like the Honda Civic Si, Mazda5, or a base Acura RSX. Other front-drives worth considering are the Chrysler PT Cruiser, Hyundai Elantra or Tiburon, Honda Civic, Nissan Sentra, or the Toyota Corolla. Of course, the Subaru Impreza or Forester would be other good choices for the 4×4 variant.

 Safety Summary

All models/years: Chronic airbag malfunctions; they deploy when they shouldn't, or don't deploy when they should. **1998**—Engine compartment fires, gas fumes in the interior, brake and power-steering failures, and excessive steering column noise. • Excessive drifting and high-speed instability because of the lack of a stabilizer bar. • Sudden acceleration. • Premature control arm failure. • Seat belt released in accident. • Rear wheel broke at the axle. • Random honking. **1998–2000**—Brakes lock up. • Vehicle continues to wander and sway at moderate speeds; side winds increase the vehicle's instability. • Gearshift dropped from Drive to Neutral while driving. • Floor mat jams the accelerator. • Engine stalls after refuelling. • Front strut assembly failure. • Inadequate headlight illumination; one side will be aimed too high, the other side, too low. **1999**—Engine compartment fire. • Loss of braking ability. • Sudden acceleration. • Cruise control self-activates. • Automatic transmission locked up while driving. • Vehicle went out of control after rear control arm failure. • At cruising speed, vehicle tends to wander all over the road. • Windshield shattered when door was closed. • Poor headlight design causes blind spot and poor visibility. • Defective engine camshaft gets inadequate oil lubrication and loses compression. • Rear seat belts aren't compatible with many child safety seats. **2001**—Sudden acceleration. • Stuck accelerator pedal. • Headlight illumination problem continues; high beam shoots skyward and is especially hazardous in rain or fog. • Rear driver-side axle sheared in half; vehicle rolled over. • Excessive front brake pad wear; premature failure of the brake proportioning valve and rear brake shoes. • Hole in the oil pan. • Failure of all four Goodyear Integrity tires. • Inside trunk release handle doesn't glow as advertised. **2002**—Fuel leakage:

> On 04/29/02 consumer discovered that vehicle was leaking fuel. Vehicle was repaired by dealer who advised consumer that the fuel lines had come loose. On 07/29/02 while driving, engine compartment caught on fire as a result of fuel leaking.

• In one deployment, airbag ripped and allowed child to be seriously injured. • Unable to shift out of Park. • While using cruise control, gas pedal suddenly went to the floor. • Left rear tire fell off while driving. • Vehicle tends to wander at highway speeds:

Vehicle wanders and sways back and forth. Vehicle was taken to dealership, and mechanic stated that all four wheels were bent. Vehicle came from factory that way. Goodyear, Integrity, P185/65R14. Right front tire had a bulge on outside.

• Early fuel pump replacement led to rotten-egg smell. • Strong sulfur smell in the interior. • Weak climate control system. • Both headlights have stray beams that project upward at a 45-degree angle; very distracting, particularly in mist. • Poor quality wiper blade. **2003**—Fire ignited because of loose fuel line. • Sudden, unintended acceleration. • Vehicle suddenly shut down while underway at 100 km/h; in another case, vehicle suddenly accelerated while cruise control was engaged. • Several owners report that a hole in the oil pan caused vehicle to stall. • When the vehicle was parked, the parking brake was released and both airbags deployed; both airbags deployed right after driver turned on the ignition switch; airbags deployed after car passed over a bump in the road; in a rear-end collision, front airbag came out, but failed to deploy; side airbag failed to deploy in a side impact; both airbags failed to deploy in a frontal collision:

> [Our] [t]hirteen-year old daughter sustained [a] severe traumatic brain injury after [a] head-on collision. Her airbag deployed, [and the] top of passenger-side airbag was completely blown apart from one side to the other, allowing her head to strike [the] dash.
>
> We both had seat belts on. I sustained bruising of [my] hips and right rib. She was in [a] coma and [is] just now beginning to move [her] left side. She still cannot sit up, stand, walk, talk coherently, eat, or do anything for herself.

• Faulty seat belt wiring could cause a fire. • Floormat catches accelerator pedal. • Brake failure when decelerating. • When brakes are applied, pedal goes soft, resulting in extended stopping distances. • When coming to a gradual stop, brakes locked up, causing extended stopping distance. • Rear welding broke away from the frame, resulting in complete loss of control. • Sudden collapse of the rear axle. • Rear control arm broke while driving at 110 km/h. • Left rear tire fell off; defective Uniroyal and Goodyear Integrity tires. • Warped wheels. • Shifter refused to go into gear while driving; transmission sometimes goes from Drive to Neutral while driving; refuses to shift out of Park. • Vehicle wanders all over the road and pulls to the left or right at moderate speeds. In windy conditions, vehicle becomes hard to steer, veering left or right. • Glow-in-the-dark inside trunk release doesn't glow in the dark because it is rarely exposed to light (owner actually crawled inside trunk to test it out). • Poor quality wiper blades; poorly designed headlights have stray beams on high beam that project upward at a 45-degree angle and low-beam headlights are too dim. • Sunlight washes out dash readings. **2004**—Vehicle crashed after suddenly accelerating on the freeway. • Engine surges when stopped at a traffic light and AC compressor is engaged. • Prematurely worn, noisy, and ineffective brakes. • Misaligned steering wheel. • Brake and gas pedals are mounted too close together. • Rotten-egg exhaust smell. • Front passenger-side windshield frame obstructs visibility. • Sun visor interferes with the rear-view mirror. • Sunroof came unglued from the metal frame. *Matrix*: **2003**—Engine surges when braking with AC engaged. • Excessive steering wander; feels a bit vague, with too much play; some torque steer (twisting) evident, especially on wet roads. • The manual shift lever's upward and forward position is counterintuitive and feels a bit ragged. • Instrument panel lights are dimmed by automatic sensor to a point where they can't be read in twilight hours, and the automatic headlights come on and go off for no apparent reason. **2004**—Clutch failures with the manual transmission. • Warped front brake rotors. • Dashboard reflected into the windshield. • Front bumper/spoiler drags on the ground over any uneven surface. Ice collects in wheel rims, throwing tire out of balance. *Vibe*: **2003**—Vibe has generated almost double the number of safety-related complaints as the Matrix, and they are mostly different complaints • Vehicle surges when foot is taken off the accelerator; several accidents caused by sudden acceleration. • Vehicle will roll while in Park. • Faulty ABS. • Dash gauges can't be read when wearing sunglasses. • Automatic headlight sensor turns the headlights on and off, about 20 times a day, depending upon sun and shade variations. • When the lights go on dashlights become unreadable. Buick Rendezvous doesn't have the problem because sensor is located in middle of dash, not near the A-pillar. • Transmission indicator isn't lit at night. 15 to 20 seconds elapse before headlights and tail lights are automatically turned on when driving away after startup. • Sunroof suddenly exploded. • Excessive condensation on interior glass. • Wet windows aren't wiped clean when rolled back up. • Refueling cannot be done without a large amount of fuel being spit out. • Rear outboard seat belts constantly tighten. • Windshield is easily cracked by small stones. **2004**—Loose driver's seat. • Instrument cluster chrome finish reflects into windshield. • Speedometer needle can't be seen on sunny days. • Headlights are too dim for night driving. • Original equipment battery is inadequate for winter startups.

Secret Warranties/Internal Bulletins/Service Tips

All models/years: Improved disc brake pad kits are described in TSB #BR94-004. • Brake pulsation/vibration, another generic Toyota problem, is fully addressed in TSB #BR94-002, "Cause and Repair of Vibration and Pulsation." • Complaints of steering column noise may require the replacement of the steering column assembly, a repair covered under Toyota's base warranty. • AM static noise on all vehicles with power antennas usually means the antenna is poorly grounded. • Toyota has developed special procedures for eliminating AC odours and excessive wind noise. These problems are covered in TSBs #AC00297 and #BO00397, respectively. **All models: 1990–2001**—Toyota has developed a special grease to eliminate clicking when the vehicle goes into Drive or Reverse. **1998**—Tips on reducing excessive engine V-belt noise. • Delayed upshift to Overdrive with cruise control engaged can be fixed by changing the cruise control ECU logic. • Water leakage into the rear cab can be plugged by installing an improved C-pillar moulding clip. • If the rear door glass malfunctions when temperatures dive, install an upgraded mounting channel insert bar. • Toyota will replace the airbag computer under a service campaign. **1998–99**—A front suspension squeaking noise can be silenced by replacing the steering rack end shaft under warranty, but Toyota tells dealers to do the repair only if the customer demands it. **1998–2000**—In an attempt to reduce brake vibration complaints, Toyota will install a new front disc brake pad kit, says TSB #BR002-00, issued March 10, 2000. **1999**—A single-cylinder misfire that causes a rough idle or the activation of the malfunction indicator light (MIL) will be fixed under Toyota's base warranty. **1999–2002**—Accessory drivebelt/belt tensioner assembly noise is addressed in TSB #EG015-01, published December 7, 2001. The service bulletin claims the squeak or rattle noise will be corrected free of charge up to 3 years/58,000 km (36,000 mi.), if the owner complains. • Vibration troubleshooting tips. • Sulfur exhaust odour remedies. • Countermeasures for vehicle pulling to one side. **2003–04**—Deformed roof moldings. • Sulfur exhaust odour countermeasures (see "Strengths and Weaknesses," above). *Matrix*: **2003**—The following items may affect the Corolla and Vibe as well. • Upper suspension tapping noise. • No airflow from centre vents. • Loose, or deformed front or rear glass door run. • AC doesn't put out sufficient cool air. • Headlights come on when turned off. • Sulfur odour in the interior. • Discoloured wheelhouse moulding. **2003–04**—Rotten-egg exhaust remedy. Console door won't stay closed. *Vibe*: **2003**—Engine lacks performance after 7000 rpm. • Transmission shifts too early when accelerating at full throttle when the engine is cold. • Harsh shifting. • Water leak from the A-pillar or headliner area. • Upper suspension tapping noise. • Low voltage display or dim lights. **2003–04**—Harsh 1–2 upshifts. • Slipping transmission. Rotten-egg exhaust remedy. **2004**—Reverse servo cover leak.

COROLLA, MATRIX/VIBE PROFILE

	1996	1997	1998	1999	2000	2001	2002	2003	2004
Cost Price ($)									
Base Corolla	13,508	13,968	14,928	15,090	15,625	15,625	15,765	15,290	15,410
Matrix	—	—	—	—	—	—	—	16,745	16,745
XR AWD	—	—	—	—	—	—	—	24,115	24,210
Vibe	—	—	—	—	—	—	—	20,995	21,150
GT AWD	—	—	—	—	—	—	—	27,000	27,140
Used Values ($)									
Base Corolla ▲	3,500	4,500	5,500	6,500	7,500	9,000	10,000	11,000	12,500
Base Corolla ▼	3,000	3,500	5,000	6,000	7,000	7,500	9,000	10,000	11,500
Matrix ▲	—	—	—	—	—	—	—	12,000	13,500
Matrix ▼	—	—	—	—	—	—	—	11,000	12,500
XR AWD ▲	—	—	—	—	—	—	—	17,000	20,500
XR AWD ▼	—	—	—	—	—	—	—	15,500	19,000
Vibe ▲	—	—	—	—	—	—	—	13,500	15,500

All ratings on a numbered scale where ⑤ is good and ❶ is bad. See pages 100–101 for a more detailed description.

Vibe ▼	—	—	—	—	—	—	—	12,500	14,500
GT AWD ▲	—	—	—	—	—	—	—	17,500	22,500
GT AWD ▼	—	—	—	—	—	—	—	16,500	21,000
Reliability	❸	❸	❸	❸	❸	❸	❸	❸	❸
Crash Safety (F)	❹	❹	❹	—	❹	❹	❹	❺	❺
Side	—	❸	❸	—	❹	❹	❹	❹	❹
Offset	—	—	❸	❸	❸	❸	❸	❺	❺
Head Restraints	—	❶	❸	❸	—	❷	❷	❸	❸
Matrix	—	—	—	—	—	—	—	❺	❺
Vibe	—	—	—	—	—	—	—	❸	❸

Toyota

ECHO ★★★★★

The Echo's so bland, it's been called "Metamucil on wheels."

RATING: Recommended (2000–04). An incredibly practical small car, if you can get by the tall, function-over-form styling. Echo represents an excellent alternative to the similarly styled, glitch-ridden Ford Focus and the soon-to-be-dropped Chrysler Neon. Slow sales have depressed resale values leading to used bargains. **Parts:** Easily found. **Maintenance/Repair costs:** Extraordinarily low. **Extended warranty:** A waste of money. **Best alternatives:** GM Firefly or Metro; Honda Civic; Hyundai Accent; Mazda Protegé; Nissan Sentra; and Suzuki Swift, Esteem, or Aerio. **Online help:** *www.autosafety.org* and *www.carsurvey.org*.

Strengths and Weaknesses

Toyota scrapped its stripped-down Tercel in favour of the year 2000 Echo, an entry-level five-passenger model that uses some of the same engine technology as the Lexus to give great fuel economy without sacrificing performance. Both two- and four-door models are available, and the car costs substantially less than the Corolla. The Echo also offers about the same amount of passenger space as the Corolla, thanks to a high roof and low floor height.

Cockpit controls and instrumentation are particularly user-friendly, located high on the dash and more toward the centre of the vehicle, rather than directly in front of the driver, where many gauges and controls would be hidden by the steering column.

The Echo is powered by a 108-hp 1.5L DOHC 4-cylinder engine featuring variable valve timing cylinder head technology. Normally, an engine this small would provide wimpy acceleration, but thanks to the Echo's light weight, acceleration is more than adequate with a manual gearbox and acceptable with the automatic.

Standard safety features include: five three-point seat belts (front seat belts have pretensioners and force limiters), two front airbags (side airbags are not available), four height-adjustable head restraints, rear child-seat tether anchors, and rear door locks.

VEHICLE HISTORY: 2003—A major restyling adds 4 cm (1.6 in.) to overall length via new front and rear sheet metal and revised bumpers, hood, front fenders, headlights, tail lights, trunk lid, and grille.

The Echo has more usable power than the Tercel and provides excellent fuel economy and lots of interior space. There's plenty of passenger room, along with an incredible array of storage areas, including a huge trunk and standard 60/40 split folding rear seats. All models are reasonably well equipped, with good-quality materials, well-designed instruments and controls, comfortable seating, easy rear access, and excellent fore and aft visibility. It's quite nimble when cornering, very stable on the highway, and surprisingly quiet for an economy car. The car hasn't changed much since its 2000 model debut and has generated almost no complaints—an amazing feat when compared with the Corolla, Camry, and Sienna quality decline since 1997.

What's there not to like? Try the tall profile and light weight, which make the Echo vulnerable to side-wind buffeting; base tires that provide poor wet traction; excessive torque steer that makes for sudden pulling to one side when accelerating; and the narrow body width, which limits rear bench seating to two adults.

 **Safety Summary**

All models/years: Airbag malfunctions. • Sudden acceleration. **2000**—Vehicle blown out of control by sidewinds. • Inoperative horn. • Brake loss said to be caused by a faulty master cylinder. • Warped brake rotors. • Brake pedal is mounted too close to the accelerator pedal. • Broken steering wheel tilt mechanism. **2001**—Partial brake loss. • Brake and gas pedals are set too close together. • Fuel line came undone; fuel line cracked. • Driver's seatbelt failed to lock in a collision. **2002**—Several incidents of sudden, unintended acceleration:

> While driving, the Echo will accelerate to 60 mph [100 km/h] without hitting the gas pedal. I have to put the vehicle in Neutral to stop it. I contacted dealer, but he cannot locate the cause.

> The sudden acceleration incident occurred three times. The dealer was unable to duplicate the problem in test driving, but removed the cruise control. The problem was not corrected by removing the cruise control.

• Sudden steering loss led to crash. • Vehicle often jumps out of Drive into Neutral. **2003**—Chronic stalling when decelerating.

Secret Warranties/Internal Bulletins/Service Tips

All models: 2000—Toyota has a Special Service Campaign (secret warranty) that allows for the free replacement of the brake booster and front brake pads on vehicles equipped with an automatic transmission. Confirmation of this campaign can be found in Toyota Service Bulletin Number TC01027, Bulletin Sequence Number 625, published December 2001, and recorded in the NHTSA database as Item Number SB625616. • MIL light may indicate a single-cylinder misfire (modify the ECM). • Probable causes for interior squeaks and rattles. • Wheel covers may click or squeak. • Excessive wind noise. • Fuel gauge and speedometer malfunctions. • Brake clicking countermeasures. • Defective airflow rotary control knob. **2000–02**—Improved carpet design. **2001**—Special Service Campaign to inspect the rear brake tubes free of charge. • Roof moulding may come loose or become deformed. **2002**—Countermeasures for vehicle pulling to one side. **2003**—Hood lock assembly will be replaced free of charge to prevent snow entry/cable rusting (see TSB #BO018-03).

	2000	2001	2002	2003	2004
Cost Price ($)					
Base	13,835	13,980	14,084	13,690	12,995
Used Values ($)					
Base ▲	5,500	7,000	8,500	9,500	10,000
Base ▼	4,500	6,000	7,500	8,500	9,000
Reliability	④	⑤	⑤	⑤	⑤
Crash Safety (F)	—	④	④	④	④
Side	—	❸	❸	❸	❸
Head Restraints	—	⑤	⑤	⑤	⑤
Rollover Resistance	—	④	④	④	④

Volkswagen

CABRIO, GOLF, JETTA ★★★

RATING: Average (1999–2004); Below Average (1993–98); Not Recommended (1985–92). These small cars are much more expensive than the competition and they age particularly badly. In addition, VW, with its Canadian headquarters located in the States, is not very generous with "goodwill" repairs. A Jetta is a Golf with a trunk; a Cabrio is a Golf without a roof. Convertibles (Cabriolets) depreciate steeply after their first five years on the market. **Maintenance/Repair costs:** Higher than average. Repairs are very dealer dependent. **Parts:** Expensive, but generally available from independent suppliers. Recall campaign parts may be back-ordered for months. **Extended warranty:** A smart idea. "Goodwill" warranty repairs are practically non-existent in Canada because of the absence of a VW head office. **Best alternatives:** Honda Civic, Hyundai Elantra or Tiburon, Mazda Protegé, Nissan Sentra, and Toyota Corolla. **Online help:** *www.autosafety.org, www. carsurvey.org, www.vwvortex.com,* and *www.MyVWLemon.com.*

⬦ Strengths and Weaknesses

On the positive side, these small imports are fun to drive and provide great fuel economy. The 1.8L gasoline engine is very peppy, and the diesel engines are very reliable and good all-around performers. Both engines are easily started in cold weather. But here's the rub: Golfs and Jettas, like the failure-prone Rabbit they replaced, aren't reliable once the warranty expires. What you save in fuel, you lose in the car's high retail price, which is carried over into the used-car market, and the ever-mounting maintenance costs as the vehicle gains years and mileage will easily wear you down.

> "…It could be the best car (VW's $119,500 Cdn. Phaeton), but I would still not buy it because it has the VW logo and because I have to go to a VW dealership where the salesmen are used to selling Jettas and Golfs…"
>
> FORMER AUDI VICE-PRESIDENT AXEL MEES (AUDI/VW FIRED HIM SEVERAL WEEKS LATER)
> SAN FRANCISCO AUDI A6 LAUNCH
> NOVEMBER 8, 2004

VW reliability is impressive—for the first three years. Then your wallet gets lighter as the brake components and fuel and electrical systems start to self-destruct. Exhaust system components aren't very durable, body hardware and dashboard controls are fragile, the paint often discolours and is easily chipped, and window regulators constantly fail:

> I bought my '96 Jetta GLS in 1999. I have replaced eight window regulators in three years, one power window motor, and I can't get the Check Engine light off for the life of me. I have also had to put the door moulding on the driver's side back door three times.

> I found that the windows falling into the door is always due to a broken window regulator, which are less than half the price if you order them from anyone other than the VW dealer, and are not hard to put in yourself.

Volkswagens have terrible quality problems that can't be repaired at the corner garage. Owners report electrical short circuits; heater/defroster resistor and motor failures; leaking transmission and stub axle seals; and defective valve-pan gaskets, head gaskets, timing belts, steering assemblies, suspension components, alternator pulleys, and brake and electrical systems. Body problems are legion, with air and water leaks, faulty catalytic converters, inoperative locks and latches, poor-quality body construction and paint, and cheap, easily broken accessories and trim items.

The redesigned 1994–96 models are a bit safer and a tad more reliable. Nevertheless, problems disclosed in service bulletins for these model years show that serious defects continue to accumulate along with the years. Powertrain failures, poor driveability, water leaks, trim defects, and premature rear tire wear are all addressed. Owners also report the following: electric door locks that take a long time to lock; paint that is easily nicked, chipped, and marked; a variety of trim defects; premature rear tire wear; and poor-quality seat cushions.

Factory defects on 1990–98 Golfs and Jettas are so numerous that they make these models very risky buys. Problems include automatic transmission, engine, suspension component, and catalytic converter failures; electrical short circuits; AC malfunctions; and fragile trim items. Body assembly and paint are second-class, leading to rattles and air leaks as the vehicles age.

VEHICLE HISTORY: 1985—Both the Golf hatchback and the Jetta's two-door and four-door sedans have more interior space. **1991**—Debut of the 2.0L 134-hp Golf GTI 16V and mandatory 5-speed manual transmission. **1992**—Upgraded diesel engine gets seven more horses (59). **1994**—Dual airbags and the top-line GLX model got a 172-horsepower V6. **1995**—Golf GTI VR6, plus two other Golf models make their debut, height-adjustable manual front seat belts with emergency tensioners, and side impact door beams. **1996**—Dashboard-mounted glove box returns and improved seat belt retractors and door locking system. **1997**—The 116-hp 4-cylinder engines got a redesigned cylinder head that cuts engine noise; the Golf GTI VR6 rides lower, thanks to new shocks, springs, and anti-roll bars; the Cabrio Highline received standard AC and a few other amenities; and a cheapened base convertible lost its standard ABS and a few other goodies. **1999**—Updated interior and exterior styling and a more powerful engine; Cabrios were given new European styling. **2001**—A 150-hp 1.8L turbo four became available for the GLS and was standard in the base GTI; and a Jetta wagon was added along with steering-mounted audio controls (on some models). **2002**—Debut of a more powerful 1.8L 4-cylinder engine, a 5-speed automatic transmission, and an optional 6-speed manual transmission; 2.8L V6 horsepower boosted to 200. **2003**—An anti-skid system standard with the V6 engine, GL got power windows, heated power mirrors, and cruise control; and GLS versions come with alloy wheels and a sunroof. **2004**—Jetta got minor styling changes and an all-wheel-drive Golf arrived.

Jettas provide slightly more comfort and better road performance than their Golf hatchback counterparts. The 1.6L 4-cylinder found on early Jettas was surprisingly peppy, and the diesel engine is very economical, although quite slow to accelerate. Diesels have a better overall reliability record than gasoline models, yet they also have serious quality shortcomings, especially with emissions components, like the mass air sensor, as these two readers relate:

> I have a 2001 VW Jetta TDI and I have been losing power. As per the dealership, they said that it is carbonization (build-up of carbon). They told me that they have to take apart and clean the EGR valve and also replace the mass air flow sensor. I was told it would cost me at least $1000 to $2000. They said that its the "ingredients in the fuel" that is causing the problem. I do know that in Alberta, there are strict guidelines that need to be followed when it comes to emissions and the sort. I feel like I am getting hosed from the dealership!!! I heard rumours that other owners in Alberta (hopefully in Canada) has had the exact same problem and that they got the work done for free. R. Y., Alberta

I bought my 2001 VW Jetta GLS TDI new, and now have about 124,000 kms. The car has been very good. I purchased an extended warranty through "Autoshield" (7 years/160,000 kms) for $2634.65. And I have used it twice. Once to replace the glow plug harness (which I understand to be a frequent problem. Condensation causes corrosion and the "Check Engine" warning light illuminates. I replaced it at 88,000 kms). The second time was at 96,000 kms; the mass air-flow "sensor" failed, causing a power loss between 3000–3200 rpms.

Other nuisance problems are that the cup holder sticks (and coffee drips down the radio stack), and the glove box breaks.

Since I bought the car, I have spent a few extra dollars on getting it oil-sprayed (Krown) and replaced the tires (Michelin Hydroedge – very good).

There is one other problem that plagues all the VWs I have seen that are more than about two years old. And that is the metal divider in the back windows that rusts prematurely. Almost without exception, every VW on a used car lot has this rusty component on both sides.

C. T.
OTTAWA

Jettas and Golfs do rust prematurely. They suffer from rapid body deterioration and increasingly frequent mechanical/electrical failures after their fourth year in service. For example, starters often burn out because they are vulnerable to engine heat; as well, sunroofs leak, door locks jam, window cranks break, and windows bind. Owners also report engine head gasket leaks, as well as water pump and heater core breakdowns. It's axiomatic that all diesels are slow to accelerate, but VW's Fourth gear often can't handle highway speeds above 90 km/h. Engine noise can be deafening when shifting down from Fourth gear.

The 1999–2004 models are more reliable, but, nevertheless, owners still report chronic automatic transmission, brake, and electrical system problems, in addition to subpar body construction and paint, leaky sunroofs, malfunctioning gauges and accessories, fragile locks and latches, bumpers that become brittle and crack as the temperature falls, defective security systems, and disagreeable interior odours. The following Toronto VW owner had this to say:

Hi Phil, I recently purchased a used 1999 VW Jetta (one of the new model types) and after talking to some co-workers there seems to be a problem with the AC in both Jettas and Golfs. The problem is that condensation builds up on one of the filters and after a little while bacteria will start to grow and then when you turn on the fan for the AC the air being pumped out starts to stink. One of my co-workers said it was so bad in her VW Jetta that she thought her husband had left his old hockey equipment in the car!

 **Safety Summary**

The NHTSA database shows that the following problems are reported repeatedly: fires; airbags that fail to deploy or cause severe injuries when they go off; airbag light stays on for no apparent reason; transmission and wheel bearing failures; transmission pops out of gear; electrical malfunctions leading to chronic stalling; self-activating alarms; lights going out; erratic cruise control operation; brake, tire, and AC failures; inadequate defrosting; AC mould and mildew smell; poor-quality body components; window regulator failure; and inoperable power windows. Also, doors may open suddenly; locks jam shut, fall out, or freeze; power window motors and regulators self-destruct; hoods suddenly fly up; cigarette lighters pop out of their holders while lit; the seat heater may burn a hole in the driver's seat; and battery acid can leak onto the power steering reservoir and cause sudden steering loss. **1998**—Engine damaged after water was ingested through the air intake system. • Transmission locked into Third gear. • ABS brake failures. • Head restraints suddenly drop down. • Inaccurate fuel gauge. **1999**—Plastic fuel line fails in cold weather. • Chronic stalling in traffic with engine warning light lit. • Headlight failure; no low beam. **2000**—Sudden acceleration. • Cracked axle. • Early replacement of the rear brake pads. • Dashboard causes excessive windshield glare. **2000–03**—Airbag cover pops off while driving. • Cracked oil pan. • Engine burns oil. • Chronic stalling in traffic. • Hard starting. • Noisy, prematurely worn brakes. • Sudden headlight failure; poor headlight illumination. • Faulty power window regulators cause windows to fall down into door panels. **2001**—Timing chain exploded. • Frequent stalling because of defective airflow sensor. • Premature constant velocity joint replacement. **2001–03**—Stalling, no-starts because of faulty ignition coils. **2002**—Fires under the bumper and in the engine compartment. • Sudden, unintended acceleration. • Many reports that the front/side airbags deployed for no reason; driver burned:

> Driving on the turnpike, the driver-side airbag deployed without any sort of impact. There is no visible damage to the vehicle, which was only two months old at the time. Fortunately the only injury was a burn from the airbag on the side of my arm. My biggest fear is knowing relatives and friends who drive Jettas and who have young children in their car. This incident could have easily been fatal.

• Brake failure. • Vehicle hesitates upon acceleration. • Engine warning light is constantly lit. • Broken window regulator; window falls into the door panel:

> On three separate occasions the driver-side front window (twice) and the passenger-side front window (once) has fallen down into the door. On the first occasion the window shattered inside the door and had to be replaced.

2003—Airbags failed to deploy. • Driver's seat burst into flames. • Vehicle will suddenly veer to the left or right. • Clutch pedal slips; vehicle won't change gears. •

Early replacement of the rear axle. **2004**—Airbags deployed for no reason. • Chronic engine stalling. • VW says engines need a special oil to prevent engine sludging. • Transmission slipping. • Tread separating from the front passenger tire.

Secret Warranties/Internal Bulletins/Service Tips

All models: 1998–99—Noisy, vibrating blower motor. • Defective instrument cluster. • Radio volume control malfunction. **1999**—Humming noise from front of vehicle when turning may be caused by the differential spider gear. • Sunroof binding or noise will be fixed with replacement slides. **1999–2000**—An engine rapping noise or throttle pedal vibration. **1999–2001**—Inoperative window regulator. • Malfunctioning instrument cluster. **2000**—Automatic transmission may go into limp mode without malfunction indicator light (MIL) activated. • Vibrating shifter. **2000–01**—Troubleshooting prematurely worn rear brake pads. **2001**—Leaking intake hoses. • Inoperative secondary air pump (blown fuse). • Troubleshooting "defective control module" indication. • Leaking transmission pan gasket. **2000–03**—Faulty ignition coils (chronic stalling, no restart) covered reluctantly by a warranty extension after VW first denied the problem existed. **2002**—Inoperative fresh air blower. • Broken armrest lid. • Defective VI radio controls.

CABRIO, GOLF, JETTA PROFILE

	1996	1997	1998	1999	2000	2001	2002	2003	2004
Cost Price ($)									
Cabrio	26,495	25,230	25,300	25,300	25,300	28,530	28,530	—	—
Golf	14,325	14,690	16,765	15,610	18,950	19,040	19,230	17,950	18,300
Jetta	17,650	18,050	18,620	18,620	21,170	21,280	21,490	24,260	24,520
Used Values ($)									
Cabrio ▲	7,000	9,000	11,000	13,000	15,000	17,000	20,000	—	—
Cabrio ▼	6,000	7,500	9,500	10,500	14,000	15,500	18,000	—	—
Golf ▲	3,000	4,000	5,500	7,000	9,000	10,000	11,500	12,500	14,500
Golf ▼	2,500	3,000	4,500	6,000	7,500	9,000	10,000	11,000	13,000
Jetta ▲	4,000	5,000	7,000	8,500	10,000	12,000	14,500	18,000	20,000
Jetta ▼	3,000	4,000	6,000	7,500	8,500	10,500	13,000	16,500	18,500
Reliability	2	2	2	3	3	3	3	3	4
Crash Safety (F)									
Golf	—	3	3	—	—	5	5	5	5
Jetta	3	3	3	—	—	3	3	3	3
Side (Jetta)	—	—	3	3	—	4	4	4	4
Offset	2	2	2	3	3	4	3	5	5
Head Restraints (F)	—	2	—	—	2	5	5	5	5
Rear	—	—	—	1	—	—	3	5	5
4d	—	1	—	3	3	3	3	3	3
Jetta	—	—	—	—	—	—	4	3	3
Rear	—	—	—	—	—	3	3	3	3
Rollover Resistance	—	—	—	—	—	4	4	4	4

MEDIUM CARS

Toyota honeymoon ending? Toyota's Camry is a good family sedan that's been plagued by serious engine and transmission problems since 1997. It's only a matter of time before *Consumer Reports* and the Canadian Automobile Association (CAA) downgrade their ratings to reflect this quality decline.

Nissan's Altima has become quite popular since its 2002 model was redesigned to combine sharp, aerodynamic styling with a sizzling high-performance engine and sophisticated handling features. Unfortunately, all of these changes make the car both unreliable and expensive to maintain.

Medium-sized cars, often referred to as "family cars," are trade-offs between size and fuel economy, offering more room and convenience features but a bit less fuel economy (9.5–11.5L/100 km) than small cars. They're popular because they combine the advantages of smaller cars with those of larger vehicles. As a result of their versatility, as well as both upsizing and downsizing throughout the years, these vehicles overlap both the small and large car niches. The trunk is usually large enough to meet average baggage requirements, and the interior is spacious enough to meet the needs of the average family (seating four people in comfort and five in a pinch). These cars are best for combined city and highway driving, with the top three choices traditionally dominated by Japanese automakers: the Honda Accord, the Mazda 626/Mazda6, and the Toyota Camry. VW's Passat has taken top honours in *Consumer Reports*' annual listing of Best Buys; however, its high MSRP and maintenance costs are a real budget buster and its safety-related defects are worrisome.

Ford's Taurus and Sable are in sales death spirals following persistent owner complaints of drivetrain deficiencies and generally poor quality control. Chrysler's Breeze, Cirrus, and Stratus have improved in quality over the past several years and generally offer the most interior space and competitive used prices, despite the fact they've been off the market for the past two years. GM is the best of the Detroit Big Three. Its models may be bland and a bit overpriced, but its quality control is better than both Ford and Chrysler and it has more models from which to choose.

MEDIUM CAR RATINGS

Recommended

Acura 1.6, 1.7L EL (1997–2004)
Acura Integra (1994–2001)
Honda Accord (2000–02)

Mazda6 (2004)
Mazda 626 (1999–2002)

Above Average

Acura CL-Series (1998–2003)
Acura Integra (1986–93)
Honda Accord (2003-04; 1990–99)
Hyundai Sonata (1999–2004)

Mazda6 (2003)
Mazda 626, MX-6 (1996–98)
Nissan Altima (1998–2001)
Toyota Camry (1985-96)

Average

Acura CL-Series (1997)
DaimlerChrysler Breeze, Cirrus,
  Stratus (1999–2000)
General Motors Bonneville, Cutlass,
  Cutlass Supreme, Delta 88, Grand
  Prix, Impala, Intrigue, LeSabre,
  Lumina, Malibu, Monte Carlo, Regal
  (2000–04; rear-drives (1984-87)
General Motors Century (1998–2004)

General Motors Achieva, Alero, Grand Am,
  Skylark (2000–04)
Honda Accord (1985–89)
Hyundai Sonata (1995–98)
Mazda 626, MX-6 (1994–95)
Nissan Altima (2002–04; 1993–97)
Toyota Camry, Solara (1997-2004)
Volkswagen New Beetle (2000–04)

Below Average

DaimlerChrysler Breeze, Cirrus,
  Stratus (1995–98)
Ford Sable, Taurus (2000–04)
General Motors Achieva, Alero, Grand Am,
  Skylark (1995–99)

General Motors Century (1997)
Volkswagen New Beetle (1998–99)
Volkswagen Passat (1998–2004)

Not Recommended

Ford Contour, Mystique (1995–99)
Ford Sable, Taurus (1986–99)
General Motors Achieva, Alero, Grand Am,
  Skylark (1985–94)
General Motors Bonneville, Cutlass,
  Cutlass Supreme, Delta 88, Grand
  Prix, Impala, Intrigue, LeSabre, Lumina,
  Malibu, Monte Carlo, Regal (1988–99)

General Motors Century, Ciera
  (1982–96)
Hyundai Sonata (1986–93)
Mazda 626, MX-6 (1985–93)
Volkswagen Passat (1989–97)

Acura

1.6, 1.7L EL ★★★★★

RATING: Recommended (1997–2004). The Honda equivalent for the revised 2001 1.7L EL is the Civic EX Sedan. The 2001 EL Premium commanded a $2,000 premium over the base version. **Maintenance/Repair costs:** Average. Repairs aren't dealer dependent. **Parts:** Average parts cost, thanks to the use of generic Honda Si parts sold through independent suppliers. **Extended warranty:** Not needed. **Best alternatives:** Honda Civic EX or Si; Hyundai Elantra wagon, Sonata, or Tiburon; Mazda 626 or Protegé; Nissan Sentra or Stanza; and Toyota Camry or Corolla. **Online help:** For the latest owner reports, service bulletins, and money-saving tips, look at "The Temple of VTEC" at *www.vtec.net/*, *www.acuraworld.com/forums/*, and *www.autosafety.org*.

 ## Strengths and Weaknesses

The first Japanese automobile built exclusively in and for the Canadian market, the EL is essentially an all-dressed Civic sedan, sold under the Acura moniker. It was a response to Canadian Acura dealers' pleas for a more affordable Acura.

VEHICLE HISTORY: 1997—Since its '97 model launch, the EL has been immensely popular—and hard to find on the used-car market. **2001**—The 1.7L 2001 model was an all-new incarnation (like the 2001 Civic) that is roomier, better equipped, and more fuel efficient, even though horsepower remains the same. **2003**—A retuned suspension and steering system for better handling and enhanced ride comfort, reduced engine vibration through improved engine mounts, and upgraded brakes. Additionally, the 2003 models were given adjustable head restraints and upgraded instrument clusters, centre console armrests, and front seats.

Based on the top-of-the-line Civic Si, the EL comes with a peppy 127-hp VTEC 1.6L 4-banger that's both reliable and economical to run. Add to this the Civic's chassis and upgraded suspension components and you have outstanding performance that's as good as or better than that of the Civic Si. Some of the 1.6 EL's weak points are: a narrow interior, with seats and seatbacks that are not to everyone's liking; emergency braking that's only average; head restraints rated "Poor" by IIHS; and excessive engine noise intruding into the passenger compartment despite upgraded soundproofing.

The EL has done quite well over the years it's been on the market, even though it hasn't changed much. No safety complaints have been reported, and the few owner complaints recorded have mostly concerned wind noise, easily dented body panels, malfunctioning accessories (AC, audio system, electrical components, etc.), and fragile trim items. Some minor turn offs with the 2001 model: The car loses power when the AC is activated; there are no stereo controls on the steering wheel; and the driver seat armrest can interfere with the gearshift lever.

Secret Warranties/Internal Bulletins/Service Tips

All models/years: Most Honda/Acura TSBs allow for special warranty consideration on a "goodwill" basis even after the warranty has expired or the car has changed hands. Referring to this euphemism will increase your chances of getting some kind of refund for repairs that are obviously related to a factory defect. Keep in mind that many Honda bulletins often apply to Acuras as well. So check out the Civic's and Accord's TSBs and safety complaints before assuming that a particular Acura problem doesn't exist or that it's your responsibility. • Acura says that it will replace any seat belt's tongue stopper button for the life of the vehicle. • Interestingly, the automatic transmission failures afflicting 2000–03 Acuras and Hondas don't seem to be much of a problem with this entry-level Acura. Still, should you have a tranny breakdown within 7 years/160,000 km, don't hesitate to cite Honda's latest transmission extended warranty to back up your claim. • Seat belts that are slow to retract will also be replaced for free, says TSB #91-050. **2003–04**—A soft brake pedal feel or any noise from the brake assembly when braking may indicate there's a problem with the brake booster master cylinder.

1.6, 1.7 EL PROFILE

	1997	1998	1999	2000	2001	2002	2003	2004
Cost Price ($)								
1.6 EL	17,800	18,800	19,800	20,005	21,500	21,700	22,000	22,200
Used Values ($)								
1.6 EL ▲	5,000	6,500	8,500	10,500	12,000	14,500	16,500	18,500
1.6 EL ▼	4,500	5,500	7,500	9,000	11,000	13,000	15,000	17,500
Reliability	⑤	⑤	⑤	⑤	⑤	⑤	⑤	⑤

Note: These vehicles have not been crash-tested.

CL-SERIES ★★★★

RATING: Above Average (1998–2003); Average (1997). Be wary of the overpriced, hard-to-find, failure-prone automatic transmission on all model years; it's one reason that the CL doesn't get a five-star rating like its little brother. **Maintenance/ Repair costs:** Lower than average. Repairs can be done practically anywhere. **Parts:** Cost is a bit higher than average, but they're not hard to find. **Extended**

warranty: Not needed since Honda/Acura already covers transmission failures via "goodwill" warranty extensions. **Best alternatives:** BMW 318, Honda Accord, Lexus SC 300, Nissan Maxima, and Toyota Camry. **Online help:** For the latest owner reports, service bulletins, and money-saving tips, look at *www.vtec.net/*, *www.acuraworld.com/forums/*, and *www.autosafety.org*.

 ## Strengths and Weaknesses

The only difference between the 2.2L CL and the 3.0L CL is the 3.0L CL's larger engine, different wheels, and larger exhaust tip. The 2.2L CL's engine was upgraded to 2.3L on the 1998 models.

These cars are stylish, front-drive, five-passenger luxury coupes that are American-designed and built. They have a flowing, slanted back end and no apparent trunk lock (a standard remote keyless entry system opens the trunk from the outside and a lever opens it from the inside). And while other Japanese automakers are taking content out of their vehicles, Acura has made the CL one of the most feature-laden cars in its class. Sure, we all know that the coupe's mechanicals and platform aren't that different from the Accord's, but when you add up all of its standard bells and whistles, you get a fully loaded medium-sized car that costs thousands of dollars less than such competing luxury coupes as the BMW 318 and the Lexus SC 300.

VEHICLE HISTORY: 1998—These cars have changed little since they were launched as 1997 models. **1998**—Debut of the 2.3L engine. **2003**—CL soldiers on with the two-door coupe and Type S coupe, equipped with stronger base 3.2L V6s.

Recent model CLs get plenty of power from the smooth-running and quiet 3.2L V6. Handling is better than average, thanks to an upgraded suspension, variable-assisted steering, and 16-inch wheels. The ride is comfortable and well controlled. Braking is first-class (35 m at 100–0 km/h). Front and rear bucket seats are supportive and easily adjusted. There's plenty of room up front, controls and most gauges are user-friendly (the navigation system and tachometer placement are the only exceptions), and the climate controls are efficient and within easy reach. Owners appreciate the large trunk with its low liftover and a locking ski pass-through that enhances the CL's cargo space.

On the down side, this is not a car for rear seat passengers. Adults will likely find their heads pressed against the top of the back-light glass, and legroom and foot-room are at a premium. Rear access is a crouch-and-crawl affair. In the trunk, lid hinges intrude into the trunk area and risk damaging cargo when the trunk is closed.

Here are some of the problems reported with the 1997–99 models: faulty transmission control unit; transmission downshift problems; chronic brake rotor pulsation and other brake problems, leading to resurfacing of brake rotors and early replacement of brake pads, rotors, calipers, and springs; repeated front-end realignments; door and wind noise leading to replacement of door; and a sunroof that won't stop at closed position, requiring replacement of sunroof switch and controller.

Owners have reported that the 2002–2003 models also have serious automatic transmission problems leading to complete failure, as the following owner relates:

> Car started free revving and erratically upshifting and downshifting with hard jerks. All malfunction indicators lit up. Almost lost control on the freeway. Was told transmission is shot on a car that is a bit over a year old.

Even if the transmission remains intact, its erratic performance creates a serious safety hazard, says another 2002 3.2 CL owner:

> The transmission downshifted by itself to a lower gear, causing the vehicle to decelerate in a dangerous manner. Sooner or later someone is going to get killed if this problem is not corrected.

Sudden, unintended acceleration and hesitation complaints are also thought to be transmission-related (see "Secret Warranties/Internal Bulletins/Service Tips").

Safety Summary

All models: 1998—When driving on a flat surface at 45 km/h, or 1500 rpm, vehicle will jerk and pull for about 30 seconds. • Transmission seals failed. • Chronic electrical shorts. • Premature shock failure. • Sudden power steering loss. • Excessive steering play because of faulty steering column coupling. • Vehicle will sometimes accelerate when slowing for a stop. **1999**—Airbags didn't deploy. • Transmission failure; inoperative gearshift because of water on the horn. • Steering locks up intermittently. • Short drivers may be seriously injured by the front airbag's deployment. **2002**—Transmission slips out of gear and suddenly downshifts, and engine surges. • Sudden, unintended acceleration, accompanied by loss of braking ability. • Window slides down into door. **2003**—Engine timing belt failure. • Stalling. • Tire tread separation.

Secret Warranties/Internal Bulletins/Service Tips

All models/years: Most Honda/Acura TSBs allow for special warranty consideration on a "goodwill" basis even after the warranty has expired or the car has changed hands. Referring to this "goodwill" will increase your chances of getting some kind of refund for repairs that are obviously related to a factory defect. • Acura says it will replace any seat belt's tongue stopper button for the life of the vehicle. • Seat belts that are slow to retract will also be replaced for free, says TSB

#91-050. **All models: 1997–98**—Power seat noise. • Power windows don't work. • Window rattling. **1998–99**—Steering wheel remote audio switches may not work properly. **2001–03**—In September 2002, Honda extended its warranties to 7 years/ 256,000 km (160,000 mi.) on automatic transmissions on about 1.2 million cars and minivans because the components may fail or wear out early. The new retro-active warranty includes 2000 and 2001 Accords, Preludes, and Odysseys; 2000–02 Acura 3.2 TLs; 2001–02 Acura 3.2 CLs; and some 2003 models of both Acura models, spokesman Kurt Antonius said. He admitted about 25,000 vehicles have experienced transmission problems, which include slow or erratic shifting. What's most disappointing about Honda's warranty extension is that it doesn't go back to cars from the 1997 model year, in which transmission breakdowns are also quite common. **2002**—Airbag light may remain lit. • Moon roof squeaks. • Seatback panel may loosen. • Missing speed sensor plug. • Troubleshooting engine oil leaks. *2.2L:* **1999**—Coolant leak from the engine block. *3.0L:* **1997–99**—A Product Update Campaign calls for the re-routing of the PCV hose to prevent the intake manifold EGR port from clogging. This is especially applicable to vehicles using fuel sold in the United States. • V6 engine oil leaks. **1997–2003**—Troubleshooting V6 engine oil leaks and rules for applying the "goodwill" warranty. **1998–99**—Troubleshooting the inadvertent activation of the MIL (malfunction indicator light). **2001–03**—A secret warranty extension covers the automatic transmission up to 7 years/ 160,000 km (100,000 mi.), says TSB #02-027, issued September 15, 2003. Although limited to the torque converter, this extension creates a benchmark for all major tranny components. • In TSB #01-017, Acura says its new revised brake pads will reduce vibration when braking. This admission means Acura should share costs for this replacement. • Brake alert lights intermittently. **2003**—Free replacement of the power control module (PCM) and fuel pressure regulator (TSB #03-017) and front engine camshaft (TSB #02-033).

CL-SERIES

	1997	1998	1999	2002	2003
Cost Price ($)					
2.2L/2.3L CL	27,800	30,000	30,900	36,000	37,800
3.0L CL	30,650	34,000	35,000	—	—
Type S CL	—	—	—	40,000	41,800
Used Values ($)					
2.2L/2.3L CL ▲	8,500	10,500	13,500	25,000	29,000
2.2L/2.3L CL ▼	8,000	9,500	13,000	24,000	28,000
3.0L CL ▲	10,500	12,500	15,500	—	—
3.0L CL ▼	10,000	11,500	15,000	—	—
Type S CL ▲	—	—	—	27,000	31,000
Type S CL ▼	—	—	—	25,000	29,000

All ratings on a numbered scale where ⑤ is good and ❶ is bad. See pages 100–101 for a more detailed description.

Reliability	④	④	④	④	④
Crash Safety (F)					
Head Restraints	❶	—	❶	❶	❶

Note: These vehicles have not been crash-tested.

 INTEGRA ★★★★★

RATING: Recommended (1994–2001); Above Average (1986–93). The Integra rating is unusually high because of the few owner complaints recorded, the car's all-around competent performance, and the ease with which it can be customized through inexpensive ground effects and other options. Interestingly, there's little price difference between used entry-level and high-end models, despite a $4,000 premium when the cars were new. **Maintenance/Repair costs:** Lower than average. Repairs can be done practically anywhere. **Parts:** Cost is a bit higher than average, but most parts can be bought from cheaper independent Honda suppliers. **Extended warranty:** Not necessary; save your money for performance tires. **Best alternatives:** Honda Accord; Mazda 626; Hyundai Elantra wagon, Sonata, or Tiburon; and Toyota Camry Solara. **Online help:** For the latest owner reports, service bulletins, and money-saving tips, look at *www.vtec.net/*, *www.acuraworld.com/forums/*, and *www.autosafety.org*.

Strengths and Weaknesses

A Honda spin-off, early Integras (1986–89) came with lots of standard equipment and are a pleasure to drive, especially when equipped with a manual transmission. The 4-speed automatic saps the base engine's power considerably, but there is usually sufficient reserve power to accomplish most tasks. Surprisingly, these early models corner better and are more agile than later 1990–93 models. The hard ride can be softened a bit by changing the shocks and adding wide tires. The front seats are very comfortable, but they're set a bit low, and the side wheelwells leave little room for your feet. Rear-seat room is very limited, especially on the three-door version.

VEHICLE HISTORY: 1986–89—Redesigned in 1989, engines became smoother running and picked up 12 more horses (130). **1990**—Four-door sedan replaced the four-door hatchback, adding a bit more interior room; and the GS debuted. **1992**—140-hp engine. **1994**—142-hp engine added variable valve timing for extra power and smoothness. **1997**—The G-SR gained a 170-hp engine, and a high-performance 195-hp Type R debuted. **1998**—A slight front-end restyling. **1999**—RS version dropped. **2000**—Return of the Type R and the addition of an upgraded 4-speed automatic transmission to the general lineup. **2001**—Emergency trunk release. **2002**—Replaced by the RSX.

For model years 1990–93, the high-revving 1.7L power plant growls when pushed and lacks guts (read torque) in the lower gears. The 1.8L engine runs more smoothly but delivers the same maximum horsepower as the 1.7L it replaced, until the '94 model year, when it gained 10 extra horses. Surprisingly, overall performance has been toned down and is compromised by the 4-speed automatic gearbox. Interior design is more user-friendly, with the front seating roomier than in previous years, but the reduced rear seating is still best for small children.

Mechanical reliability is impressive, but that's the case with most Hondas, which sell for far less, and many mechanical components are so complex that self-service can pretty well be ruled out. The Integra's front brakes may require more attention than those of other Hondas. What Integras give you in mechanical reliability and performance, however, they take away in poor quality control on body components and accessories. Water leaks, excessive wind noise, low-quality trim items, and plastic panels that deform easily are all commonplace. Owners also report severe steering shimmy, excessive brake noise, premature front brake pad wearout, and radio malfunctions.

The 1994–2001 models offer a smoother ride than previous versions. However, the powerful VTEC engine requires lots of shifting, and interior room is still problematic. Overall, there are too few improvements to justify the high prices that post-1999 models command; therefore, target cars in the 1997–99 model range for optimum savings and performance.

Owners report that some steering wheel shimmy, fit and finish deficiencies, and malfunctioning accessories continue to be problematic on later models. Only a smattering of automatic transmission defects have been mentioned, though any glitches within 7 years/160,000 km should be fixed free of charge (see Acura CL section). Premature front brake wear is also an ongoing concern, often fixed for free if the client is the least bit threatening. Squeaks and rattles frequently crop up in the door panels and hatches, and the sedan's frameless windows often have sealing problems.

Safety Summary

All models/years: No airbag deployment or inadvertent deployment, sudden acceleration, automatic transmission defects, poor headlight illumination, and chronic brake failures are common in any model years. • Prematurely warped rotors are the cause of excessive vibration and pulling. **1998**—Sudden steering lock-up. • Driver's seat belt won't loosen. • Horn failure. • Sunroof malfunctions. • Window motor inoperative. **1999**—Front windshield distorts vision. • Check Engine light comes on constantly. **2000**—Small horn buttons are difficult to activate in an emergency. • Automatic transmission failure. • Rear brake pad failure. • Steering wheel obstructs view of speedometer. **2001**—Sudden steering wheel lock-up while driving.

Secret Warranties/Internal Bulletins/Service Tips

All models/years: Most Honda/Acura TSBs allow for special warranty consideration on a "goodwill" basis even after the warranty has expired or the car has changed hands. • Vehicle cranks but won't start. • Severe and persistent steering wheel shimmy is likely because of an imbalanced wheel/tire/hub/rotor assembly. • Check Engine light constantly lit. • Headlight fogging. • Debris in blower motor (install protective screen). • Window guide channel comes loose. • Front-brake squeal countermeasures. • Reducing rattles from the rear shelf area. • Noisy power steering. • Seat belts that are slow to retract will be replaced for free, says TSB #91-050. **All models: 1992–99**—A defective seat belt tongue stopper will be replaced free of charge with no ownership, time, or mileage limitations. **1997–01**—Brake light comes on intermittently.

INTEGRA PROFILE

	1995	1996	1997	1998	1999	2000	2001
Cost Price ($)							
RS	18,595	18,795	19,500	21,000	—	—	—
LS/SE	23,095	23,245	23,800	23,800	21,800	22,000	22,500
Used Values ($)							
RS ▲	4,000	5,000	6,000	7,000	—	—	—
RS ▼	3,000	4,000	5,000	6,000	—	—	—
LS/SE ▲	5,500	6,500	7,500	8,500	9,500	12,000	14,000
LS/SE ▼	4,500	5,000	6,000	7,000	8,000	10,500	13,000
Reliability	④	④	④	④	⑤	⑤	⑤

Crash Safety (F)	—	④	—	—	—	—	—
Head Restraints	❷	—	❸	—	❸	—	❸
Rear	—	—	—	—	❷	—	—
Rollover Resistance	④	—	—	—	—	—	—

DaimlerChrysler

BREEZE, CIRRUS, STRATUS ★★★

RATING: Average (1999–2000); Below Average (1995–98). Go for the high-end, feature-laden models. Commanding a 20 percent premium when bought new, they cost little more than their entry-level cousins after a few years. Be wary of any model carrying the anemic and failure-prone 4-cylinder engine, and watch out for engine sludging with the 2.7L V6. If either engine fails, ask Chrysler to recognize its implied warranty repair obligation by extending the warranty under "goodwill." This said, these cars have fewer mechanical and safety problems, believe it or not, than the Ford competition. Nevertheless, be prepared to experience a number of nasty safety-related failures such as airbags that don't deploy, sudden acceleration, a jerky automatic transmission that suddenly drops out of gear, and loss of braking. **Maintenance/Repair costs:** Higher than average, but repairs aren't dealer dependent. **Parts:** Higher-than-average cost (independent suppliers sell for much less), but they are not hard to find. Recall parts, though, tend to dribble in; a month's wait isn't unusual (as has been the case with the transaxle oil cooler hose campaign for 2001 models). Don't even think about buying any of these cars without a 3- to 5-year supplementary warranty. **Extended warranty:** A good idea. **Best alternatives:** Acura Integra, Hyundai Elantra wagon or Sonata, Mazda 626, Nissan Altima or Stanza, and Toyota Camry. **Online help:** For the latest owner reports, safety reports, complaint strategies, and money-saving tips, look at *www.autosafety. org/autodefects.html*, *www.wam.umd.edu/~gluckman/Chrysler*, *www.daimlerchrysler-vehicleproblems.com*, and *www.allpar.com/fix/secret-warranties.html*.

⬦ Strengths and Weaknesses

Roomy and stylish, well appointed, and comfortable, the Chrysler Cirrus and Dodge Stratus were 1996 mid-sized sedan replacements for the LeBaron. The Breeze, launched as a 1996 model and dropped after its 2000 model run, is essentially a "de-contented" version of the more expensive Cirrus. For 2001, the Avenger coupe and sedan were dropped and the Stratus and the Cirrus coupe, sedan, and convert-

All ratings on a numbered scale where ⑤ is good and ❶ is bad. See pages 100–101 for a more detailed description.

ible fell under the Sebring moniker. Other improvements for the renamed models: a smoother ride and the addition of a 2.7L engine.

Most components have been used for some time on other Chrysler models, particularly the Neon subcompact and the Avenger and Sebring sports coupes. Power is supplied by one of four engines: a 2.0L 4-cylinder engine (shared with the Neon), a 2.4L 4-banger, or the recommended 2.5L and 2.7L V6. Carrying Chrysler's "cab-forward" design a step further up the evolutionary ladder, these cars have short rear decks, low noses, and massive sloping grilles. A wheelbase that's two inches longer than the Ford Taurus makes these cars comfortable for five occupants, with wide door openings and plenty of trunk space.

Judged by their styling and roominess alone, these cars would appear to be great buys. They are, in fact, high-risk choices from both a performance and a quality control standpoint. Problems reported by owners include the following: chronic automatic transmission failures; early and frequent engine head gasket failures through the 1998 models (no doubt part of the Neon engine legacy), and erratic engine operation; ABS malfunctions and sudden brake and steering loss; paint delamination and peeling; electrical short circuits; weak headlights; underperforming AC; water leaks into the trunk area and interior; easy-to-break trim items; lots of squeaks and rattles; and head restraints that are set too far back. In 1999, the manual seat height adjuster was dropped, making it difficult for short drivers to distance themselves safely from the airbag deployment. This also complicates both forward and rearward visibility, which is already seriously compromised by the cars' styling.

VEHICLE HISTORY: 1995—Avenger and Sebring coupe launched. **1996**—Horsepower boosted to 163 on the 2.5L engine. **1997**—Sebring convertible launched on Cirrus sedan platform (see "Sports Cars"). **2000**—Stratus, Avenger, and Breeze nameplates dropped. **2001**—4-cylinder engine and manual transmission are no longer available; Cirrus nameplate dropped.

 **Safety Summary**

All models: 1995–99—Upgraded engine head gasket. • Cam position sensor oil seepage. **1997–98**—NHTSA is looking into complaints of steering shaft binding. **1998**—Airbag exploded rather than inflated. • Airbags fail to deploy. • Frequent complaints of ABS failures. • Floormat jammed the steering column assembly, causing the steering to lock up. • Automatic transmission (floor console design) throw from Drive to Reverse to Park is too long, resulting in driver thinking vehicle is in Park when it's really in Reverse. • Floor shift indicator on the dash doesn't give a true reading of which gear is engaged. • Gearshift lever can be moved into Drive without putting foot on brakes to engage the transmission/brake interlock system. • High trunk lid makes it impossible to see directly behind the vehicle.

1999—Several trunk fires reported from a too-intense trunk-mounted light bulb. • Airbags failed to deploy in a collision. • Airbag deployed inadvertently, knocking driver out and causing an accident. • Sudden acceleration; stuck throttle. • Stalling upon acceleration and when foot is taken off of the gas pedal. • Steering locks up when making left-hand turns. • Automatic transmission has a short lifespan; sensors are the first to go. • Transmission lever can be shifted into Drive without first depressing brake pedal. • Cracked axle. • Dash reflects onto front windshield. • Many incidents reported of sudden brake failure without any prior warning. • While driving, brake vacuum hose separated, causing complete brake failure. • Chronic brake rotor warpage around 8,000 km (5,000 mi.), resulting in severe brake vibrations, noise, and extended stopping distance. • Engine fumes invade the cabin, causing driver drowsiness. • Frequent electrical shorts cause gauges, wipers, and windows to function erratically. • Engine, ABS, and airbag warning light often come on for no reason. • Seat belts fail to tighten. **2000**—Electrical system fire. • Brake lock-up; no airbag deployment in resulting collision. • Low-speed gear whine. • Automatic transmission has a hard 3–2 shift. • Transmission drops out of gear at 75 km/h. • Brake system failures because of loss of vacuum. • Warped brake drums and rotors; very noisy braking. • Wheel lug nuts loosen on their own. • Gas pedal sticks. • Excessive rear window fogging. • Windshield wiper doesn't clear snow adequately from driver-side windshield. • Excessive dashboard reflection onto windshield. • Driver's door jams because of faulty door panel. • Seat belts too tight. • Chronic dead battery. • Hot trunk light will burn items stored in trunk. • Space-saver spare tire is only good for a few miles and at slow speeds.

Secret Warranties/Internal Bulletins/Service Tips

ROUGH IDLE, HARD START, OR START & STALL

BULLETIN NO: 18-020-01   DATE: AUG. 17, 2001

1995–2000 Breeze/Cirrus/Stratus; 1996–2000 Sebring Convertible

Vehicle may intermittently exhibit any of the following conditions:

- Rough engine idle.
- Hard start or long crank after hot soak.
- Start and stall when started with cold engine
- Diagnostic Trouble Code (DTC) P0300, Multiple Cylinder Mis-fire.

All models/years: Anecdotal reports confirm Chrysler has a 7-year/160,000 km secret warranty covering engine head gasket failures and paint delamination, peeling, and fading (see Part Two "Paint and Body Defects," pages 71–75). • Chrysler will replace AC evaporators up to 7 years/115,000 km. **All models: 1995–98**—Repair procedure for the evaporator failure. **1995–99**—Intermittent loss of speed control. **1995–2000**—A steering column clunk or rattle can be silenced by changing the steering column retainer coupling bolt. • A poorly operating engine may only need a new EGR valve emissions component (covered by the emissions warranty). **1997–98**—Excessive cold crank time, start die-out, or weak run-up may be corrected by replacing the powertrain control module (PCM) under warranty, according to TSB #18-18-98. **1998–99**—Poor AC performance or compressor failure will be repaired under warranty or under "goodwill." **1999**—A metallic noise heard from the rear doors can be silenced by modifying the window regulator channel. **1999–2000**—No-starts and stalling may be caused by a malfunctioning sentry key immobilizer system.

BREEZE, CIRRUS, STRATUS PROFILE

	1995	1996	1997	1998	1999	2000
Cost Price ($)						
Breeze	—	18,200	18,865	19,505	21,090	—
Cirrus	22,115	23,235	24,125	24,765	22,180	22,365
LXi	24,555	25,695	26,465	26,465	24,840	25,050
Stratus	17,895	18,200	18,865	19,505	21,090	—
V6	19,750	20,100	24,060	24,475	25,025	—
Used Values ($)						
Breeze ▲	—	3,000	3,500	4,000	5,500	—
Breeze ▼	—	2,500	3,000	3,500	4,000	—
Cirrus ▲	3,000	3,500	4,000	5,000	6,000	7,500
Cirrus ▼	2,500	3,000	3,500	4,000	5,000	6,000
LXi ▲	3,500	4,000	4,500	5,500	6,500	8,000
LXi ▼	3,000	3,500	4,000	4,500	5,500	6,500
Stratus ▲	2,000	2,500	3,000	4,000	5,000	—
Stratus ▼	1,500	2,000	2,500	3,000	4,000	—
V6 ▲	2,500	3,000	3,500	4,500	5,500	—
V6 ▼	2,000	2,500	3,000	3,500	4,500	—
Reliability	❷	❷	❷	❷	❷	❸
Crash Safety (F)	❸	❸	❸	❸	❸	⑤
Side	—	—	❸	❸	❸	❸
Offset	❶	❶	❶	❶	❶	❶
Head Restraints						
Avenger	❶	—	❷	—	❷	—
Stratus (F)	❶	—	❶	—	❷	—
Stratus (Rear)	—	—	—	—	❶	—

Note: Crash ratings are applicable to all models.

Ford

bad buy **SABLE, TAURUS** ★

RATING: Below Average (2000–04); Not Recommended (1986–99). The worst of a bad lot; these cars are bargain-priced because their owners can't wait to get rid of them. Don't look for any major quality improvements from Ford. An extended bumper-to-bumper warranty is a prerequisite for anyone buying a Sable or Taurus. Of course, this extra protection will wipe out any savings realized from a low selling price. The high-performance Taurus SHO (Super High Output) is a double-whammy wallet buster. New data show it has serious engine deficiencies that can cost up to $15,000 to remedy; plus it shares most of the other generic safety- and performance-related defects that have long plagued the Taurus and Sable. Supposedly improved through a 2000 redesign, the recent models continue to generate a large volume of safety- and performance-related failures. 1999 was the last model year for Sable and the Mercury brand in Canada; they're still sold in the States, however. **Maintenance/Repair costs:** Much higher than average, but repairs aren't dealer dependent. Shopping at engine, transmission, brake, and muffler shops offering lifetime warranties can prevent some repeat repair costs. **Parts:** Average cost (independent suppliers sell for much less) and very easy to find, except for the discontinued SHO engine and Taurus parts like fuel pumps and electrical components, needed to correct chronic stalling and electrical shorts. **Extended warranty:** Nothing less than a bumper-to-bumper extended warranty will do. Even with additional protection, you're taking a huge risk with your wallet. **Best alternatives:** Honda Accord, Hyundai Elantra wagon or Sonata, Mazda 626, Nissan Sentra or Stanza, and Toyota Camry. A good alternative to the SHO and its failure-prone engine would be a Ford Mustang GT or Probe GT, or the Probe's twin, the Mazda MX-6. **Online help:** Taurus Transmission Victims: *members.aol. com/MKBradley/index.html*, *www.v8sho.com*, *www.tgrigsby.com/views/ford.htm* (The Anti-Ford Page), and *www.autosafety.org/autodefects.html*.

Strengths and Weaknesses

Although they lack pick-up with the standard 4-cylinder engine, these mid-sized sedans and wagons are competent family cars, offering lots of interior room, nice handling, a good crash rating, and many convenience features. From a performance standpoint, the best powertrain combination for all driving conditions is the 3.0L V6 hooked to a 4-speed for the family sedan. The Yamaha power plant harnessed to a manual gearbox on the high-performance SHO is a recipe for disaster. Total engine rebuilds are the norm, not the exception.

These cars are extremely risky buys and they are getting worse as they age. To see just how badly, take a look at the "Dead Ford," and NHTSA website links listed in Appendix I. Chronic engine head gasket/intake manifold and automatic transmission failures; a plethora of hazardous airbag, fuel system, brake, suspension, and steering defects; and chronic paint/rust problems are the main reasons their rating is so low this year. Owners are also reporting that engine and transmission repairs don't last: Some owners are routinely putting in new engines or transmissions every year or two.

I've recommended these cars in the past because Ford's "goodwill" programs usually compensated owners for most of the above-noted failures (except for self-destructing SHO engines) once the warranty had expired. Unfortunately, these refund programs have dried up as Ford put stonewalling over integrity. Owners are routinely faced with $3,000 engine or automatic transmission repair bills, in addition to thousands of dollars in repairs for defective fuel systems, brakes, and suspension and steering assemblies. Ford rejects many owner complaints on the grounds that repairs were done by independent agencies, the vehicle was bought used, or is no longer under the original warranty: three reasons that are often rejected by small claims court judges.

SHO

The Taurus SHO sedan, debuting in 1989, carries a Yamaha 24-valve 3.0L V6 with 220 hp; a stiff, performance-oriented suspension; and 5-speed manual transmission. As of 1993, a 4-speed automatic transmission became available. In mid-1996, a redesigned SHO debuted with a standard Yamaha 32-valve V8. Ford dropped the manual transmission at that time, a move that turned off most die-hard performance enthusiasts. The SHO is an impressive high-performance car that, unfortunately, has its own unique Yamaha-sourced engine problems in addition to carrying Ford's failure-prone automatic transmission. Both problems were well detailed in the following recent email sent to me by David S., a Cold Lake, Alberta, resident and '97 SHO owner:

> The 3.4L V8 engine found in 1996–99 Ford Taurus SHOs seems to be failing at a high rate, mostly with camshaft failures. The information on this can be found at *www.v8sho*.

com, which details fairly well the problem. The repair costs for this failure are astronomical.... Mr. Edmonston, I have to tell you my good news(?). I had to get the automatic transmission replaced (147,000 km), but using the name from your website I sent an email just to see what would happen. After a few days, I was contacted by an official who offered to pay half of the cost of the transmission. He did go through the spiel that I should have taken it to a Ford dealer, we don't usually do this, etc., but I received my cheque for $1,231 a couple of days ago.

Automatic transmission failures

Since 1991, Ford's automatic transmissions have been just as failure-prone as Chrysler's; they function erratically and are slow to shift—an annoying drawback if you need to rock the car out of a snowbank, and fairly dangerous if you need to pull out onto a busy roadway. These problems are caused principally by a cracked aluminum forward clutch piston, although dozens of other causes, including major hardware and software components, have been linked to the above failures. Breakdowns usually occur after three years of use, around the 80,000–120,000 km mark, and can cost $3,000–$3,500 to repair at the dealer, or half that much at an independent garage, (which I recommend), if no after-warranty assistance is proffered.

Poor automatic transmission performance also means sudden, unintended acceleration, as this owner of a '99 Taurus points out:

> Sudden acceleration is experienced as the vehicle shifts from First to Second gear. This occurs during stop-and-go traffic or low speed (i.e. mall parking) situations, and with the foot off both the throttle and brake. This lurch is greatly increased by even slight downhill slopes. Observation of the tachometer at this point shows the engine gaining 200 to 300 rpm, and that extra power being dumped into Second gear creates the lurch experienced. This occurs at a time when the driver is expecting a constant, predictable rate of progress and necessitates immediate braking to control the car. These dynamics are particularly frightening when turning in a tight intersection. The only assurance of smooth progress is to be braking or accelerating at these low speeds.

> Initially, my concern was for transmission longevity, which at this shift point can respond with a loud clunk and a jerk, which is felt throughout the car. However, innumerable intimidating recurrences have led me to observe that this car is a danger to other vehicles and pedestrians. Although this sudden acceleration can be anticipated intellectually, it nevertheless catches the driver off guard as attention is required elsewhere (i.e. looking for pedestrians, watching for traffic, etc.). I would not loan this vehicle to a friend and could not in good conscience sell it privately.

Engine failures

Ford's other major powertrain problem is the 3.8L engine's chronic head gasket failures, which also appear in the 1996 and later Windstars, and intake manifold defects found on other engines carried on more recent models. Head gasket symptoms include engine overheating; poor engine performance; and a thin film deposited on the inside of the windshield that cuts down on night driving visibility. Repairs range from $700 to $1,000, depending upon what other damage has occurred from overheating. Left untreated, the failure can cook your engine, requiring $3,000–$4,000 in repairs. And, even if treated in time, this defect can cause failures in emissions components (oxygen sensors and various computer modules) and other hardware malfunctions that can lead to other expensive repairs.

These engine repairs were covered by Ford's 00M09 "goodwill" engine warranty up to 7 years/160,000 km on 1994–95 Tauruses and Sables and 1995 Windstars. Owners are still angry over this warranty extension because the free engine repair didn't last, additional engine parts (including oxygen sensors) were damaged and never covered, or that they were never told about the free repairs. All of these complaints have been upheld in small claims court (see Part Two and Windstar section).

Paint delamination

Over the past decade, there have been frequent complaints of paint delamination, peeling, and premature rusting affecting Tauruses and Sables. Ford is the target of multiple class action paint lawsuits and is settling most small claims court cases, although more class actions may still be imminent.

Other problems

The 4-cylinder engine is a dog that no amount of servicing can change. It's slow, noisy, prone to stalling and surging, and actually consumes more gas than the V6. The 3.0L 6-cylinder is noted for engine head bolt failures and piston scuffing, and is characterized by hard starting, stalling, excessive engine noise, and poor fuel economy. Transmission cooler lines leak and often lead to the unnecessary repair or replacement of the transmission.

Other things to look out for: blown heater hoses, malfunctioning fuel gauge sending units, and brakes that need constant attention—they're noisy, pulsate excessively, tend to wear out prematurely, require a great deal of pedal effort, and are hard to modulate. Master cylinders need replacing around 100,000 km.

The 1988–95 models continue to have defective ignition modules, oxygen sensors, and fuel pumps, which cause rough running, chronic stalling, hard starting, and electrical system short circuits. Other problem areas include the following: biodegradable tie-rods, ball joints, coil springs, and motor mounts; an automatic transmission that is slow to downshift, hunts for Overdrive, and gives jerky performance; air conditioners that are failure-prone and can cost up to $1,000 to fix; malfunctioning heaters that are slow to warm up and don't direct enough heat to the floor (particularly on the passenger side); a defective heater core that costs big bucks to replace (buy from an independent supplier); and noisy, prematurely worn rack-and-pinion steering assemblies. Front suspension components also wear out quickly. Electrical components interfere with radio reception. The automatic antenna often sticks, electric windows short circuit, power door locks fail, and the electronic dash gives inaccurate readings. Owners report that electrical short circuits—which illuminate the Check Engine light and cause flickering lights and engine surging—are frequently misdiagnosed. Body/trim items are fragile on all cars (did somebody mention door handles?). Paint adherence is particularly poor on plastic components, weld joints, and the underside—even with mudguards. Owners also report that water leaks into the trunk through the tail light assembly and there's an annoying sound of fuel sloshing when accelerating or stopping.

VEHICLE HISTORY: 1986—Taurus and Sable debut with a wimpy 2.5L 4-cylinder, an adequately powered but failure-prone 3.0L V6, and an optional and even more unreliable 3.8L V6 (offered through 1996). 1989—SHO high-performance model, with self-destructing Yamaha engines, is introduced. 1990—Driver's side airbag. 1992—Slightly redesigned with a more rigid chassis and the dropping of the 4-banger. 1993—SHO gets an automatic transmission and engines, and transmissions start breaking down on all models. 1994—Dual front airbags; powertrain continues to self-destruct. 1995—A watershed year for engine head gasket failures and cooked engines. 1996—A terrible sales year highlighted by ugly ovoid restyling where windows look like portholes, headroom was reduced, and entry/exit became more problematic; 3.8L V6 was dropped, leaving two mediocre V6 engines to choose from. Other changes included upgraded engines, new electronic controls for the LX, better handling and ride quality, more effective soundproofing, and some transmission refinement. 1997—SHO gets a V8 and an automatic transmission. 2000—Slightly restyled with incremental improvements, like a more comfortable ride, a more powerful and quieter powertrain, upgraded airbags, adjustable pedals, seat belt pretensioners, and improved child safety seat anchors; Ford dropped the oval design and reduced sales prices in a futile effort to win back sales lost to the Japanese automakers. 2001–03—Minor upgrades as the cars are phased out.

Owners of 1996–99 models still report serious safety-related deficiencies (see "Safety Summary") and other performance-related problems, like engine and transmission seal leaks; the automatic transmission shifting erratically or not at all; front-end failures including the outer tie-rods, ball joints, and stabilizer bar links; power windows that fail one after the other and cost $300–$500 each to repair, and "possessed" windshield wipers.

Who needs a radio? Each Taurus and Sable provides a symphony of rattles, buzzes, whines, and moans to keep you company on long drives. The most annoying? The incessant snapping and creaking of the plastic in the centre console and dash from the plastic sections binding against each other when the body flexes, especially if the sun has been shining on it. The reliability of year 2000 models continues to go downhill. Fuel system failures result in surging, stalling, and a gasoline smell that invades the interior; electrical shorts cause the vehicle to suddenly shut down and not start; malfunctioning ABS, airbag, and Check Engine lights stay lit; powertrain and body components have a short lifespan; and owners have found that the restyled head restraints block rear and side visibility.

The 2001–04 models use the adequate, though dated, base 3.0L Vulcan V6; however, the high-performing 24-valve V6 provides plenty of power for most driving needs. Other nice standard features include heated outside mirrors, a 60/40 split-fold rear seatback for additional cargo space, a driver's footrest, and reserve power to operate the power windows and moon roof after the engine is shut off. Wagons get four-wheel disc brakes.

These cars are generally quiet-running, provide good handling and road holding, and offer a comfortable ride, along with better-than-average crash protection. Of course, they are also heavily discounted (we know why). Some of the minuses include insufficient storage space, limited rear headroom and access, and a history of serious transmission and engine failures. Engine intake manifold defects top the list, accompanied by sudden engine shutdown. The automatic transmission often shifts out of First gear too soon, shifts slowly, constantly bangs through the gears, and frequently chooses the wrong gear. Also expect chronic warped brake rotors, AC failures, electrical system shorts (lots of blown fuses), steering, front suspension, fuel (faulty fuel pumps), and brake system deficiencies, and extremely poor fit and finish.

Getting compensation

Canadian owners still have to threaten small claims court action to get Ford Canada to accept repairs done by independent garages, repeat failures, or failures that occur in the 100,000–160,000 km ("no man's land") range, where warranty decisions are particularly inconsistent.

Anyone who has just been blown off on the phone by a Ford Customer Assistance rep should keep in mind what one Ford whistle-blower whispered in my ear:

> The company has taken a harder line in reviewing customer claims. The only thing that gets our attention is if a small claims lawsuit is threatened or has been filed. These are kicked upstairs to Legal Affairs and are settled right away by staffers who have far more latitude and much less attitude.

 **Safety Summary**

All models/years: Tie-rod may collapse suddenly. Although the 1992 models were recalled to fix this defect, many other model years are affected and haven't been recalled. The son of a West Coast Taurus owner relates this incident:

> The right inner tie-rod, a piece of the suspension critical to the steering and thus safety of my 1992 Taurus, broke while my father was attempting to make a right turn from a stop sign. The car lost all steering control and the front wheels were seized. Fortunately, the car was barely moving, and no collision occurred.... I hope you can inform all Taurus and Sable owners of the inherent dangers lurking in their steering system.

• Front coil springs may fracture because of excessive corrosion. Ford has replaced many coils for free under a secret warranty. Interestingly, Ford's Windstars have the same problem and benefit from a 10-year extended warranty. Use that as your Taurus coil benchmark, as this Whitby, Ontario, engineer should do:

> I have a 1995 Mercury Sable that has developed two broken coil springs, on front right and rear left wheel. The fracture surfaces on the front spring show no fatigue bands and are compatible with intergranular stress corrosion or hydriding, both indicating a manufacturing defect. Microscopic examination would be required to confirm the cause of failure.

> This car has seen only light-duty service, is low mileage, and has always been garaged. I feel this is a significant safety issue. The failures have given no warning signs, and only the front one was detected during routine maintenance. The front spring has broken in two places, leaving a broken spring end only a quarter inch [0.6 cm] from the tire. I cannot easily see what is stopping it [from] going right into the tire, and suspect it would have worked its way in over the course of a few more miles. I am also concerned that a local independent mechanic says he has seen several spring failures on the Taurus/Sable, but that the local dealer's service rep has not. I note from the *Lemon-Aid* website that Transport Canada is investigating spring failures on this vehicle type.

• Strong fuel odour seeps into the interior. • Power steering suddenly failed. • These vehicles eat brake rotors, calipers, and pads every 8,000 km (5,000 mi.). • Warped rotors. • Brakes produce a grinding, growling noise in addition to an acrid smell. • Transmission slips out of Park. • Frequent complaints of sudden acceleration or high idle when taking the foot off the gas pedal, at a standstill, or when shifting into Reverse, slowly accelerating, or applying the brakes. • Chronic stalling and brake failures. • Airbag fails to deploy or is accidentally deployed. • Dash reflects onto windshield. **1998**—Accelerator and brake pedals are too close to each other. • Vehicle won't slow when accelerator pedal is released. • Faulty cruise control won't slow vehicle down. • Automatic transmission malfunctions. • Defective rotor and wiring assembly caused ABS failure. • Loss of steering when steering belt pulley and pump failed. • Defective rack-and-pinion steering spring yoke. •

Sudden steering lock-up. • Trunk lid fell on owner's head, because of defective torsion bar. • Trunk light burned garment in the trunk. • Faulty headlights. • Headlights don't give enough light to the sides. • Daytime running lights flicker because of defective module. • Dashboard reflects in the windshield, causing reduced visibility. • Heater system failed. • Driver's seat belt won't retract or lock into position. • Hatchback window suddenly exploded while vehicle was parked. **1999**—Engine fires. • Many reports of no-starts or sudden stalling caused by fuel pump failure. • Defective power-steering pump causes sudden steering lock-up. • ABS brakes locked up when applied and vehicle suddenly accelerated. • Many reports of brake pedal having been pushed to the floor with no braking effect. One '99 Taurus owner recounts the following tragic experience in his NHTSA complaint:

> Sudden brake loss, cruise control wouldn't disengage, brakes to floor, emergency brake pulled to no effect, death of four.

Every element of this owner's story is repeated throughout the NHTSA database from reports of other Taurus and Sable owners. • Cruise control fails to disengage when vehicle is going downhill. • Frequent automatic transmission failures that include: slipping, hesitation, lurching into gear, failure to engage First gear, and a defective fluid pump destroying the catalytic converter. • Transmission in Park position allowed vehicle to roll downhill. • Transmission may leak fluid onto the exhaust manifold. • Front passenger's seat belt won't retract or lock into position. • Seat belt broke. • Seat belts fail to retract in a collision. • In the morning and evening, the light tan dashboard reflects upon the windshield, reducing visibility. • Rear defroster/defogger works poorly. • Rear windshield exploded when defroster/defogger activated. • In another incident, rear windshield exploded while vehicle was underway. • Headlights dim when brakes are applied. • Trunk light bulb burned part of luggage. • Electrical system shorts lead to the erratic operation of power door locks (they unlock while vehicle is underway) and windows. • AC discharges a foul odour that causes eyes to water and burn. • Fuel tank leaks. • Vehicle will stall out when fuel gauge shows the tank is one-quarter full. In fact, the gauge is so inaccurate that it will vary its reading by a half a tank depending upon whether you are going uphill or downhill. **2000**—Over 300 safety failures have been recorded (100 complaints would be normal) for the first year of the Taurus' latest redesign. Most of the problems are similar to those reported for previous years; evidence that Ford doesn't want to spend the money or squeeze its suppliers to install better quality components. Gas fumes in the interior (driver found it exceeded CO_2 monitor limits and caused drowsiness and headaches); constantly lit warning lights; complete electrical failure; and sudden acceleration, surging, and stalling, accompanied by brake failure continue to be the most frequent complaints:

> I released the brake after stopping at a stop sign, and turned the wheel to the right, the vehicle suddenly accelerated to what seemed about 100 km/h in about 10 seconds.

The vehicle went toward the right and struck a curb, and the brakes did not appear to work. Once the vehicle came to a rest, the engine then shut off, the windshield broke, and the driver's side door wouldn't open. I suffered minor injuries.

Whatever you do, don't ignore the Check Engine light. In another recorded incident, the car didn't run away, stall, or lose its brakes; it simply exploded:

At start-up the intake manifold exploded, resulting in total destruction. Shrapnel was embedded in the insulation cover on the hood and found throughout the engine compartment. The windshield washer module on the right side was blown off and found approximately five feet [1.5 m] from the car. This vehicle has been in for service for hard starting and fuel system Check Engine light for the past year.

2001—Complaints continue unabated and echo those from previous years. • When coming to a stop, vehicle continues to accelerate because foot presses brake and gas pedal at the same time. • Car accelerated while backing up. • Airbag warning light comes on for no reason. • Rear-view mirror too low on windshield; blocks view to the right. • Early automatic transmission replacement. • Transmission clunks and jerks into gear. • Driver-side seat belt tightens by itself while driving. • Left rear wheel came off in transit; lost control of car. 2002— Engine compartment fire. • Sudden acceleration; vehicle surges and then shuts off when fuel tank is filled. • Frequent stalling, hard starts, and poor idle caused by chronic fuel pump failures or a contaminated fuel pressure sensor. • Strong fuel smell comes from the air vents (see "Secret Warranties/Internal Bulletins/Service Tips"). • Fuel gauge stuck on Full. • Fuel tank is easily punctured • Interior rear view mirror location obstructs visibility. • Seat belts may not reel out or retract. • Seat belt continually tightened around child and had to be cut. • Adjustable brake and accelerator pedals are set too close together and are often too loose. • Rear brake lines rub together. • High beam lights are too dim. • Cigarette lighter pops out and falls under passenger seat. 2003—Airbag warning light stays lit. • Rear left wheel and rim flew off because of defective lug nuts. • Engine had to be replaced because block heater was incorrectly mounted on the engine. • Engine belt tensioner shattered. • Excessive steering vibration. • Right rear wheel almost fell off because of faulty stabilizer bolt. • Firestone tire blowout. 2004—Several reports of coil spring breakage causing loss of steering control (a problem for over a decade— see below). • Chronic stalling and chirping noise coming from the wheels. • Seat belt choked passenger in a collision. • Brake failure and engine surging occur simultaneously along with a lit ABS and Traction Control warning light. • Only driver's side door has a key-operated lock. • Defective power control seat.

Secret Warranties/Internal Bulletins/Service Tips

All models/years: Many reports of sudden coil spring breakage puncturing tire and throwing vehicle out of control; no confiming TSBs, though. Writes the owner of a 1999 Taurus SE:

Driver side coil spring failed, cutting the tire in half. Not too bad at 60 km/h but would have been a disaster at 100 km/h. Seems there were "not enough failures" to require recall earlier, but ANOTHER investigation has been opened by government. Dealer said it was a 'common' failure!!! I would not drive a Taurus/Windstar until I put something other than Ford springs on them. There are also reports of similar failures in Contours, Escorts, Focus, and F-150s. Problems with Ford coil springs and corrosion date from at least 1993. So, 11 years later, they clearly have done NOTHING to fix the problem. The corrosion where my spring broke was NOT visible externally, but was clearly rusted internally at the point where it broke.

• Repeated heater core leaks. • A rotten-egg odour coming from the exhaust probably means that you have a faulty catalytic converter; replacement may be covered under the emissions warranty. • A buzz or rattle from the exhaust system may be caused by a loose heat shield catalyst. • A sloshing noise from the fuel tank when accelerating or stopping requires the installation of an upgraded tank. • Paint delamination, fading, and peeling (see Part Two "Paint and Body Defects," pages 71–75). **1994–98**—No Fourth gear may signal the need to install an upgraded forward clutch control valve retaining clip. **1994–99**—Service tips to silence wind noise around doors. **1995–99**—Tips for sealing windshield water leaks and reducing noise, vibration, and harshness while driving. **1995–2000**—A harsh 3–2 downshift/shudder when accelerating or turning may have a simple cause: air entering the fluid filter pick-up area because of a slightly low ATF fluid level. **1996–98**—Troubleshooting tips for a torque converter clutch that won't engage. • Hard starts or long cranks may be caused by a miscalibrated power control module (PCM), a faulty IAC, or a malfunctioning fuel pump. • Install a power-steering service kit to silence steering moan. • A rattle heard when accelerating may be corrected by replacing the exhaust pipe flex coupling. • Water leaking onto the passenger floor area is likely caused by insufficient sealing of the cabin air filter to the cowl inlet. **1996–99**—Frequent no-starts, long cranks, or a dead battery may be caused by excessive current drain or water entry in the ABS module connector. **1996–2001**—Inoperative power windows may need a new motor and lubrication of the glass run weather stripping. **1996–2003**—Repair tips for when the torque converter clutch doesn't engage. **1997–98**—Lack of AC temperature control may be corrected by replacing the blend air door actuator. **1999**—Owner Notification Program regarding transmission rear lube tube and bracket replacement. • Engine buzz or rattle. • Slight vibration upon acceleration. • Lack of engine braking. • Excessive spark knock with the 3.0L engine. • Engine oil pan leaks. • No Reverse engagement is likely caused by the Reverse clutch lip seals shearing or tearing during Reverse engagement in cold weather. • No 3–4 shifts or 3–4 shift shuddering. • Inoperative speed control and blower motor. • Self-activating front wipers need an upgraded multifunction switch (covered under warranty or "goodwill"). • Hard to turn ignition key. • Wagons display a false "door ajar" warning. • Intermittent loss of instrument panel illumination. • Separation between the layers of the instrument panel. • Premature deterioration of the front seat trim. • Power window binding. • Inaccurate fuel tank gauge; fuel tank causes gas pump to shut off prematurely. **2000**—Engine pan oil leaks. • Automatic trans-

INTAKE MANIFOLD GASKETS – FUEL SMELL TO THE INTERIOR

BULLETIN NO: 01-4-3

DATE: MARCH 05, 2001

2000–01 Taurus; 2001 Escape; 2000–01 Sable

SUBJECT: This article applies to 2000–01 Taurus/Sable vehicles with 3.0L 4V Duratec engine built through 4/1/2001 and 2001 Escape vehicles with 3.0L 4V Duratec engine built through 6/1/2001 only.

ISSUE: Some vehicles may exhibit a fuel odour noticed through the vents inside the vehicle. The odour may be noticed upon initial start-up after "Hot Soak." This condition produces a fuel odour only and does not involve visible fuel or include the presence of a combustible mixture. This may be caused by the lower intake manifold gaskets.

ACTION: If fuel odour condition is verified and no fuel leaks or mechanical problems are found, replace the lower intake gaskets with revised gaskets.

NO-START/HARD START/ROUGH IDLE

BULLETIN NO: 03-3-50   DATE: FEB. 17 2003

SUBJECT: DRIVEABILITY - Idle air control (IAC) valve

2000–03 Taurus; 2002 Thunderbird; 2000–03 Explorer, Ranger; 2001–03 Explorer's Sport Trac, Explore Sport; 2000–02 LS; 2000–03 Sable, Mountaineer

ISSUE: Some vehicles may exhibit driveability conditions. These may include:
^No-start/difficult to start/stall
^Low idle
^Rough idle
^High idle
^Hesitation/surge while accelerating or at steady speed
These conditions may be intermittent with no Diagnostic Trouble Codes (DTC) and no Malfunction Indicator Lamp (MIL).

mission may operate erratically. • A hissing sound may be heard coming from the intake manifold. • A growling or scraping sound may be heard during acceleration. **2000–01**—3.0L engines may exhibit a rough start or poor idle, excessive spark knock, or backfire on start-up. • 3–4 shift shudder. • The exhaust pipe contacts the rear control arm, resulting in rear end buzzing, groaning, and rattling. • Fuel smell permeates the interior (see above bulletin). **2000–03**—Power window "grunting." • No-start or hard starts (see bulletin at left). **2001**—Side airbag light may remain lit. • Rough idle. • Check Engine light remains lit. • Automatic transmission fluid leakage from the main control cover area. • Rough shifting and engine surging. • Sticking/binding ignition key lock cylinder. **2001–04**—Malfunctioning blower motor. **2002–03**—Engine noise, excessive vibration, and a rough idle may all be caused by a faulty cooling fan. **2002–05**—An inaccurate fuel gauge will be repaired under the emissions warranty (see page 52). **2003**—Transmission may not go into Reverse. • Troubleshooting transmission malfunctions. • Engine cooling-fan-induced body boom. • Rough engine idle sensation, and unusual engine noise at idle. • Incorrectly installed gear-driven camshaft position sensor synchronizer assemblies may cause engine surge, loss of power, or MIL lamp to light. • Rattling, clunking front suspension. **2004**—3.0L engine oil leaks and cold hard start, no start, and surging. • Hesitation when accelerating. • Wipers won't shut off. • Inoperative rear window defroster. • Accelerator pedal vibration. • Speedometer malfunctions. • Wheel cover and front suspension noise.

All ratings on a numbered scale where ⑤ is good and ❶ is bad. See pages 100–101 for a more detailed description.

	1996	1997	1998	1999	2000	2001	2002	2003	2004
Cost Price ($)									
Sable GS	22,595	23,595	24,395	24,595	—	—	—	—	—
LS Wagon	25,496	26,596	25,096	25,795	—	—	—	—	—
Taurus GL	22,195	23,195	—	—	—	—	—	—	—
Taurus LX	25,095	26,195	23,295	23,495	24,495	24,250	24,550	24,750	24,995
GL/SE Wagon	22,196	23,196	23,995	24,695	26,495	26,555	27,285	27,630	28,355
SHO	32,430	32,695	37,795	37,995	—	—	—	—	—
Used Values ($)									
Sable GS ▲	2,000	3,500	4,000	5,000	—	—	—	—	—
Sable GS ▼	1,500	2,500	3,500	4,000	—	—	—	—	—
LS Wagon ▲	2,500	3,500	4,000	6,000	—	—	—	—	—
LS Wagon ▼	2,000	2,500	3,000	5,000	—	—	—	—	—
Taurus GL ▲	2,000	3,000	—	—	—	—	—	—	—
Taurus GL ▼	1,500	2,000	—	—	—	—	—	—	—
Taurus LX ▲	2,500	3,500	4,000	5,500	7,500	9,500	11,500	13,500	16,000
Taurus LX ▼	2,000	3,000	3,500	4,500	6,000	8,000	9,500	12,000	14,500
GL/SE Wagon ▲	3,000	4,000	5,000	6,500	8,000	11,000	12,500	14,500	17,000
GL/SE Wagon ▼	2,500	3,500	4,000	5,500	7,000	9,500	10,500	13,000	16,000
SHO ▲	3,500	4,500	6,500	8,500	—	—	—	—	—
SHO ▼	3,000	4,000	5,500	7,000	—	—	—	—	—
Reliability	❶	❶	❶	❶	❶	❷	❷	❷	❷
Crash Safety (F)	④	④	④	⑤	—	⑤	⑤	⑤	④
Side	—	③	③	③	—	③	③	③	③
Offset	⑤	⑤	⑤	⑤	⑤	⑤	⑤	⑤	—
Head Restraints (F)	❶	❶	—	❶	③	⑤	④	③	—
Rear	—	—	—	—	—	—	③	③	—
Rollover Resistance	—	—	—	—	—	—	④	④	④

General Motors

ACHIEVA, ALERO, GRAND AM, SKYLARK ★★★

RATING: Average (2000–04), with the right powertrain set-up and an extended powertrain warranty; Below Average (1995–99); Not Recommended (1985–94). Only the Grand Am and its Alero twin survived the 1999 model year. Despite its post-2004 phase-out, the Olds Alero's resale value has remained remarkably high. Keep in mind that the 4-cylinder engines are noisy and rough-running. **Maintenance/Repair costs:** Higher than average. Repairs aren't dealer dependent. **Parts:** Higher-than-average cost, but they can be bought for much less from independent suppliers. **Extended warranty:** A toss-up. Extended powertrain coverage should be sufficient protection. **Best alternatives:** Acura Integra; Honda Accord; Hyundai Elantra wagon, Sonata, or Tiburon; Mazda 626; Nissan Altima; and Toyota Camry. **Online help:** For the latest owner reports, service bulletins, and money-saving tips, look at *www.autosafety.org/autodefects.html*, or use Google to search for GM paint delamination, piston slapping, or manifold defects.

 ## Strengths and Weaknesses

These cars originally came with a failure-prone 150-hp Quad SOHC engine, a 5-speed transaxle, and ABS. The basic front-drive platform continues to be a refined version of the Sunfire (Sunbird) and Cavalier J-body. They are too cramped to be family sedans (rear entry/exit can be difficult), too sedate for sporty coupe status, and too ordinary for inclusion in the luxury car ranks.

In their basic form, these cars are unreliable, unspectacular, and provide barely adequate performance. An upgraded 3.1L V6 power plant gives you only five more horses than the base 4-banger and frequently requires intake manifold gasket repairs covered by a 6-year/100,000 km secret warranty. There's been a lot of hype about the Quad 4 16-valve engine, available with all models, but little of this translates into benefits for the average driver. A multi-valve motor produces more power than a standard engine, but always at higher rpm and with a fuel penalty and excess engine noise.

These cars ride and handle fairly well, but mostly share chassis components with the failure-prone J-bodies. This explains why their engine, transmission, brake, and electronic problems are similar. Fortunately, manual transmissions are much more reliable and are also the better choice for fuel economy. Water leaks and body squeaks and rattles are so abundant that GM has published a six-page troubleshooting TSB that pinpoints the noises and lists fixes.

VEHICLE HISTORY: 1991–95—Potentially unsafe door-mounted front seat belts. **1992**—A major redesign offered new styling and a 3.3L V6. **1994**—A revised 3.1L V6 replaces the 3.3L V6 and a driver's-side airbag was added. **1996**—Restyled and given standard AC, dual airbags and three-point seat belts; a new twin-cam engine replaced the 2.3L Quad 4. **1998**—De-powered airbags. *Alero:* **2004**—Last model year. *Grand Am:* **1999**—Given better engines, a new platform, more standard equipment, and a restyled, more comfortable interior. **2002**—A quieter, more efficient 140-hp 2.2L base engine with 10 fewer horses than the engine it replaced, plus a revised console storage area. **2004**—A speaker upgrade.

The 2.5L 4-cylinder engine doesn't provide much power and has a poor reliability record. Avoid the Quad 4 and 3.0L V6 engines with SFI (sequential fuel injection) because of their frequent breakdowns and difficult servicing. Poor engine cooling and fuel system malfunctions are common; diagnosis and repair are more complicated than average, however. The engine computer on V6 models has a high failure rate, and the oil pressure switch often malfunctions. The electrical system is plagued by gremlins that cause gauges and controls to go haywire and result in the car shutting down on the highway. Seals and pumps in the power-steering rack deteriorate rapidly. Front brake discs, rotors, and pads need replacing every 8,000 km (5,000 mi.). Locks and headlights self-activate.

Among body deficiencies, owners note that windshield mouldings fall off, water leaks into the trunk and through the doors, door panels often need replacing, the sun visor fails to stay in place, seat cushions aren't durable, and paint defects are quite common.

Alero and Grand Am (1999–2004)

These redesigned cars aren't very impressive. The best engine choice for power, smoothness, and value retention is the 207-hp 3.4L V6; it gives you much-needed power and is quite fuel efficient. Early reports indicate that the new 2.2L engine is quieter, but its lack of power is noticeable, particularly when coupled with an automatic transmission. Stay away from the Computer Command Ride option; true, it allows you to choose your own suspension setting, but the settings aren't quite what they pretend to be.

Taking their styling cues from GM's Grand Prix, the Grand Am and its Alero twin offer a roomy, comfortable interior in two- and four-door body styles. They share the same platform and mechanical components, and the base Grand Am SE uses a 140-hp 2.2L power plant, while other trim levels use the 150-hp 2.4L Quad DOHC engine; a 170-hp 3.4L V6 engine is standard on the SE2. The upscale Alero, Oldsmobile's entry-level model, debuted in 1999 as the replacement for the slow-selling Achieva—often referred to as the "under-Achieva." The Alero shares the Grand Am's chassis and powertrains, although only the 2.2L and 3.4L V6 are offered. The V6 may be teamed with either a 5-speed manual or a 4-speed automatic transmission.

1999–2004 Grand Ams are well appointed with many standard features, including standard traction control. They have a competent V6; good steering and handling, and average quality control. Some of their disadvantages include: a mediocre ride over rough terrain; excessive 4-cylinder noise; and a noisy interior. Also, expect difficult rear seat access (coupe); awkward radio controls; rear visibility obstructed by the spoiler; problematic trunk access; annoying body creaks and rattles; and doubtful long-term powertrain reliability.

Equally well equipped, Aleros give impressive V6 acceleration (even though it's the same engine found in the Grand Am, it performs better in the Alero). You'll find logical, user-friendly gauges and controls; a fairly spacious interior for cargo and passengers; standard traction control; and a quiet-running V6 powertrain. Here's the Alero's downside: excessive 4-cylinder engine noise and torque steer; steering that's not as crisp as the Grand Am's; difficult rear seat access (coupe); and questionable long-term durability. The Alero will be dropped during the 2004 model year because of the phase-out of GM's Oldsmobile division.

Overall quality control is poor. GM's quality improvements, evident on its trucks, vans, and SUVs, weren't carried over to these passenger vehicles. Owners warn of powertrain malfunctions, including sudden transmission failure and poor shifting; engine overheating; and premature brake pad and rotor wear. The following two emails are typical of the engine and brake problems affecting recent Aleros and Grand Ams:

> I bought a '99 Alero with 55,000 km on it. After driving it for a year, I now have 95,000 km on it. Yesterday the warning light for low coolant came on and this morning I took the car to my local repair shop. He filled the reservoir (overflow) up and checked for any leaks, found none and I drove home. I quickly noticed the engine running rough, so when I got home I called him again. He checked the reservoir (overflow) again and it was already down again…. Then, he checked the oil dipstick—it was wet, steamy, and very light in colour. You probably guessed it a long time ago; all the water went into the cylinders!!! Can I not expect more than 100,000 km from the Alero's 3.4L, 6-cylinder engine!!!

> •

> Phil, I have problems with the front brakes on a 2000 Alero. I have had the rotors replaced once (28,000 km), pads twice, and there is a constant rubbing sound coming from the front end that the dealer says is the result of a rust buildup on the edge of the rotors. They told me it's something I have to live with.

Owners also mention electrical problems; suspension squeaks; and substandard body assembly that produces squeaks and rattles, water leaks, and poor paint adhesion. There are reports that the sunroof may leak water into the electrical panel, causing short-circuits. Rear visibility may be obstructed by the spoiler.

 **Safety Summary**

All models/years: Airbag failed to deploy and inadvertent airbag deployment. • Sudden acceleration and stalling. • Frequent brake failures and extended stopping distance; brake caliper seizure damages pads and rotors. • Power-steering failures and fluid leakage. • Transmission jumps out of gear. • Shoulder belt rides across driver's neck. • Erratic fuel gauge operation. • Headlights suddenly shut off or don't provide enough illumination. • Head restraints block rear vision. • Dash is reflected onto the windshield. • Water leaks everywhere. **1998–99**—Vehicle caught fire while parked. • Premature brake pad wearout and warped rotors every 4,800–8,000 km (3,000–5,000 mi.). • Cruise control is either inoperative or fails to disengage. • Chronic hesitation and stall-out, accompanied by dash lights and other electrical components going haywire. • Enhanced traction system engages when not needed. • Complete electrical system shutdown while vehicle was underway. • Rainwater leaks through the dash panel into the fuse box. • Wheel lug nuts sheared off, causing wheel to fall away. • Severe brake, steering, and body vibrations; vehicle intermittently violently jerks to one side. • Steering pump failure. • Fuel pressure regulator leaks fumes into the interior. • Sunroof exploded when side window was opened while vehicle was underway. • Windows run off their channels and shatter. • Power window motors often need replacing. • Windshield washer fluid freezes because of poor tubing design. • Locks and headlights self-activate. • Faulty fuel level sensor gives a false Empty reading. • Seat belts tend to twist when retracting. **2000**—Although there aren't an unusually large number of complaints recorded, the same problems keep appearing. They include frequent brake light burnout; poor braking or the complete loss of braking; overheated, warped brake rotors and excessive vibration when braking; chronic stalling; the trunk lid opening on its own while the vehicle is underway; and water leaks through the doors and sunroof. The sunroof leaks result in the electrical system shorting out and the vehicle shutting down. **2001**—Very few complaints reported so far; however, stalling, brake rotor warpage, and sunroof leaks appear, once again. Other problems: fire ignited at the right rear of vehicle; fuel tank is easily punctured; and rear axle bent or broken, leading to loss of control. **2002**—Frequency of safety complaints has increased substantially. • Transmission suddenly failed while cruising at speeds over 100 km/h. • Chronic stalling. • Vehicle continued accelerating after passing another car on the highway. • Car constantly surges and hesitates. • Vehicle tends to wander all over the road; pulls to one side when accelerating. • Steering shudders upon braking or acceleration; faulty power steering pump; steering feels too loose. • ABS light comes on, followed by brake failure; brake pedal set too low; parking brake failure. • Fuel pump failure. • Shoulder belts twist in their housing; in the GT two-door, they ride abnormally high on the shoulder/neck area. • Power doors lock on their own. • Headlights blink on and off. • Theft alarm sounds for no reason. • Middle rear lap seat belt is too short to secure a child safety seat and GM says an extension isn't available. • Loose driver's seat. • Windshield wipers shut off intermittently. • Rear windshield shattered when defogger was activated; side door glass shattered behind mirror for no reason. • Inside door edge is razor sharp. • Slight front impact causes the battery tray to either break off, or results in the battery sliding off the tray. *Alero*: Engine compartment fire. • Right front wheel separated because the lug nuts and bolts sheared off. • Tapped brakes to turn cruise control off and vehicle accelerated. • Rear main oil seal leak blew oil onto exhaust pipe. • Fuel tank leakage. • Water leakage onto the back of the instrument panel causes the instruments and gauges to malfunction; other electrical shorts cause instrument panel gauges and controls to fail. • Windshield water leaks cause electrical shorts.

• Hard to find horn "sweet spot" in an emergency. • Side mirror spring mounts break when passing over unpaved roads.

Secret Warranties/Internal Bulletins/Service Tips

All models/years: A rotten-egg odour coming from the exhaust may be the result of a malfunctioning catalytic converter—possibly covered by the emissions warranty. Stand your ground if GM or the dealer claims you must pay. • Tips on removing AC odours; GM has a special kit to keep AC odours at bay. • Paint delamination, peeling, or fading (see Part Two "Paint and Body Defects," pages 71–75). • Reverse servo cover leaks. **1990–2000**—Countermeasures for water collecting in the tail lights. **1995–98**—A steering squeak or squawk may be reduced by installing a rack-and-pinion service kit. **1996–98**—Install a seat belt webbing stop button if the seat belt latch slides to the anchor sleeve. • Passenger compartment water leaks can be plugged by applying silicone sealer to the top vent grille assembly. **1997–98**—Hard starting or a weak or dead battery may signal the need to repair the B+ stud and/or starter wiring. **1999–2000**—No Third or Fourth gear may signal a defective direct clutch piston. • Upgraded pads and rotors will fix brake pulsation/vibration. • A wet front or rear carpet may mean the front door water deflectors need to be replaced. • Simply changing the radiator cap may cure your hot-running engine. *Skylark*: **1995–98**—Intermittent Neutral/loss of Drive at highway speeds can be fixed by replacing the control valve body assembly. *Grand Am, Alero*: **1998–2003**—Automatic transmission flaring. **1999**—Hesitation or lack of power when accelerating on vehicles equipped with the 3.4L engine may simply require reprogramming the power control module (PCM). • Paint chipping from the Grand Am SE's rocker panel and lower quarter panel can be prevented by installing upgraded driver- and passenger-side rocker mouldings. **1999–2001**—A front-end clunk or rattle can be silenced by replacing the brake pedal assembly under warranty. • Water leak troubleshooting. • Wind rush from the front windshield. **1999–2002**—Excessive pedal or steering wheel pulsation when braking can be eliminated by using GM's Front Pad Kit #18044437, says TSB #00-05-23-002A. **1999–2004**—Faulty rear lights cost up to $300 to repair, but GM will cover the cost through a secret warranty, a recall (SUVs included), and its implied warranty obligations. • Poor automatic transmission performance, slipping. • Faulty front door window glass and power window motor. • Front wheel tire noise may be silenced by replacing Goodyear Eagle tires. **2000**—If the vehicle stalls, hesitates, or won't start, you may need to replace the modular fuel sender strainer. **2000–01**—If the Check Engine light comes on, it may mean the fuel-sender-to-tank O-ring is defective.

STOP/TAIL LAMPS INTERMITTENTLY INOPERATIVE

BULLETIN NO: 00-08-42-007B   **DATE:** JUNE 17, 2004

Stop/Tail Lamp(s) Inoperative or Intermittent and/or Water in Lamp (Replace Circuit Board/Gasket and/or Lamp Assembly)

1997–2003 Malibu; 2004 Classic; 1999–2004 Grand Am

CONDITION: Some customers may comment that a stop and/or tail lamp may not work correctly, or that the tail lamp has water in it.
CAUSE: This condition may be caused by the circuit board and/or gasket.

1997–2002 Malibu; 1997–99 Cutlass; 1999–2002 Alero, Grand Am

CONDITION: Some customers may comment on a pulsation condition felt in the brake pedal and/or steering wheel during a brake apply. In some cases, it may be noted that the pulsation condition has reoccurred in 5,000-11,000 km (3,000-7,000 mi.) after having had the brakes serviced, tires rotated, or any type of servicing that required wheel removal.

CAUSE: Pulsation is the result of brake rotor thickness variation causing the brake caliper piston to move in and out of the brake caliper housing. This hydraulic "pumping/pulsing" effect is transmitted through the brake system and may be felt in the brake pedal. In severe cases, this condition may also transmit through the vehicle structure and other chassis system components such as the steering column or wheel. The major contributor to rotor thickness variation is excessive lateral run-out of the rotor, causing the brake pads to wear the rotor unevenly over time.

CORRECTION: Confirm that the brake pads have the number 1417 printed on the edge of the pad backing plate (refer to the illustration). This indicates the correct brake pads have been previously installed. The brake pads contained in Front Pad Kit, P/N 18044437, are the only brake pads that should be used on these vehicles. If the number 1417 is not present, or if the number is not legible, replace the brake pads. If the correct pads were previously installed, verify the brake pad thickness. If the brake pad friction material thickness is 4.6 mm (0.18 in.) or greater, re-use the pads. If the friction material thickness is less than 4.6 mm (0.18 in.), install new brake pads contained in Front Pad Kit P/N 18044437.

If the rotor thickness is less than 25 mm (0.98 in.), install a new rotor. If rotor thickness is greater than 25 mm (0.98 in.), refinish the rotor.

Replace existing front brake rotors and pads, if necessary, with new components indicated in the table following the applicable Service Manual procedures and the service guidelines contained in Corporate Bulletin Number 00-05-22-002.

• Install a fuel tank sender kit under warranty if the fuel gauge gives inaccurate readings. • TSB #01-06-01-005 allows for free 3.1L engine piston replacement to cure an engine ticking noise. **2000–03**—Firm transmission shifts and shudders or transmission slips or fails to shift. • Loss of power steering. • Noisy front suspension. • Inaccurate fuel gauge readings. • Front door window glass comes out of run channel and wind noise from rear of vehicle. **2001–04**—Silencing a creaky door. **2001–05**—Harsh upshifts. **2002**—No-starts, harsh transmission shifts. • Transmission fluid leakage. • Premature failure of the transaxle converter pump. • A Customer Service Campaign will pay for the inspection and correction of a transaxle converter bearing failure, detailed in TSB #01031. • Remedy for suspension noise or malfunctions. • Shift indicator doesn't show correct gear selection. • Engine alerts stay lit. • Brake pedal, underbody, or suspension clunk or rattle noise. • Door creaking. • Windshield glass distortion. **2002–04**—Poor transmission performance can be caused by a defective driven sprocket support assembly. **2003**—Poor shifting and inaccurate gauges. **2004**—No-starts, stalling. • Transmission growl or howl when accelerating from a stop. • Trunk water leaks.

ACHIEVA (CALAIS), ALERO, GRAND AM, SKYLARK PROFILE

	1996	1997	1998	1999	2000	2001	2002	2003	2004
Cost Price ($)									
Achieva S	19,925	20,735	21,200	—	—	—	—	—	—
Alero	—	—	—	20,995	20,445	21,335	21,745	22,285	22,335
Grand Am	18,000	19,035	19,610	21,795	20,625	20,915	21,405	21,640	21,885
Skylark	20,035	21,220	22,965	—	—	—	—	—	—
Used Values ($)									
Achieva S ▲	3,000	3,500	4,000	—	—	—	—	—	—
Achieva S ▼	2,000	3,000	3,000	—	—	—	—	—	—
Alero ▲	—	—	—	5,500	6,500	8,500	10,000	12,000	14,000
Alero ▼	—	—	—	4,500	5,500	7,000	8,500	10,500	12,000
Grand Am ▲	4,000	4,500	5,000	6,000	7,000	9,000	11,000	13,000	15,000
Grand Am ▼	3,500	4,000	4,500	5,000	6,000	8,000	9,500	11,500	13,500
Skylark ▲	4,000	4,500	5,000	—	—	—	—	—	—
Skylark ▼	3,500	4,000	4,500	—	—	—	—	—	—
Reliability	②	②	③	③	③	③	③	③	③
Crash Safety (F)									
Achieva 2d	④	—	—	—	—	—	—	—	—
Achieva 4d	⑤	—	—	—	—	—	—	—	—
Grand Am 2d	—	④	—	—	—	④	④	④	④
Grand Am 4d	④	⑤	—	④	④	④	④	④	④
Skylark 2d	—	④	—	—	—	—	—	—	—
Skylark 4d	④	⑤	—	—	—	—	—	—	—
Side									
Achieva 4d	—	①	①	—	—	—	—	—	—
Grand Am 2d	—	—	—	—	—	①	①	①	①
Grand Am 4d	—	—	①	①	③	③	③	③	③
Skylark 4d	①	①	—	—	—	—	—	—	—
Offset	—	—	—	—	①	①	①	①	—
Head Restraints	①	—	①	—	②	—	③	③	—
Alero	—	—	—	—	—	—	—	②	—
Rollover Resistance	—	—	—	—	—	—	④	④	—

BONNEVILLE, CUTLASS, CUTLASS SUPREME, DELTA 88, GRAND PRIX, IMPALA, INTRIGUE, LESABRE, LUMINA, MALIBU, MONTE CARLO, REGAL   ★★★

RATING: Average (2000–04); Not Recommended for front-drives (1988–99); Average for rear-drives (1984–87). Although these GM models are generally classed as medium-sized cars, some of them move in and out of the large car class as well. Overall, the Intrigue, Malibu, Monte Carlo, and Grand Prix provide the

All ratings on a numbered scale where ⑤ is good and ❶ is bad. See pages 100–101 for a more detailed description.

best quality at the highest depreciation rate (for used-car bargain hunters). Nevertheless, use some of the savings for extra powertrain protection, or get close to the service manager's daughter. **Maintenance/Repair costs:** Higher than average, but repairs aren't dealer dependent. **Parts:** Higher-than-average cost (independent suppliers sell for much less), but not hard to find. Nevertheless, don't even think about buying one of the front-drives without a supplementary 3- to 5-year powertrain warranty. **Extended warranty:** Yes, mainly for the engine and automatic transmission. **Best alternatives:** Acura Integra; Honda Accord; Hyundai Elantra wagon, Sonata, or Tiburon; Mazda 626; and Toyota Camry. **Online help:** The Center for Auto Safety has a huge database of service bulletins and owner complaints at *www.autosafety.org/autodefects.html*, or, once again, you can use Google to search for GM paint delamination, engine piston slapping, or manifold defects.

 ## Strengths and Weaknesses

The following problems are common to all models: no-start or no-crank conditions caused by defective ignition and start switch assembly; hot engine idles poorly; engine oil pan leaks; harsh shifting, harsh 1–2 upshifts; poor engine performance and transmission slipping (clean out debris in valve body and case oil passages); some transmissions may produce a grinding or growling noise when engaged on an incline with the engine running and the parking brake not applied; delayed shifts, slips, flares, or extended shifts in cold weather; erratic shifting; excessive vibration on smooth roads; generator whine, hum, moan, or vibration; premature alternator failure; steering vibration, shudder, or moan during parking manoeuvres.

Body assembly on all models is notoriously poor and is no doubt one of the main reasons why GM has lost so much market share over the past decade. Premature paint peeling and rusting, water and dust leaks into the trunk, squeaks and rattles, and wind and road noise are all too common. Accessories are also plagued by problems, with defective radios, power antennas, door locks, cruise control, and alarm systems leading the pack. Premature automatic transmission failures and excessive noise when shifting have been endemic up to the 1998 model year. Since then, the company's powertrain problems have been less frequent. Engine intake manifold gaskets, though, have a high failure rate and are covered by a 6-year/100,000 km secret warranty (see five confidential GM service bulletins on pages 229–232).

Rear-drives

The rear-drives are competent and comfortable cars, but they definitely point to a time when handling wasn't a priority and fuel economy was unimportant. Nevertheless, interior comfort is impressive, overall reliability is pretty good, repairs are easy to perform, defects aren't hard to troubleshoot, and cheaper independent garages can service them quite easily. Electrical malfunctions increase proportionally with extra equipment. The AC module and condenser and wheel bearings (incredibly expensive) also have short lifespans. The rear edge of trunk lids, roof areas above doors, and the windshield posts rust through easily.

Front-drives

Front-drive technology is not GM's proudest achievement, so it's not surprising to see the company embrace rear-drives in its post-2004 models. Its front-drives, phased into the lineup in the '80s, are a different breed of car: less reliable and more expensive to repair than rear-drives, with a considerable number of mechanical (e.g., brake, steering, and suspension components) deficiencies directly related to their front-drive configuration. Nevertheless, acceleration is adequate, fuel economy is good, and they're better at handling than their rear-drive cousins—except in emergencies, when their brakes frequently lock up or fail, notwithstanding ABS technology. The Detroit Big Three's front-drive designs and manufacturing weaknesses make for unimpressive high-speed performance, a poor reliability record, and expensive maintenance costs. That's why most fleets and police agencies use rear-drives when they can get them. They've seen the rear-drives' safety and operating cost advantages. Interestingly, Chrysler, Ford, and GM have announced a return to rear-drive full-sized cars by 2005.

Medium-sized front-drives aren't particularly driver-friendly. Many models have a dash that's replete with confusing push buttons and gauges that are washed out in sunlight or reflect annoyingly upon the windshield. At other times, there are retro touches, like the Intrigue's dash-mounted ignition, that simply seem out of place. The keyless entry system often fails, the radio's memory is frequently forgetful, and the fuel light comes on when the tank is just below the $1/2$ fuel-level mark. The electronic climate control frequently malfunctions and owners report that warm air doesn't reach the driver-side heating vents. Servicing, especially for the electronic engine controls, is complicated and expensive, forcing many owners to drive around with their Service Engine, airbag, and ABS warning lights constantly lit.

Other major problem areas found over the past decade: engine head gasket leaks; plastic intake manifold cracking; automatic transmission failures and clunking; leaking and malfunctioning AC systems (due mainly to defective AC modules); faulty electronic modules; rack-and-pinion steering failure; weak shocks; excessive front brake pad wear; warping rotors; seizure of the rear brake calipers; rear brake/wheel lock-up; myriad electrical failures requiring replacement of the computer module; leaking oil pan; and suspension struts.

The base 2.3L and 2.5L engines found on pre-'95 models provide insufficient power. The more powerful 3.1L V6 is peppier, but it's seriously hampered by the 4-speed automatic transaxle. The high-performance 3.4L V6, available since 1991, gives out plenty of power, but only at high engine speeds. Overall, the 3.8L V6 is a more suitable compromise. One major powertrain problem found over the past decade involves the 3.1, 3.4, and 3.8L V6 engines: specifically, engine head gasket leaks and plastic intake manifold cracking. These engine defects affect almost all GM and Saturn models, as well as Ford's 1994–2002 lineup (see the Crown Victoria, Grand Marquis, and Town Car section). The intake manifold failure may cause extensive engine damage in a short period of time, as this GM service manager whistle-blower told *Lemon-Aid*:

> One problem that I do not see mentioned on your website involves late 1990s full-sized GM cars (LeSabre, Delta 88, Bonneville) with the 3.8L (VIN K) engine. GM has released a TSB regarding a poorly designed intake manifold that actually melts from EGR heat. Their cure is to replace the upper and lower intake manifold at a cost of approximately $1,000 to the consumer.
>
> What the TSB does not reveal is that by the time most consumers are aware that there is a problem, irreversible engine damage has occurred. This is because when the intake fails, coolant leaks internally into the crankcase, therefore contaminating engine oil. The only way to know that this is happening is to check the oil on a daily basis. Once enough coolant is lost, the vehicle overheats and by that time, there are several quarts of coolant in the oil (and a wiped out engine). I know of many defects on various cars, but this one bothers me the most as the consumers have no way to protect themselves. Most of these folks (the LeSabre and Delta 88 crowd, who are mostly elderly) are driving around in mechanical time bombs.

Elderly, or not, the owners of these cars are not meekly paying for engine repairs caused by factory-related goofs and penny-pinching. Many are demanding that GM pay for its mistake up to 7 years or 160,000 km (see sample complaint letters in Part Two). When this demand is sent by registered letter, fax, or email to the company's Legal Affairs department in Oshawa, Ontario, GM usually makes a "goodwill" offer to partially cover the repair. Lemon-Aid knows of no intake manifold claim that has been litigated, although there has been a notable Canadian CAMVAP arbitration 3.4L engine victory (see below) and a class action lawsuit over the 3.8L engine was recently filed in New Jersey (see: *www.sheller.com/Practice.asp?PracticeID=143*):

> Phil: This consumer class action was filed on August 18, 2004 in the Superior Court of New Jersey. The Complaint alleges that the Defendants, General Motors, manufactured, marketed, and sold numerous vehicles with a defective 3.8 liter V6 engine. The Complaint states that the K engine is prone to coolant leakage, which leads to overheating, continual coolant replacement and ultimately engine failure. Symptoms include a milky substance on the oil dipstick or oil fill cap, a strong and unpleasant odor while operating the vehicle, and coolant puddles beneath the vehicle when parked.
>
> Additionally, the Complaint discusses General Motors response to the problem, termed "Customer Satisfaction Program – Engine Coolant Leak #03034". The Complaint alleges

that the repair is only a temporary remedy and is designed to hide the problem until after the consumer's warranty has expired. The Complaint lists owners and lessees of Buick Park Avenue, Buick Regal, Chevrolet Impala, Chevrolet Monte Carlo, Pontiac Bonneville and Pontiac Grand Prix from the model year 2000, 2001, and 2003 as those affected by the defective K Engine and to be included in the Class. It is important to note that while we have only filed a lawsuit in NJ, we are investigating the filing of other lawsuits across the country.

•

Jo Ann's 1999 Oldsmobile Silhouette—A Victory Story!

I am the original owner of a 1999 Oldsmobile, Silhouette minivan.

Before any major problems occurred the van would leave small fluid leaks on the garage floor. At 91,000 km it was finally obvious that the lower intake manifold gasket was leaking and was repaired for $976.00. At 113,000 km the camshaft split in two and at that time the engine had to be replaced. Cost for the engine replacement was $6,600.00. My mechanic felt that the intake manifold gasket had been leaking internally before it was finally detected and the mixing of the antifreeze and oil directly resulted in the seizing of the bearings which caused the camshaft to split.

I contacted the dealership where I purchased the vehicle as well as the local GM dealership and received no help whatsoever. The dealerships denied knowing of any problem with the intake manifold gasket leaks or the possibility of the camshaft splitting. I then contacted General Motors head office in Oshawa, Ontario and was told that they would not accept any responsibility for the problem and that they were not aware of any gasket defect.

The local GM dealership suggested I approach CAMVAP, which is an arbitration company that is funded by car manufacturers. They were extremely supportive and sent me an information package detailing the steps to be completed before attempting arbitration. GM head office said I could have my repairs/engine replacement done by my own mechanic but a GM dealership would have to assess the damage and confirm what the problem was. After the van was evaluated by the dealership my mechanic installed a new engine.

I gathered all receipts for routine maintenance, intake manifold gasket, and engine replacement repairs and proceeded with arbitration through CAMVAP. The hearing was held at a local hotel and there was a GM representative, an arbitrator, my mechanic and myself in attendance. We were able to provide enough evidence from my mechanics testimony and copies of other testimonials off the Internet to support my claim. The arbitrator's decision was sent to me within two weeks and ruled in my favour. General Motors had to compensate me for the total cost of the gasket and engine replacement. Even though the van was considerably over the recognized warranty the arbitrator believed that the gasket was defective from the time of purchase and was directly related to the engine failure. The only options I had were to proceed with arbitration or go to small claims court. There is no fee for arbitration but you can only try one method...if arbitration fails you cannot then go to small claims.

Apparently the new engine has the same type of gasket as the original one and I am just waiting for the same problems to occur. In the meantime I am currently looking for a new vehicle and definitely not a GM with a 3.4 L engine.

Note: See Secret Warranties 1995–2004 for copies of incriminating GM service bulletins.

Additionally, owners report a high number of automatic transmission failures and clunking; leaking and malfunctioning AC systems (mainly because of defective AC modules); poor engine performance and myriad electrical shorts, requiring the early replacement of various computer modules; rack-and-pinion steering failure; weak shocks; excessive front brake pad wear; warping rotors; seizure of the rear brake calipers; rear brake/wheel lock-up; leaking oil pan; and suspension struts.

Other deficiencies: The instruments and steering column shake when the car is travelling over uneven road surfaces; and lots of road and wind noise comes through the side windows, thanks to the inadequately soundproofed chassis. Seating isn't very comfortable because of the lack of support caused by low-density foam, knees-in-your-face low seating, and the ramrod-straight rear backrest. The ride is acceptable with a light load, but when fully loaded, the car's back end sags and the ride deteriorates. Owners report that 3.8L engines won't continue running after a cold start, the exhaust system booms, 3T40 automatic transmissions may have faulty Reverse gears, and the instrument panel may pop or creak.

On one hand, 2002–04 models do have a nice array of standard features; a good choice of powertrains that includes a supercharged 3.8L engine; a comfortable ride; and an easily accessed and roomy interior. On the other hand, they continue to have noisy engines at high speeds; rear seating that's uncomfortable for three; bland styling; and obstructed rear visibility because of a high-tail rear end. Most importantly, these cars are hobbled by a chintzy powertrain warranty that's clearly insufficient, knowing GM's past engine and transmission deficiencies. Imagine having to pay $3,000–$5,000 for a new engine or transmission just as your used-car "bargain" passes its fifth year.

Intrigue

Strikingly similar to the Alero, the Oldsmobile Intrigue is GM's replacement for the Cutlass Supreme and represents the most refined iteration of the W-body shared by the Century, Grand Prix, Lumina, and Regal. It's more luxurious than the Lumina and performs as well as the Accord, Camry, and Maxima. Its rigid chassis has fewer shakes and rattles than are found on GM's other models, and its 3.8L engine provides lots of low-end grunt but lacks the top-end power that makes the Japanese competition so much fun to toss around. '99 versions got a torquier

3.5L V6 coupled with standard traction control. This engine's a bit more refined, but it's still not smooth, and the automatic transmission still struggles to get past its first two gears. Year 2001 models dropped standard traction control and added automatic headlights.

1995–2004 Impala, Lumina, and Monte Carlo

These models are popular two- and four-door versions of Chevy's "large" mid-sized cars, featuring standard dual airbags, ABS, and 160-hp V6 power. The Monte Carlo was formerly sold as the Lumina Z34. Powertrain enhancements have increased horsepower and fuel efficiency. Each car has been given a slightly different appearance and a distinct personality. A 3.1L V6 is the standard engine, a standard 3.4L 210-hp V6 powers the coupe and is optional with the LS Lumina, and a 3.8L V6 equips the more upscale versions. The 2004 SS came with a supercharged 3.8L engine.

VEHICLE HISTORY: 1996—The 3.4L got a slight horsepower boost, and all-disc braking was adopted on the Monte Carlo Z34 and upscale versions of the LS. **1997**—A better-performing transmission, mated to the 3.4L engine, gives smoother shifts. **1998–99**—Few changes, except for the addition of the 3.8L V6 to the Monte Carlo Z34 and Lumina LTZ. *Bonneville:* **1992**—A slight restyling and plastic front fenders. **1994**—Dual airbags and more SSE features. **1995**—A 205-hp 3.8L engine. **1996**—A more powerful supercharged engine and restyled front and rear ends. **2000**—Restyled similarly to the Buick LeSabre, with a larger wheelbase and longer platform, but with less headroom. Also new this year: standard front seat side-impact airbags, four-wheel disc ABS brakes, a tire-inflation monitor, and an anti-skid system (SSEi). **2001**—SLE given standard traction control. **2003**—Revised bucket seats. **2004**—Arrival of a 275-hp V8 and the dropping of the 240-hp V6. *Impala:* **2001**—Standard OnStar with the LS and emergency inside trunk release on all. **2002**—Standard dual-zone climate controls and a cassette player. **2003**—OnStar and a driver-side airbag become optional. **2004**—A new SS model equipped with a 240-hp supercharged V6. *Lumina:* **2000**—Lumina's standard 3.1L engine got a bit more torque and a small horsepower boost, in addition to more standard equipment. This was the Lumina's last year before it was replaced by the Impala. But the Monte Carlo soldiered on, having been reworked and brought out on the Impala platform for 2000. It was carried over unchanged. *Malibu:* **1998**—Aluminum wheels. **1999**—Automatic, brighter headlights and tail lights and added soundproofing. **2000**—A restyled front end and no more four-cylinder engine. **2001**—Standard power door locks and defogger and an improved sound system and remote keyless entry. **2002**—A CD player and floormats. **2003**—ABS becomes optional. **2004**—Completely redesigned. The sedan uses Saab's 9-3 platform and a base 145-hp four-cylinder engine (a 200-hp V6 comes with the LS and LT) hooked to a four-speed automatic transmission. A Maxx hatchback uses the same power-train, but adds a sliding rear seat, with a reclining seatback, a cargo cover that transforms into a tailgate table, a glass skylight, 4-wheel disc brakes, and head-protecting curtain side airbags. *Monte Carlo*: **2001**—Standard driver-side airbag, traction control, OnStar, and emergency inside trunk release. **2002**—Standard dual-zone climate controls and a rear seat centre shoulder belt. **2003**—Remote keyless entry for the LS. **2004**—A supercharged 3.8L SS.

Except for the automatic transmission upgrade, owners report that newer versions still have some of the same shortcomings seen on earlier front-drive models. For example, in spite of some noise reduction progress, body construction is still below par, with loose door panel mouldings, poorly-fitted door fabric, and misaligned panels. Other common problems: fuel pump whistling, frequent stalling, vague steering, premature paint peeling on the hood and trunk, heavy accumulation of hard-to-remove brake dust inside the honeycomb-design wheels, and front tires that scrape the fenders when the wheel is turned. Despite its own recent redesign, the 3.1L engine isn't entirely problem-free. Faulty intake manifold gaskets (a chronic problem affecting the entire model lineup; see "Secret Warranties/Internal Bulletins/Service Tips"), electronic fuel-injection systems, and engine controls have created many problems for GM owners. The 4-speed automatic transmission still has some bugs. The front brakes wear quickly, as do the MacPherson struts and shock absorbers. Steering assemblies tend to fail prematurely. The electrical system is temperamental. The sunroof motor is failure prone. Owners report water leaks from the front windshield. Front-end squeaks may require the replacement of the exhaust manifold pipe springs with dampers.

1997–2004 Cutlass and Malibu

These two front-drive, medium-sized sedans are slotted in between the Cavalier and Lumina in both size and price. They are boringly-styled cars that use a rigid body structure to cut down on noise and improve handling. Standard mechanicals include a 2.4L twin-cam 4-cylinder engine or an optional 3.1L V6. There's plenty of passenger and luggage space. Although headroom is tight, the Malibu can carry three rear passengers and gives much more legroom than either the Cavalier or Lumina. 1998 was the Cutlass' last model year, while its Malibu twin continues on.

Other points to consider: The base 4-cylinder is loud, handling isn't on par with the Japanese competition, there's lots of body lean in turns, outside mirrors are too small, there's no traction control, and the ignition switch is mounted on the dash (a throwback to your dad's Oldsmobile).

In model year 2004, there are two vehicles thought of as Malibu. The "old" Malibu (N Body) was called Malibu through model year 2003. In 2004, it was renamed the Classic. The "new" Malibu (Z Body) is called Malibu in 2004. The redesigned 2004 Malibu's engine feels underpowered for highway cruising, with constant shifting with the four-cylinder hooked to the four-speed automatic transmission (only set-up available). Good handling, but the ride is a bit firm. Its tires don't inspire confidence. Interior seating is okay up front, but knees-to-chin in the rear. Maxx version excels at providing rear seating comfort.

In addition to the generic front-drive problems listed previously, owners also report the following: early failure of the intake manifold gasket (see "Secret Warranties/Internal Bulletins/Service Tips"); fuel-injector deposits that cause chronic stalling, poor idling, or hard starts; excessive vibration at any speed; the transmission doesn't lock when the key is in the accessory position; steering is very loose; backfires caused by defective computer modules; premature suspension strut failures (vehicle bottoms out with four or more passengers aboard); excessive AC noise; and the high-beam light switch fails intermittently.

 **Safety Summary**

All models/years: Airbag failed to deploy. • Sudden engine failure or overheating (faulty intake manifold). • Vehicle suddenly accelerates or stalls in traffic. • Brake failures. • Frequent loss of braking and premature rotor warpage and pad wearout. • Vehicle rolls downhill when parked on an incline. • Dash reflection in the windshield obstructs view. • Automatic trunk flies up and falls down on one's head. • Improper headlight illumination. • Horn is difficult to activate because of the hand pressure required. **1998**—Sudden acceleration; faulty fuel pressure regulator suspected. • Power seat puts occupant too close to airbag. • Headrest can't be raised high enough for someone over six feet tall. • Engine hesitates when accelerating. • Flexible hose line from fuel pump rests against sharp metal edge of the heat shield. • Trunk popped open while driving. **1998–99**—Automatic transmission and electrical system failures. **2000–01**—Sudden electrical shutdown. • Exhaust/gas fumes in the interior. • Automatic transmission failure. • Hard, noisy shifting. • Excessive vehicle vibration while underway. • Front control arm breakage. • Blurred windshield. • Tires mounted on aluminum wheels tend to leak air. • Vehicle wanders or "floats" on the highway. • Heater gives out insufficient heat. • Headlight switch overheats. *Bonneville*: **2000–01**—Battery located in the back of the rear seat went bad, causing sulfuric acid fumes to escape into the passenger compartment, making passengers ill. • Weak spring design allowed trunk lid to fall on person's head, causing injury. **2002**—Engine mount failure causes excessive vibration. • Tilt steering locks. • Outside rear-view mirror vibration. • Loose head restraints. **2003**—Defogger was activated and fire ignited. • Fire erupted in the rear deck speaker. • Shifter can be moved without key in the ignition or brakes applied. *Impala*: **2003**—Frequent complaints of dash area and engine compartment fires. • Front harness wires overheat; excessive current load from fuel pump may burn the ignition block wire terminal; inhalation injuries caused by the melting of the wiring harness plastic. • Electrically heated seat burned the driver's back. • The connection that goes to the brake pedal piston collapsed, causing total brake failure. • Chronic stalling; engine sputters, hesitates; Service Engine and battery lights come on (dealer unable to correct problem). • When traction control is activated, wheel slip computer is also activated and security system kills the engine and prevents it from being restarted. • Driver's side wheel fell off. • Vehicle jerks when passing over rough pavement. • Car rolls back at a stop. • Excessive steering wheel vibration. • Fuel sloshes in tank when accelerating or stopping. • Left and right control arm, lower control arm, ball joint, and steering failure. • AC refrigerant leaks into car interior. • Driver's seat adjuster failed, causing seat to suddenly move backward, causing loss of vehicle control. • The rubber seal on the windows, which sometimes acts as a squeegee when lowering and raising the window, has been replaced with a new design, which allows road salt to enter and short-circuit the window mechanism. • Front driver's side windshield wiper doesn't clean the windshield completely; poor design allows dirty windshield washer fluid to be deflected off the windshield and cuts the view out of the side windows. • A hazy film collects on the inside of all the windows (usually a sign of intake manifold gasket failure). **2004**—Crankshaft position sensor failures cause vehicle to stall and not restart. • Vehicle can be shifted out of Park without applying the brakes. • Vehicle hydroplanes easily, wanders all over the road, and jerks to one side when braking. • Steering wheel suddenly jerked to one side and resisted driver's pull in the other direction. • Unreliable steering assembly replaced twice. • Defective front-end suspension. • Lights dim when power windows are raised or lowered. • Poorly-designed daytime running lights blind oncoming drivers. • Fuel tank failures. • Moisture in headlights reduces illumination (dealer says defect affects all Impalas). • Static electricity shocks occupants as they leave the vehicle. *LeSabre*: **2000–01**—Under-hood fire erupted as driver was parking car. • When the fuel tank is full, fuel leaks from the top. • False airbag deployment injured driver. • Airbag deployment when key inserted into the ignition. • Car stalled because fuel lines leaked. • Cruise control cable disconnects from cruise control module, jamming the accelerator cable to full throttle. • Accelerator cable popped out of its bracket, causing vehicle to go to full throttle. • Brake pedal went all the way to the floor because of missing brake shaft retainer clip. • When applying brakes, pedal becomes very hard, resulting in extended stopping distance. • Sudden steering loss. • Excessive highway wander. • Shoulder belt crosses at driver's neck. • Hard-to-read speedometer. • Difficulty seeing dashboard controls because of dash-top design. • ABS and service light come on for no reason. • Intermittent windshield wiper failure. • Horn is hard to operate, unless driver balls her hand into a fist and pounds on it. • Water leaks into interior through the dash. • Headlight design creates a shadow, impeding visibility. **2003**—Engine surging while driving on the highway. • Brake pedal goes almost to the floor without stopping the vehicle. **2004**—Wipers fail intermittently. • Uncomfortable seats are too slippery. • Headlight failure. • Excessive vibration, especially when car is put into Reverse. *Monte Carlo*: **1995–2001**—Under-hood fires. • Airbag deployment caused driver's shirt to catch on fire. • Side airbag flap material falls off, leaving a large hole. • Side airbag falls out of its mounting. • Extremely poor wet traction. • Although GM TSB asks dealers to re-weld the subframe engine cradle, owners say that the fix isn't effective. • Early fuel pump and water pump failures. • Dash gauges go haywire from chronic electrical shorts. • Check Engine, ABS, and airbag lights stay lit despite dealers' best troubleshooting attempts. • Shoulder belt crosses at neck and seat belts don't retract properly. • Horn is hard to access. **2002**—Fire ignited from overheated seat heater. • Sudden steering loss; excessive steering effort required. • Vehicle rolls back on an incline. • Excessive brake pulsation. • Constant headlight flickering. **2003**—Fire ignited in the trunk area. • Engine cradle mounting welds came apart from the steering gear. • Hard shifting. • Automatic transmission slips in First gear because of faulty pressure valve. • Sudden loss of braking. • Because brake pedal sits a bit higher than it would on other makes, foot can easily slip under the pedal. • Bent stabilizer bar. • Driver and passenger seat belts tighten up progressively to the point where they are extremely uncomfortable. • Horn takes excessive force to activate; malfunctions in the winter. • Tail light failures. • Sunroof cracks. • Rear ground effects moulding separates from the rest of the body. **2004**—Mushy brakes; pedal went to the floor when brakes were applied. • Warped dash and radio face gets extremely hot.

Secret Warranties/Internal Bulletins/Service Tips

All models/years: Keep in mind that some of the following service bulletins may apply to more than one model and to subsequent model years. • Reverse servo cover seal leak (transmission). **All models: 1993–2003**—AC-induced odours can be eliminated by using a coil coating kit. • A rotten-egg odour coming from the exhaust is probably caused by a malfunctioning catalytic converter (covered by the emissions warranty). • Paint delamination, peeling, or fading (see Part Two "Paint and Body Defects," pages 71–75). **1993–2004**—TSB #01-08-42-001A covers the causes and remedies for moisture in the headlights. **1995–2001**—Troubleshooting engine oil pan leaks. **1995–2004**—Five GM service bulletins confirm a pattern of engine intake manifold gasket defects, which are covered by a 6-year/100,000 km secret warranty:

ENGINE COOLANT – CONSUMPTION/LEAK

BULLETIN NO: 01-06-01-007A   DATE: JULY 2001

SUBJECT: Engine Coolant Consumption or Coolant Leak (Inspect For Material Degradation/Replace Intake Manifolds)

1995–97 Buick Riviera; 1995–98 Buick LeSabre, Park Avenue; 1996–98 Buick Regal; 1998 Chevrolet Lumina, Monte Carlo; 1995–96 Oldsmobile Ninety-Eight; 1995–98 Oldsmobile Eighty-Eight; 1998 Oldsmobile Intrigue; 1995–98 Pontiac Bonneville; 1997–98 Pontiac Grand Prix
with 3.8L Engine (VIN K - RPO L36)

CONDITION: Some owners may comment on excessive engine coolant consumption, or an engine coolant leak near or under the throttle body area of the upper intake manifold.
CAUSE: Upper intake manifold composite material may degrade around the EGR stove pipe and could result in an internal or external coolant leak.
CORRECTION: Follow the upper intake manifold removal instructions found in the Engine Unit Repair Section of the Service Information Manual.

Here's a second "smoking gun" GM internal service bulletin admitting to poor-quality engine intake manifolds. Notice that this defect has existed over ten model years and imagine how many owners have paid thousands of dollars to fix this problem, which GM admits here is clearly its own fault (see following bulletin).

ENGINE OIL OR COOLANT LEAK

BULLETIN NO: 03-06-01-010A

DATE: APRIL 2003

Engine oil or coolant leak
(install new intake manifold gasket)

2000–2003 Buick Century; 2002–03 Buick Rendezvous; 1996 Chevrolet Lumina APV; 1997–2003 Chevrolet Venture; 1999–2001 Chevrolet Lumina; 1999–2003 Chevrolet Malibu, Monte Carlo; 2000–2003 Chevrolet Impala; 1996–2003 Oldsmobile Silhouette; 1999 Oldsmobile Cutlass; 1999–2003 Oldsmobile Alero; 1996–99 Pontiac Trans Sport; 1999–2003 Pontiac Grand Am; 2000–03 Pontiac Grand Prix, Montana
2001–03 Pontiac Aztek with 3.1L or 3.4L V6 engine (VINs J, E - RPOs LGB, LA1)

CONDITION: Some owners may comment on an apparent oil or coolant leak. Additionally, the comments may range from spots on the driveway to having to add fluids.
CAUSE: Intake manifold may be leaking allowing coolant, oil or both to leak from the engine.
CORRECTION: Install a new-design intake manifold gasket. The material used in the gasket has been changed in order to improve the sealing qualities of the gasket. When replacing the gasket, the intake manifold bolts must also be replaced and torqued to a revised specification The new bolts will come with a pre-applied threadlocker on them.

In service bulletin 03034, GM admits to a special "voluntary" program to refund engine repair costs. Although referred to by GM as a "recall," this free repair isn't under Transport Canada's jurisdiction and isn't part of the safety recall process, which usually has an 8-year repair period with notification sent out by the automaker. It is important to note that GM takes responsibility for this engine failure and specifically includes Canadian owners in retroactive payouts to independent repair agencies, also promising to offer free courtesy transportation.

All of the above benefits should be cited whenever an extended or "goodwill" warranty is offered by any automaker, or whenever a claim is filed in small claims court.

The fourth GM bulletin, No. 03-06-01-016, lists several of the symptoms indicating an intake manifold gasket failure and under what conditions a more thorough repair should be undertaken. The nuts are also listed as having been upgraded for better retention; another liability admission by GM.

CUSTOMER SATISFACTION PROGRAM ENGINE COOLANT LEAK

PROGRAM NO: 03034   DATE: JULY 7, 2003

All 2000–2002 and Certain 2003 Chevrolet Impala, Monte Carlo; Pontiac Grand Prix, Bonneville; and BuickRegal, LeSabre, Park Avenue Equipped with 3.8L V6 Engine.

THIS RECALL IS IN EFFECT UNTIL JULY 31, 2005.

CONDITION General Motors has decided that all 2000-2002 and certain 2003 Chevrolet Impala, Monte Carlo; Pontiac Grand Prix, Bonneville; and Buick Regal, LeSabre, Park Avenue model vehicles equipped with 3.8L (RPO L36–VIN Code K) engines, may have a condition in which engine coolant may leak at the upper intake manifold throttle body gasket, or at the upper intake manifold to lower intake manifold gasket. This condition may result in a low engine coolant level and higher engine operating temperatures.

CORRECTION Dealers are to replace the three throttle body fastener nuts and add cooling system sealant to the radiator tank.

VEHICLES Involved are all 2000-2002 Chevrolet Impala, Monte Carlo; Pontiac Grand Prix, Bonneville; and Buick Regal, LeSabre, Park Avenue model vehicles equipped with 3.8L (RPO L36–VIN Code K) engines

CUSTOMER REIMBURSEMENT FOR CANADA

All customer requests for reimbursement of previously paid coolant leaks that were repaired by replacing the upper intake manifold/gasket, throttle body nuts or throttle body gasket are to be submitted by July 31,2004. All reasonable customer paid receipts should be considered for reimbursement. The amount to be reimbursed will be limited to the amount the repair would have cost if completed by an authorized General Motors dealer.

Dealers are to ensure that these customers understand that shuttle service or some other form of courtesy transportation is available and will be provided at no charge. Dealers should refer to the General Motors Service Policies and Procedures Manual for Courtesy Transportation guidelines.

GENERAL MOTORS PRODUCT PROGRAM CUSTOMER REIMBURSEMENT PROCEDURE

If you have paid to have this condition corrected by replacing the upper intake manifold/gasket, throttle body nuts, or throttle body gasket before August 8, 2003, you may be eligible to receive reimbursement. Requests for reimbursement may include parts, labor, fees and taxes. Reimbursement may be limited to the amount the repair would have cost if completed by an authorized General Motors dealer. Your claim will be acted upon within 60 days of receipt. Letters will be sent to known owners of record located within areas covered by the US National Traffic and Motor Vehicle Safety Act. For owners outside these areas, dealers should notify customers using the attached suggested dealer letter.

In the most recent bulletin, No. 04-06-01-017, GM says that its revised intake manifold gasket is more "robust," and adds 2004 models to the afflicted models list. This is another admission of liability under the implied warranty statutes. Note: Internet references include *www.gmtechlink.com* (Dutch, English, French, and Spanish text available); *www.talkaboutautos.com/group/alt.autos.chevrolet. malibu/messages/5867.html; www.impalasuperstore.com/naisso/forum2002/topic. asp?TOPIC_ID=19173𤿱 and www.alldatapro.com.*

LOSS OF COOLANT, MILKY COLORED OIL

BULLETIN NO: 03-06-01-016   DATE: MAY 21, 2003

2000–2003 LeSabre, ParkAvenue, Regal; 2000–2003 Chevrolet Impala, Monte Carlo; 2000–2003 Bonneville; 2000–2003; Grand Prix with 3.8L V6 Engine.

CONDITION: Some owners may comment on a loss of coolant, coolant odor, having to add coolant or a milky substance on either the oil dipstick or oil fill cap. Additionally, owners may indicate that there are signs of coolant loss left on the ground where the vehicle is normally parked.

CAUSE: Condition may be due to coolant leaking past intermediate intake or throttle body gaskets.

CORRECTION: The upper intake manifold should not be replaced for a coolant leak condition, unless a rare instance of physical damage is found. Even if the throttle body surface shows a slight warpage, the upper intake should not be replaced unless a drivability concern is noted or a relevant engine DTC, such as a code for an unmetered air leak, is set and the upper intake manifold can clearly be shown as the cause of the concern.

Thoroughly check for any external leaks. If no external leaks are found, then replace the intermediate intake manifold gasket and the throttle body gasket. When changing the throttle body gasket, the nuts that retain the throttle body should be replaced with a new design that improves torque retention. Medium strength thread locker should be applied to the studs before installing the new nuts.

REDESIGNED UPPER INTAKE MANIFOLD AND GASKETS

BULLETIN NO: 04-06-01-017   DATE: MAY 26, 2004

1995–1997 Riviera; 1995–2004 Park Avenue; 1996–2004 Regal; 1997–2004 LeSabre; 1998–1999 Lumina; 1998–2004 Monte Carlo; 2000–2004 Impala;
1995–1996 Ninety-Eight; 1995–1999 Eighty-Eight; 1998-1999 Intrigue;
1995–2004 Bonneville; 1997–2003 Grand Prix with 3.8L V6 Engine

New upper intake manifold and gasket kits have been released. These new kits will provide the dealer with the ability to get exactly what is necessary for a correct repair. In addition some of the gaskets have been updated to a more robust design.

Don't break out the champagne yet over GM's apparent recognition of its engine defects. This 2003 LeSabre owner says GM's intake manifold fix is no fix at all:

> I recently received a letter from GM stating that there may be a problem with coolant leaks around gaskets at the upper intake manifold or at the lower intake manifold which might "cause high engine temperatures." The letter says it is a "voluntary customer satisfaction program." The suggested fix is to take the vehicle in to the local dealer and have them

change some of the fasteners and then "add cooling system sealant" to the radiator. It seems to me that putting cooling system sealant in a brand new car (and thus reducing the life of the radiator) is an unacceptable fix for a possible gasket problem.

1997–98—A rough-running engine may be fixed by changing the plug wires. **1997–99**—A low-speed steering shudder or vibration may be corrected by replacing the steering pressure and return lines with revised "tuned" hoses. • Front disc pads have been upgraded to reduce brake squeal. • A shaking sensation at cruising speed may be fixed by replacing the transmission mount. **1997–2000**—Front disc brake pulsation will be corrected by installing upgraded pads and rotors, says TSB #00-05-23-002. • An automatic transmission oil leak can be fixed by installing an upgraded part. **1998**—A wet right rear floor signals the need to reseal the stationary glass area. • Engine runs rough. • Power-steering shudder and vibration. • Front suspension scrunch/pop. • Reducing AC odours. • Inaccurate speedometer. **1998–99**—Power-steering shudder/vibration may be fixed by replacing the pressure pipe/hose assembly. **1999–2000**—No Third and Fourth gear may mean the direct clutch piston assembly needs to be replaced. • An engine that runs hot, overheats, or loses coolant may only need an upgraded radiator cap (check this before authorizing any expensive repairs). **1999–2004**—Poor performance, slipping transmission. **2000–01**—TSB #01-06-01-005 allows for free 3.1L engine piston replacement to cure an engine ticking noise. • Reduced AC performance; AC makes a tick-tock noise. • Eliminating an air vent whistling noise or a steering vibration, shudder, or moan. **2001**—Remedies for delayed automatic transmission shifts (see bulletin found in Century "Secret Warranties"). **2001–02**—Poor engine performance and erratic shifting. • Intermittent no-start. **2001–04**—Erratic shifting, slipping transmission. **2001–05**—Harsh 1–2 upshifts. **2004**—Noisy blower motor. *Cutlass* and *Malibu*: **1997–99**—Front disc brake pulsation will be corrected by installing upgraded pads and rotors, says TSB #00-05-23-002. **1997–2003**—Inoperative tail lights due to water intrusion. • Automatic transmission flaring. **1999–2002**—Troubleshooting tips for plugging water leaks into the trunk and interior. **2000–01**—Faulty fuel gauge. **2002**—Dash rattling correction. **2003**—Firm shifts, no downshifts, shudder. **2004**—Noisy steering column and lack of steering assist. • Wind noise caused by the transmission shift cable. • Ignition key hard to remove in cold weather. • Instrument panel rattle or buzz.

A/T – OIL LEAK FROM VENT
BULLETIN NO: 01-07-30-032A   **DATE:** JAN. 2002

SUBJECT: Transmission Oil Leaking From Transmission Vent (Replace Transmission Case Cover Gasket/Channel Plate Gasket With New Design Gasket)

1997–99 Buick Riviera; 1997–2001 Buick Park Avenue; 1998–2001 Buick LeSabre; 1999–2001 Buick Regal; 2000–01 Buick Century; 1997–2001 Chevrolet Lumina, Monte Carlo; 1999–2001 Chevrolet Venture; 2000–01 Chevrolet Impala; 1997–99 Oldsmobile Eighty Eight; 1998–2001 Oldsmobile Intrigue; 1999–2001 Oldsmobile Silhouette; 2001 Oldsmobile Aurora (with 3.5L Engine); 1997–2001 Pontiac Bonneville, Grand Prix; 1999–2001 Pontiac Montana; With Hydra-Matic 4T65-E Automatic Transmission (RPOs MN3, MN7, M15, M76).

BONNEVILLE, CUTLASS, CUTLASS SUPREME, DELTA 88, GRAND PRIX, IMPALA, INTRIGUE, LESABRE, LUMINA, MALIBU, MONTE CARLO, REGAL PROFILE

	1996	1997	1998	1999	2000	2001	2002	2003	2004
Cost Price ($)									
Bonneville	29,440	31,175	33,255	29,000	30,740	32,065	32,365	33,430	34,345
Cutlass Supreme	25,285	26,355	—	—	—	—	—	—	—
Delta 88 LSS	30,190	32,185	32,950	32,515	—	—	—	—	—
Grand Prix	23,940	26,305	26,035	27,489	28,050	28,110	28,050	28,277	28,125
Impala	30,675	—	—	—	24,595	24,490	24,875	26,020	26,810
Intrigue	—	—	27,998	27,994	28,365	28,450	28,365	—	—
LeSabre	29,560	32,370	33,100	28,845	30,465	32,120	32,960	33,720	33,935
Lumina	21,455	22,340	22,980	23,074	—	—	—	—	—
Malibu	—	19,995	20,595	20,895	22,050	22,495	22,760	22,980	22,370
Malibu Maxx	—	—	—	—	—	—	—	—	26,320
Monte Carlo	23,625	24,275	24,895	24,715	26,090	26,165	26,525	27,620	28,200
Regal	25,035	27,795	28,410	27,695	29,120	28,895	29,080	29,980	29,975
Used Values ($)									
Bonneville ▲	4,500	5,500	7,000	9,500	10,500	13,000	17,000	20,000	23,000
Bonneville ▼	3,500	4,500	6,000	8,000	9,000	12,000	15,500	18,500	22,000
Cutlass Supreme ▲	3,500	4,500	—	—	—	—	—	—	—
Cutlass Supreme ▼	2,500	3,500	—	—	—	—	—	—	—
Delta 88 LSS ▲	4,500	5,500	7,000	9,000	—	—	—	—	—
Delta 88 LSS ▼	3,500	4,500	5,500	8,000	—	—	—	—	—
Grand Prix ▲	4,000	5,000	6,500	8,500	10,000	12,000	14,500	18,000	20,500
Grand Prix ▼	3,000	4,000	5,000	7,000	8,500	10,500	13,000	16,500	19,000
Impala ▲	—	—	—	—	9,000	11,000	13,000	15,000	18,000
Impala ▼	—	—	—	—	7,500	9,500	11,500	13,500	16,500
Intrigue ▲	—	—	6,500	8,000	9,500	12,000	14,500	—	—
Intrigue ▼	—	—	5,500	6,500	7,500	10,500	13,000	—	—
LeSabre ▲	4,500	6,000	7,500	9,500	11,500	13,500	17,000	20,000	22,500
LeSabre ▼	4,000	5,000	6,500	8,500	10,000	12,000	15,500	18,500	21,000
Lumina ▲	2,500	3,500	5,000	6,500	—	—	—	—	—
Lumina ▼	2,000	3,000	4,000	5,000	—	—	—	—	—
Malibu ▲	—	3,500	4,500	5,500	6,500	8,000	10,500	12,500	14,500
Malibu ▼	—	3,000	3,500	4,500	5,500	6,500	9,500	11,000	13,500
Malibu Maxx ▲	—	—	—	—	—	—	—	—	17,000
Malibu Maxx ▼	—	—	—	—	—	—	—	—	15,500
Monte Carlo ▲	4,000	5,000	6,500	7,500	9,500	12,000	14,000	16,500	19,500
Monte Carlo ▼	3,000	4,000	5,500	6,500	8,000	10,500	12,500	15,000	18,000
Regal ▲	3,500	4,500	6,500	7,500	9,500	12,000	14,500	18,000	21,000
Regal ▼	3,000	4,000	5,500	6,500	8,500	11,000	13,000	16,500	19,000

Reliability	2	2	2	3	3	3	3	3	3
Crash Safety (F)									
Bonneville 4d	5	5	5	—	—	4	4	4	4
Cutlass 4d	—	—	—	4	4	—	—	—	—
Cutlass Supreme 2d	4	—	—	—	—	—	—	—	—
Delta 88 4d	4	—	—	—	—	—	—	—	—
Grand Prix 4d	—	4	—	—	—	4	4	4	3
Impala	—	—	—	—	5	5	5	5	5
Intrigue	—	—	4	4	4	—	—	—	—
LeSabre 2d	4	—	—	—	—	—	—	—	—
LeSabre 4d	—	4	4	4	—	—	4	4	4
Lumina 4d	5	5	4	4	4	4	—	—	—
Malibu	—	4	4	4	4	4	4	4	4
Monte Carlo	4	4	—	—	—	5	5	—	5
Regal 2d	4	—	—	—	—	—	—	—	—
Regal 4d	—	—	—	4	4	4	4	4	4
Side									
Bonneville 4d	—	—	—	—	—	4	4	4	4
Grand Prix	—	—	—	—	—	—	2	2	3
Impala	—	—	—	—	4	4	4	4	4
Intrigue	—	—	—	—	—	3	3	—	—
LeSabre 4d	—	—	3	3	4	4	4	4	4
Lumina	—	4	4	4	4	4	—	—	—
Malibu	—	1	1	1	2	2	3	3	4
Monte Carlo	4	4	—	—	—	3	3	—	3
Regal 4d	—	—	3	3	3	3	3	3	3
Head Restraints									
Bonneville	—	1	—	1	5	5	5	1	1
Cutlass	—	1	—	1	—	—	—	—	—
Cutlass Sup.	—	1	—	—	—	—	—	—	—
Grand Prix	—	—	—	—	—	—	—	3	1
Intrigue	—	—	—	1	—	1	1	—	—
LeSabre 4d	—	1	—	1	—	—	—	1	1
Lumina	—	1	—	1	—	—	—	—	—
Malibu	—	2	—	2	—	2	2	2	3
Malibu Classic	—	—	—	—	—	—	—	1	1
Monte Carlo	—	1	—	1	—	2	2	2	2
Regal 4d	—	—	—	1	—	1	1	1	1
Offset									
Bonneville 4d	—	—	—	—	5	5	5	5	5
Cutlass 4d	—	3	3	3	—	—	—	—	—
Grand Prix 4d	—	3	3	3	3	3	3	3	—
Impala	—	—	—	—	5	5	5	5	5
Intrigue	—	—	3	3	3	3	3	—	—

All ratings on a numbered scale where 5 is good and 1 is bad. See pages 100–101 for a more detailed description.

LeSabre 4d	—	—	—	—	⑤	⑤	⑤	⑤	⑤
Lumina 4d	⑤	⑤	⑤	⑤	⑤	⑤	—	—	⑤
Malibu	—	—	—	—	—	—	—	③	⑤
Malibu/Classic	—	③	③	③	③	③	③	③	③
Regal 4d	—	③	③	③	③	③	③	③	③
Rollover Resistance									
Bonneville	—	—	—	—	—	—	—	⑤	⑤
Grand Prix	—	—	—	—	—	—	—	④	④
Impala	—	—	—	—	—	④	④	④	④
LeSabre	—	—	—	—	—	—	—	⑤	⑤
Lumina 4d	—	—	—	—	—	④	—	—	—
Malibu	—	—	—	—	—	—	④	④	④
Monte Carlo	—	—	—	—	—	—	—	—	④
Regal	—	—	—	—	—	—	—	④	④

CENTURY, CIERA ★★★

RATING: Average (1998–2004); Below Average (1997); Not Recommended (1982–96). With the older models, the same failure-prone components were used year after year. The 1996 Century isn't in the same league as the revised 1997 version, which adopted the W-platform used by the Chevrolet Lumina, Pontiac Grand Prix, and 1998 Oldsmobile Intrigue. The '97 is more refined, but also more glitch-ridden during the first year of its redesign. A 1996 Ciera is cheaper, but you won't have the important mechanical and body upgrades offered by its 1998 replacement, the '98 Oldsmobile Cutlass. The new Cutlass is an upgraded mid-sized sedan similar to the new Malibu (be careful not to confuse the new Cutlass with the Cutlass Supreme, a 10-year-old model that was replaced by the Intrigue, which is equipped like the Century). **Maintenance/Repair costs:** Higher than average, but repairs aren't dealer dependent. **Parts:** Higher-than-average cost (independent suppliers sell for much less), but not hard to find. Nevertheless, don't even think about buying one of these front-drives without a 3- to 5-year comprehensive warranty. **Extended warranty:** Yes, for the powertrain. **Best alternatives:** Acura Integra; GM Cavalier or Sunfire (Sunbird); Honda Accord; Hyundai Elantra wagon, Sonata, or Tiburon; Mazda 626 or Protegé; Nissan Sentra or Stanza; and Toyota Camry. **Online help:** Owner reports and service bulletins can be found at *www.autosafety. org/autodefects.html*, or you can use Google to search for GM paint delamination, engine piston slapping, or manifold defects.

 ## Strengths and Weaknesses

The Century and Ciera were always outclassed by the competition because of their lack of high-quality components and their less-than-fresh styling. Nevertheless, these cars have always been popular with fleet buyers and car rental agencies because they were useful as comfortable family sedans and wagons. Handling and other aspects of road performance varied considerably depending on the suspension and powertrain chosen. But overall reliability remained a constant: abysmally poor.

The 1988–96 models are particularly unreliable. The 2.5L 4-cylinder engine suffers from engine-block cracking and a host of other serious defects. The 2.8L V6 engine hasn't been durable either; it suffers from premature camshaft wear and leaky gaskets and seals, especially the intake manifold gasket, a problem carried over to GM's entire 2003 model lineup (see "Secret Warranties/Internal Bulletins/Service Tips" on pages 000–000). The 3-speed automatic transmission is weak and the 4-speed automatic frequently malfunctions. Temperamental and expensive-to-replace fuel systems (including the in-tank fuel pump) afflict all models/years, causing chronic stalling, hard starting, and poor fuel economy (use the emissions warranty as leverage to get compensation). Fuel system diagnosis and repair for the 3.0L V6 are difficult, and the electronic controls are often defective. Air conditioners frequently malfunction, and the cooling system is prone to leaks.

Prematurely worn power-steering assemblies are particularly commonplace. Brakes are weak and need frequent attention because of premature wear and dangerously rapid corrosion; front brake rotors warp easily; excessive pulsation is common; and rear brake drums often lock up, particularly when damp. Shock absorbers and springs wear out quickly. Rear wheel alignment should be checked often. Electric door locks frequently malfunction. Water leaks onto carpeting. Premature and extensive surface rust—caused by poor paint application, delamination, and defective materials—is common for all years. Far more disturbing are the scattered reports of severe undercarriage/suspension rusting, possibly making the vehicles unsafe to drive—and costing lots of money to correct, as this owner of a 1990 Century relates:

> Recently I was doing an oil change on my car and I noticed a small divot in the engine cradle (or subframe). I poked at it and put my finger right through it! I discovered that the cradle was rotted on both sides near the idler arm. The car is only eight years old and has only 112,000 km on it. I have had it into two collision repair places and they both said they have never seen a rotted engine cradle. One man has been in the business 25 years!

VEHICLE HISTORY: 1982–96—Early 125–150-hp V6 engines replaced by a 3.3L V6 in 1989. A failure-prone 4.3L diesel engine was carried over from 1982–85 (beware!). A 3.1L V6 came on the scene in 1994 along with a driver-side airbag and ABS. **1997**—Given a complete make-over that included the following: a spunkier 160-hp 3.1L V6 engine; gobs of room and trunk space (rivalling that of the Taurus, Concorde, Accord, and Camry); sleeker styling; a much quieter interior; and an upgraded, standard ABS system that produces less pedal pulsation. Engine noise was also reduced, although insufficient firewall insulation means a considerable amount of noise still gets into the interior. Other new features included upgraded door seals, steering-wheel-mounted radio controls, and additional heating ducts for rear passengers. **1998**—Reduced-force airbags. **1999**—Adoption of a revised ABS system, better traction control, and an enhanced suspension to reduce body roll. **2000**—Given a small horsepower boost to 175. **2003**—Given a minor face-lift and a freshened interior. **2004**—Standard four-wheel disc brakes.

On the downside, the post-'96 Century's engine intake manifold gaskets have a short lifespan (see preceding Bonneville, Grand Prix, *et al.* section), the speed-dependent power steering is too light and vague, and its suspension and handling are more tuned to comfort than to performance. The front air deflector shield has also been the object of many complaints. Its low placement causes the shield to hit the roadway whenever passing over a small dip or bump. Furthermore, the bumper pulls off when passing over parking blocks.

Overall reliability has improved a bit since the 1997 model changeover glitches were corrected. However, powertrain breakdowns are still commonplace, and fit and finish remain subpar, particularly when compared with the Japanese competition. The 2000–04 models aren't much improved. They continue to have premature engine head gasket failures, "piston slap" noise, early transmission breakdowns, electrical system and computer module malfunctions, and front and rear brakes that rust easily, wear out early, with discs that warp far too often. Shock absorbers and MacPherson struts wear out or leak prematurely. The power rack-and-pinion steering system degenerates quickly after three years and is characterized by chronic leaking. Poor body fit, particularly around the doors, leads to excessive wind noise and water leaks into the interior. Door locks also freeze up easily.

 Safety Summary

All models/years: Vehicle suddenly accelerates on its own. • Horn buttons difficult to access and depress because of their small size. • Dash reflection in windshield causes poor visibility. • Headlights provide poor visibility. • Head restraints won't stay in the raised position. **1998**—Idle surge after releasing brake because of faulty oxygen sensor. • Leaking lower intake manifold. • Engine oil pan leakage. • Chronic stalling. • Transmission shifts erratically. • Transmission hard to put into Reverse; faulty gearshift lever. • Sudden loss of electrical power. • Climate control switch failures. • Excessive brake vibrations. • Headlight switch failure. • Windshield wiper arm failures. • Water leaks into trunk. • Horn blows on its own when car is not running. **1999**—Engine fire upon start-up. • Chronic engine hesitation when accelerating or changing gears. • Cruise control failed to disengage. • Premature transmission failure: Won't go into Reverse; shift lever hangs up; Drive gear won't hold vehicle when stopped on an incline. • Seat belt trapped child around waist; child had to be cut free. • Front right window suddenly exploded. • Tire jack won't hold vehicle's weight. **2000**—Engine replaced twice. • Transmission has a tendency to shift often, whether it's necessary or not. • If vehicle is driven with the windows down, there is a loud, shaking noise and the vehicle vibrates violently. • Steering wheel heats up when the radio and headlights are on. • Driver's seat leans to the side. • Large head restraints block vision. • Low beams don't illuminate the highway adequately; the light spreads only to the side end of the front fender, resulting in poor visibility. • Air scoop/spoiler hits or scrapes the ground. • If vehicle is parked on uneven ground, the doors stick because of body flexing. • Driver-side window suddenly exploded, as from decompression, while underway. • Wipers can't be aligned. **2001**—Brakes failed. • Transmission won't hold vehicle parked on an incline. • Cannot drive car with rear windows down because the air pressure hurts eardrums. **2002**—Sun visors are hard to use. • Gas pedal may be mounted too low for some drivers. • Reverse and tag lights fail because of frayed wiring at trunk hinge. **2003**—Sudden brake failure. • Car rolls backward when stopped in gear on an incline. • Passenger-side windshield wiper channels water directly in the line of vision on the upstroke, temporarily blocking driver's vision. • Vent behind shifter handle becomes very hot when heater is on. • Gear shift lever continually sticks. • Water leaks onto the interior carpet. • Air dam deflector on the front of the vehicle is mounted too low and hits the road on dips. **2004**—Airbag failed to deploy. • Excessive cabin noise when driving with the windows down. • Fuel sloshes in the gas tank.

Secret Warranties/Internal Bulletins/Service Tips

All models/years: An upgraded low level fuel sensor will fix a fluctuating fuel gauge that bedevils GM's entire car lineup; it's an expensive repair that's covered by a GM "goodwill" warranty, if you insist on it. • Reverse servo cover seal leak (transmission). **1993–2003**—A rotten-egg odour coming from the exhaust is probably the result of a malfunctioning catalytic converter; replacement cost may be covered by the emissions warranty. • Eliminate AC odours by installing an evaporator cooling-coil coating kit. • Paint delamination, peeling, or fading (see Part Two "Paint and Body Defects," pages 71–75). **2001**—Delayed automatic transmission shifting (TSB #01-07-30-014). **2001–04**—Erratic shifting, slipping transmission. **2001–05**—Harsh 1–2 upshifts. *Century*: **1994–98**—A cold engine tick or rattle heard shortly after start-up may be fixed by replacing the piston/pin assembly. **1997–99**—A low-speed steering shudder or vibration may be corrected by replacing the steering pressure and return lines with revised "tuned" hoses. • Front disc pads have been upgraded to reduce brake squeal. • A shaking sensation at cruising speed may be fixed by replacing the transmission mount. • TSB #00-03-06-001 gives a comprehensive listing of common front-end noises and what's needed to silence them. • Install a new steering wheel inflatable restraint module to make it easier to sound the horn. **1997–2001**—Binding auto-

---

A/T – DIFFICULT SHIFT LEVER OPERATION

BULLETIN NO: 01-07-30-017   DATE: APRIL 2001

SUBJECT: Transmission Shift Lever is Difficult to Move (Replace Shift Lever)

1997–2001 Buick Century

CONDITION: Some owners may comment that the transmission range selector lever is difficult to move/shift.

CAUSE: The original shift lever may not impart enough mechanical advantage on the shift linkage to provide low enough effort when shifting gears.

---

matic transmission shift lever (see TSB 01-07-30-017). **1998**—A wet right rear floor signals the need to reseal the stationary glass area. **1998–2000**—Simply changing the radiator cap may cure your hot-running engine and prevent coolant loss. **2000–01**—GM's TSB says the best way to eliminate an engine ticking noise is to replace the engine's pistons (covered by a secret warranty, of course). **2000–02**—Exhaust system ping, snap. • Poor transmission performance. • No-start remedy. **2003**—Firm shifts, no downshifts, shudder.

CENTURY, CIERA PROFILE

	1996	1997	1998	1999	2000	2001	2002	2003	2004
Cost Price ($)									
Century	23,820	24,545	25,215	25,199	25,570	25,200	25,325	25,820	26,300
Ciera S/SL	23,625	—	—	—	—	—	—	—	—
Used Values ($)									
Century ▲	3,500	4,500	5,500	7,000	9,500	11,500	13,000	15,000	17,000
Century ▼	3,000	3,500	4,500	6,000	8,500	10,000	11,500	13,500	15,500
Ciera S/SL ▲	2,000	—	—	—	—	—	—	—	—
Ciera S/SL ▼	1,000	—	—	—	—	—	—	—	—
Reliability	❷	❷	❷	❷	❸	❸	❸	❸	❸
Crash Safety (F)									
Century 4d	④	—	—	④	④	④	④	④	④
Side (Century 4d)	—	—	③	③	③	③	③	③	③
Offset	—	③	③	③	③	③	③	③	③
Head Restraints (F)	—	❶	—	❶	—	❷	❷	❶	❶
Rear	—	—	—	—	—	❶	❶	❶	❶
Rollover Resistance	—	—	—	—	—	—	—	④	④

Note: 1995 Ciera earned a four-star frontal crashworthiness rating.

Honda

ACCORD ★★★★

RATING: Above Average (2003–04, 1990–99); Recommended (2000–02); Average (1985–89). With the 16-valve 4-cylinder engine or V6, the Accord is one of the most versatile compacts you can find. Think of it as a better-performing Toyota Camry, with similar high-quality components and powertrain defects covered by extended warranties. The 2003 and 2004 models have been down-rated because of redesign glitches. These include the powertrain problems already noted, and numerous reports of sudden acceleration and stalling, brake failures, and airbag malfunctions that cause the devices to go off when they shouldn't and not deploy when they should. **Maintenance/Repair costs:** Lower than average. Repairs aren't dealer dependent. Recall repairs may be delayed. **Parts:** Higher-than-average cost, but they can easily be found for much less from independent suppliers. **Extended warranty:** Not needed. **Best alternatives:** Acura Integra; Hyundai Elantra wagon, Sonata, or Tiburon; Mazda 626; and Toyota Camry. **Online help:** Owner complaints and service bulletins can be found at *www.autosafety.org/autodefects.html* and helpful owner forums can be found at "The Temple of VTEC" at *www.vtec.net/*, *www.kbb.com*, *www.edmunds.com*, *www.carforums.com/forums*, and *www.cartrackers.com/Forums*.

 ## Strengths and Weaknesses

Fast and nimble without a V6, this is the mid-sized sedan of choice for drivers who want maximum fuel economy and comfort along with lots of space for grocery hauling and occasional highway cruising. With the optional V6, the Accord is one of the most versatile mid-sized cars you can find. It offers something for everyone, and its top-drawer quality and high resale value mean there's no way you can lose money buying one.

The Accord doesn't really excel in any particular area; it's just very, very good at everything. It's smooth, quiet, mannerly, and competent, with outstanding fit and finish inside and out. Other strong points: comfort, ergonomics, impressive assembly quality, reliability, and driveability. Some of its weak points: insufficient torque with the base engine on early models makes for constant highway downshifting; the automatic transmission tends to shift harshly and slowly (covered by a "goodwill" warranty); rear passenger room is tight; and the aforementioned safety-related complaints reported to NHTSA.

Despite all the foregoing praise, this hasn't always been a great car. During the '80s, Accords were beset with severe premature rusting, frequent engine camshaft and crankshaft failures, and severe front brake problems. Engines leaked or burned oil and blew their cylinder head gaskets easily, and carbureted models suffered from driveability problems through 1986. If left untreated, rust perforations will develop unusually quickly. Especially vulnerable spots are front fender seams; door bottoms; and areas surrounding side-view mirrors, door handles, rocker panels, wheel openings, windshield posts, front cowls, and trunk and hatchback lids.

VEHICLE HISTORY: 1990–93—More room and additional power through a new and quieter 2.2L 4-cylinder engine. Rear seating space remains inadequate, the added weight saps the car's performance, and the automatic transmission shifts harshly at times. Owners report prematurely worn automatic transmissions, constant velocity joints, and power-steering assemblies, and numerous air and water leaks.

1994—Redesign adds dual airbags, increases interior room and boosts 4-cylinder horsepower from 125–130 to 145. **1995**—Addition of a 175-hp 2.7L V6. The automatic transmission still works poorly with the 4-cylinder, producing acceleration times that are far from impressive, and owners still complain of excessive road noise and tire whine. Nevertheless, no significant reliability problems have been reported with that redesign. **1996**—Slightly restyled, the trunk opening was enlarged, and a rear-seat pass-through feature increased cargo space. **1998**—Substantially reworked, with more powerful engines (150–200 hp), including a new 200-hp 3.0L V6, a more refined suspension and automatic transaxle, upgraded ABS, additional interior space, and more glass; wagon version dropped. **1999**—ABS on the LX. **2000**—Side airbags with all V6-equipped models. **2001**—A restyled exterior, dual side airbags, V6 traction control, and improved soundproofing. **2003**—This larger, totally restyled model offers a V6 and 6-speed manual tranny combo, increased 4-cylinder and V6 horsepower (160 and 240, respectively), and increased fuel economy.

Confidential technical service bulletins show that the 1994–97 models are susceptible to AC malfunctions, engine oil leaks, the Check Engine light coming on for no reason, transmission glitches, power-steering pump leaks, windows falling off their channels, and numerous air and water leaks. Usually, these problems are simple to repair and Honda customer relations staff are helpful; however, Honda staffers and dealers are reluctant to admit their mistakes and may be getting a bit too arrogant in their dealings with the public. Witness the company's failure to publicly disclose its 1994–97 engine oil leak problems, which now affect the 2004 Accord and Odyssey.

Bulletins and owner complaints relating to the reworked 1998–2000 models show a surprisingly large number of factory-related powertrain and body defects, undoubtedly a result of the Accord's redesign. Some of those deficiencies, which affect both safety and performance: chronic lurching, hesitation, and stalling while on the highway, accompanied by the Check Engine light coming on; hard starting; frequent transmission failures; poor tracking that allows vehicle to wander; defective rear-computerized motor mounts; electrical shorts; coolant and brake master cylinder leakage; ABS and AC failures; and poor radio reception.

Body and accessory problems for these same model years include a plethora of squeaks, creaks, groans, and rattles; wind noise; water leaks; fuel gauge defects; paint chipping, bubbling, and peeling on hood, trunk, and roof (Honda blames it on bird droppings); leaky sunroof; windshield with vertical lines of distortion; driver-side mirror that shakes excessively; faulty fuel sending unit makes for inaccurate fuel readings (when full, indicates three-fourths full); and the speedometer off by 10 percent.

Owners of 2001 and 2002 models report that sudden, unintended acceleration remains a serious problem and can occur at any time, as the owner of this 2001 Accord relates:

> While taking the car through a car wash, vehicle accelerated and ran into two other cars and through a fence.

Other performance-related problems include automatic transmission breakdowns, expensive and frequent servicing of the brake rotors and pads, and electrical glitches.

The 2003 redesign has contributed to a serious decline in quality through the 2004 model year. Over 200 safety-related have been registered by NHTSA, when a quarter of that number would be normal. Sadder still, Honda promised us better-performing, more durable transmissions in its redesigned 2003s. The company lied (fortunately, an extended warranty now covers tranny breakdowns up to eight years).

Other problems related to this last redesign: a rotten-egg smell in the cabin; coolant in the engine oil pan; frequent hard starts; erratic transmission shifts; brake shuddering, grinding, and squealing; warped brake rotors; a popping noise when accelerating; a steering column ticking; a hole in the AC condenser; defective CD changer; stereo speaker hum; windshield creaks in cold, dry weather; the moon roof doesn't close all the way; non-stop rattles, squeaks, and vibrations in door panels, tops of windows, rear shelf, and in the B-pillars around the top seat belt anchor; wrinkled, bubbling, door window moulding; rear headliner becomes unglued, defective paint; roof water leaks; and the headliner sags in the rear.

The aforementioned increase in engine, transmission, and brake failures is worrisome. Nevertheless, CAA surveys have shown that customer satisfaction is an impressive 88 percent, compared to 85 percent for both the Toyota Camry and Mazda 626. Keep in mind that Honda puts a "goodwill" clause in almost all of its service bulletins, allowing service managers to submit any claim to the company long after the original warranty period has elapsed.

Safety Summary

All models/years: Sudden acceleration, stalling. • Airbags fail to deploy or deploy for no reason. • Check Engine light is always on. • Excessive windshield glare. • AC failure. • Premature front/rear brake wear. • Gas and brake pedals are too close together and often get pressed at the same time. • Faulty power windows. • Seat belt continually ratchets tighter. **1998**—Defective rear computerized motor mounts on '98 and '99 models. • ABS brake light comes on continually. • Frequent brake failures. • Sudden brake lock-up. • Brake master cylinder failures. • Floormat bunches under the brake pedal. • Engine oil leakage. • Power-steering fluid leakage, causing sudden loss of steering control. • Vehicle rolled back when parked. • Automatic transmission gears disengage and make a loud noise when engaging. • Transmission fails to engage at slow speeds. • Transmission fails to fully lock up in Overdrive. • Transmission hunts for the right gear. • Clutch pedal failure. • Automatic transmission parking mechanism failure. • Because of the design of dashboard lights, it's hard to read odometer, digital clock, and radio indicator. • Can't see high beam indicator light in the daytime. • Light tan dash reflects too much sunlight into the eyes. • Instrument panel lights are too bright at night and can't be dimmed enough. • To activate horn, driver must remove hand from steering wheel. • Fuel gauge shows two-thirds full when the gas tank is full, or indicates an empty tank with warning light on while 19L (5 gal.) remain in the tank. • Poor seat belt design allows for belt to wrap around the release lever and get stuck, or causes seatback to suddenly recline. • Seat belts get trapped underneath the seatback electric switch. • Rear passenger-side door won't unlock. • Sunroofs and headliners often need replacing. **1999–2000**—Airbag deployment caused extensive neck and head injuries. • Sudden brake loss. • Emergency brakes failed to hold on hill, allowing car to roll into lake. • Brake master cylinder leakage. • Driver's seatback suddenly fell back. • Steering knuckle broke while driving. • Bolt that holds the lower control arm assembly broke away from the frame, causing wheel to come out of fender. • Many complaints of chronic lurching, hesitation, and stalling while on the highway, accompanied by Check Engine light coming on (dealers say they can't duplicate the problem). • Engine sputters at half throttle. • Hard starting. • Frequent transmission failures. • Vehicle doesn't track well; wanders all over the road. • Exhaust pipe runs under oil pan plug, causing dripped oil to burn off exhaust. • Seat belts fail to retract or continually tighten up, choking occupant. • Right front passenger window exploded while driving. • Windshield has vertical lines of distortion. • Driver-side mirror shakes excessively. **2001**—Excessive front-end vibration and wandering over the highway. • Automatic transmission leaks and jerks into gear. • Rear stabilizer bar links broke. • Vehicle rolls back when stopped on an incline. • Complete brake loss. Check Engine and airbag lights remain lit. • Incorrect fuel gauge readings. • The front windshield has a UV protective coating that gives the windshield a wavy appearance. **2002**—Car suddenly shuts down in traffic because of a defective immobilizer system. • Automatic transmission failures. • Seat belt wouldn't retract or continually tightens; child had to be cut free. • Child safety seat can't be installed because buckle latch is located too far into the seat. • Partial brake failure, brakes fail to "catch" at first, then suddenly grab. • Vehicle pulls sharply when braking. • Electrical short caused CD player overheating and battery sparking. • Trunk lid may suddenly fall. **2003**—Sudden, unintended acceleration while car is in motion or when put into Reverse. • Axle suddenly snapped. • Front and side curtain airbags deployed for no reason. • Severe pulling to the right. • Power steering groan believed to be caused by the steering pump. • Console overheats and smells burnt. • Keys overheat in the ignition. • Complete brake failure. • ABS and traction control lights stay lit and corrective parts aren't easily found. • Frequent Michelin tire blowouts. • Rear vision is obstructed by head restraints, high rear deck, and roof pillar. **2004**—Several reports of fires igniting in the insulation material:

> While driving vehicle caught fire. Dealership found that the sound deadening material came too close to the heat of the engine.

Complete brake failure; brake alert is constantly lit. • Seatbelt failed to retract in a rear-end collision. • Frequent no-starts. • Once underway, vehicle constantly pulls to the right. • Excessive on-road vibration. • Passenger-side mirror slipped off. • Steering pulls to one side while driving. • Distorted windshield:

> A new windshield was installed and that one was also distorted. In total, five replacement windshields were ordered but they all had the same defect.

• Side window shattered after morning moisture was wiped off. • Side airbag deployed for no reason. • If you put your purse on the front passenger-side seat, the airbag is disabled. • Same thing occurs if driver's 90-pound daughter sits in the same seat. • Key sticks in the ignition. • Two-month wait for transmission recall appointment.

Secret Warranties/Internal Bulletins/Service Tips

All models/years: Steering wheel shimmy is a frequent problem, and is taken care of in TSB #94-025. A slow-to-retract seat belt will be replaced for free under Honda's lifetime warranty, says TSB #03-062. • Deformed windshield moulding. **All models: 1998**—Creak from the rear shelf area, headliner, windshield, and rear window. • Front ABS wheel sensor harness rubs against wheel. • Rattle from rear stabilizer bar. • If the brake system indicator stays on, install an improved master cylinder reservoir cap float. • An inaccurate fuel gauge must be replaced with an upgraded unit. • Tips on eliminating wind noise from the top of the front windshield and a creaking noise from the rear shelf, headliner, and windshield area. • Coolant leakage from the radiator drain plug may require the replacement of the drain plug/O-ring assembly. • Rear door water leaks may be plugged simply by removing excess weather stripping. **1998–99**—A clutch pedal squeak or groan is likely caused by insufficient lubrication of the piston cup seal. • Noisy rear wheel bearings are covered by a "goodwill" replacement program; look for a partial refund under TSB #99-040. **1998–2000**—Manual transmission bangs in Reverse. **1998–2001**—Tips on silencing a moon roof squeak (eligible for "goodwill" consideration). **1998–2004**—V6 engine oil leaks (an extension of a problem first noticed on 1994–97 models). **1999**—Glove box door rattles, wheels clicking, and clutch pedal and rear wheel bearing noise. • Loose AC, heater, temperature, and fan control knobs. • Inaccurate fuel gauge. **1999–2000**—Engine hard starts. • Coolant leaks from the water passage near the EGR valve. • PCM needs to be recalibrated under warranty to prevent malfunction indicator light (MIL) from coming on for no reason. • TSB #00-038 says a transmission shudder or judder will be fixed for

V6 ENGINE OIL LEAKS

BULLETIN NO: 01-009   DATE: FEB. 20, 2004

1998–03 Accord V6—ALL; 1999–03 Odyssey—ALL; 2003 Pilot—ALL

SYMPTOM: An oil leak from the front, middle, or rear of the engine.

PROBABLE CAUSE: The cast aluminum engine block may be porous in spots.

CORRECTIVE ACTION: Depending on the location of the leak, seal it with JB Weld or 3-Bond-coated sealing bolts.

OUT OF WARRANTY: Any repair performed after warranty expiration may be eligible for goodwill consideration by the District Parts and Service Manager or your Zone Office. You must request consideration, and get a decision, before starting work.

PRODUCT UPDATE CAMPAIGN – A/T NO-REVERSE CONDITION

BULLETIN NO: 03-042   DATE: JULY 31, 2003

PRODUCT UPDATE: No-Reverse condition

BACKGROUND: If a vehicle is stuck in snow and the transmission is shifted several times between a Forward drive gear and Reverse (at wheel speeds above 12 mph [19 km/h]), a no-Reverse condition can develop.

free under a "goodwill" program. **1999–2003**—Automatic transmission malfunctions and failures will be fixed or replaced under a more recent and comprehensive "goodwill" extended warranty program (see Part Two). **2001**—Windshield hum or whine. • Cracked, damaged foglight lens. • The horn plate bolts on the driver's airbag may not have been properly torqued and could cause a rattle in the steering wheel. **2003**—"Goodwill" campaigns to replace automatic transmissions and MICU units that regulate door locks, trunk alarm, etc. • Corrective action for coolant leakage into the engine oil pan; oil leaks at the cylinder head cover. • A faulty air intake air breather pipe hose may cause the engine warning light to remain lit. Its replacement is covered by a special Honda Product Update Campaign. • Engine clicking or ticking at idle. • An automatic transmission that won't go into Reverse is eligible for a free correction under another Honda "goodwill" campaign (TSB #03-042). • Automatic transmission leaks on the cooler lines. • Hard starts. • Troubleshooting calipers, rotors, and pads, following complaints of excessive brake vibration (wait a minute, weren't these the same chronic problems present before Honda's much-vaunted 2003 brake upgrade?):

> My 2003 Accord has been in the Honda dealer with problems with the front brakes (warped rotors). After having the front rotors resurfaced and pads replaced twice, it was found that the front calipers were hanging up. My car just turned 17,000 miles [27,200 km] and it has had problems with the front brakes since it had 8,000 miles [12,800 km], at that time I was told by the dealer that I was "riding" my brakes and they would only take care of this problem for me at no cost just this "one time." I feel Honda knows

that 2003 Accords have brake problems and Honda puts the blame on everyone else except themselves. My vehicle has now been in the Honda dealer for two weeks because they are unable to locate new calipers. From talking with other 2003 Accord owners and reading information on other websites, [I know] I'm not alone with this problem.

• Troubleshooting ABS brake light illumination. • Inaccurate gauges and odometer. • Vehicle pulls to the right. • Excessive steering vibration. • Noisy power steering countermeasures. • Investigating owner reports of cracked windshields. • Doors don't unlock in cold weather. • Poor AC cooling. • Rear shelf rattling. • Dash or pillar creaking or clicking. • Roof water leak fix. • Roof moulding channel leaks water. • Wrinkled door window moulding. • Remedies for front brake noise or judder when braking. 2003–04—Remedies for a sulfur smell in the interior. • If the brake pedal is stiff, a new booster vacuum hose may be required. 2004—Excessive engine vibration in idle. • Noisy steering. • No starts and faulty power windows. • Door rattles. • Wheel bearing humming or growling. • Heater blower overheats or blows a fuse.

ACCORD PROFILE

	1996	1997	1998	1999	2000	2001	2002	2003	2004
Cost Price ($)									
LX	20,295	20,995	23,800	23,800	23,000	22,800	23,000	25,000	25,100
EXi/EX	22,995	23,495	26,800	26,801	31,300	30,800	31,100	32,500	32,900
Used Values ($)									
LX ▲	6,000	7,000	8,500	10,500	12,500	14,000	16,500	19,500	21,500
LX ▼	5,000	6,000	7,000	9,000	11,000	13,000	15,000	18,000	20,000
EXi/EX ▲	7,500	8,500	10,000	12,500	15,500	18,000	21,000	24,000	27,500
EXi/EX ▼	6,500	7,500	9,000	10,500	14,000	16,000	19,500	23,000	26,000
Reliability	4	4	4	4	5	5	5	4	4
Crash Safety (F)	—	4	4	4	—	5	5	5	5
4d	4	4	4	4	4	5	5	5	5
Side (2d)	—	—	—	3	3	4	4	5	4
4d	—	2	4	4	4	4	4	5	5
Offset	3	3	3	3	3	3	3	5	5
Head Restraints (F)	2	3	3	—	3	3	4	1	1
Rear	1	2	2	—	2	2	3	1	1
Rollover Resistance	—	—	—	—	5	5	5	4	4

All ratings on a numbered scale where ⑤ is good and ❶ is bad. See pages 100–101 for a more detailed description.

Hyundai

RATING: Above Average (1999–2004); Average (1995–98); Not Recommended (1986–93). The 1994 model year was skipped. These cars haven't registered one-tenth the number of safety complaints as the higher-rated Honda Accord. For maximum savings, I suggest you buy a 1999–2003 version, with some of the original warranty left, plan to keep it at least five years to shake off the depreciation, and put some of the savings on the purchase price into a comprehensive supplementary warranty to protect yourself when the warranty ends. **Maintenance/Repair costs:** Higher than average. Repairs aren't dealer dependent. **Parts:** Higher-than-average cost, and often back-ordered. **Extended warranty:** An extended powertrain warranty would be a smart buy. **Best alternatives:** Acura Integra, GM Cavalier or Sunfire, Honda Accord, Hyundai Elantra wagon or Tiburon, Mazda 626, and Toyota Camry. **Online help:** For the latest owner reports, service bulletins, and money-saving tips, look at *www.automotiveforums.com/vbulletin/f741*, *www.autosafety.org/autodefects.html*, *www.kbb.com*, *www.edmunds.com*, *www.carforums.com/forums*, and *www.cartrackers.com/Forums*.

Strengths and Weaknesses

This mid-sized front-drive sedan was built under Mitsubishi licensing, but its overall reliability isn't anywhere near as good as what you'll find with Mitsubishi's cars and trucks sold in Canada under the Chrysler and Eagle monikers. Acceleration is impressive with the manual gearbox, but only passable with the automatic. Handling and performance are also fairly good, although emergency handling isn't confidence inspiring, particularly because of the imprecise steering and excessive lean when cornering. As with other Hyundai models, the automatic transmission performs erratically, the engine is noisy, and reliability is a problem—it's way below average for the 1989–93 models; the 1995–98 models are moderately improved.

VEHICLE HISTORY: 1995—Redesigned for additional interior room, more horsepower, and an upgraded automatic transmission. Nevertheless, acceleration with the automatic is still below average with the 4-banger, and the automatic gearbox downshifts slowly. (The manual transmission is still more reliable and fuel efficient.) **1996**—More standard features, like air conditioning, power steering, a split folding rear seatback, liquid-filled engine mounts, and additional sound-proofing. **1999**—Arrived with a redesigned body and suspension, side airbags, two new engines, and a huge price increase that's not reflected in its low resale value. **2000**—Side airbags and larger wheels. **2001**—A new grille and additional standard features of minor importance. **2002**—GL given four-wheel disc brakes. **2003**—Standard front-side airbags.

Throughout the Sonata's history, Hyundai technical service bulletins are replete with references to automatic transmissions that exhibit what Hyundai describes as "shift shock," as well as delayed shifting. In addition to the tranny problems, owners of pre-1995 models report poor engine performance (hard starting, poor idling, stalling); the engine runs hot, and when you're stopped at a traffic light, it shakes like a boiling kettle; the #3 spark plug often needs replacing or cleaning; rough engine rattle; high oil consumption (1L every two to three months); excessive front brake pulsation and premature wear; steering defects (when the steering wheel is turned to either extreme, it makes a sound like metal cracking); cruise control malfunctions and electrical short circuits; battery life of only 18 months; malfunctioning lights; radio failures; falling interior roof liner; faulty hood locks; rotten-egg smell coming from the catalytic converter; broken muffler; faulty resonator; defective exhaust pipe; poor door and window sealing (water leaking into the interior when the car is washed); and premature paint peeling and rusting.

The 1995–2004 Sonatas have elicited very few quality-control and safety complaints and represent the better buys in this group, following the '95 and '99 models' redesign. However, automatic transmissions, brakes, airbags, steering, and fuel- and electrical-system components still top the list of parts most vulnerable to premature failure or malfunctioning. Airbag and Check Engine lights are constantly lit, and fit and finish continue to be only average.

 **Safety Summary**

All models/years: Airbags don't deploy when they should or deploy when they shouldn't. • Frequent automatic transmission failures. • Hyundai may not offer a seat belt extension for large occupants. **1999**—Complete brake failure. • Airbag warning light comes on for no reason. • Sudden alternator failure causes entire vehicle to shut down. • **2000**—Driver-side airbag deployed when driver slammed the door. • Airbag light stays lit, and corrective parts are on national back order. • Sudden brake loss; brakes don't hold in a panic situation. • Warped front brake rotors produce excessive steering shimmy. • Stalls when in low gear or when decelerating (recall campaign didn't remedy the problem). • Power-steering leaks and early replacement. • Window often comes off its track. • Power window caught child's head and neck. • Headlights dim when AC engages. **2001**—Hood flew up and shattered windshield. • Engine sleeves can come loose, causing pistons to smash spark plugs. • Engine bucks and hesitates before rpm suddenly increase and car takes off. • Frequent stalling upon deceleration. • Faulty crankshaft position sensor is blamed for the poor engine performance. • Automatic transmission may suddenly shift into Neutral, or the shift lever sometimes pops out of gear. **2002**—Problems getting recall work done. • Axle (U-bolt) failed while car was underway. • Seat belt latch releases when jostled by passenger's elbow.

2003—Driver-side seat belt buckle suddenly released. • Large rear-view mirror obstructs the view. **2004**—Airbags failed to deploy. • Gas fumes enter the cabin. • Stalling because of faulty throttle sensor. • Complete brake loss. • Seat belt came loose during a collision.

Secret Warranties/Internal Bulletins/Service Tips

All models/years: Troubleshooting tips for delayed engagement of the automatic transmission. • Harsh shifting when coming to a stop or upon initial acceleration is likely caused by an improperly adjusted accelerator pedal switch TCU. • A faulty air exhaust plug could cause harsh shifting into Second and Fourth gears on vehicles with automatic transmission. • Brake pedal pulsation can be corrected by installing upgraded front discs and pads. • Troubleshooting tips for reducing brake noise. **All models: 1989–98**—Revised measures to reduce AC odours. **1995–98**—Harsh shifting might be fixed by installing an upgraded transaxle control module (TCM) under a "goodwill" warranty. • If wind noise makes a "kazoo" sound, try installing an additional drip rail moulding. **1995–99**—Tips are offered on getting the automatic transmission to shift properly. **1999**—Shudder or vibration during acceleration can be eliminated by correcting a sticking inboard CV-tripod joint assembly. • A humping/knocking noise heard from the left front side of the vehicle on hard right turns may be caused by the left rear corner of the transaxle mounting bracket base touching the body. • Tips on silencing front wheel bearing noise. **1999–2000**—No-starts, hard starting, or erratic idling may all be caused by a canister purge valve that's stuck open. • Correcting hard manual shifting into First or Second gear and shudder on acceleration (CV joints). **1999–2001**—Correcting erratic shifts. • Key sticks in ignition cylinder. • Silencing gear whine. **2000**—Rear suspension produces a metallic rubbing noise. **1999–2002**—Harsh, delayed shifts. **2000–01**—Correcting droning or rumbling brake noise at freeway speeds. **2001–02**—Hyundai will fix a noisy rear suspension by replacing the rear stabilizer bar bushing. **2002**—Troubleshooting poor shifting and torque converter clutch malfunctions. • 2–3 shift flare. • Erratic operation of the automatic climate control. **2003**—Harsh shifts into Drive or Reverse. • Sticks in Second gear. **2004**—Engine hesitation requires a reprogrammed PCM.

SONATA PROFILE

	1996	1997	1998	1999	2000	2001	2002	2003	2004
Cost Price ($)									
Base	16,595	16,995	17,495	19,495	19,995	20,495	21,195	21,595	22,395
Used Values ($)									
Base ▲	3,500	4,000	5,000	6,000	7,500	8,500	11,500	14,000	16,000
Base ▼	3,000	3,500	4,500	5,000	6,000	6,500	10,000	12,500	15,000

Reliability	3	3	3	3	4	4	4	4	4
Crash Safety (F)	3	3	3	—	—	—	4	4	4
Side	—	1	1	—	4	4	4	4	4
Offset	1	1	1	3	3	3	3	3	3
Head Restraints	1	1	—	3	—	1	1	1	1
Rear	—	—	—	1	—	—	—	1	1
Rollover Resistance	—	—	—	—	—	—	5	5	5

Mazda

best buy | 626, MX-6, MAZDA6 | ★★★★★

RATING: *Mazda6*: Recommended (2004); Above Average (2003). *626*: Recommended (1999–2002); *626, MX-6*: Above Average (1996–98); Average (1994–95); Not Recommended (1985–93). Why a higher rating for the latest models than for the Accord? Simple. Accords aren't discounted, so you'll pay a lot more for a used model than for a 626, which costs a lot less now that the Mazda6 has hit the showrooms. Furthermore, the Accord's latest revision has compromised quality, while the latest 626/Mazda6 duo seem to have no more than an average number of first-year production snafus. Make sure the car fits your size: Tall drivers should be wary of the low headrests, which can be hazardous in a col-

All ratings on a numbered scale where 5 is good and **1** is bad. See pages 100–101 for a more detailed description.

lision, and short drivers will want to ensure they can see adequately without getting dangerously close to the airbag housing, particularly on pre-1998 models that carried fully powered airbags. **Maintenance/Repair costs:** Higher than average. Repairs aren't dealer dependent. Mazda suggests changing the engine timing chain after 100,000 km. **Parts:** Easily found, but sometimes costly. Although Mazda has promised to cut prices, you should still compare prices with independent suppliers. **Extended warranty:** An extended powertrain warranty is recommended as protection against automatic transmission breakdowns and other factory-related defects. **Best alternatives:** Acura Integra; GM Cavalier or Sunfire; Honda Accord; Hyundai Elantra wagon, Sonata, or Tiburon; and Toyota Camry. **Online help:** Owner reports, customizing tips, performance upgrades, and service bulletins can be found at *www.automotiveforums.com/*, *www.autosafety.org/autodefects.html*, *www.kbb.com*, *www.edmunds.com*, *www.carforums.com/forums*, and *www.cartrackers.com/Forums*.

Strengths and Weaknesses

Although far from being high-performance vehicles, these cars ride and handle fairly well and still manage to accommodate four people in comfort (except for the MX-6 coupe/Ford Probe). The 1988–92 versions incorporated a third-generation redesign that added a bit more horsepower to the 4-banger. Apart from that improvement, these cars have changed little over the years and are still easy riding, fairly responsive, and not hard on gas. On the downside, the automatic transmission downshifts roughly, the power steering is imprecise, and the car leans a lot in turns.

Four-wheel steering was part of the sedan's equipment in 1988, and it was added exclusively to the MX-6 a year later. Wise buyers should pass over this option and look instead for anti-lock brakes and airbags on 1992 LG and GT versions. The manual transmission is a better choice because the automatic robs the engine of much-needed horsepower, as is the case with most cars this size. A passenger-side airbag was added to all '94 models.

A mid-sport and mid-compact hybrid, the MX-6 (Ford Probe) is a coupe version of the 626. It has a more sophisticated suspension, more horsepower, and better steering response than its sedan alter ego. The 1993 model gained a base 2.5L 165-hp V6 power plant. Overall reliability and durability are on par with the 626.

The 1995–97 models offer improved performance, handling, and overall reliability, plus reasonable fuel economy. Owners still complain, though, of subpar body construction, electrical system and cruise control glitches, dim headlights, brakes and AC compressors that wear out prematurely, and automatic transmissions that shift poorly and are prone to premature failure. The Check Engine light comes on and goes off repeatedly because of oil spilling into the airflow sensor or the intake manifold gasket leaking. Expect jerky downshifts when the 4-cylinder is at full throttle. Shocks and struts (MacPherson) aren't very durable and are expensive to replace (especially when the model is equipped with the electronic adjustment feature).

Body problems include windshield mouldings that flake and fall off; door and hatchlocks that often freeze up; the right side of the dash is often loose; the interior door panel pulls away; interior colours fade; headliner rattles; and the metal surrounding the rear wheelwells is prone to rust perforation, as are hood, trunk, and door seams. The paint seems particularly prone to chipping. The underbody and suspension components on cars older than five years should be examined carefully for corrosion damage. The exhaust system rarely lasts more than two years, and wheel bearings fail repeatedly within the same period.

VEHICLE HISTORY: 1998—Attractive Millenia-type styling, a longer wheelbase and larger cabin, a reinforced body to keep creaks and rattles to a minimum, and more powerful engines. **1999**—A larger selection of standard accessories. **2000**—Restyled and substantially improved with a small horsepower boost (5), enhanced handling, steering, and interior appointments. **2001**—Improved sound system, an emergency trunk release, and user-friendly child safety seat anchors. **2003**—Arrival of the Mazda6. **2004**—A four-door hatchback and wagon were added.

Owners of 1998–2002 models report malfunctioning automatic transmissions, engine head gasket failures, fuel system glitches that cause sudden acceleration and stalling, faulty airbags, and electrical shorts that result in the Check Engine light staying lit and engine stalling, or shutdown.

Other complaints point out that shifting isn't all that smooth, nor is the automatic gearbox very reliable; the car is hard-riding over uneven pavement; there's too much body lean in turns; excessive torque steer (pulling) to the right often occurs when accelerating; road noise intrudes into the cabin; the rear spoiler blocks rear visibility; and the trunk opening isn't conducive to loading large objects. As if that wasn't enough, Mazda has a history of automatic transmission and fit and finish deficiencies; and scheduled maintenance overcharges (check out the CBC TV *Marketplace* archives).

Mazda6

The 2003 and 2004 Mazda6 is offered with two power plants: an impressive 160-hp inline 4-cylinder that equals the Accord's entry-level engine, and a 220-hp V6 that trumps the Camry's 192 horses, but comes up a bit short when compared with the 240 horses unleashed by the Accord and Altima. Either engine can be hooked to a 5-speed manual or automatic transmission that also offers a semi-manual "Sport Shift" feature.

Don't get the idea that this is a warmed-over 626. It's set on an entirely new platform and carries safety and convenience features never seen by its predecessor, like two-stage airbags and a chassis engineered to deflect crash forces away from occupants. Wider than the Accord, the Mazda6's interior allows for a comfortable ride and carries an unusually large trunk.

During its first year on the market, there have been few owner complaints. However, some owners mention interior clunks that are omnipresent and a number of driveability concerns that include poor engine and transmission performance (a chronic problem), a rotten-egg smell that pervades the interior, window motor failures, rust-like stains in the door sashes and trunk lids, and waits of a month or more for replacement parts.

 ## Safety Summary

All models/years: The 626's different iterations have registered far fewer complaints than their Asian, European, or American counterparts. • Head restraints may be too low. One Canadian neurologist told *Lemon-Aid* that early 626 head restraints are set too low and cannot extend to a safe level; he says there is an additional two inches required for a six-foot-tall occupant. The doctor maintains his '97 Mazda 626 (and other model years) cannot be safely operated by a driver over 5'10". • Inadvertent airbag deployments or airbags that failed to deploy in a collision. • Frequent automatic transmission malfunctions and failures. **1998**—Sudden, unintended acceleration. • Front axle pulled out of the transmission. • Steering rack gear broke in two without prior warning. • Sudden automatic transmission downshifts. • Frequent transmission failures. • Many reports of tire tread separation. • Poor braking leads to extended stopping distance. • Driver's seat is so low that it must be brought dangerously close to the airbag housing for maximum visibility. **1999**—Left lower strut bolts loose, bent, and broken, causing the driver-side wheel to fall. • Premature tire wear. • When AC engages, engine hesitates and causes car to jerk. • Automatic transmission shift shock. • Transmission fails upon deceleration, it downshifts harshly, O/D light flashes, and then engine compartment starts to fill with transmission fluid. • Headlights dim intermittently. • Excessive vibration at low speeds. • Seat belts won't properly secure a child safety seat. **2000**—Cylinder head failures at the #2 cylinder. • 4-cylinder engine stumbles badly in cold weather. • Automatic transmission jerks during 2–1 shift, lurches into gear because of sudden high revs, and sometimes won't go into gear. • Cracked passenger-side rear axle. • Check Engine light stays on. **2001**—Automatic transmission jerks into gear. • Seat belts fail to retract. **2002**—Airbag failed to deploy. • Driver's side seat belt unlatched during an accident. • Transmission failures; jerky automatic transmission shifts. • Loose front wheel bearing. • AC constantly blows cold air. • Excessive right side vibration when vehicle is underway. • Bridgestone tire tread separation.

Secret Warranties/Internal Bulletins/Service Tips

All models/years: Non-turbo models that idle roughly after a warm restart could have fuel vapourizing in the distribution pipe (TSB #023/87R). • Excessive rear brake squealing can be reduced with improved brake pads (TSB #015/89-11). • Excessive vibrations felt in the brake pedal, steering wheel, floor, or seat when applying the brakes can be fixed by installing a redesigned brake assembly. • TSB #50901898 gives tips for eliminating wind noise around doors. **All models: 1997–98**—Wind noise around doors. • Inoperative speedometer. • Steering wheel slightly off centre. • Brake pulsation repair. • Dead battery troubleshooting. • Tips on fixing faulty sunroofs, a seat belt warning buzzer that sounds for no reason, rough automatic transmission shifts, excessive idle vibration, rear brake squeal, coolant leaks, and hard-to-close trunk lid. **1998–2000**—Tips on silencing a rear-end tapping noise, and preventing AC odours. **1998–2002**—Remedy for mildew odour. **2000**—Troubleshooting an MIL light that won't go off. **2002**—Rough idle, hesitation, and stumble. • Grinding, rubbing noise at front of vehicle. • Tips to silence wind noise around doors. *Mazda6*: **2003**—Seat fails to heat. • Doors hard to close in cold weather. • Sticking traction control system switch. Trunk lid staining. • Wind noise around doors. **2004**—Engine surging ar 80 km/h. Hesitation or rough idle at high altitude. • Remedies for brake judder and moan. Special Service Program #60 to replace the fan control module. • Special Service Program for evaporative emission system leak monitoring failure. • Special Service Program for O_2 sensor failure. • Front suspension popping, clunking.

626, MX-6, MAZDA6 PROFILE

	1996	1997	1998	1999	2000	2001	2002	2003	2004
Cost Price ($)									
626	19,365	19,995	19,995	20,140	20,140	23,175	23,470	—	—
MX-6	22,780	23,325	—	—	—	—	—	—	—
Mazda6	—	—	—	—	—	—	—	24,295	24,395
Used Values ($)									
626 ▲	4,000	4,500	6,000	7,500	9,500	11,000	14,500	—	—
626 ▼	3,000	4,000	4,500	6,000	8,000	9,500	13,500	—	—
MX-6 ▲	4,500	5,000	—	—	—	—	—	—	—
MX-6 ▼	4,000	4,500	—	—	—	—	—	—	—
Mazda6 ▲	—	—	—	—	—	—	—	18,500	20,000
Mazda6 ▼	—	—	—	—	—	—	—	17,500	18,500
Reliability	❷	❸	❸	❹	❹	❹	❹	❹	❹
Crash Safety (F)	❹	—	❹	❹	❹	❹	❹	❺	❺
Side (626 4d)	❷	❸	❸	❸	❸	❸	❸	❸	❸
Offset	—	—	❸	❸	❺	❺	❺	❺	❺
Head Restraints	—	❶	—	❶	—	❶	❶	❶	❶
Rollover Resistance	—	—	—	—	—	—	—	❺	❺

All ratings on a numbered scale where ❺ is good and ❶ is bad. See pages 100–101 for a more detailed description.

Nissan

ALTIMA ★★★

RATING: Average (2002–04, 1993–97); Above Average (1998–2001). Here's the Altima dilemma: Until 1997, these cars were fairly reliable, though so-so performers. Thereafter, performance was improved incrementally as prices remained quite reasonable. Then, the totally new, high-performance and stylish 2002 Altima changed everything. Sure, it's a great highway performer, but few can pay the $24,000–$30,000 entry fee. Moreover, safety- and performance-related defects are extraordinarily frequent and difficult to diagnose. And finally, word has gotten around that these redesigned models are troublesome and resale value has plummeted. Writes this owner of a 2003:

> Is it possible that Nissan's commitment to quality, customer service, and related policies to customer satisfaction are only window dressing, and is it possible that they have adopted Ford's policies to quality and customer satisfaction?

> Nevertheless, at my "wit's end" with the Altima, and after less than two years of problem-plagued ownership, last night I visited a local Hyundai dealer, only to learn that the black book value of my 2003 Altima is only $15,000.

Hopefully, later iterations will be built better, and dealer mechanics will become more competent in troubleshooting these rather sophisticated machines.

Watch out for early model bargains: The 140-hp 4-cylinder engine barely provides the necessary versatility needed to match the competition. Although the SE gives the sportiest performance, the less expensive GXE is the better deal from a price/quality standpoint. You will need an extended powertrain warranty, though, to protect you from automatic transmission failures on 1998–2001 models, and a more extensive warranty to protect you from post-2001 Altima defects. **Maintenance/Repair costs:** Higher than average. Repairs are dealer dependent. **Parts:** Owners complain of parts shortages on the 2002 and later versions; parts on earlier models are relatively inexpensive. **Extended warranty:** A comprehensive extended warranty is a must-have for all model years. **Best alternatives:** Acura Integra; later model GM Cavalier or Sunfire; Honda Accord; Hyundai Elantra wagon, Sonata, or Tiburon; Mazda 626, or Mazda6; and Toyota Camry. **Online help:** For the latest owner reports, service bulletins, and money-saving tips, look at *www.autosafety.org/autodefects.html*, *www.alldata.com*, *www.kbb.com*, *www.edmunds.com*, *www.carforums.com/forums*, and *www.cartrackers.com/Forums.*

Strengths and Weaknesses

The 1993–97 Altima's wheelbase is a couple of inches longer than the Stanza's, and the car is touted by Nissan as a mid-size, even though its interior dimensions put it in the compact league. The small cabin seats only four, and rear-seat access is difficult to master because of the slanted roof pillars, inward-curving door frames, and narrow clearance.

Expect only average acceleration and fuel economy with the pre-2002 4-cylinder engine. It has insufficient top-end torque and gets buzzier the more it's pushed. In order to get the automatic to downshift for passing, for example, you have to practically stomp on the accelerator. Manoeuvrability is good around town, but twitchy on the highway. There are no reliability problems reported with the 16-valve power plant, however, the 5-speed manual transmission is sloppy and the automatic transmission's performance has been problematic through the '97 model year; later years through 2001 are a better choice from a reliability and fuel-economy standpoint. The uncluttered under-hood layout makes servicing easy. Body assembly is only so-so, with more than the average number of squeaks and rattles.

The 2002–04 redesigned models are shaped like Passats with Maxima hearts, and provide scintillating V6 acceleration, flawless automatic transmission operation, good braking, well laid-out instruments and controls, and better-than-average interior room and craftsmanship.

Highway handling isn't impressive. The 4-cylinder engine isn't as refined as the competition and is noisy when pushed, and the V6 acceleration overpowers this car and causes excessive rear-end instability and steering pull to one side. Brakes tend to lock up on wet roads; interior appointments lack panache; there's limited rear headroom; expect snug rear seating for three adults, and obstructed rear visibility; the dashboard reflects onto the windshield; dash gauges wash out in sunlight; and parts are often back-ordered. Quality problems multiply as these cars age. Says this owner of a 2003 Altima:

> I have reported: abysmal floating, wander, and continual correction at highway and in-town speeds; an overabundance of torque steer; and exorbitant amounts of buffeting leading to excessive driver correction and fatigue, uncertainty, and fear.

> I have reported intermittent clanks in the front end when getting into the vehicle and coming to a stop, all of which cannot seem to be duplicated by Nissan techs or service managers. This is further exacerbated by well known and documented facts that the rear struts are faulty and are commonly replaced, faulty front struts also require replacement, and there is a fix for faulty front suspension components. I have previously reported the handling characteristics to that of a full-size minivan towing a boat or trailer driving behind a transport truck. Certainly not the same characteristics communicated by Nissan. I have

also reported the ride to be extremely harsh. Traversing bumpy roads with or without occupants in the rear seat, the ride is unstable. Road noise and small cracks and bumps are also amplified and quite apparent.

The car's 175-hp 2.5L 4-cylinder engine is almost as powerful as the competition's V6 power plants and the optional 245-hp 3.5L V6 has few equals among cars in this price and size class. And when you consider that the Altima is much lighter than most of its competitors, it's obvious why this car produces sizzling (and sometimes uncontrollable) acceleration.

Owners report engine surging, stalling, and hard starting, possibly because of a defective engine crank sensor or throttle switch (on national back order); annoying and hazardous dash reflection onto the windshield; electrical glitches and excessive brake wear, noise, and pulsations. Snow builds up in the small wheelwells, making steering difficult and causing excessive shimmy; clutch pressure plate throw-out bearing and flywheel may fail when downshifting into Fourth gear; noisy, failure-prone rear shocks; ABS warning light stays lit; and there is lots of ignition noise in the radio speakers.

VEHICLE HISTORY: 1993—Altima debuts with a 140-hp 2.4L 4-cylinder engine, a driver's airbag, and poorly designed, uncomfortable motorized shoulder belts. **1994**—Dual airbags and no more motorized belts. **1995**—Freshened styling. **1998**—Slightly restyled with a slightly larger interior, de-powered airbags, and degraded handling. **2000**—Slightly restyled again to look longer and wider; engine got five more horses (155 hp); and suspension/chassis enhancements improved handling somewhat and made for a quieter ride. **2002**—Completely revised with two high-performance engines (a 180-hp 2.5L 4-cylinder and an optional 240-hp 3.5L V6), a larger interior, and a more supple ride combined with sportier handling. Quality declines. **2003**—Inconsequential trim changes.

Altimas have always had a fairly good reliability reputation; problem areas with early models were prematurely worn, noisy front brakes, fuel system malfunctions, transmission and electrical system failures, and body glitches. 1998–2001 models have generated fewer complaints, but owners still report sudden acceleration and stalling; front brakes locking up or failing completely; failure of the airbags to deploy; transmission breakdowns; and poor body fit and finish, notably water leaks (mainly in the trunk) and body squeaks and rattles.

Safety Summary

1998—Stalling when accelerating. • Rear seats won't lock upright. • Windows rattle excessively. • Wheel cover failure. **1999**—Several incidents where engine or electrical fires ignited while vehicle was parked. • Sudden acceleration. • Vehicle unstable on wet roadway. • Airbags failed to deploy. • Airbag light comes on for no reason. • Gearshift lever sticks in Park. • Transaxle snapped in half, taking suspension and steering knuckle with it. • Sudden tire separation; Continental-General tires gradually lose air. • Chronic brake problems. • Driver's seat moves forward when braking. **2000**—Exhaust fumes enter vehicle. • Dashboard burst into flames while vehicle was underway. • Vehicle continues to accelerate when slowing down to a stop, or when put into Reverse. • Chronic stalling. • Automatic transmission won't stay in gear. • The rear wheelwell inner fender has sharp, jagged edges. • Firestone Affinity tire blowout. • All windows have a film on them that makes it difficult to see at night or during rainy weather. • Windshield cracks frequently. **2001**—Sudden, unintended acceleration. • Engine will suddenly shut down. • Engine motor mount failure. • Airbags failed to deploy. • Automatic transmission makes a grinding or clunking noise when shifting. • Defective sway bar bushing. • Wheel fell off, causing vehicle to slam into a wall. **2002–03**—Safety defects become more common as these cars age. Dealerships said to be aware of redesigned Altima's tendency to catch fire. One on occasion, fire erupted after collision; fire ignited because of a faulty fuel injection system on another occasion, and also ignited while vehicle was cruising on the highway. • Airbags failed to deploy. • Vehicle was idling and then suddenly went into Reverse and accelerated as groceries were unloaded from the trunk (dash indicator showed car in Park). • Driver run over by his own car when it slipped into Reverse. • Sudden acceleration when brakes are applied. • Transmission slips and engine hesitates when accelerating. • Chronic stalling. • Windshield distortion. • Exhaust pipe hanger pin catches debris that may ignite. • Crankshaft position sensor failure. • Tail lights constantly fail. • Battery suddenly blew up. • Seat belt fails to retract. • Instrument panel gauges wash out in sunlight. **2004**—Sudden stalling and hard starts. • Excessive vibration once underway. • Rear windshield shattered as door was closed. • Rear seat belt will not slacken when pulled gently. • Right front tire fell off vehicle.

Secret Warranties/Internal Bulletins/Service Tips

All models/years: Diagnostic and correction tips for brake vibration and steering wheel shimmy. • TSB #NTB99-028 outlines the procedures necessary to fix slow-to-retract seat belts. • TSB #NTB00-037a covers possible causes of the vehicle

---

ENGINE WON'T CRANK IN PARK/WILL CRANK IN NEUTRAL

BULLETIN NO: EL02-028; NTB02-083   DATE: JULY 30, 2002

2002–2003 Altima (L31) - with automatic transmission

SYMPTOMS: If an applied vehicle shows all of the following symptoms:

^Engine does not crank when the gear shift selector lever is in Park (P) position,

^Engine does crank when the gear shift selector lever is in Neutral (N),

^Incident usually happens if the engine is at normal driving temperature rather than cold,

The Service Procedure has two steps: Part A - Check the Park/Neutral Switch Adjustment, adjust if necessary; Part B - Adjust the Automatic Transmission Control Cable, at the Slotted Transmission Control Arm. Remove any play or "slack" in the cable.

pulling to the side. **1998–2000**—Troubleshooting a rattling in the engine compartment. • Tips for eliminating brake vibration and shudder. **1999–2000**—A sunroof that jams when opening rearward requires a readjustment of the sunroof links. • Guidelines as to what constitutes suspension strut leakage qualifying for warranty coverage are found in TSB #NTB99-001. • Remedies for a noisy automatic transmission. **2002–03**—Hard starting (see bulletin on previous page). • Chronic loss of power:

HESITATION ON ACCELERATION

BULLETIN NO: EC03-003; NTB03-022   DATE: MARCH 15, 2003

2002–03 Maxima (A33) only with manual transmission; 2002–03 Altima (L31) only with V6 (VQ35) engine and manual transmission

SYMPTOMS: An Applied Vehicle has a momentary hesitation when accelerating between 2000 and 3000 rpm.
ACTIONS: Replace the Mass Airflow Sensor; Perform ECM reprogramming.

• Excessive engine noise:

ENGINE BUZZ

BULLETIN NO: BT02-007A; NTB02-037A   DATE: NOV. 6, 2002

2002–03 Altima,

SYMPTOMS: buzz noise at 2500–2700 rpm, moderate load
ACTIONS: Locate the automatic transmission breather tank and repair as shown in the Service Procedure.

• Fuel sloshing noise:

FUEL TANK SLOSH/CLUNK NOISE

BULLETIN NO: FE02-001; NTB02-103   DATE: OCT. 10, 2002

2002 and 2003 Altima (L31)

SYMPTOMS: If an Applied Vehicle has "slosh" or "clunk" noise from the rear of the vehicle under the following conditions:
^ The fuel tank is 3/4 full to completely full, and
^ When braking,
^ Driving at low speeds over bumps, or
^ Accelerating at low speeds,
ACTIONS: The Service Procedure will direct you to install the following parts:
^ Fuel Tank
^ Fuel Tank Baffle inside fuel tank
^ Shim Pads on top of fuel tank
^ Insulation Pad under the rear seat

INTERMITTENT CLUNKING NOISE

BULLETIN NO: FA02-003; NTB03-002   DATE: JAN. 6, 2003

SUBJECT: Clunk noise from front suspension

2002–03 Altima

SYMPTOMS: An intermittent (difficult to duplicate) "clunk" noise coming from the front suspension area when:

^first accelerating or,

^applying the brakes or,

^going over bumps.

ACTIONS: Check/Tighten the torque on the front suspension components.

• Suspension noise (see bulletin left). • Front door trim fabric separation. • Low power, poor running, and MIL light stays lit. • Inoperative AC/warm air flows from vents. • Poor heater performance. • AC temperature isn't adjustable. • AC drain hose may leak into interior. Howling noise when clutch is released. • Rear suspension and radio speaker noise. • Sunroof wind noise and water leaks. • Water leakage on front floor area. • Wind noise from doors. • Sunroof won't close at highway speeds. • Faulty airbag warning light. • Wheel cover squeak, click. • Automatic transmission slips in Reverse and won't brake when in Drive 1 range, also makes a clicking noise. • Headliner rattle. • Poor heater performance. • Fuel tank slosh noise. **2002–04**—The control valve assembly may be the culprit responsible for erratic shifting. • Front door windows noise. • Grease streaks on front door glass. **2004**—Hard starts, no-starts may signal the need for a new fuel pump assembly. • Engine won't crank in low temperatures. • Alternator noise after engine shut off. • Window noise when activated.

ALTIMA PROFILE

	1996	1997	1998	1999	2000	2001	2002	2003	2004
Cost Price ($)									
XE/S	20,598	20,798	19,398	19,898	19,998	19,998	23,498	23,798	23,798
GXE/SE	23,498	21,398	21,998	22,698	22,698	22,698	27,698	24,675	24,298
Used Values ($)									
XE/S ▲	2,000	3,000	4,500	6,000	7,500	9,000	10,000	15,000	19,500
XE/S ▼	1,500	2,000	3,000	4,500	6,000	7,500	9,000	14,000	18,000
GXE/SE ▲	3,000	4,500	6,000	8,000	9,500	11,000	12,000	16,000	20,500
GXE/SE ▼	2,000	3,500	5,000	7,000	8,500	10,000	11,000	15,000	18,500
Reliability	4	4	4	4	4	4	2	2	3
Crash Safety (F)	4	4	3	3	—	4	4	4	4
Side	—	—	3	3	3	3	3	3	3
Offset	—	—	—	—	2	2	5	5	5
Head Restraints	—	2	—	2	1	1	3	3	3
Rear	—	—	—	—	—	—	2	2	2
Rollover Resistance	—	—	—	—	—	—	4	4	4

All ratings on a numbered scale where **5** is good and **1** is bad. See pages 100–101 for a more detailed description.

Toyota

CAMRY, SOLARA ★★★

RATING: Average (1997–2004); Above Average (1985–96). The Solara, a two-door Camry clone, is outrageously overpriced when bought new; however, the 1999–2001 models are veritable bargains because of their rapid depreciation. Of the three model years, I'd go for the 2001 Solara (its third year out) for a few thousand more and a better build quality. The 1996 LE V6 sedan and 2001 version are the best Camrys from a quality/price standpoint. Just a word of caution: 1997–2004 model Camrys and Solaras have elicited an unusually high number of safety complaints that are carried over from one model year to the next. The complaints include sudden acceleration; engine compartment fires; V6 engine failures from sludge buildup; automatic transmission breakdowns; transmission interlock failures, which allow a parked vehicle to roll away; severe wandering at highway speeds; loss of braking; and poor headlight illumination. There is nothing you can do to prevent these failures, and you may have to force Toyota to pay for their correction. **Maintenance/Repair costs:** Higher than average, but repairs aren't dealer dependent. **Parts:** Parts can be more expensive than for most other cars in this class, making it worth your while to shop at independent suppliers. Parts availability is excellent. **Extended warranty:** Not needed for 1996 and earlier models; essential for 1997 and later vehicles. **Best alternatives:** The Acura Integra; Honda Accord; Hyundai Elantra wagon, Sonata, or Tiburon; and Mazda6 or 626. **Online help:** Owner feedback, service bulletins, and complaint strategies can be accessed at *www.autosafety.org/autodefects.html*, *www.automotiveforums.com/*, *www.kbb.com*, *www.edmunds.com*, *www.carforums.com/forums*, *www.cartrackers.com/Forums*, and through Google, using "engine sludge" as the key word.

 ## Strengths and Weaknesses

The Camry is a Japanese Oldsmobile (the old rear-drive kind). Safety complaints aside, it's an excellent small family hauler because of its spacious, comfortable interior, good fuel economy, and impressive reliability and durability. Just make sure you change the oil more frequently than Toyota, (or Lexus for that matter), suggests for its V6 engine (see engine sludge comments below).

The 1985–93 models have few problems, although they're far from perfect. Main areas of concern are failure-prone cylinder head gaskets; suspension and electrical system failures; defective starter drive and ring gear; leaking low-pressure and high-pressure power-steering lines; outer CV boots that split, causing grease to leak; premature brake wear; and some paint peeling and rusting.

Premature brake wear, and excessive noise and vibrations are persistent problems with all Toyota vehicles up to the current models. Stung by consumer criticism that owners were charged for useless repairs, Toyota published a "Brake Repair" service bulletin (POL94-18) in October 1994, which set the benchmark for after-warranty assistance that can still be used today by savvy owners. Toyota states that premature brake wear and noise will be fixed under warranty for the first 12 months/24,000 km (15,000 mi.), and that vibrations will be attended to, under warranty, for up to 3 years/ 80,000 km (50,000 mi.). Front suspension bushings wear out quickly, leading to clunking and squeaking noises when driving over bumps or stopping quickly. There's also the so-called Camry chop (exceptionally rough rides when passing over uneven roadways) reported by owners of 1992–94 models. Cruise control fails frequently on all years.

1995–96 Camrys are the most reliable and reasonably priced, but they too have their shortcomings. Owners report premature brake failures and excessive brake vibration and wear; faulty window regulators; smelly ACs; and myriad rattles, clunks, and groans that seem to come from everywhere. There is also an annoying surging and shuddering when decelerating, likely caused by a faulty PCM computer module. These cars exhibit the beginnings of automatic transmission problems (such as automatic transmissions that slip out of gear when parked), but nowhere near the number of chronic breakdowns seen with 1997–2003 Camrys.

1994–96 model body problems include excessive wind noise coming from the front windshield, back doors, and sunroof. Trim items rust and fall off, door handles pull away, and mufflers have a short lifespan. No reports of rust perforation problems, but weak spots are door bottoms, rear wheel openings, and trunk and hatchback edges. There are complaints concerning premature rusting on cars painted white.

"De-contenting" hit Toyota's 1997 lineup hard, resulting in many changes that cheapened the Camry and precipitated a huge increase in owner complaints over problems that had never appeared on Toyota vehicles before. One of the worst problems first showing up in 1997, and continuing through the year 2000 models, is engine sludge buildup leading to engine failures that may cost as much as $7,000 to correct (see full report in the Sienna minivan section). Toyota has also admitted to engine head gasket leaks for the first time. Other changes you'll note on 1997 and later models are less expensive S-rated tires on models with 4-cylinder engines, cheaper heating/ventilation system components, no more assist handles for front occupants, no more chrome trim around the windshield, one door seal instead of three (greater chance for wind and water leaks), fewer airbag sensors, an LCD odometer, a distributorless ignition with the 4-cylinder, and a windshield-embedded antenna. Owners report the 1997 models have limited rear visibility (because of the side pillars and high trunk lid), less steering "feel," and more squeaks and rattles than in previous versions.

Quality problems continue to plague the 1997–2002 models. Specifically, owners report that both the engine head gasket and automatic transmission are failure-prone (to Toyota's credit, both problems are covered by an extended "goodwill" warranty), frequent hesitation or stalling out when accelerating or braking; front power windows often run off their channels; the steering wheel vibrates excessively; brake pulsation is a constant irritant, brake components (calipers, rotors, pads, master cylinder, and the ABS valve) wear out early; the AC self-destructs; warning lights constantly come on; the charcoal canister needs early replacement (covered by the emissions warranty, if you insist on it); the suspension "bottoms out" when carrying four adults; struts leak and are noisy; and the moon roof is prone to water leaks and wind noise.

VEHICLE HISTORY: 1992—No more AWD; only a hatchback and wagon are offered with a 130-hp 2.2L 4-banger or a 185-hp 3.0L V6, plus a driver's airbag. **1997**—Totally redesigned to be taller, longer, wider, more powerful, and cheaper (in both senses of the word). Gone are the coupe and station wagon variants. The wheelbase was extended by 5 cm, giving backseat passengers more room. Other changes: It's powered by a base 2.2L 133-hp 16-valve 4-cylinder engine (taken from the Celica) and an optional 3.0L 24-valve V6 that unleashes 194 horses. Either engine can be mated to a 5-speed manual or an electronically controlled 4-speed automatic. ABS and traction control is standard on all V6-equipped Camrys, rear seats have shoulder belts for the middle passenger, low beam lights are brighter. **1998**—Optional side airbags and an improved anti-theft system. **1999**—Debut of the Solara; adjustable front headrests; new upholstery. **2000**—Slightly restyled: Given larger tires and a small horsepower boost (4-cylinder engines). The following year's models remained unchanged. **2002**—Car gets larger and now carries a 157-hp 2.4 4-cylinder engine. **2003**—Power-adjustable foot pedals are offered. **2004**—SE version gets a 225-hp 3.3L V6, hooked to a revised 5-speed automatic, improved fuel injection, and additional soundproofing. Standard foglights and an in-dash 6-CD changer are new to the XLE and XLE V6. *Solara*: This year's redesign makes it much larger than its predecessor, but interior space remains practically the same. It also gets the new 3.3L V6 coupled to a 5-speed sequential-shift automatic transmission.

Solara

Introduced in the summer of 1998 as a '99 model, the Solara is essentially a longer, lower, bare-bones, two-door coupe or convertible Camry with a sportier powertrain and suspension and a more stylish exterior. But don't let this put you off. Most new Toyota model offerings, like the Sienna, Avalon, and RAV4, are Camry derivatives. Year 2000 models returned unchanged, except for the addition of a convertible version and three additional horses; 2001s were carried over without any significant improvements.

Relatively rare on the used-car market, a base model Solara will cost you $3,000–$4,000 more than an entry-level Camry sedan. And if you get one with the Sienna and Lexus ES 300's V6 power plant, you're looking at a few thousand dollars more. You have a choice of either a 4- or 6-cylinder power plant. Unfortunately, vehicles equipped with a V6 also came with a gimmicky rear spoiler and a headroom-robbing moon roof. The stiff body structure and suspension, as well as tight steering, make for easy, sports car-like handling, with lots of road feel and few surprises.

Safety Summary

All models/years: Airbag fails to deploy or is accidentally deployed. • Sudden acceleration when braking, shifting, or parking. • Stalling, then surging when accelerating or braking. • Car rolls away when parked on an incline. • Owners report that Firestone original equipment tires fail prematurely. • Vehicle wanders all over the road or drifts into oncoming traffic. **1998**—Several reports of engine fires. • Vehicle stalled, oil light came on, and fire ignited in engine compartment. • Overly soft suspension allows the chassis to scrape the roadway when passing over a small bump. • Frequent ABS brake failures. • Excessive brake noise and extended stopping distances. • Transmission gearshift lever went from Neutral to Drive without pressing button. • Airbag service indicator light stays on. • Engine malfunction light stays on. • Inadequate night illumination from headlights: Low beam halogen headlights don't carry very far; dark spot cast from left headlight results in poor visibility; and metal deflector inside the concealed headlights blocks out all light beyond 10 m. • Electrical system failure; running lights won't shut off. • Lock design allows for occupants to be temporarily locked in vehicle if someone gets out before them and locks the doors. • Power door locks fail intermittently. • Front restraints lock up when vehicle is parked on an incline. • Sun visors are too small to block the sun, and they cut visibility. • Back windshield shattered. • Fumes from inside the vehicle fog up the windshield. • Gas tank makes sloshing noise when brakes are applied. • General Tire wears excessively on the inside tread. • Frequent complaints of moon roof leaks, which may cause electrical short. • Doors have to be slammed shut. **1999**—471 safety-related incidents logged into NHTSA's database. Incredible as it may seem, the Camry continues to have serious safety-related defects that aren't much different from what's been recorded for previous model years. They include, in order of frequency: sudden unintended acceleration; airbags not deploying during a collision; inadvertent airbag deployment, injuring occupants; complete brake failure or extended stopping distances caused by poor braking; sudden acceleration; chronic engine hesitation when accelerating or stalling; engine, airbag, and ABS warning light come on constantly; optically distorted windshield; and the transmission won't hold when stopped on a hill. **2000**—312 safety-related incidents logged into NHTSA's database. **2001**—156 safety-related incidents logged into NHTSA's database. • Under-hood fire (left side) while vehicle was parked overnight. • Fire ignited from underneath vehicle while driving. • Excessive grinding noise and long stopping distances associated with ABS braking. • Brake pedal went to floor but no braking effect. • ABS brakes suddenly locked up when coming to a gradual stop. • Defective rear brake drum. • Vehicle tends to drift to the right at highway speeds. • Excessive steering wheel vibrations at speeds over 100 km/h. • Entire vehicle shakes excessively when cruising. • Vehicle's weight is poorly distributed, causing the front end to lift up when the vehicle's speed exceeds 90 km/h. • Suspension bottoms out too easily, damaging the undercarriage. • Too-compliant shock absorbers make for a rough ride over uneven terrain. • Rear suspension noise at low speeds. • Automatic transmission slippage. • With engine running and transmission in Park position, car rolled down a hill. Two small girls inside of car jumped out, but one was run over. • Car rolled backward after it was put into Park and ignition key was removed. • Vehicle parked overnight had its rear window suddenly blow out. • Windshield distortion is a strain on the eyes. • Floor-mounted gear shift indicator is hard to read. • Seat belts are too tight on either side and tighten up uncomfortably with the slightest movement. • Shoulder belt twists and won't lie straight. • Leaking suspension struts and strut rod failure. • Trunk lid may suddenly collapse. • Faulty driver's window track. • Driver-side door latch sticks. • Sulfuric acid odour enters the interior. • Fuel tank makes a sloshing noise when three-quarters full. • Clunking noise heard from rear of vehicle when gas tank is half full. • Tire jack collapsed during change of tire. **2002**—An astounding 471 owner complaints up to December 2004. • Starter caught on fire in the parking lot; under-hood fire (left side) while vehicle was parked overnight; fire ignited from underneath vehicle while driving. • Airbags failed to deploy:

> My brother was involved in a fatal crash in a new 2002 Toyota Camry XLE. The accident occurred in North Carolina and is being investigated by the highway patrol. The car left the highway and rolled over, eventually impacting a tree. The car was equipped with front, side, and side curtain airbags. No airbag deployed in this accident. I believe the lack of airbag deployment was contributory to my brother's death.

• Inadvertent airbag deployment. • Faulty cruise control caused vehicle to suddenly accelerate. • Sudden acceleration without braking effect. • Brake pedal went to floor with no braking effect. • ABS brakes suddenly locked up when coming to a gradual stop. • Defective rear brake drum. • Many owners complain of poor brake pedal design:

> Arm that holds up brake pedal is interfering with the driver's foot. Driver stated if consumer had a large size foot, it could easily get wedged and stuck on brake pedal. Foot gets caught between the floormat and the brake arm, needs to be redesigned.

• Front right axle broke six months after car was purchased. • High rear end cuts rear visibility. • Turn signal volume is too low. **2003**—265 safety-related complaints registered by NHTSA. **2004**—129 safety-related complaints are logged into NHTSA's database; almost twice as many as usual. Fire ignited in the side wheelwell. • Airbags failed to deploy; deployed inadvertently. • Sudden, unintended acceleration when braking, shifting from Park to Reverse, or pulling into a parking space:

> Difficulty shifting from Park to Reverse, then upon shifting into Drive the car accelerated uncontrollably, would not stop, collided with a mobile home, airbags did not deploy, resulting in the death of one passenger and injury of driver.

> •

> While parking the car, the steering locked turning the car to the right. The car accelerated and surged despite depressing the brake (same as ODI PE04021), the car broke a metal flag pole, damaged a retaining wall, and fell seven feet into a major street. The airbags did not deploy.

• Steering U-joint bearing fell out. • Brake and gas pedal are mounted too close together. • Brake pedal goes all the way to the floor and braking distance is increased. • Many complaints that the car drifts to the left into oncoming traffic:

> If you don't keep constant pressure on the steering wheel the car will go left at an alarming rate. The amount of drift is so bad that if you remove your hand from the wheel, the steering wheel will turn left by itself. The amount of auto wheel turn is between 3 to 12 inches.

• When in Drive on a hill, the vehicle rolls backward. When shifted into Reverse, vehicle went forward. • Transmission shudders when shifted from First to Second gear. • When accelerating, engine and transmission will hesitate for up to 4 seconds, then surge forward. This has been a problem over several model years and also includes the Lexus ES 300/330. • Poorly designed, misadjusted headlights cause a blinding glare. • Backup lights are too dim. • Airbags are disabled even when a heavy adult sits in the seat. • Inside cabin hood release latch not attached to release mechanism. • The bumpers are easily dented. • Several cases where a Firestone/Bridgestone tire sidewall unravelled. • Unstable tire jack. • Odometer over-registers by 3 percent (affects warranty, etc.). • Electronic gas mileage calculator is off by 2 km per litre (4.5 miles per gallon). Dealer said they are all off and that no repair is being contemplated.

Secret Warranties/Internal Bulletins/Service Tips

All models/years: To reduce front brake squeaks on ABS-equipped vehicles, ask the dealer to install new, upgraded rotors (#43517-32020). • Owner feedback over the last decade and dealer service managers who wish to remain anonymous tell me that Toyota has a secret warranty that will pay for replacing front disc brake components that wear out before 2 years/40,000 km. If you're denied this coverage, threaten small claims court action. • Toyota has a special kit to reduce AC odours. **All models: 1990–2000**—Measures to eliminate front brake clicking. **1997–98**—A front suspension groan can be fixed by replacing the front spring bumper. • Steering rack bushing noise. **1997–99**—Fuel door operation improvement. • Tips on reducing steering noise. • New front brake pad kits will reduce brake grinding or groaning, says bulletin #BR001-99. • To enhance headlight performance, the alignment process has been modified. **1997–2000**—Silencing steering rack end noise. **1997–2001**—Engine oil sludge will be corrected for free up to February 28, 2003. • Trunk leaks will be fixed under Toyota's base warranty.

TRUNK WATER LEAKS

BULLETIN NO: B0028-00

DATE: NOV. 3, 2000

1997–2001 Camry (U.S.); 1998–2001 Sienna; 1999–2001 Solara; 2001 Avalon

OVERVIEW: A field fix is available for incidents of moisture and odours permeating into the vehicle. The Quarter Panel Air Duct flaps may have become loose or missing. Replacing the Quarter Panel Air Duct will remedy the condition.

1998–99—Door glass that runs off its channel is a common factory-related problem that Toyota admits is covered under its base warranty. Here's the catch: The dealer isn't authorized to upgrade the channel (a half-hour procedure) unless the customer asks for the service. **1999–2000**—Seat movement, or no movement of seat adjustment. **2000–01**—Wheel bearing dust deflector ticking noise. **2001**—Troubleshooting a false MIL warning. **2002**—Special Service Campaign to replace the driver-side front airbag. • Automatic transmission shift quality improvements. • Catalytic converter heat shield rattle. • Free replacement of the JBL amplifier addresses popping noise. • Gas cap sticks. • Campaigns to repair the washer reservoir tank; remove coil spring spacers. • Tips on eliminating sulfur exhaust odours. *Solara*: Water leaking into the trunk area. • Poor durability of rear-view mirrors. **2002–03**—Harsh automatic transmission shifts:

LIGHT THROTTLE SECOND–THIRD GEAR SHIFT SHOCK/SHUDDER

2002–03 Camry

OVERVIEW: Some 2002 and 2003 model year V6 Camry vehicles produced at TMMK may exhibit a triple shock (shudder) during the 2–3 upshift under "light throttle" acceleration. Follow the repair procedure in this bulletin to adjust the condition on applicable vehicles.

• Excessive brake vibration:

BULLETIN NO: BR006-02   DATE: DEC. 24, 2002
FRONT BRAKE VIBRATION

2002–03 Camry (V6 XLE & V6 SE)

OVERVIEW: Under certain usage conditions, some 2002–03 model year Camry vehicles may exhibit front brake vibration. The rotor and pad have been improved to correct this condition. The new rotor and pad must be installed as a set. The revised parts have been introduced into production.

• Sliding roof repair tips (TSB #BO002-03). • Power front seat feels loose (TSB #BO004-03). • Poor AC/heating:

BULLETIN NO: AC001-03   DATE: APRIL 15, 2003
AC – BLOWER VOLUME GRADUALLY DIMINISHES

SUBJECT: AC performance & durability improvement
2002–03 Camry

OVERVIEW: Some 2002–03 model year Camry owners may experience a condition where the blower volume gradually decreases after about 1.5 hours of driving. It has been determined that, in hot high humidity conditions, the AC system evaporator is freezing over, blocking the airflow path. There may be some instances where this condition may affect the AC compressor and clutch assembly. An in-line thermistor resistor harness is now available to correct this concern.

2002–04—Fuel door hard to open. • Remedy for rotten-egg smelling exhaust. *Camry*: 2002–04—Intake manifold rattle (see image on following page). **2003**— Poor shift quality, can be corrected by updating the ECM calibration (TSB #TC008-03). **2004**—Correction for vehicle drifting into oncoming traffic:

VEHICLE PULLING TO THE LEFT

BULLETIN NO: ST002-04   DATE: FEB. 4, 2004

'04 Avalon, Camry & Solara

This service bulletin is to inform you of the repair procedure for the 2004 model year Avalon, Camry and Solara vehicles pulling to the left. Please use these repair methods in conjunction with the Repair Manual instructions. This repair is covered under the Toyota Comprehensive Warranty. This warranty is in effect for 36 months or 36,000 miles, whichever occurs first, from the vehicle's in-service date. Warranty application is limited to correction of a problem based upon a customer's specific complaint.

TOYOTA

Technical Service BULLETIN

June 3, 2004

Title:
INTAKE MANIFOLD NOISE

Models:
'02 – '04 Camry

Bulletin No.: EG0/8-04

TSB REVISION NOTICE:
July 13, 2004: The Applicable Warranty information has been changed.
All previous versions of this TSB should be discarded.

Some 2002 – 2004 model year Camry vehicles with the 2AZ-FE engine may experience the following condition:

- A rattle noise from the engine area, most noticeable at idle or on light acceleration.

The noise may be caused by the intake air as it flows through the intake manifold. The intake manifold has been modified to improve this condition.

- **2002 – 2004** model year **Camry** vehicles equipped with **2AZ-FE engines** produced **BEFORE** the Production Change Effective VINs shown below.

MODEL	PLANT	PRODUCTION CHANGE EFFECTIVE VIN
Camry	TMMK Line 1	4T1BE3#K#4U262489
	TMMK Line 2	4T1BE3#K#4U790816

PREVIOUS PART NUMBER	CURRENT PART NUMBER	PART NAME	QTY
17120-0H010	Same	Manifold Assembly, Intake	1

1. Verify noise is from the intake manifold.
2. Replace intake manifold following instructions on the Toyota Technical Information System (TIS), 2002 – 2004 model year Camry Repair Manual: *Engine Mechanical*.
3. Verify that the noise is not present after repair.

Warranty Information

OP CODE	DESCRIPTION	TIME	OFP	T1	T2
170011	R & R Intake Assembly	1.2	17120-0H010	91	50

Applicable Warranty*:
This repair is covered under the Toyota Comprehensive Warranty. This warranty is in effect for 36 months or 36,000 miles, whichever occurs first, from the vehicle's in-service date.

* Toyota says warranty application is limited to correction of a problem based upon a customer's specific complaint.

• Engine running lean. • Vibration during 1–2 upshift. • Accessory drivebelt squeal; belt tensioner rattle. Excessive sulfur dioxide odour. • MIL warning light constantly comes on. • ECU updated calibration.

	1996	1997	1998	1999	2000	2001	2002	2003	2004
Cost Price ($)									
Camry Coupe	20,488	—	—	—	—	—	—	—	—
Base Sedan CE	21,138	21,178	21,348	21,680	22,180	24,565	—	—	—
LE	24,718	25,458	25,268	26,508	27,070	27,695	23,755	24,800	24,800
LE V6	29,858	—	—	—	—	—	27,585	27,070	27,070
Wagon V6	32,178	—	—	—	—	—	—	—	—
Base Solara	—	—	—	26,245	26,665	27,580	28,175	28,175	28,800
V6	—	—	—	29,815	30,270	33,075	33,990	34,290	27,777
Used Values ($)									
Camry Coupe ▲	6,500	—	—	—	—	—	—	—	—
Camry Coupe ▼	5,500	—	—	—	—	—	—	—	—
Base Sedan CE ▲	5,000	6,000	8,000	10,500	12,500	13,500	—	—	—
Base Sedan CE ▼	4,000	5,000	6,500	9,000	11,000	12,000	—	—	—
LE ▲	7,500	9,500	11,500	13,500	15,500	17,000	17,000	18,000	21,000
LE ▼	6,500	8,500	10,000	12,000	14,000	16,000	15,500	18,000	18,500
LE V6 ▲	7,500	—	—	—	—	—	21,000	20,500	22,500
LE V6 ▼	7,000	—	—	—	—	—	18,500	19,000	21,000
Wagon V6 ▲	8,000	—	—	—	—	—	—	—	—
Wagon V6 ▼	7,000	—	—	—	—	—	—	—	—
Base Solara ▲	—	—	—	11,000	13,500	16,500	18,500	20,000	22,000
Base Solara ▼	—	—	—	9,000	12,000	15,000	17,000	18,500	20,500
V6 ▲	—	—	—	12,500	14,500	16,500	19,000	23,500	25,000
V6 ▼	—	—	—	11,000	13,000	15,000	16,500	20,000	22,000
Reliability	5	3	3	3	4	3	3	3	3
Crash Safety (F)	4	4	4	4	4	4	5	5	4
Side	—	3	3	3	4	3	2	3	4
Solara	—	—	—	3	3	3	3	3	5
Offset	3	5	5	5	5	5	5	5	5
Head Restraints	3	—	3	3	—	4	2	2	2
Solara	—	—	—	3	—	3	3	3	3
Rollover Resistance	—	—	—	—	—	5	4	4	4

All ratings on a numbered scale where ⑤ is good and ❶ is bad. See pages 100–101 for a more detailed description.

Volkswagen

RATING: Average (2000–04); Below Average (1998–99). The New Beetle is an expensive trip down memory lane carried along on a Golf/Jetta platform. Personally, I don't think it's worth it—with or without its speed-activated spoiler and dash-mounted bud vase. And, interestingly enough, I'm not alone in my opinion. VW new-car sales are down by about 20 percent and used Beetle prices have nosedived. Another negative is the large number of safety-related complaints registered by NHTSA involving electrical fires, chronic stalling, and transmission failures. **Maintenance/Repair costs:** Average, but only a VW dealer can repair these cars. **Parts:** Easily found, since they're taken mostly from the Golf parts bin. Body parts are harder to find. **Extended warranty:** A good idea. **Best alternatives:** Acura Integra; GM Cavalier or Sunfire; Honda Accord; Hyundai Elantra wagon, Sonata, or Tiburon; Mazda 626; Nissan Sentra; and Toyota Camry. **Online help:** For the latest owner reports on their Beetle love/hate relationships, service bulletins, and money-saving tips, look at www.myvwlemon.com, www.vwvortex.com, www.autosafety.org/autodefects.html, www.alldata.com, www.kbb.com, www.edmunds.com, www.carforums.com/forums, and www.cartrackers.com/Forums.

 ## Strengths and Weaknesses

The New Beetle was a hands-down marketing and public relations winner when the model was reintroduced as a 1998 model after being absent since 1979.

Why so much emotion for an ugly German import that never had a functioning heater, was declared "Small on Safety" by Ralph Nader and his Center for Auto Safety, and carried a puny 48-hp engine? The simple answer is that it was cheap; it was the first car most of us could afford as we went through school, got our first jobs, and dreamed of…getting a better car. Time has taken the edge off the memories of the hardship the Beetle made us endure—like having to scrape the inside windshield with our nails as our breath froze—and left us with the cozy feeling that the car wasn't that bad after all.

But it was.

Now VW has resurrected the Beetle and produced a competent front-engine, front-drive, compact car, set on the chassis and running gear of the Golf hatchback. It's much safer than its predecessor, but oddly enough, it is still afflicted by many of the same deficiencies that we learned to hate with the original. Again, without the turbocharger, the 115-hp base engine is underwhelming when you get it up to cruising speed (the 90-hp turbodiesel isn't much better), there's still not much room for rear passengers, engine noise is disconcerting, radio buttons and power accessory switches located on the door panels aren't user-friendly, front visibility is hindered by the car's quirky design, and storage capacity is at a premium.

On the other hand, the powerful, optional 1.8L turbocharged engine makes this Beetle an impressive performer; the heater works fine; steering, handling, and braking are quite good; and the interior is not as spartan or tacky as it once was.

VEHICLE HISTORY: 2000—Addition of a 150-hp turbocharged 4-cylinder engine, firmer suspension, and improved theft protection. **2001**—Larger exterior mirrors and a trunk safety release. **2002**—Introduction of the 180-hp Turbo S, with a new Electronic Stabilization Program. **2003**—Convertible and turbodiesel arrive. **2004**—Upgraded, head-protecting airbags and front head restraints; improved spoiler, and new wheels. The GLX model has been axed.

In a nutshell, here are the New Beetle's strong points: standard side airbags; easy handling; sure-footed, comfortable though firm ride; impressive braking; comfortable and supportive front seats with plenty of headroom and legroom; and a cargo area that can be expanded by folding down the rear seats.

On the minus side: Serious safety defects have been reported by owners (see NHTSA data below), powertrain performance is unimpressive, and body construction is second-rate. Specific owner gripes: The base engine runs out of steam around 100 km/h; diesel engines lack pep and produce lots of noise and vibration; faulty O_2 sensor causes the Check Engine light to come on; frequent electronic control module (ECM) failures; axle oil pan and oil pump failures; delayed shifts from Park to Drive, or failure to shift into Fourth gear; car is easily buffeted by crosswinds; optional high-mounted side mirrors, large head restraints, and large front roof pillars obstruct front and rear visibility; limited rear legroom and headroom; difficult rear entry/exit; excessive engine and brake noise; early brake component replacement; malfunctioning dash gauges; awkward-to-access radio buttons and door panel-mounted power switches; faulty window regulators; skimpy interior storage and trunk space; interior vent louvre loosens and breaks; hatchback rattles and sometimes fails to open; AC disengages when decelerating; front lights retain water and short out; and the low-slung chassis causes extensive undercarriage damage when going over a curb.

Safety Summary

1998—Driver's head restraint sits too high and can't be lowered, seriously restricting rear visibility. • Oil pan hole leaked oil and caused vehicle to stall. • Sudden loss of power while driving at 100 km/h, forcing driver to reset computer by restarting the vehicle. • While driving at any speed, vehicle goes into emergency mode and suddenly slows down to about 20 km/h. • Instrument cluster failure. • Vehicle was smoking under the hood because a faulty hose leaked oil onto the engine. • While stopped at a traffic light, vehicle exploded into flames and was a total loss. **1999**—Vehicle caught fire on inside of ignition switch box. • Another fire reportedly ignited in the wiring harness behind the dashboard. • Brake and accelerator pedals are too close together. • Sudden, unintended acceleration, and steering locked up. • Cruise control wouldn't disengage when brakes were applied. • Airbags failed to deploy. • Airbag warning light often comes on for no reason. • Sudden tread separation on the low-profile sporty tires. • When brakes are applied in a panic stop, one of the rear wheels will lock up along with one of the front wheels, causing vehicle to go into a spin. • Chronic hesitation and stalling on the highway (one fatality reported). • Vehicle won't start when facing down on a slope. • Frequent automatic transmission breakdowns. • Clutch failure causes vehicle to stall. • Left-side driveshaft cracked twice. • Driver's seat broke in a collision, causing severe injuries. • Driver-side seat came off its track and fell into back seat. • Tire jack fails to hold vehicle. • Cracked battery leaked acid onto power-steering fluid reservoir. • Vehicle shakes and shudders when driven with the sunroof fully open. • Headrest cannot be adjusted down to permit driver to see through rear and side windows; it's also quite uncomfortable for short drivers. **2000–01**—Many complaints of prolonged hesitation when accelerating. • Steering suddenly locked up. • Prematurely worn rear brake pads (TSB #00-01, November 27, 2000). • Low-mounted fuel tank is easily punctured. • Mass airflow sensor and secondary air injection pump motor failures. • Back glass suddenly shattered. • Windows fall into door channel because of defective regulators. • Hard to keep rear window free of rain, snow, or dew. • Windshield distortions impede vision. • Airbags failed to deploy. • Airbag warning light stays lit constantly. • Rear seat belted passengers hit their heads on the unpadded side pillars. **2002**—ABS failure. • Window goes up and down on its own. • Brake fluid leakage. • Harsh downshifts; vehicle loses power (mass airflow sensor is suspected cause):

> Car downshifts extremely hard when coming to a stop, causing driver and passengers to be lunged forward in their seats. Dealer states that this is a characteristic of the car. Problem is intermittent and increases when vehicle is warmed up. On one occasion downshift occurred so hard that I thought I was just rear-ended by another car. I bought the car for my wife and now she is afraid to drive it.

2003—Sudden acceleration, stalling. • Side airbag deployed for no reason. • Driver-side airbag failed to deploy. • Punctured fuel tank leaked fuel. • Steering wheel lock-up; excessive shake, constant pulling to the right (torque steer). • Back glass suddenly exploded. • Rear windshield is hard to see through. • Dash warning lights come on constantly for no apparent reason. • Head restraints still sit too high to be comfortable and obstruct rear visibility. • Open sunroof sucks exhaust into the cabin. • Left front strut slipped down through the spindle, causing the spindle to hit the wheelwell. **2004**—Airbags failed to deploy. • Complete transmission failure. • Wiper suddenly quit working. • Airbag warning light comes on constantly. • Annoying beep when seat belt isn't buckled. • Driver-side window lowers on its own. • On convertible models, the windows catch on the top when the doors are opened.

Secret Warranties/Internal Bulletins/Service Tips

All models/years: Lousy radio reception. **1998–99**—An erratic-shifting automatic transaxle is likely caused by an improper throttle angle setting. VW will correct the problem under its base warranty. • Troubleshooting tips on silencing instrument panel, front door lock/latch, and door speaker squeaks or rattles. • Possible causes and fix for wind noise or whistle coming from the instrument panel. • Diagnosing humming noise from front of vehicle when cornering. • No adjustment of airflow from centre air outlets. • Throttle pedal and shifter lever vibration or knocking vibration. **1998–2002**—Troubleshooting a noisy blower motor. • Malfunctioning instrument cluster. • Hood emblem chrome peeling off. • Faulty window regulator repair tips. **2000–01**—Prematurely worn rear brake pads. **2001**—Inoperative secondary oil pump. **2002**—Transmission appears to leak fluid. • Inoperative fresh air blower motor. **2003–04**—Erratic performance of manual transmission Reverse gear. **2000–01**—Turn signal blinks too fast. **2004**—Hard starting, no-starts, rough running when wet; may emit light gray smoke. • Front-seat passenger airbag disabled when full-sized passenger is seated. • Inoperative rear window heating element. • Monsoon radio amplifier doesn't automatically switch off.

NEW BEETLE PROFILE

	1998	1999	2000	2001	2002	2003	2004
Cost Price ($)							
Base	19,940	21,500	21,950	21,950	21,950	23,210	23,690
Used Values ($)							
Base ▲	7,000	8,500	10,000	12,000	14,500	17,500	19,500
Base ▼	6,000	7,000	8,500	10,500	13,000	16,000	18,000
Reliability	②	②	③	③	③	③	③
Crash Safety (F)	—	④	④	④	④	④	④
Side	—	⑤	⑤	⑤	⑤	⑤	⑤
Offset	⑤	⑤	⑤	⑤	⑤	⑤	⑤
Head Restraints (F)	④	④	—	④	④	④	③
Rear	③	③	—	—	③	③	—
Rollover Resistance	—	—	—	—	—	④	④

All ratings on a numbered scale where ⑤ is good and ❶ is bad. See pages 100–101 for a more detailed description.

RATING: Below Average (1998–2004); Not Recommended (1989–97). Don't listen to the car journalists who love European cars. They don't pay for service visits. Read owner opinions and you'll see that the Passat is a big disappointment. Word has gotten out that these cars are over-hyped for their performance prowess, that they aren't very dependable, and that they cost a lot to maintain. Consequently, Passats have lost their lustre to Japanese luxury cars and now depreciate quickly. But beware; their low price won't cover the extraordinarily high repair bills you'll get from Otto and Hans. But, if you're a risk-taker, protect your wallet somewhat by staying away from pre-'98s and insist upon a comprehensive extended warranty. **Maintenance/Repair costs:** Much higher than average. Most major repairs are dealer dependent. **Parts:** Parts and service are more expensive than average; long waits for parts are commonplace. **Extended warranty:** Yes, principally for the powertrain. **Best alternatives:** Acura Integra, Audi A4 or A6, and the Honda Accord. **Online help:** For owner feedback detailing the "dark side" of VW ownership go to *www.myvwlemon.com*, *www.vwvortex.com*, *www.autosafety.org/autodefects.html*, *www.alldata.com*, *www.kbb.com*, *www.edmunds.com*, *www.carforums.com/forums*, *www.cartrackers.com/Forums*, and through Google, using "VW coil pack stalling," or "engine sludge" in your search.

Strengths and Weaknesses

This front-drive compact sedan and wagon uses a standard 2.0L engine and other mechanical parts borrowed from the Golf, Jetta, and Corrado. However, a 2.8L V6 became the standard power plant beginning with the '99 wagon. Its long wheelbase and squat appearance give the Passat a massive, solid feeling, while its styling makes it look sleek and clean. As with most European imports, it comes fairly well appointed.

As far as overall performance goes, the Passat is no slouch. The multi-valve 4-cylinder engine is adequate, and its handling is superior to that of most of the competition. The 2.8L V6 provides lots of power when revved and is the engine that works best with an automatic transmission.

VEHICLE HISTORY: 1990—Debuts with a 134-hp 2.0L 4-cylinder engine. **1993**—A 172-hp 2.8L V6 powered the GLX. **1994**—4-cylinder engines were axed. **1995**—Redesigned model adopted dual airbags, a restyled interior, rear headrests, a softened suspension, and a much-improved crashworthiness rating; 4-cylinder engine returned and a TDI wagon and sedan debuted. **1998**—Based upon the Audi A4 and A6, this model offers more usable interior space, better handling, and better engine performance with its 150-hp turbocharged 1.8L engine and 190-hp 2.8L V6. **2000**—An AWD model, heated front seats, a brake wear indicator, and an improved anti-theft ignition. **2001**—Mid-year changes included a new nose, upgraded tail lights and dash gauges, chassis improvements, and the debut of a 170-hp engine alongside a new W8, 270-hp AWD luxury car. **2002**—Given a 134-hp 2.0L turbocharged diesel coupled to either a front-drive, or an all-wheel-drive powertrain. Also new: a 5-speed automatic transmission with manual capability. **2003**—W8 given a 6-speed manual transmission.

Passats are infamous for automatic transmission failures, engine ignition coil/fuel system stalling and no starts, and engines gummed up by oil sludge; all costly-to-repair items covered by secret warranties. Even when they're operating as they should, the Passat's manual and automatic gearboxes leave a lot to be desired. For example, the 5-speed manual transmission gear ranges are too far apart: There's an enormous gap between Third and Fourth gear, and the 4-speed automatic shifts poorly with the 4-banger. Also, owners report that the transmission won't shift from lower gears, as well as problems with clutch slave cylinder leaks, front brakes (master cylinder replacements, brake booster failure, rotor warpage, premature wear, and excessive noise), MacPherson struts, and fuel and electrical systems as the car ages. Owners mention defective tie-rod and constant velocity joint seals that allow debris to enter into system, effectively causing premature wearout of internal components; engines often leak oil; early replacement of the power-steering assembly; and fuel and computer module problems that lead to hard starts and chronic stalling.

On the body side, there's a helicopter-type wind noise when cruising with the windows or sunroof open; sunroof rattles; front spoiler and rear trim fall off; a persistent water leak from the pollen filter; interior trim and controls are fragile; heated seats are a pain in the…well, you know; driver's seat memory feature fails; door speakers are frequently replaced; fuel gauge malfunctions, indicating fuel in tank when it's empty; windshields may be optically distorted; rear-view passenger-side mirrors are too small and cause several blind spots.

Owners report that VW dealer servicing is the pits. Cars have to be brought in constantly to fix the same problem, recall campaign repairs are often slow because parts aren't available, and warranty coverage is spotty because VW headquarters doesn't empower or pay dealers sufficiently to take the initiative. Competent servicing and parts are particularly hard to find away from the larger cities, and many of the above-mentioned deficiencies can cost you an arm and a leg to repair.

 **Safety Summary**

1998—Engine head gasket/manifold leaks, car stalls, and turbo blows:

> I wanted to advise you of problems I am having with my VW '98 Passat. I see you have the Passat listed in your book as a good buy. I am writing to get you to consider changing your recommendation.

I just got off the phone with the National Safety Transportation Board. They are racking up calls on the Passat. Seems I am not the only one who has a Passat that stalls out with no warning for no apparent reason. I now have $2,400 into trying to fix the problem, and no solution has been found. It is a miracle I have not been in and/or caused an accident. The other NHTSA complaints are identical to mine.

In addition, my turbo and manifold blew out, to the tune of $1,500, due to extreme heat. I live in Maine, take great care of the car, and have been told by two dealers that the turbo and manifold should not have blown at 64,000 miles [100,000 km]. To boot, they said there is nothing I can do to prevent it from blowing again. The NHTSA also said there were a number of complaints for blown turbos. My mechanic said the folks at the VW parts warehouse in Boston have had so many calls to replace manifolds and turbos on Passats, that they have the parts list pinned up over their phones.

I don't think this is a good sign for what is becoming a number-one sedan choice in America, and hope you warn potential buyers in your next edition and on your website. My next stop is the *myvwlemon.com* site—thanks for the link!

L.C.
PORTLAND, MAINE

• Erratic transmission performance. • Gas tank can't be filled without the pump shutting off repeatedly. • AC re-circulation switch failure. • Serious blind spots caused by the small size and narrow view of the three mirrors. • Front seats move back and forth when vehicle is braking or accelerating. • Total electrical-system failure. **1999**—Electrical fire. • Airbags failed to deploy. • Airbag light comes on for no reason. • Sudden, unintended acceleration. • Cruise control doesn't disengage, or engages on its own. • Accelerator pedal fails to return after full throttle. • Chronic stalling on the highway. • Early transmission clutch failure. • Clutch depressed to the floor and gear stayed engaged. • Front suspension's lower right arm failure caused by a faulty bushing. • Front left wheel came off when making a turn. • Premature failures of the Michelin MXV4 tire; when rear tires blow out, they wreak havoc on vehicle's undercarriage (wheelwell and well lining), in some cases causing the fuel tank to leak. • Other complaints of ruptured fuel tanks. • Oil line ruptured while driving. • Missing power steering cap caused fluid to leak out. • Driver's seat has excessive fore and aft movement. • Windshield cracked while vehicle was parked in direct sunlight. **2000**—More reports of fire erupting in the engine compartment. • Excess raw fuel flows out of the exhaust system. • Hard starts and chronic stalling. • Check Engine light comes on intermittently and then engine shuts down. • While cruising, vehicle speeds up; when brakes applied, it slows down, until foot is taken off the brake, then it surges again. Owners describe it this way:

Dangerous situation. When accelerating from a complete stop, vehicle does one of three things: 1) gasps for gas and goes nowhere (dangerous when making left-hand turns), or 2) tries to move ahead like a carbureted car with vapour lock, or 3) performs normally.

• Braking doesn't disengage cruise control. • Hesitation and long delays when accelerating. • Automatic transmission suddenly drops out of gear. • Airbags failed to deploy; airbag warning light stays lit. • Many complaints of windshield distortion (there's an accordion effect where letters and objects expand and contract as they pass by). • Passenger window suddenly exploded just after being rolled up. • Windshield wipers cut out. • Plastic engine nose shield fell off. • Rear tire failure damaged the fuel-filler neck, causing a fuel leak. **2002**—An incredible number of automatic transmission malfunctions, breakdowns, and early replacements. • Transmission vibration and noise. • Premature CV joint failure. • Oil pan is easily punctured because of low ground clearance. • Some electrical and fuel system glitches cause chronic stalling; ignition coils still seem to be a primary cause of this stalling and loss of engine power. • Gas pedal remained stuck to the floor. • Brakes don't grab as well when vehicle is cold, premature brake wear, and noisy braking. **2003**—Several reports that fire ignited in the engine compartment. • Excess raw fuel flows out of the exhaust system. • Hard starts and chronic stalling. • Check Engine light comes on intermittently and then engine shuts down. • While cruising, vehicle speeds up, when brakes applied, it slows down until foot is taken off the brake, when it surges again. • Vehicle runs out of fuel despite the fuel gauge showing a quarter-tank of gas. • Braking doesn't disengage cruise control. • Hesitation, long delays when accelerating. • Automatic transmission suddenly drops out of gear; airbags failed to deploy or deploy for no reason. One VW employee told U.S. federal investigators he was fired for complaining about the airbag hazard:

> The driver-side head airbag (air curtain) of a 2003 Volkswagen Passat W8 sedan deployed spontaneously while I was driving the car...a few minutes later, when the car was stopped, the steering wheel airbag deployed spontaneously...I suffered a permanent wrist injury and am suffering from post-traumatic stress syndrome...the incident, which happened during a test drive, was reported to the management of the VW dealership for which I was working and to VW of America by the management.

• Airbag warning light stays lit. • Many complaints of windshield distortion (accordion effect). • Passenger window suddenly exploded just after being rolled up. • Windshield wipers cut out. • Plastic engine nose shield fell off. • Rear tire failure damaged the fuel-filler neck, causing a fuel leak. • Super-heated seats. **2004**—Vehicle lurches forward when braking or accelerating:

> When slowing to a stop transmission/drivetrain occasionally will demonstrate a jarring and potentially dangerous "clunk" as if the transmission is dropping out of the car. The car also lurches forward slightly. We have read that some dealers tell their customers the problem is due to a faulty transmission control module. Our dealer said they could do nothing, denying ever hearing about the problem. We contacted VW-USA and they said they had no knowledge of such a problem. This is clearly untrue!!! There are complaints of this problem all over the Internet. VW is setting itself up for tremendous liability issues should injuries occur because of this problem.

All ratings on a numbered scale where Ⓢ is good and ❶ is bad. See pages 100–101 for a more detailed description.

• Engine seized because of oil sludging. • Transmission control module failure, clutch failure, hard shifting, and gears slam into place with a clunking sound. • Automatic transmission tends to hesitate and then jumps forward. • Loss of power steering, grinding noise. • Prematurely worn rear brake pads. • Electrical short circuits shut off lights. • Insufficient space between the footrest and clutch pedal; foot gets trapped. • Windshield wiper collects snow and ice in wiper groove. • Tire tread separation; defective valve stems.

Secret Warranties/Internal Bulletins/Service Tips

All models/years: Failure-prone, malfunctioning automatic transmissions. **1995–99**—An erratic-shifting automatic transmission may be caused by an improper throttle angle setting. **1998–99**—Tips on fixing a door speaker rattle or vibration. • VW says a delayed upshift after a cold start is normal and a wait of 40 seconds isn't too long (typical of company logic: "Our cars are perfect, our customers aren't."). **1998–2000**—Defective fresh air control lever light affects operation of heating/AC system. **1998–2001**—Malfunctioning radio volume control and instrument cluster. **1999**—Engine cranks, but won't start. • Malfunctioning windshield wipers. • Engine misfire. **2000–01**—Airbag warning light remains lit. **2001**—Noisy sunroof. • Broken armrest lid latch. **2003**—Updates for the ECM and TCM modules. • AC musty odours.

PASSAT PROFILE

	1996	1997	1998	1999	2000	2001	2002	2003	2004
Cost Price ($)									
Base	27,230	28,620	28,450	29,100	29,100	29,500	29,550	29,550	29,550
Used Values ($)									
Base ▲	5,500	6,500	8,500	11,500	14,000	16,500	19,000	22,000	25,500
Base ▼	4,000	5,500	7,000	10,000	12,500	15,000	17,500	20,500	23,500
Reliability	2	2	2	2	2	3	3	3	3
Crash Safety (F)	4	4	—	—	5	5	5	5	5
Side	—	—	—	—	4	4	4	4	4
Offset	1	1	5	5	5	5	5	5	5
Head Restraints	—	1	2	2	—	1	1	1	1
Rear	—	—	1	1	—	—	—	—	—
Rollover Resistance	—	—	—	—	—	—	—	4	4

LARGE CARS

These are the cars you're most likely to see in your rear-view mirror with their red and blue lights flashing. Quintessential highway cruisers for travelling salespeople, law enforcement agencies, large families, and retirees, full-sized American cars are icons of a time long passed. No longer able to compete with high fuel costs and more versatile minivans and small sport-utilities, most of these "land yachts" have been axed or are being phased out, as is the case with Ford's Crown Victoria and Grand Marquis.

The Crown Victoria and Grand Marquis are cheap and plentiful gas-guzzlers. True, they aren't as reliable as the Asian competition, but repairs aren't as costly, either.

DaimlerChrysler is bringing back the rear-drive wagon with its new Magnum. The rear-drive configuration has been a winner in the past, but with a mishmash of doubtful-quality Mercedes parts, long-term dependability is less than reassuring.

Chrysler has stayed in the game with its spacious and attractively styled Concorde, Intrepid, and 300M sedans. Unfortunately, these family sedans are several notches below Ford and GM when it comes to dependability and highway performance. Chrysler hopes to climb back up the performance and quality ladder with its new 2005 rear-drive Magnum wagon equipped with a Hemi engine. Initial reports aren't all that positive.

Owners once had to pay a premium for these behemoths, which usually came fully loaded with performance and convenience features, but they were happy to do so because these vehicles offer considerable comfort and stability at high speeds. They also depreciate relatively quickly (making them great used-car bargains), they can seat six adults comfortably, and they're ideal for motoring vacations. Repairs are a snap and can be done almost anywhere, and there's a large reservoir of reasonably priced replacement parts sold through independent agencies.

The downside? Atrocious fuel economy, mediocre highway performance, and handling that's neither precise nor exciting. The interior is comfortable but not as versatile as a minivan or SUV, seniors find entry and exit physically challenging, and you don't get as commanding a view of the road as in other, taller vehicles.

LARGE CAR RATINGS

Average

DaimlerChrysler 300M, Concorde, Intrepid
(2002–04)
Ford Cougar, Thunderbird (1985–97)

Ford Crown Victoria, Grand Marquis
(1996–2004)

Not Recommended

DaimlerChrysler Concorde, Intrepid,
LHS, New Yorker, Vision (1993–2001)

Ford Cougar, Thunderbird (1999–2002)

Station Wagons (Full-Sized)

If passenger and cargo space and carlike handling are what you want, a large station wagon may not be the answer. A used minivan, van, light truck, downsized SUV, or compact wagon can fill the same niche and be just as cheap, and it will probably still be around a decade from now. Once-popular rear-drive, full-sized wagons—like the GM Caprice and Roadmaster (both axed in 1996)—have lost out to the van and minivan craze.

Some disadvantages of large station wagons include difficulty in keeping the interior heated in winter, atrocious gas consumption, sloppy handling, and poor rear visibility. Rear hatches and rear brake supporting plates tend to be rust-prone.

DaimlerChrysler

300M, CONCORDE, INTREPID, LHS, NEW YORKER, VISION	★★★

RATING: Average (2002–04); Not Recommended (1993–2001). Like most Chryslers, these poor quality cars are more style than substance. Recent models get a better rating not because they're better built, but because they're better protected with a 7-year powertrain warranty to protect you from chronic engine failure (particularly the 2.7L Mitsubishi V6) and automatic transmission breakdowns. They are also dirt-cheap, because no one wants cars that are no longer built. Although these cars are bargain priced, factory glitches can steal away most of your savings. Be especially wary of the discontinued LHS, New Yorker, and Vision. Parts are rare and mechanics cringe when these hard-to-service cars arrive in their service bay. **Maintenance/Repair costs:** Higher than average, but most repairs aren't dealer dependent. **Parts:** Higher-than-average cost (independent suppliers sell for much less), but not hard to find. **Extended warranty:** If you can't get the original Chrysler powertrain warranty, don't give these cars a second glance. In fact, what you really need is bumper-to-bumper protection—a $2,000–$3,000 extra. **Best alternatives:** GM Bonneville, Caprice, LeSabre, or Roadmaster; Ford's early Cougar, T-Bird, Crown Victoria, or Mercury Grand Marquis. **Online help:** *www.datatown.com/chrysler, www.wam.umd.edu/ ~gluckman/Chrysler/index.html, www.daimlerchryslervehicleproblems.com, intrepidhorrorstories.blogspot.com,* and *www.autosafety.org/autodefects.html.*

 ## Strengths and Weaknesses

These full-sized cars share the same chassis and offer most of the same standard and optional features. They provide loads of passenger space and many standard features, such as four-wheel disc brakes and independent rear suspension. Since their 1998 redesign, base models are equipped with a failure-prone 2.7L V6 aluminum engine that delivers 200 hp. Higher line variants get a more powerful 3.2L V6 225-hp power plant or a 242-hp 3.5L V6. Earlier models also carried a 3.3L 153-hp 6-banger, but 70 percent of buyers chose the 3.5L for its extra horses. Both engines provide plenty of low-end torque and acceleration, but this advantage is lost somewhat when traversing hilly terrain: The smaller V6 power plant strains to keep up.

These cars have better handling and steering response than the Sable, Taurus, or GM mid-sized front-drives, but the difference is marginal when you tote up the $3,000–$10,000 cost of powertrain, brake, and AC repairs.

Furthermore, these cars can be as unsafe as they are unreliable. Read the following owners' experiences, which are both scary and typical:

> Travelling on the freeway at 100 km/h, my 1999 Chrysler 300M's rear windshield was sucked out and flew to the side of the road. I had no prior problems with the windshield. Entire rear windshield and casing flew off.

> •

> My 2000 Concorde accelerated on its own. I had to hit a tree to stop the car. The airbags did not deploy upon impact. Tires continued spinning after impact, until I turned off the ignition.

Owner reports confirm that there are chronic problems with engine sludge gumming up the works of the 2.7L engine, leaking 3.3L engine head gaskets, and noisy lifters that wear out prematurely around 60,000 km. Water pumps often self-destruct and take the engine timing chain along with them (a $1,200 repair). Engine surging and unintended acceleration are also frequent refrains affecting all model years. However, the one recurring safety problem affecting almost all model years concerns the steering system. Says *www.daimlerchryslervehicleproblems.com*:

> Chrysler has been under investigation by NHTSA for more than 55,000 warranty claims for steering problems with these vehicles and 1,450 reports of steering control problems, some including complete loss of steering control....

> Many consumers have also paid over $1,200 (U.S.) for replacement steering assemblies.... Common symptoms of steering problems with these vehicles are typically loose steering, excessive play in the steering, vibration, wandering, steering out of alignment, clunks, rattle, rubbing, or binding.

The 4-speed LE42 automatic transmission is a spin-off of Chrysler's failure-prone A604 version, and owner reports show it to be just as unreliable. Owners tell of chronic glitches in the computerized transmission's shift timing and other computer malfunctions, which result in early replacement and driveability problems (stalling, hard starts, and surging).

Body problems abound, with lots of interior noise; uneven fit and finish with misaligned doors and jagged trunk edges; poor-quality trim items that break or fall off easily; exposed screw heads; faulty door hinges that make the doors rattle-prone and hard to open; distorted, poorly mounted windshields; windows that come off their tracks or are misaligned and poorly sealed; power window motor failures; and steering wheel noise when the car is turning.

AC failures are commonplace and costly to repair. The problem has become so prevalent that Chrysler has a little-known warranty extension that will pay for the replacement of the evaporator up to seven years. Chrysler has tried to limit compensation to certain models only, but the company is stuck with its 7-year benchmark, first announced over a decade ago, which owners can now cite for any AC failure (see page 58).

VEHICLE HISTORY: 1994—Debut of a sporty LHS and redesigned New Yorker equipped with variable-assist power steering; Concorde gets the touring suspension and a small horsepower boost (eight). **1997**—New Yorker dropped along with the 3.3L V6 on the base LX model. **1998**—Concorde and Intrepid were completely redesigned, given two new V6s (a 200-hp 2.7L and a 225-hp 3.2L), ABS, traction control (on the LXi), and dual front airbags. **1999**—Improved steering and ride. **2000**—Suspension upgrades, a freshened instrument panel, and standard variable-assist steering on the LXi. **2001**—Steering-mounted audio controls, a rear seat centre shoulder belt, and an internal trunk release. **2002**—A 300M Special performance model comes with a new grille, upgraded ABS, and more user-friendly child safety seat anchors. Concorde got the LHS's styling and most of the other LHS amenities, including a 250-hp 3.5L V6, leather trim, high-tech gauges, ABS, traction control, and 17-inch alloy wheels. The LXi acquired the 3.2L V6 with a 234-hp variant of the 3.5L V6. **2003**—Intrepid gets a 244-hp 3.5L V6, Concorde horsepower goes to 250, and the 300M's power is boosted to 255 hp. All adopted rear-drive in late-2004 models. It'll be fun to watch Chrysler badmouth front-drives to promote its new rear-drive models.

300M and LHS

These two models represent the near-luxury and sport clones of the Chrysler Concorde. Although they use the same front-drive platform as the Concorde, their bodies are shorter and they're styled differently. In fact, the 300M is the shortest of Chrysler's mid-sized sedans. Both cars are powered by a 253-hp 3.5L V6 mated to Chrysler's AutoStick semi-automatic transmission. Mechanical and body deficiencies generally mirror those of the Concorde and Intrepid.

 Safety Summary

All models/years: No airbag deployment in a collision. • 2.7L engine suddenly self-destructs because of excess oil sludge and overheating. Owners describe the failure this way:

> The primary symptom is that the car heater, for no reason, does not blow hot air. If this has been happening it is likely that your car engine has been overheating and causing sludge to build up in the top half of the engine. Ultimately your engine will fail with very little warning. Some symptoms are: car starts to burn oil, very light traces of white smoke from exhaust, and the engine may seem to run a little rough at idle.

Examine your oil fill cap to see if there is any buildup of a black grease-like gunk. If you see this, ask a mechanic to check for a sludge buildup. If sludge is present your engine may fail with little or no warning. Cost for repairs averages $6,500 (U.S.).

Two excellent websites that cover this problem from a Canadian and an American perspective are *intrepidhorrorstories.blogspot.com/2003_11_01_intrepidhorrorstories_archive.html* and *www.autosafety.org/article.php?did=961&scid=122*. Interestingly, Mercedes-Benz recently settled a class action lawsuit for $32 million (U.S.) over engine sludge breakdowns affecting its 1998–2001 lineup of luxury cars. See *www.legalnewswatch.com/news_182.html*.

• Engine rod bearing failure. • Engine surging and sudden, unintended acceleration. • Many reports of sudden transmission failures, often because of cracked transmission casings. • Transmission fluid leakage caused by defective transmission casing bolt. • Gas fumes enter the interior. • Windshields are often distorted and may fall out while vehicle is underway. • A high rear windowsill obstructs rear visibility. • Headlights may be too dim for safe motoring, cut out completely, or come on by themselves. Defrosting is also inadequate, allowing ice and moisture to collect at the base of the windshield. Chrysler has a fix for these two problems that requires the installation of a new headlight lens and small foam pads into the defroster outlet ducts. • Both ABS and non-ABS brakes perform poorly, resulting in excessively long stopping distances or the complete loss of braking ability. • Brake rotors rust prematurely and warp easily, and pads have to be changed every 15,000 km. • The overhead digital panel is distracting and forces you to take your eyes from the road. • The emergency brake pedal catches pant cuffs and shoelaces as you enter or exit the vehicle. **1998**—Reports of sudden acceleration when shifting into Reverse. • When transmission relay fails, it causes a harsh downshift to Second gear while at highway speeds. **1999**—Vehicle suddenly accelerated when shifted into Reverse at a car wash. • The bolt that holds the fan and engine pulley came loose, resulting in complete loss of steering ability. • Brakes continually lock up, grind when applied, and result in extended stopping distance. • Vehicle will suddenly shudder or lurch violently while underway at cruising speed. • Fuel smell invades the interior. • Shifter pin to interlock cable broke off, causing the ignition key to be removable while vehicle is in gear. • Frequent failure of the power window motors. **2000–01**—Transmission won't shift to Reverse and engine stalls. • Side seat belts don't retract. • Front and rear windshields distort view; there may be an annoying reflection on the inside of the windshield, particularly evident on vehicles with beige interiors. **2002**—Yikes! Transmission malfunctions continue unabated:

> Transmission intermittently bumps, shifts, or slams into gear. [It happens] [w]hen driving at around 40–50 mph [65–80 km/h] and flooring it to accelerate then letting off the accelerator pedal. There is sometimes a bang or bump, sometimes harsh feeling in the front end or transmission. This is sometimes so hard that passengers feel it and complain. Bump is sometimes felt on deceleration in lower gears nearing a stop.

• Steering drifts; sometimes takes undue effort or squeaks and clunks. • Seat belt button is too sensitive; belt is easily unlatched inadvertently. *300M:* **1999**—Airbags suddenly deployed for no reason when changing lanes. • Transmission jumped from Park to Reverse with engine running. • Driver's son took shifter out of Park without key in ignition, and vehicle rolled down hill. • Vehicle constantly shakes and shimmies; wobbles and bobbles on the highway. **2001**—Sudden stalling in traffic. • Unstable driver's seat. • Fuel tank easily overflows. **2002**—Brake failure, then engine surges. • No-starts. • Sunroof exploded. • Right front wheel disconnected from vehicle. **2003**—Sudden brake and automatic transmission failure. • Surging when stopped. • Rear visibility compromised by narrow rear windows in the 300M. **2004**—Steering wheel vibration and clicking. • Automatic rear-view mirror operates erratically. • Trunk collects water, interferes with spare tire access.

Secret Warranties/Internal Bulletins/Service Tips

All models/years: A rotten-egg odour coming from the exhaust is probably caused by a malfunctioning catalytic converter; this is covered by Chrysler's original warranty and by the emissions warranty. Don't take no for an answer. The same advice goes for all the squeaks and rattles and the water and wind leaks that afflict these vehicles. Don't let Chrysler or the dealer pawn off these problems as maintenance items. They're all factory related and should be covered for at least five years. **All models: 1993–98**—Delayed transaxle engagement can be corrected through upgraded hardware and software components. **1993–99**—Troubleshooting tips for trunk water and dust leaks. • Paint delamination, peeling, or fading (see Part Two "Paint and Body Defects," page 71–75). **1993–2000**—If the vehicle leads or pulls at highway speeds, TSB #02-16-99 suggests a whole series of countermeasures, including replacing the engine mounts if necessary. Chrysler will apply the base warranty to this repair. • Loose or noisy steering may be corrected by servicing the inner tie-rod bushings or by simply replacing the tie-rod. • Harsh, erratic, or delayed transmission shifts can be corrected by replacing the throttle position sensor (TPS) with a revised part. **1993–2001**—More tips on fixing loose or noisy steering. **1995–99**—More troubleshooting tips are offered on diagnosing and fixing trunk water leaks. **1998–99**—A rough idle or poor driveability may require the testing and replacing of the EGR valve and power control module (PCM). • An engine hiss noise can be silenced by replacing the throttle body assembly. • Delayed shifts and other transmission malfunctions affecting a broad range of models are addressed in TSB #21-03-98. This is proof positive that Chrysler's transmission woes are far from over. • Troubleshooting tips for no hot air or lack of cold air. • Poor heater performance may mean the PCM should simply be reprogrammed. • Window sticks in the up position. • Countermeasures for correcting excessive road noise and a variety of squeaks, rattles, and squawks. • Troubleshooting tips for correcting water leaks on top and/or under floor carpets. • Poor AM radio reception can be fixed by installing a new electronic backlight module. **1998–2000**—Poor AC performance can be fixed by first carrying out Customer Satisfaction Recall #857 and then reprogramming the PCM. • Repair procedures are outlined for reattaching the rear door trim panel. • Guidelines for silencing wind noise emanating from the sunroof and the area in front of the B-pillars. • Front suspension strut squeaking can be stopped by installing a revised front strut striker cap. **1998–2001**—Loose driver's seat. • Window sticks in the up position. **1998–2004**—Remedy

---

STEERING – LOOSE FEEL/ CLUNKING ON TURNS

BULLETIN NO: 19-001-01   MARCH 23, 2001

OVERVIEW: This bulletin provides service procedures and parts information for the inner tie-rod bushings.

1993–2001 (LH) Concorde/Intrepid/LHS/New Yorker/Vision/300M

SYMPTOM: Loose feel or clunk in the steering wheel as the wheel is moved from side to side.

DIAGNOSIS: Observe the inner tie-rod to steering gear attaching point while moving the steering wheel from side to side. If there is movement between the gear and inner tie-rod, perform the repair.

for a 3.5L engine that stumbles or misfires, according to TSB #09-002-03. • Rear headliner sags or rattles. • Erratic AC operation:

AC – ERRATIC OPERATION

BULLETIN NO: 24-009-01   **DATE: AUG. 3, 2001**

1998 - **2002** (LH) LHS/300M/Concorde/Intrepid

NOTE: PERFORM CUSTOMER SATISFACTION RECALL NO. 857, REPROGRAM PCM, FOR 2000 MODEL YEAR VEHICLES BUILT PRIOR TO AUGUST 30, 1999 (MDH 0830XX).

SYMPTOM/CONDITION: Erratic operation of the AC and heater systems including: lack of cold air, lack of hot air, unrequested mode change (Automatic Temperature Control [ATC] only), no control of mode or temperature control or dithering/tapping blend door noise. These symptoms may be accompanied by the following Diagnostic Fault Codes (DTCs): Blend Door Feedback, Blend Door Stall, A/C Control Mode Door Input Shorted To Battery, In-Car Temp Sensor Failure, ATC Messages Not Received, or Mode Door Stall.

Remedy for an engine ticking noise (TSB #09-002-04). **1999–2002**—Snapping sound when opening or closing door. **2000–01**—Erratic engine idle. • Front strut noise. • Front suspension or steering gear rattle. • Vehicle leads or pulls. • Speaker screw contacts door seal. **2000–04**—Fuel tank slow to fill; this has been a chronic problem affecting five model years:

FUEL SYSTEM – FUEL TANK SLOW TO FILL

BULLETIN NO: 14-001-03   **DATE: JAN. 24, 2003**

2000–04 (LH) LHS/300M/Concorde/Intrepid

OVERVIEW: This bulletin involves correcting any or all of the following items as necessary:
^Kinked/plugged fuel tank vent lines
^Replacing the fuel tank control valve
^Replacing the Leak Detection Pump (LDP) filter
^Unplugging or replacing the fuel tank fill tube assembly

• Rear strut squeaks. **2001**—Troubleshooting automatic transmission surge, sag, and shift bump complaints (TSB #18-007-01). **2002**—Transaxle limp-in, engine misfire, engine no-start. • Discoloured window moulding. **2002–04**—Vehicles equipped with a 3.5L engine that has a rough idle when cold may need the PCM re-calibrated or replaced; a free service under the emissions warranty (see TSB #18-042-03). **2003**—Engine stumbling or misfire. • Defective PCM. • Delayed or temporary loss of transmission engagement after initial start-up. • Transmission goes into "limp" mode. • Harsh 4–3 downshift. • Headliner sag or rattle. • Front brake noise or pulsation. • Poor AC performance. • Rear strut squeaks. • Wind noise from sunroof or B-pillar when driving. **2003–04**—Harsh downshifts. • Poor transmission shifting:

AUTOMATIC TRANSMISSION DELAYED ENGAGEMENT

BULLETIN NO: 21-007-04   DATE: MAY 11, 2004

OVERVIEW: This bulletin involves replacing the front pump assembly in the transmission and checking the Transmission Control Module (TCM) for the latest software revision level.

2004 Pacifica; 2003-2004 Sebring Convertible/Sebring Sedan/Stratus Sedan; 2003 Liberty; 2003-2004 300M/Concorde/Intrepid; 2003 Neon/SX2.0; 2003 PT Cruiser; 2003 Town & Country/Caravan/Voyager; 2003 Wrangler.

300M, CONCORDE, INTREPID, LHS, NEW YORKER, VISION PROFILE

	1996	1997	1998	1999	2000	2001	2002	2003	2004
Cost Price ($)									
300M	—	—	—	39,150	39,675	40,900	39,900	40,335	40,910
Concorde	26,005	26,815	26,915	27,635	28,115	28,485	29,690	30,240	30,775
Intrepid	22,980	24,055	24,395	25,060	25,520	25,910	25,765	25,095	25,615
LHS	38,420	40,500	40,500	41,150	41,370	41,655	—	—	—
New Yorker	34,490	—	—	—	—	—	—	—	—
Vision	23,770	24,775	—	—	—	—	—	—	—
Used Values ($)									
300M ▲	—	—	—	9,000	11,500	14,500	18,000	22,000	26,000
300M ▼	—	—	—	7,500	10,000	13,000	16,000	20,000	23,000
Concorde ▲	3,500	5,000	6,000	7,000	9,000	11,000	14,000	16,000	19,000
Concorde ▼	3,000	4,000	5,500	6,500	7,500	9,000	12,000	14,500	17,500
Intrepid ▲	3,000	4,000	5,500	7,000	8,500	10,000	12,000	14,500	16,500
Intrepid ▼	2,500	3,500	5,000	6,000	7,000	8,500	11,000	13,000	15,000
LHS ▲	5,000	6,000	7,000	9,000	12,000	15,000	—	—	—
LHS ▼	4,000	5,000	6,500	7,500	10,500	13,000	—	—	—
New Yorker ▲	4,500	—	—	—	—	—	—	—	—
New Yorker ▼	3,500	—	—	—	—	—	—	—	—
Vision ▲	3,000	4,000	—	—	—	—	—	—	—
Vision ▼	2,500	3,000	—	—	—	—	—	—	—
Reliability	❶	❶	❶	❶	❶	❷	❸	❸	❸
Crash Safety (F)	④	④	—	④	④	④	④	④	④
300M	—	—	—	—	—	③	③	③	④
Side	④	④	—	④	④	④	④	④	④
Offset	—	—	—	—	③	③	③	③	③
LHS/300M	—	—	—	❶	❶	③	③	③	③
Head Restraints (F)	—	❶	—	③	—	❶	③	③	③

All ratings on a numbered scale where ⑤ is good and ❶ is bad. See pages 100–101 for a more detailed description.

Rear	—	—	—	❷	—	—	❷	❷	❷
300M (F)	—	—	—	❷	—	❷	❶	❶	❶
Rear	—	—	—	❶	—	—	—	—	—
Intrepid	—	❶	—	—	❷	❹	❹	❹	❹
Rear	—	—	—	—	—	—	❸	❸	❸
LHS	—	❶	—	❷	—	❸	—	—	—
Vision	—	❶	—	—	—	—	—	—	—
Rollover Resistance									
300M	—	—	—	—	—	—	❹	❹	❹
Concorde	—	—	—	—	—	—	—	❺	❺
Intrepid	—	—	—	—	—	—	—	❺	❺

Note: All these vehicles are practically identical and should have similar crashworthiness scores, even though not every model was tested each year.

Ford

COUGAR, THUNDERBIRD

RATING: Not Recommended (1999–2002); Average (1985–97). For readers wondering how the Cougar could go from Average to Not Recommended, remember that we are reviewing distinctly different vehicles. The early rear-drives improved over the years; however, the 1999–2002 front-drive iteration carries all of the deficiencies of Ford's front-drives, coupled with the Contour's and Mystique's own subset of problems. As a first-year vehicle, the Cougar's quality control suffered even more (see "Safety Summary" and "Secret Warranties/Internal Bulletins/ Service Tips"). **Maintenance/Repair costs:** About average, and most repairs aren't dealer dependent. **Parts:** Moderately priced (independent suppliers sell for much less), and not hard to find for rear-drives. Front-drive parts, however, are more expensive and not as easily found. And with both the Contour and the Cougar taken off the market, they will likely become rarer. **Extended warranty:** No. **Best alternatives:** GM Caprice, LeSabre, or Roadmaster; Ford's early Cougar, T-Bird, Crown Victoria, or Mercury Grand Marquis. **Online help:** *www.autosafety.org/auto-defects.html* and *www.blueovalnews.com.*

Strengths and Weaknesses

These are no-surprise, average-performing, two-door, rear-drive luxury cars that have changed little over the years. Handling and ride are far from perfect, with considerable body lean and rear-end instability when taking curves at moderate speeds or on wet roadways.

Overall reliability of these models has been average, as long as you stay away from the turbocharged 4-cylinder engine and watch out for 3.8L V6 engine head gasket failures and automatic transmission glitches.

True, these cars offer lots of power, but excessive noise and expensive repairs are the price you pay when they're pushed too hard. Front suspension components wear out quickly, as do power-steering rack seals. Owners of recent models have complained of ignition module defects, electrical system bugs, premature front brake repairs, steering pump hoses that burst repeatedly, erratic transmission performance, early AC failures, defective engine intake manifolds, numerous squeaks and rattles, faulty heater fans, and failure-prone power window regulators.

VEHICLE HISTORY: *Thunderbird:* **1989**—Thunderbird is trimmed down and equipped with a fully independent suspension, and a 3.8L V6; a 210-hp Super Coupe (SC) model debuts. **1991**—A 200-hp 5.0L V8 arrives. **1994**—A 4.6L V8 debuts along with dual front airbags and restyled front and rear ends. **1996**—Super Coupe is dropped and more restyling tweaks are added. **1997**—Four-wheel disc brakes and dash/interior touch-ups. **2004**—Revised interior trim, restyled wheels, and a new garage opener. *Cougar:* **1999**—First year on the market. **2000**—Interior trunk release handle; no more driver's door map pockets. **2001**—Interior and exterior styling revisions. **2002**—35th Anniversary Edition Package.

1999–2002 Cougar

Essentially a Contour spin-off, this Cougar's main attributes are its attractive styling and pleasant handling. Owners have to accept, however, mediocre acceleration with the base models, problematic transmission performance, a four-seater with a narrow, claustrophobic interior, limited rear seat room, obstructed rear visibility, an ugly and superfluous trunk-lid spoiler, and excessive interior noise.

The front-drive Cougar, restyled as a hatchback, is equipped with a 16-valve, 125-hp 2.0L inline-four and a 24-valve, 170-hp 2.5L V6, later replaced with an upgraded 200-hp power plant and optional ABS and side airbags. It shares the Contour's chassis (with 2.5 cm added), base 4-banger, and V6, but its suspension and steering are much tighter. Emergency handling is acceptable, but it's not in the same league as Japanese sedans. The firm suspension and quick, responsive steering make the Cougar both nimble and stable when cornering under speed, especially with the optional Sport Group's rear disc brakes and larger wheels (you'll have to put up with a harder, noisier ride, though). The car is also quite peppy around town, with a good amount of low-end torque. Braking is also good, with little fading after successive stops.

Acceleration is only so-so with the base 4-cylinder or V6 engine, and they both run roughly; the 4-banger is not as refined or fun to push as the Japanese competition. The 170-hp V6 lacks passing or merging power; 0–100 km/h takes about 10 seconds. The automatic transmission tends to hunt for the proper gear when going over hilly terrain, and there's no way to lock out Overdrive in Fourth gear. The 5-speed hooked to the V6 also shifts roughly. The base suspension doesn't absorb bumps very well and the optional Sports Group tires produce a busy, jostling ride on any surface that's less than perfect. Steering is also a bit heavy in city traffic.

Owner-reported problems include chronic engine stalling; automatic transmission failures accompanied by slipping or hunting during the 1–2 shift; humming and clanking noises; manual transmission hard to shift from one gear to another; electrical glitches; engine increases rpm when shifting; chronic stalling, rough running, and hard starts; premature front and rear brake wear and a low grinding noise or squeak heard when the brakes are applied; misaligned trunk lid, sunroof, door, and side windows jamming; door latch failures; doors that lock and unlock themselves; faulty driver-side door weather stripping that produces excessive wind noise; and water leakage into the interior (be wary of car washes).

2002–04 Thunderbird

After a brief hiatus, the Thunderbird name returned affixed to a $56,775 retro-styled, two-seat, rear-drive convertible that looks nothing like its 1955–57 namesake or the $25,095 '97 model it replaced (now worth about $5,000). This T-Bird shares variations of the engine and chassis used by the Lincoln LS and Jaguar S-Type, as well as their 5-speed automatic transmission. Power is supplied by a retuned 280-hp 3.9L V8.

The car is way overpriced. Sure, you get lots of bells and whistles for your $50,000+, but other cars offer just as much for far less money. Second, this is one dull-looking luxury roadster with few features that distinguish it from half a dozen cheaper imports of the same genre. Other minuses: a tiny, shallow trunk; a cheap-looking, boring instrument panel; limited headroom; an unwieldy folding top cover; and excessive air turbulence when driven with the top down. Ford wants you to believe that the new Thunderbird iteration is true to the heritage of its classic forebears and represents good value for your money. Unfortunately, this Thunderbird proves just the opposite. Head restraints are rated "Poor" by IIHS, the official launch and delivery was delayed several times because of factory-related problems, the base MSRP is double what a Thunderbird cost just a few years ago, and the car was discontinued in 2005.

All models/years: Airbags failed to deploy. • Inadvertent airbag deployment. • Transmissions are noisy, won't shift properly, and frequently won't shift at all. • Frequent reports of sudden brake failures, front brake rotor warpage, and noisy brakes. • Brake pedal sinks below the accelerator pedal level, causing driver to depress the accelerator. • Power window regulator failures. • Electric door locks are failure-prone. • Speedometer and fuel gauge work erratically. • Horn is hard to activate. **1999**—Driver's airbag deployed after collision and seat belt failed to lock up. • Sticking throttle causes sudden, unintended acceleration. • Cruise control wouldn't disengage. • Chronic hesitation or stalling (electrical shorts or a faulty fuel pump, fuel regulator, intake gaskets, or idle air control (IAC) solenoid are the prime suspects). • No-start caused by faulty ignition or starter. • Transmission failures. • While driving at 110 km/h, transmission downshifted on its own. • Sudden brake failure (locked up). • Total brake failure when ABS brake master cylinder exploded. • Brake pads, calipers, and rotors need replacing after only 32,000 km (20,000 mi.). • Power steering fails and dash lights go out when car is driven through a rain puddle. This may be caused by the serpentine belt getting wet. • Plastic fuel tank is prone to early disintegration, contributing to stalling. • Gas tank seal swells and breaks, spilling fuel. • Fuel tank wiring harness melted. • Brake lights don't come on when brakes are applied. • Electrical failures tend to blow out the fuel pump. • On another occasion, dash lights suddenly came on, engine died, and brakes and steering ability were gone. • Steering failures because of a broken suspension strut or the tie-rod bolt shearing off. • Wheel may crack, causing a tire blowout. • Lug nut wrench doesn't work. • Trunk won't open or close, and remote release is useless. • Inadequate rear windshield defogger. **2000–01**—Broken stabilizer bar bracket allowed wheel to drop under car. • Intermittent brake failure. • Automatic transmission hesitates, as it hunts for the correct gear and then shifts with a jerk. • Faulty seal causes fuel tank leakage. • Fuel smell in the interior comes in through the vents; fuel also leaked onto the ground. • Engine hangs in higher rpm when foot is taken off the gas pedal and clutch is depressed. • Lights flicker and loss of all electrical power. • Headlight failures. • Airbag and engine warning lights stay lit. • Key won't work in the ignition. • Hard to find a child safety seat that fits in the rear. • The silly, non-functional rear spoiler is distracting and cuts rearward vision. **2001**—Engine compartment fire erupted while in traffic. • Gas fumes permeate interior through the air vents. • Broken rear stabilizer bar bracket. • Instrument panel light dims when braking. • Brake lights often fail. *Cougar*: **2002**—Gas fumes seep into the cabin. • Chronic stalling. • Transmission failed. • Frequent failure of the sway bar bushing. • Brakes were applied; vehicle hesitated, then surged forward. • Fuel pump failures; incorrect fuel gauge reading. *Thunderbird*: **2002**—Water leaked onto the airbag housing. • Frequent stalling, especially when making a left turn. • Driver's seat belt failed to release. • Sun visor can't be tilted toward the driver or passenger. • Convertible top flew up while car was underway. **2003**—Erratic shifting. • Transmission failure. • ABS failure; vehicle hopped all over the road. • Front brake caliper came off and locked up wheel. • Vehicle accelerated when brakes were applied. **2004**—Passenger-side rear airbag deployed for no reason, burning passenger. • Wrench light came on and car would not move.

Secret Warranties/Internal Bulletins/Service Tips

All models/years: Ford's "goodwill" warranty extensions cover engine and transmission breakdowns up to about seven years. There's nothing like a small claims court action to focus Ford's attention. The same advice applies if you notice a rotten-egg odour coming from the exhaust. **All models: 1993–2002**—Paint delamination, peeling, or fading (see Part Two). **1993–2000**—Brake vibration diagnosis and correction. **1999**—Three bulletins target automatic transmission failures, suggesting that either the Overdrive/Reverse ring gear be replaced or an upgraded transaxle assembly be installed. • Front brake groaning during city driving can be silenced by installing revised brake pads under warranty, says TSB #99-8-9. **1999–2000**—Engine hesitation and a rough idle may be corrected by reprogramming the PCM. • Engine knock. • An exhaust sulfur odour evident just after highway cruising may signal the need to replace the catalytic converter under the emissions warranty. Transmission won't shift into any forward gear. • Automatic transmission fluid leaks. • Water leaks and wind noise troubleshooting tips. **1999–2001**—No forward gear:

NO FORWARD GEAR ENGAGEMENT

BULLETIN NO: 00-18-2   **DATE: SEPT. 04, 2000**

1994–97 Probe; 1994–2000 Contour; 2001 Escape; 1994–2000 Mystique; 1999–2001 Cougar

ISSUE: Some vehicles may exhibit no forward gear ranges due to the misalignment of the forward/coast clutch cylinder snap ring with respect to the legs of the forward clutch piston.

ACTION: During assembly of the forward/coast clutch cylinder, the gap in the select fit retaining ring should be located midway (i.e., 45 degrees) between adjacent legs of the forward clutch piston.

• Rear brakes moan or groan:

REAR BRAKES MOANING/GROANING NOISE

BULLETIN NO: 00-26-5   **DATE: DEC. 25, 2000**

1999–2001 Cougar

ISSUE: Some vehicles equipped with rear disc-brakes may exhibit a "moaning/groaning" noise on initial brake application (cold soak). This may be caused by the rear brake pads vibrating in the caliper. Braking performance is not affected by this condition.

ACTION: Install revised rear disc brake service kit.

Frank M. Ligon
Director
Service Engineering Operations
Ford Customer Service Division

Ford Motor Company
P. O. Box 1904
Dearborn, Michigan 48121

May 2004

TO: All U.S. Ford and Lincoln Mercury Dealers

SUBJECT: Extended Coverage Program 04N02: Supplement #1
Certain 1999 through 2002 Model Year Cougar Vehicles
Fuel Delivery Module – New Design

Ref: Extended Coverage Program 04N02: Dated April 2004
Certain 1999 through 2002 Model Year Cougar Vehicles
Fuel Delivery Module

PURPOSE OF THIS SUPPLEMENT

- Notify dealers of the availability of the new design fuel delivery module.
- Revised technical instructions for the new design fuel delivery module.
- Revised labor times and part information.
- Special required cutting tool – (same cutting tool supplied and used for 03N01).

PROGRAM TERMS

This program extends the coverage of the fuel delivery module (FDM) to 10 years from the original warranty start date of the vehicle, with no limit on the number of miles that the vehicle has been driven. This program provides one-time replacement coverage, and is automatically transferred to subsequent owners.

VEHICLES COVERED BY THIS PROGRAM

Certain 1999 through 2002 model year Cougar vehicles built at the Flat Rock Assembly Plant from May 25, 1999 through November 30, 2001. Affected vehicles are identified in OASIS.

REASON FOR PROVIDING ADDITIONAL COVERAGE

Some of the affected vehicles may experience engine hesitation, loss of power, surging, and other similar symptoms as a result of contamination of the fuel pump. Because the contamination of the fuel pump is progressive, it may ultimately become sufficiently blocked to cause the engine to stall completely. Although the symptoms noted above can occur under a variety of driving conditions, they are most likely to occur when there is less than one-quarter tank of fuel and/or when the driver is attempting to accelerate while making a turning maneuver (such as entering a highway through a cloverleaf) or while driving uphill.

This 10-year fuel pump warranty can be used as a benchmark for claims relating to any automaker's vehicles.

• Brake warning light stays lit. **1999–2002**—Harsh, delayed upshifts. • Repeated failure of the heater core. • There's a 10-year secret warranty on fuel pumps, says Blue Oval News at *www.blueovalnews.com/2004/recalls/cougar.04no2.htm*. According to this website, Ford told its dealers that it has extended the warranty on 1999–2002 Mercury Cougar fuel delivery modules (FDM) to 10 years from the original warranty start date. The new warranty (warranty code 04N02) will apply regardless of how many kilometres the vehicle has been driven. Ford is replacing the fuel pumps because they can become contaminated and cause engine hesitation, loss of power, and surging. According to Ford's instructions to its dealers, should a consumer "inform a dealership that their vehicle exhibits stalling, engine hesitation, loss of power, surging, or other similar symptoms, replace the FDM. There is no need for further diagnostics prior to FDM replacement. Owners are not to be charged for any diagnostics or repairs in relation to the FDM replacement." If the repairs have already been completed, Ford Motor Company will refund owner-paid repairs (see previous page). **2000**—Airbag light remains lit. • Low Engine Coolant lamp on for no apparent reason. • Automatic transmission fluid leakage. • Water leak or wind noise at the upper corner of the B-pillar. **2002–05**—Water leaks from convertible top. **2003**—No-starts, discharged battery. • Harsh shifting. **2003–04**—Steering noise, vibration. **2004**—Rough-running, misfiring engine. • Harsh shifts. • Driveline vibration. • Rear brake squealing.

COUGAR, THUNDERBIRD PROFILE

	1995	1996	1997	1999	2000	2001	2002	2003	2004
Cost Price ($)									
Cougar	22,095	23,495	24,995	19,995	20,595	23,655	26,995	—	—
T-Bird	22,995	23,595	25,095	—	—	—	51,550	56,615	56,775
T-Bird SC	28,697	—	—	—	—	—	—	—	—
Used Values ($)									
Cougar ▲	3,500	4,500	5,000	7,500	9,000	11,500	14,000	—	—
Cougar ▼	3,000	4,000	4,500	6,000	7,500	9,500	12,500	—	—
T-Bird ▲	4,000	4,500	5,000	—	—	—	32,000	37,000	42,000
T-Bird ▼	3,500	4,000	4,500	—	—	—	29,000	34,000	39,000
T-Bird SC ▲	5,000	—	—	—	—	—	—	—	—
T-Bird SC ▼	4,000	—	—	—	—	—	—	—	—
Reliability	③	③	③	②	②	②	②	②	③
Crash Safety (F)	⑤	⑤	⑤	—	—	—	④	—	④
Side	—	—	③	—	—	③	⑤	—	⑤
Cougar	—	—	—	—	—	—	—	③	⑤
Head Restraints	❶	—	❶	—	—	—	❶	❶	❶
Cougar (F)	❶	—	❶	❷	—	❷	❷	—	—
Cougar (Rear)	—	—	—	❶	—	❷	❷	—	—
Rollover Resistance	—	—	—	—	—	—	—	—	⑤

CROWN VICTORIA, GRAND MARQUIS ★★★

RATING: Average (1996–2004). Downgraded from five to three stars because of an increasing number of powertrain failures and safety-related deficiencies. Don't waste your money buying a 1998 or 1999 version if you can find a low-mileage

1995. It'll cost much less, give you most of the same features, and have a more durable engine intake manifold. The Marquis is a slightly more luxurious version that costs a bit more but gives little of consequence for the extra expense. **Maintenance/Repair costs:** Average, but some electronic repairs can be carried out only by Ford dealers. **Parts:** Higher-than-average cost (independent suppliers sell for much less), but they're not hard to find. **Extended warranty:** Yes, invest in an extended powertrain warranty. **Best alternatives:** Buick LeSabre; early Ford Thunderbird or Cougar; GM Caprice or Roadmaster; Toyota Avalon. **Online help:** *www.autosafety.org/autodefects.html, www.tgrigsby.com/views/ford.htm, www.flaming-fords.info, www.crownvictoriasafetyalert.com,* and *www.blueovalnews.com.*

 ## Strengths and Weaknesses

These rear-drive cars are especially well suited to seniors, who will appreciate the roomy interiors and oodles of convenience features (although entry and exit may require some acrobatics). The high crash protection scores and ease of servicing are also major advantages. Handling, though, is mediocre, and can be downright scary on wet roads where the car can quickly lose traction and fishtail out of control. Passing over small bumps is also a white-knuckle affair; the car bounces around, barely controllable.

Both the 4.6L and 5.0L V8s provide adequate though sometimes sluggish power, with most of their torque found in the lower gear ranges. The Lincoln Town Car shares the same components and afflictions as the Crown Vic and Grand Marquis.

As is the case with most full-sized sedans, high insurance premiums and fuel costs have walloped the resale value of all three models, making these cars incredibly good used buys. The only caveat is to make sure the undercarriage, powertrain, electronics, and brakes are in good shape before you ink a deal.

VEHICLE HISTORY: 1995—Restyled and given standard heated outside mirrors and a new interior treatment. **1997**—Improved steering and rear air suspension (a horror to diagnose and repair). **1998**—More power steering and suspension improvements. **1999**—ABS and a new stereo system. **2000**—An emergency trunk release, user-friendly child safety seat anchorages, and an improved handling package for quicker acceleration; last model year for the Crown Victoria in Canada, as the Grand Marquis continues alone. *Grand Marquis:* **2001**—A small horsepower boost, minor interior improvements, adjustable pedals, seat belt pre-tensioners, and improved airbag systems. **2002**—Traction control to offset the car's notoriously poor wet-weather traction. **2003**—A revised frame and upgraded suspension, plus the debut of a high-performance Marauder—equipped with a 302-hp V8, sport suspension, and exclusive trim.

On the downside, a number of factory-related problems appear year after year. These include failure-prone fuel pump, sender, fuel filter, and fuel hose assemblies; ignition module and fuel cut-off switch malfunctions that cause hard starting and frequent stalling; brakes (rotors, calipers, and pads), shock absorbers, and springs that wear out more quickly than they should; and chronic front suspension noise when passing over small bumps. Inadequate inner fender protection allows road salt to completely cover engine wiring, brake master cylinder, and suspension components; frequent inspection and cleaning is required. Hubcaps frequently fall off. Finally, there is such a high number of safety-related complaints concerning brake and fuel lines, suspension, and steering components that an undercarriage inspection is a prerequisite to buying models three years or older. Other annoying body defects include poor fit and finish, trunk leaks, subpar interior materials, and flimsy plastic trim.

 **Safety Summary**

All models/years: Fuel line and electrical fires. • Sudden, unintended acceleration. • Cracked intake manifolds cause loss of coolant (see "Secret Warranties/Internal Bulletins/Service Tips"). • Airbags fail to deploy, or deploy for no reason. • ABS brake failures. • Premature brake rotor warpage and pad wearout cause excessive brake noise (grinding), vibration, and extended stopping distance:

> Fleet of 15 police cars, Crown Victoria had the front brake, rotors, and pads replaced every 20,000 miles [32,000 km]. There is a premature wear of brake parts.

• Brake and accelerator pedals mounted too close together. **All models: 1992–2001**—Rear-end impact may puncture fuel tank; two TSB repairs already carried out. **1998**—NHTSA investigators are looking into reports that the inertia fuel cut-off switch operates when it shouldn't, stalling the vehicle. • Sudden loss of power; stalling. • Traction control engages for no reason, causing loss of power and control. • Steering too sensitive when changing lanes, making it easy to lose control. • Dome light switch is poorly designed; it can be activated only by the driver because of its location. • Loss of lighting caused by sudden electrical system failure. • Rubber hose leading from the fuel tank is easily hit when going over a bump or pothole. **1999**—Sudden stalling while underway (fuel inertia cut-off switch self-activates when vehicle hits a pothole or goes over a small bump). • Steering shaft failure when turning. • Cracked rear trailing-arm assembly frames. • Transmission jumps from Park into gear. • Sticking front calipers cause vehicle to veer to the right or left. • Premature wear of the lower control arm. • Headlights aren't bright enough. • Loose rear outer door handles. • Driver's seat misalignment places steering wheel and gas/brake pedals too far to the right. **2000**—Oversensitive steering causes vehicle to wander. • Power window failures in cold weather. • Headlights short out intermittently. **2001**—When the car is driving in rainy weather, water gets into the engine compartment, causing the water pump to throw the fan belt and leading to loss of control of the vehicle. • Frequent complaints of little traction on wet roads. • ABS failure leading to brake lock-up or loss of braking ability. • Spongy brakes sink to floor with little braking effect. • Vehicle moves forward when shifted into Reverse. • Vehicle rolls back when stopped on an incline. • Windshield wipers fail intermittently and easily freeze up in sleet. **2002**—38 Crown Victoria complaints centred on the powertrain, fuel tank fire fears, cracked wheel rims, and poor rainy weather performance:

> Ford has stopped installing splash shield (p/n [part number] fsvy*8327*a) under motor of Crown Victoria. This causes the fan belt to come off when it is raining. Car loses all accessories including power steering/alternator, and water pump. Car can not be driven over 4 blocks due to overheating. This will place elderly people on side of road in rain (or they will crash because they will not be able to turn the car without power steering).

• 37 Grand Marquis complaints centred on sudden acceleration, cruise control not disengaging, and tire sidewall separation (Michelin and others). **2003**—Vehicle struck from behind exploded into flames. • Tire tread separation. • Missing upper control arm bolt. • Brake booster failed. • Fan belt comes off in rainy weather, causing overheating and loss of power steering, water pump, and other accessories. • Horn "sweet spot" too small; horn takes too much effort to sound. • Sunlight causes a reflection of the defrost vents onto the windshield and poor dash panel illumination. **2004**—Transmission slips; shifted into Reverse on its own. • Excessive steering vibration may be caused by original equipment wheels and faulty tires. • Turn signal fails intermittently.

Secret Warranties/Internal Bulletins/Service Tips

All models: 1985–2002—Repeated heater core failure. **1990–2001**—Correcting a radio whine or buzz in the speakers. **1992–2001**—Measures to protect fuel tank from puncturing and fuel from igniting during a rear-end collision. **1993–2001**—

An exhaust buzz or rattle may mean you have a loose catalyst or muffler heat shield. • Paint delamination, peeling, or fading (see Part Two "Paint and Body Defects," pages 71–75). **1994–99**—Tips on preventing wind noise around the doors. **1995–99**—Tips on reducing noise, vibration, and harshness, as well as plugging windshield water leaks. **1996–2001**—The following intake manifold coolant leakage bulletin traces the problem back to 1996 models and shows that Ford is at fault. It can help you to get a repair refund if Ford refuses to extend its 1998–2001 Special Service Campaign (see picture above and following bulletin) to these earlier models, or says that time period or mileage makes you ineligible for compensation.

1997–98—Lack of AC temperature control may require a new air door actuator. **1997–99**—Delayed upshifts may require a new 2–3 accumulator along with a

ENGINE INTAKE MANIFOLD LEAKAGE

BULLETIN NO: 02-2-2

DATE: FEB. 04, 2002

1996–97 Thunderbird; 1996–2001 Crown Victoria, Mustang; 2002 Explorer; 1996–2001 Town Car; 1996–97 Cougar; 1996–2001 Grand Marquis.

ISSUE: Some vehicles may exhibit an intake manifold crossover (first runner) coolant seepage condition. This may be caused by a crack in the intake manifold coolant crossover.

ACTION: Inspect the suspect intake manifold for a coolant leak at the first runner crossover area. If coolant seepage is found in this area, order the appropriate service kit.

revised piston. • A rough idle or exhaust system resonance can be fixed by installing an exhaust system mass damper. **1998–99**—A pull or drift when braking in rainy weather can be corrected by installing upgraded front brake linings that are less sensitive to water, says TSB #98-13-4. • A poorly performing AC that also makes a thumping noise may need a new suction accumulator and suction hose assembly. **1998–2000**—Ford Special Service Campaign 00B60 (January 31, 2002) allowed for the free installation of control arm reinforcing brackets or new control arms, regardless of mileage. Ask for a partial refund. **1998–2001**—A Ford Special Service Campaign will replace the engine mounts free of charge on vehicles in fleet service. **1998–2002**—In a separate campaign, the automaker has extended the intake manifold warranty to seven years, without any mileage limitation. This campaign is in response to complaints of coolant leakage leading to engine over-heating. **1998–2002**—Inoperative shift interlock. **1998–2005**—Troubleshooting engine misfires (TSB #04-16-1). **1999–2001**—Correcting a 2–1 shift clunk noise. **1999–2002**—Engine head gasket leakage:

ENGINE OIL LEAK FROM R/H CYLINDER HEAD GASKET

BULLETIN NO: 03-6-2

DATE: MARCH 31, 2003

1999–2002 Crown Victoria, Mustang; 1999–2001 E Series, Expedition, F-150, Super Duty F Series; 2000–01 Excursion; 1999–2002 Town Car; 1998–99 Navigator; 1999–2002 Grand Marquis

ISSUE: Some vehicles equipped with the Romeo-built 4.6L 2V engine or 5.4L 2V Windsor and 5.4L Supercharged engine may exhibit an oil leak or oil weepage from the cylinder head gasket at the right hand rear or the left hand front of the engine. Oil weepage is not considered detrimental to engine performance or durability. An oil leak may be caused by metal chip debris lodged between the head gasket and the block, chip debris between the cylinder head and the head gasket, or by damage to the cylinder head sealing surface that occurred during the manufacturing process.

ACTION: Once an oil leak is verified with a black light test at the head gasket joint, replacement of the head gasket can be performed. If the head was damaged by chip contamination, the head should be replaced. A revised "Service-Only" gasket is now released for both of these cases.

2000–01—Troubleshooting a ticking noise in First gear. 2000–03—Excessive engine grinding noise:

2000–04—Lack of cooling or low airflow from the vents. 2001—Correcting a 3–4 shift flare. 2001–02—Front-end accessory drivebelt slips off water pump pulley when splashed with water (TSB #02-5-4). 2003—Ford says rear axles "may be noisy, or exhibit rear axle shaft and/or axle bearing premature wear. This is caused by excessive load, temperature, and inadequate lubrication." Ford will replace the axle bearings under dealer operation code 030505A. • Water in the headlights and erratic headlight operation. • Inaccurate fuel gauge. • Power steering assist calibration. • Excessive power steering pump noise. • Front wheel area click or rattle. • Anti-theft system may cause the transmission to stick in Park or the steering wheel to lock. • Defective front coil springs may cause the vehicle to have a harsh ride or the suspension to sit low in the front. Ford will install free revised front coil springs: #3W1Z-5310-EA and #3W1Z-5310-HA. • Cracked wheel rims. Call 1-800-325-5621 to replace the affected wheel(s) up to five years or 240,000 km (150,000 mi.) from the vehicle's warranty start date. 2001–04—Tips on silencing engine ticking (includes replacing the cylinder head):

Sigh; it's the same old engine troubles. Use the service bulletin above to avoid arguments as to who pays for the repair.

2003–04—Countermeasures for suspension squeaking or rubbing. • Excessive engine vibration at idle. • An engine knock after a cold start can be silenced by installing a free exhaust shield kit, says TSB #04-2-1. • Ignition lock cylinder binding. • AC rattling. **2004**—Vehicle won't shift into Overdrive.

CROWN VICTORIA, GRAND MARQUIS PROFILE

	1996	1997	1998	1999	2000	2001	2002	2003	2004
Cost Price ($)									
Crown S/LTD	27,195	29,895	30,995	31,895	32,095	—	—	—	—
Grand Marquis GS	30,295	32,195	32,895	33,695	31,195	34,125	35,120	35,800	36,720
Used Values ($)									
Crown S/LTD ▲	4,000	5,000	7,000	9,000	11,500	—	—	—	—
Crown S/LTD ▼	3,500	4,500	5,500	7,500	12,500	—	—	—	—
Grand Marquis GS ▲	4,500	5,500	7,500	9,500	12,000	14,500	17,000	21,000	25,000
Grand Marquis GS ▼	4,000	5,000	6,000	8,000	10,000	13,000	15,500	19,000	23,000
Reliability	3	3	3	3	3	3	3	4	4
Crash Safety (F)	4	5	5	5	5	5	5	5	5
Side	—	—	4	4	4	5	4	4	4
Offset	—	—	—	—	—	—	—	5	5
Head Restraints	—	1	—	1	—	1	1	2	2
Rollover Resistance	—	—	—	—	—	5	5	5	5

LUXURY CARS

Luxury Lemons

Money doesn't buy you love—and it doesn't buy you quality and reliable performance in a luxury car, either. Ask any Cadillac, Jaguar, Lincoln Continental, Mercedes, or Saab owner. They now know that more dependable and better-performing cars can be bought for half the price from other automakers. Heck, surveys show even the Germans prefer Japanese brands over their own.

Audi of America, Inc.

3800 Hamlin Road
Auburn Hills, MI 48326
Tel. (248) 754-5000

August 2004

Subject: Warranty Extension for 1997 - 2004 Model Year Audi A4 Sedan, Avant, or Cabriolet
Equipped with 1.8L Turbo Engine

Dear Audi Owner,

We are writing to inform you that Audi is providing a warranty extension covering certain "oil sludge" related repairs on 1997 - 2004 model year Audi A4 equipped with 1.8L Turbo engines. Our records show that you are the owner of one of these vehicles.

What is the Issue?
Some Audi owners have reported engine component problems resulting from a condition known as "oil sludge." Engine oil sludge occurs when old, dirty engine oil thickens and cannot continue to provide adequate engine lubrication. This condition occurs primarily when the engine is operated at oil change intervals beyond those prescribed in your owner's manual, or when oil with lower quality than Audi recommended standard is used.

A vehicle with engine oil sludge may exhibit **a constantly or occasionally illuminated Red Engine Oil Pressure Warning light.**

Please note that other conditions may also cause this symptom and that the presence of this symptom does not necessarily mean oil sludge exists in your engine.

Smart luxury shoppers are picking BMW, Lexus, and Porsche.

Pardon my Slip

Used luxury cars can be great buys if you ignore all the hype, you know how to separate symbol from substance, and you're smart enough to know that most of the

Imagine, a $67,000 2002 Cadillac Seville with a slipping transmission.

high-end models don't give you much more than the lower-priced entry-level versions. For example, the Lexus ES 300 is a Toyota Camry with a higher sticker price; the Audi A4 isn't much different from the Volkswagen Passat; Lincoln's front-drive Continental uses mostly junky Ford Taurus and Sable power-trains; and the Acura 3.2 TL, Infiniti I35 (formerly called the I30), and Jaguar X-

Lincoln's front-drive Continental was merely a warmed-over Taurus with serious powertrain problems.

Type are fully loaded, high-tuned versions of the Honda Accord, the Nissan Maxima, and the European Ford Mondeo, respectively.

Both high- and low-end models project a flashy cachet; come loaded with high-tech safety, performance, and comfort features; and can be bought, after three years or so, for half of what they sold for new. Furthermore, if you can get servicing and parts from independent garages, you'll save even more. On the downside, there are overpriced luxury lemons out there (like the Lincoln Continental and the Cadillac Allanté and Catera, for example) that aren't built anymore and are unreliable, with hard-to-service engines and transmissions and servicing costs that rival Neiman Marcus.

Mercedes-Benz owners, for example, can't say they weren't warned. Over a decade ago, a $5-million study conducted over five years by the Massachusetts Institute of Technology said that the German automaker made lousy cars by committing the same assembly-line mistakes as American automakers—allowing workers to build poor-quality vehicles and then fixing the mistakes at the end. As one reviewer of *The Machine that Changed the World*, by James P. Womack, Daniel T. Jones, and Daniel Roos (HarperCollins, November 1991), wrote:

This study of the world automotive industry by a group of MIT academics reaches the radical conclusion that the much vaunted Mercedes technicians are actually a throwback to the pre-industrial age, while Toyota is far ahead in costs and quality by building the automobiles correctly the first time.

Readers of my *Lemon-Aid SUVs, Vans, and Trucks* guides know from the internal service bulletins that I quote extensively that Mercedes' C-Class compacts and M-Class sport-utilities have been plagued by serious factory defects (running the gamut from powertrain failures to fit and finish deficiencies). However, a confidential January 2002 quality survey leaked to the press confirms that Mercedes' quality problems now affect its entire vehicle lineup.

Automakers and Customer Satisfaction

AUTOMAKERS WITH THE HIGHEST CUSTOMER SATISFACTION

1. Toyota	13. Volvo	25. Rover
2. Subaru	14. Jaguar	26. Audi
3. Honda	15. Citroen	27. Opel
4. Mazda	16. Kia	28. Chrysler
5. Nissan	17. Skoda	29. Smart
6. Mitsubishi	18. Lancia	30. Fiat
7. Suzuki	19. Daewoo	31. Volkswagen
8. Porsche	20. Peugeot	32. Mercedes
9. Saab	21. Ford	33. Land Rover
10. Hyundai	22. Seat	
11. BMW	23. Renault	
12. Daihatsu	24. Alfa Romeo	

German drivers know their cars, and they give the worst quality marks to European automakers.

The survey, commissioned by European automakers from TUV, a German auto-inspection and research association, ranked Mercedes twelfth in quality control, just behind GM's much-maligned Opel (you have to be European to appreciate what a slap in the face this represents to Mercedes-Benz). A few weeks earlier, J.D. Power & Associates had released an American-based study of 156,000 car owners that showed that five-year-old Mercedes vehicles had a higher-than-average number of problems (engine oil sludge being foremost on 1998–2001 models). Power subsequently lowered the company's rating for quality control to "fair" from "good."

Now, several years later, German drivers have apparently reached the same conclusion as Power. The 38,454 members of ADAC, Germany's largest automotive club, who responded to a December 2003 survey put Volkswagen as number 31, Mercedes as number 32, and Land Rover as number 33 among the 33 brands polled on overall customer satisfaction.

Industry insiders believe Mercedes' quality problems are symptomatic of a malaise affecting many luxury car builders: rushing too many new models into production and building cheaper, smaller, bare-bones knock-offs of popular models.

Traditionally, the luxury-car niche has been dominated by American and German automakers. During the past decade, however, buyers have gravitated towards Japanese models. This shift in buyer preference has forced Chrysler out of the market, made Ford drop its problem-plagued Lincoln Continental, and has GM returning to rear-drive Cadillacs.

Okay, so you're well advised to choose a Japanese model, but doesn't that mean you'll have to dig deep in your wallet, wiping out most of your expected savings from buying used? Not necessarily. You don't always have to spend a lot to get true luxury and ironclad reliability. Smart buyers can pick up a fully equipped 2000 Toyota Camry or Avalon for between $13,000 and $16,000, or about half of what these models originally cost. Or, to look at it from a different perspective: Each car costs less than what a new 2001 Ford Focus ZTS sold for three years ago. Similar savings are realized by the purchase of a Honda Accord, Nissan Maxima, or Mazda 929, all of which offer similar equipment, reliability, and performance to Acura, Infiniti, and Lexus models, but for much, much less.

It's sad but true: There aren't any American luxury cars that can match an equivalent Japanese model for overall reliability, durability, and value. And this isn't because Japanese products are that well made; far from it, as anyone who's purchased a transmission-challenged Lexus will attest. No, it's simply because GM, Ford, and Chrysler's vehicles are so poorly made that they make everyone else's look better. This fact has been reflected in the head-spinningly high depreciation rates and plummeting market share seen with most large-cum-luxury cars put out by the Big Three. GM's rear-drive Cadillac DeVille and Lincoln's Town Car come closest to meeting the imports in overall reliability and durability, yet they still come nowhere near the quality level of many entry-level imports. Examples of lousy American luxury cars abound: The Chrysler front-drive New Yorker and LHS are unremarkable and are plagued by serious powertrain reliability problems, and most GM Cadillacs have been characterized by innovative, albeit unreliable, technology like variable-cylinder engines (the 4-6-8 engine), cobbled-together diesel power plants, and poorly engineered, high-maintenance, low-quality front-drive components.

What does this foretell for the future of used luxury cars? Prices for American entries will plummet as high fuel and insurance costs take their toll. A flood of off-lease cars will further cut into prices and give buyers a wider choice among imports and the Detroit Big Three. Finally, we'll likely see the renaissance of rear-drives, with Cadillac, Ford, and Chrysler leading the parade.

LUXURY CAR RATINGS

Recommended

BMW 5 Series (1992–2003)
BMW M Series (1997–2004)
BMW Z4 (2003-04)

Infiniti I30 (2000–03)
Lexus ES 300, GS 300, LS 400,
   SC 400 (1996–2001)

Above Average

Acura RL (1996–2004)
Acura TL (1996–99)

Infiniti I30 (1997–99)
Infiniti I35 (2002–04)

Audi A4, A6 (100), A8, S6
TT Coupe (1996–99)
BMW 3 Series (2001–04)
BMW Z3 (1996–2002)
Ford/Lincoln Mark VII, Mark VIII
(1995–98)
General Motors Aurora (2001–03)
General Motors Cadillac Brougham,
Fleetwood rear-drive (1993–96)

Infiniti J30 (1994–97)
Infiniti Q45 (1991–96; 2001–04)
Lexus ES 300, GS 300, LS 400,
SC 400 (2002–04; 1990–95)
Nissan Maxima (1989–2001; 2003)
Toyota Avalon (1995–2004)
Volvo 900 series (1989–96)

Average

Acura TL (2000–04)
Audi A4, A6 (100), A8, S6, TT Coupe
(2000–04)
BMW 3 Series (1994–2000)
BMW 5 Series (1985–91; 2004)
Ford/Lincoln LS (2000–03)
Ford/Lincoln Mark VII, Mark VIII
(1994)
Ford/Lincoln Town Car (1995–2004)
General Motors 98 Regency,
Park Avenue (1998–2004)
General Motors Cadillac Brougham,
Fleetwood rear-drive (1984–92)
General Motors Cadillac Concours,
DeVille (2002–04)

General Motors Aurora (1995–99)
General Motors Riviera (1995–99)
Infinity I30 (1996)
Infiniti J30 (1993)
Infiniti Q45 (1997–2000)
Kia Magentis (2003–04)
Mercedes-Benz 300 series,
400 series, 500 series,
E-Class (1985–91)
Nissan Maxima (2002; 2004; 1986–88)
Volvo 900 series, S80, S90, V90
(1997–2004)
Volvo 850, C70, S40, S70, V40,
V70 (1993–2004)

Below Average

BMW 3 Series (1984–93)
Ford/Lincoln Continental (1988–2002)
Ford/Lincoln Mark VII, Mark VIII
(1986–93)
Ford/Lincoln Town Car (1988–94)
General Motors 98 Regency,
Park Avenue (1991–97)

General Motors Cadillac Catera,
Eldorado, Seville (1992–2004)
General Motors Concours, DeVille,
(1985–2001)
Kia Magentis (2001–04)
Mercedes-Benz 300 series, 400 series,
500 series, E-Class (1992–2004)
Mercedes-Benz C-Class (1994–2004)

Not Recommended

Audi 90, A6 (100), S6 (1984–95)
General Motors 98 Regency, Park
Avenue (1985–90)

General Motors Cadillac Eldorado,
Seville (1986–91)
General Motors Riviera (1986–93)
Infiniti G20 (1994–2002)

Acura

RATING: Above Average (1996–2004). Basically a fully loaded, longer, wider, and heavier TL, equipped with a larger engine that produces less horsepower than its smaller brother. Watch out for the failure-prone, notchy 6-speed manual transmission. Resale value is high on all Acura models. **Maintenance/Repair costs:** Average, and most repairs are dealer dependent. **Parts:** Most mechanical and electronic components are easily found and moderately priced. Some reports that recall repairs are often delayed because corrected parts aren't available (transmission/transfer case, for example). Body parts may be hard to come by and can be expensive. **Extended warranty:** No, save your money. **Best alternatives:** Consider the departed Acura Legend, BMW's 5 Series, Infiniti's I30 or I35, and the Lexus GS 300/400. You may want to take a look at the TL sedan: It's not as expensive, and it's a better performer, though passenger room is more limited. **Online help:** *www.cbel.com/acura_cars* and *www.acurasucks.com/Main.htm.*

 Strengths and Weaknesses

Good, though not impressive, acceleration that's smooth and quiet in all gear ranges; exceptional steering and handling; comfortable ride; loaded with goodies; top-quality body and mechanical components. The steering can be numb, however, and manual and automatic transmissions are sometimes problematic.

The 3.5 RL is Honda's—oh, I mean, Acura's—flagship sedan. It's loaded with innovative high-tech safety and convenience features one would expect to find in a luxury car. These include heated front seats, front and rear climate controls, a rear-seat trunk pass-through, xenon headlights (get used to oncoming drivers flashing you with their headlights), "smart" side airbags, ABS, traction control, and an anti-skid system. The 3.5L 210-hp V6 mated with a 4-speed automatic transmission provides good acceleration that's a bit slower and more fuel-thirsty than the TL, partly because of the RL's extra pounds. The car handles nicely, with less firm a ride than the TL, although steering response doesn't feel as crisp. Interior accommodations, which fit four occupants, are excellent up front and in the rear because of the RL's use of a larger platform than the TL's.

VEHICLE HISTORY: 1996—RL replaces the Legend. **1998**—A sportier suspension, alloy wheels, and a three-point rear centre seat belt. **1999**—Side airbags, high-intensity discharge headlights, larger brakes, and a retuned suspension. **2000**—A Vehicle Stability Assist system and upgraded side airbags. **2001**—An in-trunk emergency opener. **2002**—A small horsepower boost (15), OnStar assistance, wider tires, larger brakes, and more sound deadening. **2003**—Improved child safety seat anchors, wheels, and tail lights. **2004**—Minor equipment upgrades.

Owner-reported problems: a failure-prone, misshifting manual transmission, noisy transmission engagement, frequent stalling, malfunctioning accessories, electrical shorts, premature brake wear, and front-wheel liner cracking.

Safety Summary

All models/years: It's interesting to note that the RL has had remarkably few complaints registered by NHTSA. **All models: 1998**—Premature wearout of the front and rear brake pads around 24,000 km (15,000 miles). **1999**—ABS failed to respond, resulting in rear-end collision. **2000**—Vehicle suddenly stalls when decelerating or cruising on the highway; transmission replaced, but problem returned. • Premature transmission replacements. **2001**—Transmission shifts poorly when accelerating or decelerating; vehicle stalls at slower speeds. • 6-speed manual transmission misshifts when going from Third to Fourth gear; it engages Second gear instead, causing extensive engine damage. • In cold weather, Second gear is hard to engage and produces a grinding noise. • Sometimes transmission pops out of Second gear. • Cracked front wheelwell liners. **2002**—Extensive engine damage caused by downshifting into Second gear, grinding:

> Very bad "grind" going into Second gear, when the transmission is cold. It takes about 25 minutes of driving until it starts to shift smoothly. The colder the weather is outside, the worse the problem. You can feel the gears grinding in the transmission. I have a petition with over 60 signatures from other RSX owners. This problem can be very dangerous if you are trying to get into Second gear and the transmission is grinding so bad it locks you out.

• Chronic stalling when decelerating. **2003**—Vehicle suddenly stalled while exiting a freeway. • Dashboard display is unreadable in daylight. • Seat belt did not restrain driver. **2004**—Xenon headlights are blinding.

Secret Warranties/Internal Bulletins/Service Tips

All models/years: Like Honda's, most of Acura's TSBs allow for special warranty consideration on a "goodwill" basis, even after the warranty has expired or the car has changed hands. Referring to this euphemism will increase your chances of getting some kind of refund for repairs that are obviously factory defects. • Seat belts that fail to function properly during normal use will be replaced for free under the company's lifetime seat belt warranty. • Diagnostic procedures and correction for off-centre steering wheels. **All models: 1996–98**—A growling or whining coming from the rear wheels can be fixed by replacing the hub bearing unit. • Brake squeal during light application can be fixed by replacing the front pads. **1996–2000**—

Moon roof rattles can be silenced by replacing the moon roof glass. **1996–2002**—Intermittent electrical shorts.

1997–2001—Master cylinder clutch fluid leakage. **1999**—A navigation system that locks up or resets can be corrected by rewriting the unit's software; a remanufactured unit may also be considered. **1999–2000**—A squeaking, creaking driver's seat is addressed in TSB #00-010. **2000**—Troubleshooting noisy automatic transmissions. • Moon roof rattles. • Driver's seat noise. • Steering wheel clunk. **2000–01**—Stability Assist may activate too soon. • Engine starts and dies when ignition is released. **2000–02**—Low-speed stalling. **2003**—Airbag light comes on for no reason. • Troubleshooting automatic transmission malfunctions. **2004**—Sticking fuel filler cap.

SECURITY/ELECTRICAL SYSTEM– INERMITTENT PROBLEMS

BULLETIN NO: 98-028   **DATE: OCT. 1, 2001**

1996–2001 3.5 RL; 2002 3.5 RL

SYMPTOMS: The security system sounds intermittently while the vehicle is parked. The door locks cycle while driving. The instrument panel lights remain on.

PROBABLE CAUSE: Water is leaking into the front pillars. The water is getting into the connectors for the under-dash fuse relay box, the driver's multiplex control unit, or the door lock actuator, causing a short circuit.

RL PROFILE

	1996	1997	1998	1999	2000	2001	2002	2003	2004
Cost Price ($)									
Base	52,300	54,600	55,000	52,000	52,000	53,000	54,000	55,000	55,800
Used Values ($)									
Base ▲	7,000	9,000	11,500	15,000	18,000	22,000	28,000	34,000	40,000
Base ▼	5,500	7,500	10,000	13,500	16,500	20,000	26,000	32,000	38,000
Reliability	④	④	⑤	⑤	⑤	⑤	⑤	⑤	⑤
Crash Safety (F)	—	—	—	④	④	④	④	④	④
Side	—	—	—	—	—	—	—	—	④
Offset	③	③	③	③	③	③	③	③	③
Head Restraints	—	②	—	②	—	❶	❶	❶	❶
Rollover Resistance	—	—	—	—	—	—	—	④	④

TL   ★★★

RATING: Average (2000–04); Above Average (1996–99). Every year that these Acuras are redesigned, quality takes a hit. **Maintenance/Repair costs:** Average cost, but many repairs are dealer dependent. **Parts:** Higher-than-average cost (some independent suppliers sell for much less under the Honda name), but not hard to find. **Extended warranty:** Not needed. **Best alternatives:** Consider the

Acura Integra, Audi A4, BMW's redesigned 3 Series, Infiniti's redesigned I30 or I35, the Mazda Millenia, and the Lexus ES 300. You may want to take a look at Acura's CL coupe: It's not as expensive, and it's as close as you can get to the Accord with lots of standard bells and whistles thrown in. **Online help:** "The Temple of VTEC" at *www.vtec.net/, www.acuraworld.com/forums/, www.cbel.com/acura_cars,* and *www.autosafety.org/autodefects.html.*

 ## Strengths and Weaknesses

The TL has impressive acceleration, handles well, rides comfortably, and is well put-together, with quality mechanical and body components. However, the suspension may be too firm for some, and the vehicle has uncomfortable rear seating, excessive road noise, and problematic navigation system controls.

Filling the void left by the discontinued Vigor, the TL combines luxury and performance in a nicely styled front-drive five-passenger sedan that uses the same chassis as the Accord and CL coupe. Base models will likely carry an adequate, though unimpressive, 2.5L inline 5-cylinder engine. Performance enthusiasts will opt for versions equipped with the more refined 3.2L 225/270-hp V6 mated with a 6-speed manual transmission and a firmer suspension introduced with the 2004 model. It provides impressive acceleration (0–100 km/h in just over 8 seconds) in a smooth and quiet manner, without any fuel penalty. Handling is exceptional with the firm suspension, but can be a bit tricky when pushed. Bumps are a bit jarring and the ride is somewhat busier than other cars in this class, but this is a small price to pay for the car's high-speed performance.

VEHICLE HISTORY: 1998—TLs came with a bit more standard equipment than in previous years. 1999—2.5L engine was dropped and practically everything else was upgraded. 2000—Enhanced performance features that include a better-performing 5-speed transmission, a free-flowing intake manifold, side airbags, and depowered front airbags. 2002—A new performance version based on the CL Type S, a minor face-lift, new wheels and headlights, and more comfortable seat belts. 2004—New styling, 10 more horses, and more standard safety features. Although the length is shorter by 6.3 inches, interior room remains unchanged, despite the addition of head-protecting curtain side airbags. Other changes include a six-speed manual tranny, a sportier suspension, high-performance tires, Brembo front brakes, and a limited-slip differential.

Interior accommodations are better than average up front, but rear occupants may discover that legroom is a bit tight and the seat cushions lack sufficient thigh support. The cockpit layout is very user-friendly, due in part to the easy-to-read gauges and accessible controls (far-away climate controls are the only exception). Standard safety features include ABS, traction control, childproof door locks, three-point seat belts, and a transmission/brake interlock.

Common complaints involve chronic automatic and manual transmission failures (covered by a goodwill warranty), engine surging and stalling, malfunctioning airbags and accessories, electrical shorts, premature brake wear, and poor body fits. Owners point out that the window regulator may need replacing, the ignition switch buzzes, the trunk lock jams, and the rear bumper is often loose.

 ## Safety Summary

All models/years: Horn is difficult to locate in emergency situations. • Airbags fail to deploy in a collision. • Sudden, unintended acceleration. **All models: 1998–2001**—Clutch master cylinder fluid leakage. **1999**—Airbags deployed in a collision and severely burned driver's hands. • Seat belt failed to retract in a collision, allowing driver to hit windshield. • Transmission fails to downshift or upshift. • Front rotors warp within 160,000 km (10,000 miles). • Door locks operate erratically. • Wiper blades leak graphite, smearing windshield. • Instrument panel is washed out in sunlight, making odometer practically invisible. **2000**—Brake pedal feels spongy, and it's easy to confuse brake and gas pedals. **2001**—Automatic transmission failures that leave the engine revving high (like when passing), but the car doesn't accelerate (it actually slows down). **2002**—Driver's seat belt unreeled during accident. • Automatic transmission failures at high speed. • Transmission grinds when shifting from First to Second gear. **2004**—Side airbags failed to deploy. • Erratic automatic transmission shifting. • Stability control activated right front brake, causing the vehicle to swerve suddenly. • Excessive steering wheel shake and chassis vibration may be caused by a defective transmission torque converter. • Cracked alloy wheel rim caused tire failure. • Headlight low beam creates a dark/blind spot. • Multiple malfunctions with the hands-free phone system. • Windshield is easily broken. • Many complaints of hydroplaning and excessive vibration from the Bridgestone Turanza EL42 tires:

> This tire exhibits unsafe characteristics in wet weather, with noticeable drift and hydroplaning in any amount of standing water, even as little as 1/16 inch. In heavy rains, even with no standing water present, the tire seems incapable of dispersing water as quickly as it falls, again leading to vehicle instability. From a ride quality point of view the tire is also unsatisfactory in that it flat spots every morning, especially in cool weather but even in warmer weather as well.

•

Many users complaining about the tires; see *edmunds.com*. 2005 model no longer uses Bridgestone, changed to Michelins.

Secret Warranties/Internal Bulletins/Service Tips

All models/years: Like Honda's, most of Acura's TSBs allow for special warranty consideration on a "goodwill" basis, even after the warranty has expired or the car

312

has changed hands. Referring to this euphemism will increase your chances of getting some kind of refund for repairs that are obviously factory defects. • Seat belts that fail to function properly during normal use will be replaced for free under the company's lifetime seat belt warranty. • Diagnostic procedures and correction for off-centre steering wheels. **All models: 1996–98**—A growling or whining coming from the rear wheels can be fixed by replacing the hub bearing unit. • Brake squeal during light application can be fixed by replacing the front pads (eligible for "goodwill"). **1999**—A navigation system that locks up or resets can be corrected by rewriting the unit's software; a remanufactured unit may also be considered. **1999–2000**—A squeaking, creaking driver's seat is addressed in TSB #00-014. • A wrinkled rear door sash trim will be covered under a "goodwill" policy, even if correction was done by an independent body shop. • Tips on replacing a leaking torque converter. • Troubleshooting moon roof creaks. **1999–2002**—Front, middle, or rear engine oil leaks likely caused by a too-porous cast aluminum engine block (TSB #01-041). • Loose front seat back panel. **2000**—Excessive cranking when restarting. • Faulty front and rear water passage gaskets at the cylinder head can cause a coolant leak next to the EGR valve. • Radiator/condenser fan runs continuously, discharging battery. • Vehicle clunks when going over bumps. **2000–01**—MIL (malfunction indicator light) and airbag warning light may stay lit for no apparent reason. • V6 engine oil leaks. • Speed sensor plug may be missing. • Panic alarm activates inadvertently. • Brake pedal pulsation. • Windshield wiper smearing and streaking. **2001**—A booming sound may be heard when the moon roof is opened while the car is underway. • Moon roof squeaks. • Climate control changes intermittently. **2000–03**—Honda extended its warranties to 7 years/160,000 km (100,000 miles) on automatic transmissions (see CL section, pages 189–193). **2004**—A lit ABS warning lamp may indicate that there's moisture in the sensor.

TL PROFILE

	1996	1997	1998	1999	2000	2001	2002	2003	2004
Cost Price ($)									
Base	34,900	36,600	37,000	35,000	35,000	36,000	37,000	37,800	40,800
Used Values ($)									
Base ▲	7,000	8,500	10,000	12,500	15,500	18,500	22,000	27,000	32,000
Base ▼	6,000	7,500	9,000	11,000	14,000	17,000	20,500	25,000	30,000
Reliability	4	4	4	4	3	4	4	3	3
Crash Safety (F)	4	4	4	—	—	4	4	4	5
Side	—	—	—	—	—	4	4	4	4
Offset	—	—	—	5	5	5	5	5	5
Head Restraints	—	1	—	1	—	1	1	1	2
Rollover Resistance	—	—	—	—	—	—	5	4	4

All ratings on a numbered scale where 5 is good and 1 is bad. See pages 100–101 for a more detailed description.

Audi

RATING: Average (2000–04); Above Average (1996–99); Not Recommended (1984–95). Rating has been dropped because of poor wet weather braking performance and serious transmission and ignition coil pack failures. The 1997 V6-equipped A4 is a price/performance bargain in this series, while the 2000 TT is an excellent buy considering it sells for about half the price ($27,000) originally charged. A second series model will be more dependable. **Maintenance/Repair costs:** Higher than average, and almost all repairs have to be done by an Audi dealer. Long delays for recall repairs. **Parts:** Way higher-than-average cost, and independent suppliers have a hard time finding parts. Don't even think about buying one of these front-drives without a 3- to 5-year supplementary warranty backed by Audi. **Extended warranty:** A good idea, considering how badly past engine, coil pack, and sludge problems were handled by Audi in Canada. VW and its different divisions work from the States. **Best alternatives:** Acura Integra, TL or RL; BMW 3 Series; Infiniti I30/I35; and Lexus ES300. TT Coupe shoppers may also want to look at the BMW Z3 Series, Honda S2000, and Mazda Miata. **Online help:** *www.audiworld.com, www.audi-tt.org, www.vwvortex.com, MyAudiTTsucks.com,* and *www.robertfarago.com/tac* (The Truth About Cars).

Strengths and Weaknesses:

Audi's best-selling line, these cars are attractively styled and comfortable to drive, handle well, and provide a fairly comfortable interior. But you'd better know how to separate the wheat from the chaff, since some model years can be wallet-busters.

The early '90 models, including the old 90 and 100, have a worse-than-average reliability record and are plagued by mechanical and electrical components that don't stand up to the rigors of driving in cold climates. Look for the better-built and more recent A4 and A6 models. Although most dealers don't want to service these relics, many independent garages (staffed by former VW mechanics) will go the extra mile to keep them on the road.

The 1996 and later models are the pick of the Audi litter (dating from when all-wheel drive became an optional feature on all entry-level models). The A6, the reincarnation of the 100 series, is packed with standard features, and is a comfortable, spacious, front-drive or all-wheel-drive luxury sedan that comes with dual airbags and ABS. It uses the same V6 power plant as the A4, its smaller sibling, but has 47 additional horses. Unfortunately, the engine is no match for the car's size (0–100 km/h in 13 seconds), and steering and handling is decidedly trucklike. The

A8, the first luxury car with an all-aluminum body, competes with the BMW 7 Series and the Mercedes S-Class. Equipped with a WHO 174-hp 2.8L V6 or a 300-hp V8, the A8 is an above-average buy. Its drawbacks: It comes with a high price, its steering is a bit imprecise for an Audi, and its aluminum body can only be repaired by an Audi dealer.

The S6 is a solid performer with its turbocharged 227-hp 2.2L 5-cylinder engine. Its reliability is better than average and its sports performance leaves the A6 in the dust. It may be equipped with a sports suspension, a turbocharger, and four-wheel drive.

VEHICLE HISTORY: 1994—Airbags became a standard feature. *A4:* **1997**—The A4 V6 sedan was renamed the 2.8 and joined a new entry-level A4 1.8T. An improved 190-hp DOHC V6 also debuted that year. **1998**—The addition of the A4 2.8 V6 wagon equipped with a 5-speed Triptronic transmission. **1999**—Addition of an A4 1.8 wagon, and the base 1.8 model received additional insulation. **2000**—A high-performance S4 joined the A4 lineup, and A4 2.8s were given a power-assisted front passenger's seat. The S4 is a limited-production, high-performance spin-off that carries a 227-hp turbo-charged rendition of the old 5-cylinder power plant. **2001**—The base 1.8L engine got 20 extra horses; an all-new 2001 S4 sedan and Avant, featuring a 250-hp 2.7L twin-turbocharged V6, also joined the lineup. **2002**—A4 was totally revamped, getting a roomier interior, a 10-hp boost to the base engine, and a 3.0L all-aluminum, 5-valve-per-cylinder, 220-hp V6 engine, hooked to a new 6-speed manual transmission. Other features: a more rigid body, an upgraded independent rear suspension, and brake assist. **2003**—Addition of a convertible. **2004**—More high-performance models and greater all-wheel drive availability. *A6:* **1999**—Carried over with minor changes. **2000**—Addition of two performance sedans and side curtain airbags (standard on the 4.2). **2001**—2.7T and the 4.2 A6 models got Audi's electronic stabilization program, which prevents fishtailing and enhances traction control. **2002**—Debut of all-wheel drive, a 2.7L engine, and adjustable air suspension. **2003**—The new RS6 debuts equipped with a 450-hp 4.2L V8; the sporty S6 Avant adds a more powerful V8, sport suspension, and special trim, the 2.7T gets 17-inch wheels. On the downside, front passenger-seat memory is no more, and steering-wheel shift buttons are gone. **2004**—A V8 for the all-road quattro and a new sports model, the 2.7T S-line sedan. *TT:* **2001**—A two-passenger softtop Roadster debuts; addition of Electronic Stability Program (ESP), a rear spoiler, and a 225-hp turbocharged 4-cylinder engine. **2002**—A new radio with in-dash CD. **2003**—All-wheel drive now only found on uplevel models; a revised grille. **2004**—A 250-hp 3.2L V6 Quattro model hooked to a new Direct Shift Gearbox—a clutchless manual that can shift like an automatic.

These alphabetically named cars are conservatively styled, often slow off the mark (in spite of the V6 addition when hooked to an automatic), and plagued by electrical glitches. The 4-speed automatic shifts erratically (delayed and abrupt engagement), and the 2.8L V6 engine needs full throttle for adequate performance. Handling is acceptable, but the ride is a bit firm and the car still exhibits considerable body roll, brake dive, and acceleration squat when pushed. Handling is on a par with the BMW 3 Series, and acceleration times beat out those of the Mercedes.

Overall quality control improved markedly with the 1996–99 model years and then started going downhill. Through the 2004 models, there have been an inordinate number of safety- and performance-related defects reported by owners. The electrical system is the car's weakest link and it has plagued Audi's entire lineup for the past decade. Normally, this wouldn't be catastrophic; however, as the cars become more electronically complex, with more functions handled by computer modules, you're looking at some annoying glitches to say the least (particularly, chronic ignition coil pack failures, resulting in stalling or no-starts). Other "annoyances": the transmission suddenly downshifting or jerking into forward gear, brake failures in rainy weather, premature brake wear and grinding when in Reverse, fuel system malfunctions leading to surging and stalling, early lower control arm replacement, steering grinds, defective mirror memory settings, distorted windshields, and body glitches head the list of things likely to go wrong. Furthermore, servicing is still spotty because of the small number of dealers in Canada and the fact that these cars are extremely dealer-dependent; owners report long servicing delays.

90

These cars were launched in 1988 as entry-level Audis, sharing the same wheelbase and powertrain components. Equipped with an efficient but wimpy 4-cylinder (dropped in 1991) or the more powerful 2.3L 5-cylinder engine, four-wheel disc brakes, and galvanized body panels, these small sedans are leagues ahead of Audi's mid-1980s vehicles. The 1991 models are clearly a better choice; they use an improved 4-speed automatic transmission hooked up to a more powerful engine. 1992 was basically a carryover year in which unsold 1991 models were recycled. Audi's first convertible, the Cabriolet, first appeared in 1994. It's essentially a 90 model set on a shorter wheelbase with a standard automatic transmission. The 90 was redesigned in 1995 (replacing both the 80 and the old 90) as the Sport 90, a stylish sporty version that was more show than go—it was dropped shortly thereafter. Common problems include AC, electrical system, and brake malfunctions. Although bargain-priced, these cars should be shunned because of the poor parts supply, unwillingness of mechanics to troubleshoot and service them (it takes even more skill and patience with older models), and the general poor quality of replacement parts.

TT Coupe

The best of the Audi lineup, the TT Coupe is a sporty front-drive hatchback with 2+2 seating, set on the same platform used by the A4, Golf, Jetta, and New Beetle. A two-seat convertible version, the Roadster, was launched in the spring of 2000. The base 180-hp 1.8L engine (lifted from the A4) is coupled to a manual 5-speed, while the optional engine uses a 6-speed manual transaxle. Shorter and more firmly sprung than the A4, the TT's engines are turbocharged.

More beautifully styled and better handling than the Prowler, the TT comes with lots of high-tech standard features that include four-wheel disc brakes, airbags everywhere, traction control (front-drive models), a power top (Quattro), a heated-glass rear window, and a power-retractable glass windbreak between the roll bars (convertible). An alarm system employs a pulse radar system to catch prying hands invading the cockpit area.

Problem areas reported by owners: premature transmission failures and grinding of the Second gear synchronizers, excessive brake noise, electrical shorts causing dash gauges and instruments to fail, premature wheel bearing failure, and steering wheel clunks.

 Safety Summary

All models/years: Extremely poor wet braking on later models, caused by water contaminating the brake rotor and disc; braking delay is almost two seconds. • Chronic stalling. • Many cases of distorted windshields. **1998**—Stuck gas pedal. • Premature transmission failure; car pops out of gear. • Front and rear brake rotor and pad failed. • Premature upper and lower control arm failures (50 complaints found on *www.audiworld.com*). • Sunroof opens by itself. **1999**—Sudden, unintended acceleration when backing up. • Vehicle will roll away even though parking brake is engaged. • Brakes suddenly locked up. • Engine loses power when shifting. • Door locks don't work. • Airbag failures. • Headlights burn out prematurely and don't provide sufficient illumination. • Booming noise heard if the sunroof or any window is open when car is underway. **2001**—Brakes fail to stop vehicle. • Headlights blind oncoming drivers. • Hood latch broke, allowing hood to smash into windshield. **2002**—Frequent coil pack failures forced Audi to pay for their replacement, but the problem continues on other models (see *www.audiworld.com/search/index.html*):

> I have been in contact with close to 100 other 2002 Audi owners through the AudiWorld website and the coil pack problem is a serious issue. The ignition coil packs have been failing on at least 10 percent of the 2002 vehicles and Audi says they are all isolated cases. When they fail the car barely runs and can create a lot of personal safety issues.

I have learned that Audi had a product recall for this exact problem, however my 2003 A4 components are not covered by those under recall. I was told I have the "newer" versions of the ignition coils already in my car. While they might be newer, they sure haven't solved the underlying problem! Two blown igition coils in less than 2 months and i can't get the MFR to replace the other 2 coils that I'm certain will go out at some point soon too.

• Sudden acceleration. • No airbag deployment. **2003**—Stuck accelerator pedal. • No-starts believed to be caused by instrument cluster or steering lock/ignition cylinder failures. • Ignition coil packs continue to blow (see above complaint). • Stalling believed to be caused by a defective fuel pump. CVT hesitates before engaging. • Parking brake failed to hold. • Outside mirrors don't automatically readjust. • Ice glazes the brake rotors. • Frequent failure of the windshield wiper motor and washer. • Faulty Pirelli tires. • Doors fill with water when it rains. **2004**—Sudden, unintended acceleration. • Stuck accelerator caused sudden acceleration. • Tire jack stand collapsed. • Pirelli tire tread separation. • Convertible top failures. *A6 Sedan:* **1998–99**—During refuelling, gasoline spits back violently from the filler pipe. **2003**—Car fails to start (not coil-related, they say). • Sudden acceleration. • Airbags failed to deploy. • Numerous complaints of delayed braking; no brakes in rainy weather; parking brake failure; and premature replacement of the front brake rotors. • Sudden headlight failure. • Blue-white headlights blind oncoming drivers. **2004**—More Pirelli tire failures. *TT Coupe:* **2000**—Engine compartment howling or moaning heard when accelerating. • Periodic grinding of the Second gear synchronizers is a common failure, said to affect many Audi and VW models. • Parking brake failure. • Engine exploded following a computer malfunction. • Electrical short causes vehicle to lose power. • Fuel gauge shows full, even though fuel is low. **2001**—Defective fuel gauge gives false reading (A6 models recalled for the same defect). • All windshields have some kind of visual distortion (anything viewed, especially straight lines, is distorted). Audi has a secret warranty to replace the windshields for free, regardless of mileage. • Sudden clutch failure (Audi paid half the replacement cost). • Central computer failure causes door locks to jam, trapping occupants. • Sudden windshield wiper failure. **2002**—Xenon headlights don't adequately light the roadway.

Secret Warranties/Internal Bulletins/Service Tips

All models/years: Defective catalytic converters that cause a rotten-egg smell may be replaced free of charge under the emissions warranty. • Inoperative radio; dash light is too dim. • Underbody wind noise. **2001–03**—Faulty ignition coils cause sudden stalling/no-starts; replacement coils will be installed free of charge without prior ownership or mileage restrictions; consequential damages (towing, alternate transport, ruined vacation, etc.) will also be refunded if you stand your ground (see following bulletin).

2002–04—Broken, missing audio knobs will be replaced free of charge (TSB #04-05, April, 2004). *A4, A6, S6*: **1996–2004**—Moisture accumulation in headlights is Audi's responsibility (TSB #03-03, November, 2003). *A4, A6*: **1998–2000**—Diagnostic and repair procedures for disc brake squeal, an engine that will crank but not start, and engine misfires. **1999**—AC doesn't provide enough cooling. • Tips to silence rear window creaking or popping. **2002–03**—Automatic transmission jerks going into Reverse. *A4*: **2002**—Poor AM band reception. **2002–04**—Oil leak at camshaft adjuster. **2004**—3.0L engine misfiring troubleshooting tips. *A6*: **1997–2001**—Erratic engine idle fluctuation. **1998–2002**—Inoperative fresh air control lever. **2000**—Automatic transmission goes into limp mode and won't shift. **2001**—Inoperative self-levelling system. • Stained D-pillar trim. **2003**—Inoperative keyless entry transmitter and faulty fresh air control lever light. *TT*: **2004**—Front stabilizer bar upgrade to reduce noise.

90, A4, A6 (100), A8, S6, TT COUPE PROFILE

	1996	1997	1998	1999	2000	2001	2002	2003	2004
Cost Price ($)									
A4	36,250	31,600	32,700	32,700	32,990	33,785	37,225	37,310	34,435
A6 (100)	48,904	49,270	48,800	48,880	49,170	49,835	54,235	51,740	51,950
A8	—	89,840	90,540	90,540	86,250	86,500	86,500	86,500	97,750
S6	61,400	63,550	—	—	—	—	—	88,500	—
TT	—	—	—	—	49,500	50,400	50,400	48,650	49,975
Used Values ($)									
A4 ▲	6,500	8,500	10,500	12,000	15,000	19,500	24,000	27,500	29,000
A4 ▼	5,500	7,000	9,000	10,500	13,500	18,000	22,500	26,000	27,500
A6 (100) ▲	9,000	10,000	13,000	17,000	21,500	27,000	34,000	41,000	45,000
A6 (100) ▼	7,500	9,000	11,500	15,500	19,500	25,000	32,000	39,500	43,000
A8 ▲	—	15,000	17,500	20,000	27,000	35,000	47,000	60,000	77,000
A8 ▼	—	13,500	15,500	18,500	25,000	33,000	45,000	58,000	64,000
S6 ▲	11,000	13,000	—	—	—	—	—	—	—
S6 ▼	10,000	11,500	—	—	—	—	—	—	—
TT ▲	—	—	—	—	21,000	25,000	30,000	36,500	42,000
TT ▼	—	—	—	—	19,500	23,000	28,000	34,500	40,000
Reliability	❷	❷	❸	④	④	④	④	④	④

All ratings on a numbered scale where ⑤ is good and ❶ is bad. See pages 100–101 for a more detailed description.

Crash Safety (F)

A4	④	④	—	—	—	—	④	④	④
A6 (100)	⑤	⑤	—	—	—	—	—	—	—
A8	—	—	⑤	⑤	⑤	⑤	⑤	⑤	⑤
Side (TT)	—	—	—	—	—	⑤	⑤	⑤	⑤
A4	—	—	—	—	—	—	⑤	⑤	⑤
Offset (A6)	—	—	❸	❸	❸	❸	❸	❸	❸
A4	—	—	—	—	—	—	⑤	⑤	⑤
Head Restraints									
A4 (F)	—	❶	—	❸	—	⑤	⑤	⑤	❶
A4 (Rear)	—	—	—	—	—	❸	—	—	❶
A6	—	❶	—	❸	—	⑤	⑤	⑤	⑤
A8	—	❶	—	❸	—	❸	❷	❷	⑤
TT Coupe	—	—	—	—	—	—	❸	❸	❸
TT Roadster	—	—	—	—	—	⑤	⑤	⑤	⑤
Rollover Resistance									
A4	—	—	—	—	—	—	④	④	④
TT	—	—	—	—	—	—	—	⑤	⑤

BMW

3 SERIES, 5 SERIES, M SERIES, Z3 ★★★★☆

RATING: *3 Series*: Above Average (2001–04); Average (1994-2000); Below Average (1984–93). *5 Series*: Recommended (1992–2003); Average (1985–91; 2004); there was no 1996 version. *M Series*: Recommended (1997–2004). Z3: Above Average (1996–2002). Z4: Recommended (2003-04). Sorry, but *Lemon-Aid* can't jump on the "BMW is best" bandwagon for every model year. First of all, there's no reason why the 2004 series should cost $10,000 more than the previous year's model. Also, owner feedback and internal service bulletins show these cars come with a performance and quality reputation that far exceeds what they actually deliver. Some of the websites listed below show the dark side of the BMW driving experience.

Maintenance/Repair costs: Higher than average, but many repairs can be done by independents who specialize in BMW repairs. Unfortunately, these experts are usually concentrated around large urban areas. **Parts:** Higher-than-average cost, and they're often back-ordered. **Extended warranty:** Not needed. **Best alternatives:** Yes, there are a number of credible alternatives to the Z Series, like the AWD 3 Series, an A4 Quattro, or a Mazda6. Also look at the Acura Integra, TL, and

RL; Infiniti I30 or I35; Mazda Millenia; and the Toyota Avalon. *Wagons*: Get a Mercedes E-Class. Sure, BMW makes better sedans, but the E-class gives a more comfortable ride, offers a huge trunk, a flat floor and a low loading sill, and doesn't infuriate you with a confusing, high-tech, iDrive gizmo. **Online help:** *www. straight-six.com, www.mwerks.com, www.bmwnation.com, www.roadfly.org, yoy.com/ auto/m3_failure_index.html, www.bmwboard.com,* and *www.bmwlemon.com.*

 ## Strengths and Weaknesses

3 Series

The 3 Series vehicles exhibit great 6-cylinder performance with the manual gearbox, and ride and handling are commendable. The 318's small engine is seriously compromised, however, by an automatic transmission. The 325e is more pleasant to drive and delivers lots of low-end torque. Through 1998, rear passenger and cargo room is limited. After a redesign of the '99 models, passenger and cargo space was increased.

The 1991 and later models provide peppy 4-cylinder acceleration only with high revs and a manual transmission. Keep in mind that city driving requires lots of manual gear shifting characterized by an abrupt clutch. If you must have an automatic, look for a used model with the 6-cylinder engine. The larger 1.9L 4-cylinder that went into the mid-'96 models doesn't boost performance all that much.

Although the 1997 models come with traction control, it is not very effective in giving these vehicles acceptable wet pavement traction. A problem since the early '90s, the rear end tends to slip sideways when the roadway is wet (much like Ford's rear-drive Mustang). Smart shoppers will opt for the improved 2000 models, keeping in mind that rear interior room is still a joke—unless you happen to be sitting there. Various upgrades make the 2001 and later models the best choice.

VEHICLE HISTORY: 1998—Given a 2.5L inline 6-cylinder and side airbags. **1999**—Revamped with a better-performing base engine and 2.8L 6-banger, and a more refined transmission and chassis. **2000**—A redesigned lineup of coupes, convertibles, and wagons; the hatchback is gone. **2001**—Received an engine upgrade, larger brakes and wheels, and optional 4×4 capability. High-performance M3 coupe returned with a 330-hp engine. **2002**—M3 got a new 6-speed sequential manual transmission; entire lineup got recalibrated steering, reshaped headrests, and an in-dash CD player. **2003**—Coupes and convertibles are restyled, along with a transmission upgrade and a new sedan performance package. **2004**—Expanded availability of the sequential manual transmission.

Handling with all model years is still tricky on wet roads, despite the ASC+T traction control; rear seat access is problematic; rear passenger space continues to be disappointing; and styling is the essence of bland. Brakes, electrical system, and some body trim and accessories are the most failure-prone components. Engine overheating is a serious and common failure.

5 Series

Essentially a larger, more powerful 3 Series, the 5 Series has made its reputation by delivering more performance in a larger, more versatile interior. There is no problem with rear seat or cargo room with the 5 Series Bimmer. Handling and ride are superb, although these weighty upscale models do strain when going over hilly terrain if they have the automatic gearbox.

5 Series owners report numerous electrical and fuel glitches, faulty turn signal indicators, starter failures, self-activating emergency flashers, rotten-egg odours from the exhaust, and excessive steering wheel or brake vibration.

Overall reliability was very poor with early Bimmers, but has improved as of late. Nevertheless, whenever a problem does arise, repair costs are particularly high because of the small number of dealers, the relative scarcity of parts, and the acquiescence of affluent owners. Electrical and fuel system, automatic transmission, and front brake failures are the primary weak spots of the 1984–93 models. Chronic engine surging at idle and a rotten-egg smell from the exhaust are also commonplace. Door seams, rocker panels, rear-wheel openings, and fender seams are particularly prone to rust. Check the muffler bracket for premature wear, and weather seals and door adjustments for leaks.

The '94 and later models still have reliability problems affecting the automatic and manual transmissions, brakes, and fuel and electrical systems. Additionally, owners report that premature brake wear causes excessive vibration and noise when the brakes are applied. Some reports of water leaks through the doors. Year 2000–03 models are plagued by cooling fan malfunctions, leading to engine overheating and fires; airbag malfunctions; a manual transmission that's hard to shift into Second gear, pops out of gear, and grinds when shifting; automatic transmission screeches when shifting; steering degradation when braking at slow speeds; and front door water leaks.

The 2004 models are scary. Equipped with BMW's iDrive, which uses a console "joystick" knob to control entertainment, navigation, communication, and climate functions, this system both annoys and distracts drivers who aren't that techno-savvy.

VEHICLE HISTORY: 1989—Based on the 7 Series, the new 5 sits on a longer wheelbase than earlier models. Two rear-drive sedans were available: the 525i with a 2.5L 6-cylinder engine, and the 535i, whose 3.4L 6-cylinder engine developed 208 hp. **1990**—A driver-side airbag arrives. **1991**—The 525i gained a more powerful engine; 535i's automatic transmission got a shorter final-drive ratio and reprogrammed management system, producing quicker acceleration; M5 came with a 310-hp 3.5L engine. **1993**—Engines got variable valve timing. **1994**—V8 engines for the 530i sedan and wagon, and 540i sedan; passenger-side airbags; the 535i and the M5 are dropped. **1997**—The redesigned model is longer and comes with an enlarged V6 or V8 engine, dual front and side airbags, anti-lock brakes, and traction control. **1998**—Head protection system introduced. **1999**—Station wagons get both 6-cylinder and V8 power, xenon headlights, memory for power seats and mirrors, Park Distance Control that warns of obstacles when backing up, and a self-levelling rear suspension for wagons. Standard on V8 models and newly optional for 528i versions was BMW's Dynamic Stability Control. **2000**—Return of the high-performance M5 sedan; 528i versions get a standard anti-skid system; rear side airbags for the M5. **2001**—525i sedan and wagon debut. **2002**—540i's V8 got an extra 8 hp. **2003**—A sunroof for all 6-cylinders and a new Sport Package with the manual-transmission 540i sedan. **2004**—Redesigned with new styling, new features, and a more powerful V8. 545i 6-Speed was given a sport suspension teamed with run-flat tires, plus Active Steering and Active Roll Stabilization to counteract body lean. All models have BMW's controversial iDrive, console "joystick" to control entertainment, navigation, communication, and climate functions. Critics say that the iDrive takes a McGill Engineering degree to operate it and that it's a safety hazard. 545i and 545i 6-Speed models use a 4.4-liter V8 with 325 hp, up from 290 in last year's 540i. The wagon is gone.

M Series

Launched in 1997 as a four-door model, the M3 is a high-performance coupe equipped with a potent 240-hp 3.0L engine, a manual shifter, firmer suspension, and 17-inch tires.

VEHICLE HISTORY: 1997–2000—Re-designated the M Series. **2000**—The M5 is mostly a renamed 540i sports sedan. **2001**—Arrival of a new 315-hp inline six, Dynamic Stability Control, and a tighter suspension (watch those kidneys), while the M3 returned in a convertible and coupe format, equipped with a high-performance 333-hp engine. **2002**—All models were given a modified aluminum suspension, wider 18-inch tires and wheels, a new limited-slip differential, and a refreshed interior.

Overall M3 reliability is quite impressive; however, these cars have one fatal flaw. Their engines self-destruct. In fact, 112 failed engines have been registered with the *yoy.com/auto/m3_failure_index.html* website, which dubs the power plant "The Engine of Damocles."

Except for in AutoWeek (*autoweek.com*), little has been reported about possible main bearing or connecting rod problems with M3 engines built in 2001 and 2002. Nevertheless, the problem is real, has been confirmed by BMW, and is extensively documented online at *members.roadfly.com*. Many owners have had engines replaced with no explanation of what went wrong.

Other reported problems: loud clunking from the rear end when shifting or decelerating, said to be caused by a faulty driveshaft attachment at the differential, and poor paint application and delamination.

Z Series

BMW's first sports car, the Z3 is a two-seater based on the 3 Series platform that debuted in early 1996. Its 138-hp 1.9L four-banger is outclassed by the competition (like the non-S Boxster, the 3.2L V-6 SLK, or Honda S2000), and you have to get the revs up past 3000 rpm to get adequate passing torque. The 2001 model, with its 2.5L, 184-hp six-cylinder engine, is an all-around better performer and offers more features at a fairly depreciated price.

Dynamic Stability Control, large 17-inch wheels, and Dunlop SP Sport performance tires don't enhance handling as much as BMW pretends they do: Get used to lots of steering corrections.

The Z4 is a more feature-laden convertible equipped with an inline 6-cyl engine and a standard manual softtop. It still carries a base 184-hp 2.5L engine coupled with a 5-speed manual transmission; the higher-end Z4 3.0i has a 225-hp 3.0 mated to a 6-speed manual gearbox Run-flat tires, ABS, and an anti-skid system are standard features.

In 2000, BMW launched its $195,000 super-luxury Z8, a limited-production, fully equipped model with a power softtop, removable hardtop, a body made largely of aluminum, and a 4.9L V8, hooked to a mandatory 6-speed manual transmission. The car lasted four model years and is now worth about $80,000.

VEHICLE HISTORY: 1996—BMW's Z3 1.9L roadster arrived on the scene. 1997—An optional 2.8L engine was added, along with standard traction control. 1998—Standard rollover bars and upgraded sport seats. 1999—Standard side airbags (318Ti excepted) and a new 2.8 coupe. A 2.5L inline six replaced the 1.9L 4-cylinder engine. 2000—A slight restyling and standard Dynamic Stability Control. 2001—Debut of the Z8. Roadsters and coupes adopted a 3.0L power plant (instead of the 2.8L), and bigger brakes and wheels were added. Also, the 2.5L engine was tweaked to unleash 14 additional horses. 2003—Launch of the Z4; the Z8's last model year.

Owners report frequent stalling when decelerating, faulty right-side seat switches, and a squeaking, popping noise from the driver's door or in the shoulder area of the convertible top.

 **Safety Summary**

All models/years: Sudden acceleration. • Airbag malfunctions include bag deploying inadvertently, failing to go off in an accident, and a constantly lit warning light. • Transmission pops out of gear. **All models: 2002**—Many incidents where cooling fan failure caused engine to overheat, or a fire to ignite (see *www.bimmer.org*); airbag failed to deploy; and the premature replacement of the front control arms. *318*: **1998**—Finger was cut off when caught in the power window. • Glass came out of door channel. • Headlights provide poor illumination of the roadway. • Severe suspension hop when passing over small bumps. • Car's rear end slides out during turns. • Incorrect fuel gauge readings. **1999**—Front plastic grille piece fell off car and damaged the windshield. • Automatic transmission failures. • Seat belt doesn't retract as it should. • Horn sounds when vehicle is put in Reverse. • Headlights come on and off intermittently. • Several incidents of fire erupting when high beams were activated. • Heated seats get too hot. **2000**—Poor wet braking. • Faulty steering damper and control arms. • Seat belt warning light stays on. • Seat belt doesn't retract properly. • Drivebelts may suddenly fail. **2001**—Fire ignited because of defective fan assembly. • Defective cooling fan causes engine to overheat; seen as a widespread problem on the bulletin board at *www.roadfly.org/bmw*. • Premature replacement of the control arms. • Defective gas pedal assembly causes jerky acceleration. BMW will replace it on a case-by-case basis. *320*: **2002**—Distorted windshield. *323*: **2002**—Premature failure of the magnesium-alloy control arms and steering damper. • Airbag light stays on for no reason. • Poor steering when braking at slow speeds. • Sudden acceleration while cruising. • In rainy weather brakes stiffen as they are applied, leading to extended stopping distance. • Faulty sunroof. *325i*: Transmission failure within five days of purchase. • Electrical system fire. • Steering column is kinked to the left. • Right door airbag deployed even though vehicle was hit on the left. • Sunroof glass suddenly exploded (several incidents reported):

> Urgent—my 2002 325i's first sunroof glass exploded on me on 1/25/02. The replacement glass has two surface hairline cracks and two hairline cracks beneath the surface of the glass. This cannot be an isolated incident. Please examine your sunroof carefully for defects. No one at BMW is taking this seriously enough.

• Doors lock without prior warning. *328*: **2002**—Sudden acceleration; when accelerating, engine cuts out, then surges forward (suspected failure of the throttle assembly). • Severe engine vibrations after a cold start as Check Engine light comes on. • If driver wears a size 12 shoe or larger, when foot is flush against the accelerator pedal, the top of the shoe rubs up against the panel above the pedal, preventing full pedal access. • Rear quarter blind spot with the convertibles. *330i*: **2002**—Side airbag deployed when vehicle hit a pothole. • Vehicle overheats in low gear; tires lose air. • Vehicle slips out of Second gear when accelerating. *M3*: **1998**—Brake failure. • Airbags failed to deploy. • Chronic horn failures. • Rearview mirror blocks a substantial portion of the field of vision. • Inadvertent deployment of side airbags. **1999**—ABS failure. **2001**—Rear-end clunking, leading to failure of the driveshaft attachment at the differential (confirmed by other complaints on *www.roadfly.org/bmw*). *Z3:* **1998**—Defective rear stabilizer bar. • Automatic transmission jumps out of gear. • Intermittent headlight and instrument cluster failures. • Rear-view mirror creates a huge blind spot. **1999**—Seat belts don't spool out or retract as they should. **2000**—Computer keeps engine at high revs when throttle is released. • Passenger-side seat belt jams. **2000–01**—Faulty speedometer. **2001**—Engine stalls when decelerating. • Interior and exterior lights dim when AC engages. • Passenger seat belt doesn't fit snugly. • Driver's seat rocks to and fro. • Incorrect speedometer readings. • Exterior and interior lights dim and engine loses power when AC is engaged.

Secret Warranties/Internal Bulletins/Service Tips

All models/years: Rear sway bar links may come off the sway bar. • Front brake squeal. • Steering wheel buzz. • Door brake doesn't hold. • Driver's seat is loose. **All models: 1996–99**—Frequent crankshaft position sensor failures result in chronic Check Engine light illumination. This can be corrected by changing the sensor and installing an adapter harness under warranty or under a BMW "goodwill" policy. **2001–04**—Engine cylinder head oil leaks. *3 Series:* **1998**—A no-start condition may signal that the oil level sensor is faulty. • A clunk heard during downshifts, when releasing the accelerator pedal, or when shifting into Reverse is likely caused by excessive axial clearance at the transmission output. • Inoperative sunroof. **1998–2000**—Hard shifts or no shifts can be corrected by exchanging the valve body. **1999**—Tips for improving AM radio reception. • An inoperative cruise control may need a new brake light switch (strange but true). **1999–2000**—Guidelines for plugging manual transmission oil drain plug leaks. **2000**—Idle speed and headlight brightness fluctuate when seat heater is activated. • Low airflow through vents. • Erratic automatic transmission shifting. **2002**—Incorrect fuel gauge readings. • Rattling, tapping engine noise. • Troubleshooting navigation system malfunctions. • No 1–2 upshift. **2003**—Harsh 3–2 and 2–1 downshifts (reprogram EGS module). **2004**—Delayed Park to Drive shift. • Low oil level false alert. Numerous malfunctions of telematics components. *5 Series:* **All models/years**—Centre dash humming or buzzing when accelerating. • Water inside of headlamp. • Erratic performance of the navigation system. **1996**—Oil level sensor may give an incorrect reading. **1997**—Airbag light stays lit for no reason. **1998**—A no-start condition may signal that the oil level sensor is faulty. *525i:* **2000**—No 1–2 upshift. *540:* **1999**—Air mass meter warranty extended to 7 years/120,000 km (75,000 miles). **2002**—Rattling, tapping engine noise. • Passenger-side airbags may not line up with the dash. • Steering groaning and grinding. • Troubleshooting navigation system malfunctions. *M Series:* **2001–03**—After a plague of self-destructing engines, BMW put out SIB #11-04-02 in June 2003 that extended the warranty to 6 years/161,000 km (100,000 miles) on all 6-cylinder engines, initiated a Service Action to replace key components free of charge, and recalibrated software for easier cold starts. Owner repair bills were also paid retroactively, including demands for consequential damages.

	1996	1997	1998	1999	2000	2001	2002	2003	2004
Cost Price ($)									
318ti	25,900	26,900	27,800	27,800	—	—	—	—	—
318i 4d	30,900	32,300	33,300	—	—	—	—	—	—
Convertible	42,900	43,900	44,900	45,900	—	—	—	—	—
320i 4d	—	—	—	—	—	33,900	34,500	34,900	34,950
325i, 328i	43,900	46,900	47,900	50,902	44,900	37,950	41,200	39,300	39,450
Convertible	55,300	57,900	58,900	58,900	—	52,500	52,800	53,400	—
323 Coupe	—	—	39,900	—	—	—	—	—	—
M3 2d	—	61,900	62,900	62,900	62,900	69,800	73,500	73,800	73,950
M5 4d	—	—	—	—	102,650	104,250	105,500	105,500	—
Z3 1.9L/2.3L	38,900	40,500	41,500	43,900	45,901	46,900	47,200	—	—
Z3 2.8L	—	49,900	51,900	52,900	54,900	55,900	56,200	—	—
Z4 2.5L	—	—	—	—	—	—	—	51,500	51,800
Z4 3.0L	—	—	—	—	—	—	—	59,500	59,900
Z8	—	—	—	—	190,000	190,000	195,000	195,000	—
Used Values ($)									
318ti ▲	6,500	8,500	10,000	11,500	—	—	—	—	—
318ti ▼	5,500	7,500	9,000	10,500	—	—	—	—	—
318i 4d ▲	8,000	10,000	12,500	—	—	—	—	—	—
318i 4d ▼	6,500	8,500	10,500	—	—	—	—	—	—
Convertible ▲	10,000	12,500	15,000	17,500	—	—	—	—	—
Convertible ▼	8,500	11,000	13,500	16,000	—	—	—	—	—
320i 4d ▲	—	—	—	—	—	18,000	21,500	25,500	28,500
320i 4d ▼	—	—	—	—	—	16,500	20,000	24,000	26,500
323 Coupe ▲	—	—	13,000	—	—	—	—	—	—
323 Coupe ▼	—	—	11,500	—	—	—	—	—	—
325i, 328i ▲	9,000	11,000	13,500	18,000	20,500	21,000	25,000	30,000	33,000
325i, 328i ▼	8,000	9,500	12,000	16,500	19,000	19,500	23,500	28,500	31,500
Convertible ▲	12,500	15,000	18,500	23,000	—	31,000	36,000	42,000	—
Convertible ▼	11,000	13,500	17,000	21,500	—	29,000	34,000	40,000	—
M3 2d ▲	—	15,000	19,000	24,000	28,000	37,000	45,000	54,000	60,000
M3 2d ▼	—	13,000	17,500	22,000	26,000	35,000	43,000	52,000	58,000
M5 4d ▲	—	—	—	—	42,000	54,000	68,000	80,000	—
M5 4d ▼	—	—	—	—	40,000	52,000	65,000	77,000	—
Z3 1.9L/2.3L ▲	10,000	12,500	16,000	18,500	24,000	28,000	32,000	—	—
Z3 1.9L/2.3L ▼	8,500	11,000	14,500	17,000	22,000	26,000	30,000	—	—
Z3 2.8L ▲	—	13,500	17,000	20,000	25,000	29,000	33,000	—	—
Z3 2.8L ▼	—	11,000	15,500	18,500	23,000	28,000	31,000	—	—
Z4 2.5L ▲	—	—	—	—	—	—	—	39,000	44,000
Z4 2.5L ▼	—	—	—	—	—	—	—	36,500	42,000
Z4 3.0L ▲	—	—	—	—	—	—	—	46,000	51,000
Z4 3.0L ▼	—	—	—	—	—	—	—	44,000	48,000

All ratings on a numbered scale where ⑤ is good and ❶ is bad. See pages 100–101 for a more detailed description.

Z8 ▲	—	—	—	—	80,000	100,000	120,000	154,000	—
Z8 ▼	—	—	—	—	77,000	95,000	115,000	150,000	—
Reliability	③	③	④	④	④	⑤	⑤	⑤	⑤
Crash Safety (F)	—	—	—	—	—	—	④	④	④
328i	④	④	—	—	—	—	—	—	—
Side	—	—	—	—	—	—	—	③	③
Offset	—	—	—	—	⑤	⑤	⑤	⑤	⑤
Head Restraints	—	❶	—	②	③	③	❶	❶	❶
M3	—	—	—	—	②	②	②	②	②
Convertible	—	—	—	❶	—	—	—	—	—
Z3	—	❶	—	③	—	③	—	—	—
Z4	—	—	—	—	—	—	⑤	⑤	⑤
Rollover Resistance	—	—	—	—	—	—	④	④	④

5 SERIES PROFILE

	1996	1997	1998	1999	2000	2001	2002	2003	2004
Cost Price ($)									
525i, 528i	—	54,900	56,200	57,200	55,500	54,700	55,200	55,500	65,500
Used Values ($)									
525i, 528i ▲	—	14,000	16,000	20,000	24,000	29,000	35,000	42,000	52,000
525i, 528i ▼	—	12,500	14,500	17,500	22,000	27,000	33,000	40,000	49,000
Reliability	⑤	⑤	⑤	⑤	⑤	⑤	⑤	⑤	④
Crash Safety (F)									
Offset	—	⑤	⑤	⑤	⑤	⑤	⑤	⑤	⑤
Head Restraints (F)	—	③	—	③	—	⑤	⑤	⑤	❶
Rear	—	②	—	—	—	—	—	—	—
Rollover Resistance	—	—	—	—	—	—	—	—	—

Ford/Lincoln

CONTINENTAL, LS, MARK VII, MARK VIII, TOWN CAR ★★☆

RATING: *Continental*: Below Average (1988–2002). *LS*: Average (2000–03). *Mark VII, Mark VIII*: Above Average (1995–98); Average (1994); Below Average (1986–93). *Town Car*: Average (1995–2004); Below Average (1988–94). In a nutshell:

Rear-drives, yes; front-drives, no. Although early front-drive Continentals are dirt-cheap, their low quality makes them risky buys. Ford dropped the Continental after its 2002 model year, so servicing problems will likely increase as well. The rear-drive Town Car and LS are the best choices for quality and performance, but you are still taking a substantial risk. The Mark series isn't a bad choice either, particularly in view of its incredibly low cost. **Maintenance/Repair costs:** Higher than average, and they must be done by a Ford or Lincoln dealer. **Parts:** Higher-than-average cost, but not hard to find (except for electronic components and body panels). **Extended warranty:** Yes for the front drive Continental; no for any of the rear drives. **Best alternatives:** Acura Integra, or RL; Cadillac DeVille; and Infiniti I30 or I35. **Online help:** *www.autosafety.org/autodefects.html* and *www.blue-ovalnews.com*.

⟨⚒⟩ Strengths and Weaknesses

These large luxury cruisers are proof that quality isn't proportional to the money you spend. Several designer series offer all the luxury options anyone could wish for, but the two ingredients most owners would expect to find—high quality and consistent reliability—are sadly lacking, especially with the front-drive versions. All models, however, have poor-quality automatic transmissions, electrical systems, brakes, body hardware, and fit and finish. NHTSA-recorded safety complaints also target more front-drive than rear-drive Lincolns, with engine, transmission, airbag, and brake failures cropping up repeatedly over the years—and increasing in severity and frequency.

Continental (front-drive)

When the Continental went front-drive from 1988 until its end in 2002, what was a mediocre luxury car became a luxury lemon with serious safety-related deficiencies. The frequency and cost of repairs increased considerably, and parts became more complex, complicating easy diagnosis and repair. The automatic transmission tends to self-destruct, particularly on 1988–2000 models; engine head gaskets blow (see Part Two); electrical components are unreliable, with intermittent loss of all electrical power; stopping performance is compromised by premature brake wear and wheel lock-up; and body hardware is an embarrassment. The redesigned 1995 Continental featured a new V8 power plant, more aerodynamic styling, and fibreglass panels. However, engine, transmission, electrical system, and brake problems actually worsened.

VEHICLE HISTORY: 1991—15 additional horses (155) and an upgraded 4-speed automatic transmission. **1992**—A passenger-side airbag and five more horses (160). **1994**—A slight restyling and suspension improvements. **1995**—A new 260-hp V8 and 4-speed automatic transmission; restyled, including dual airbags, anti-lock braking, automatic climate control, and an air-filtration system. **1996**—Anti-theft alarm. **1997**—Traction control added and failure-prone air springs dropped.

1998—A shorter nose and 2.5 cm less rear legroom. **1999**—Front side airbags and a 15-hp boost to 275 hp. **2000**— Rear child-seat anchors and an emergency trunk release.

These cars don't offer the kind of trouble-free driving one would normally expect in a luxury vehicle selling for over $40,000. The automatic levelling air-spring suspension system makes for a stiff ride (especially on early models), while still allowing the Continental to "porpoise" because of its heavy front end. The Continental's anemic V6 powertrain is poorly suited to a car of this heft. The engine hesitates in cold weather and the automatic transmission shifts roughly.

Mechanical defects include frequent engine flywheel and transmission forward clutch piston replacements; failure-prone ABS, electrical, suspension, and steering systems; and glitch-ridden electronic modules, causing hard starts and sudden stalling. The mass of electrical gadgets increases the likelihood of problems as the cars age. For example, automatic headlight doors fail frequently, and the electronic antenna and power windows often won't go up or down. The computerized dashboard is particularly failure-prone.

Other reliability complaints concern transmission fluid leakage caused by misplaced bolts, rough upshifting caused by a defective valve body, and air conditioning and heating that sometimes work in reverse.

Town Car

The rear-drive Town Car is the best of a bad lot, sharing most of its parts with the Crown Victoria and Grand Marquis. Its only saving grace is that, thanks to its rear-drive configuration, it's relatively inexpensive to repair and parts aren't hard to find. Nevertheless, the Town Car is still afflicted by many generic problems that appear year after year. Some of the more common problems are safety-related defects; engine head gaskets warped because a plastic part in the intake manifold has failed; transmission, AC, and electrical glitches; biodegradable tie-rod ends; and body hardware deficiencies.

VEHICLE HISTORY: 1990—Restyled to look less square. **1991**—The 4.6L V8 replaced the 5.0L; a new front suspension; and four-wheel disc brakes. **1993**—Dual airbags. **1994**—Dual exhausts. **1995**—Restyled; electronically adjustable steering, and seats have extra travel. **1995**—Slightly restyled, and steering improvements. **1996**—Engine upgraded and revised climate controls. **1997**—Steering refinements, but loss of dual exhausts cuts horsepower by 20 (drops to 190 hp). **1998**—Redesigned for a faster, lower, and stiffer ride. **1999**—Side airbags. **2000**—Improved child seat anchorages and a trunk emergency escape release. **2001**—25 horses added to engine, adjustable pedals, and seat belt pretensioners; the following model year got few changes. **2003**—Restyled; a revised frame, suspension, and steering system; and 17-inch tires. Also new: four-wheel, fully assisted ABS disc brakes, front-side airbags, an upgraded navigation system, and a 14-hp boost. **2004**—Standard rear obstacle-detection system; base Executive model dropped.

Incidentally, Ford will pay for intake manifold failures long after the warranty has expired—if you are a fleet customer (taxi, limousine, and law enforcement). Others are routinely denied after-warranty assistance. Unfair? You bet. Stupid? Absolutely! One owner of a '97 Lincoln afflicted with this malady had this to say:

> Ford has extended a no-charge coverage for this part for seven years and no mileage limitation, and it's automatically extended to subsequent owners. This should be extended to all owners of vehicles equipped with this defective part. Ford customer service has rejected [my] claim when contacted by telephone. They have not replied to two requests [sent] by mail.

LS

Lincoln's latest iteration, the LS rear-drive sedan, comes with a high-performance 200-hp variant of the Taurus 3.0L V6, mated with an optional manual or a standard automatic gearbox. Also available: a 250-hp 3.9L V8, based on that of the Jaguar XK8 coupe, coupled to a semi-automatic transmission. Both engines are identical, but the Lincoln produces 30 fewer horses than the Jag equivalent. There is very little difference between the 2000 and 2001 models, except that the 2001 carries standard traction control. The 2002s came back unchanged.

The LS offers a lot for a reasonable base price. The V6 version is priced in the range of the BMW 3 Series, Lexus ES 300, and Mercedes C-Class, while delivering standard equipment and interior space that rivals the 5 Series, GS, and E-Class.

Lincoln's return to rear-drive has opened up a Pandora's box of powertrain, AC, electrical system, and body glitches. Owners report jerky transmission shifting, excessive drivetrain and body noise and vibrations, inconsistent braking response, and erratic AC performance.

Safety Summary

All models/years: Sudden, unintended acceleration; gas pedal sticks. • Loss of braking. • Inadvertent deployment of airbags, or airbags don't deploy when they should. • Gas and brake pedal are mounted too close together. • Sudden loss of electrical power. • Severe pull and vibration when braking. • Brake failures caused by premature wear of rear drums and rotor warpage. • Steering control degrades or locks up when car passes through puddles. • Annoying reflections onto the front windshield. • Horn is hard to activate. • Mirrors vibrate excessively and don't adjust easily. *Continental*: **1998**—Cracked high-pressure plastic line on top of engine caused fuel to spew out and catch fire. • Several complaints that engine coolant leaks and bubbles up onto the engine compartment, risking a fire. •

Premature engine timing chain failure. • Cruise control speeds up when vehicle goes downhill. • Frequent stalling and no-starts likely caused by a sensor failure. • Sudden steering failure. • Right front wheel assembly came off as vehicle came to a stop. • Power-steering pump fails periodically. • Front suspension failed as vehicle came to a stop. • Interior lights fail, smoke. • Many complaints that the interior ventilation system leaks exhaust fumes. **1999**—Brake line ruptured. • Headlights fail to adequately light side of the road. • Visual image speedometer can't be seen by colour-blind drivers. **2000**—Warning lights come on constantly and car's central computer module often malfunctions. • Brakes don't work well; require extended stopping distance. • Side-view mirror can't be adjusted properly because of a design defect. **2001**—Car suddenly accelerated while in Reverse; brake/transmission interlock not connected. • Driver's foot can be snared by two console cables when going from the gas pedal to the brakes. • Instrument panel washes out in bright sunlight. **2002**—Sudden forward acceleration when shifter placed into Reverse. • While in Park with the brakes applied, vehicle rolled back into another car. • Sticking, binding shoulder belt. *LS*: **2000–01**—Lurching, hesitating automatic transmission shifting. • Brakes fail during the first five minutes after a cold start. • Brake pedal becomes hard and resists application or turns mushy and goes to the floor. • Warning lights come on for no reason. • Defective steering causes violent swerving from side to side. • Automatic door locks engage by themselves, locking out driver. **2002**—Sudden shutdown while on the highway. *Town Car*: **1998**—Traction control engages at the wrong time, making driver lose control of the vehicle. • Fuel may spit out of filler pipe when refuelling. • Easy to get foot stuck on accelerator pedal because of placement of partition. • Fuse panel location interferes with applying the brake pedal. • Rear-view mirror creates a large blind spot. • Passenger-side door won't open close to a curb because of the car's low stance. **1999**—Loss of all electrical power while cruising on the highway. • Chronic stalling. • Head restraints won't lock into position. **2000**—Vehicle suddenly accelerates when cruise control is engaged and brakes are applied. The following NHTSA report is rather typical of other similar complaints:

> Driver was going 75 mph [120 km/h] with cruise control set. When approaching a curve, driver applied the brakes to slow down, and as brake pedal was pressed, vehicle [sped] up. Driver was coached from limousine service on a two-way radio how to control vehicle. Driver turned off cruise control switch and vehicle returned to normal.

• Inadvertent airbag deployment. • Frequent brake failures (brake pedal will fade and not hold). • Horn is hard to activate. • Vehicle pulls hard to one side when braking. • Faulty trunk light bulb ignited clothing in trunk. • Power windows fail intermittently. **2001**—Sudden acceleration when brakes are applied. • Inadvertent airbag deployment:

> Passenger side airbag deployed at 70 mph [110 km/h] with no impact to vehicle. Lost control of vehicle temporarily and crossed traffic to other side of road. Regained control after crossing back to original lane shoulder and braking hard. Very frightening experi-

ence considering the noise, surprise, and dust from the airbag deploying. Only good thing was that no traffic was coming in other lane.

• NHTSA is looking into side-impact airbags deploying for no reason. Seventy-six complaints and nine injuries reported. • Frequent brake failures. • Wheel lug studs break off at the hub. • Ignition locks up when key is inserted. • Broken driver's seat. • Headlights can't be aimed properly. • Brake and accelerator pedal set too close together. Dash reflects onto windshield. 2002—Repeated brake master cylinder failures. • Brake pedal not responsive until pressure is reapplied. • Head restraints set too low. • While driving, sunroof blew off. 2003—Sudden, unintended acceleration. • Complete brake failure. • Brake light causes an annoying reflection onto the rear windshield. • Hood latch snapped while driving. 2004—No airbag deployment. • Sudden, unintended acceleration; many reports that the vehicle accelerated when brakes were tapped. • Poor braking. • Sunshine reflects on dashboard metal strip creating an annoying glare.

Secret Warranties/Internal Bulletins/Service Tips

All models: 1985–2002—Repeated heater core leaks. **1993–99**—Paint delamination, peeling, or fading (see Part Two "Paint and Body Defects," pages 71–75). *Continental*: **1984–94**—A hum from the air suspension system can be corrected by replacing the compressor isolators with upgraded parts. **1994–99**—Tips on plugging door, window, and moon roof wind noise. **1995–98**—No Fourth gear may mean you have a defective forward clutch control valve retaining clip. • Condensation buildup on the inside of windows may be stopped by installing an upgraded pressure cycling switch. • An intermittent shifting into Neutral or loss of forward or Reverse gear is likely caused by a defective forward clutch piston (a problem that has haunted Ford and Lincoln for over 12 years). • Front brake groaning, moaning, or squealing can be silenced by installing upgraded brake pads under the bumper-to-bumper warranty. **1995–99**—Troubleshooting tips for silencing a creak or pop while turning or braking and wind noise coming from the side doors. **1996–98**—No-starts may be because of fuel pump wire chafing. **1997–98**—Lack of AC temperature control. **1998**—Inaccurate fuel gauge readings. **1998–99**—Steering wheel vibration/moaning can be fixed by installing a longer power steering hose. **1999**—No Reverse engagement with the automatic transmission may be caused by torn Reverse clutch lip seals. Ford will cover the repair under a special "goodwill" policy (see Part Two). **1998–2002**—Hard to turn ignition switch. **1999–2002**—Engine hesitation, surging, and bucking can be fixed under warranty by reprogramming the PCM.

ENGINE CONTROLS – ENGINE HESITATION/SURGING/BUCKING

BULLETIN NO: 02-13-5   DATE: JULY 08, 2002

SUBJECT: Driveability – Hesitation, bucking or surge felt during steady speeds between 40–60 mph (64–96 km/h)

1999–2002 Lincoln Continental

ISSUE: Some vehicles may exhibit a hesitation, buck or surge during a steady state operation at 40–60 mph (64–96 km/h). This may be caused by the Powertrain Control Module (PCM) calibration.

LS: **2000–01**—Frequent bulletin references to automatic transmission defects producing delayed engagement (PCM module seen as likely culprit), driveline vibration and buzz/clunk/drone, and fluid leakage. • Trunk may suddenly open. • Inaccurate ambient temperature display. • Inoperative AC dual zone heater. • ABS, airbag, and Service Engine lights come on for no apparent reason. • Noisy front power windows. • Steering wheel "nibble," hum, or boom noise. • 3.9L oil leak from the bell housing area. • Poor braking on V6-equipped models. • V6 engine noise on acceleration and highway drone noise. • Hard starts or no-starts. • Instrument panel squeaks and rattles. **2000–02**—Inoperative power windows. • Oil pan drain plug leaks. • Correction for a noisy suspension. **2000–03**—Inoperative defroster. **2000–05**—Troubleshooting engine misfires. • Inoperative defroster. **2001–02**—A faulty cooling fan is the likely cause of engine overheating. **2003**—Harsh shifting. **2003–04**—Moisture in the Reverse tail light. • Steering gear noise, vibration. **2004**—Harsh upshifts. Mark VII, Mark VIII: **1985–99**—An exhaust buzz or rattle may be caused by a loose heat shield catalyst. **1986–94**—The in-tank fuel pump is the likely cause of radio static. Install an electronic noise RFI filter (#F1PZ-18B925-A). **1993–94**—A squeak or chirp coming from the blower motor can be stopped by installing an upgraded blower motor. • Automatic transmissions with delayed or no forward engagement, or a higher engine rpm than expected when coming to a stop, are covered in TSB #94-26-9. *Town Car:* **2001**—Rear-end impact may puncture fuel tank; two TSB repairs already carried out. **2001–04**—Engine ticking. **2003**—Premature wear of the axle shaft or axle bearing. • Erratic AC blower motor operation. • Blower motor whistling. • Inaccurate fuel gauge. • Power steering assist calibration; excessive power steering pump noise. • Front wheel area click or rattle. • Anti-theft system may cause the transmission to stick in Park or a locked steering wheel. • Rear parking brake clicking. • Poor AM radio reception. **2003–04**—Cold start engine knocking. • Suspension squeaking and rubbing. • Erratic operation of the AC blower. **2004**—Exhaust manifold to converter leak.

CONTINENTAL PROFILE

	1995	1996	1997	1998	1999	2000	2001	2002
Cost Price ($)								
Continental Ex.	50,995	51,896	49,995	51,995	52,795	52,895	51,920	52,900
Used Values ($)								
Continental Ex. ▲	4,500	5,500	6,500	8,000	10,500	15,000	20,000	23,000
Continental Ex. ▼	4,000	5,000	6,000	6,500	8,500	12,500	18,500	21,000
Reliability	❷	❷	❷	❷	❷	❷	❷	❸
Offset	❸	❸	❸	❸	❸	❸	❸	❸
Head Restraints	❶	—	❶	—	❶	—	❷	❷

LS PROFILE

	2000	2001	2002	2003	2004
Cost Price ($)					
LS	40,595	40,870	42,300	42,500	43,750
Used Values ($)					
LS ▲	13,500	17,000	22,500	28,000	32,000
LS ▼	12,000	15,500	21,000	26,500	30,500
Reliability	3	3	3	4	4
Crash Safety (F)	5	5	5	—	5
Side	—	4	4	4	4
Offset	5	5	5	5	5
Head Restraints	1	2	2	3	3
Rollover Resistance	—	5	5	5	5

MARK VII, MARK VIII PROFILE

	1991	1992	1993	1994	1995	1996	1997	1998
Cost Price ($)								
Mark VII, VIII	38,895	41,010	43,968	47,995	50,996	51,895	53,695	56,595
Used Values ($)								
Mark VII, VIII ▲	2,500	3,000	3,500	4,000	5,000	6,000	7,500	9,500
Mark VII, VIII ▼	2,000	2,500	3,000	3,500	4,500	5,500	6,500	8,000
Reliability	2	2	2	2	2	3	3	3
Head Restraints	—	—	—	—	1	—	1	—

Note: The Mark series hasn't been crash-tested by NHTSA.

TOWN CAR PROFILE

	1996	1997	1998	1999	2000	2001	2002	2003	2004
Cost Price ($)									
Town Car	44,895	45,895	50,195	52,195	51,495	53,970	53,445	55,205	57,645
Used Values ($)									
Town Car ▲	6,000	7,500	9,500	11,500	15,500	21,500	26,000	33,000	39,000
Town Car ▼	5,000	6,000	8,000	10,000	14,000	19,500	24,000	31,000	37,000
Reliability	4	4	4	4	4	4	4	5	5
Crash Safety (F)	4	4	—	—	4	5	5	5	5
Side	—	—	—	4	4	4	4	5	5
Head Restraints	—	1	—	1	—	1	1	2	2
Rollover Resistance	—	—	—	—	—	—	—	5	5

All ratings on a numbered scale where 5 is good and 1 is bad. See pages 100–101 for a more detailed description.

General Motors

RATING: Average (1998–2004); Below Average (1991–97); Not Recommended (1985–90). **Maintenance/Repair costs:** Higher than average, but repairs aren't dealer dependent. **Parts:** Higher-than-average cost (independent suppliers sell for much less), but not hard to find. Nevertheless, don't even think about buying one of these front-drives without a 3- to 5-year extended warranty backed by the automaker. **Extended warranty:** A must-have. **Best alternatives:** Acura Integra and RL; Cadillac DeVille; Infiniti I30 and I35; Nissan Maxima; and Toyota Avalon. **Online help:** *www.autosafety.org/autodefects.html*.

 ## Strengths and Weaknesses

Full-sized luxury sedan aficionados love the flush glass, wrap-around windshield and bumpers, and clean body lines that make for an aerodynamic, pleasing appearance. But these front-drive cars are more than a pretty package; they provide lots of room (but not for six), luxury, style, and—dare I say—performance. On one hand, plenty of power is available with the 205-hp 3.8L V6 engine and the 240-hp supercharged version of the same power plant. On the other hand, owners decry the cars' ponderous handling, caused partly by a mediocre suspension and over-assisted steering with the base model; obstructed rear visibility; hard braking accompanied by severe nosedive; and interior gauges and controls that aren't easily deciphered or accessed.

Although the 1991–96 Park Avenue and '98 Regency were improved over the years, they compiled one of the worst repair histories among large cars. Main problem areas are the engine, automatic transmission, fuel system, steering, brakes, electrical system (including defective PROM and MEMCAL modules), starter and alternator, and badly assembled, poor-quality body hardware. The 3.0L V6 engine is inadequate for cars this heavy, and the 3.8L has been a big quality disappointment.

Under-hood servicing is complicated. Other problems: Automatic transmission and engine computer malfunctions are common, the fuel-injection system is temperamental, window mechanisms are poorly designed, the power-steering assembly is failure-prone, there are frequent electrical failures, front brake pads and rotors require frequent replacement, and shock absorbers leak or go soft very quickly. Extensive surface corrosion has been a problem because of poor and often incomplete paint application at the factory.

VEHICLE HISTORY: *Park Avenue:* **1991**—A horsepower boost tied to a revised 4-speed automatic transmission, an updated chassis, anti-lock braking, a driver-side airbag, and height-adjustable seat belts. **1992**—Debut of the supercharged Ultra. **1993**—A slightly more powerful base engine. **1994**—Dual airbags were added and the Ultra's supercharged engine gained 20 hp. **1995**—Base engines boosted to 205 hp; fresh interior and exterior styling. **1996**—All models get variable-assist steering and the Ultra gains 20 more horses. **1997**—Park Avenue and Ultra were redesigned to include a reworked powertrain, a stiffer body, improved interior amenities, upgraded four-wheel disc brakes, and an upgraded ventilation system. **1998**—De-powered airbags. **1999**—A tire-monitor gauge for the Ultra. **2000**—StabiliTrak stability control was added. **2002**—Steering wheel controls for the climate and sound system. **2003**—Ultra gets side VentriPorts, a new grill, and chrome exhaust tips.

Plenty of power is available with the 205-hp 3.8L V6 engine and the Aurora's 240-hp supercharged power plant. It does 0–100 km/h in under nine seconds (impressive, considering the heft of these vehicles), and improves low- and mid-range throttle response. Both the Park Avenue and Ultra use a stretched version of the more rigid Riviera and Aurora platform. The revised 1998–2004 models continue to have serious engine intake manifold and transmission problems in addition to airbag, AC, fuel, and electrical system failures. Poor fit and finish is characterized by leaks, squeaks, rattles, moans, and whines.

 **Safety Summary**

All models: 1998—Chronic stalling and loss of electrical power, particularly when braking. • Vehicle also suddenly accelerates when braking. • With cruise control engaged, vehicle picks up speed when going downhill. • Faulty fuel sending unit; fuel gauge failure. • Cracked engine head gasket. • Transmission failures. • Brakes or steering fail in rainy weather. • ABS failure may be caused by defective computer module. • Steering failure caused by broken serpentine belt. • Premature failure of brake rotors, pads, and calipers. • Goodyear tire tread separation. • Faulty air level ride filled up rear shocks so that rear end stuck up high in the air. • Seat belts jam in the retractor; fail to extend or retract. • Door locks don't work properly. • Windshield dash glare. **1999**—Sudden acceleration after vehicle jumped from Park into Drive. • Frequent stalling; Check Engine light comes on. • Loss of steering because of premature steering pump failure. • Brake rotor overheating and warpage creates excessive vibration and pulling to one side when brakes are applied. • Transmission jerks when going from Reverse to Drive. • Airbag light comes on for no reason. • Shoulder belt twists in retractor. • Premature failure of Goodyear tires. • Keys won't lock or unlock the doors. • Battery often goes dead. **2000**—Airbags deploy when they shouldn't and fail to deploy when they should. • Steering may suddenly lock up. • Excessive steering wheel vibrations numb hands. • Horn is hard to activate, especially in cold weather. • Front seat lapbelts may be too short; GM will give owners a free extension if they sign a waiver of liability. •

Windshield wipers suddenly quit working. **2001**—Sudden, unintended accelera-tion. • Delayed and extended shifts, slippage in cold weather; early replacement. • Intermittent windshield wiper shut-off. • Trunk lid fell on driver's head. • Excessive dash reflection onto windshield. • Hard to find horn button in an emergency. • Windshield wiper malfunctions. • Driver's seat belt locks up. **2002**—Intermittent horn failure in cold weather. **2003**—Multiple brake failures. • Chemical used to combat AC mold may cause an allergic reaction.

Secret Warranties/Internal Bulletins/Service Tips

All models/years: Automatic transaxles on front-drive models equipped with V6 engines are particularly failure-prone. • Reverse servo cover leak. **All models: 1993–2002**—AC odours can be reduced by applying a cooling-coil coating or by installing a special kit. • A rotten-egg odour coming from the exhaust is probably caused by a malfunctioning catalytic converter and may be covered under GM's emissions warranty. • Paint delamination, peeling, or fading (see Part Two "Paint and Body Defects," pages 71–75). **1995–2001**—Engine oil pan leaks. **1997–99**—Excessive brake noise can be reduced by installing upgraded pads and rotors. **1997–2001**—Troubleshooting steering vibration, shudder, or moan. **1998**—A fuel gauge that gives inaccurate readings probably needs a new fuel level sensor. • Rattling from the rear may mean the fuel tank strap is loose or defective. **1998–99**—Low power, stalling, or stumbling when accelerating can be cured by re-calibrating the PCM. **1998–2000**—A hard-to-shift gear-shift lever may need a new cable assembly. **1999–2000**—An engine that runs hot, overheats, or loses coolant may simply need a new radiator cap. • Transmission whine in Park or Neutral may be silenced with a new drive sprocket support bearing. • Slips, harsh upshift or garage shifts, and launch shudders have a variety of causes and correc-tions, says TSB #00-07-30-002. • Diagnostic procedures for an engine that runs hot, overheats, or loses coolant are outlined in TSB #00-06-02-001. **1999–2001**—Tips on correcting excessive engine vibration and silencing generator whine, hum, and moan. **2000–01**—Inoperative power sunroof. **2000–03**—GM admits it has a "goodwill" warranty covering engine intake manifold failures (see Impala, Monte Carlo rating on page 231):

> I recently received a letter from GM stating that there may be a problem with coolant leaks around gaskets at the upper intake manifold or at the lower intake manifold which might "cause high engine temperatures." The letter says it is a "voluntary customer satisfaction program." The suggested fix is to take the vehicle in to the local dealer and have them change some of the fasteners and then "add cooling system sealant" to the radiator. It seems to me that putting cooling system sealant in a brand new car (and thus reducing the life of the radiator) is an unacceptable fix for a possible gasket problem.

2001—Delayed and extended shifts, slippage in cold weather. **2001–02**—Poor engine performance and erratic shifting (TSB #02-07-30-013). **2001–04**—Transmission slippage and harsh 1–2 shifts. **2002–03**—Door lock falls into door panel. **2003**—Erratic automatic transmission shifting. • Transmission grind/growl when vehicle is parked on an incline. • Defective front outer tie-rod ends.

98 REGENCY, PARK AVENUE PROFILE

	1996	1997	1998	1999	2000	2001	2002	2003	2004
Cost Price ($)									
Park Avenue	38,150	40,865	41,850	41,060	42,075	43,000	43,700	45,790	47,550
98 Regency	36,610	—	—	—	—	—	—	—	—
Used Values ($)									
Park Avenue ▲	5,000	6,000	7,500	10,000	13,500	16,000	21,500	27,500	31,000
Park Avenue ▼	4,000	5,000	6,000	8,500	12,000	14,000	19,500	25,500	29,000
98 Regency ▲	5,500	—	—	—	—	—	—	—	—
98 Regency ▼	4,500	—	—	—	—	—	—	—	—
Reliability	②	②	③	③	③	④	④	④	④
Crash Safety (F)	—	—	—	—	—	④	④	④	④
Side	—	—	—	—	—	④	④	④	④
Offset	—	⑤	⑤	⑤	⑤	⑤	⑤	⑤	⑤
Head Restraints									
Park Avenue	—	❶	—	❶	—	❶	❶	❶	❶
Rollover Resistance	—	—	—	—	—	—	—	④	④

AURORA, RIVIERA ★★★★

RATING: *Aurora:* Above Average (2001–03); Average (1995–99). There was no year 2000 model. Now that GM is phasing out its Oldsmobile division, Aurora resale values are falling rapidly, making the second-series, revamped 2001 and 2002 excellent used buys. *Riviera:* Average (1995–99); Not Recommended (1986–93). GM skipped the 1994 model year and introduced an all-new 1995 version. **Maintenance/Repair costs:** Higher than average, but repairs aren't dealer dependent. **Parts:** Higher-than-average cost (independent suppliers sell for much less), but not hard to find. GM's phase-out won't affect availability or costs, since these vehicles use the same generic parts found on many other GM products. **Extended warranty:** Yes; powertrain repairs alone can cost double what you will pay for an extra warranty. **Best alternatives:** Acura Integra, TL, or RL; Cadillac DeVille, Fleetwood, and Brougham; Ford Crown Victoria or Mercury Grand Marquis; Mercedes E-Class; Nissan Maxima; and Toyota Avalon. **Online help:** *www.auto-safety.org/autodefects.html.*

All ratings on a numbered scale where ⑤ is good and ❶ is bad. See pages 100–101 for a more detailed description.

Strengths and Weaknesses

Although the redesigned 1988–93 cars got performance, handling, and ride upgrades, they kept the same low level of quality control, with multiple design and manufacturing defects, including serious fuel injection, engine computer, and electrical system problems that haven't been solved to this day. One particularly poor design was the complex Graphic Control Center, which used an oversensitive video screen and small push buttons. It's both distracting and expensive to repair. The automatic transmission is notoriously failure-prone, and brakes wear out prematurely and perform poorly. Surface rust and poor paint quality are the most common body complaints on all years. Shock absorbers wear out quickly, and the diesel engine seldom runs properly.

VEHICLE HISTORY: 1995—Riviera was totally redesigned with standard dual airbags, ABS, a 3.8L V6, and a supercharged variant. **1997**—Additional standard features and a smoother-shifting automatic transmission. **1998**—A supercharged engine arrives. **1999**—Traction control.

Overall, 1995–99 models offer many more luxury features but continue the checkered repair history. As with many of its front-drives during the latter half of the '90s, GM improved quality somewhat, but there are still many generic deficiencies affecting the automatic transmission (torque converter constantly engages and disengages), engine, fuel and electrical systems, computer modules, AC compressor, brakes (rotor warpage and premature pad replacement), steering, suspension, and fit and finish. Trunk wheelwell leaks are common. Because of their problematic brakes, these cars usually have a pronounced low-speed shudder/vibration and severe pull that intensifies when passing over uneven terrain or when braking.

Aurora

This front-drive Olds luxury sedan is aimed at the Acura, Infiniti, and Lexus crowd. It uses the same basic design as the Riviera but doesn't share the same major mechanical features or popular styling. Because it's a relatively new entry into the Oldsmobile line, GM took more care in the selection of mechanical, electronic, and body components. This has made the Aurora more reliable and glitch-free than GM's other vehicles, which continue to be hobbled with poor-quality components and subpar fit and finish. Too bad that this progress is for naught, as Aurora folded along with the entire Oldsmobile line.

VEHICLE HISTORY: 1997—Larger front brakes. **1999**—Additional engine mounts to damper vibration. **2001**—A new platform and now equipped with a 3.5 V6 or 4.0L V8 engine. **2001**—The mid-year addition of an automatic load levelling suspension. **2002**—GM phase-out of the V6 in favour of a V8. **2003**—Last model year sees all models powered by a V8.

The Aurora's main advantages are its sporty handling and unusual aero styling. In contrast to the Riviera, the Aurora seats only five and offers a 4.0L V8 derived from the Cadillac 4.6L V8 Northstar engine. Acceleration is underwhelming (this is a heavy car) but adequate for highway touring. Road and wind noise are omnipresent, and the rear trunk's small opening compromises the large trunk's ability to handle odd-sized objects.

The 1995–2000 Auroras have similar quality failings to those of the Riviera, but they're not as extensive and they generally become less common with the 2001 through 2003 models. Nevertheless, owners of these recent models complain of engine coolant leaks, chronic electrical and fuel supply glitches, harsh shifting, drivetrain vibration, brake failures and high maintenance costs, and water leaks through the front corner moulding.

Safety Summary

Aurora: **1995–2001**—Chronic stalling. • Horn is hard to access and operates erratically. • Headlights short out or come on inadvertently. **1999**—Water is sucked up into engine when car passes over puddles. • Power steering loses power at low speeds. • Lost all electrical power, including interior and exterior lights. • Exhaust fumes enter interior. **2001**—Total brake failure. • Will not go into First gear when cupholder is extended. • Electrical shorts cause complete electrical shutdown or erratically operating interior and exterior lights and gauges. • Reflection of the defrost grate is very distracting to short drivers. • Head restraints block rear vision. • Windshield wipers fail intermittently. **2001–03**—Loss of engine coolant. **2002**—Severe front-end vibration at 100 km/h; not tire related. • Headlights flicker. **2003**—Vehicle suddenly accelerated when started up and placed into Reverse. • Sudden loss of steering. • When turning, feels like tire is rubbing underbody. • High headrest obstructs rear visibility. • Interior and exterior lights go out periodically. • Rear tail lights dim intermittently. • ABS and traction control warning lights come on for no reason. • Will not go into First gear with cupholder extended. • Defrost grate reflects upon the windshield. *Riviera:* **1998**—Engine mount failure. • Brakes don't stop vehicle; frequent rotor replacement. • Horn won't blow at times.

Secret Warranties/Internal Bulletins/Service Tips

All models: 1993–99—AC odours can be reduced by applying a cooling-coil coating. • A rotten-egg odour coming from the exhaust is likely the result of a malfunctioning catalytic converter, covered by GM's emissions warranty. • Paint delamination, peeling, or fading (see Part Two "Paint and Body Defects," pages 71–75). **1995–96**—Intermittent Neutral/loss of Drive at highway speeds can be fixed by replacing the control valve body assembly. **1995–98**—A noise, growl, or vibration from the front when making a right turn or when accelerating may signal the need to replace or reposition the rear transaxle mount. **1995–99**—Floor pan corrosion perforation in the battery compartment can be corrected by installing a GM repair kit. **1997–99**—Excessive front brake noise can be reduced by installing upgraded pads and rotors. **1998**—A fuel gauge that gives inaccurate readings probably needs a new fuel level sensor. • Rattling from the rear may mean the fuel tank strap is loose or defective. **1998–99**—A clunk, rattle, or metal-to-metal noise coming from the front of the vehicle can be silenced by installing anti-slip/friction material between the engine frame and the stabilizer shaft insulator. **1999**—Curing front strut squeaks. *Aurora:* **1995–99**—A cold engine knock or ticking may be caused by excessive carbon deposits in the engine. • A steering shudder at idle or during parking may be fixed by installing an anti-shudder power-steering outlet hose assembly. **1996–99**—GM has an enhanced crankshaft rear seal to use for complaints related to leaking or poor sealing. **1997–98**—Excessive front brake noise can be reduced by installing upgraded pads and rotors. **1998**—Harsh or delayed gearshifts may require the installation of an enhanced garage shift package. • Accessory drive noise may be caused by a misaligned accessory drive pulley. • Delayed or no engine braking in D3 may require the replacement of the forward and coast latch piston assemblies. **1998–99**—Diagnostic and repair tips for a faulty cruise control and speedometer. **1999–2000**—Overheating or coolant loss may be corrected by simply replacing the radiator cap and polishing the radiator filler neck. **2000–01**—If there's a sudden loss of power when accelerating, the transmission fluid pressure switch may be defective. **2000–02**—Seatback squeaks. • Poor shifting. **2001**—Cooler fitting coolant leaks. • Delayed Reverse engagement. **2001–02**—Shake, vibration at cruising speed. • Tilt steering sticks. • Noisy steering. • Inoperative heated seat. **2003**—Intermittent no-start, no-crank condition. • Engine overheating in cold weather. • Sudden engine shutdown. • Harsh shifting remedy. • Automatic transmission grind/growl when vehicle is parked on an incline. • Poor transmission and engine performance may be caused by debris in the transaxle valve body and case oil passages, says TSB #02-07-30-013. • Incorrect First gear ratio; delayed Reverse engagement; harsh shifting upon start-up; transmission whining noise and cooling line leaks; leakage from the quick-connect fitting at the case cover; no Fourth gear, or slipping in Fourth gear; oil leakage from the oil level sensor; and intermediate shaft clunk. • Water contamination of the ABS sensor. • Excessive vibration on smooth roads. • Broken sunroof deflectors. • Faulty windshield wipers. • Horn blows on its own, or refuses to blow. • Loose, sagging attachment arms/straps in the rear compartment seatback trim panel.

AURORA PROFILE

	1995	1996	1997	1998	1999	2001	2002	2003
Cost Price ($)								
Aurora	43,020	43,695	46,045	47,250	46,190	39,590	40,030	46,590
Used Values ($)								
Aurora ▲	4,500	5,500	6,500	8,500	10,500	15,500	20,000	27,500
Aurora ▼	3,500	4,500	5,500	7,000	9,000	13,500	18,000	25,000

Reliability	③	③	③	③	③	③	③	④
Crash Safety (F)	③	③	③	③	③	④	④	④
Side	—	—	—	—	—	③	③	③
Offset	—	—	—	—	—	⑤	⑤	⑤
Head Restraints	❶	—	❶	—	❶	⑤	⑤	⑤

RIVIERA PROFILE

	1993	1995	1996	1997	1998	1999
Cost Price ($)						
Riviera	30,790	39,525	40,700	42,415	44,950	44,125
Used Values ($)						
Riviera ▲	3,500	4,000	5,000	6,500	8,500	10,500
Riviera ▼	3,000	3,500	4,500	5,500	7,000	9,000
Reliability	②	③	③	③	③	③
Head Restraints	—	❶	—	❶	—	❶

CADILLAC CATERA, ELDORADO, SEVILLE ★★

RATING: Below Average (1992–2004); Not Recommended (1986–91). 2001 was the Catera's last model year; only the Seville carries on through 2004. **Maintenance/ Repair costs:** Higher than average; Catera repairs are more expensive because they are dealer dependent. Long delays for recall repairs on all models. **Parts:** Higher-than-average cost (independent suppliers sell for much less), but most parts aren't hard to find. **Extended warranty:** Don't buy any of these cars without a 3- to 5-year supplementary warranty. **Best alternatives:** Acura Integra and RL; Cadillac DeVille, Brougham, or Fleetwood; Ford Crown Victoria or Mercury Grand Marquis; and the Mercedes E-Class. **Online help:** *www.autosafety.org/autodefects. html* and *www.supremecourt.nm.org/pastopinion/VIEW/98ca-020.html.*

Strengths and Weaknesses

Front-drive Cadillacs are unreliable, cobbled-together embarrassments. The biggest tip-off that GM was conning us with these front-drives was in 1987, when GM sold gussied-up V6-equipped Cavaliers as Cadillac Cimarrons. They flopped, and Infiniti and Lexus carved out a huge chunk of the American luxury car market that they have never given up. Even though later Cadillacs used many of the same mechanical components as the Riviera and Toronado, they continued to be no match for the Asian competition because of their poor quality and complexity.

All ratings on a numbered scale where ⑤ is good and ❶ is bad. See pages 100–101 for a more detailed description.

Catera

Assembled in Germany and based on the Opel Omega, the rear-drive, mid-sized Catera comes with a 200-hp V6 engine, 4-speed automatic transmission, 16-inch alloy wheels, four-wheel disc brakes, a limited-slip differential, traction control, and standard dual front airbags. The conservatively styled Catera (the uninspired styling has Lumina written all over it) was designed to compete with the BMW 328i, Lexus ES 300, and Mercedes-Benz C280. It was also a flop.

VEHICLE HISTORY: 1998—De-powered airbags. **1999**—More complex electronics and emissions systems to meet federal standards. **2000**—Slight styling changes, side airbags, improved throttle control, and a retuned suspension.

Cateras have a quiet, spacious, and comfortable interior, responsive handling, fine-tuned suspension, and almost non-existent lean or body roll when cornering. On the downside, the steering system lacks balance and allows the vehicle to wander; the controls aren't easy to figure out, some gauges are hard to read, and the driver's rear view is hindered by the large rear head restraints and narrow back windshield. Furthermore, owners report chronic stalling and hard starts, possibly because of a malfunctioning idle control valve; the transmission hunts for the right gear; dash warning lights are constantly lit. Body fit and finish is subpar: Panels are often misaligned, squeaks and rattles are omnipresent, and wind and water leaks are commonplace. Two other performance problems reported by many owners: When you pass over a large expansion joint, the floor pan vibrates annoyingly, and if you drive over a bump when turning, the steering wheel kicks back in your hands.

A few other points you may wish to consider: GM dealers are notoriously bad when it comes to understanding and repairing European-transplanted cars (just ask any Saab owner). As well, low-volume cars generally don't have an adequate supply of replacement parts in the pipeline until they've been on the market for a while. Add in the Catera's European connection and the fact it has just been dropped by GM, and you'd best be ready to endure lots of mechanic head-scratching, long service waits, and high parts costs for those repairs not covered under warranty.

It's a safe bet that these cars will be less reliable and more troublesome than the competition. GM first learned that lesson with the British-built, failure-prone Vauxhall Firenza it unleashed on an unsuspecting Canadian public in the '70s. A few years later, it settled out of court on several class actions that I piloted, and paid a $20,000 fine to the federal government for misleading advertising. (On a nationally advertised road trip across Canada, GM said the cars excelled. Truth is, they were a disaster. They required a team of engineers just to get started.)

Eldorado and Seville

Sitting on the same platform as the front-drive Eldorado, the Seville has European-style allure with a more rounded body than the Eldorado. Apart from that, since its redesign in 1992, its engine, handling, and braking upgrades have followed the Eldorado's improvements in lockstep fashion.

Although the base 4.9L V8 provides brisk acceleration, the 32-valve Northstar V8, first found on the 1993 Touring Coupe, gives you almost 100 more horses, with great handling and a comfortable ride. Overall, the Touring Coupe or Sport Coupe will give you the best powertrain, handling, and braking features. Of course, you'll have to contend with poor fuel economy, rear visibility that's obstructed by the huge side pillars (a Seville problem as well), confusing and inconvenient climate controls, and a particularly complex engine that's failure-prone and a nightmare to troubleshoot.

VEHICLE HISTORY: 1998–2001—The only real change was the Eldorado's Northstar engine tweaking for year 2000 models. *Seville*: **2002**—An upgraded suspension. **2004**—300-hp engine is dropped; Seville replaced by the STS.

These cars have generic deficiencies that fall into common categories: poorly calibrated and failure-prone engines, transmissions, and fuel and ignition systems; a multiplicity of electrical short circuits; and sloppy body assembly using poor-quality components. Specifically, engines and fuel systems often produce intermittent stalling, rough idling, hesitation, and no-starts; the Overdrive automatic is prone to premature failure; oil pumps fail frequently; front brakes and shock absorbers wear out quickly; paint is often poorly applied, fades, or peels away prematurely; fragile body hardware breaks easily (front bumper cracks are commonplace); and there are large gaps between sheet-metal panels and doors that are poorly hung and not entirely square. Other body problems include cracking of front outside door handles, door rattles (Eldorado), poor bumper fit, loose sun visor mounting, rear tail light condensation, fading and discolouring appliqué mouldings (Seville), interior window fogging, creaking body mounts, water leaking into trunk from licence plate holder (Eldorado), noisy roof panels and seatback lumbar motors, and a creaking noise at the front-door upper hinge area.

 ## Safety Summary

Catera: **1997–2001**—Chronic stalling. • Frequent wheel alignments. • Defective brake rotors cause excessive vibration and pull. • Premature tire wear. • Vehicle wanders and pulls to one side. • Door locks don't work and key sticks in the ignition. • Windshield wipers are inadequate in heavy rain. **1998**—Engine head gasket failures. **1999**—Accelerator can be floored and vehicle will only creep forward. • Head restraints block vision. • Loss of steering. • Excessive vehicle wandering. •

Door latch sticks in the closed position. **2000**—Chronic stalling. • Hesitant shifting. • Defective ignition switch. **2001**—Airbags failed to deploy. • Gas pedal sticks. • Sudden stalling. • Fuel line is exposed to road debris. • Windshield orange peel pattern. • Tires may wear out quickly because the wheels pitch in slightly. *Eldorado, Seville*: **1986–2001**—A plethora of electrical short circuits, front axle, ABS brake, and steering failures. • Sudden, unintended acceleration. • Airbag malfunctions (deploying for no reason and injuring occupants). • Brake rotors and pads always need changing. • Excessive vibration at all speeds. • Poor headlight illumination. *Eldorado*: **2002**—No airbag deployment. • Front tires wore out prematurely. *Seville*: **1999**—Front control arm snapped. • Tie-rod end came apart. • Loss of power steering when driving in the rain. • Front and rear lights collect water. **2000**—Seat belt retractors don't work properly. • Excessive drifting at any speed. • Brake caliper locked up. **2001**—While driving, passenger-side wheel collapsed because of a missing suspension bolt. • Steering column rubbing noise is heard when making a right turn. **2002**—Chronic stalling in traffic. • Many reports of excessive vibration (suspension, driveshaft, wheels, and tires replaced). • Noisy, erratic transmission shifting. **2003**—Display panel can be hard to see. **2004**—Headlights cause too much glare.

Secret Warranties/Internal Bulletins/Service Tips

All models: Reverse servo cover leak. **1993–99**—A cold engine knock or ticking may be caused by excessive carbon deposits in the engine. • AC odours can be reduced by applying a cooling-coil coating. • Defective catalytic converters that cause a rotten-egg smell in the interior may be replaced free of charge under the emissions warranty. • Paint delamination, peeling, or fading (see Part Two "Paint and Body Defects," pages 71–75). **1996–2003**—Excessive oil consumption may be caused by dirty piston rings, says GM TSB #02-06-01-009B. **1997–98**—Brake noise on these models can be reduced by installing upgraded pads and rotors. **1998**—Harsh or delayed gearshifts may require the installation of an enhanced garage shift package. • Accessory drive noise may be caused by a misaligned accessory drive pulley. • Delayed or no engine braking in D3 may require the replacement of the forward and coast latch piston assemblies. **1998–99**—Diagnostic and repair tips for a faulty cruise control and speedometer. • Front-end clunks and rattles can be silenced by judicious use of anti-friction materials. **1998–2003**—Water, musty smell in rear compartment. • Inoperative seat heater. **1999–2000**—An engine that runs hot, overheats, or loses coolant may simply need a new radiator cap. • Steering column clunk. **1999–2004**—Repair tips for a slipping automatic transmission. **2000–01**—If there's a sudden loss of power when accelerating, the transmission fluid pressure switch may be defective. **2000–02**—Power steering noise. • No power when accelerating; 1–2 shift concerns. **2001**—Intermittent inoperative instrument panel (requires replacement of the I/P cluster assembly). • Cooler fitting coolant leaks. • Delayed Reverse engagement. **2001–03**—Loss of engine coolant. • Steering clunk remedy is to replace the intermediate shaft. **2001–05**—Harsh upshifts. **2003**—Erratic transmission performance. *Catera*: **1997**—Oil leakage from the engine timing cover can be corrected by installing a new oil pump gasket. **1997–2001**—Coolant loss; engine overheating. • Rear compartment noise. • Steering column squeak. • Key can't be removed from the ignition lock cylinder. *Eldorado, Seville*: **1996–2003**—Excessive oil consumption can be corrected with new piston rings, if a new ring-cleaning process doesn't work (TSB #02-06-01-009C).

CADILLAC CATERA, ELDORADO, SEVILLE PROFILE

	1996	1997	1998	1999	2000	2001	2002	2003	2004
Cost Price ($)									
Catera	—	42,690	43,250	42,310	42,635	42,485	—	—	—
Eldorado	50,745	52,015	53,000	52,660	53,455	56,600	57,450	—	—
Seville	55,635	57,000	59,900	59,195	60,195	58,710	59,450	62,045	63,400
Used Values ($)									
Catera ▲	—	6,000	8,500	10,500	13,500	16,000	—	—	—
Catera ▼	—	4,500	7,000	9,500	12,000	14,000	—	—	—
Eldorado ▲	5,500	7,500	10,500	13,000	15,000	21,500	29,000	—	—
Eldorado ▼	5,000	6,000	9,000	11,000	13,000	20,000	31,000	—	—
Seville ▲	8,000	9,500	11,500	15,500	18,000	23,000	31,000	40,000	45,000
Seville ▼	7,000	8,000	10,000	13,500	16,000	21,000	28,000	37,000	43,000
Reliability	2	2	2	3	3	3	3	3	3
Offset									
Catera	—	5	5	5	5	5	—	—	—
Seville		1	1	—	—	5	5	5	5
Head Restraints									
Catera		—	3	—	2	—	3	—	—
Eldorado		—	1	—	1	—	1	1	—	—
Seville		—	1	—	1	1	1	1	1

Note: Reliability figures apply to the Eldorado and Seville only; Catera reliability information is given in the text. No crash test data is available.

CADILLAC CONCOURS, DEVILLE ★★★

RATING: Average (2002-04); Below Average (1985–2001); Interestingly, a new Concours is sold at a premium over the DeVille, but the difference narrows considerably as the vehicles age. There are two major safety problems affecting 1995–99 models: inadvertent side and front airbag deployment, and chronic stalling in traffic. **Maintenance/Repair costs:** Higher than average, and most repairs must be done by a dealer. Long delay for recall repairs. **Parts:** Higher-than-average cost, but not hard to find. All of these front-drives require a 3- to 5-year supplementary warranty. **Extended warranty:** A good idea for the front drives,

All ratings on a numbered scale where 5 is good and 1 is bad. See pages 100–101 for a more detailed description.

because these Cadillac parts are so darned expensive and there are not a lot of independent suppliers. **Best alternatives:** Acura Integra and RL; Infiniti I30 or I35; and Toyota's Avalon. **Online help:** *www.autosafety.org/autodefects.htm*l.

 ## Strengths and Weaknesses

Although they have better handling and are almost as comfortable as older, traditional Caddies, these front-drive luxury coupes and sedans aren't worth considering because of their dismal reliability and overly complex servicing. Redesigned 1995–99 versions have posted fewer complaints; however, they are still far below the industry norm for quality and reliability. As with the Eldorado and Seville, you get the best array of handling, braking, and performance features with the post-1996 versions, but reliability remains a problem and Cadillac fuel economy is an oxymoron. Also, the dash controls and gauges are confusing and not easily accessible, and the rear view is obstructed by the high trunk lid and large side pillars.

VEHICLE HISTORY: 1996—DeVilles were given the Northstar V8 and an upgraded automatic transmission and suspension. The Concours received 25 additional horses along with improved steering and suspension. **1997**—Substantially reworked and given new styling, side airbags, and an upgraded interior. **1998**—De-powered airbags. **2000**—A number of high-tech improvements, including refinements to the V8 engine, Night Vision, Rear Parking Assist, and StabiliTrak traction control. **2002**—An enhanced suspension.

The 4.3L V6, 4.1L V8, and 4.5L V8 engines and 4-speed automatic transmission suffer from a variety of terminal maladies, including oil leaks, premature wear, poor fuel economy, and excessive noise. The electrical system and related components are temperamental. Steering is noisy, the suspension goes soft quickly, and the front brakes often wear out after only 18 months/20,000 km. Problems with the digital fuel injection and engine control systems are very difficult to diagnose and repair. Poor body assembly is characterized by premature paint peeling and rusting, excessive wind noise in the interior, and fragile trim items.

 ## Safety Summary

DeVille: **1998**—Inadvertent side airbag deployment. • Wheel flew off car after wheel studs failed. • Vehicle suddenly accelerated, killing one person and injuring others. • Accelerator sticking. • Cruise control self-activates. • Chronic stalling while underway. • Can't read speedometer in daylight. • Many complaints of front and rear brake rotor warpage and premature pad and caliper failure. • Sudden loss of power steering. • Vehicle tends to wander all over the road. • Leaking engine oil coolant. • Windshield washer fluid doesn't pump high enough. • Gas tank sensor failure causes inaccurate fuel readings. • Interior lights frequently malfunction. **1999**—Airbags explode when vehicle is started, idles, accelerates, or is parked. Several occupants have been injured. • Incidents where front and side airbags failed to deploy in a collision. • Engine overheating, loose head bolts, and excessive oil consumption. • Stalling when coasting or coming to a stop. • Vehicle rolls backward when in gear. • Fuel tank leaks fuel. • Premature warpage of the front and rear brake rotors. • Failure-prone ignition and electronic control module. • Tire flew off while vehicle was underway. • Factory-equipped jack inadequate to support vehicle. • Instrument panel lighting hard to read in daylight. • Power door locks operate erratically. • Windshield wipers won't come on unless turned on High. • Driver's seat belt constantly tightens up. **2000**—Sudden, unintended acceleration and chronic stalling. • Steering locked up. • Automatic transmission jolts when shifting. • Airbags deploy inadvertently. • A shroud may impede accessing brake pedal. • Frequent crankshaft sensor failure. • Digital instrument panel can't be read in daylight. • Sun visor blocks out overhanging traffic lights. • Horn is hard to access. **2001**—Transmission doesn't shift all the way into Drive; it pops out of gear and allows vehicle to roll down an incline. • Brake pedal goes to the floor without braking. • Steering wheel emits a grinding sound. • Side mirror creates a huge blind spot. **2002**—Sudden acceleration in Reverse. • Driver's side wheel fell off. • Chronic stalling after refuelling. • Seat belts are too short for some occupants. • Shoulder belt fits short drivers poorly. • Distorted windshield. • Airbag light stays lit. **2003**—Intermittent stalling. • Total brake failure. • Instrument panel shuts down. • Sun visor obstructs vision. • Tire jack collapsed. **2004**—Emergency flashers and turn signal lights burn out early.

Secret Warranties/Internal Bulletins/Service Tips

All models/years: Defective catalytic converters that cause a rotten-egg smell in the interior may be replaced free of charge under the emissions warranty. • Reverse servo cover seal leak. • Paint delamination, peeling, or fading (see Part Two "Paint and Body Defects," pages 71–75). **All models: 1996–2003**—Excessive oil consumption can be corrected with new piston rings if a new ring-cleaning process doesn't work (TSB #02-06-01-009C). **1998**—Harsh or delayed gearshifts may require the installation of an enhanced garage shift package. • Delayed or no engine braking in D3 may require the replacement of the forward and coast latch-piston assemblies. **2001**—Intermittent inoperative instrument panel (requires replacement of the I/P cluster assembly). • Cooler fitting coolant leaks. • Delayed Reverse engagement. **2000–02**—Loss of power when accelerating. • 1–2 shift concerns. • Noisy steering. • Steering column rubbing noise. • Scratched door glass. • Parking brake won't release; warning lamp stays lit. **2001–03**—Loss of engine coolant. **2001–05**—Harsh upshifts. **2003**—Erratic transmission shifting. *All models with 5.7L engines*: **1997–98**—Excessive front brake noise can be reduced by installing upgraded pads and rotors. **1998–99**—Diagnostic and repair tips for a faulty cruise control and speedometer. • Front-end clunks and rattles can be silenced by a judicious use of anti-friction materials. **1999–2000**—An engine that runs hot, overheats, or loses coolant may simply need a new radiator cap. *DeVille*: **2000–04**—Remedies for excessive vibration, shaking while cruising. • Troubleshooting rear suspension noise. **2003**—Intermittent no-starts; no electrical power (align engine wiring junction block; TSB #06-03-009). **2003–04**—Right rear door air leak.

CADILLAC CONCOURS, DEVILLE PROFILE

	1996	1997	1998	1999	2000	2001	2002	2003	2004
Cost Price ($)									
Concours	54,340	56,985	58,600	57,490	—	—	—	—	—
DeVille	48,125	49,400	50,495	49,710	51,995	51,895	52,555	54,925	56,235
Used Values ($)									
Concours ▲	8,000	10,500	11,500	14,000	—	—	—	—	—
Concours ▼	6,500	9,000	10,000	12,500	—	—	—	—	—
DeVille ▲	6,000	7,500	9,000	10,500	13,000	21,500	27,000	34,000	40,000
DeVille ▼	5,000	6,000	8,000	11,500	15,000	19,500	25,500	33,000	38,000
Reliability	❷	❷	❷	❷	❷	❷	❸	❸	❸
Crash Safety (F)									
Concours	❸	—	—	—	—	—	—	—	—
DeVille	❸	④	④	④	❸	❸	❶	❶	④
Side (DeVille)	—	④	④	④	④	④	④	④	④
Head Restraints (F)	—	❶	—	❷	—	❷	❷	❷	❷
Rear	—	—	—	—	—	❶	❶	—	—
Rollover Resistance	—	—	—	—	—	—	⑤	⑤	⑤

Infiniti

G20, I30/I35, J30, Q45 ★★★★

RATING: *G20*: Not Recommended (1994–2002). *I30*: Recommended (2000–03); Above Average (1997–99); Average (1996). *I35*: Above Average (2002–04). *J30*: Above Average (1994–97); Average (1993). *Q45*: Above Average (2001–04, 1991–96); Average (1997–2000). The 1997–99 Q45s were made more cheaply, came with fewer standard features, and were equipped with a smaller, less powerful engine than previous models. The 2002 I35 exhibits a disturbingly high number of performance- and safety-related defects; other Infinitis, however, demonstrate impressive reliability and quality control. **Maintenance/Repair costs:** Higher than average, and repairs must be done by either an Infiniti or a Nissan dealer. **Parts:** Higher-than-average cost, but not hard to find (except for body panels and the lighting assembly on the I30t):

In late October I noticed that one of my headlights would periodically cut out and I was left with just the daytime running light in that particular headlight. It wasn't doing this consistently and I assumed it was probably just a problem with the bulb or perhaps a loose connection/wire.

When I took it in to the dealer for my next service in mid-Feb I asked them to check it out. They found the problem [...] but told me that it couldn't be repaired and that the part wasn't sold separately. Instead the entire light assembly needed to be replaced with the light assembly costing $1,500.00 and with taxes and labour the cost would exceed $1,800.00.

```
###########         LIGHTS                      ##TECH#(S)#3023#########
COMPLAINT:   HEADLIGHT BULB AND RPM TACK LIGHTS DIM AS CAR WARMS UP
             TACK IS WORKING KNOW
             BULB STILL GOES DOWN. STAYS OFF UNTIL CAR IS RESTARTED
CAUSE:       HEADLITE ACTUATOR WORN OUT
CORRECTION:  MUST REPLACE COMP ASS. AS ACTUATOR NOT SOLD PARTS 1500.00
             PLUS LABOUR AND TAX

PARTS------QTY---FP-NUMBER--------------DESCRIPTION--------LIST PRICE-UNIT PRICE-
                                                      JOB # 2 TOTAL PARTS      0.00

                                          JOB # 2 TOTAL LABOR & PARTS         0.00
..............................................................................
MISC------CODE-------DESCRIPTION----------------------CONTROL NO--------      1.37
JOB # A          SS  SHOP SUPPLIES                                            1.37
                                                      TOTAL - MISC

COMMENTS--------------------------------------------------------------

TRYING TO FIND USED HEADLITE ASSEMBLY

TAX SUMMARY----------------------------------------------------------
GST    2.33                        PST    2.00
```

Extended warranty: Not necessary. **Best alternatives:** The fully equipped Honda Accord, Mazda Millenia or 929, Nissan Maxima, and Toyota Camry or Avalon are better buys from a price/quality standpoint, but they don't have the same luxury cachet. Also consider the Acura Integra, Legend, or RL, and the Mercedes E-Class. **Online help:** *www.carsurvey.org/*.

 ## Strengths and Weaknesses

With its emphasis on sporty handling (diluted somewhat with the '97 and later model years), the Infiniti series takes the opposite tack from the Lexus, which puts the accent on comfort and luxury. Still, the Infiniti comes fully equipped and offers owners the prestige of driving a comfortable and nicely styled luxury car that's more reliable than what's offered by Lexus, though not quite as refined.

G20

The least expensive Infiniti, the 1994–96 G20 is a front-drive luxury sports sedan that uses a base 2.0L 140-hp 16-valve, twin-cam, 4-cylinder power plant to accelerate smoothly, albeit noisily, through all gear ranges. Dual airbags came on line midway through the 1993 model year, and ABS is standard. Towing capacity is 450 kg (1,000 lb.). Cruise control is a bit erratic, particularly when traversing hilly terrain. Unlike the engine, the automatic transmission is silent, and power is reduced automatically when shifting. Steering is precise and responsive on the highway. However, the rear end tends to swing out sharply following abrupt steering changes. Early Infiniti G20s rode a bit too firmly, which led to the suspension being softened on the 1994 model. Thereafter, drivers say that the suspension bounced and jiggled occupants whenever the car went over uneven pavement or the load was increased.

VEHICLE HISTORY: 1999—Returning after a three-year hiatus, the '99 G20 wasn't worth the wait. It's basically a package of unfulfilled expectations with its wimpy 2.0L 140-hp engine, firmer ride, and ordinary styling. On the positive side, the car does handle and ride better. **2000**—A bit more horsepower and an upgraded transmission. **2001**—Standard leather seats and a power sunroof.

1999 and later G20s aren't as refined as their entry-level Lexus counterparts in interior space, drivetrain, or convenience features. The 140-hp engine's lack of low-speed torque means that it has to work hard above 4000 rpm—while protesting noisily—to produce brisk engine response in the higher gear ranges. The automatic transmission shifts roughly, particularly when passing, the power steering needs more assist during parking manoeuvres; and the dealer-installed foglights cost an exorbitant $500 to replace. Tall drivers will find the legroom insufficient, and rear passengers will feel cramped. Trunk space is limited by the angle of the rear window.

Owner complaints target automatic transmission failures, engine coolant leaks, prematurely worn brake rotors and brake pads, excessive noise when braking, malfunctioning power seats, and clunky springs and shock absorbers.

J30

Introduced as an early 1993 model and dropped in 1997, the rear-drive, four-door J30 and its high-performance variant, the I30, are sized and priced midway between the G20 and the top-of-the-line Q45. The J30 uses a modified version of the Nissan 300ZX's 3.0L 210-hp V6 engine. Although the vehicle is replete with important safety features and it accelerates and handles well, its engine is noisy, passenger and cargo room have been sacrificed to styling, and fuel economy is underwhelming.

The J30 comes with a standard airbag (or dual airbags, depending on the model year), ABS, and traction control. It has changed very little over the years, meaning that there's no reason to choose a more recent model over a cheaper older version.

Quality problems include airbag malfunctions (inadvertent deployment and failure to deploy), cracked exhaust manifold, leaking fuel injection system, and excessive vibration when accelerating.

Introduced as an early '96 model, the I30 is a sport sedan spin-off of the Nissan Maxima with additional sound-deadening material and a plushier interior. The car has a roomy interior, but its ride is unimpressive and handling is compromised by excessive body lean when cornering. Engine and road noise is omnipresent. The redesigned year 2000 model adds rear seatroom and reduces body lean considerably. I35s have a quieter and better performing engine, a much improved ride, and more responsive handling.

VEHICLE HISTORY: I30s come loaded with standard safety, performance, and comfort features, notably a 190-hp 3.0L V6 engine with dual camshafts and anti-lock brakes. **1996–99**—Models changed little, except for front side airbags and new headlights and tail lights added to the '98s. **2000**—Represents the best value from a price/performance perspective. It was entirely revamped with more conservative styling, 37 more horses, and a larger cabin. Head restraints were also upgraded, suspension improved, larger wheels were added, and high-intensity headlights adopted. **2002**—Renamed the I35 and given a larger V6 engine, new styling, and more standard features.

Incredibly, the recently minted I35 has elicited more performance-related complaints than its I30 predecessor, which was no paragon of quality control. This same phenomenon has been noted with Nissan's new Altima models, which continue to have serious factory-related glitches four years after the model's launch.

I30 owners report chronic suspension failures; drivetrain vibration and clunking; faulty steering; and defective transverse links, springs and struts. I35s are known for hesitation and surging when accelerating, electrical shorts, excessive front-end play, vibration, drivetrain noise, loose steering, rattling noises, incorrect fuel gauge reading, and inoperative seat memory buttons.

Q45

Faster and glitzier than other cars in its category, this luxury sedan provides performance, while its chief rival, the Lexus LS 400, provides luxury and quiet. Up to the '96 model, the Q45 used a 32-valve 278-hp 4.5L V8 tire-burner not frequently found on a Japanese luxury compact. It accelerates faster than the Lexus, going 0–100 km/h in 7.1 seconds without a hint of noise or abrupt shifting. Unlike the base engine of the G20, though, the Q45's engine supplies plenty of upper-range torque as well. The suspension was softened in 1994, but the car still rides much more firmly than its Lexus counterpart. The four-wheel steering is precise, but the standard limited-slip differential is no help in preventing the car's rear end from sliding out on slippery roads, mainly because of the original equipment "sport" tires, which were designed for 190 km/h autobahn cruising. There's not much footroom for passengers, and cargo room is disappointing. Fuel economy is nonexistent. ABS is standard, but a passenger-side airbag wasn't available before 1994.

VEHICLE HISTORY: 1994—Redesigned, including a restyled front end, a chrome grille, and an updated instrument panel. **1997**—A downsized 4.1L V8 set on a smaller platform, effectively changing the character of the car from a sporty performer to a highway cruiser. **1998**—Front seat belt pretensioners. **2002**—A new 4.5L V8 producing 340 hp (up from 266). The transmission is a 5-speed automatic with a manual shift mode. High-end electronics are standard, including traction control (TCS), Vehicle Dynamic Control (VDC), Electronic Brake Force Distribution (EBD), tire pressure monitors, high-intensity xenon headlights, and Voice Control for the climate control and eight-speaker Bose 300-watt audio system, including a six-disc CD changer. **2003**—A rear-axle upgrade for faster and smoother acceleration. **2004**—A rear-view camera.

The Q45 has been exceptionally reliable throughout its model run, despite some reports of premature AC failures, power steering problems, excessive wind noise around the A-pillars, sunroof wind leaks, tire thumping, cellular telephone glitches, faulty CD players, and a popping sound from the radio. Owners say that the paint scratches and flakes off so easily that it has to be constantly touched up.

Technical service bulletins list the following defects affecting the 1994–96 models: AC not blowing cold, front brake pad noise, low or rough idle, doors locking and unlocking themselves, and windshield cracking. You may also be interested in reviewing other helpful bulletins that contain troubleshooting tips for AC compressor leaks and noise, brake clunking noises and pedal pulsation, booming/drone noise and vibration, cold-weather hard starts, rough idle, suspension noise, Code 45 driveability alerts, and brake shudder and steering-wheel shimmy.

Safety Summary

G20: **1999**—Carbon monoxide poisoning. • When car is put into Reverse, driver's seat reclines without warning. **2001**—Foul odour emitted by AC. • Brake failure. • Brake rotors glaze over and need turning. • Airbags failed to deploy. *I30/I35:* **1998**—Airbag malfunctions. • Side window blew out. • Brake failure. **1999**— When using the turn signal, it's easy to turn off the headlights. • Airbag light stays on continuously. • Water seeps inside the vehicle from beneath. **2000**—Sudden, unintended acceleration. • Transmission jerks when shifting. • Premature wear of brake rotors. • Sunlight washes out gauges. • Headlight aimed too low. **2001**—Rear suspension failed. • Sudden, unintended acceleration. • Cruise control wouldn't disengage when brakes were applied. **2002**—Airbags failed to deploy. Steering wheel pulls sharply to one side when accelerating. • Poor braking. • Stalling. *Q45:* **1996**—Airbag indicator flashes because of ECM failure. • Premature failure of the shock absorber and power window. **1997**—Owner alleges that vehicle design causes the vehicle to hydroplane. • Airbag warning light comes on for no reason. •

When car is put into Reverse, driver's seat reclines without warning. • Severe front-end vibration continued after tires were replaced. **1998**—Airbag failed to deploy. • Accelerator pedal stuck while vehicle was stopped. **2000**—Excessive vibration starts at 100 km/h. **2001**—Sudden acceleration when vehicle was shifted into Reverse gear. **2002**—Excessive vibration caused by bent original-equipment wheels.

Secret Warranties/Internal Bulletins/Service Tips

All models/years: Troubleshooting tips to correct hard starts. • Vehicles with sunroofs may have wind noise coming from the sunroof area because of a small pinhole in the body sealer at the rear C-pillar. • Windshield cracking. • Erratic operation of the power antenna requires that the antenna rod be replaced. • Slow retraction of the front seat belt can be fixed by wiping off any residue found on the seat belt D-ring. *G20:* **1999**—Excessive blower noise can be reduced by installing a new cover. • Coolant leakage may be caused by a defective intake manifold expansion plug. • Replace the window glass run rubber if window makes a popping sound when opened. **1999–2000**—Countermeasures for front-end clunks when turning or braking. **1999–2001**—Power seat won't move or makes a grinding noise. • Shock absorbers that clunk will be replaced under warranty. **2000**—Engine lacks power; stuck in Third gear. • Correcting a brake judder. • Cloudy, scratched instrument cluster lens. • Parcel shelf rattle or buzz. • Low idle or dies when put into gear. • Preventing a rotten-egg smell emitted by the exhaust. **2001–02**—Rear brake caliper clunk, rattle, or knock. • Defroster not flush, rattles. *I30/I35:* **1996–1998**—If either one of the front power seats won't move, check for a broken power seat drive cable. **1996–2000**—Excessive blower noise can be reduced by installing a new cover. **2000–01**—No-starts may be caused by a faulty engine wire harness. • Transmission slippage. • Brake judder (vibration) is covered by a 4-year/97,000 km (60,000 mi.) warranty, says TSB #ITB00-063b. • Troubleshooting tips to correct self-locking doors. **2000–04**—Poor transmission performance. **2001**—Remedy for a low/no idle after a cold start. **2001–02**—Rear brake caliper clunk, rattle, or knock. **2002**—Faulty sunroof. **2002–03**—Upgraded brake pads to reduce brake judder or other anomalies. *Q45:* **1997–99**—A lumbar support mechanism that's inoperative should be replaced with an upgraded support mechanism. • If either one of the front power seats won't move, check for a broken power seat drive cable. • Excessive blower noise can be reduced by installing a new cover. • TSB #ITB98-062 gives an exhaustive listing for a variety of squeak

ABNORMAL SHIFTING

BULLETIN NO: ITB04-014   DATE: MARCH 10, 2004

2000–2004 I30/I35

IF YOU CONFIRM: An Applied Vehicle equipped with an automatic transaxle has ALL of the following conditions:

- Abnormal shifting (like: slip "shift shock" no shift improper shift timing)
- Transmission fluid is not burnt
- No excessive debris in oil pan*
- The incident is listed as an A/T internal fault as per the Electronic Service Manual (ESM) diagnostic procedure

DO NOT replace the transaxle assembly.

Instead first replace the control valve assembly (valve body) of the incident transmission.

and rattle repairs. **1997–2000**—TSB #ITB00-010 gives a detailed list of brake judder countermeasures. **1998–99**—An automatic transmission that produces a "double thump" noise when coming to a stop likely needs a new transmission control module (TCM). **2002**—Engine hesitation. • Steering pull to the right; excessive vibration. • Difficult to move shift lever. • Front suspension noise. • Rear power seat grinding noise. • Door sash rusting. • Inoperative rear sunshade. • Trunk lid hard to close. • Hard to read oil gauge. • Smoke from tailpipe. • Airbag light stays lit. • Loose driver's seat cushion. • Poor AC performance. • Inoperative headlight low beam. **2002–03**—Incorrect shifting. • Navigation system stuck in "please wait" mode. • Upgraded brake pads to reduce brake judder or other anomalies. **2002–04**—Remedy for engine knocking after a cold start.

G20, I30/I35, J30, Q45 PROFILE

	1996	1997	1998	1999	2000	2001	2002	2003	2004
Cost Price ($)									
G20	31,440	—	—	29,950	29,950	29,900	29,900	—	—
I30/I35	40,600	40,600	41,000	41,350	41,950	39,900	39,500	39,700	41,200
J30	51,600	52,600	—	—	—	—	—	—	—
Q45	72,000	65,000	66,500	71,000	71,000	70,000	73,000	74,900	75,500
Used Values ($)									
G20 ▲	4,000	—	—	9,000	11,500	13,500	16,000	—	—
G20 ▼	3,000	—	—	7,500	10,000	12,000	14,500	—	—
I30/I35 ▲	6,500	8,000	9,000	12,000	15,000	18,500	22,000	27,000	31,000
I30/I35 ▼	6,000	6,500	8,000	10,500	13,500	17,000	20,500	25,500	29,500
J30 ▲	7,500	9,500	—	—	—	—	—	—	—
J30 ▼	7,000	8,000	—	—	—	—	—	—	—
Q45 ▲	9,500	10,500	13,000	14,500	19,000	25,000	35,000	46,000	54,000
Q45 ▼	9,000	9,500	11,500	13,500	17,500	23,000	33,000	44,000	52,000
Reliability	④	⑤	④	④	④	④	④	④	④
Crash Safety (I30/I35)	—	—	④	—	④	④	④	④	④
J30	—	④	—	—	—	—	—	—	—
Side (I30/I35)	—	—	④	—	④	④	④	④	④
Offset									
I30/I35	❶	③	③	③	③	③	③	③	③
J30	—	—	—	—	③	③	—	—	—
Q45	—	②	②	②	②	②	—	⑤	—
Head Restraints									
G20	—	—	—	②	—	❶	❶	—	—
I30/I35	—	②	—	②	⑤	⑤	⑤	⑤	—
J30	—	❶	—	—	—	—	—	—	—
Q45	—	❶	—	❶	⑤	⑤	⑤	⑤	—
Rollover Resistance (I35)	—	—	—	—	—	—	④	④	④

Kia

MAGENTIS ★★

RATING: Below Average (2001–04). Consider buying a competitor with more refinement and a proven history for reliability and good quality control. **Maintenance/ Repair costs:** Average. **Parts:** Average cost, but parts aren't widely available yet. **Extended warranty:** A good idea only if the car will be kept more than five years. **Best alternatives:** A loaded Honda Accord, Nissan Maxima, or Toyota Camry. **Online help:** *www.mycarstats.com/auto_complaints/KIA_complaints.asp.*

 Strengths and Weaknesses

Sold in the States as the Optima, this front-drive, five-passenger sedan is basically a Hyundai Sonata without traction control. The Magentis comes with a twin-cam 138-hp 2.4L 4-cylinder or optional 170-hp 2.7L V6 hooked to a 4-speed automatic transmission (V6s have the Sonata's separate gate for manual shifting and four-wheel ABS). Other standard features: front seat belt pretensioners, a tilt steering column, independent double wishbone front suspension and independent multi-link rear suspension, 60/40 split folding rear seat, and tinted glass.

The Magentis is nicely appointed, provides good V6 performance, handles well, and rides comfortably. There's also plenty of front headroom and better-than-average fuel economy with regular fuel. The car is a bit better built than Kia's other models, but fit and finish is still inferior to other Asian makes. Still, performance and reliability are expected to be similar to the Sonata.

Unfortunately, this car has some major weaknesses that include a wimpy 4-cylinder engine, a poorly performing 4-speed automatic transmission, mediocre braking, limited rear headroom, considerable body lean when turning, faulty door locks that trap occupants, excessive wind and tire noise, a small trunk opening, and a weak dealer network. Owner complaints deal primarily with poor servicing, sudden acceleration, stalling, brake failure, premature brake pad and rotor wear, electrical shorts, and subpar fit and finish.

MAGENTIS PROFILE

	2001	2002	2003	2004
Cost Price ($)				
LX	20,995	21,295	22,250	22,250
LX V6	23,995	24,295	25,750	25,750
SE/EX V6	27,995	29,095	28,750	28,750
Used Values ($)				

All ratings on a numbered scale where ⑤ is good and ❶ is bad. See pages 100–101 for a more detailed description.

LX ▲	8,500	10,500	13,000	15,000
LX ▼	7,500	9,500	11,500	13,500
LX V6 ▲	9,500	12,500	15,000	17,500
LX V6 ▼	8,500	11,000	13,500	16,000
SE/EX V6 ▲	11,500	14,500	17,500	20,000
SE/EX V6 ▼	10,500	13,000	16,000	18,500
Reliability	❷	❸	❸	❸
Crash Safety (F)	—	—	④	④
Side	—	—	—	④
Offset	❸	❸	❸	❸
Head Restraints	❶	❶	❶	❶
Rollover Resistance	—	—	⑤	⑤

Lexus

ES 300, GS 300, 430, LS 400/430, SC 400/430 ★★★★

RATING: Above Average (2002–04; 1990–95); Recommended (1996–2001). A bit more refined than the Infinitis, Lexus' lineup offers first-class performance and better-than-average reliability, with the exception of recent powertrain defects.

The two latest model years have been downgraded because of serious design deficiencies relating to sudden acceleration, chronic engine/transmission stumble, shudder, and surge, and dash gauges that are unreadable during daylight hours. **Maintenance/Repair costs:** Higher than average, and repairs must be done by either a Lexus or a Toyota dealer. **Parts:** Higher-than-average cost, but not hard to find (except for body panels). **Extended warranty:** Not necessary. **Best alternatives:** A fully equipped Legend, Honda Accord, or early Nissan Maxima and Toyota Camry will provide airbags, comparable highway performance, and reliability at far less initial cost, but you don't get the Lexus *cachet*. Nevertheless, if you do pay top dollar for a used Lexus, its slow rate of depreciation virtually guarantees that you'll get much of your money back. **Online help:** *us.lexusownersclub.com, us.lexusownersclub.com/forums/index.php?act=ST&f=7&t=3584&, www.carsurvey.org/manufacturer_Lexus.html,* and *yotarepair.com/Automotive_News.html* (for Lexus engine sludge and other repair hints, search for "Toyota engine sludge" on Google).

Strengths and Weaknesses

These are benchmark cars known for their impressive reliability and performance. Sports cars, they're not. But if you're looking for your father's Oldsmobile from a Japanese automaker, these luxury cars fill the bill. Like the Acuras and Infinitis,

Lexus models all suffer from some automatic transmission failures, engine sludge buildup (*www.autooninfo.info/VCC200310ToyotaEngineReliability.htm*), early rear main engine seal and front-strut replacement (front-struts are often replaced under a secret warranty), front brake, electrical, body, trim, and accessory deficiencies, most of which are confirmed by confidential technical service bulletins.

ES 300

Resembling an LS 400 dressed in sporty attire, the entry-level ES 300 was launched in 1992 to fill the gap between the discontinued ES 250 and the LS 400. In fact, the ES 300 has many of the attributes of the LS 400 sedan but sells for much less money. A five-passenger sedan based on the Camry but 90 kg (200 lb.) heavier and with a different suspension and tires, it comes equipped with a standard 3.0L 24-valve engine that produces 181–210 horses, coupled to either a 5-speed manual or a 4-speed electronically controlled automatic transmission. Like some Infiniti models, however, the ES 300 hesitates and surges when accelerating. Headroom is also surprisingly limited for a car this expensive.

VEHICLE HISTORY: *ES 300/330:* **1994**—Dual airbags and a new 3.0L 6-cylinder that boosted horsepower (3) to 188. **1995**—A new front air intake, standard foglights, and new brake/signal lights. **1997**—A restyled interior and exterior, increased interior dimensions, improved centre rear seat belt, and horsepower increased to 200. **1998**—De-powered airbags, along with side airbags and an upgraded anti-theft system. **1999**—Horsepower increased to 210, upgraded automatic transmission, and traction control. **2000**—Restyled front ends and tail lights, and improved child safety seat anchors. **2001**—An emergency trunk release. **2002**—A longer, taller body; new 5-speed automatic transmission; improved brakes, steering, and suspension; and more standard luxury features; no more standard traction control. **2004**—ES 330 debuts with 15 extra horses and larger head-protecting side airbags.

On April 3, 2003, Toyota issued a press release admitting engine sludge problems with its 1997–2002 Toyota and Lexus vehicles equipped with 3.0-liter IMZ V-6 engines and all 1997–2001 Toyota vehicles powered by 5SFE 2.2-liter 4-cylinder engines. The automaker pledged to cover claims with an extended warranty. For a vehicle this well made, government-reported safety-related defects are surprisingly omnipresent. These include airbag-induced injuries; sudden acceleration; an unreliable powertrain that surges, stumbles, stalls, and shifts erratically; ABS and Goodyear tire failures; excessive vibration when underway; interior window fogging; unreadable dash gauges; and poor AC performance.

GS 300

The rear-drive GS 300 is a step up from the front-drive ES 300 and just a rung below Lexus' top-of-the-line LS 400. It carries the same V6 engine as the ES 300, except that it has 20 more horses. This produces sparkling performance at higher speeds, though the car is disappointingly sluggish from a start. Fuel economy is sacrificed for performance, however, and the base suspension and tires pass noisily over small bumps and ruts. Visibility is also less than impressive, with large rear pillars and a narrow rear window restricting the view. There's not much usable trunk space, either, and the liftover is unreasonably high.

VEHICLE HISTORY: 1996—A light rear-end restyling and a 5-speed automatic transmission. **1998**—Restyled once again and given an upgraded V8. **2000**—A new brake assist system and more user-friendly child safety seat anchors. **2001**—Substantially upgraded with a 300-hp 4.3L V8, upgraded transmission controls, standard side curtain airbags, smart airbags, an emergency trunk release, and a host of other convenience features. **2002**—A revised navigation system.

Owner complaints have centred around brake failures, electrical and fuel system malfunctions resulting in unintended sudden acceleration and hesitation, electrical shutdown, wheel bearings, excessive front-end vibration, and fragile wheel rims.

LS 400, LS 430

The Lexus flagship, the LS 400 rear-drive arrived in 1990 with a 250-hp 4.0L V8. It outclasses all other luxury sedans in reliability, styling, and function. Its powerful engine provides smooth, impressive acceleration and superior highway passing ability at all speeds. Its transmission is smooth and efficient. The suspension gives an easy ride, without body roll or front-end plow during emergency stops, delivering a major comfort advantage over other luxury compacts. Other amenities: antilock brakes, a driver-side airbag, and automatic temperature control.

VEHICLE HISTORY: 1993—A passenger-side airbag and interior/exterior restyling. **1995**—Increased interior and exterior dimensions, a more powerful engine, and a better-performing drivetrain for quicker acceleration. **1997**—Side airbags. **1998**—An improved V8, a new 5-speed automatic transmission, Vehicle Skid Control (VSC), and a host of interior upgrades. **2001**—Totally redesigned with a sleeker body, a 4.3L V8, an upgraded suspension, and a more spacious, reworked interior. Additional safety and comfort features have also been added. **2002**—Navigation system upgrade.

The brakes don't inspire confidence, owing to their mushy feel and average performance. Furthermore, there's limited rear footroom under the front seats, and the rear middle passenger has to sit on the transmission hump. This car is a gas-guzzler that thirsts for premium fuel.

Owner complaints deal mainly with sudden, unintended acceleration; stalling caused by a faulty throttle sensor; traction control causing vehicle to swerve (usually to the left) unexpectedly; failure of the VSC to activate; main computer failures; spongy brakes; electrical glitches; and door locks that stick shut, trapping occupants.

SC 300, SC 400/430

These two coupes are practically identical, except for their engines and luxury features. The cheaper SC 300 gives you the same high-performance 6-cylinder engine used by the GS 300 and Toyota Supra, while the SC 400 uses the 4.0L V8 engine found in the LS 400. You're likely to find fewer luxury features with the SC 300 because they were sold as options. Nevertheless, look for an SC with traction control for additional safety during poor driving conditions. On the downside, V8 fuel consumption is horrendous, rear seating is cramped, and trunk space is unimpressive. Also, invest in a good anti-theft device, or your Lexus relationship will be over almost before it begins.

VEHICLE HISTORY: 1993—A passenger airbag. **1995**—Slightly restyled. **1996**—Given the LS 400's V8. **1998**—SC got the 4.0L V8 engine, while the SC 300 continued to use the previous year's inline-six, but ditched its 5-speed manual transmission. Other upgrades: variable valve timing, a more refined 5-speed automatic transmission, a new anti-theft system, and de-powered airbags. **1999**—American-sold models got larger brakes.

 **Safety Summary**

All models: 1997–2002—Engine warranty extended to 8 years to cover engine oil sludge claims (*www.autosafety.org/*). *ES 300/330*: **All years**—Sudden, unintended acceleration. **1998**—Vehicle accelerated as brakes were applied. • **1999**—Rear seat belts don't hold a child safety seat firmly. • Vehicle suddenly swerves from one lane to another. • Excessive oil consumption, blue smoke comes from the tailpipe, PCV valve is clogged up, and head gasket has failed (all symptomatic of Toyota's "oil sludge" problem, covered in the Sienna section). **2000**—Sudden, unintended acceleration when in Reverse. • Engine stalls or won't accelerate in traffic. • Vehicle suddenly downshifts from Fourth to First in heavy traffic; jerky shifting. • Rolls backward when transmission is in Drive. • Swerves left on a straight road. • Rear-view mirror doesn't move, resulting in poor visibility. **2001**—Engine fire erupted from what investigator said was fuel leaking from a rubber hose that had disconnected from the fuel filter. • Car suddenly accelerated as driver slowed coming to a stop sign, and again when pulling into a parking space. • Traction control engages much too easily when merging into traffic. • Vehicle started up and began moving down the street in Reverse, despite the fact that there was no key in the ignition cylinder and the vehicle was left in Park. • Vehicle hesitates when applying accelerator after decelerating; computer replacement is said to be on national back order. **2002**—Airbags failed to deploy. • Impossible to read speedometer and other gauges in sunlight; they have red needles against a black background. • Won't go into gear properly. • Fuel cap won't screw off. • Warped brake rotors. • Defective Goodyear Eagle tires (sidewall bubbling). **2002–03**— Chronic engine/transmission surging and stalling not fixed by computer module recalibration, switching to premium fuel, etc. (see NHTSA complaint below):

> The transmission of the 2003 Lexus ES 300 is subject to major hesitation, particularly in crowded intersections and with lack of acceleration. Very noticeable when traveling about 27 mph [43 km/h] and then needing to move, there is major delay in the signal telling the engine and transmission to work together and move the car. This vehicle is new with about 1,000 miles [1,600 km]. It cannot make up its mind to upshift or downshift and this delay will mean a major crash someday. Around 40 mph [64 km/h] it wants to upshift to the Fifth gear, and just below that hunts to go back to Fourth.

> The manufacturer says, as he did for the 2002 models, that a software fix is being prepared. They stated the problem from the 2002 was fixed. Evidently that is not the case. They now tell me that a fix is coming year-end. How many accidents will occur by then? Dealer says that the car will learn from the driver, but that is not working, and hesitation from 0–5 mph [0–8 km/h], from 27–45 [43–72 km/h], etc. Is very pronounced. If you "floorboard" it from slow speeds, its hesitation is great, and car almost dies. Lexus says "don't do that", but from car creation to now, car movement meant add more gas, not the reverse. My safety depends on it.

GS 300: **1998**—Vehicle surges or suddenly accelerates. • After yaw sensor replacement, as per recall, yaw sensor failure caused an accident. • Rear brake caliper plate for brake pads fell off after brake pins dislodged. • Poor low beam illumination. • Trunk lid falls down unexpectedly. **1999**—Sudden, unintended acceleration and unexpected delayed acceleration. • Airbags failed to deploy. • Wheels break under normal driving conditions. • Complete brake failure. • Excessive vibration at highway speeds. **2002**—Fire ignited from fuel filter leak. • Sticking accelerator. • Vehicle started without key. • Traction control engages too easily. • Inadequate headlight illumination. • Digital dash indicator washes out in sunlight.

Secret Warranties/Internal Bulletins/Service Tips

All models: 1990–2000—Eliminating brake clicking when changing direction of travel (requires a special grease recommended by Toyota/Lexus). *ES 300/330:* **1996–99**—A knocking noise from under the floor in the rear of the car can be fixed by following the field fix outlined in TSB #SU005-96. **1997–99**—New front brake pads have been developed to reduce brake grind and groan. **1997–2000**— Front suspension noise may be silenced by installing an upgraded suspension support, says TSB #SU002-99. **1997–2001**—Turn signal flashes erratically. **1999**— Excessive engine noise when idling at normal operating temperature. • If the vehicle shudders during a 2–3 shift, try changing the transaxle valve body under warranty, before moving on to other repairs. • Rear suspension squeaks and groans.

VEHICLE PULLS TO THE LEFT
BULLETIN NO: ST003-04   **DATE: FEB. 4, 2004**

VEHICLE PULL IMPROVEMENT
PROCEDURE

'04 ES 330

This service bulletin is to inform you of the repair procedure for the 2004 model year ES 330 vehicles pulling to the left.

APPLICABLE WARRANTY: This repair is covered under the Lexus Comprehensive Warranty. This warranty is in effect for 48 months or 50,000 miles, whichever occurs first, from the vehicle's in-service date. Warranty application is limited to correction of a problem based upon a customer's specific complaint.

• New, improved brake pads will reduce rear brake squeaks. • Tips on troubleshooting a false MIL alert. **1999–2001**—Information on correcting automatic transmission fluid leaks. **2000–01**—Procedures for obtaining a free seat belt extender. **2002**—Harsh 2–3 shift. • Tilt steering hard to move from down position. • Troubleshooting steering pull and interior squeaks and rattles. • Coil spring creaking. • Heat shield rattles. • No sound from amplifier. • Gas cap sticks. **2002–03**—TSB #TC004-03, issued August 4, 2003, gives recalibration instructions for correcting erratic shifting. This free repair is in effect for 96 months or 128,000 km (80,000 mi.), and is limited to the correction of a problem based upon a customer's specific complaint. • Unreadable dash gauges will be corrected free of charge under TSB #EL001-03, issued January 23, 2003. • A shim kit will reduce front brake vibration, says TSB #BR002-02, issued December 24, 2002. • A gas cap sticking fix is detailed in TSB #EG003-02, issued February 8, 2002. • Body creak or snap from top of front windshield. **2004**—Troubleshooting tips for a malfunctioning front seat occupant seat belt sensor. • Vehicle pulls into oncoming traffic. *GS 300*: **1998–2000**—Front window wind noise. • Noisy seat belt retractor. **1998–2001**—Glove box rattling. **2000–02**—Front stabilizer bar noise. **2001–02**—Front coil spring clicking. **2002**—No sound from amplifier. • Steering pull troubleshooting. *LS 400, LS 430*: **1998–99**—An upgraded blower motor that is better at maintaining blower speed will be installed under warranty. **1999–2000**—Countermeasures to reduce steering noise and improve smoothness. **2000**—Moon roof water leaks. **2001**—Moon roof rattle and rear corner air leak. • Instrument panel rattling. • Rear seat and luggage compartment creaking. • False illumination of the MIL (malfunction indicator light). **2002**—No sound from amplifier. • Steering pull troubleshooting.

ES 300, GS 300, LS 400/430, SC 400/430 PROFILE

	1996	1997	1998	1999	2000	2001	2002	2003	2004
Cost Price ($)									
ES 300/330	45,600	42,960	43,820	44,235	43,995	44,000	43,400	43,800	43,800
GS 300	71,400	71,400	58,900	59,220	59,420	60,700	60,700	61,700	61,700
LS 400/430	78,700	78,700	78,300	78,690	78,950	80,000	81,900	82,800	83,200
SC 400/430	82,000	83,000	84,000	—	—	—	84,000	85,500	86,800

All ratings on a numbered scale where ⑤ is good and ❶ is bad. See pages 100–101 for a more detailed description.

Used Values ($)

ES 300/330 ▲	9,000	11,000	12,500	14,500	19,000	22,500	27,500	33,000	37,000
ES 300/330 ▼	8,000	9,500	11,000	13,000	17,500	21,000	26,000	31,000	35,000
GS 300 ▲	11,500	13,000	15,000	19,500	24,500	31,000	39,000	45,000	51,000
GS 300 ▼	10,500	12,000	13,500	18,000	23,000	29,000	36,000	43,000	49,000
LS 400/430 ▲	15,000	17,000	19,000	25,500	32,000	41,000	52,000	62,000	70,000
LS 400/430 ▼	13,500	16,000	17,500	23,000	30,000	38,000	50,000	59,000	66,000
SC 400/430 ▲	16,500	18,000	20,000	—	—	—	55,000	65,000	73,000
SC 400/430 ▼	15,500	17,000	19,000	—	—	—	52,000	63,000	70,000

Reliability	5	4	4	4	4	4	4	4	4
Crash Safety (F)									
ES 300/330	5	—	4	4	—	—	—	5	5
GS 300	3	3	—	—	—	—	—	—	—
Side (ES 300/330)	—	—	5	5	—	5	—	5	5
Offset									
ES 300/330	—	—	—	—	—	—	5	5	5
GS 300	—	—	—	5	5	5	5	5	5
LS 400/430	5	5	5	5	5	5	5	5	5
Head Restraints									
ES 300/330	—	3	—	3	—	3	3	3	1
GS 300	—	—	—	3	5	5	5	2	2
LS 400/430	—	2	—	3	—	2	2	2	2
SC 400/430	—	1	—	1	—	—	5	5	5
Rollover Resistance									
(ES 300/330)	—	—	—	—	—	—	—	4	4

Mercedes-Benz

300 SERIES, 400 SERIES, 500 SERIES, E-CLASS ★★★

RATING: Below Average (1992–2004); Average (1985–91). Mercedes' quality has deteriorated over the past decade because of the increased complexity of mechanical and electronic components. Beware of engine oil sludge. **Maintenance/Repair costs:** Higher than average, but many repairs can now be done by independent garages. **Parts:** Higher-than-average cost and limited availability. **Extended warranty:** A good idea for recent models. **Best alternatives:** Acura Integra or RL; Ford Crown Victoria or Mercury Grand Marquis; Infiniti I30; Mazda Millenia; and Toyota's Avalon. **Online help:** *benzworld.org, www.mercedes-benz-usa.com, www.mercedesproblems.com, www.troublebenz.com, www.lemonmb.com, www.car-survey.org,* and *www.oil-tech.com/32million.htm.*

Strengths and Weaknesses

These cars were once ideal mid-sized family sedans until Mercedes started churning out feeble downsized models and installed failure-prone electronic components in its cars. Nevertheless, the E-class sedans are the best of a bad lot and are relatively reliable, depreciate slowly, and provide all the interior space that the early 190 series and present-day C-Class leave out. Their major shortcoming is a weak dealer network that limits parts distribution and drives up parts and servicing costs.

If you'd like to drive one of these cars but are of an economical frame of mind, choose the 260E—it offers everything the 300 does, but for much less. The 300CE is a coupe version, appealing to a sportier crowd, while the 300TE is the station wagon variant.

VEHICLE HISTORY: *E Series*: **1997**—A new 5-speed automatic transmission, and the E420 got a V8 engine. **1998**—The addition of a station wagon and all-wheel drive. The 300D added a turbocharger for extra power; the E320 came with a new 3.2L V6. Other additions: a BabySmart child protection system, Brake Assist, and an electronic Smart Key feature. **1999**—A new side-impact head protection feature. **2000**—Diesel dropped; a new all-wheel-drive E430 with standard side airbags was added. All models got new wheels, Touch Shift (an auto-manual device), and Electronic Stability. **2001**—One-touch opening sunroofs. **2003**—A E320 Special Edition sedan. **2004**—Increased availability of all-wheel drive, a revamped wagon body style, and a new 7-speed automatic transmission.

Quality control has traditionally been better than average with the 300 and higher series; however, it has followed a downward trend during the last decade. Owners point out recurring problems with the fuel and electrical systems, causing lights, instruments, and gauges to shut off and the trunk lid to open when the engine is shut down. Other common problems: premature rusting of the doors, engine won't shut off; stalling and engine surging; engine problems caused by a stretched timing chain; 1998–2001 oil sludging (see "Secret Warranties/Internal Bulletins/Service Tips"); computer module failures (for both engine and transmission); erratically performing and noisy transmission; leaking transmission transfer case; excessive power steering; and front window noise.

 ## Safety Summary

300 series: **1998**—Sudden, unintended acceleration while on the highway. • Airbag failed to deploy in a collision. • While parking, steering went out and car caught on fire. • Total loss of braking; pedal went to floor. • Premature failure of the automatic transmission, tie-rod, belt tensioner, fuel pump, fuel level sensor, oxygen sensor, windows, power-assisted sunroof, electric seats, turn signal switch, and brake lights. • Power seat suddenly moved back and reclined while vehicle was in traffic. **1999**—Sudden acceleration when turning or decelerating to exit the freeway. • Engine fuel line leakage. • Sunroof electrical fire. • Fuel pump failures. • Inaccurate fuel gauge says tank is full, but almost 23L more (five gallons) can be pumped. • Sudden stalling while underway, especially when going over a bump in the road. • Excessive vibration when decelerating. • Transmission leaks oil, disengages, and then suddenly locks up. • ABS suddenly activated, throwing vehicle to side of the road. • Self-activating door locks. • Severe window hazing in rainy weather. **2000**—Panic stops may produce a brake pedal stiffness and loss of braking ability. • Premature brake booster failure. • Poor acceleration said to be caused by fuel injection control module. • Fuel gauge still gives false low readings. • Horn blows on its own, and warning lights are constantly lit. **2001**—Side airbags deploy inadvertently. The following owner of a 2001 300E recounts his surprise at the time:

> While driving down the highway, my passenger side curtain and rear side door airbags deployed for no reason at all…. It scared the hell out of me and nearly caused me to crash the car.

• Water enters the automatic transmission control module, preventing the transmission from changing gears. • Vehicle hesitates when accelerating with gas pedal halfway depressed, then it lurches forward. **2002**—Steering locked up while turning. • Total electrical failure in traffic leading to vehicle shutdown. • Stalling when accelerating. • Windows don't stay up. **2003**—Faulty gateway module and software cause failure in the braking system and tire pressure feedback. • Electrical failures can leave the vehicle with no rear brakes and limited use of the front brakes. • Erratic transmission shifts. **2004**—Airbags failed to deploy. • Vehicle lurched forward without accelerator depressed. • Engine oil leaks. • Frequent automatic transmission failures and fluid leaks. • Total brake failure. • Intermittent failure of the radar-controlled cruise control. • Mirrors tilt down when backing up, but don't tilt up until car goes forward at 14 km/h.

Secret Warranties/Internal Bulletins/Service Tips

All models/years: Engine surges at full load. • Vacuum pump oil supply modified through the introduction of a second bore in oil spray nozzle. This helps reduce complaints that engine won't shut off. • Airbag Service Campaign. **All models: 1986–98**—Fuel pump relay failures. **1998**—Engine rattle countermeasures. **1998–2004**—Free engine repairs or replacement if afflicted by engine oil sludge, following the O'Keefe class action settlement in April 2003. Order No: S-B-18.00/16a, published December 2003, gives all the details on the problem and Mercedes' payout rules. **2000**—A Special Service Campaign will replace, free of charge, side airbags that may deploy if the vehicle is left in the sun. **2003**—Piston slap engine noise. **2004**—ABS buzzing. • Steering leaks. • Sliding roof rack cover cracks. • Wheelhouse water drain modification. • Rear axle rumbling. • No-starts. • Exhaust system rattling, hissing, and humming.

	1996	1997	1998	1999	2000	2001	2002	2003	2004
Cost Price ($)									
300ED	58,500	59,950	59,950	59,950	—	—	—	—	—
320E 4d	64,750	65,900	66,450	66,750	67,150	67,900	68,350	69,950	72,050
420E, 430	72,500	73,300	73,950	74,250	74,750	75,750	76,150	—	—
500E/S	132,500	132,950	117,900	122,900	112,851	114,650	116,950	81,500	83,500
Used Values ($)									
300ED ▲	13,000	14,500	16,500	19,000	—	—	—	—	—
300ED ▼	11,500	13,500	15,000	17,500	—	—	—	—	—
320E 4d ▲	14,000	15,000	17,500	21,000	28,000	33,000	43,000	54,000	61,000
320E 4d ▼	13,000	15,500	16,000	19,500	26,500	31,000	41,500	52,000	58,000
420E, 430 ▲	15,000	17,000	19,000	23,000	31,000	37,000	46,000	—	—
420E, 430 ▼	14,000	15,500	17,500	21,000	29,000	34,000	44,000	—	—
500E/S ▲	18,000	22,000	25,000	33,000	39,000	52,000	65,000	61,000	70,000
500E/S ▼	16,000	19,000	23,000	31,000	36,000	49,000	60,000	59,000	67,000
Reliability	③	③	③	③	③	③	③	③	③
Crash Protection									
Offset	—	③	③	③	⑤	⑤	⑤	⑤	⑤
Head Restraints (4d)	—	⑤	—	③	—	⑤	⑤	⑤	③
Wagon	—	—	—	—	—	③	③	—	—

RATING: Below Average (1994–2004). These cars no longer outclass the Detroit Big Three in reliability and comfort, but the word is just getting around now because Mercedes has had a free ride from a fawning automotive press that has ignored its quality and safety shortcomings. Keep in mind that you'll have to keep your car much longer to amortize its higher cost. **Maintenance/Repair costs:** Higher than average, and most repairs must be done by a Mercedes dealer if you don't live in an area where independent shops have sprung up. Look out for engine oil sludge (see page 365) **Parts:** Higher-than-average cost. Parts are highly dealer dependent and relatively expensive. **Extended warranty: Best alternatives:** Acura Integra or RL; BMW 3 Series; Infiniti I30; and Toyota Avalon. **Online help:** *forums.mbnz.org/ forums, www.mercedesproblems.com, www.troublebenz.com, www.lemonmb.com, and www.carsurvey.org.*

All ratings on a numbered scale where ⑤ is good and ❶ is bad. See pages 100–101 for a more detailed description.

Strengths and Weaknesses

Replacing the power-challenged, and bland 190-series, the 1994 C-Class gained interior room and two new engines: a base 147-hp 2.2L and a 194-hp 2.8L 6-cylinder—a real powerhouse in this small car when coupled to the manual 5-speed transmission. The 4-speed automatic is a big disappointment—it requires a lot of throttle effort to downshift and prefers to start out in Second gear. Although this series got small incremental power increases and additional features over the years, you don't see a major redesign until 2001. Unfortunately, the new engines and other features added at that time only add to the cars' poor reliability: engine and road noise is still bothersome, and interior space is still inadequate. Since then, these cars have coasted on the Mercedes name and been touted mainly as fuel-sippers with a high-end cachet. That's poor recompense for what little the car actually offers.

VEHICLE HISTORY: 1997—C-Class replaced the standard 2.2L engine with the more robust 2.3L (C230) and revised headlights. **1998**—A new 2.8L engine (C280), BabySmart car seats, Brake Assist, and side airbags. **1999**—Models got the SLK's 2.3L supercharged engine, replacing the C230's normally aspirated power plant, a better-performing drivetrain, and standard leather upholstery. **2000**—A Touch Shift auto-manual transmission, stability control, and Tele-Aid, a communications system for calling for assistance. **2001**—Completely revamped, gaining two new engines, additional safety features, and more aerodynamic styling. **2002**—Additional rear room and storage space, more high-performance features, a wagon, and an AWD sedan and wagon.

Keep in mind that owner surveys give the entry-level C-Class cars a just better-than-average rating, while the 300 and higher series have always scored way above average in owner satisfaction. C-Class owners report frequent problems with sudden, unintended acceleration, drivetrain noise and vibration, and slipping or soft shifts. Engines (oil sludge), brakes, and the AC electrical system and computer-controlled electronic componentry (telematics) is glitch-prone, hell to diagnose, and expensive to repair.

 Safety Summary

1998—Airbag warning light came on and then airbag suddenly exploded. • Transmission fluid leakage. • Faulty gas gauge sensor. • Rear suspension bouncing makes it difficult to maintain directional control. • Inoperative windshield wipers. • Car is very vulnerable to side-wind buffeting. • Window failures. **1999**—Vehicle suddenly accelerated and brakes couldn't stop it. • Brakes failed on incline. **2000**—Sudden acceleration when pulling into a parking space. • Automatic transmission slips when the vehicle is cold, sticks in gear, and shifts abruptly. **2001**—Unintended acceleration. • Vehicle suddenly stopped by the highway as engine self-destructed. **2002**—Many reports of sudden loss of power, stalling. • Airbags failed to deploy. •

Wide rear quarter panel blind spot (C240). • Multiple electrical short circuits. • Differential failure. • Vehicle wanders over highway. • Driver seat and side rear-view mirror fail to return to preset position. **2003**—Sudden engine surging. • Fuel gauge failure and loss of power. • Faulty fuel tank causes engine warning light to stay lit. • No throttle response and strong fuel smell pervades the interior. • Vehicle jerks when accelerating. • Weak wheels are easily bent. • Poor wiper performance. **2004**—Airbags failed to deploy. • Loose driver's seat. • Windshield wipers fail intermittently. • Auto-dimming rear-view mirror sometimes turns pitch black.

Secret Warranties/Internal Bulletins/Service Tips

All models/years: Excessive engine valve train noise may be caused by a stretched timing chain. After 48,000 km, the camshaft and timing chain drive should be checked carefully, especially if excessive noise is heard. • Water in the oxygen sensor connector in the front passenger wheelwell. • Ignition key difficult to remove. • Clicking from the front door lock trim. **All models: 1997–04**—Engine oil sludge refund guidelines. **1998–2001**—Free engine repair or replacement for oil sludge. **1999**—Hesitation after a cold start and rough 1–2 and 2–3 shift during warm-up. **1999–2000**—If the brake pedal is hard to apply, replace the brake booster and crankcase vent hoses. **2001**—Troubleshooting hard starts and poor engine performance. **2002–03**—Lack of power, engine hesitation. **2004**—Engine oil leaks through the cylinder head bolt threads. • Steering leaks. • Suspension rumbling. • Exhaust rattling, hissing, and humming.

C-CLASS PROFILE

	1996	1997	1998	1999	2000	2001	2002	2003	2004
Cost Price ($)									
220	35,995	—	—	—	—	—	—	—	—
230	—	36,950	37,550	37,950	38,450	—	33,950	34,450	35,290
240	—	—	—	—	—	37,450	37,950	38,450	41,290
280	49,995	50,995	49,950	49,950	49,950	—	—	—	—
Used Values ($)									
220 ▲	9,000	—	—	—	—	—	—	—	—
220 ▼	7,500	—	—	—	—	—	—	—	—
230 ▲	—	9,500	11,500	13,000	16,500	—	20,000	25,500	29,000
230 ▼	—	8,500	10,000	12,000	15,000	—	19,000	24,000	27,500
240 ▲	—	—	—	—	—	19,000	23,000	28,000	32,000
240 ▼	—	—	—	—	—	17,000	22,000	26,000	31,000
280 ▲	12,000	13,500	15,500	18,000	21,000	—	—	—	—
280 ▼	11,000	12,500	14,000	16,500	19,500	—	—	—	—
Reliability	❸	❸	❸	❸	❸	❸	❸	❸	❸

All ratings on a numbered scale where ❺ is good and ❶ is bad. See pages 100–101 for a more detailed description.

Crash Safety (F)									
C220, C230	④	④	—	—	—	—	—	—	—
Side									
C230	—	❸	❸	❸	—	—	—	—	—
Offset	—	—	—	—	—	⑤	⑤	⑤	⑤
Head Restraints (F)	—	❷	—	❸	—	⑤	⑤	⑤	❸
Rear	—	—	❷	❷	—	—	—	—	—

Nissan

<table>
<tr><td>MAXIMA</td><td align="right">★★★</td></tr>
</table>

RATING: Average (2002; 2004; 1986–88); Above Average (1989–2001; 2003). Redesigned 1995–2001 versions offer a peppier engine, more rounded styling, a slightly longer wheelbase, and fewer factory-related problems. The 2002 and 2004 model redesigns did not go as well, and overall quality has been seriously compromised. **Maintenance/Repair costs:** Higher than average, but repairs can be done practically anywhere up to the 2001s. Thereafter, you are totally dependent upon field fixes, a mountain of service bulletins, and "goodwill" warranties to tackle complicated factory-related goofs. **Parts:** Higher-than-average cost, but easy to find. Xenon headlights are frequently stolen from the car because they are easily accessed and can cost $800 each to replace. **Extended warranty:** A must-have for 2002 and 2004 models. **Best alternatives:** Acura Integra and RL; Infiniti I30; Mazda Millenia; and Toyota Avalon. **Online help:** www.mycarstats.com/auto_complaints/NISSAN_complaints.asp and www.consumeraffairs.org/automotive/nissan.html.

 ## Strengths and Weaknesses

These front-drive sedans are very well equipped and nicely finished, but cramped for their size. Although the trunk is spacious, only five passengers can travel in a pinch (in the literal sense). The 6-cylinder, 190-hp engine, borrowed from the 300ZX in 1992, offers sparkling performance; the fuel injectors, however, are problematic. The '93 models got standard driver-side airbags, and the Maxima remained unchanged until the 1995 model's redesign and a second redesign of the year 2000 version.

Early Maximas are less expensive to buy, but more costly to maintain—for example, the exhaust manifold, a component that commonly fails, will set you back $300–$500 to replace on 1993–96 models. Owners report that the '95 Maxima's suspension was cheapened to the detriment of both the ride and the handling.

Minor electrical and front suspension problems afflict early Maximas. Brakes and engine timing belts need frequent attention in all years. Newer models have a weak automatic transmission and the ignition system can malfunction. There have also been reports of cooked transmissions caused by a poorly designed transmission cooler. Mechanics say that this breakdown can be avoided by installing an externally-mounted transmission cooler with a filter and replacing the transmission filter cooler at every oil change.

Owners report that the V6-equipped Maxima is sometimes hard to start in cold weather because of the engine's tendency to flood easily. The cruise control unit is another problematic component. When it's engaged at moderate speeds, it hesitates or drifts to a lower speed, acting as if the fuel line was clogged. It operates correctly only at much higher speeds than needed. Owners say that a new fuel filter will not correct the problem. Additionally, though warped manifolds were once routinely replaced under a "goodwill" warranty, Nissan now makes the customer pay. The warpage causes a manifold bolt to break off, thereby causing a huge exhaust leak. Most fuel-injector malfunctions are caused by carbon clogging up the injectors; there are additives that you can try that might reduce this buildup. There have also been internal problems with the coil windings on the fuel-injectors. Your best bet is to replace the entire set.

Nissan has had problems with weak window regulators for some time. If the window is frozen, don't open it. The rubber weather stripping around the window is also a problem. It cuts easily and causes the window to go off-track, which in turn causes stress on the weak regulators. Driver-side window breakage is common and can cost up to $300 to repair. Costly aluminum wheels corrode quickly and are easily damaged by road hazards. There have been a few reports of surface rust and paint problems. Pre-1990 Maximas suffer from rust perforation on the sunroof, door bottoms, rear wheelwells, front edge of the hood, and bumper supports. The underbody should also be checked carefully for corrosion damage. Premature wearout of the muffler is a frequent problem; it's often covered by Nissan's "goodwill" warranty, wherein the company and dealer will contribute 50 percent of the replacement cost.

VEHICLE HISTORY: 1995—A longer wheelbase (adding to interior room), a new 3.0L engine, and more rounded styling. They compete well with fully equipped Camrys, entry-level Infinitis, and Lexus models. Nevertheless, tall passengers will find the interior a bit cramped, and the automatic transmission is often slow to downshift and isn't always smooth. **1997**—Models got a new front-end restyling. **2000**—Version was redesigned to offer more power, interior space (particularly for rear-seat passengers), and safety/convenience features. **2001**—Carried over relatively unchanged, except for an Anniversary edition equipped with a 227-hp 3.0L V6 taken from the Infiniti I30. **2002**—Completely revamped, featuring a 260-hp 3.5L V6 coupled to a 6-speed manual or 4-speed automatic transmission; revised interior trim, larger front brakes, new front-end styling, a power driver's seat, xenon headlights, and 16-inch wheels. **2003**—GLE gets standard front side air-bags. **2004**—Another redesign adds to the size and weight, along with five more horses. Once again, quality takes a big hit.

Each Maxima redesign has been followed by an increase in owner complaints, a normal occurrence with most revamped vehicles. Usually after a year or two, quality rebounds and complaints diminish. This hasn't happened with the Maxima because of a close succession of major changes over the past three years.

Recent redesigns have hobbled the powertrain. Owners have difficulty controlling the engine speed with the gas pedal; there's engine popping and knocking when accelerating; surging or stalling when braking or decelerating; and transmission malfunctions galore. Premature front brake pad wear and rotor warpage; a choppy, jarring suspension; excessive front-end vibrations; faulty ignition coils; and inadequate headlight illumination continue to be major problems.

The 2004 revamped Maxima has even worse quality problems, as confirmed on the *Maxima.Org* website and by "Craig," a *Lemon-Aid* correspondent and Maxima owner:

> Phil: attached is my "master listing" of the 6th generation Maxima problems. Many owners are mad as hell the quality has dropped so much from previous versions of the cars. As well, many owners are sick and tired of inept dealers, who cannot fix the problems.
>
> A few problems, such as brake and wheel shimmy, orange peel paint and broken struts, and the "skyview" roof window known for spontaneous shattering, seem to have no Nissan solution. Here are the links: *http://www.harjothundal.com/maximaorg/04maxskyview2.pdf* and *http://www.harjothundal.com/maximaorg/04maxskyview3.pdf*.

Quality Issues List

Brake shimmy or judder when braking from highway speed

Wheel shimmy between 45 and 65 mph when driving

Glove box misalignment

Left turn signal won't return to center position

Orange peel paint

Grill peeling

Shift plate scratches too easily

Display screen scratches too easily, is foggy or has condensation inside

Rear parcel shelf vibrating and/or noise

Broken strut(s)

Harsh automatic shifting (especially when cold) with 5 speed auto

Gear grind from 1st to 2nd

Slow seat heaters

Instrument cluster plastic protectors peel

Weak radio reception

Windows slow to roll down

Side mirrors won't reposition

Seat shifting

Rear speaker "beeping"

Screeching sound – loose heat shield at 2000 rpm

Transmission failure

Air bag warning label on visor bubbling up

Sunroof deflector hitting glass

Door trim pieces easily get rub marks

HID lights – high beam won't return to low beam

HID lights – burn out prematurely

Fog lights – burn out prematurely

Car won't start (loose fuel pump connector at fuse panel)

Right floorboard soaked floor

Liquid running sound in A/C system, especially after cold start

Stiff doors after sitting for awhile

Skyview roof exploding

Armrest won't stay down and cup holder comes out of track

Leaking sunroof

Plastics flexing and squeaking inside cabin

Stereo buttons on steering wheel don't work

This is clearly a situation where one cure definitely does not fit all. It seems the dealers lean toward all the "usual suspects" before they resort to the steering rack friction adjustment that has cured the shimmy for some of the most persistent cases. Hard starting can be traced in some cases to a loose fuel pump connector at the fuse panel.

 ## Safety Summary

All years: Airbag failed to deploy. • Sudden loss of power, resulting in inoperative brakes and steering. • Chronic stalling. • Erratic transmission performance. • ABS failures. **1998**—Vehicle intermittently accelerates while braking. • Frequent windshield wiper failures. **1999**—Airbags failed to deploy. • Throttle "shock" and transmission hesitation. • Frequent ignition coil failures. • Vehicle pulls constantly to the left. • Cruise control resume feature doesn't work. • Power door locks cycle from lock to unlock. **2000**—Early replacement of the catalytic converter (alerted by Check Engine light) and the #6 ignition coil. Stand your ground; both are covered by extended warranties. • Poor headlight illumination. • A chlorine-type smell permeates the interior. **2001**—Engine compartment fire. • Steering lock-ups and loss of brakes. **2002**—Vehicle suddenly swung to the right. • Steering wheel overheats. • Sudden acceleration in Reverse with gearshift lever indicating Drive. • ABS and traction control malfunction every time car is washed. • Front wheels lock up or get no power; ABS light remains lit. • Car has pronounced hesitation upon acceleration:

> When driving vehicle out of a parking lot, at about 15 mph [24 km/h], I pressed gas pedal and car did not respond (there seems to be no traction on wheels for about 10 seconds), then "slip" light starts flashing for about 3 seconds. After this, vehicle starts getting traction again and light stops flashing.

• Vehicle accelerates when foot taken off accelerator. • Defective mass air sensor or crank sensor causes sudden loss of power and transmission bucking and jerking. • Vehicle rolled backward when parked on an incline. • Right front wheel buckled when brakes were applied. • While parking, vehicle surged when brakes were applied, and car hit a brick wall. • Faulty air control valve causes sudden acceleration. • Suspension transverse link failed, causing loss of control; owners report that cars not in the recall have the same defect. • Lower control arm failure like in recall notice, but car isn't among those recalled. • Chronic brake failures. • Xenon headlights are easily stolen and expensive to replace:

> Headlights easily stolen on Nissan Maxima 2002, 2003. I have a 2002 Maxima Se and the other day, my headlights were stolen while the car was parked outside my mother-in-law's house. I found out this has been an ongoing problem with this vehicle and Nissan isn't telling anyone about this problem when purchasing this vehicle [...] the way the lights are connected they are easily stolen and will be an ongoing problem as long as you own this vehicle. Nissan will retrofit new lights at the owner's expense, about $300.00.

• Moisture collects in the headlights. • Windshield wiper doesn't work in cold weather; fluid line freezes up. • Sunroof opens on its own, allowing rain and debris to enter. • Front passenger side window won't stay closed. • Back window suddenly shattered. • Rear quarter window air leaks. • Trunk water leaks. • Original tires leak air. • Hood and front bumper paint chipping. **2003**—O_2 sensor failure. • Hard to read instrument panel lights. • Passenger-side airbag deployed on its own. • Paint chips easily. • Xenon headlight thefts. **2004**—Excessive steering wheel shimmy. • Vehicle underway at 100 km/h when suddenly the steering wheel locked up and the brakes failed. • While vehicle was in motion, the front wheels locked up, causing extensive undercarriage damage. • Vehicle suddenly swerved out of control; vehicle suddenly accelerated in Reverse when put into Drive. • Sudden acceleration upon start-up (a faulty air control valve is suspected). • Unable to control engine speed with the accelerator pedal. • Vehicle stalls without warning in cold weather (suspect the computer module). • Fuel leaks from seal when over-filled. • Excessive front-end vibrations. • Strong bleach-type odour permeates the interior. • Many complaints that the headlights are poorly designed, placing the high beams too high for adequate visibility; drivers complain they can't see between the high and low beams. • Trunk lid and latch are hazardous when raised. • Several incidents where the skyview roof shattered:

> While driving a 2004 Maxima, out of nowhere the glass roof exploded outward. Glass covered me and the backseat of the car. Nothing hit the car. I went under no overpasses, there were no other vehicles around me at the time. I nearly lost control of the car and suffered minor scratches to forehead and arm from the shattered glass. I strongly feel that this was some sort of defect and want this documented as to prevent further injury to other driver's of this make vehicle.

• Sunroof opens and closes on its own. • Steering wheel overheats in direct sunlight. • The driver-side windshield washer may not work in cold weather. • Tire tread separation.

Secret Warranties/Internal Bulletins/Service Tips

All models/years: Defective catalytic converters that cause a rotten-egg smell may be replaced free of charge under Nissan's emissions warranty; the same principle applies to EVAP canister charcoal leakage. • TSB #P195-006 looks at the many causes and remedies for excessive brake noise. • Troubleshooting MIL light alerts. **All models: 1995–98**—An inoperative power seat may require a new drive cable. **1995–99**—Blower motor noise can be cured by installing a new blower motor cover. • A front brake groan when stopping is addressed in TSB #99-032. • A rear brake groan or hum can be fixed by readjusting the parking brake cable. • If the rear brakes squeak or squeal when cold, replace the rear brake pads with upgraded ones. • Guidelines for correcting steering pull or drift. • Tips on eliminating a foul odour emanating from the sunroof sunshade. **1996–99**—Diagnostic tips for fixing a front seat belt that's slow to retract. **1998–99**—An On-Off transmission throttle shock can be attenuated by installing an upgraded ECM. **1999**—Guidelines for correcting rocker panel creaking or popping. **2000**—Low idle or stalling in gear. • Excessive brake vibration countermeasures. • Right front strut noise. • Rear bumper scratched by trunk lid. • Tips on silencing interior squeaks and rattles and front brake groan. **2000–01**—Automatic transmission gear slippage. **2000–02**—Doors may intermittently lock by themselves. **2000–03**—Driver's seat won't go forward or backward. • Abnormal shifting (the control valve assembly is the likely culprit, says TSB #NTB04-035). **2001–02**—Rear brake caliper clunk, rattle, or knock. • Rear suspension bottoms out (also an Infiniti problem). • Hood vibration. **2002**—Erratic sunroof operation. • Radio ignition static. • Driver's power seat won't move forward or backward. • Clutch howling. **2002–03**—Hesitation upon acceleration. • Lack of engine power. • Sunroof operates on its own. **2003**—Navigation screen stuck on "please wait." • Troubleshooting brake noise and judder. **2004**—Cold upshift shock; abnormal shifting. • Hard start after a cold soak. • Front brake noise. • AC gurgling noise. • Exhaust ticking noise. • Water leaks from roof. • Headlamp fogging.

MAXIMA PROFILE

	1996	1997	1998	1999	2000	2001	2002	2003	2004
Cost Price ($)									
Base	27,998	27,998	27,998	28,598	28,598	29,000	32,900	32,900	34,500
Used Values ($)									
Base ▲	5,500	7,000	8,000	10,000	13,000	15,000	18,000	22,000	27,000
Base ▼	5,000	6,000	7,000	8,500	11,500	14,000	16,500	20,500	25,500
Reliability	④	④	⑤	⑤	⑤	⑤	⑤	⑤	❸
Crash Safety (F)	④	④	④	④	—	④	④	④	⑤

All ratings on a numbered scale where ⑤ is good and ❶ is bad. See pages 100–101 for a more detailed description.

PART THREE • LUXURY CARS

374

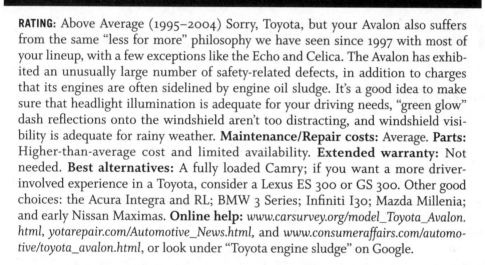

Side	—	4	4	4	—	4	4	4	4
Offset	1	3	3	3	3	3	3	3	5
Head Restraints (F)	—	2	2	3	3	5	5	5	1
Rear	—	—	—	2	—	—	—	—	—
Rollover Resistance	—	—	—	—	—	—	4	4	4

Toyota

AVALON ★★★★

RATING: Above Average (1995–2004) Sorry, Toyota, but your Avalon also suffers from the same "less for more" philosophy we have seen since 1997 with most of your lineup, with a few exceptions like the Echo and Celica. The Avalon has exhibited an unusually large number of safety-related defects, in addition to charges that its engines are often sidelined by engine oil sludge. It's a good idea to make sure that headlight illumination is adequate for your driving needs, "green glow" dash reflections onto the windshield aren't too distracting, and windshield visibility is adequate for rainy weather. **Maintenance/Repair costs:** Average. **Parts:** Higher-than-average cost and limited availability. **Extended warranty:** Not needed. **Best alternatives:** A fully loaded Camry; if you want a more driver-involved experience in a Toyota, consider a Lexus ES 300 or GS 300. Other good choices: the Acura Integra and RL; BMW 3 Series; Infiniti I30; Mazda Millenia; and early Nissan Maximas. **Online help:** *www.carsurvey.org/model_Toyota_Avalon. html*, *yotarepair.com/Automotive_News.html,* and *www.consumeraffairs.com/automotive/toyota_avalon.html*, or look under "Toyota engine sludge" on Google.

 ## Strengths and Weaknesses

This near-luxury four-door offers more value, interior space, and performance than do other cars in its class that cost thousands of dollars more. A front-engine, front-drive, mid-sized sedan based on a stretched Camry platform, the six-passenger Avalon is bigger than the rear-drive Cressida it replaced and similar in size to the Ford Taurus. Sure, there's a fair amount of Camry in the Avalon, but it's quicker on its feet than the Camry, better attuned to abrupt manoeuvres, and 5 cm (2 in.) longer. In fact, there's more rear-seat legroom than you'll find in either the Taurus or the new Chevrolet Lumina. It's close to the Dodge Intrepid in this respect.

VEHICLE HISTORY: 1997—More power, torque, and standard features. **1998**—Seat belt pretensioners, side airbags, new headlamps and tail lights, and a new trunk lid and grille. **2000**—Restyled and considerably improved. It's more powerful, roomier, and full of more high-tech safety and convenience features. **2003**—More styling upgrades and revised gauges.

Quality control is better than average, though steering, suspension, and fuel system components are failure-prone, and many owners have complained of engine sludge forcing them to spend thousands of dollars for engine repairs (now covered by a "goodwill" extended warranty, shown below in 1997–2002 "Secret Warranties/Internal Bulletins/Service Tips" section). Owners also have some performance gripes that include numerous electrical system glitches, premature front brake repairs and suspension strut failures, power steering that's a bit too light, hydroplaning, excessive body lean, and under-steer when cornering. Body construction and assembly are fairly good, although rattles are commonplace for all model years (see *www.carsurvey.org/viewcomments_review_35534.html*), trunk leaks have been reported on the '99 models, and paint flaking has afflicted some 2001–03 models. Except for some engine sludge complaints, premature brake wear, and body and accessories glitches (wind noise, AC, and audio system malfunctions), the 2002–03s have had few problems.

 ## Safety Summary

All years: Airbags failed to deploy in an accident. • Sudden, unintended acceleration. • Bridgestone/Firestone, Dunlop, and Michelin tire failures. **1998**—Vehicle caught fire at fuel filler neck when getting gas. • Gas tank fuel hose leaks fuel. • Airbag deployment caused severe chest and chin injuries. • Front seat reclined suddenly when vehicle was hit from the rear. • Engine surges and drops rpm rapidly and unexpectedly when engaging cruise control or when taking foot off the gas pedal. • Power-steering pump failure and fluid reservoir leakage. • Early replacement of brake pads, calipers, and rotors. • Front suspension bangs and clanks when going over a bump of any size, and rear suspension bottoms out. • Constant vibration in steering wheel and accelerator while driving caused by fuel pressure regulator. • Loose driver's seat. • Kick panel falls off repeatedly. **1999**—Airbag warning light comes on for no reason. • Cruise control operates erratically. • Brake pedal went to floor with little effect. • Car shifts poorly (hesitates and jerks) when you let off the gas and then accelerate, or do a rolling stop. **2000**—Automatic transmission slippage. • Brake pedal went to the floor with no braking effect. • Driver's seat rocks back and forth. • Steering wheel off-centre. • Airbag light stays lit. • Dash lights and gauges reflect onto windshield. • Inadequate headlight illumination. • Horn failure. **2001**—Excessive highway wandering. • Engine surging at idle. • Flex hose came off the charcoal canister, causing warning light to come on when refuelling. • Front and rear suspension bottoms out when carrying four adults. • Insufficient steering feedback. • Jerky acceleration. • Sudden failure of the instrument and information panel lighting and headlights. • Driver's side-view mirror has a small viewing area. • At night, the instrument panel lights and gauges reflect a green glow onto the windshield. **2002**—Cruise control doesn't slow car when going downhill. • Vehicle veers to the left at high speeds; vehicle wanders left and right. • Driver-side seat belt doesn't retract. • Dash lights reflect onto the windshield. • Vehicle emits a strong sulfur odour, which Toyota bulletins claim is normal. **2003**—Extended braking distance caused by improperly installed brake lines. • Front brakes appear to apply themselves. • Steering wheel blocks view of speedometer; hard to read gearshift position gauge at night. • Panel glass overheats while driving. • Incorrect readings from the fuel range finder. **2004**—Sudden acceleration. • Rear wheel seized while vehicle was underway. • Stalling when AC is activated.

Secret Warranties/Internal Bulletins/Service Tips

All models: 1990–2000—Brake pad clicking may be corrected by use of a special Toyota-recommended grease; however, some owners say it's not very effective. **1995–2000**—A power-steering squeak can be silenced by installing a new rack end shaft. **1997–99**—Front suspension noise can be eliminated by changing the suspension support. **1997–2002**—Extended warranty will pay for engine sludge damage up to eight years, without any mileage limitation. **2000**—Roof leaks water. • Sliding roof and door mirror noise. **2000–01**—Measures to reduce instrument panel luminosity. • Wheel bearing ticking noise. • Door popping and creaking. **2000–04**—Fuel door hard to open. **2003**—Blank navigation screen. **2004**—Correction for vehicle tendency to pull to the left.

AVALON PROFILE

	1996	1997	1998	1999	2000	2001	2002	2003	2004
Cost Price ($)									
XL	33,368	33,718	34,688	35,605	36,595	36,370	38,365	—	—
XLS	35,778	36,188	37,868	42,515	43,800	44,710	45,135	45,560	45,830
Used Values ($)									
XL ▲	5,500	7,000	9,000	11,500	15,000	17,000	21,000	—	—
XL ▼	5,000	6,000	7,500	10,000	13,500	16,000	19,000	—	—
XLS ▲	6,500	8,500	10,000	12,500	16,000	20,000	23,000	31,000	36,000
XLS ▼	5,500	7,500	9,000	11,000	14,500	18,500	21,500	29,000	34,000
Reliability	④	⑤	⑤	⑤	⑤	⑤	⑤	⑤	⑤
Crash Safety (F)	④	④	④	—	❸	❸	④	④	④
Side	—	⑤	⑤	—	④	④	④	④	④
Offset	❷	❷	❸	❸	⑤	⑤	⑤	⑤	⑤
Head Restraints (F)	❶	❶	❸	❸	❸	❶	❶	❶	❶
Rear	—	—	❶	❶	—	—	—	—	—
Rollover Resistance	—	—	—	—	—	—	④	④	④

Volvo

RATING: Average (1993–2004). Surprisingly, for a car company that emphasizes its commitment to safe cars, the 850 and 70 series have quite a few safety-related defects reported by owners, including engine and seat fires, loss of steering, sudden acceleration, transmission failures, electrical shorts, light failures, and tire blowouts. As if this weren't bad enough, Ford's cost-cutting and sadistic customer relations have left many new and used buyers leery of getting a Volvo. **Maintenance/Repair costs:** Higher than average, and repairs must be done by a Volvo dealer. **Parts:** Higher-than-average cost and limited availability. **Extended warranty:** A good idea, considering that even some of the most mundane repairs can be costly to perform. **Best alternatives:** Don't waste your money on a 1997 850; the 1996 models are virtually identical. The 1998 model 850s were renamed the C70, S70, and V70; they also have a disappointingly high number of safety-related deficiencies reported to the U.S. federal government. Other choices: Acura Integra and RL; BMW 3 or 5 Series; Infiniti I30; Mazda Millenia; early Nissan Maximas; and Toyota Avalon. **Online help:** *www.volvospy.com, www.consumeraffairs.com/automotive/volvo.htm, www.consumeraffairs.com/automotive/volvo_fires.html,* and *www.carsurvey.org.*

 ## Strengths and Weaknesses

Bland, but practical to the extreme, with plenty of power, good handling, and lots of capacity. For 1997, the 850 GLT got a bit more lower-end torque, while the turbo version was upgraded with electrically adjusted front passenger seats and an in-dash CD player. The base 850 sedan uses a 2.4L 24-valve, 168-hp 5-cylinder engine hooked to a front-drive powertrain. (An all-wheel-drive version is available only in Canada and Europe.) Wagons use the same base power plant, hooked to a 5-speed manual or optional 4-speed electronic automatic. GLTs have a torquier, turbo variant of the same power plant that boosts horsepower to 190.

The sports sedan T5 is a rounder, sportier-looking Volvo that delivers honest, predictable performance but comes up a bit short on the "sport" side. Volvo's base turbo boosts horsepower to 222, but its new T-5R variant uses an upgraded turbocharger that boosts power to 240 horses—for up to seven seconds. Passenger space, seating comfort, and trunk and cargo space are unmatched by the competition. Braking on dry and wet pavement is also exemplary. The ride of both the sedan and the wagon deteriorates progressively as the road gets rougher and passengers are added. Turbo versions are particularly stiff, and passengers are constantly bumped and thumped.

The 850 hasn't escaped the traditional AC, electrical system, and brake problems that afflict its predecessors. Additionally, owners have complained that the early models have uncomfortable seat belts, insufficient rear travel for the front seats, and many body hardware deficiencies.

70 series and 90 series

Making its debut for the 1998 model year, the 70 series is basically the discontinued 850 using a nom de plume. The letters S, V, and C preceding the numerical designation stand for sedans, wagons, and coupes. The 90 series is a re-designated rear-drive 960, and, as with the 70 series, sedans are indicated by an S and wagons by a V. Both the 70 and 90 series are carried over relatively unchanged, except for their names.

With the front-drive 70 series, all-wheel drive is offered with the wagons, and the base 2.4L 5-cylinder engine comes with three horsepower ratings: 168, 190, and 236 hp. Only two transmissions are available: a manual 5-speed (relatively rare) and an automatic 4-speed. Handling is superb, with the suspension dampened somewhat for a more comfortable ride than what many European imports offer. AWD performs flawlessly, road and body noise are muted, and the cars are well appointed with a full array of standard safety features, with the exception of traction control, which is optional.

On the downside, rear seating is cramped for three adults, and the instrument panel appears overly busy, with a confusing array of gauges, instruments, and controls on the centre console. Plus, the three rear head restraints induce claustrophobia while severely restricting rear visibility.

The 90 series has plenty of room for three rear seat passengers and its 181-hp V6 performs very smoothly and fairly quietly, providing plenty of power for passing and merging. The car's tight turning circle makes parking a snap, and the suspension has been tuned for comfort rather than performance. Still, handling is quite good. Once again, the large rear head restraints obstruct rear visibility.

As far as quality control and dealer servicing are concerned, Volvo technical service bulletins and owner complaints indicate that factory defects on all models have been on the rise for the past five years. For example, the cars' electrical system may shut down in rainy weather or when the car is passing over puddles; headlights, turn signal lights, and other bulbs burn out monthly; dash lights suddenly go berserk when the car drives through puddles; power window switches and locks fail constantly; wheels are easily bent; the turn signal lever doesn't return; airbags deploy for no reason; and springs are noisy.

The above defects clearly show that there's less stringent quality control at the factory level since Ford acquired the company and that Volvo is counting on Ford and

Volvo dealers to repair their engineering mistakes. On the other hand, Volvo has improved service and warranty relations by accelerating service training programs. But the effort may be too little, too late: Volvo sales have plummeted and many dealers are trying to bail out before Ford's mismanagement ruins them.

C70

The C70's strong points: good acceleration with lots of torque, exceptional steering and handling, first-class body construction and finish, and predicted better-than-average reliability. Its weak points: difficult rear seat entry/exit, some engine turbo lag, excessive engine noise, a jarring suspension, and an uncertain future.

Seating four comfortably, this luxury coupe and convertible is based on the 850 (pardon, S70) platform, and marketed as a high-performance Volvo. It comes with two turbocharged engines: a base 2.4L 190-hp inline 5-cylinder and a 2.3L 236-hp variant. Either engine can be hooked to a 5-speed manual or a 4-speed automatic transmission. Of the two engines, the 190-hp appears to offer the best response and smoothest performance. Acceleration is impressive, despite the fact that the car feels underpowered until the turbo kicks in at around 1500 rpm—a feature that drivers will find more frustrating with a manual shifter than with an automatic. Steering and handling are first class, fit and finish above reproach, and mechanical and body components are top quality.

The only things not to like are turbo lag, tire thumping caused by the high-performance tires, excessive engine and wind noise, and power-sliding rear seats that require lots of skill and patience.

S40 and V40

Volvo's latest small sedan and wagon come with a 1.9L 150-hp turbocharged 4-cylinder engine coupled to an automatic transmission. Two side airbags, anti-lock brakes, air conditioning, cruise control, and power windows are also standard. The 2001 model got a minor facelift, an upgraded engine and 5-speed automatic transmission, side-curtain airbags, and some handling improvements; 2002s were carried over unchanged.

These models have generated an unacceptably high number of complaints concerning chronic brake repairs, automatic transmission failures, fuel system malfunctions leading to poor driveability, and myriad electrical shorts and body defects.

 **Safety Summary**

All models: 1998—Passenger-side airbag suddenly deployed while vehicle was parked. • Frontal and side airbags failed to deploy in a collision. • Right front wheel assembly disengaged from car while vehicle was underway, causing loss of control and an accident. • Vehicle suddenly accelerated; brakes locked up. • Stalling while underway caused by defective air mass sensor. • A piece of the vacuum brake system came loose, causing engine rpm to surge and spontaneously locking up the brakes. • Transmission randomly fails to engage in Reverse gear, or kicks strongly when going into Reverse. • Frequent battery failures caused by battery not holding its charge. • Headlights and other lights burn out frequently. • Two incidents where the front turn signal socket smouldered and charred. • Driver's seat belt doesn't retract when disconnected. • Continental tires tread separation. • Frequent tire blowouts. • Wheels are easily bent, causing excessive vibration. • Defective door lock pin makes it difficult to open or close door. • Weak trunk lid struts allow lid to fall. • Dashboard causes excessive glare on windshield. • Tall front seats and head restraints obstruct visibility. **1999**—Sudden acceleration when applying brakes. • Vehicle shuts down when making a left turn. • Airbags failed to deploy. • While underway, driver seat suddenly moved backward. • Fuel fumes leak into interior. • Brake pedal locks up. • Chronic light failures. • Automatic door locks and trunk lock fail to open. • Automatic gas tank door jams shut. • Tailpipe extends beyond bumper, burning occupant. • Inside door handles pinch fingers. *C70:* **2001**—Power window noise. *S40, V40:* **2001**—Under-hood electrical fire. • Cracked fuel regulator pump spilled fuel onto hot engine and spread fumes into the interior. • Sudden, unintended acceleration when vehicle put into Drive. • Chronic stalling attributed to faulty idle control valve and air mass meter. • Complete loss of braking. • Brake pedal hard to depress, reducing brake effectiveness. • Brakes don't stop vehicle in a reasonable distance. • Brake pedal is too close to the gas pedal. • Brake pedal snapped, went to the floor while going downhill. • When applying the brakes in cold weather, pedal won't depress, causing extended stopping distance (dealer confirmed vacuum pump motor was defective). • Premature replacement of the front and rear rotors and pads:

> I have a 2001 S40 with 30,000 miles [48,000 km] on it. I have had nothing but problems with the brakes and headlamps. I have replaced the front brakes and rotors three times. I have replaced the rear rotors once and the pads twice. The headlamps constantly blow out. I wrote Volvo and they tell me the brakes go because of the material they use. Apparently it is soft. Too bad they did not tell me I would incur these expenses before I leased it.

• Vehicle pulls to the left when accelerating or coming to a stop. • Repeated automatic transmission failures. • Airbag light stays lit. • Faulty forward/backward seat adjustment. • Noisy engine and sunroof. **2002**—Sudden, unintended acceleration. • Airbags failed to deploy. • Annoying reflection of the dash into the windshield (see *www.volvospy.com*). • ABS failure. • Rear brake pads wore out prematurely and ruined the rotors. • Horn is hard to activate. **2003**—Transmission slips from 2nd to 3rd and shifts harshly:

This transmission slipping usually lasts for 2 to 3 secs and this loss of power can easily put me into a major accident.

• Faulty engine fuel line. • Michelin tire blowout allegedly because of a factory defect. *V40:* More complaints that the pedal won't depress, causing total brake loss or extended stopping distance and premature wearout of the front brake pads (around 20,000 km). • A new wiring harness is available to extend the life of low-beam headlight bulbs. • Under a special program, Volvo will replace the front door window to prevent excessive noise. This replacement is contingent upon a customer complaint. • Correction for front seat whining or creaking. **2002**—Poor braking with ABS. • Dash reflects onto windshield. *S70, V70:* **2000**—Airbags failed to deploy. • Vehicle suddenly pulls to one side while cruising. • Unexpected total loss of power. • Engine sputters and then shuts off. • Prematurely worn front stabilizer link rod. • Considerable brake fade at start-up. • Driver's window stuck in the down position. • AC allows exhaust fumes into the vehicle. • Chronic light failures. *V70:* **2001**—Excessive reflection of beige dash onto windshield. • Engine stalls in traffic; dealer says problem is caused by a "weak" fuel pump. • Engine mounts broke. • Manual transmission clutch sticks in cold weather. • Vehicle can roll away when parked on an incline. • Brake pedal is too close to gas pedal. • Front door indent doesn't hold door open. • Sunroof blew in while going through a car wash. • Rear tailgate door won't lock. • Coffee spilled from cupholder and shorted airbag computer. • Frequent bulb failures. **2002**—Shoulder belt crosses at neck. • Sunroof broke and fell into roof liner. **2003**—Emergency brake bracket comes apart. • Tires continually wear out prematurely. **2004**—Pirelli P6 tire sidewall bubbles and cracks. • Fuel gushes out when refuelling. • Vehicle pulls to the right. • Loose steering caused by prematurely worn out tie-rod.

Secret Warranties/Internal Bulletins/Service Tips

All models/years: Check the valve cover nuts at every servicing interval to prevent oil leakage. • Free front seat belt extenders available. **All models: 1996–99**—Automatic transmission final drive whining sound can be eliminated by putting a damper on the driveshaft. **1997–99**—Rear axle whining countermeasures. • Automatic transmission final drive whining correction tips. **1998–2000**—Installation of protective door lock covers. **1999**—Measures to reduce upper windshield moulding noise. **2000**—Special Service Campaign to service the engine oil filler grate. *850, S70, V70:* **1997–99**—There are at least a half-dozen bulletins addressing water leaks affecting the C70. • Rear axle whining countermeasures. **1997–2000**—Automatic transmission final drive whining correction tips. • **1998–2000**—Power-window noise can be silenced by following the procedures outlined in TSB #8330033. • Poor FM reception (static) can be improved by modifying the ground strap. **1998–2001**—Upgraded rear brake pads will be installed under warranty for more efficient and quieter braking. • Special Service Campaign provides for the free replacement of the headlight wiper stop lug. **2001**—Special Service Campaign to upgrade service life of headlights; free bulb replacement. *C70*: **2001**—Rough cold start; long cranking time, tachometer jump, and engine warning light activated. *S40, V40*: **2000**—Engine oil filler neck may be faulty. • Ticking noise may be heard from the canister purge valve. • The malfunction light (MIL) stays on while driving. **2001**—Exhaust manifold retaining nuts may be loose or missing. • Engine oil filler neck may be faulty. • A ticking noise may be heard from the canister purge valve. • The malfunction indicator light (MIL) stays on while driving. **2002**—Uneven idle. *S70, V70, C70*: **1997–2000**—Reducing power seat lateral movement. **1998–2000**—Special Service Campaign to upgrade service life of headlights; free bulb replacement. • Another campaign provides for the free replacement of the headlight wiper stop lug. **1999–2003**—Suspension resonance, vibration. **1999–2004**—Brake, exhaust system resonance, vibration. • Front seat loose, noisy. *C70*: **1998–2002**—Uneven idle. *S60, V70*: **2001**—Uneven idle. **2001–04**—Brake, exhaust system resonance, vibration. • Front seat noise, rocking. **2002–04**—Engine knock, rattle, and reduced power.

850, C70, S40, S70, V40, V70 PROFILE

	1996	1997	1998	1999	2000	2001	2002	2003	2004
Cost Price ($)									
850	29,995	31,995	—	—	—	—	—	—	—
Turbo	41,695	43,995	—	—	—	—	—	—	—
TLA/AWD	48,695	48,495	—	—	—	—	—	—	—
C70	—	—	54,675	49,995	50,595	52,995	49,995	59,595	63,995
S40	—	—	—	—	—	31,400	31,495	31,495	31,495
S70	—	33,995	34,995	35,195	—	—	—	—	—
V40	—	—	—	—	—	32,400	32,495	32,495	32,495
V70	—	—	33,295	36,295	36,495	37,495	37,995	37,995	37,995
Used Values ($)									
850 ▲	6,000	8,500	—	—	—	—	—	—	—
850 ▼	5,000	7,000	—	—	—	—	—	—	—
Turbo ▲	8,000	10,000	—	—	—	—	—	—	—
Turbo ▼	7,000	9,000	—	—	—	—	—	—	—
TLA/AWD ▲	9,000	11,000	—	—	—	—	—	—	—
TLA/AWD ▼	8,000	10,000	—	—	—	—	—	—	—
C70 ▲	—	—	11,500	14,000	18,500	22,500	28,000	44,000	52,000
C70 ▼	—	—	10,000	13,000	17,000	20,000	26,000	42,000	50,000
S40 ▲	—	—	—	—	—	15,000	18,500	22,000	25,000
S40 ▼	—	—	—	—	—	13,500	17,000	20,000	23,000
S70 ▲	—	9,500	11,500	14.000	—	—	—	—	—
S70 ▼	—	8,000	10,000	12,500	—	—	—	—	—
V40 ▲	—	—	—	—	—	16,000	19,000	22,000	26,000
V40 ▼	—	—	—	—	—	14,000	17,500	20,500	24,000

V70 ▲	—	—	10,500	12,500	15,000	18,000	22,000	27,000	30,000
V70 ▼	—	—	9,500	11,000	13,500	16,500	20,500	25,000	28,500
Reliability	5	5	4	4	4	4	4	4	4
Crash Safety (F)									
850	5	5	—	—	—	—	—	—	—
S40	—	—	—	—	—	—	—	—	4
S70	—	5	5	5	—	—	—	—	—
Side									
850	4	—	—	—	—	—	—	—	—
S40	—	—	—	—	—	—	5	5	5
S70	—	4	4	4	—	—	—	—	—
Offset (850/S70)	5	5	5	5	5	—	—	—	—
S40	—	—	—	—	—	—	5	5	5
S60	—	—	—	—	—	5	5	5	5
Head Restraints									
850	—	5	—	—	—	—	—	—	—
C70	—	—	—	5	—	5	—	5	5
S40/V40	—	—	—	—	—	5	5	5	5
S70	—	—	—	5	—	—	—	—	—
V70	—	—	—	5	—	5	5	5	5

900 SERIES, S80, S90, V90 ★★★

RATING: Average (1997–2004); Above Average (1989–96). The 1998 model 900s were renamed the S90 and V90, and have apparently inherited similar brake and electrical deficiencies. The model was renamed the S80 for the 1999 model year. It's interesting to note that the 960 series becomes cheaper to acquire than the 940 as the years progress. Unfortunately, as the revamped Volvos have aged, their reliability and safety have become more problematic. **Maintenance/Repair costs:** Higher than average, and repairs must be done by a (Ford) Volvo dealer. Yikes! **Parts:** Higher-than-average cost and limited availability. **Extended warranty:** A wise purchase simply to avoid expensive surcharges as Ford and Volvo mechanics and claims agents tap dance around who pays for warranty repair costs. **Best alternatives:** Acura Integra, TL, or RL; BMW 3 Series; Infiniti I30; Mazda Millenia; early Nissan Maxima; and Toyota Avalon. **Online help:** www.volvospy.com, www. consumeraffairs.com/automotive/volvo.htm, and www.carsurvey.org.

⬦ Strengths and Weaknesses

On one hand, these cars are practical to the extreme, with plenty of power, good handling, lots of carrying capacity, many standard safety features, and impressive crashworthiness ratings and accident injury claim data. On the other hand, weak

All ratings on a numbered scale where 5 is good and 1 is bad. See pages 100–101 for a more detailed description.

points include a jarring ride with vehicles equipped with 16- and 17-inch wheels; limited rear visibility; excessive engine, wind, and road noise; fuel-thirstiness (turbo models); declining quality control and increased frequency of safety-related deficiencies; and limited availability, causing soaring resale prices for recent reworked models with little room for negotiating.

Having debuted as essentially repackaged 760s, the flagship 900 Series rear-drive sedans and wagons have a much better reliability record than do the 240 and 700 Series, and have been on par with the 850, S70, and V70 over the last few model years. Both the 940 and 960 offer exceptional roominess and comfort, and are capable of carrying six people with ease. The wagon provides lots of cargo space and manages to do it in great style. Some owner gripes: The base 114-hp 2.3L engine is overpowered by the car's weight, excessive fuel consumption with the turbo option, and excessive road and wind noise at highway speeds. The 1996 960s were given front seat side-impact airbags and upgraded door locking.

Most of the 900 and 90 Series' deficiencies are identical to those seen in the S70s with some exceptions, like miscalibrated engine computer modules that cause random misfiring; rotten-egg and other exhaust odours that permeate the interior even after the catalytic converter is replaced; ignition switch, rear spring, and climate control unit failures; excessive on-road shudder/vibration, drifting, and hard steering; frequent fuel leaks; children suffering burns from the extended tailpipe; battery boiling over, causing acid to spray into engine compartment; and seat belts that catch in the door after failing to retract properly. Drivers also report that the front bumper is too low; it hits the wheel stop in parking lots, causing extensive bumper and wheelwell damage. Also, brakes continue to require frequent and expensive maintenance because of the poor durability of front and rear pads and the premature warpage of the brake rotors (15,000–30,000 km).

VEHICLE HISTORY: 1999—The S80 is a redesign of the S90 and offers several interesting new features, like a powerful 268-hp, transverse inline 6-cylinder engine and a sophisticated automatic transmission called the Geartronic—a 4-speed automatic with a feature for manually changing gears if one so desires. Additionally, the car is chock-full of safety features, has the largest interior of any Volvo, gives impressive performance and handling, and is attractively styled. **2001**—Dual-stage airbags and 16-inch wheels. **2002**—Engine tweaks give more power at lower rpm and the base engine drops a few horses. An in-trunk emergency release and new alloy wheels. **2004**—Refreshed styling, new gauges, and the addition of all-wheel drive.

Unfortunately, the S80's defects closely resemble the problems reported on prior years' models (see "Safety Summary") and seriously undermine Volvo's much-touted safety claims.

 **Safety Summary**

All models: 1998—Engine fire. • Airbags didn't deploy in a collision. • Fuel system leak (T-junctions and clamps replaced). • Other fuel leaks reported, where owners claim problem may relate to the fuel expansion tank or its hoses. • Vehicle suddenly accelerated. • Tire tread separation. Premature failure of the headlight, tail light, turning signal, driveshaft, front and rear brake pad and rotor, tailgate struts, window switches, and door locks. • Turn signal bulbs are scorched and plastic melted. • Total loss of braking ability. • Inappropriate placement of the tailgate handle causes one to pull the tailgate close to one's face, causing nose injury. • Brakes didn't work on an incline after vehicle stalled out. **1999**—Electrical short caused under-hood fire. • Another fire occurred as vehicle was backing into a parking space. • Airbags deployed inadvertently while car was in Park. • Vehicle suddenly accelerated while parking. • Accelerator pedal became stuck when passing another vehicle on the highway. • Several incidents where electrical switches continually malfunction, console and console knobs are hot to the touch, and tapes have melted in the tape deck. • Chronic short circuits of headlights and turn signal lights, leading to lights constantly burning out; wires melted in turn signal socket. • Engine wire harness cracked and fell apart; shorted out near engine and radiator. • Fuel pump leaks and other unspecified leaks from the gas tank area. • Fuel tank wouldn't accept fuel. • Fuel line sprayed small amounts of fuel from impact with a rock. It should have some kind of protective shield. • Tire tread separation. • Transmission grinding and vibration when underway. • Suddenly stalled while turning. • Steering wheel locks up when making a left turn. • Total brake failure and excessive brake fade after successive braking. • Defective steering rack replaced by dealer. • Front wheel fell off the axle. • Sudden ball joint failure also causes premature tire wear. • Chronic front end shimmy. • Subframe bushing problem. • Clunking sound when automatic transmission is put into Reverse. • Power windows operate erratically. **2000**—Severe glare onto windshield from beige dash. • Airbags failed to deploy. • Chronic stalling; refuses to accelerate on turns. • Signal light blown; housing melted. • Excessive front-end vibration, accompanied by a thumping or humming sound. • Broken right front ball bearing. • Brakes fail to stop car when applied shortly after start-up. • When stopped on an incline, vehicle will roll back even though transmission is set in Drive. • Front head restraints block view, and front seat belt retractor locks unexpectedly. • Poorly anchored fuel filler could spill fuel in an accident. **2001**—Engine compartment electrical fire. • Fuel tank leakage. • Vehicle doesn't track in a straight line. • Rough terrain causes vehicle to bounce and veer off in one direction. • Vehicle jolts forward when accelerator pedal is depressed. **2002**—Transmission doesn't hold on a hill. • Dash glares onto the windshield. • Child safety seat anchor may not be installed. **2003**—Fuel tank cracked. **2004**—Sudden stalling on the highway.

Secret Warranties/Internal Bulletins/Service Tips

All models/years: Check the valve cover nuts at every servicing interval to prevent oil leakage. • New steering components will reduce power steering knocking. • AC evaporator odours can be controlled by installing a new fan control module. • Tips on silencing noise from the manual front seats. **All models: 1992–98**—Oil pump leaks are usually because of loose pump retaining screws. **1997–99**—Rear axle whining countermeasures. • Automatic transmission final drive whining correction tips. • Upgraded rear brake pads to reduce grinding. • Upgraded weather stripping to reduce upper windshield moulding noise. • Installation of protective covers for door locks. • Improvements for door handle operation in cold weather. **1998**—Service Campaign #83 provides for the free replacement of faulty AC compressors. Service Campaign #83A and 83B provide for the free replacement of the front panel to prevent it from interfering with the AC. *S80:* **1999**—Uneven throttle. **1999–2000**—Automatic transmission shudder during upshift. **1999–2001**—New rear brake pads have been developed to reduce vibration. • Power seat movement on acceleration and deceleration. • Loose A-pillar trim. • Subframe bushing knocking noise. **1999–2003**—Suspension resonance, vibration. **1999–2004**—Brake, exhaust system resonance, vibration. **2000**—Free engine oil grate inspection. **2002–04**—Engine knock, rattles, and low power.

900 SERIES, S80, S90, V90 PROFILE

	1996	1997	1998	1999	2000	2001	2002	2003	2004
Cost Price ($)									
960	46,400	47,400	—	—	—	—	—	—	—
S90	—	—	47,400	—	—	—	—	—	—
V90	—	—	49,075	—	—	—	—	—	—
S80	—	—	—	49,995	55,995	54,395	54,395	54,895	54,895
Used Values ($)									
960 ▲	7,500	9,000	—	—	—	—	—	—	—
960 ▼	6,500	8,000	—	—	—	—	—	—	—
S90 ▲	—	—	10,500	—	—	—	—	—	—
S90 ▼	—	—	9,000	—	—	—	—	—	—
V90 ▲	—	—	11,500	—	—	—	—	—	—
V90 ▼	—	—	10,000	—	—	—	—	—	—
S80 ▲	—	—	—	13,000	17,000	21,500	28,000	36,000	42,000
S80 ▼	—	—	—	11,500	15,500	20,000	26,500	34,500	40,000
Reliability	④	③	③	③	③	④	④	④	④

Crash Safety (F)									
960	—	④	—	—	—	—	—	—	—
S80	—	—	—	—	—	⑤	⑤	⑤	⑤
Side (S80)	—	—	—	—	—	⑤	⑤	⑤	⑤
Offset (S80)	—	—	—	—	⑤	⑤	⑤	⑤	⑤
Head Restraints									
960/S90	—	⑤	—	—	—	—	—	—	—
S80	—	—	—	⑤	⑤	⑤	⑤	⑤	⑤
Rollover Resistance	—	—	—	—	—	—	—	⑤	⑤

All ratings on a numbered scale where ⑤ is good and ❶ is bad. See pages 100–101 for a more detailed description.

SPORTS CARS

Forbidden Love

Yes, we all know that these small, low cars with high-powered engines and seating for two are a dangerous choice for young drivers and scream out "mid-life crisis" when driven by pony-tailed, open-shirted, middle-aged men. They're astronomically expensive to insure, and they beg to be driven too fast.

But they are so much fun to drive, especially for those of us who missed our chance to own one in our youth because we were too poor, practical, and preoccupied with our Corollas and Cavaliers to give in to our primeval instincts.

If driving performance is important to you now, consider getting an agile, fun-to-drive small car, such as mid-1990s versions of the Acura Integra, Honda Civic, Mazda Miata, and Nissan Sentra SE-R. If you want to be a little more in your face, however, it's hard to lose money with a "muscle car" sportster built through 1974 (see Appendix III, "Bargain Beaters").

There are three kinds of sports cars to consider: the traditional two-seater roadster, styled much like the MGB of the early '70s or Mazda's Miata; sporty coupes and hatchbacks, like the Japanese Acura Integra, Honda Civic, Mazda MX-3, and Toyota Celica, which offer sportier styling, performance, and handling than their entry-level versions and are more versatile and cheaper to maintain than traditional sports cars; and muscle cars, which feature large engines and a few more creature comforts. The best deals in the last category are the V8-equipped Ford Mustang and the GM Camaro and Firebird.

Other notable recommended sports models are the Audi TT (a stylish Golf in drag); BMW Z3 (a looker that lacks the precise steering of a Miata); BMW Z4 (better steering and an upgraded suspension that equals the Boxster's); Mazda6 (plenty of horsepower to challenge, and with a stick shift not found on the Accord and the Camry); and the Mazda3.

Although Hyundai's Tiburon is more "show" than "go," it will give you some sports car thrills without the high repair bills. See Appendix II, page 498.

The Internet offers a comprehensive forum that goes into numbing detail as to what makes a good sports car at *www.sportscarforums.com*. Different cars are rated, service tips are given, and the age-old feud between Camaro/Firebird and Mustang owners is omnipresent.

Most sports cars, or "high-performance vehicles" as they're euphemistically named, don't offer the comfort or reliability of a Honda Civic, a Toyota Celica, or even a Hyundai Tiburon. Instead, they sacrifice reliability, interior space, and a comfortable suspension for speed, superior road handling, and attractive styling. They also need a whole slew of expensive high-performance packages, because many entry-level sports cars aren't very sporty in their basic form. Remember, too, that used sports cars often have serious accident damage that may not have been repaired properly, resulting in serious tracking problems because of a bent chassis.

Used, fully loaded sporty cars usually sell at a fraction of their original cost, and very few end up as collectibles. Most models that have been taken off the market—like the Toyota Supra, Nissan 300ZX, and Chevrolet Corvette ZR1—aren't likely to become collectors' cars with soaring resale values. Even discontinued Japanese sports cars like the Nissan 1600, which are usually in high demand, haven't done nearly as well as some of the British roadsters taken off the market at about the same time.

Like early Mustangs, 2002 and earlier GM Camaros and Firebirds can be fun cars to drive and make you a tidy profit as well, once they have been tricked out with some relatively inexpensive options. Not only are they relatively reliable and cheap to maintain, but their resale prices are fairly stable and there's plenty of used stock to choose from. But don't expect them to appreciate in value any time soon (although the early muscle versions are now breaking away from the pack).

Horsepower Hypocrisy

Sports car buffs usually equate performance thrills with high horsepower ratings, even though there are many other handling features that need to be considered. Nevertheless, automakers are just as fixated on horsepower and aren't above falsifying the figures to get a leg up on the competition. In 1999, Ford suckered over 5,000 Mustang SVT Cobra owners with 270-hp Cobras that they claimed had 320 horses. Two years later, Ottawa's Competition Bureau found Hyundai had boosted its ratings between 4 and 9 percent on its entire lineup for over a decade, and that Hyundai-owned Kia's 2001–02 model figures were also suspect. Again in 2001, Mazda claimed that the Miata's horsepower had jumped from 140 to 155. When owners found that the 2001 version was no quicker than the 2000 model, Mazda quickly revised its numbers down to 142.

But Mazda is still playing with horsepower figures: Its 2004 RX-8 is less powerful than originally thought. First presented as having a 250-hp engine, the number was dropped slightly to 247. Then Mazda restated its horsepower rating to a still-optimistic 238 and offered customers $500 and free basic maintenance for four years or 80,000 km (50,000 mi.), or a refund.

SPORTS CAR RATINGS

Recommended

General Motors Camaro, Firebird,
 Trans Am (1997–2002)

Mazda Miata (1990–2004)
Toyota Celica (2001–04; 1995–99)

Above Average

DaimlerChrysler Avenger, Sebring
 (2002–04)

Toyota Celica (2000; 1986–94)

Average

DaimlerChrysler Avenger, Sebring
 (2000–01)
Ford Mustang (1996–2004)

General Motors Camaro, Firebird,
 Trans Am (1994–96)
General Motors Corvette (1997–2004)

Below Average

DaimlerChrysler Avenger, Sebring
 (1995–99)
Ford Mustang (1980–95)

General Motors Camaro, Firebird,
 Trans Am (1992–93)
General Motors Corvette (1994–96)

Not Recommended

Ford Cobra (1999–2003)
General Motors Camaro, Firebird,
 Trans Am (1982–91)

General Motors Corvette (1977–93)

DaimlerChrysler

AVENGER, SEBRING ★★★★

RATING: Above Average (2002–04); Average (2000–01); Below Average (1995–99).
The Avenger and its more luxuriously appointed Sebring twin have had fewer factory-related defects than other new Chrysler designs, though this is faint praise
indeed. Drive a hard bargain, because the money you save will be eaten up in
transmission, engine head gasket, engine sludging (1998–2002 models), and AC
evaporator repair bills unless you get the 7-year powertrain warranty, threaten
small claims court action, or use your service manager successfully in getting
"goodwill" assistance. The Sebring convertible is an attractively styled bargain
ragtop. **Maintenance/Repair costs:** Average. Avenger repairs must be done by a
Chrysler dealer. **Parts:** Average cost and availability. **Extended warranty:** Yes, if

Chrysler's base warranty has expired. **Best alternatives:** Ford Mustang or Probe, GM Camaro or Firebird, Hyundai Tiburon, Mazda Miata, Nissan 240SX, and Toyota Celica. **Online help:** *www.autosafety.org/autodefects.html, www.datatown. com/chrysler, www.wam.umd.edu/~gluckman/Chrysler/index.html, www.daimlerchrys- lervehicleproblems.com,* and *intrepidhorrorstories.blogspot.com.*

 Strengths and Weaknesses

These coupes, sedans, and convertibles are good buys mainly because they've had fewer new-model "teething" problems than other Chrysler-built vehicles. Sebring is a reasonably priced luxury model equipped with standard amenities, including AC, bucket seats, and a tilt steering wheel, while the Stratus fills the sporty coupe niche with standard tinted glass and an awesome sound system.

These front-drives use powertrains and platforms from Mitsubishi's Eclipse and Galant, and also share most safety features and mechanical components, including standard dual airbags and a 150-hp 2.4L 4-banger along with a 2.7L V6, a 200-hp 3.0L V6, and a 3.5L V6.

VEHICLE HISTORY: 1995–99—Minor restyling touches and the dropping of the 4-cylinder engine in mid-1999. **2000**—Sebring convertible's suspension was retuned to give a more comfortable ride, and the same year's base Avenger was given additional standard equipment—notably, the ES's 2.5L V6 and automatic transmission. **2001**—The redesigned Sebring added a sedan, a more powerful V6, and a premium sound system. The Avenger was dropped. **2002**—Sebrings were joined by a 200-hp 2.7L, V6 R/T sedan equipped with a manual 5-speed gearbox. **2003**— Addition of four-wheel disc brakes. **2004**—Restyled front ends.

Acceleration is fairly good, though noisy, with the base 4-cylinder engine and a manual transmission; however, the 3.0L and 3.5L V6 are the engines of choice to overcome the power-hungry automatic transmission and to avoid a persistent 4-cylinder engine head gasket defect affecting all model years through 1999. Handling is better than average, and the ride is generally comfortable, except for a bit of choppiness because of the firm suspension.

The 2.7L V6 would normally be a good alternative to the small 4-cylinder; however, it is subject to early engine primary timing chain tensioner and tensioner O-ring failures and oil sludging on 1998–2002 models—a problem covered by a secret "goodwill" warranty. Owners also report automatic transmission failures, grinding when shifting, shuddering from a stop, and defaulting to Second gear; engine oil leaks; loss of steering and a clanking or rattling heard when turning over rough pavement; premature suspension replacement, brake wear and brake failures; ignition, electrical system, and power control module (PCM) glitches; sunroof malfunctions; and sloppy body construction (water leaks and lots of wind noise) as the areas most needing attention. Would you believe that the driver's seat motor burns out because it doesn't have a fuse? Replacement cost: $2,000!

The convertible top can fly off on early models, leaks water and air, and operates erratically. A faulty window regulator allows the window to run off its track. Poor design and sloppy construction allow water into the vehicle when window is partly opened; rear windshield sealant lets water leak into vehicle; wheel rims are easily bent and leak air from normal driving; there's excessive brake dust; a black goo oozes from body panels and the undercarriage; side door mouldings melt; and the airbag coating peels.

 Safety Summary

All models: 1995–99—Mitsubishi-built Avengers have had few safety-related incidents reported to NHTSA. Sebring safety failures over the same period were frequent and serious. *Sebring*: **1996–1999**—Engine head gasket failures occur around 100,000 km; covered by a "goodwill" warranty. **1998**—More of the same old complaints, like electrical short circuits, brake, and airbag complaints. • Reports concerning sudden acceleration, loss of steering control caused by the floormat blocking the steering column, bent wheel rims causing tire blowouts, seat belt lock-up, and alternator/battery failures have increased. • One new item: many complaints that the side door panel cladding falls off while cruising. **1998–2002**—2.7L engine oil sludging has generated over 1,000 complaints and is covered by a secret warranty similar to the head gasket failures seen with earlier models (see "Service Tips," below). • Timing chain failures with the same engine. **1999**—Vehicle caught fire after hitting bumper of other car at 8 km/h (5 mph). • Other fire reported from a leaking fuel hose. • Front airbags failed to deploy upon impact. • Many incidents where the throttle stuck while engaging Reverse. • Premature replacement of the lower lateral sway bar. • Automatic transmission rebuild after 61,000 km (38,000 mi.). • Split transmission line. • Delayed, noisy transmission shifting. • Slipped into Reverse and rolled downhill, despite being in Park with ignition off. • Constant velocity joint flew off in heavy traffic on Interstate. • Brakes don't grab sufficiently; complete loss of braking caused by loss of vacuum. • Defective rear defroster clip. • Windshield wipers suddenly stop working. • Convertible boot flew off while vehicle was underway. • Brake failure and extended stopping distance caused by defective wheel speed sensor, modulator, or master cylinder and brake pad disintegrating, causing rotor scoring. • Automatic transmission slipped out of gear while vehicle was cruising at 120 km/h; suddenly went to 50 km/h. • Transmission fluid leakage through a crack in the transmission case. • Driver's seat belt often unlatches and seatback side latch may fail. **2001**—Brake failure accompanied by sudden, unintended acceleration. • Brake caliper bolt fell off. • Brake and accelerator pedals are too close to each other. • Window shattered when convertible top was lowered. **2002**—When putting vehicle into Reverse, it sometimes surges forward. • Engine stalls out after fill-ups. • Sudden brake failure. • Suspension feels loose at higher speeds when passing over bumps or potholes. • Steering wheel catches and pulls right when turning. • Back windows suddenly exploded. • Brake and gas pedals are too close together. • Coupes have the driver's seat set at an angle that's disorienting. **2003—** Sudden loss of steering. • Driver's airbag deployed for no reason. • Tapping brakes locks them up. • Rodents can get into the heater blower area. • Headlights dim and shut off intermittently. **2004—**Airbags failed to deploy. • Sudden, unintended acceleration when stopped or accelerating. • Engine overheating and stalling. • Transmission slippage; not engaging the gear selected, and shifting to a higher and then a lower gear, making the car surge. • Annoying cricket noise and whistle when shifting. • Steering failure. • Excessive steering shake at idle. • Seat heater overheated. • Windshield wiper switch broke away from steering column. • Dash lights flicker and headlights may suddenly go off. • Horn may not work properly.

Secret Warranties/Internal Bulletins/Service Tips

All models: 1995–98—Delayed transaxle engagement can be corrected by installing an upgraded trailing-arm bushing. **1995–2001—**Front coil spring creak, pop, or squeak can be silenced by putting in coil spring insulators. • Intermittent loss of speed control can be prevented by installing new speed sensors. • Wind noise coming from the front windshield area is caused by wind lifting the windshield moulding at the glass. • Tips on reducing excessive front brake pulsation or shudder. • Paint delamination, peeling, or fading (see Part Two "Paint and Body Defects," pages 71–75). **1997–99—**New software will prevent the transmission from shifting erratically or falling into a Second gear "limp" mode. *Sebring:* **1996–99—**Upgraded engine head gasket. **1996–2000—**Steering wheel clunk or rattle. • Wet carpet (convertible). **1998–2002—**The 2.7L V6 engine sludging "goodwill" warranty isn't confirmed by any service bulletin, yet. Nonetheless, Chrysler spokesman Sam Locricchio told AutoWeek on September 3, 2004, that the automaker is working hard to "find a reasonable and appropriate resolution" of individual complaints. This problem may not go away. Chrysler hasn't shown any production changes that guarantee that the engine will not sludge up on the estimated 10 percent of 2005 Chrysler 300 and Dodge Magnums that are sold with the same V6 engine (mounted front-to-back rather than sideways). **2001—**Rough 2.7L engine idle. • Automatic transmission bump, sag, and surge. • Rear suspension squawk. **2001–02—**Moderate to severe highway engine surge. • Exhaust rattle, vibration. • Low or no cabin heat. • Loose, warped front door trim panel. **2001–03—**Erratic AC operation. **2001–04—**Poor AC operation. • Suspension, body pop or clunk noise. • Window fogging. **2002—**Hard to remove fuel cap. **2003—**Horn blows on its own. • Rear brake clunk. **2003–04—**Delayed gear engagement. • Harsh downshifts. **2004—**Driveability improvements: Engine stumbles, runs rough; idle fluctuation, or surge when at idle or coming to a stop. • Harsh 4–3 downshifts. • Low-speed transmission bumps. • New spark plug for 2.4L engine. • Pop/clunk sound from front of vehicle; engine snapping noise. • Steering column click. • Revised suspension lateral control links. • Door clunk noise. • Power seat won't adjust; front seat movement. • Intermittent loss of accessories. • Customer Satisfaction No. C30 relative to the PCM connector seal. • Window fogging.

AVENGER, SEBRING PROFILE

	1996	1997	1998	1999	2000	2001	2002	2003	2004
Cost Price ($)									
Avenger	18,954	18,780	19,280	20,360	—	—	—	—	—
Avenger V6	22,544	23,820	24,320	23,545	—	—	—	—	—
Sebring	19,514	21,420	21,500	23,380	26,525	—	—	—	—
Sebring V6	25,538	24,135	24,360	28,675	26,525	30,095	27,380	27,795	28,415
Convertible	25,210	27,030	27,530	32,100	32,585	33,595	33,580	34,515	35,855
Used Values ($)									
Avenger ▲	4,000	4,500	5,000	6,500	—	—	—	—	—
Avenger ▼	3,000	4,000	4,500	5,000	—	—	—	—	—
Avenger V6 ▲	4,500	5,000	5,500	7,000	—	—	—	—	—
Avenger V6 ▼	4,000	4,500	5,000	5,500	—	—	—	—	—
Sebring ▲	4,500	5,500	7,000	9,000	—	—	—	—	—
Sebring ▼	4,000	4,500	6,000	7,500	—	—	—	—	—
Sebring V6 ▲	4,000	5,000	6,000	7,500	8,500	11,000	12,500	15,000	18,000
Sebring V6 ▼	3,500	4,500	5,000	6,000	7,000	9,500	11,500	13,500	16,500
Convertible ▲	5,500	6,500	8,500	10,500	12,500	14,500	18,000	21,500	24,000
Convertible ▼	5,000	5,500	7,500	9,000	11,000	13,500	16,500	20,000	22,500
Reliability	2	2	3	3	3	3	4	4	4
Crash Safety (Avenger)	5	5	—	—	—	—	—	—	—
Sebring 2d	—	5	—	—	—	4	4	4	—
Sebring 4d	—	—	—	—	—	5	5	5	5
Sebring cvt.	—	4	—	—	—	3	3	3	3
Side (Sebring)	—	—	—	—	—	3	3	3	3
Sebring 4d	—	—	—	—	—	3	3	3	3
Sebring cvt.	—	—	—	—	—	3	3	3	3
Offset	—	—	—	—	—	3	3	3	3
Head Restraints (Avenger)	—	2	—	2	—	—	—	—	—
Sebring 2d	—	1	—	3	—	2	3	2	2
Sebring (Rear)	—	—	—	2	—	1	2	—	—
Rollover Resistance	—	—	—	—	—	5	5	5	5
Sebring 2d	—	—	—	—	—	—	—	4	4
Sebring cvt.	—	—	—	—	—	—	—	5	5

Ford

MUSTANG, COBRA ★★☆

RATING: *Mustang*: Average (1996–2004); Below Average (1980–95); *Cobra*: Not Recommended (1999–2003). Here's the problem: Ford has alienated its parts suppliers and reduced reliability through unrealistic price-cutting and last-minute, poorly thought-out component changes. Mustangs don't perform well on wet roadways and they have had a frighteningly high number of safety-related mechanical failures (chronic stalling, especially). Additionally, new crash data indicates the vehicles may be fire-prone following collisions at moderate speeds. GM's Camaro and Firebird are the Mustang's traditional competition as far as performance is concerned and represent the better buy. Ford has the price advantage, with a base Mustang costing a bit less than the cheapest Camaro, but it lags from a performance standpoint. The GM models also offer more sure-footed acceleration, crisper handling, standard ABS, a 6-speed transmission, and more comfortable rear seats. All 4-cylinder Mustangs should be shunned. **Maintenance/Repair costs:** Average, particularly because repairs can be done anywhere. **Parts:** Average cost, and parts are often sold for much less through independent suppliers. Some parts are continually back ordered, particularly if involved in recall repairs (cruise control components, for example). **Extended warranty:** A good idea for the powertrain. Best alternatives: Ford Probe, GM Camaro or Firebird, Hyundai Tiburon, Mazda Miata, and Toyota Celica. **Online help:** *www.autosafety.org/autodefects.html, forums.mustangworks.com, www.flamingfords.info, www.tgrigsby.com/views/ford.htm, www.antiauthority.com/cobra/service/#links, www.flatratetech.com, and www.blueovalnews.com.*

Strengths and Weaknesses

This is definitely not a family car. A light rear end makes the car dangerously unstable on wet roads or when cornering at high speeds. But for those who want a sturdy and stylish second car, or who don't need room in the back or standard ABS, the 1999–2000 Mustang is a pretty good sports car buy. Base models come equipped with a host of luxury and convenience items, which can be a real bargain once the base price has sufficiently depreciated—say, after the first three or four years. Off-lease models are particularly good buys these days.

1994–2004

These models got more powerful engines, better brakes, additional airbags, and a more rigid chassis to reduce rattles and water leaks (which didn't work). Unfortunately, Ford's performance- and safety-related problems are carried over year after year (see "Safety Summary"). Engines and transmissions are even more unreliable than before: Both the V6 and V8 have a propensity for chronic surging and stalling; blowing engine intake manifold and head gaskets; failed motor mounts; ticking and rattling at 3000 rpm until the car shifts into Second gear; poorly shifting automatic transmission, especially from First to Second gear; differential howling or whining (ring and pinion failure); engines that die when decelerating; fuel system glitches, highlighted by frequent fuel injector malfunctions; faulty differential carrier bearings; and prematurely worn clutch pressure plates. Owners also frequently complain of electrical short circuits causing instrument panel shutdown; the early replacement of brake rotors, pads, and calipers; and unbelievably poor fit and finish highlighted by paint defects, premature rusting, wind noise, water leaks, and clunks and rattles.

VEHICLE HISTORY: 1993—Cobra debuts. **1994**—The 4-banger replaced with a V6. Four-wheel disc brakes, dual airbags, and a more rigid chassis are added. No more hatchbacks. Mustangs now carry a base 3.8L V6 and an optional 4.6L V8. In addition, the high-performance limited edition Cobra variation delivers 90 more horses than the stock 4.6L V8 offers. The single- and twin-cam V8 options make the Mustang a powerful—if somewhat unsophisticated—street machine. V6 models are an acceptable compromise, even though the engines fail to deliver the gobs of power most performance enthusiasts expect. **1996**—A 4.6L V8 with upgraded spark plugs, and the Cobra received a 305-hp variant of the same power plant. **1998**—GT got a 10-hp performance boost. **1999**—Got fresh styling and another horsepower boost. That year, the V6 models also got suspension and steering gear upgrades; Ford also admitted that its 1999 SVT Cobra delivered up to 50 hp less than the 320-hp advertised. **2000**—Improved child safety seat anchoring. **2001**—GT models received hood and side scoops and larger wheels. All models got an upgraded centre console, blacked-out headlights, and spoilers. **2002**—New 16-inch alloy wheels; sporty Cobra stays home this year. **2003**—Three 4.6L V8 models: the GT with 260 hp, the new Mach 1 with 305 hp, and the 390-hp supercharged SVT Cobra. **2004**—Commemorative 40th anniversary badges.

 **Safety Summary**

All models/years: Regularly equipped Mustangs, like most rear-drive Fords, don't handle sharp curves or wet pavement very well. The rear end swings out suddenly, and the car tends to spin uncontrollably. Traction is easily lost and braking is hardly reassuring. • Serious concerns have been raised about the Mustang's fuel system failing safety integrity standards and about the tendency of the convertible's doors to jam shut in a 57 km/h frontal collision. • Transmission allows vehicle to roll away when parked on an incline; emergency brake disengages. • Airbag failed to deploy; inadvertent airbag deployment. • Sudden acceleration because of a stuck throttle. • Brake failure and premature replacement of the brake master cylinder. • Excessive vehicle vibration when accelerating. • Side windows fall off their tracks. **1998–99**—Fuel tank leaks. • Engine compartment fires. • Hood flew up unexpectedly while vehicle was underway. • Frequent stalling, hesitation, and power loss. • No airbag deployment; airbag-induced injuries. • Parking brake doesn't hold (traced to a broken ratchet assembly). • Brake pedal goes to floor without braking. • Steering system failure. • Right ball joint fractured, causing wheel to turn inward. • Tire sidewall tread separation. • Seat belt continually tightens up. • Other repeats of '97 problems: transmission, braking, and engine failures. • New problems: fire ignited in the centre console and dash areas, defective seat belt retractor and poor design allows belt to slip out of guide, stalling caused by fuel pump or fuel relay cut-off switch failure, and original equipment tire blowouts (sidewall splits). **2000**—There's an unusually large number of safety complaints recorded by NHTSA for year 2000 models. • Fumes from airbag deployment made passengers ill and temporarily blinded them. • Alternator melted battery wires; car caught on fire. • Automatic transmission sticks in Reverse. • Convertible top unlatches and flips up while vehicle is underway. • Hood flew up. • Head restraints sit too low. • Many reports of rear axle failures. • Brake calipers and lines were replaced to correct brake fluid leakage. • Multiple function switch failure causes headlights to suddenly go out. **2001**—Lower control arm came off. • Sudden brake lock-up. • Loose brake rotor responsible for collision. • Foot hits fuse box when engaging clutch pedal. • Seat belt retracted unexpectedly, nearly choking occupant, who had to be cut free. • Driver's seat rocks back when driving. **2002**—Fire ignited in the wiring harness under dash area. • Chronic stalling when coasting or braking, or when clutch is depressed. • Serpentine belt came off, causing loss of power steering and brakes. • Wheel lug nuts fell off. • Sudden acceleration. • Sudden loss of steering when making a left-hand turn. • Car left on an incline with transmission in Park and motor shut off rolled down after 10 minutes and hit a tree. • Airbags failed to deploy in a frontal collision. • Emergency brake ratchet assembly broke, making mechanism inoperable. • Gas spills out of fuel tank because clamps not sufficiently tightened. • Left front wheel fell off when the lower control arm and ball joint became loose. • Defective transmission spider gear. • Stuck gas pedal. • Seat belt continually tightens up when worn. • A light rear end makes the car dangerously unstable on wet roads or when cornering at moderate speeds. **2003**—Poorly designed speaker wires caused rear seat fire. • Airbags failed to deploy. • Gas pedal sticks. • Chronic stalling when decelerating. • Automatic transmission failures. • Loss of brakes. • Seat belt ratchets tighten. • Premature Goodyear tire blowout. • Water leaks through side windows. **2004**—Airbag failed to deploy. • Faulty rear differential; it whines and is wobbly when making turns. • Seatback collapsed from a rear-ender accident; seatback bolt broke while driving. • Head restraints don't adjust enough. • A fuel smell permeates the interior.

⌕ Secret Warranties/Internal Bulletins/Service Tips

All models/years: Paint delamination, peeling, or fading (see Part Two "Paint and Body Defects," pages 71–75). • Ford 7-year "goodwill" warranty extensions usually cover engine and transmission components. • Cold hesitation when accelerating, rough idle, long crank times, and stalling may all signal the need to clean out excessive intake valve deposits. These problems also may result from the use of fuels that have low volatility, such as high-octane premium blends. • Excessive oil consumption is likely caused by leaking gaskets, poor sealing of the lower intake manifold, defective intake and exhaust valve stem seals, or worn piston rings; install new guide-mounted valve stem seals for a better fit, as well as new piston rings with improved oil control. • A buzz or rattle from the exhaust system may be caused by a loose heat shield. • A thumping or clacking heard from the front brakes signals the need to machine the front disc brake rotors. **All models: 1985–2002**—Repeated heater core failures. **1994–98**—Loose rocker panel mouldings. **1994–2000**—Hood may be difficult to close. **1996–2001**—Manual transmission may stick in Reverse, or pop out of Reverse. **1997–99**—Delayed or no 2–3 upshift may be caused by a leaking accumulator seal. • Road noise or dust/water leaks in the luggage compartment can be fixed by sealing the wheelhouse flange. **1997–2000**—Automatic transmission fluid leaks at the radiator can be stopped by installing an O-ring on the transmission oil cooler fitting. **1998–99**—Tips for spotting abnormal ABS braking noise. **1999–2000**—An erratically operating front windshield wiper probably has a faulty multifunction switch. Replace it under warranty, says TSB #00-9-6. • Same thing goes for an inaccurate speedometer. **1998–2002**—Guidelines for replacing defective ignition lock cylinders. **1999–2001**—Troubleshooting a downshift clunk and a driveline whine upon coastdown. **1999–2003**—Cracked roof ditch material. **1999–2004**—Exhaust leak repair may be covered by "goodwill" (see bulletin above). **2000–01**—First gear ticking. **2001–02**—Some vehicles equipped with a 4.6L engine may exhibit a FEAD belt jump-off toss (see bulletin below). **2001–03**—Wind noise from the A-pillar area. **2001–04**—4.6L engine rattle. • AC panel vents rattle. **2002**—Service tips for reports of premature engine failure. • Air leaks in the intake manifold or engine. • Ford has found that engine cylinder heads often still leak after having been repaired. • Engine runs roughly after stopping. • In 4.6L engine, oil leaks from the head gasket area. • Oil pressure gauge shows low oil or no oil. • 3.8L engine may run roughly at idle; same engine may cause AM radio speaker interference. • Automatic transmission fluid leak near the radiator. • Manual transmission clashes or grinds. • Transmission ticking heard when First gear is engaged. • Rear whine heard during coastdown from 100 km/h. • Vehicles equipped with a 5-speed manual transmission may stumble or hesitate when cold. • Driveline

---

LEAKS FROM R/H EXHAUST PIPE

ARTICLE NO: 04-10-3   DATE: MAY 25, 2004

EXHAUST LEAK—RIGHT SIDE EXHAUST PIPE—3.8L AND 3.9L ENGINES 1999–2004 MUSTANG

ISSUE: Some 1999–2004 Mustang LX vehicles equipped with a 3.8L or 3.9L engine may exhibit an exhaust leak. The condition will typically be present on the right side exhaust pipe.

ACTION: To service order and install the appropriate service kit based on transmission type. The Kit contains a new inlet pipe condensation shield and exhaust hanger.

ACCESSORY DRIVE BELT— SLIPS OFF PULLEY WHEN WET

BULLETIN NO: 02-5-4   DATE: MARCH 01, 2002

2001–02 Crown Victoria, Mustang, Grand Marquis, And Town Car

ACTION: Verify condition. Replace the Water Pump Pulley and/or Tensioner assembly as necessary.

vibration; electrical problems include erratic operation of turn signals, hard starting, and illuminated ABS warning lamp. • A shorted coil/open PCM fuse may result in no-starts or rough running. • Climate control stays in the defrost mode. • Inoperative door window because of faulty window regulator; inoperative door glass. • Defective ignition-switch lock cylinder. **2003–04**—Hard to shift, rattling manual transmission. • Ford will install four revised hood scoop insulators (#2L7Z-9P686-AA) to eliminate a rattle emanating from the hood of the vehicle. *Cobra*: **2003**—Defective engine cylinder heads or valve guides (replacement cylinder head part number is 3R2Z-6049-GA). **2004**—Intermittent loss of power, no-starts. • Engine overheating. • Manual transmission gear whine. • Driveline clunk during gear changes or quick acceleration. • Squealing noise from the steering assembly. • Front suspension squeaking noise when vehicle passes over bumps. • Inoperative rear window defroster. • Thump noise when AC clutch engages.

General Motors

best buy CAMARO, FIREBIRD, TRANS AM ★★★★★

RATING: Recommended (1997–2002); Average (1994–96); Below Average (1992–93); Not Recommended (1982–91). Camaro and Firebird were dropped for the 2003 model year. What a goofball decision! GM should have axed its money-losing Saturn and Saab divisions and kept Oldsmobile and the Camaro and Firebird. Fun to drive and easily repaired, these cars are more reliable than the Mustang, despite having elicited similar safety-related complaints such as airbag deployment injuries, sudden acceleration, brake failures, and steering loss. Be especially wary of brake rotor warpage, requiring rotor replacement every two years (about a $300 job). Bargain hunter alert: The 1996 Camaro and Firebird are essentially the same as the more expensive 1997 versions. A V8-equipped Camaro or convertible is the best choice for retained value a few years down the road. But you can do quite well with a used base coupe equipped with the performance handling package and high-performance tires. **Maintenance/Repair costs:** Average, and repairs can be done by any independent garage. **Parts:** Reasonably priced and easy to find. **Extended warranty:** A waste of money; instead, spend an extra $100 getting the car checked out thoroughly *before* you buy it. **Best alternatives:** Ford Mustang or Probe, Hyundai Tiburon, Mazda Miata, and Toyota Celica. **Online help:** *www. autosafety.org/autodefects.html* and *www.sportscarforums.com.*

Strengths and Weaknesses

Camaros and Firebirds are rear-drive muscle cars that perform better than the Mustang and produce excellent crash protection scores and reasonable resale values. They also take the lead over the Mustang with their standard ABS and slightly better reliability record. Their overall performance varies a great deal depending on the engine, transmission, and suspension combination in each particular car. Base models equipped with the V6 power plant accelerate reasonably well, but high-performance enthusiasts will find them slow for sporty cars. Handling is compromised by poor traction on wet roads, minimal comfort, and a suspension that's too soft for high-speed cornering and too bone-jarring for smooth cruising. The Z28, IROC-Z, and Trans Am provide smart acceleration and handling, but at the expense of fuel economy—a small drawback when you tote up the savings from buying used.

VEHICLE HISTORY: 1987—Relatively unchanged since its last redesign in 1982. **1990**—A driver-side airbag, tilt steering wheel, tinted glass, intermittent wipers, and halogen headlights. The IROC-Z debuted with a standard limited-slip differential and 16-inch alloy wheels. **1991**—V8-equipped Z28 returned after a 3-year hiatus and the IROC-Z was axed. **1993**—Totally redesigned and given a more aerodynamic body style. Dimensions were slightly enlarged, weight was added, power boosted, and the dashboard was reworked. Dual airbags and ABS also became standard safety features. Convertible dropped. **1994**—Convertible returned with an upgraded top and a 6-speed gearbox. **1995**—Added a 3.8L V6 engine. **1996**—3.8L engine used as the base power plant, the 5.7L V8 gained 10 extra horses, and a new high-performance SS option was offered for the first time on the Z28. **1997**—GM offered a 30th birthday styling package for the Camaro and some interior upgrades, V6 engine dampening for smoother running at high speeds, optional Ram Air induction, and racier-looking ground-effects body trim for the Firebird. **1998**—Got a minor facelift, and the Z28 and SS both received a slight horsepower boost. **1999**—Electronic throttle control on V6-equipped versions and a new Zexel Torsion differential used in the limited-slip rear axle. **2000**—Camaros and Firebirds got alloy wheels and an improved throttle response for cars equipped with the manual transmission. **2001**—Z28 and SS models were given five more horses and restyled chrome wheels. **2002**—Improved ride quality and dashboard layout.

Performance and reliability problems are still commonplace. Much like Ford's embarrassing 4-banger, the puny and failure-prone 2.5L 4-cylinder power plant was the standard engine up until 1986—part of the legacy of an earlier fuel crisis and the subsequent downsizing binge. The turbocharged V8 offered on some Trans Am models should be viewed with caution because of its many durability problems. Body hardware is fragile, poor paint quality and application are common problems that lead to premature rusting, and squeaks and rattles are legion. Body integrity is especially poor on cars equipped with a T-roof. Areas particularly vulnerable to rusting are the windshield and rear wheel openings, door bottoms, and rear quarter panels. The assorted add-on plastic body parts found on sporty versions promote corrosion by trapping moisture along with road salt and grime. Also note that the Camaro's flat seats don't offer as much support as the better-contoured Firebird seats.

These cars are also plagued by chronic fuel-system problems, especially on the Crossfire and multi-port fuel-injection controls. Automatic transmissions, especially the 4-speed, aren't durable. The standard 5-speed manual gearbox has a stiff shifter and a heavy clutch. Clutches fail frequently and don't stand up to hard use. The 2.8L V6, used through 1989, suffers from leaky gaskets and seals and premature camshaft wear. The larger 3.1L 6-cylinder has fewer problems. However, malfunctioning dash gauges and electrical problems are common, and exhaust parts rust quickly. Dual outlet exhaust systems on V8 engines are expensive to replace. Front suspension components and shock absorbers wear out very quickly.

Of this grouping, you should stick with the 1996–2003 models for the best performance and price. All of these cars are much better overall performers than previous models, and additional standard safety features are a plus. These sporty convertibles and coupes are almost identical in their pricing and in the features they offer (the Firebird has pop-up headlights, a more pointed front end, a narrower middle, and a rear spoiler). As noted above, both cars got a complete make-over in 1995, making them more powerful and aerodynamic, with less spine-jarring performance.

As one moves up the scale, overall performance improves considerably. The V8 engine gives these cars lots of sparkle and tire-spinning torque, but there's a fuel penalty to pay. A 4-speed automatic transmission is standard on the 5.7L-equipped Z28; other versions come with a standard 5-speed manual gearbox or an optional 6-speed. Many of these cars are likely to have been ordered with lots of extra performance and luxury options, including a T-roof package guaranteed to include a full assortment of creaks and groans.

Not everything is perfect, however. Owners report premature automatic transmission failures, a noisy base engine, and excessive oil consumption with the larger engine. Fuel economy is unimpressive, the AC malfunctions, front brakes (rotors and pads, mostly) and MacPherson struts wear out quickly, servicing the fuel-injection system is an exercise in frustration, electrical problems are common, gauges operate erratically, and body problems are common. These include door rattles, misaligned doors and hatch, a sticking hatch power release, and poor fit and finish. Owners also complain that the steering wheel is positioned too close to the driver's chest, the low seats create a feeling of claustrophobia, visibility is limited by wide side pillars, and trunk space is sparse with a high liftover.

 **Safety Summary**

All models/years: Early brake rotor warpage and pad replacement. One dealer mechanic explains the problem this way:

> The rotors are not thick enough and have insufficient air to cool them. ASE-certified independent mechanics and dealership employees (unofficially) buy slotted "racing" rotors or use ceramic non-metal pads from other sources. This has apparently gone on since 1998 on both Firebirds and Camaros.

• Airbag malfunctions. • Seat belts fail to lock up. **All models: 1997–98**— Prematurely worn brake pads and warped or cracked rotors, sudden acceleration, no airbag deployment, and failure of the emergency brake to hold are all recurring problems. **1998**—Dash fire. • Axle seal, tie-rod, serpentine belt, fuel pump, brake caliper bolt, AC blower motor, fuel gauge, and wiper failures. **1999**—Interestingly, both the Camaro and the Firebird have about one-third fewer safety-related complaints registered against them by NHTSA than does the Ford Mustang. • Airbags failed to deploy on impact. • Cracked fuel tank leaks fuel. • Accelerator pedal sticks. • Prematurely warped front brake rotors jerk to one side when brakes are applied and cause pulsation, excessive noise, and extended stopping distance. • Many incidents of clutch slippage at low mileage. • Frequent complaints that the stock shifter causes misshifts. • Electrical system shorts cause instrument panel and assorted gauges and lights to operate erratically. • Turn signal lights don't flash, headlights often dim to about 50 percent of their intended brightness, heater slows down, and power windows run slowly. **2000**—Engine surging and stalling. • Electrical wires melted. • Emergency brake failed to hold vehicle; came off in driver's hand. • Rear brake lock-ups and chronic pad and rotor failures. • T-top flew off vehicle. • Seat belt failed to retract in an emergency stop. • Headlights flicker or suddenly go out. • Horn collects water, which muffles sound. • Front end pulls to the right. • Headrests are set too low (same complaint heard from Mustang owners). • Replacement windshields are seriously distorted along the bottom edge. • Windows leak water. • Premature power-window motor failures. • Severe vibration when accelerating. **2001**—Premature automatic transmission failure. **2002**—Airbags failed to deploy. • Premature brake rotor wear causes excessive shudder, vibration. • Design causes front windshield distortion. • Early headlight failures.

Secret Warranties/Internal Bulletins/Service Tips

All models/years: Eliminate AC odours by applying an evaporator core cooling coil coating. • A rotten-egg odour coming from the exhaust is probably the result of a malfunctioning catalytic converter, which may be covered by the emissions warranty. • Paint delamination, peeling, or fading (see Part Two). • GM guidelines to dealers on troubleshooting exterior lamp condensation complaints. • Oil leaks between the intake manifold and engine block are most often caused by insufficient RTV bonding between the intake manifold and cylinder block. • Reverse servo cover seal leaks. **All models: 1993–2002**—GM has a special kit to prevent AC odours in warm weather. **1994–98**—GM guidelines for repairing front brake problems. **1997–2002**—Radio speaker buzz or rattle. **1998**—Tips on eliminating roof panel ticking. **1998–2000**—An engine that loses coolant or runs hot may simply need a new radiator cap or the radiator filler neck polished. • Install upgraded disc pads to eliminate rear brake chirp or groan and front brake squeal when braking. • Silence accessory drivebelt chirping or squeaking by installing a new double row idler pulley, generator bracket, and serpentine belt. **1998–2002**—Water runs out of front lower corners of rear hatch. • Engine spark knock remedy. **1999**—If the convertible top closes with difficulty, it may be because the headliner is too short. **1999–2001**—Excessive oil consumption (see Corvette "Secret Warranties/Internal Bulletins/Service Tips"). **1999–2002**—Poor transmission performance, slipping. **2000**—Repair tips for fixing an inoperative or erratically operating antenna. **2000–02**—Clogged injectors are the likely cause of poor engine performance. • Delayed shifting. **2001–02**—Tips for troubleshooting an engine that cranks but won't run. • Engine knocking or lifter noise. • Slipping or missing Second, Third, or Fourth gear. • Remedy for harsh upshifts. • Rear brake rattling. **2002**—Intermittent no-start caused by fuel pump and fuel gauge wiring harness short. • Harsh automatic transmission shifts. • Automatic transmission pump leaks. • Quarter trim panels pull away. • Troubleshooting guide for correcting wind noise and water leaks. • Exhaust ping. • Radiator cap may not hold sufficient vacuum. • Rattling door handles. • Noisy, faulty clutch pedal. *Models with 2.5L engines:* **All years:** Spark knock can be fixed with a new PROM module (#12269198), if the emissions warranty applies. • Frequent stalling may require a new MAP sensor (TSB #90-142-8A). **3.8L V6: 1996–98**—These engines have a history of low oil pressure caused by a failure-prone oil pump. A temporary remedy is to avoid low-viscosity oils and use 10W-40 in the winter and 20W-50 for summer driving.

CAMARO, FIREBIRD, TRANS AM PROFILE

	1995	1996	1997	1998	1999	2000	2001	2002
Cost Price ($)								
Camaro/RS	18,995	20,195	22,075	22,790	23,100	26,065	26,120	26,995
Z28	23,650	25,530	27,270	27,840	28,670	31,630	29,540	30,785

All ratings on a numbered scale where ⑤ is good and ❶ is bad. See pages 100–101 for a more detailed description.

Convertible	26,045	28,365	29,080	29,795	30,105	38,270	38,585	39,225
Firebird	19,795	20,955	23,120	24,580	24,865	27,605	26,915	27,695
Trans Am	27,390	28,755	30,780	34,080	34,750	35,505	35,815	36,365
Used Values ($)								
Camaro/RS ▲	4,500	5,000	6,000	7,000	8,500	10,000	12,500	15,000
Camaro/RS ▼	3,500	4,500	5,000	6,000	8,000	8,500	11,000	14,000
Z28 ▲	5,000	6,000	7,000	8,000	9,000	12,500	15,500	18,500
Z28 ▼	4,000	5,500	6,000	7,000	8,000	11,000	14,000	17,000
Convertible ▲	7,500	9,000	10,000	12,000	14,500	17,000	19,000	23,000
Convertible ▼	7,000	8,000	9,000	11,000	13,000	15,500	17,500	21,500
Firebird ▲	5,000	5,500	6,500	8,000	9,500	11,000	13,000	14,500
Firebird ▼	4,500	5,000	6,000	7,000	8,500	10,000	12,000	13,500
Trans Am ▲	6,000	7,000	8,000	9,000	11,000	14,000	17,500	21,500
Trans Am ▼	5,500	6,000	7,500	8,000	9,500	12,500	16,000	19,500
Reliability	③	④	④	④	④	④	⑤	⑤
Crash Safety (Camaro)	⑤	⑤	⑤	④	④	④	④	④
Side (Camaro)	—	—	③	③	③	③	③	③
Head Restraints	❶	—	❶	—	❶	—	❶	❶

CORVETTE ★★★

RATING: Average (1997–2004); Below Average (1994–96); Not Recommended (1977–93). The cheaper 1996 Corvette won't have the cachet or the mechanical and body refinements of the redesigned 1997 version. If you choose the 1997 model, try to get a second-series car that was made after June 1997. Keep in mind that premium fuel and astronomical insurance rates will further drive up your operating costs. And don't discount the serious safety-related problems you're likely to experience on 1997–2001 models. They run the gamut of sudden steering lock-up when underway, electrical shorts causing vehicle shutdown, a non-functioning parking brake, brake failures caused by premature rotor warpage (around 16,000 km), and seat belts that jam in the retractor. The locked-up steering is particularly scary because it apparently has carried over to year 2001 models, and traffic accident investigators may simply conclude that a resulting accident was because of driver inexperience or unsafe driving. **Maintenance/Repair costs:** Higher than average, although most repairs can be done by any independent garage. Long waits for recall repairs. **Parts:** Pricey, but easy to find. Surprisingly, it is often easier to find parts for older Corvettes through collectors' clubs than it is to find many of the high-tech components used today. **Extended warranty:** By all means; just saving the diagnostic fees will pay for the warranty. **Best alternatives:** Ford Mustang or Probe, GM Camaro or Firebird, Mazda Miata, and Toyota Supra. **Online help:** *www.corvetteforum.com* and *www.carreview.com*.

Strengths and Weaknesses

Corvettes made in the late '60s and early '70s are acceptable buys, mainly because of their value as collector cars and their uncomplicated repairs. Unfortunately, the Corvette's overall reliability and safety have declined over the years as its price and complexity have increased. GM has chosen to update its antiquated design with high-tech, complicated add-ons rather than come up with something original. Consequently, the car has been gutted and then retuned using failure-prone electronic circuitry. Complicated emissions plumbing, braking, and suspension systems have also been added in an attempt to make the Corvette a fuel-efficient, user-friendly, high-performance vehicle—a goal that General Motors has missed by a large margin.

The electronically-controlled suspension systems have always been plagued by glitches. Servicing the different sophisticated fuel-injection systems is a nightmare—even (especially) for GM mechanics. The noisy 5.7L engine frequently hesitates and stalls, there's lots of transmission buzz and whine, the rear tires produce excessive noise, and wind whistles through the A- and C-pillars. These, and the all-too-familiar fibreglass body squeaks and paint delamination (yes, fibreglass delaminates), continue to be unwanted standard features throughout all model years. The electronic dash never works quite right (speedometer lag is one example).

Ownership of more recent Corvette models does have its positive side. For example, the ABS vented disc brakes, available since 1986, are easy to modulate and fade-free. The standard European-made Bilstein FX-3 Selective Ride Control suspension can be pre-set for touring, sport, or performance. Under speed, an electronic module automatically varies the suspension setting, finally curing these cars of their earlier endemic oversteering, wheel spinning, breakaway rear ends, and other nasty surprises.

All used Corvettes are high-risk buys, but the 1977–93 models have been particularly troublesome. These models are notorious for complicated and failure-prone safety, emissions, and performance "innovations" that were routinely brought in one year and dropped shortly thereafter, making for difficult troubleshooting and hard-to-find parts. There's also a greater chance you'll get stuck with a turned-back odometer or an accident-damaged car, written off by the insurance company and then resold through wholesalers, auctions, body shops, or their employees. All these scams can be detected by running a Carfax check online or by fax (see Part One).

Another precaution: Get a GM-backed supplementary warranty, or look for a recent model that has some of the original warranty left. The frequency of repairs and the high repair costs make maintenance outrageously expensive. Following are some of the things that can put a large dent in your wallet if they haven't been fixed already.

A substantial redesign was carried out in mid-1997. The transmission was moved back, creating a roomier cockpit; the interior was made much more user-friendly; structural improvements reduced body flexing (a problem with most convertibles) and made for a more rigid hatchback; and a new aluminum 340-hp LSI V8 engine arrived on the scene. The '98 and '99 versions are pretty much carryovers of the redesigned '97 and aren't worth a higher price. A high-performance hardtop model was launched for the '99 model year. Year 2000 models returned unchanged; however, the 2001 Corvette got a horsepower boost, an Active Handling performance upgrade, and was joined by a high-performance Z06 variant. For 2002, the Z06 got a 20-hp boost to 405 hp, enhanced rear shocks, aluminum front stabilizer bar links, high-performance brake pads, and new aluminum wheels. The 2003s got 50th anniversary decals and not much else, while the 2004 models were simply given additional commemorative trim options.

Owners admit the redesigned '97 models offer improved performance, better handling, and additional safety features, but they still find fault with the stiff ride, poor fuel economy, and excessive interior noise. From a reliability standpoint, these 1997 and later models are more refined, but serious engine and transmission problems remain. You can expect chronic engine stalling and surging, excessive engine oil consumption, an oily black buildup on the exhaust tips and catalytic converter failures within the first five years. A real hair-raiser is the tendency of steering columns on 1977 through 2001 models to suddenly lock while the vehicle is underway or parked. This continues to be a a widespread hazard, despite a recent recall, says the following Corvette owner:

> This item has failed on an estimated 3,000 Corvettes throughout the U.S. Please see Internet site *www.corvetteforum.com*. As a safety professional, I see this as a hazard that Chevrolet needs to address with more severity. The loss of steering control because the steering wheel locks can lead to property loss, as well as death.

·

> The consumer's vehicle experienced the same problem as stated in NHTSA recall #04V060000 which states that on certain passenger vehicles equipped with electronic column lock systems (ED), when the ignition switch is turned to lock, the EDI prevents turning of the steering system when the vehicle is started. The vehicle is designed so that if the column fails to unlock when the vehicle is started and the customer tries to drive, the fuel supply will be shut off so that the vehicle cannot move when the vehicle cannot be steered. The dealership indicated that the consumer's vehicle was not included in the recall.

Other performance deficiencies make the car unsafe: The active handling system often malfunctions and makes the vehicle veer into traffic or spin out of control;

faulty electronic and electrical systems cause it to abruptly shut down; the brake, suspension, and AC systems are unreliable; and body accessories and electronics suddenly short out.

Deficiencies on the post-2000 models: The engine is excessively noisy; the cabins overheat; the driver's seat moves while driving; the trunk door warps; seat belts twist easily and tend to pull down uncomfortably against the shoulder; the passenger seat belt jams and won't extend or retract; smelly exhaust fumes enter the cabin, causing watery eyes and dizziness; excessive heat buildup from catalytic converters deforms rear bumper assembly and heats up the interior even more; the glass rear-view window limits rear vision; and front and rear wheel weights sometimes fly off the wheels.

Servicing the different sophisticated fuel-injection systems isn't easy, and may be the primary reason why so many owners complain of having to take their Corvettes back to the shop repeatedly to correct poor engine and transmission performance.

Safety Summary

1997–98—Sudden loss of power, engine shuts down, and warning lights come on everywhere. • Defective throttle control module, parking brake, brake rotors and pads, seat belt retractors, fuel line clips, and Check Engine light. **1997–2001**—NHTSA is looking into 350 complaints, 24 crashes, and 10 injuries related to steering column lock-ups; GM admits it has processed 24,000 warranty claims and sent its dealers three bulletins about the problem. • **1998**—Fuel tank leakage. • No airbag deployment. • Transmission failure, leaks. • Emergency brake won't hold. • Excessive vibrations when driving. • Poor headlight illumination. **1999**—Sudden, unintended acceleration. • Fuel tank leaks when gassing up; vehicle caught fire as raw fuel was ignited by the catalytic converter. • Fuel pump failures. • Parking brake won't hold car. • Chronic premature warpage of the brake rotors. • Front lapbelts jam in the retractor. • Electrical shorts caused headlights to stick open, rear-view mirror assembly melted, and a plethora of other electronic glitches led to vehicle shutdown. • Engine serpentine belt and tensioner failures. • Poorly anchored driver's seat and warped trunk door. **2000–01**—Catalytic converter caught fire. • When fuel tank is full, fuel leaks from the top of the vent. • Fuel leaks from the fuel lines near the firewall inside the engine compartment. • Chronic stalling; fuel-injector failures cause vehicle to shudder and stall. • Engine dies while driving in the rain and brakes don't work. • Early failure of the engine serpentine belt and tensioner. • If one wheel loses traction, the throttle closes, starving the engine. • Brakes drag and lock up; brake pedal doesn't spring back; overheated rotors are common. • Car is nearly uncontrollable at time of brake lock-up. • Seat belt doesn't retract properly when reeling it out and tightens up progressively when driving. • Driver's seat rocks. • Foot easily slips off clutch and brake pedals. **2002**—Sudden stalling on the highway accompanied by brake

All ratings on a numbered scale where ⑤ is good and ❶ is bad. See pages 100–101 for a more detailed description.

failure. • Erratic transmission performance (shifts to Fourth before entering Second gear; won't shift into Second when going uphill). • Horn is hard to access since it's just a small indentation on the steering wheel. **2003**—Sudden engine surge while underway. • When accelerating from a stop, vehicle fails to shift from First to Second gear and stalls out. • Constant leak and failure of rear differential and suspension system. • Leaking oil pan gasket. • Annoying dash reflection onto the windshield. • Driver seat belt locks up. **2004**—Defective steering despite recall. • Fuel leaks found outside of the car at the fuel tank, fuel pump seal, and the interconnecting hoses; fuel tank was replaced. • Fuel leakage from the cross-over pipe. • Sudden stalling caused by faulty fuel pump.

Secret Warranties/Internal Bulletins/Service Tips

All models/years: A rotten-egg odour coming from the exhaust is probably caused by a defective catalytic converter, which may be covered by the emissions warranty. • Clearcoat paint degradation, whitening, and chalking, long a problem with GM's other cars, is also a serious problem with the fibreglass-bodied Corvette, says TSB #331708. It too is covered by a secret warranty for up to six years (see Part Two). • Reverse servo cover seal leak. **All models: 1993–2002**—GM has a special kit to prevent AC odours in warm weather. **1995–2000**—Guidelines for repairing brake rotor warpage. **1997–98**—What to do when the Low Engine Coolant light comes on. • Silence a muffler insulator rumble noise by installing upgraded insulators. • Countermeasures to eliminate water leaks above the door glass and door glass rattles. **1997–99**—A no-start condition can be corrected by reprogramming the power control module (PCM). • TSB #99-06-02-016 has the remedy for a low coolant light that comes on at start-up. • Shift boot squeaking can be silenced by installing a new shift boot assembly. • Accessory drive squeaks can be corrected by installing a new idler pulley assembly. **1997–2000**—Repair tips for an inaccurate fuel gauge. **1997–2001**—Sound system speakers make the door panel rattle or buzz. **1997–2002**—Tips on correcting water leaks in various areas. • Loose driver's seat. **1997–2003**—Inoperative AC. **1997–2004**—Remedy for a leaking rear differential (see bulletin at right). **1998–2000**—Tips on correcting a faulty rear window defogger. • An inoperative or noisy window motor can be corrected by replacing the window regulator and motor assembly. **1998–2002**—Engine spark knock remedy. **1999**—

REAR DIFFERENTIAL FLUID LEAK
BULLETIN NO: 03-04-20-006   DATE: NOV. 18, 2003
Fluid Leak at Rear Axle (Replace Left Differential Side Cover O-Ring and Left Axle Shaft Seal, Add Sealant to Side Cover Flange)
2004 Cadillac XLR and 1997–2004 Chevrolet Corvette

Rattling from the left fuel tank area can be silenced by installing a fuel tank foam insulator pad. **1999–2000**—An engine that runs hot or loses coolant may simply need a new radiator cap or polishing of the radiator filler neck. **1999–2001**—Wind noise around the B-pillar. **1999–2002**—Poor transmission performance; SES light lit. • Excessive oil consumption (see following bulletin). **2000**—Reducing exhaust boom. • Repair tips on fixing an inoperative or erratically

HIGHER THAN NORMAL OIL CONSUMPTION

BULLETIN NO: 01-06-01-023A   **DATE: JUNE 2002**

1999–2001 Camaro, Firebird; 1999–2002 Corvette with 5.7L engine.

CONDITION: Some owners may comment on higher than expected oil consumption. When checked, the oil consumption could be in the range of 700–1000 km/L (400–600 miles per quart). On the LS6 engine only, the technician may find oil behind the engine throttle plate and in the intake manifold.

ACTION: Replace the engine valley cover if oil is found behind the throttle body or in the intake manifold before replacing the piston ring.

operating antenna. • Left headlight door may not remain closed. **2000–04**—Delayed automatic transmission shifts. **2001**—Incomplete brake pedal return can be fixed by replacing the vacuum brake booster. **2001–02**—Slipping or missing Second, Third, or Fourth gear. **2002**—Engine knock. • Erratic fuel gauge or radio operation. • False Service Engine light illumination. • Harsh transmission shifts; 2–4 band and 3–4 clutch damage; transmission pump leaks. • Light brake drag; brake light remains lit. • B-pillar wind noise. **2001–03**—Engine knock or lifter noise. **2001–05**—Harsh upshifts. **2002–04**—Exhaust system jingle noise. **2004**—Erratic idle, idle surge, rough running, stalling. • Coolant leak from head cup plugs. • Transmission fluid leaks; inoperative Second, Third, and Fourth gears. • Rear axle side cover oil leak. • Poor automatic transmission shifting, slipping. • Transmission squawk, grunt, rattle, growl, or buzz noise. • Intermittent or inoperative fuel gauge TSB #01659, January 2004. • Wind noise or water leak at top of door glass. • Tire wander. • Seat belt won't release from retractor. • Blotches in all glass. • Inoperative Twilight Sentinel automatic headlight control.

CORVETTE PROFILE

	1996	1997	1998	1999	2000	2001	2002	2003	2004
Cost Price ($)									
Base	48,080	48,895	50,430	53,870	60,050	61,400	62,400	68,120	69,940
Convertible	56,335	—	58,430	60,850	66,965	68,315	69,665	74,120	75,940
Used Values ($)									
Base ▲	18,000	21,000	27,000	30,000	33,000	36,000	42,000	49,000	57,000
Base ▼	16,000	19,000	25,000	28,000	31,000	34,000	40,000	46,000	52,000
Convertible ▲	21,000	—	29,000	33,000	36,000	39,000	44,000	52,000	63,000
Convertible ▼	19,000	—	27,000	30,000	34,000	37,000	42,000	48,000	61,000
Reliability	②	②	③	③	③	③	③	③	③
Head Restraints (F)	—	—	—	③	—	③	③	③	③
Rear	—	—	—	—	—	②	②	②	②

All ratings on a numbered scale where ⑤ is good and ❶ is bad. See pages 100–101 for a more detailed description.

Mazda

RATING: Recommended (1990–2004). There was no 1998 model. An almost-perfect sports car, except for its poor braking performance on rain-slicked roadways. **Maintenance/Repair costs:** Below-average costs, and most repairs aren't dealer dependent. **Parts:** Average cost, with good availability. **Extended warranty:** A waste of money. **Best alternatives:** Ford Mustang or Probe, GM Camaro or Firebird, Hyundai Tiburon, Nissan 200SX, and Toyota Celica. **Online help:** *www.miata.net, www.straight-six.com,* and *www.miataforum.com.*

Strengths and Weaknesses

The base 1.6L engine delivers adequate power and accelerates smoothly. Acceleration from 0 to 100 km/h is in the high 8-second range. The 5-speed manual transmission shifts easily and has well-spaced gears; the 6-speed adds 27 kg (60 lb.) and isn't that impressive. The vehicle's lightness, precise steering, and 50/50 weight distribution make this an easy car for novice drivers to toss around corners.

VEHICLE HISTORY: 1995–98—The Miata changed very little. **1999**—Some handling upgrades and additional standard features. **2001**—A slight horsepower boost, a restyled interior and exterior, 15-inch wheels, seat belt pretensioners, improved ABS, and an emergency trunk release. **2003**—16-inch V-rated tires and strut-tower braces. **2004**—Debut of the MazdaSpeed, equipped with a 178-hp turbocharged engine, 6-speed manual transmission, sport suspension, and 17-inch wheels.

Owners' top performance gripes target the same characteristics that make other sports car enthusiasts swoon: inadequate cargo space, cramped interior for large adults, excessive interior noise, and limited low-end torque that makes for frequent shifting.

Owners also say that it's important to change the engine timing chain every 100,000 km. Other reported problems: crankshaft failures, leaky rear-end seals and valve cover gaskets, rear differential seal failure, a leaking or squeaky clutch, hard starts and stalling, torn drive boots, transmission whining in upper gear ranges, engine and exhaust system rattles, electrical system glitches, brake pulsation, valvetrain clatter on start-up (changing oil may help), prematurely worn-out shock absorbers and catalytic converter, the softtop cover comes off or breaks, and minor body and trim deficiencies.

 **Safety Summary**

ALL MODELS/YEARS: Used Miatas will likely have some collision damage; make sure you run a Carfax check online or by fax (see Part One). **1999**—Airbags failed to deploy upon impact. • While passing another car on the highway, accelerator cable and the cable adjuster assembly disengaged from the horseshoe bracket that holds the cable. • Transmission suddenly failed, causing both rear wheels to seize. • Keizer aluminum wheel cracked, damaging brake caliper, rotor, and fender. • Performs poorly on wet roads. • At highway speeds, vehicle tends to wander all over the roadway. **2000**—In heavy rain, stepping on the brakes results in a 2-second delay before braking; must continually pump the brakes. • Airbags deployed two minutes after collision. • Convertible top latches may inadvertently open while vehicle is underway. • Hard shifting and stiff shifter at Neutral causes gear hunting, grinding, and rattling. • Gas pump shuts off before tank is filled. **2001**—Vehicle rolled down hill despite being parked with emergency brake engaged. **2002**—Interior can heat up to 130 degrees because exhaust system is mounted too close to the centre console. **2003**—Poor headlight illumination. **2004**—Seat belt locks up during normal driving.

Secret Warranties/Internal Bulletins/Service Tips

All models/years: TSB #006/94 gives all of the possible causes and remedies for brake vibration. • TSB #N00198 addresses complaints that the steering wheel is off-centre. • Other bulletins address the issue of musty AC odours. **All models: 1990–99**—Paint damage caused by the trunk rubber cushions will be repaired under the base warranty. Ask for pro rata compensation if the warranty has expired. **1999**—A hard-to-start engine may have debris accumulated at the fuel pressure regulator valve area, causing the valve to stick open. • Engine rattling may be caused by premature wear of the engine thrust bearing or the engine harness clips rubbing against the car's frame. • Muffler rattling may be silenced by installing an upgraded unit. **1999–2002**—Additional tips on reducing AC odours. **1999–2003**—Clutch chatter on cold start-up. **2002**—Clutch chatter during cold takeoff on manual transmission-equipped vehicles. • Fuelling difficulty caused by gas pump shutting off early. • The 6-speed manual transmission won't shift into Fifth gear or Reverse. **2004**—Door rattling.

MIATA PROFILE

	1995	1996	1997	1999	2000	2001	2002	2003	2004
Cost Price ($)									
Base	21,820	24,210	24,695	26,025	26,995	27,605	27,695	27,695	27,895
Used Values ($)									
Base ▲	5,000	6,000	7,500	11,000	13,000	15,000	18,000	20,000	23,000
Base ▼	4,500	5,500	7,000	9,500	11,500	14,000	16,500	18,500	21,000

All ratings on a numbered scale where ⑤ is good and ❶ is bad. See pages 100–101 for a more detailed description.

Reliability	4	5	5	5	5	5	5	5	5
Crash Safety (F)	4	4	—	—	—	4	—	—	—
Side	—	—	—	—	—	3	—	—	—
Head Restraints	—	**1**	—	**1**	—	3	3	3	3
Rear	—	—	—	—	—	2	2	2	—

Toyota

CELICA ★★★★★

RATING: Recommended (2001–04, 1995–99); Above Average (2000, 1986–94). The 1996 and 1997 models are practically identical; choose the cheaper version. The reworked 2000 model has been downgraded because of its many factory-related deficiencies. Keep in mind that the 1989–96 GTS is far superior to the GT, with its 135-hp DOHC 2.0L engine, firmer suspension, better-equipped interior, ABS, and sportier feel. All handle competently and provide the kind of sporting performance expected from a car of this class. The extra performance in the higher-line versions does come at a price, but this isn't a problem, given the high resale value and excellent reliability for which Celicas are known. Few safety-related complaints or recalls. **Maintenance/Repair costs:** Average, and most repairs can be done at any garage. **Parts:** Reasonably priced and easy to find. **Extended warranty:** No; you'd be throwing your money away. **Best alternatives:** Ford Mustang or Probe, GM Camaro or Firebird, Hyundai Tiburon, and Nissan 200SX. **Online help:** *www.toyotanation.com.*

◈ Strengths and Weaknesses

Redesigned 1994 models are full of both show and go, with more aerodynamic styling, an enhanced 1.8L that gives more pickup than the ST's 1.6L, and better fuel economy. Among the upgraded models available, smart buyers should choose a used 1994 ST for its more reasonable price, smooth performance, quiet running, and high fuel economy.

Owner gripes target the excessive engine noise, limited rear seat room, and inadequate cargo space. Pre-1994 models get the most complaints regarding brakes, electrical problems, AC malfunctions, and premature exhaust wearout. The 1994 models may have a manual transmission that slips out of Second gear, as well as hard starts caused by a faulty airflow meter (#22250-74200). Areas vulnerable to early rusting include rear wheel openings, suspension components, the area surrounding the fuel-filler cap, door bottoms, and trunk or hatchback lids.

VEHICLE HISTORY: 1995—A GT convertible debuts. **1996**—Extra sound insulation and add-on skirts. **1997**—GT given five more horses and the notchback GT is axed. **1998**—ST dropped and GT given more standard features. **1999**—GT Sport Coupe is dropped. **2000**—Crisper handling, a new 180-hp engine, and a 6-speed gearbox (GT-S). **2003**—Hatchback coupes are slightly restyled.

All late-model Celicas offer decent reliability and durability, with three major exceptions: engine sludging; an engine-blowing, self-destructing 6-speed gearbox; and premature, costly brake repairs:

> Toyota has a big problem with their 6-speed in the new Celica. They even told me about it at Toyota. The malfunction is that when trying to shift from Third to Fourth gear, the transmission will slip into Second instead of Fourth. This then causes the engine to be blown.
>
> This is a very dangerous situation if trying to merge with traffic on Interstate at around 70–75 mph [113–120 km/h] and suddenly your car decelerates instantly to around 50 mph [80 km/h]. They need to do something about it before someone gets seriously hurt....

Servicing and repairs are straightforward, and parts are easily found. The front-drive series performs very well and hasn't presented any major problems to owners. Prices are high for Celicas in good condition, but some bargains are available with the base ST model.

Some common problems over the years include engine failure caused by engine oil sludge (1997–2001 models), a problem covered by Toyota "goodwill" (see Sienna); brake pulsation and pulling to one side; rear defroster terminals breaking on convertibles; sunroof leaks; erratic CD changer performance; and smelly AC emissions.

Another subset of problems shows up on the redesigned 2000 and later models. This includes engine failures while driving ("weak" valves blamed); stalling after a cold start; engine knocking; excessive oil consumption; early replacement of the belt tensioner and airflow meter; the aforementioned failure-prone 6-speed transmission; insufficient AC cooling; lights dim and heater lags when shifted into idle; seat belt tabs that damage door panels; interior panels separating; driver's window catches and doesn't go all the way up; drivebelt squeaks when turning; a squeaking gear shift lever; a grinding noise emanating from the front wheels and brakes; paint peeling; and limited rearward visibility. The audible reverse alarm isn't Toyota's brightest idea. Audible only inside the vehicle, it adds a forklift cachet to your Celica.

Safety Summary

All models/years: Even if your vehicle has 4×4 capability, it's imperative to fit it with snow tires in order to avoid dangerous control problems on snow and ice. **All models: 1999**—Convertible top and sunroof leaks. **2000**—A huge increase in safety-related complaints. • Fuel leak caused by a broken hose. • No airbag deployment. • Seat belts didn't hold driver in place in a frontal collision. • Cruise control suddenly slows car down without warning. • Constant stalling. • Won't shift into Overdrive. • Clutch and accelerator pedal stick to the floor. • Excessive steering wheel play. • At 100 km/h, vehicle pulls to one side. • Passenger-side wheel suddenly locked up, causing an accident. • Shield protecting wires and fuel lines came off and caused extensive AC valve damage. • Spoiler fell off because of loose bolts. **2000–01**—Without a lockout on the 6-speed gear shift, car can be inadvertently shifted from Fifth to Second gear. **2001**—Engine failures. **2002**—Airbags failed to deploy. **2003**—Hood latch failure. • Fuel leak because of defective valve clamp. • Inoperative cruise control. • Steering tends to over-correct.

Secret Warranties/Internal Bulletins/Service Tips

All models/years: Toyota TSB #TC002-01 confirms misshifts with the 6-speed tranny. • Troubleshooting updates for steering pulling complaints are found in TSB #ST005-01. • Older Toyotas with stalling problems should have the engine checked for excessive carbon buildup on the valves before any extensive repairs are authorized. • Owner feedback and dealer service managers (who wish to remain anonymous) confirm the existence of Toyota's secret warranty that will pay for replacing front disc brake components that wear out before 2 years/40,000 km. • To reduce front brake squeaks on ABS-equipped vehicles, ask the dealer to install new, upgraded rotors (#43517-32020). **All models: 1990–2000**—Toyota has put out a special grease to minimize brake clicking. **2000**—GT-S automatic transmission fluid leaks. • Loose outer door handle. • Sunshade improvements. • Cruise control shock can be attenuated by replacing the ECU. • Moon roof creaking. • Squeak and rattle service tips. **2000–01**—Drivebelt and engine squealing. • Enhanced sunroof durability. **2000–02**—Insufficient rear hatch support. **2003**—Throttle body motor malfunctions. • Fuel tank check valve Special Service Campaign.

CELICA PROFILE

	1996	1997	1998	1999	2000	2001	2002	2003	2004
Cost Price ($)									
Base	27,968	28,528	34,138	34,475	23,980	24,140	24,645	24,645	24,650
Used Values ($)									
Base ▲	7,000	9,000	11,000	12,500	13,000	14,500	16,500	18,500	21,000
Base ▼	6,000	7,500	9,500	12,000	11,500	13,000	15,000	17,000	19,500

Reliability	4	5	5	5	5	5	5	5	5
Crash Safety (F)	—	—	—	—	—	4	4	4	4
Side	—	—	—	—	—	3	3	3	3
Head Restraints	—	2	—	3	—	5	5	5	5
Rear	—	—	—	2	—	—	—	—	5
Rollover Resistance	—	—	—	—	—	—	—	5	5

All ratings on a numbered scale where 5 is good and 1 is bad. See pages 100–101 for a more detailed description.

MINIVANS

No More "Mommy-mobile"

Like sport-utilities, minivans fall into two categories: upsized cars and downsized trucks. The upsized cars are "people-movers." They're mostly front-drives, they handle like cars, and they get great fuel economy. The Honda Odyssey and Toyota Sienna are the best examples of this kind of minivan. Following Toyota's upgrades last year and Honda's 2005 Odyssey improvements, their road performance surpasses that of the front- and rear-drive minivans built by DaimlerChrysler, Ford, and General Motors.

GM's Astro and Safari and Ford's Aerostar are downsized trucks that are dirt-cheap used choices. Using rear-drive, 6-cylinder engines, and heavier mechanical components, these minivans handle cargo and passengers equally well. On the negative side, their fuel economy is no match for the front-drives, and their highway handling is more trucklike. Overall, rear-drive GM and Ford minivans are much more reliable performers than the front-drive Ford Windstar/Freestar or Chrysler minivans. As AWDs, though, they'll keep you in the repair bay for weeks.

Rear-drive vans are also better suited for towing trailers in the 1,600–2,950 kg (3,500–6,500 lb.) range. Most automakers say their front-drive minivans can pull up to 1,600 kg. (3,500 lb.) with an optional towing package (often costing almost $1,000 extra), but don't you believe it. Owners report white-knuckle driving and premature powertrain failures caused by the extra load. It just stands to reason that Ford, Chrysler, and GM front-drives equipped with engines and transmissions that blow out at 60,000–100,000 km under normal driving conditions are going to meet their demise much earlier under a full load.

Declining quality

Quality control has always been a serious problem with minivans and vans. In the 60s, VW minivans were unreliable rustbuckets that spent more time in the service bay than they spent on the road. To this day, the VW EuroVan is more of a curiosity than a credible transporter.

Chrysler

But Chrysler minivans did catch on from their debut in 1984, when they were seen as fairly reliable and efficient people-haulers. Thanks to Chrysler's 7-year bumper-to-bumper warranty, much of the sting was taken out of repair costs. Since then, these minivans have dominated the market, despite their biodegradable engines, automatic transmissions, brakes, and air conditioners. In fact, it's amazing how little Chrysler's defect patterns have changed during the past two decades.

Ford

Ford's minivans have gone from bad to worse. Its first minivan, the 1985–97 Aerostar, was fairly dependable, although it did have some recurring tranny, brake, and coil spring problems. Collapsing coil springs may cause tire blowouts on all model years, although 1988–90 models are covered by a regional recall. Other years fall under a "goodwill" program, as this *Lemon-Aid* reader reports:

> On vacation in Washington, our 1995 Aerostar blew a tire that was worn right through from the left rear coil spring (broken in two places). The right rear coil spring is broken, as well. I showed Dams Ford in Surrey, B.C. the broken spring and they have "graciously" offered to replace the tire or repair the right side at no cost to us.

INTAKE MANIFOLD OIL/COOLANT LEAK

BULLETIN NO: 03-06-01-010B   DATE: OCT. 24, 2003

2000–2003 Century; 2002-2003 Rendezvous; 1996 Lumina APV; 1999–2001 Lumina; 1997–2003 Venture; 1999–2003 Malibu, Monte Carlo; 2000–2003 Impala; 1996–2003 Silhouette; 1999 Cutlass; 1999–2003 Alero; 1996–1999 Trans Sport; 1999–2003 Grand Am, Montana; 2000–2003 Grand Prix; 2001–2003 Aztek with 3.1L or 3.4L V-6 Engine.

CONDITION: Some owners may comment on an apparent oil or coolant leak. Additionally, the comments may range from spots on the driveway to having to add fluids.
CAUSE: Intake manifold may be leaking allowing coolant, oil or both to leak from the engine.
CORRECTION: Install a new design intake manifold gasket. The material used in the gasket has been changed in order to improve the sealing qualities of the gasket.

Ford's quality decline continued with the Mercury Villager, a co-venture that also produced the Nissan Quest. The Villager/Quest duo lasted through the 2000 model year. Quest continued on its own with minimal changes to its 2001 through 2003 models; the 2004 Quest was totally redesigned. First year models were so glitch-prone that Nissan sent over 200 engineers to the States to correct the factory-related deficiencies.

Then Ford brought out the 1995 Windstar—one of the poorest quality, most dangerous minivans ever built. Renamed the Freestar, its failure-prone power-train, suspension (broken coil springs), electrical, fuel, and braking systems can put both your wallet and your life at risk.

Ford has compounded the Windstar's failings by its hard-nosed attitude toward customer complaints, and by refusing warranty coverage for what are clearly factory-induced defects. Fortunately, there's been a flood of Canadian small claims court decisions that have come to Ford owners' aid when Ford wouldn't. These Canadian courts say Ford and its dealers must pay for engine and transmission repairs, even if the original warranty has expired (see page 80).

General Motors

GM's minivans and vans have also been seriously bug-afflicted. Plagued by faulty engine intake manifolds and diesel engine injectors, clunky, failure-prone automatic transmissions, defective brake and fuel systems and subpar fit and finish, they are no better than Detroit's other contenders.

Asian

Asian competitors don't make perfect machines either, as a perusal of NHTSA-registered safety complaints, service bulletins, and online complaint forums will quickly confirm. Asian companies, looking to keep costs down, have also been bedevilled by chronic engine and automatic transmission failures, sliding door malfunctions, catastrophic tire blowouts, and electrical malfunctions.

A word of warning about Nissan. Yes, the company has made fairly dependable vehicles—including minivans—for the past three decades. However, the newly redesigned Quest minivan has been an exception, along with recent Altimas and Maximas, which both use similar components. Interestingly, the Murano and Titan have so far escaped a large number of factory-related glitches.

Volkswagen

And finally we come back to where we started—Volkswagen. Its 1979 Vanagon and 1993 EuroVan/Camper have never been taken seriously since they came to North America in 1950 as the Transporter cargo van and the nine-seat, 21-window Microbus. A reputation for poor overall quality, puny engines, and insufficient parts and servicing support continues to drive buyers away.

Getting more for less

Most minivans are overpriced for what is essentially an upgraded car or downsized truck, and motorists needing a vehicle with large cargo- and passenger-carrying capacity should consider a Chrysler, Ford, or GM full-sized van, even if it means sacrificing some fuel economy. You just can't beat the excellent forward vision and easy-to-customize interiors that these large vans provide. Furthermore, parts are easily found and are competitively priced because of the large number of independent suppliers.

Please remember that the following minivan ratings may differ somewhat from those in *Lemon-Aid* New Cars and Minivans because of the use of more current data and an additional review of the ratings by the author. Also, some minivans that are no longer built, like the Ford Aerostar and Nissan Axxess, are given mini-ratings in Appendix II.

MINIVAN RATINGS

Above Average

DaimlerChrysler PT Cruiser (2002–04)
Honda Odyssey (2003–04)

Mazda MPV (2002–04)
Toyota Sienna (1998–2003)

Average

DaimlerChrysler Caravan, Voyager,
  Grand Caravan, Grand Voyager,
  Town & Country (2002–04)
DaimlerChrysler PT Cruiser (2001)
Ford Villager/Nissan Quest (1997–2002)
General Motors Astro, Safari
  (1996–2004)

Honda Odyssey (1996–2002)
Kia Sedona (2002–04)
Mazda MPV (2000–01)
Toyota Previa (1991–97)
Toyota Sienna (2004)

Below Average

DaimlerChrysler Caravan, Voyager,
  Grand Caravan, Grand Voyager,
  Town & Country (1998–2001)
Ford Freestar (2004)
Ford Villager/Nissan Quest (1995–96)
General Motors Astro, Safari
  (1985–95)

General Motors Lumina, Lumina APV,
  Montana, Silhouette, Trans Sport,
  Venture (1997–2004)
Mazda MPV (1988–98)
Nissan Quest (2004)

Not Recommended

DaimlerChrysler Caravan, Voyager,
  Grand Caravan, Grand Voyager,
  Town & Country (1984–97)
Ford Villager/Nissan Quest
  (1993–94)

Ford Windstar (1995–2003)
General Motors Lumina, Lumina APV,
  Montana, Sihouette, Trans Sport
  Venture (1990–96)

DaimlerChrysler

CARAVAN, VOYAGER, GRAND CARAVAN, GRAND VOYAGER, TOWN & COUNTRY

RATING: Average (2002–04); Below Average (1998–2001); Not Recommended (1984–97). Let's get this straight: Chrysler, Ford, and GM minivans are at the bottom of the heap as far as quality and dependability are concerned. Chrysler, however, has the best warranty for engines and transmissions, and only its transmissions are seriously defective. Ford and GM, on the other hand, have serious transmission and engine problems, covered by a much shorter warranty. That's why the Chrysler lineup has been given a higher rating than those of the other two Detroit automakers. **Maintenance/Repair costs:** Maintenance and repair costs are average during the first three years and then rise dramatically thereafter. Parts are reasonably priced when bought and installed by independent suppliers. **Parts:** Easy to find, reasonably priced parts. Independent garages offer cheaper parts, provide longer warranties, and will often give expert testimony when the replaced component is found to be poorly manufactured. This is especially important with transmission and ABS repairs, since an independent will furnish you with proof to get a "goodwill" refund from Chrysler or a small claims court settlement. **Extended warranty:** The 7-year Chrysler powertrain warranty is ideal, but it has only been a standard feature for the past few years. If it's expired, opt for the same warranty sold through Chrysler, if possible. If you're buying the warranty from a dealer, bargain it down to about one-third of the $1,500 asking price. Forget the bumper-to-bumper extended warranty; it's simply too expensive. **Best alternatives:** Honda's Odyssey should be your first choice. Toyota's 2003 or earlier models are a good second choice, inasmuch as the 2004 version is still working through its redesign glitches. The Mazda's 2002 and 2003 MPV is also a good used alternative. GM and Ford front- and rear-drive minivans aren't credible alternatives because of their failure-prone powertrains, brake, suspension, and steering problems, electrical short-circuits and subpar body work. Full-sized GM and Chrysler rear-drive cargo vans are more affordable and practical buys if you intend to haul a full passenger load or do some regular heavy hauling, you are physically challenged, you use lots of accessories, or you take frequent motoring excursions. Don't splurge on 2003 or 2004 Chrysler luxury minivans like the Town & Country: They will cost up to $15,000 more than a base Caravan and only be worth a few thousand more after five years on the market. **Online help:** *www.geocities.com/ plumraptor, www.autosafety.org/autodefects.html, www.datatown.com/chrysler, www.wam. umd.edu/~gluckman/Chrysler/index.html,* and *www.daimlerchryslervehicleproblems.com.*

⟨⚡⟩ Strengths and Weaknesses

Cheap and plentiful, these versatile minivans offer a wide array of standard and optional features that include AWD (dropped for 2005), anti-lock brakes, child safety seats integrated into the seatbacks, flush-design door handles, and front windshield wiper/washer controls located on the steering column lever for easier use. Childproof locks are standard, and the front bucket seats incorporate vertically adjustable head restraints. The Town & Country, a luxury version of the Caravan, comes equipped with a 3.8L V6 and standard luxury features that make the vehicle more fashionable for upscale buyers.

Chrysler's minivans continue to dominate the new- and used-minivan market, though they're quickly losing steam because of market cooling and better quality products from Japanese and South Korean automakers. Nevertheless, they offer pleasing styling and lots of convenience features at used prices that can be very attractive. They can carry up to seven passengers in comfort, and they ride and handle better than most truck-based minivans. The shorter-wheelbase minivans also offer better rear visibility and good ride quality, and are more nimble and easier to park than truck-based minivans and larger front-drive versions. Cargo hauling capability is more than adequate.

Caravans also give you a quiet and plush ride, excellent braking, lots of innovative convenience features, user-friendly instruments and controls, a driver-side sliding door, and plenty of interior room. Depreciation is much faster than with pickups, SUVs, and Japanese minivans.

Don't make the mistake of believing that Chrysler's Mercedes connection means you'll get a top-quality minivan. You won't. In fact, owner complaints and service bulletins tell me that the 2004–05 minivans will likely have similar powertrain, electrical system, brake, suspension and body deficiencies as previous versions. The following *Lemon-Aid* reader's email is rather typical:

> My 2003 Dodge Caravan is a piece of garbage. My new Caravan had a recall for a part in the transmission. It is noisy, rough running, and it doesn't get the 21–27 mpg [8–11 km/L] as advertised. 12 mpg [5 km/L] is more realistic.

These minivans pose maximum safety risks because of their chronic electronic, mechanical, and body component failures. Owners report bizarre defects, like seat belts that may strangle children, airbags that deploy when the ignition is turned on, transmissions that jump out of gear, or sudden stalling and electrical short-circuits when within radar range of airports or military installations.

Recently launched minivans continue to exhibit an array of serious mechanical deficiencies that belie Chrysler's so-called commitment to quality improvement. Some of the more serious and most common problems include the premature wearout of the engine tensioner pulley, automatic transmission speed sensors, engine head gaskets, motor mounts, starter motor, steering column glitches, front brake discs and pads (the brake pad material crumbles in your hands), front rotors and rear drums, brake master cylinder, suspension components, exhaust system components, ball joints, wheel bearings, water pumps, fuel pumps and pump wiring harnesses, radiators, heater cores, and AC units. Fuel injectors on all engines have been troublesome, the differential pin breaks through the automatic transmission casing, sliding doors malfunction, engine supports may be missing or not connected, tie-rods may suddenly break, oil pans crack, and the power-steering pump frequently leaks. Factory-installed Goodyear tires frequently fail prematurely at 40,000–65,000 km.

Since 1996, Chrysler's V6 engines have performed quite well—far better than the similar engines that equip Ford and GM minivans. Nevertheless, some owners have reported engine oil sludging and head gasket failures, hard starts, stalling, serpentine belt failures and power steering pump hose blowouts (which cause loss of power steering).

Chrysler's A604, 41TE, and 42LE automatic transmissions, phased in with the 1991 models, are a reliability nightmare that can have serious safety consequences (see "Safety Complaints"). Imagine having to count to three in traffic before Drive or Reverse will engage, limping home in Second gear at 50 km/h, or suddenly losing all forward motion in traffic.

Catastrophic transmission failures are commonplace because of poor engineering, as the following reader discovered:

> My '99 Grand Voyager had a complete differential failure at 104,000 km. The retaining pin sheared off, which allowed the main differential pin to work its way out and smash the casing and torque converter.
>
> In our case this is what happened. The gear bit, the pin spun, shearing the retaining pin off. With the centrifugal force the main pin worked its way out of the housing and smashed a 2" x 4" [4 cm x 10 cm] hole through the bell housing and nearly punctured the torque converter. In my opinion this is a design flaw that should have been corrected 10 years ago. From my research I have determined that the transaxle identification number matches the original A604 transaxle. I was shocked that they would still use these in 1999.

Fit and finish has gotten worse over the past two decades. Body hardware and interior trim are fragile and tend to break, warp, or fall off (door handles are an example). Premature rust-out of major suspension and steering components is a major safety and performance concern. Paint delamination often turns these solid-coloured minivans into two-tone models with chalky white stripes on the hood and roof.

Chrysler knows about this problem and often tries to get claimants to pay half the cost of repainting (about $1,500 on a $3,000 job), but will eventually agree to pay the total cost if the owner stands fast or threatens small claims court action.

And as the minivan takes on its albino appearance, you can listen to a self-contained orchestra of clicks, clunks, rattles, squeaks, and squeals as you drive. Giving new meaning to the phrase "surround sound," these noises usually emanate from the brakes, suspension and steering assemblies, poorly anchored bench seats, and misaligned body panels.

VEHICLE HISTORY: 1991—Restyled second generation models offered all-wheel drive, ABS, and a driver-side airbag (all optional); body was rounder and the glass area was increased. **1992**—Standard driver-side airbag. **1993**—Upgraded front shoulder belts and bucket seat tilts forward to ease entry/exit. **1994**—Passenger-side airbag, side door guard beams, a redesigned dash, and new bumpers and mouldings. **1996**—Third generation models have more aerodynamic styling, a driver-side sliding door, roll-out centre and rear seats, a longer wheelbase, standard dual airbags and ABS (ABS later became optional on base models), and a more powerful 150-hp 2.4L 4-cylinder engine. **1998**—The 3.0L V6 engine was paired with a better-performing 4-speed automatic transmission and the 3.8L V6 got 14 additional horses (180). **2000**—A new AWD Sport model (it was a sales flop) and standard cassette player and AC. **2001**—A small horsepower boost for the V6s, front side airbags, adjustable pedals, upgraded headlights, and a power-operated rear liftgate. **2002**—Fuel tank assembly redesigned to prevent post-collision fuel leakage, a tire air-pressure monitor, and a DVD entertainment system. **2003**—AutoStick transmission dropped; standard power liftgate on the Grand eX and ES models. **2004**—Not much new, except for a tire-pressure warning monitor, enhanced audio, and new keyless entry options.

There's an abundance of used Chrysler minivans on the market selling at bargain prices. However, very few have any original warranty coverage left, "goodwill" repair refunds are spotty, and guidelines are vague. Don't even consider the 4-cylinder engine—it has no place in a minivan, especially when hooked to the inadequate 3-speed automatic transmission. It lacks an Overdrive and will shift back and forth as speed varies, and it's slower and noisier than the other choices. The 3.3L V6 is a better choice for most city-driving situations, but don't hesitate to get the 3.8L if you're planning lots of highway travel or carrying four or more passengers. Since its introduction, it's been relatively trouble-free, and it's more economical on the highway than the 3.3L, which strains to maintain speed. The sliding side doors make it easy to load and unload children, install a child safety seat in the middle, or remove the rear seat. On the downside, they run the risk of exposing kids to traffic, and they're a costly, failure-prone option. Child safety seats integrated into the rear seatbacks are convenient and reasonably priced, but Chrysler's versions have had a history of tightening up excessively or not tightening enough, allowing the child to slip out. Try the seat with your child before buying it. You may wish to pass on the tinted windshields as well; they seriously reduce visibility. Be wary of models featuring all-wheel drive and ABS brakes: The powertrain isn't reliable and is horrendously expensive to repair, and Chrysler's large number of ABS failures is worrisome. Ditch the failure-prone Goodyear original equipment tires and remember that a night drive is a prerequisite to check out headlight illumination, which many call inadequate.

 **Safety Summary**

All models/years: Sudden, unintended acceleration; owners report that cruise control units often malfunction, accelerating or decelerating the vehicle without any warning. • Airbag malfunctions.

Get used to the term "clockspring." It's an expensive little component that controls some parts within the steering wheel and, when defective, can result in the airbag warning light coming on or cause the airbag, cruise control, or horn to fail. It has been a pain in the butt for Chrysler minivan owners since the 1996 model year. Chrysler has extended its warranty for 1996 through 2000 model year minivans in two separate recalls and replaced the clockspring at no charge. Apparently, the automaker has found that the part fails because it was wound too tight or short-circuited from corrosion.

• Defective engine head gaskets, rocker arm gaskets, and engine mounts. • Engine sags, hesitation, stumble, hard starts, or stalling. • No steering/lock-up. • Carbon monoxide comes through air vents. • Brakes wear out prematurely, or fail completely. • Transmission fails, suddenly drops into low gear, won't go into Reverse, delays engagement, or jumps out of gear when running or parked. • One can move the automatic transmission shift lever without applying brakes. • Several incidents where ignition was turned and vehicle went into Reverse at full throttle, although transmission was set in Park. • ABS failure caused an accident. • Many complaints of front suspension strut towers rusting, then cracking at the weld seams; jig-positioning hole wasn't sealed at the factory. • Brakes activated by themselves while driving. • Prematurely warped rotors and worn-out pads cause excessive vibrations when stopping. • Seatbacks fall backward. • Rear windows fall out or shatter. • Power window and door lock failures. • Sliding door often opens while vehicle is underway, or jams, trapping occupants. • Weak headlights. • Horn often doesn't work. • Several incidents where side windows exploded for no apparent reason. • Adults cannot sit in third-row seat without their heads smashing into the roof as the vehicle passes over bumps. **1996–2002**—Steering may emit a popping or ticking noise. **1998**—Engine overheating. • Right rear tail light caught fire. • Frequent replacement of the steering column and rack and pinion; in one incident, the steering wheel separated from the steering column. • Front suspension strut failure. • Many reports of defective liftgate gas shocks. • Many incidents reported of electrical short circuits and total electrical system failure. • Difficult to see through windshield in direct sunlight. • Defroster vent reflects in the windshield, obscuring driver's vision. • Poor steering-wheel design blocks the view of instruments and indicators. • Rear-view mirror often falls off. • Horn hard to find on steering hub. **1999**—Instrument panel fire. • Faulty speed sensors cause the automatic transmission to shift erratically and harshly. • Five-year-old was able to pull shift lever out of Park into Drive without engaging brakes. • Sudden tie-rod breakage, causing loss of vehicle control. • Chronic steering pump and rack failures. • Poor braking performance: brake pedal depressed to the floor with little or no effect; excessive vibrations or shuddering when braking. • Rusted-through front brake rotors and rear brake drums. • Power side windows fail to roll up. • Dash gauges all go dead intermittently. **2000**—Gas tank rupture. • Engine camshaft failure. • Although the owner's manual says vehicle should have a transmission/brake interlock, the feature is lacking (see "Secret Warranties/Internal Bulletins/Service Tips"). • Cruise control malfunctions. **2000–01**—Sudden loss of engine power, accompanied by fuel leakage from the engine compartment. • Emergency parking brake may not release because of premature corrosion. • Right front brake locked up while driving, causing the vehicle to suddenly turn 90 degrees to the right; same phenomenon when braking. • Transmission shift lever blocks the driver's right knee when braking. • Fifth-wheel assembly fell off while vehicle was underway. • Instruments are recessed too deep into the dash, making it hard to read the fuel gauge and speedometer, especially at night. **2001–02**—Engine camshafts may have an improperly machined oil groove. • Snow and water ingestion into rear brake drum. • Inaccurate fuel tank gauge drops one-quarter to one-half while driving. • Faulty power seat adjuster. • Difficult to remove fuel cap (install a new seal); this free repair applies to all of the 2002 vehicle lineup. **2002**—Adults cannot sit in third-row seat without their heads bumping into the roof as the vehicle passes over bumps. • Airbags deployed for no reason. • Airbag light comes on randomly and clock spring defect disabled the airbag. • Middle-seat seat belt unbuckles on its own. • Headlights come on and off on their own. **2003**—Exposed electrical wires under the front seats. • Excessive steering vibration. • Seat belts unlatch themselves. • Missing suspension bolt caused the right side to collapse. • Wiper blades stick together. **2004**—Chronic stalling. • Airbag clockspring failed, causing cruise control to malfunction. • Seat belts don't latch properly.

Secret Warranties/Internal Bulletins/Service Tips

> **BULLETIN NO: 23-044-02**   **DATE: OCT. 14, 2002**
>
> **SUSPENSION/BODY –**
> **STRUT TOWER CORROSION**
>
> **SUBJECT:** NS Strut Tower Corrosion
> **OVERVIEW:** This bulletin involves correcting a corrosion staining, surface corrosion, or corrosion perforation condition at the top of the strut tower(s).
>
> 1996–2000 NS Town & Country/Voyager/ Caravan
>
> **SYMPTOM/CONDITION:** Cosmetic corrosion or perforation at upper strut tower(s) usually between the strut and upper load path beam inner panel (inner fender).

All models/years: If pressed, Chrysler will replace the AC evaporator for free up to seven years. Other AC component costs are negotiable. **1993–2002**—Paint delamination, peeling, or fading (see Part Two "Paint and Body Defects," pages 71–75). • A rotten-egg odour coming from the exhaust may be the result of a malfunctioning catalytic converter, probably covered under the emissions warranty. **1995–98**—Possible causes of delayed transmission engagement (TSB #21-07-98). **1996–99**—A serpentine belt that slips off the idler pulley requires an upgraded bracket. • Upgraded engine head gasket. • Oil seepage from the cam position sensor. **1996–2000**—Strut tower corrosion (see bulletin at left). • Cruise control that won't hold the vehicle's speed when going uphill may have a faulty check valve. • Countermeasures detailed to correct a steering column click or rattle. • Airbag warning light stays lit. **1996–2001**—AWD models must be equipped with identical tires; otherwise, the power transfer unit may self-destruct. • A suspension squawk or knock probably means the sway bar link needs replacing under Chrysler's "goodwill" policy (5 years/100,000 km). **1996–2005**—Rusted, frozen rear brake drums.

REAR DRUM WATER/SNOW INGESTION/FREEZING

BULLETIN NO: 05-002-04　　　　　　　　　　　　　　　　　　　　**DATE: FEB. 17, 2004**

SNOW/WATER INGESTION INTO REAR BRAKE DRUM

This bulletin involves installing a revised rear drum brake support (backing) plate and possible replacement of the rear brake shoes and drums.

2001–2005 Town & Country/Voyager/Caravan; 1996–2000 Town & Country/Caravan/Voyager; 1996–2000 Chrysler Voyager (International Markets)

SYMPTOM/CONDITION: While driving through deep or blowing snow/water, the snow/water may enter the rear brake drums causing rust to develop on the rear brake drum and shoe friction surfaces. This condition can lead to temporary freezing of the rear brake linings to the drums. This symptom is experienced after the vehicle has been parked in below freezing temperatures long enough for the snow/water to freeze inside of the rear brake drums. When the parking brake has been applied the symptom is more likely to occur.

• Roof panel is wavy or has depressions. **1997–98**—Engines that run poorly or stall may need the powertrain control module (PCM) reprogrammed under the emissions warranty. **1997–2000**—If the ignition key can't be turned or cannot be removed, TSB #23-23-00 proposes four possible corrections. **1997–2001**— Rear brake noise (see following bulletin).

REAR BRAKE HOWL/MOAN

BULLETIN NO: 05-003-01　　　　　　　　　　　　　　　　　　　　**DATE: APRIL 20, 2001**

OVERVIEW: This bulletin involves replacing the rear disc brake adapters.

1997–2001 Voyager/Caravan/Town & Country

SYMPTOM/CONDITION: During low speed and/or low speed turns such as a parking lot manoeuvre, with no brake pedal pressure applied, a low frequency howl/moan noise is heard from the rear brake area.

1998—A faulty radiator fan relay may cause the engine to overheat; replace it with a new relay and reprogram the PCM under Customer Satisfaction Notice #771. **1998–99**—Front brakes continue to wear out quickly on front-drive minivans. Owners report that Chrysler pays half the cost of brake repairs for up to 2 years/40,000 km. • Silence a chronic squeaking noise coming from underneath the vehicle by installing a new strut pivot bearing. **1998–2000**—Troubleshooting AC compressor failure. **1999–2000**—Measures to prevent the right-side sliding door trim panel from hitting the quarter panel when the door is opened. **2000**— Delayed shifts. **2000–01**—Poor starting. • Rear disc brake squeal. • AC compressor failure, loss of engine power when switching on the AC, serpentine belt chirping, and spark knock can all be traced to a miscalibrated PCM. • No heat on front right side because of a defective blend air door. • AC compressor squeal. • Rear bench seat rattle or groan. • Hood hinge rattle. • Inoperative overhead reading lamp and rear wiper. • Noisy roof rack and power-sliding door. **2001–02**—Engine surging at highway speeds. • Engine knocking. • Engine sag and hesitation caused by a faulty throttle position sensor (TPS). • Engine mount grinding or clicking. • Steering wheel shudder; steering column popping or ticking. • Poor rear AC performance. • AC leaks water onto passenger-side carpet. • Wind or water leaks at the rear quarter window. • High-pitched belt-like squeal at high engine rpm. • Sliding door reverses direction. • Incorrect fuel gauge indicator. • Loose tail light. • Flickering digital display. **2001–03**—Rear brake rubbing sound. • Oil filter leaks with 3.3L and 3.8L engines (confirmed in TSB # 09-001-03):

> On February 25, 2003, my 2002 Grand Caravan lost almost all of its engine oil which resulted in engine failure. At no time did the vehicle's warning sensors indicate any problem with the engine. The failure was the result of a leak in the filter gasket of the FE292 Mopar oil filter. Documentation from the oil filter manufacturer indicates that the oil filter gasket overhangs the inside diameter of the adapter head by .1 cm/side [.045 in./side].

2001–04—AC water leaks. **2002**—Transmission slips in First or Reverse gear. • Airbags deployed for no reason. • Airbag light comes on randomly and clock spring defect disabled the airbag. • Power-steering fluid leakage. • Middle-seat seat belt unbuckles on its own. • Rear side vent window exploded while driving. • Erratically operating power sliding door or liftgate. • Headlights come on and off on their own. • Noisy engine and transmission. **2002–03**—Sliding door or liftgate malfunctions. **2003**—Troubleshooting water leaks. • Three bulletins relating to automatic transmission malfunctions: delayed gear engagement, harsh 4–3 downshift, and excessive vibration and transfer gear whine. **2004**—Rough idle, hesitation, and hard starts. • Accessory drivebelt chirping. • Front suspension rattling. **2004–05**—Warm engine rough idle. • Transmission ticking.

CARAVAN, VOYAGER, GRAND CARAVAN, GRAND VOYAGER, TOWN & COUNTRY PROFILE

	1996	1997	1998	1999	2000	2001	2002	2003	2004
Cost Price ($)									
Caravan	18,840	19,885	20,255	24,230	24,970	24,885	25,430	25,430	27,620
Grand Caravan	20,320	21,465	23,160	25,890	26,665	29,505	28,875	29,295	30,190
Town & Country	38,280	40,350	41,040	41,260	41,815	41,150	40,815	42,705	44,095
Used Values ($)									
Caravan ▲	3,500	4,500	5,500	7,000	9,000	11,500	14,000	16,000	19,000
Caravan ▼	3,000	4,000	5,000	6,000	7,500	10,000	12,500	15,500	17,500

All ratings on a numbered scale where ⑤ is good and ❶ is bad. See pages 100–101 for a more detailed description.

Grand Caravan ▲	4,000	5,000	6,000	7,500	9,500	12,500	15,500	18,000	21,000
Grand Caravan ▼	3,500	4,500	5,500	6,000	8,000	11,000	14,000	16,500	19,500
Town & Country ▲	4,500	5,500	7,000	9,500	12,500	15,000	21,000	25,500	29,000
Town & Country ▼	4,000	5,000	5,500	8,000	11,000	13,500	19,500	24,000	28,000
Reliability	❶	❶	❷	❷	❷	❷	❸	❸	❸
Crash Safety (F)									
Caravan	—	④	③	—	④	④	④	④	④
Grand Caravan	③	③	③	④	④	④	④	④	④
Town & Country	—	④	③	—	—	—	—	④	④
Town & Country LX	③	③	③	④	④	④	④	④	④
Side									
Caravan	—	—	—	⑤	⑤	④	④	④	④
Grand Caravan	—	—	—	⑤	⑤	④	⑤	⑤	⑤
Town & Country LX	—	—	—	⑤	⑤	④	⑤	⑤	④
Offset (Grand Caravan)	❷	❷	❷	❷	❷	❶	❸	❸	❸
Town & Country	❷	❷	❷	❷	❷	❶	❸	❸	❸
Rollover Resistance	—	—	—	—	—	❸	❸	❸	—

Note: Voyager and Grand Voyager prices and ratings are almost identical to those of the Caravan and Grand Caravan.

PT CRUISER ★★★★

RATING: Above Average (2002–04); Average (2001). The 2002 and later models' powertrain warranty makes a big difference in the Cruiser's rating. Nevertheless, despite its hot-rod flair, this Neon spin-off's popularity is waning, with sales down 25 percent. Similar hard times have hit other "nostalgia" cars, like the VW New Beetle and resurrected Ford Thunderbird; only the Mini Cooper has remained popular. **Maintenance/Repair costs:** Average, until the 5-year mark, when first-year glitches and the warranty's expiration will likely hike maintenance and repair costs. This is another reason to buy a supplementary powertrain warranty or to choose a 2002 or later version protected by Chrysler's 7-year warranty. **Parts:** Reasonably priced, since many parts come from the Neon generic parts bin. Body parts are another matter. Expect long delays and high costs. **Extended warranty:** A good idea if you don't have Chrysler's original 7-year powertrain warranty. **Best alternatives:** Try Mazda's MPV minivan, or the following wagons: VW's Jetta wagon, the Subaru Legacy Outback Limited, or the Volvo V40. Sport-utilities worth considering are the Subaru Forester, Honda CR-V EX, GM Tracker, Hyundai Santa Fe, and Suzuki Grand Vitara. Not much to choose from the American stable. The Escape is riddled with factory-related defects and uses poor quality powertrains, and the Liberty is both unreliable and rollover-prone, say NHTSA's safety complaint log, *Autoweek*, and Germany's *Auto Bild* magazine ("Wie gefährlich ist der Jeep?" or "How dangerous is the Jeep?"). GM's Astro and Safari will do in a pinch if rear-drive brawn is needed. **Online help:** *www.ptcruiser.org, www.ptcruiserlinks.com, www.data-town.com/chrysler, www.wam.umd.edu/~gluckman/Chrysler/index.html, www.daimlerchryslervehicleproblems.com,* and *www.autosafety.org/autodefects.html.*

 ## Strengths and Weaknesses

Cobbled together with Neon parts and engineering, the PT Cruiser is essentially a fuel- and space-efficient hatchback mini-minivan. It's noted for excellent fuel economy (regular fuel), nimble handling around town, good braking, lots of interior space, easy access, a versatile cargo area, many thoughtful interior amenities, slow depreciation, and unforgettable hot-rod styling.

Forget about hot-rod power with the base engine, though. The 2.4L 150-hp, 4-cylinder power plant is not very smooth running and, when matched with the automatic transmission, struggles when going uphill or merging with freeway traffic. This requires frequent downshifting and lots of patience—accelerating to 100 km/h takes about 9 seconds. Costlier turbocharged models will give you plenty of power, but you risk some steep repair bills. The automatic transmission doesn't have much low-end torque, either, forcing early kickdown shifting and deft manipulation of the accelerator pedal. High-speed handling is competent, but not impressive; hard cornering produces an unsteady, wobbly ride because of the car's height. Count on a firm ride with lots of engine, wind, and road noise in the cabin area. ABS braking is acceptable, when the system functions as it should.

VEHICLE HISTORY: 2002—A CD player and underseat storage bin. **2003**—A new 215-hp turbocharged GT and 17-inch wheels. **2004**—A second optional turbo is unveiled with 40 less horses (180) than the 220-hp GT.

Reliability has been surprisingly good so far, although there have been some drivetrain complaints that include faulty valve cover gaskets causing oil burning, and automatic transmission failures and erratic shifting (forcing the drivetrain to gear down to "limp mode") caused by faulty powertrain control modules:

> I have had my transmission go out twice now. The first time the whole tranny had to be replaced, second time it just lost all its fluid. The 41TE transmission is one of the worst transmissions ever made. Go to any search engine and type in 41TE and all the websites talking about the problems with the tranny will come up. DC has known of the problems since 1989 and doesn't care.

Writes another owner of a 2001 PT Cruiser:

> Transmission control unit went out on the freeway in stop-and-go traffic. Tranny went into failsafe (Second gear) so I drove it to the dealership for repairs. Took one

day (they had the part in stock). Two days later, my wife's Dodge Caravan had the same part go out on her.

Premature failure of the power-steering pump and the steering unit are also frequent problems that can result in costly repairs once the warranty expires.

Windshield stress cracks are another PT Cruiser specialty reported on the Internet by owners in Australia, Canada, and the United States. Chrysler is replacing the windshields under a "goodwill" program while insisting that its unlucky windshields just happen to be "rock prone."

Other owner complaints read like an anthology of common Chrysler defects: annoying wind noise when driving with the rear window or sunroof open; drivetrain whine; moisture between clearcoat and paint that turns the hood a chalky white colour; and water leaks through the passenger-side window.

 ## Safety Summary

2001—Some side wind instability. • Tall drivers beware: The windshield is uncomfortably close, and its styling makes it difficult to see overhead traffic lights. • The three small and recessed instrument pods are difficult to read in the daylight. • Wide pillars obstruct one's view. • When parked, transmission slipped out of gear and vehicle rolled down driveway. • Hot exhaust may melt the rear bumper. • Oil blows through tailpipe. • Engine suddenly shuts down when vehicle passes through a large puddle. • Sudden loss of all electrical power. • Chronic stalling caused by a faulty ignition coil. • Defective powertrain control module (PCM). • Steering wheel loosens on its shaft. • Excessive vibration caused by out-of-round tires or a loose suspension. • Steering column popping or cracking sound. • Head restraints won't stay in position; they tend to drift up. • Headlights flicker from bright to dim. • Low beam headlight may suddenly go out. • Only part of the headlight beam illuminates the roadway. **2002**—Sudden, unintended acceleration. • Gas pedal went to floor with no acceleration. • Airbags deployed for no reason, or failed to deploy. • Suddenly shifts into First gear while cruising. • Sudden brake lock-up. • Headrests are too high, block vision. • Optima battery leaks acid. • White powder leaks from airbag. • Hard-to-read speedometer. **2003**—Airbags failed to deploy. • Chronic engine overheating. • Sudden front axle/bearing seizure threw car out of control and caused $7,000 damage to the drivetrain. • Other automatic transmission failures while car was underway. • Premature failure of the clutch assembly. • Headlights flicker when braking. • Chrysler misleads buyers by telling them that the car has a rear stabilizer bar when really it's just a beefed-up axle (see *www.petitiononline.com/2003stab/petition.html*). • Sudden, unintended acceleration while stopped at a traffic light or when braking. • Self-activating door locks and seat heater. • Third brake light gasket doesn't sit flush to the windshield. • Goodyear Eagle tire sidewall blew out.

Secret Warranties/Internal Bulletins/Service Tips

All models/years: 2001—Hard starting caused by a faulty fuel pump module. • Hard starting in cold weather because of the 5-volt regulator failure in the SBEC PCM. • A faulty transmission control module (TCM) may cause harsh shifting. • MIL (malfunction indicator light) comes on because of a faulty TCM harness connector or a defective evaporator purge flow monitor. • Poor acceleration and spark knock. • Because of a delamination problem, the accessory drivebelt for the power steering pump and AC compressor may need replacement. • Left or right floor latch on rear seat won't release. • Fuel gauge won't indicate full. • Missing or loose roof luggage rack stanchion. • Airbag pads fall off. • Airbag rattles. • Ticking noise caused by faulty rear body exhauster. • Discoloured B- and C-pillar door appliqués. • Wind buffeting with the windows and/or sunroof open or partially opened. • The front door water dam may contact the speaker and create a buzzing or humming. **2001–02**—Highway speed surge. **2001–03**—Alarm sounds for no reason. • Transmission slips in Reverse or First gear. • Moisture accumulation in headlights. • High-speed engine surging. **2002–03**—Steering column clicking. **2003**—Turbo engine hesitation, loss of boost, and screeching. • Delayed gear engagement. • Harsh 4–3 downshift. • Rear windshield washer nozzle leak. • Warning lights come on for no reason. • Warped rear bumper.

PT CRUISER PROFILE

	2001	2002	2003	2004
Cost Price ($)				
Base	23,665	23,850	22,500	24,360
Limited	27,180	27,305	27,420	28,800
Turbo	—	—	27,700	31,350
Used Values ($)				
PT Cruiser ▲	13,000	14,000	15,500	17,500
PT Cruiser ▼	11,500	12,500	14,000	16,000
Limited ▲	13,500	15,500	17,500	20,000
Limited ▼	12,500	14,000	16,000	18,500
Turbo ▲	—	—	18,500	21,000
Turbo ▼	—	—	17,000	19,500
Reliability	④	④	④	④
Crash Safety (F)	❷	④	④	④
Side	④	④	④	—
Head Restraints	⑤	⑤	⑤	⑤
Rollover Resistance	④	④	④	—

Ford

bad buy **WINDSTAR/FREESTAR** ★★

RATING: *Windstar*: Not Recommended (1995–2003). Infamous for atrocious quality control, stonewalled complaints, and life-threatening defects. *Freestar*: Below Average (2004). Freestar is a warmed-over Windstar, with its own serious quality control problems. Windstars have similar transmission, brake, and AC failures to the Chrysler and GM competition, and their engines aren't very reliable. Unfortunately, Ford doesn't protect its owners with a 7-year powertrain warranty like Chrysler does, hence the different ratings for the two vehicles. **Maintenance/ Repair costs:** Average while under warranty; outrageously higher than average thereafter, primarily because powertrain breakdowns are not covered by warranty or are insufficiently covered by parsimonious "goodwill" gestures. **Parts:** Reasonably priced parts are easy to find. Independent suppliers are lured by attractive profits sustained by parts that apparently have a high failure rate, like brake master cylinders and speedometers. Digital speedometers are often defective and can cost almost $1000 to repair. **Extended warranty:** Definitely, and don't leave home without it. A Saint Christopher medallion would also help. **Best alternatives:** You still can't beat the Japanese for minivan reliability and performance. Honda's Odyssey and the 2003 or earlier Toyota Sienna are the best choices if you don't mind spending a few thousand dollars more. You can cut costs and get fairly good reliability from recent Mazda MPVs and GM's Astro or Safari. Some full-sized GM (Chevy Van and Vandura) or Chrysler rear-drive cargo vans might be a more affordable and practical buy. Even an older Ford Aerostar rear-drive minivan may fit the bill if the automatic transmission, electrical system, and brakes check out okay. **Online help:** *www.tgrigsby.com/views/ford.htm, ca.geocities.com/windstar-woes,* and *www.autosafety.org/autodefects.html.*

 ## Strengths and Weaknesses

Ford can call it the Windstar or the Freestar; the fact remains that owners call it garbage.

Sure, the Windstar combines an impressive five-star crash safety rating, plenty of raw power, an exceptional ride, and impressive cargo capacity. But these minivans have failure-prone engines, self-destructing automatic transmissions, "do you feel lucky today?" brakes, and unreliable electrical systems. Particularly scary is Ford's admission that Windstar's suspension includes poor-quality coil springs that frequently break, blow out the front tire, and make the minivan uncontrollable. As solace, Ford says it will pay for coil breakage up to ten years on vehicles registered in rust-prone regions.

And, as another counterpoint to Ford's Windstar crashworthiness boasting, there's a frightening archive of Windstar safety-related failures compiled by the U.S. Department of Transportation's NHTSA. Besides the many coil spring failures already noted (these have affected almost all of Ford's vehicles for practically a decade), owners report sudden acceleration, stalling, steering loss, windows exploding, wheels falling off, horn failures, sliding doors that open and close on their own, and vehicles rolling away while parked.

Other safety-related deficiencies include the lack of head restraints for all seats on early Windstars, and a digital dash that's often confusing, failure-prone, and expensive to replace. Optional adjustable pedals help protect drivers from airbag injuries. Be careful, though; some drivers have found that these are set too close together and seem loose. Drivers must also contend with mediocre handling, restricted side and rear visibility, and an abundance of clunks, rattles, and wind and road noise.

Freestar is a very small step up from the Windstar.

VEHICLE HISTORY: 1996—45 more horses added to the 3.8L engine (200), a smaller 3.0L V6 powers the GL, upgraded seat belts, and a tilt-slide driver-side seat to improve rear seat access. **1998**—A wider driver-side door, easier rear seat access, and new front styling. **1999**—A bit more interior space; the third-row bench got built-in rollers; improved steering and brakes (compromised by rear drums, though); ABS; an anti-theft system; new side panels; a new liftgate; larger headlights and tail lights; and a revised instrument panel. **2001**—The base 3.0L V6 is gone, an upgraded automatic transmission, a low-tire-pressure warning system, "smart" airbags, new airbag sensors, and a slight restyling. **2002**—Dual sliding doors. **2003**—An optional anti-skid system. **2004**—Freestar arrives, and flops.

Freestar: Too little, too late

In 2004, Windstar was reincarnated and renamed the Freestar. Sales almost immediately nosedived about 22 percent from the Windstar's 2003 poor sales figures, as shoppers saw through the masquerade and fled.

Built on a modified Taurus platform, Freestar gives you the same uninspired, though predictable, carlike handling characteristics of Ford's mid-size family sedans. You'll encounter many of the horrific engine, automatic transmission, electrical, suspension, and brake system problems experienced by Taurus and Sable owners.

Freestar does feature some upgrades in safety, interior design, steering, ride, and performance, but it still lags far behind the Japanese competition for overall performance and dependability. Entry-level LX models came with a 200-hp 3.9L V6, based on the Windstar's 3.8L engine. Uplevel SE and top-line limited models got a new 201-hp 4.2L V6, also derived from the 3.8L. It comes with larger four-wheel disc brakes and an optional "safety canopy" side-curtain airbag system that offers protection in side-impact collisions and rollovers for all three rows of seating. There's also better access to the third-row seat, which folds flat into the floor.

Engine and transmission failures

Engine and transmission failures are commonplace. The 3.0L engine is overwhelmed by the Windstar's heft and struggles to keep up, but opting for the 3.8L V6 may get you into worse trouble. Even when it's running properly, the 3.8L knocks loudly when under load, and pings at other times. Far more serious is the high failure rate of 3.8L engine head gaskets shortly after the 60,000 km mark. Ford's 7-year/160,000 km Owner Notification Program only covers '95s, so owners are asked to pay $1,000 to $3,000 for an engine repair, depending upon how much the engine has overheated. Transmission repairs seldom cost less than $3,000.

Early warning signs are few and benign: The engine may lose some power or overheat; the transmission pauses before downshifting or shifts roughly into a higher gear. Owners may also hear a transmission whining or groaning sound, accompanied by driveline vibrations. There is no other prior warning before the transmission breaks down completely and the minivan comes to a sudden banging, clanging halt.

> Phil, I just want to thank you for saving us at least $1,500. The transmission in our '98 Windstar went bang with only 47,300 miles [75,700 km]. After reading

about Ford's goodwill adjustment, we were told by our local Ford dealer that owner participation would be $495. We received a new rebuilt Ford unit installed. Believe it or not, I am a fairly good mechanic myself and this came with no warning! We even serviced the transmission at 42,000 miles [67,200 km] and found no debris or evidence of a problem.

Ford admits automatic transmission glitches may afflict its 2001 Taurus, Sable, Windstar, and Continental. In a March 2001 Special Service Instruction (SSI) #01T01, Ford authorized its dealers to replace all defective transaxles listed in its TSB, which describes the defect in the following manner:

> The driver may initially experience a transaxle "slip" or "Neutral" condition during a 2–3 shift event. Extended driving may result in loss of Third gear function and ultimately loss of Second gear function. The driver will still be able to operate the vehicle, but at a reduced level of performance.

Ford's memo states that owners weren't to be notified of the potential problem (they obviously didn't count on *Lemon-Aid* getting a copy of their memo).

Brakes are another Windstar worry. They aren't reliable, and calipers, rotors, and the master cylinder often need replacing. Other frequent Windstar problems concern no-starts and chronic stalling, believed to be caused by a faulty fuel pump or powertrain control module (PCM); electrical system power-steering failures; hard steering at slow speeds; excessive steering wheel vibrations; sudden tire tread separation and premature tread wear; advanced coil spring corrosion, leading to spring collapse and puncturing of the front tire (only 1997–98 models were recalled); rear shock failures at 110 km/h; left-side axle breakage while underway; exploding rear windshields; power-sliding door malfunctions; and failure-prone digital speedometers that are horrendously expensive to replace. There have also been many complaints concerning faulty computer modules; engine oil leaks; AC failures; and early replacement of engine camshafts, tie-rods, and brake rotors and calipers.

Getting compensation

Since 1997, I've lobbied Ford to stop playing "Let's Make a Deal" with its customers and to set up a formal 7-year/160,000 km engine and transmission warranty similar to its 1994–95 model 3.8L engine extended warranty and emission warranty guidelines (see "Secret Warranties/Internal Bulletins/Service Tips" on page 441). I warned the company that failure to protect owners would result in huge sales losses by Ford as the word spread that its vehicles were lemons.

In the ensuing three years, under the capable leadership of Ms. Bobbie Gaunt, president of Ford Canada, hundreds of engine and transmissions claims were amicably settled using my suggested benchmark.

But it didn't last. Ford USA got wind of it and squashed the Canadian initiative. Interestingly, the three top Ford Canada executives who pleaded the Canadian case have since left the company. And Jac Nasser, Ford USA's CEO, who rejected additional protection for owners, was fired shortly thereafter when he tried a similar move with Firestone claimants. (No, Nasser isn't one of my favourite auto executives.)

As I predicted, Ford's sales have plummeted, small claims court judgments are pummeling the company, and owners are vowing to never again buy any Ford product:

> Hi Phil: I just wanted to let you know that I did have to go to small claims court to nudge Ford into action. In pretrial settlement proceedings, the Ford representative at first gave me an offer of $980 for my troubles. I countered with the actual cost of $2,190 to replace my '96 Windstar's transmission. He did not like that idea, and we went back into the court setting. After instruction from the judge, I began to copy my 200+ pages (for the judge as evidence) of documentation for why this is a recurring problem with Ford transmissions (thank you, by the way, for all the great info).
>
> I think it made him a little scared, so I asked if he would settle for $1,600 (a middle ground of our original proposals) to which he accepted. My transmission costs were $2,190, so I basically paid about $600 for a new transmission (not a Ford replacement, either).
>
> Anyway, I figured a guaranteed $1,600 was better than not knowing what would happen in court. Thanks for your help!

Ford's denial of owner claims has been blasted in small claims court judgments across Canada over the past few years. Judges have ruled that engines and transmissions (and power-sliding doors) must be reasonably durable long after the warranty expires, whether the vehicle was bought new or used, notwithstanding that it was repaired by an independent, or that had the same problem repaired earlier for free. The three most recent engine judgments supporting Ford owners are *Dufour v. Ford Canada Ltd, Schaffler v. Ford Motor Company Limited and Embrun Ford Sales Ltd.*, and *John R. Reid and Laurie M. McCall v. Ford Motor Company of Canada* (see Part 2).

Automatic transmission lawsuits have also been quite successful. They are often settled out of court because Ford frequently offers 50–75 percent refunds if the lawsuit is dropped. For one *Lemon-Aid* reader's tips on beating Ford, see pages 77–79.

Dangerous doors

We noted previously that Ford has been slammed by the courts for allowing dangerously defective sliding doors to go uncorrected year after year. Typical scenarios reported by owners include: a sliding door slammed shut on a child's head while the vehicle was parked on an incline; passengers are often pinned by the door; the door reopens as it is closing; and the door often pops open while vehicle is underway. • Driver's finger broken in closing manual sliding door; the handle is too close to the door jam and the hazard has been reported on the Internet since 1999:

> I am writing about our 2003 Ford Windstar. Our passenger automatic sliding door frequently pops open after it appears to have latched shut. It has opened by itself on three occasions while the van was in drive. Recently my three year old daughter almost fell out of the van headfirst onto concrete because the door popped back open as soon as it "latched" shut. The van has been in to repair this problem seven times without success. We first started having problems with both doors within the first 2 weeks of purchase. The times the door has popped back open are way to numerous to count.

•2003 Windstar automatic sliding door opens by itself—no command; door will not power open; door lock assembly freezes. The door has opened itself while the vehicle is in motion—very scary and dangerous for my children. This is a problem Ford has known about but have not been proactive about fixing (see Ford TSB article 03-6-8).

Mental distress (door failures)

In *Sharman v. Formula Ford Sales Limited, Ford Credit Limited, and Ford Motor Company of Canada Limited*, Ontario Superior Court of Justice, No: 17419/02SR, 2003/10/07, Justice Sheppard awarded the owner of a 2000 Windstar $7,500 for mental distress resulting from the breach of the implied warranty of fitness, plus $7,207 for breach of contract and breach of warranty. Problem: The Windstar's sliding door wasn't secure and leaked air and water after many attempts to repair it. Interestingly, the judge cited the Wharton decision (see page 48), among other decisions, as support for his award for mental distress.

 **Safety Summary**

All models/years: These are the most dangerous minivans on the market. 1998 Windstar owners have logged over 1,549 safety-related complaints in the NHTSA database, compared to the 708 incidents registered against Chrysler's 1998 Caravan, which had more than double the sales. And it gets worse the further back you go. **1995–98**—The following is a short summary of problems carried over year after year; I don't have the space to list many other reported defects.

Nevertheless, you can easily access NHTSA's website (see Appendix I) for the details of thousands of other Windstar complaints. • Airbag failed to deploy. • Severe injuries caused by airbag deployment. • Sudden acceleration and chronic stalling. • Control arm and inner tie-rod failures cause the wheel to fall off. • Sudden steering lock-up or loss of steering ability. • Engine head gasket failures. • Loose or missing front brake bolts could cause the wheels to lock up or the vehicle to lose control. • Chronic ABS and transmission failures. • Almost a dozen reports that the vehicle jumps out of Park and rolls away when on an incline, or slips into Reverse with the engine idling. • Transmission and axle separation. • Faulty fuel pump, sensor, and gauge. • Built-in child safety seat is easy to get out of, but the securing seat belts are too tight; child almost strangled. • Faulty rear liftgate latches; trunk lid can fall on one's head. • Horn doesn't work properly. **1999**—This is a summary of the several hundred complaints in the NHTSA database. Keep in mind that many of these defects have been found in previous model year Windstars, but may not have been included because of space limitations. • Airbag failed to deploy. • While parked, cruising, turning on the ignition, or when brakes are applied, vehicle suddenly accelerates. • Stuck accelerator causes unintended acceleration. • Chronic stalling caused by fuel vapour lock or faulty fuel pump. • Check Engine light constantly comes on because of a faulty gas cap or over-sensitive warning system. • Front passenger-side wheel fell off when turning at a traffic light; in another reported incident, dealer found the five lug nuts had broken in half. • Vehicle pops out of gear while parked and rolls away. • Frequent transmission failures, including noisy engagement, won't engage forward or Reverse, slips, or jerks into gear. • Transmission jumped from Park to Reverse and pinned driver against tree (similar transmission problems have affected Ford vehicles for almost three decades). • Sudden loss of power steering, chronic leakage of fluid, and early replacement of steering components, like the pump and hoses. • Excessive brake fade after successive stops. • When brake pedal is depressed, it sinks below the accelerator pedal level, causing the accelerator to be pressed as well—particularly annoying for drivers with large feet. • ABS module wire burned out. • Complete electrical failure during rainstorm. • Horn button "sweet spot" is too small and takes too much pressure to activate; one owner says, "Horn doesn't work unless you hit it with a sledgehammer." • Windshield suddenly exploded when car was slowly accelerating. • Sliding door opens and closes on its own, sticks open or closed, or suddenly slams shut on a downgrade. • Sliding door closed on child's arm. • Door locks don't stay locked; passenger-side door opened when turning, causing passenger to fall out. • Many complaints that the side or rear windows suddenly exploded. • Rear defogger isn't operable (lower part of windshield isn't clear) in inclement weather when windshield wipers are activated. • Windshield wipers fail to clear windshield. • Water pours from dash onto front passenger floor. • Floor cupholder trips passengers. • Continental General tires lose air and crack between the treads. • Unspecified original equipment tires have sudden tread separation. • Large A-pillar (where windshield attaches to door) seriously impairs forward visibility, hiding pedestrians. • Seat belts aren't as they're described in owner's manual (supposed to be automatically retractable). • Two incidents where flames shot up out of fuel tank filler spout when gassing up. **2000**—Vehicle caught on fire while parked. • Sudden, unintended acceleration while stopped. • Chronic stalling; engine shuts down when turning. • Sometimes cruise control won't engage or engages on its own. • Right passenger-side wheel came off because of lug nut failure. • One Ingersoll, Ontario owner of a year 2000 Windstar recounts the following harrowing experience:

> Last week, as my wife was running errands, the support arm that goes from the rear crossmember (not an axle anymore) up under the floor, broke in half. The dealer replaced the whole rear end as it is one welded assembly. If she had been on the highway going 80 km/h she would probably have been in a bad accident.

• Check Engine light constantly comes on for no reason. • Driver heard a banging noise and Windstar suddenly went into a tailspin; dealer blamed pins that "fell out of spindle." • Transmission jumped out of gear while on highway. • Many reports of premature transmission replacements. • Transmission lever can be shifted without depressing brake pedal (unsafe for children). • After several dealer visits, brakes still spongy, pedal goes to floor without braking, and emergency brake has almost no effect. • When braking, foot also contacts the accelerator pedal. • Emergency brake is inadequate to hold the vehicle. • Dealers acknowledge that brake master cylinders are problematic. • Joints aren't connected under quarter wheel weld; one weld is missing and three aren't properly connected. • Passenger door opened when vehicle hit a pothole. • While underway, right-side sliding door opens on its own and won't close (see "mental distress" judgment on page 48). • When parked on an incline, sliding door released and came crashing down on child. • Hood suddenly flew up on the freeway. • Steering failed three times. • Power-steering pump whines and lurches. • Steering wheel is noisy and hard to turn. • Rear side windows, liftgate window, and windshield often explode suddenly. • When the interior rear-view mirror is set for night vision, images become distorted and hard to see. • Windshield wipers are unreliable. • Second-row driver-side seat belt buckle wouldn't latch. • Original equipment tire blowouts and sidewall bulging. • Driver must hunt for right place to push for horn to work. **2000–01**—Harsh 3–2 shifting when coasting then accelerating. • Transmission fluid leakage. • 3.8L engine hum, moan, drone, spark knock, and vibration. • Power-steering grunts or shudders during slow turns and leaks fluid. • Faulty self-activating wipers and door, trunk, and ignition locks. **2001**—Airbag may suddenly deploy when the engine is started. • Transmission shudder during 3–4 shifts. • Transmission fluid leaks from the main control cover area. • Power-steering grunt or notchy feel when turning; leaks. • Drifting or pulling while driving. • Rear drum brakes drag or fail to release properly. • Fogging of the front and side windows. • Twisted seatback frame. **2002**—Airbags failed to deploy. • Sudden automatic transmission failure. • Gas and brake pedal are set too close. • Back door won't open or close properly. • Both sliding doors won't retract. • Child can shift transmission without touching brake pedal. **2003**—Wheel suddenly broke away. • Airbags failed to deploy. • Sudden, unintended acceleration when braking.

• Engine surging. • Chronic stalling from blown fuel pump fuses. • Coolant leak from the timing cover gasket. • Advanced tracking system engages on its own, causing vehicle to shake violently. • Automatic transmission suddenly seized. • Steering wheel locked up. • Interior windows are always fogged up because of inadequate defrosting. • Brake and gas pedals are mounted too close together. • Gas pedal arm pivot causes the pedal to flip almost horizontally, exaggerating any pedal pressure. • Body seams not sealed; water intrudes into floor seat anchors. • Driver's seat poorly anchored. • Dashboard glare onto the windshield. • Check tire warning light comes on for no reason. • Tire jack collapsed. Freestar: **2004**— Sudden loss of steering. • Airbag light stays on, may not deploy. • A-frame dropped out of the tie-rod collar. • Front axle suddenly broke while underway. • Left inner brake pad fell apart and locked up brake. • Dealer had to change pads and rotor. • Sliding door closed on a child, causing slight injuries. • Broken plastic running board broke, blocking sliding door operation, locking occupants inside the vehicle. • Headliner-mounted DVD screen blocks rear-view mirror.

Secret Warranties/Internal Bulletins/Service Tips

All models/years: Engine Intake Manifolds: Engine oil mixed with coolant or coolant loss signals the need for revised engine lower intake manifold side gaskets and/or front cover gaskets. The internal bulletin shown here can go a long way in getting a repair refund for any Ford model up to 7 years/160,000 km, since it shows that the defect is factory-related, an upgraded part has been devised, and the problem is covered by the much-longer emissions warranty. • An exhaust buzz or rattle may be caused by a loose catalyst or heat shield. • Sliding door malfunctions. • Buzzing noise in speakers caused by fuel pump. • A malfunction indicator light (MIL) lit for no reason may simply show that the gas cap is loose. • If the power-sliding door won't close, replace the door controller; if it pops or disengages when fully closed, adjust the door and rear striker to reduce closing resistance. • Front wipers that operate when switched off need a revised multi-function switch (covered under service program and recall). **1995–98**—A parking brake that won't release needs a new parking pawl actuating rod. • Power door locks that grind or won't work may need a new front door lock actuator. • Tips on finding and silencing instrument panel buzzing, rattling, squeaking, chirping, and ticking. • The front-end accessory drive belt (FEAD) slips in wet weather, causing a reduction in steering power-assist. • Water leakage onto carpet or headliner in rear cargo area is a factory-related defect

---

ENGINE COOLANT LOSS/ OIL CONTAMINATION

BULLETIN NO: 99-20-7   DATE: OCT. 04, 1999

3.8L AND 4.2L ENGINE—LOSS OF COOLANT; ENGINE OIL CONTAMINATED WITH COOLANT

1996–1997 THUNDERBIRD; 1996–1998 MUSTANG, WINDSTAR; 1997–1998 E-150, E-250, F-150; 1996–1997 COUGAR

This may be caused by the lower intake manifold side gaskets and/or front cover gaskets allowing coolant to pass into the cylinders and/or the crankcase.

ACTION: Revised lower intake manifold side and front cover gaskets have been released for service.

WARRANTY STATUS: Eligible Under The Provisions Of Bumper To Bumper Warranty Coverage And Emissions Warranty Coverage

covered in TSB #98-5-5. **1995–99**—Tips for correcting excessive noise, vibration, and harshness while driving; side door wind noise; and windshield water leaks. **1995–2000**—A harsh 3–2 downshift/shudder when accelerating or turning may mean that the transmission is low on fluid. • Diagnostic tips on brake vibration, inspection, and friction material replacement. **1995–2002**—Silencing suspension noise. **1995–2003**—Engines that have been repaired may have an incorrectly installed gear driven camshaft position (CMP) sensor synchronizer assembly. This could cause poor fuel economy, loss of power, and engine surge, hesitation, and rough running. **1996–98**—Harsh automatic 1–2 shifting may be caused by a malfunctioning electronic pressure control or the main control valves sticking in the valve body. • Unwanted airflow from the AC vents can be stopped by replacing the evaporator case baffle. • An intermittent Neutral condition when coming to a stop signals the need to replace the forward clutch piston and the forward clutch cylinder. • Black soot deposits on the right rear quarter panel can be avoided by installing an exhaust tailpipe extension. **1996–2003**—Tips on troubleshooting automatic transmission faulty torque converters. **1997–98**—A rattling or clunking noise coming from the front of the vehicle may be caused by a loose front tension strut bushing retainer. **1998**—Lack of AC cooling may be caused by refrigerant leak at the P-nut fitting. • AC may have a loose auxiliary climate control fan switch. • A Low Fuel light lit for no reason signals the need for an upgraded fuel tank and sender assembly. • An inaccurate metric speedometer requires a new speedometer gear. • Squeaks and creaks from the left rear of the driver's seat can be silenced by lubricating the lateral stability bracket. • Chronic stalling can be corrected by reprogramming the PCM. • Excessive vibration at highway speeds may require new rear brake drums. **1998–99**—Tips on spotting abnormal ABS braking noise, although Ford says that some noise is inevitable. **1999**—No Reverse engagement may be caused by torn Reverse clutch lip seals. • To improve the defogging of the driver-side door glass, install a revised window demister vent. **1999–2003**—Things that go beep in the night (see the bulletin at left). • Bulletin No. 04-2-3, published 02/09/04, goes into excruciating detail on finding and fixing the sliding door's many failures. • Inoperative rear window defroster. **2001**—Ford admits automatic transmission defects (slippage, delayed shifts) in Special Service Instruction #01T01. **2001–02**—Service tips for reports of premature engine failures. • Vacuum or air leaks in the intake manifold or engine system causing warning lamps to

---

PARKING ASSIST-FALSE ACTIVATION

BULLETIN NO: 04-7-1   **DATE: APRIL 19, 2004**

FALSE ACTIVATION OF WARNING TONE

1999–2003 WINDSTAR; 1999–2004 EXPLORER; 2000–2004 EXCURSION, EXPEDITION; 2001–2004 F SUPER DUTY; 2003–2005 ESCAPE; 2004 F-150; FREESTAR; 2000–2004 NAVIGATOR; 2002–2003 BLACKWOOD; 2003–2004 AVIATOR; 1999–2004 MOUNTAINEER; 2004 MONTEREY

Various 1999–2005 vehicles equipped with the Parking Aid reverse sensing system (RSS) may sound a warning tone when the vehicle is in reverse, even though there are no objects behind the vehicle. This condition may also occur on vehicles equipped with the forward sensing system (FSS) when vehicle is in reverse or drive. **ACTION:** The condition MAY NOT be due to proximity sensor(s) malfunction but may be a normal operation characteristic, or due to sensor contamination (sensor being covered with dirt).

light. • Concerns with oil in the cooling system. • Engine cylinder heads that have been repaired may still leak coolant or oil from the gasket area. • Hard starts; rough running engines. • Shudder while in Reverse or during 3–4 shift. • Transmission fluid leakage. • Power-steering fluid leaks. • Brake roughness and pulsation. • Rear brake-drum drag in cold weather. • Fogging of the front and side windows. • False low tire warning. • Repeated heater core failures. • Troubleshooting MIL warning light. **2001–03**—Remedy for a slow-to-fill fuel tank. **2002**—Automatic transmission fluid leaking at the quick connect for the transmission cooler lines. • MIL light comes on, vehicle shifts poorly, or vehicle won't start. • Instrument panel beeping. • Buzz, groan, or vibration when gear selector lever is in Park. • Some vehicles may run roughly on the highway or just after stopping. • Defective ignition switch lock cylinders. • Anti-theft system operates on its own. • Battery may go dead after extended parking time. • Sliding doors rattle and squeak. • Steering system whistle/whine. • Loose rear wiper arm. **2003**—Front-end grinding popping noise when passing over bumps or making turns. • Airbag warning light stays lit. • Inoperative rear window defroster. **Freestar: 2004**—Transmission has no 1–2 upshift (TSB #04-15-12). • False activation of parking assist. (Remember, I said this optional safety device would drive you nuts with false warnings.) • Bulletin No. 04-2-3, published 02/09/04, lists ways to find and fix sliding door's many failures. • Loose rear door trim.

WINDSTAR/FREESTAR PROFILE

	1996	1997	1998	1999	2000	2001	2002	2003	2004
Cost Price ($)									
Freestar/Base	—	—	—	—	—	—	—	—	27,295
SE	—	—	—	—	—	—	—	—	29,695
SEL	—	—	—	—	—	—	—	—	27,295
Windstar/Base	23,495	24,495	24,495	24,295	—	—	—	—	—
LX	27,495	28,995	28,995	28,195	25,995	26,750	25,995	26,195	—
SEL	—	—	—	36,195	36,195	33,190	33,685	37,015	—
Used Values ($)									
Freestar/Base ▲	—	—	—	—	—	—	—	—	16,500
Freestar/Base ▼	—	—	—	—	—	—	—	—	15,000
SE ▲	—	—	—	—	—	—	—	—	18,000
SE ▼	—	—	—	—	—	—	—	—	15,000
SEL ▲	—	—	—	—	—	—	—	—	23,500
SEL ▼	—	—	—	—	—	—	—	—	22,000
Windstar/Base ▲	3,500	4,500	5,500	6,500	—	—	—	—	—
Windstar/Base ▼	3,000	4,000	4,500	5,500	—	—	—	—	—
LX ▲	4,000	5,000	6,000	7,000	9,000	11,000	13,500	16,500	—
LX ▼	3,500	4,500	5,500	5,500	8,000	9,500	12,000	15,000	—
SEL ▲	—	—	—	7,500	10,000	12,500	15,500	20,000	—
SEL ▼	—	—	—	6,000	8,500	11,000	14,000	18,500	—

Reliability	❶	❶	❶	❶	❷	❷	❷	❸	❸
Crash Safety (F)	⑤	⑤	⑤	⑤	⑤	⑤	⑤	⑤	⑤
Side	—	—	—	⑤	④	⑤	④	④	④
Offset	⑤	⑤	⑤	❸	❸	❸	❸	❸	⑤
Head Restraints (F)	❶	❶	—	❸	—	⑤	⑤	⑤	⑤
Rear	—	—	—	❶	—	❸	❸	❸	⑤
Rollover Resistance	—	—	—	—	—	④	④	④	④

Ford/Nissan

VILLAGER, QUEST ★★

RATING: *Quest*: Below Average (2004). Even though it's larger, more powerful, and better-appointed than the old Villager, the 2004's redesign was badly done. Engineering goofs and poor-quality body and electrical components are everywhere. On top of that, Nissan servicing and warranty support has soured. *Villager and Quest*: Average (1997–2002); Below Average (1995–96); Not Recommended (1993–94). There was no 2003 model. Best used for city commuting, rather than long highway journeys. **Maintenance/Repair costs:** Higher than average. Costs can be kept down by frequenting independent repair agencies, but the 2004 Quest is highly dealer dependent. **Parts:** Both Ford and Nissan dealers carry parts, which are moderately priced. The exceptions to this rule: broken engine exhaust manifold studs (a frequent problem through 1996), AC, and electrical components. **Extended warranty:** Yes, it's essential for the "orphaned" Villager, and good backup for the glitch-ridden 1993–96 and 2004 Quest. **Best alternatives:** Other minivans worth considering are the Honda Odyssey, the 2002–04 Mazda MPV, or a 2003 or earlier Toyota Sienna (Toyota's 2004 reworked model had similar quality bugs). **Online help:** *www.mycarstats.com/auto_complaints/MERCURY_complaints. asp* and *www.autosafety.org/autodefects.html.*

Strengths and Weaknesses

Smaller and more carlike than most minivans, the pre-2004 Villager and Quest are sized comfortably between the regular and extended Chrysler minivans. These minivans' strongest assets are a 170-hp 3.3L V6 engine that gives them carlike handling, ride, and cornering; modular seating; and reliable mechanical components. Nissan borrowed the powertrain, suspension, and steering assembly from the

Maxima, mixed in some creative sheet metal, and left the job of outfitting the sound system, climate control, dashboard, steering column, and wheels to Ford. This has resulted in an attractive, not overly aero styled minivan.

These fuel-thirsty minivans are quite heavy, though, and the 3.0L and 3.3L engines have to go all out to carry the extra weight. GM's 2.8L engines produce more torque, but the Villager/Quest powertrain set-up trails the Odyssey in acceleration and passing. Other minuses: The interior looks cheap, the control layout can be a bit confusing, suspension is too soft, and rear-seat access can be difficult.

VEHICLE HISTORY: 1996—Annoying motorized shoulder belts were dropped, a passenger-side airbag was added, and the dash and exterior were slightly restyled. *Villager*: **1999**—The Pathfinder's 3.3L V6 debuts, giving the Villager and Quest an additional 19 horses. The Villager gained a fourth door, more interior room, a revised instrument panel that's easier to reach, restyled front and rear ends, and improved shifting, acceleration, and braking. The suspension was retuned to give a more carlike ride and handling, the old climate control system was ditched for a more sophisticated version with air filtration. Mercury's top-of-the-line model, the Nautica, was dropped. *Quest*: **1999**—A larger platform, standard ABS brakes, a driver-side sliding rear door, upgraded headlights, and rear leaf springs. The second row of seats can be removed and the third row is set on tracks. **2000**—An improved child safety seat anchoring system. An entertainment centre with a larger screen is standard on all Quest models, as well as a stabilizer bar on the GLE. **2001**—A slightly restyled exterior and upgraded dashboard. **2002**—Restyled wheels. **2004**—Totally redesigned and made less reliable.

1994–2003 problems

Most owner-reported problems involve excessive brake noise and premature brake wear, door lock malfunctions, interior noise, and driveline vibrations. There have also been many reports of engine exhaust manifold and crankshaft failures that cost up to $7,000 to repair. Other problems include electrical shorts; brake failures because of vibration, binding, or overheating; premature wear of the front discs, rotors, and pads; chronic stalling, possibly because of faulty fuel pumps or a shorted electrical system; and loose

NISSAN LOW QUALITY SCORES

Nissan's Titan, Armada, and Quest fared poorly in the J.D. Power Initial Quality Study released in April 2004.

	PROBLEMS PER 100	SEGMENT	RANK
Titan	166	Light-duty full-sized pickup	Last (9 in segment)
Armada	209	Full-sized SUV	Last (7 in segment)
Quest	243	Compact van	Last (13 in segment)

Source: J.D. Power and Associates

steering and veering at highway speeds. Other common problems include film buildup on windshield and interior glass; a sulfur smell from the exhaust system; poor AC performance or compressor failures, accompanied by musty, mildew-type AC odours; and recurring fuel pump buzzing heard through the radio speakers.

Body integrity has been subpar and disappointing up to and including the 2004 models. Owners complain of doors opening and closing on their own, and poorly fitted panels that produce a cacophony of wind noise, squeaks, and rattles, as well as water leaks. Paint defects are legion and there have been some reports of premature rusting on the inside sliding door track.

2004 Quest

A totally different minivan than its predecessor, the 2004 Quest is one of the largest and priciest minivans on the road. Based on the Altima/Murano platform, it offers a more powerful engine, and all the standard high-tech safety, performance, and convenience features one could want. Its long wheelbase allows for the widest opening sliding doors among front-drive minivans, rear seating access is a breeze, and a capacious interior allows for flexible cargo and passenger configurations that can easily accommodate 4'×8' objects with the liftgate closed. Standard fold-flat third-row seats and fold-to-the-floor centre-row seats allow owners to increase storage space without worrying about where to store the extra seats, although third-row headrests must be removed before the seats can be folded away.

Although it feels a bit heavy in the city, the revamped Quest is still very carlike when it's driven on the highway. Ride and handling are enhanced by a new four-wheel independent suspension, front and rear stabilizer bars, and upgraded antilock brakes.

Safety features include standard head curtain supplemental airbags for outboard passengers in all three rows, supplemental front-seat side-impact airbags, standard traction control and ABS brakes with brake assist.

2004 problems

Fit and finish deficiencies are still the number one complaint and have become even more common than in previous models. In its Customer Satisfaction Initiative Bulletin #BT04-014, Nissan pledged to fix a number of mechanical and body defects for free to eliminate squeaks and rattles and to improve window and door operation—as long as a June 2005 deadline is respected (they can't be serious!). Skyroof leaks are quite common, and owners also complain of malfunctioning engines, transmissions, and brakes.

Safety Summary

All models/years through the 2003 model: Airbags fail to deploy. • Inadvertent airbag deployment. • Vehicle suddenly accelerated forward. • Sudden stalling caused by faulty fuel pump. • Steering wander and excessive vibration. • Chronic ABS failures; brake pads and rotors need replacing every 5,000 km. • Brake failures (extended stopping distance, noisy when applied). Brake and accelerator pedals are the same height, so driver's foot can easily slip and step on both at the same time. • Cycling or self-activating front door locks failures; occupants have been trapped in their vehicles. **1997–99**—Gas fumes leak into the interior. • Gas pedal sticks. **2000**—Vehicle tends to lurch forward when the AC is first engaged. • Weak tailgate hydraulic cylinders. • Instrument panel's white face hard to read in daylight hours. **2000–01**—Missing seat belt latch plate stopper button. • Shift indicator is misaligned because shift-lock cable plate is broken. • 22-month-old child was able to pull the clasp apart on integrated child safety seat. • Seat belts don't retract properly. • Rear window on liftgate door shattered for unknown reason (replaced under warranty). • Power steering fluid leakage caused by O-ring at rack gear splitting. **2002**—Stuck accelerator pedal. • Excessive vibration at highway speeds. • Leaking front and rear struts degrade handling. • Steering wheel is off-centre to the left. • Continental tire tread separation. **2003**—No data. **2004**—Sudden, unintended acceleration. • Sliding door trapped child; adults also trapped; door continuously pops open. • Reflection of dash on windshield. • Automatic transmission won't downshift. • Dome light fuse blows continuously. • Ineffective windshield washers.

Secret Warranties/Internal Bulletins/Service Tips

1993–98—Automatic transmission whining when accelerating may be caused by a faulty transaxle support bracket and insulators. **1993–2000**—Paint delamination, peeling, or fading (see Part Two "Paint and Body Defects," pages 71–75). **1993–2002**—Repeat heater core failure. **1995–99**—Tips for correcting windshield water leaks and excessive noise, vibration, and harshness. **1996–2002**—Power door locks that intermittently self-activate are a common occurrence that's covered in TSB #98-22-5. **1997–98**—Tips on silencing rattles and creaks. • Hard starts, no-starts, stalling, or an exhaust rotten-egg smell can be corrected by replacing the power control module (PCM) under the emissions warranty. **1997–99**—An exhaust buzz or rattle may be caused by a loose catalyst or muffler heat shield. **1999–2002**—Side windows pop open. • Rear AC blows warm air. **1999–2004**—Cooling system leaks/overheating. **2004**—Troubleshooting abnormal shifting. • Side windows pop open. **2004**—No-start, hard start remedies. • Silencing a ticking engine/exhaust noise. • Tips on correcting an abnormal shifting of the automatic transmission. • Skyroof water leaks (TSB #BT03-045). • AC blows out warm air from floor vents. • Leaks, overheating cooling system. • Guidelines on troubleshooting brake complaints.

	1996	1997	1998	1999	2000	2001	2002	2004
Cost Price ($)								
Villager GS	23,695	24,295	24,595	24,595	24,595	—	—	—
Villager LS	28,095	29,195	29,495	29,495	29,495	—	—	—
Quest GXE/S	30,598	30,898	30,898	27,798	30,498	30,498	30,698	32,900
Quest GXE/SL	25,598	25,598	25,598	32,498	33,498	35,198	35,198	36,600
Used Values ($)								
Villager GS ▲	5,000	6,000	7,500	9,000	10,500	—	—	—
Villager GS ▼	4,000	5,000	6,000	7,500	9,000	—	—	—
Villager LS ▲	5,000	6,500	8,500	10,000	12,000	—	—	—
Villager LS ▼	4,500	5,000	7,000	8,500	10,500	—	—	—
Quest GXE/S ▲	5,500	6,000	8,500	9,500	12,500	15,000	18,000	23,000
Quest GXE/S ▼	5,000	5,500	8,000	8,500	11,500	13,500	16,500	21,500
Quest XE/SL ▲	6,000	7,000	7,500	10,500	13,000	16,000	19,500	25,000
Quest XE/SL ▼	5,000	6,500	7,000	9,000	12,000	14,500	18,000	23,500
Reliability	③	④	④	④	④	④	④	③
Crash Safety (F)	④	④	—	—	④	⑤	⑤	⑤
Side	—	—	—	—	⑤	⑤	⑤	⑤
Offset	②	②	②	❶	❶	❶	❶	⑤
Head Restraints	②	②	—	②	—	❶	❶	②
Rear	②	②	—	❶	—	❶	❶	②
Rollover Resistance	—	—	—	—	—	④	④	④

General Motors

<table>
<tr><td style="background:black;color:white">**ASTRO, SAFARI**</td><td style="background:black;color:white">★★★</td></tr>
</table>

RATING: Average (1996–04); Below Average (1985–95). These vehicles are more mini-truck than minivan. Believe it or not, these run-of-the-mill minivans are beginning to look quite good when compared to the problem-plagued Chrysler, GM, and Ford front-drive minivans and the overpriced Asian competition. (VW and Mercedes? Not even in the running.) They have fewer safety-related problems reported to the government, are easy to repair, and cost little to acquire. Stay away from the unreliable all-wheel-drive models; they're expensive to repair and not very durable. **Maintenance/Repair costs:** Average. Any garage can repair these rear-drive minivans. **Parts:** Good supply of cheap parts. A large contingent of inde-

All ratings on a numbered scale where ⑤ is good and ❶ is bad. See pages 100–101 for a more detailed description.

pendent parts suppliers keeps repair costs down. Parts are less expensive than they are for other vehicles in this class. **Extended warranty:** A wise choice, but not essential; a powertrain-only warranty is all you'll need. Most repairs will be surprisingly cheap, but one rebuilt automatic transmission can set you back $3,000. **Best alternatives:** As with the Aerostar, the classified ads are jam-packed with sellers wanting to unload their Astros and Safaris simply because their vehicles have high mileage or because the owners run small businesses and now need larger vans. Whatever the reason, you can find some real bargains if you're patient. Honda's Odyssey should be your first choice, though; early Nissan and Toyota minivans also have good handling and are reliable and economical people-carriers; unfortunately, they lack the Astro's considerable grunt, essential for cargo hauling and trailer towing. Also consider getting a later-model Ford Aerostar (watch the tranny, though). **Online help:** *www.autosafety.org/autodefects.html*.

Strengths and Weaknesses

More a utility truck than a comfortable minivan, these boxy, rear-drive minivans are built on a reworked S-10 pickup chassis. As such, they offer uninspiring handling, average-quality mechanical and body components, and relatively high fuel consumption. Both the Astro and Safari come in a choice of either cargo or passenger van. The cargo van is used either commercially or as an inexpensive starting point for a fully customized vehicle. The Safari is identical to the Astro, except for a slightly higher base price.

With the right options, the Astro and Safari have the advantage of being versatile cargo-haulers when equipped with heavy-duty suspensions. In fact, Astro's 2,500 kg (5,500 lb.) trailer-towing capability is 900 kg (2,000 lb.) more than that of the front-drive Venture. The base 4.3L V6 gives acceptable acceleration, but the High Output variant of the same engine (first available in the 1991 model) is a far better choice, particularly when it's mated to a manual gearbox. The full-time AWD versions aren't very refined, have a high failure rate, and are expensive to diagnose and repair.

VEHICLE HISTORY: 1991—A more powerful V6; and lap/shoulder belts. **1993**—Base engine gained 15 hp. **1994**—Driver-side airbag, side-door guard beams, plus a centre-mounted rear stop lamp was installed in the roof. **1995**—Lightly restyled front end, extended bodies, and a 190-hp engine. **1996**—Passenger-side airbag, a new dash, engine torque cut by 10 lb.-ft., and more front footroom. **1997**—Upgraded power steering. **1998**—An improved automatic transmission. **1999**—A reworked AWD system. **2000**—Only seven- and eight-passenger models available; engine made quieter and smoother, while the automatic transmission was toughened up to shift more efficiently when pulling heavy loads; and a larger fuel tank was installed. **2001**—A tilt steering wheel; cruise control; CD player; remote keyless entry; power windows, mirrors, and locks. **2002**—A rear heater on cargo models. **2003**—Upgraded four-wheel disc brakes.

The 1985–95 versions suffer from failure-prone automatic transmissions, poor braking systems, failure-prone AC compressors, and fragile steering components. The early base V6 provides ample power, but also produces lots of noise, consumes excessive amounts of fuel, and tends to have leaking head gaskets and failure-prone oxygen sensors. These computer-related problems often rob the engine of sufficient power to keep up in traffic. While the 5-speed manual transmission shifts fairly easily, the automatic takes forever to downshift on the highway. Handling isn't particularly agile on these minivans, and the power steering doesn't provide the driver with enough road feel. Unloaded, the Astro provides very poor traction, the ride isn't comfortable on poor road surfaces, and interior noise is rampant. Many drivers find the driving position awkward (no left legroom) and the heating/defrosting system inadequate. Many engine components are hidden under the dashboard, making repair or maintenance awkward. Even on more recent models, highway performance and overall reliability aren't impressive. Through the 2000 model year, the 4-speed automatic transmissions are clunky and hard shifting, though they're much more reliable than Ford or Chrysler gearboxes.

Other owners report that the front suspension, steering components, computer modules, and catalytic converter can wear out within as little as 60,000 km. There have also been lots of complaints about electrical, exhaust, cooling, and fuel system bugs; inadequate heating/defrosting; failure-prone wiper motors; and axle seals wearing out every 12–18 months.

Body hardware is fragile, and fit and finish is the pits. Water leaks from windows and doors are common but hard to diagnose. Squeaks and rattles are legion and hard to locate. Sliding-door handles often break off and the sliding door frequently jams in cold temperatures. The hatch release for the Dutch doors occasionally doesn't work, and the driver-side vinyl seat lining tears apart. Premature paint peeling, delamination, and surface rust are fairly common.

The 1995–99 models are a bit improved, but they still have problems carried over from earlier years, with stalling, hard starts, and expensive and frequent automatic transmission, power-steering, wheel bearing, brake pad, caliper, and rotor repairs heading the list.

Year 2000–04 models are a bit more reliable and better performing, inasmuch as they underwent considerable upgrading by GM. Nevertheless, buyers should pay extra attention to the following areas: excessive vibration transmitted through the AWD; automatic transmission clunk; poor braking performance (brake pedal hardens and brakes don't work after going over bumps or rough roads) and expensive brake maintenance; electronic computer modules and fuel system glitches that cause the Check Engine light to remain lit; hard starts, no-starts, or chronic stalling, especially when going downhill; heating and AC performance hampered by poor air distribution; electrical system shorts; and sliding door misalignment and broken hinges.

 Safety Summary

All models/years: NHTSA has recorded numerous complaints of dashboard fires. Power steering locks up or fails unexpectedly, components wear out quickly, and steering may bind when turning. Seat belt complaints are also common: seat belts tighten up unexpectedly, cannot be adjusted, or have nowhere to latch. **1995–98**—Vehicle continues to accelerate after foot is removed from accelerator. • Frequent stalling. • Erratic engine performance because of blocked catalytic converter. • Vehicle jerks to one side when braking. • Front wheels lock up when turning the steering wheel to the right from a stop while in gear. • Steering stuck when turning. • Fresh-air ventilation system allows fumes from other vehicles to enter interior compartment. • With jack almost fully extended, wheel doesn't lift off ground. • Spare tire not safe for driving over 60 km/h. • Horn buttons require excessive pressure to activate. • Driver-side window failure. • Sliding door suddenly fell off. • Front passenger door won't close. • Passenger-side door glass fell out. • Rear hatch latch release failed. • Rear hatch hydraulic rods are too weak to support hatch. • Front passenger's seat reclining mechanism failed. • Poor traction. • Parked in gear and rolled downhill. • Transmission failures. • Left rear axle seal leaks, causing lubricant to burn on brake lining. • Sudden wheel bearing failure. • AC clutch fell apart. • Alternator bearing failure. **1999**—Very few safety-related complaints, compared with most other minivans. Many of the 1999 model problems have been reported by owners of earlier model years. • Hard shifting between First and Second gear; transmission slippage. • Delayed shifting or stalling when passing from Drive to Reverse. • Leaking axle seals. • Rear cargo door hinge and latch slipped off, and door opened 180 degrees. • Floor mat moves under brake and accelerator pedals. • Brake pedal set too close to the accelerator. • Fuel gauge failure caused by faulty sending unit. **2000**—Brake and gas pedals are too close together. • When brakes are applied, rear wheels tend to lock up while front wheels continue to turn. • Vehicle stalls when accelerating or turning. • Astro rolls back when stopped on an incline in Drive. • Sliding door slams shut on an incline or hinges break. • Extensive damage caused to bumper and undercarriage by driving over gravel roads. **2001**—Sudden acceleration. • Chronic stalling. • Sudden total electrical failure, especially when going into Reverse. • Brake pedal set too high. • Differential in transfer case locked up while driving; defective axle seals. • Vehicle rolls backward on an incline while in Drive (dealer adjusted transfer case to no avail). • Fuel gauge failure. • Faulty AC vents. • Water can be trapped inside the wheels and freeze, causing the wheels to be out of balance. **2002**—Airbag failed to deploy. • Sticking gas pedal. • Brake pedal goes to floor without braking. • Seat belts in rear are too long; don't fit children or child safety seats. • Driver-side window failures. • Sliding-door window blew out. • Uniroyal spare tire sidewall cracks. **2003**—Harsh, delayed shifting. • On a slight incline, sliding door will unlatch and slam shut. • Intermittent windshield wiper failure. 2004—Rear driver-side window exploded.

Secret Warranties/Internal Bulletins/Service Tips

1993–99—Tips on getting rid of AC odours. • Defective catalytic converters may cause a rotten-egg smell eligible for an emissions warranty refund. 1993–2005—GM says that a chronic driveline clunk can't be silenced and is a normal characteristic of its vehicles. • Paint delamination, peeling, or fading (see Part Two "Paint and Body Defects," pages 71–75). 1995–2000—Dealer guidelines for brake servicing under warranty. 1995–2004—Booming interior noise at highway speeds. 1996–98—Rough engine performance may be caused by a water-contaminated oxygen sensor, and a rough idle shortly after starting may be caused by sticking poppet valves. 1996–2000—Hard start, no-start, backfire, and kickback when starting may be corrected by replacing the crankshaft position sensor. • A rough idle after start and/or a Service Engine light that stays lit may mean you have a stuck injector poppet valve ball that needs cleaning. 1996–2001—Poor heat distribution in driver's area of vehicle (install new heat ducts). • Exhaust rattle noise. 1996–2003—Engine noise remedy: see the bulletin below. 1996–2004—Silence a boom-type noise heard during engine warm-up by installing an exhaust dampener assembly (TSB #00-06-05-001A). 1997–98—An engine ticking noise that appears when the temperature falls may require an EVAP purge solenoid valve. 1997–99—A hard start, no-start, and rough idle can be fixed by replacing the fuel tank fill pipe assembly and cleaning the SCPI poppet valves. 1999—Steering column squeaking can be silenced by replacing the steering wheel SIR module coil assembly. 1999–2000—If the engine runs hot, overheats, or loses coolant, try polishing the radiator filler neck or replacing the radiator cap before letting any mechanic convince you that more expensive repairs are needed. • A popping or snapping sound may emanate from the right front door window area. 1999–2004—Automatic transmission malfunctions may be caused by debris in the transmission (Bulletin No. 01-07-30-038B). 2001—Harsh automatic transmission shifts. • 2–4 band and 3–4 clutch damage. • Steering shudder felt when making low-speed turns. • Excessive brake squeal. • Wet carpet/odour in passenger footwell area (repair evaporator case drain to cowl seal/open evaporator case drain). • Delayed shifts, slips, flares, or extended shifts during cold operation (replace shift solenoid valve assembly). 2002—Automatic transmission slips, incorrect shifts, and poor engine performance. • Service Engine Soon light comes on, no Third or

---

ENGINE RATTLE

BULLETIN NO: 03-06-01-024B DATE: MARCH 04, 2004

RATTLE NOISE IN ENGINE (INSTALL TIMING TENSIONER KIT)

1996–2003 Chevrolet Astro, Blazer, Express, S-10, Silverado; 1996–2003 GMC Jimmy, Safari, Savana, Sierra, Sonoma; 1996–2001 Oldsmobile Bravada with 4.3L V6 Engine

CONDITION: Some customers may comment on a rattle-type noise coming from the engine at approximately 1800 to 2200 RPMs.

CAUSE: The spark, rattle-type noise may be caused by torsional vibration of the balance shaft.

CORRECTION: Install a new tensioner assembly kit.

Fourth gear, and loss of Drive. • Slipping or missing Second, Third, or Fourth gear. • Inadequate heating. • Roof panel has a wavy or rippled appearance. • Water leak in the windshield area. **2002–03**—Engine runs rough or engine warning light comes on. • Sliding door difficult to open. **2003**—Hard starts, rough idle, and intermittent misfiring. • Transfer case shudder. • Right rear door handle breakage. **2004**—Silencing a suspension pop.

ASTRO, SAFARI PROFILE

	1996	1997	1998	1999	2000	2001	2002	2003	2004
Cost Price ($)									
Cargo	23,475	25,110	25,110	23,290	24,015	24,465	—	—	26,390
CS/base	25,285	26,920	26,920	23,839	25,675	26,440	27,255	27,600	27,615
Used Values ($)									
Cargo ▲	3,500	4,500	5,000	7,000	8,500	10,000	—	—	18,000
Cargo ▼	3,000	4,000	4,500	6,000	7,000	9,000	—	—	16,500
CS/base ▲	4,000	5,000	6,000	8,000	9,500	11,500	15,000	17,000	19,000
CS/base ▼	3,500	4,500	5,000	6,500	8,000	10,000	13,500	16,000	18,000
Reliability	❷	❷	❸	❸	❸	❹	❹	❹	❹
Crash Safety (F)	❸	❸	❸	❸	❸	❸	❸	❸	❸
Side	—	—	—	—	—	—	—	❺	❺
Offset	❶	❶	❶	❶	❶	❶	❶	❶	❶
Head Restraints (F)	❷	❷	—	❷	—	❷	❷	❶	❶
Rear	❶	❶	—	—	—	—	—	—	—
Rollover Resistance	—	—	—	—	—	❸	❸	❸	—

LUMINA, LUMINA APV, MONTANA, SILHOUETTE, TRANS SPORT, VENTURE ★ ☆

RATING: Below Average (1997–2004); Not Recommended (1990–96). These minivans have been down-rated this year for three reasons: serious automatic transmission and engine head gasket failures; deteriorating reliability combined with an inadequate warranty (Chrysler's warranty is better); and safety defects that include sliding doors crushing and injuring children. These minivans are almost as bad as Ford's Windstar/Freestar and actually make Chrysler's minivans look good. **Maintenance/Repair costs:** Average costs, except for powertrain glitches where GM dealers force on customers more expensive engine and tranny repairs in order to be eligible for GM goodwill refunds. Engine intake manifold gaskets, automatic transmissions, ABS, and the electrical system are all high-maintenance items with an equally high failure rate around the fifth year of ownership. **Parts:** The same parts are used on many other GM models, so they're reasonably priced and not hard to find. **Body parts** are likely to be more problematic and costly. **Extended warranty:** Definitely needed for both the engine and automatic transmission. **Best alternatives:** Honda Odyssey, Nissan Quest or Axxess, and Toyota Sienna. **Online help:** *www.gm-v6lemons.com* and *www.autosafety.org/autodefects.html.*

 ## Strengths and Weaknesses

These minivans have more carlike handling than GM's Astro and Safari. Seating is limited to five adults in the standard models (two up front and three on a removable bench seat), but this can be increased to seven if you find a vehicle equipped with optional modular seats. Seats can be folded down flat, creating additional storage space.

As with most minivans, be wary of vehicles equipped with a power-assisted passenger-side sliding door; it's both convenient and dangerous. Despite an override circuit that should prevent the door from closing when it is blocked, a number of injuries have been reported. Furthermore, the doors frequently open when they shouldn't, and can be difficult to close securely.

All models and years have had serious reliability problems—notably engine head gasket and intake manifold defects; electronic module (PROM) and starter failures; premature front brake component wear, brake fluid leakage, and noisy braking; short circuits that burn out alternators, batteries, power door lock activators, and the blower motor; AC evaporator core failures; premature wearout of the inner and outer tie-rods; automatic transmission breakdowns; abysmal fit and finish; chronic sliding door malfunctions; and faulty rear seat latches. Other problems include a fuel-thirsty and poor-performing 3-speed automatic transmission; a poorly mounted sliding door; side-door glass that pops open; squeaks, rattles, and clunks in the instrument panel cluster area and suspension; and wind buffeting noise around the front doors. The large dent- and rust-resistant plastic panels are robot-bonded to the frame, and they absorb engine and road noise very well, in addition to having an impressive record for durability.

VEHICLE HISTORY: 1994—A shortened nose, APV designation is dropped, driver-side airbag arrives. **1996**—3.4L V6 debuts, and the Lumina was replaced by the Venture at the end of the model year. **1997**—Dual airbags and ABS. **1998**—The sliding driver-side door is available on more models. **1999**—A 5-hp boost to the base V6 engine (185), de-powered airbags, an upgraded automatic transmission, a rear-window defogger, and heated rear-view mirrors. **2000**—Dual sliding rear side doors. **2001**—Slightly restyled, a fold-flat third-row seat, driver-side power door, and a 6-disc CD player; cargo version dropped. **2002**—Nothing major; optional AWD and DVD entertainment centre. **2003**—Optional ABS and front side-airbags.

By the way, don't trust the towing limit listed in GM's owner's manual. Automakers publish tow ratings that are on the optimistic side—and sometimes they even lie. Also, don't be surprised to find that the base 3.1L engine doesn't handle a full load of passenger and cargo, especially when mated with the 3-speed automatic transmission. The ideal powertrain combo would be the 4-speed automatic coupled to the optional 3800 V6 (first used on the 1996 versions). These minivans use a quiet-running V6 power plant similar to Chrysler's top-of-the-line 3.8L 6-cylinder, providing good mid-range and top-end power. The GM engine is hampered by less torque, however, making for less grunt when accelerating, and frequently down-shifting out of Overdrive when climbing moderate grades. The electronically controlled 4-speed automatic transmission shifts smoothly and quietly—one advantage over Chrysler and Ford.

This advantage is lost, however when you consider that the 1996–2004 models have chronic powertrain problems highlighted by engine manifold, head gasket, and camshaft failures along with frequent automatic transmission breakdowns and clunky shifting (covered by a 6-year/100,000 km secret warranty):

> Our '97 Venture has less than 100,000 km and the engine has seized, with broken cam shafts. I am looking at paying $4,000.

The 1996 and later models are less rattle-prone because of a more rigid body structure than that of their predecessors. However, fit and finish quality is still wanting. The front windshield is particularly prone to leak water from the top portion into the dash instrument cluster (a problem affecting rear-drive vans as well and covered by a secret warranty):

> Our 2002 Venture has a poorly fitted windshield and a misaligned dash and hood, as well as quarter panels, front doors, and the sliding rear door on the passenger side. I have inspected other 2002 and 2003 Chevrolet Ventures and have seen the same windshield fit errors.

Other troublespots include EGR valve failures, electrical glitches, excessive front brake noise and frequent repairs (rotors and pads), early wheel bearing failure, assorted body deficiencies, including paint peeling and blistering paint, blurry front windshield, air constantly blown through the centre vent, failure-prone AC condensers, and "eccentric" wipers:

> My wife and I have had these wipers reset twice and the motor replaced once already. Seems every time there is snow in the wiper seat, they will not rest in their designated resting position and end up resting in the upright position, requiring service or motor replacement. Dealer keeps saying to my wife "you must have forced them or bent them" neither of which she has done. Last week in Ottawa at my workplace parking lot I noticed no shortage (5 of 8) of Montanas with the wipers resting in the deficient vertical position.

 **Safety Summary**

All years: Fire may ignite around the fuel-filler nozzle or within the ignition switch. • Tie-rod failures may cause loss of steering control. • Sudden steering loss in rainy weather or when passing through a puddle (serpentine belt slippage). • Chronic brake failures or excessive brake fade. • Airbags malfunction. • Sliding doors suddenly open, close, come off their tracks, jam shut, stick open, injure children, and rattle during highway driving. • Transmission failures; slips from Drive into Neutral; and won't hold gear on a grade. • Some front door-mounted seat belts cross uncomfortably at the neck, and there's a nasty blind spot on the driver's side that requires a small stick-on convex mirror to correct. **1995–99**—Headlight assembly collects moisture, burns bulb, or falls out; seatback suddenly collapses; windshield wipers fail intermittently; accelerator and brake pedals are too close together; fuel slosh/clunk when vehicle stops or accelerates (replacement tank is useless); self-activating door locks lock occupants outside or inside; door handles break inside the door assembly; horn is hard to access; window latch failures. **2000–2001**—Fire ignited under driver's seat. • Windshield suddenly exploded outward while driving with wipers activated. • Firestone tire blowout. • Faulty fuel pump causes chronic stalling, no-starts, surging, and sudden acceleration. • Snapped rear control arm:

> In May we were driving our 2002 Pontiac Montana with 6 adults inside (luckily), on a small two-lane road, doing about 50 or 60 km/h. Suddenly, the right rear control arm snapped and the rear axle rattled and shook.
>
> Our mechanic said in 28 years he had never seen such a thing happen. If we'd been going 120 on a 400 highway we'd be dead.
>
> The dealer we bought it from paid all the costs for a used part to be installed, even thought there was no warranty, but our mechanic suggested we photograph the parts he had removed. He was surprised at the thinness of the metal of the control arm. Also that the control arm is welded to the axle, so it can't be replaced without replacing the entire component. New, they are $2000!
>
> KITCHENER, ONTARIO

• Steering idler arm fell off because of missing bolt. • Brakes activate on their own, making it feel as if van is pulling a load. • Loose fuel tank because of loose bolts/bracket. • Fuel tank cracked when passing over a tree branch. • Plastic tube within heating system fell off and wedged behind the accelerator pedal. • Bracket weld pin that secures the rear split seat sheared off. • Centre-rear lap seat belt isn't long enough to secure a rear-facing child safety seat. • Children can slide out of the integrated child safety seat. • Electrical harness failures result in complete electrical shutdown. • Headlights, interior lights, gauges, and instruments fail intermittently (electrical cluster module is the prime suspect). • Excess padding around horn makes it difficult to depress horn button in an emergency. • Weak-sounding horn. • Frequent windshield wiper motor failures. • Heater doesn't warm up vehicle sufficiently. • Antifreeze smell intrudes into interior. • Premature failure of the transmission's Fourth clutch. • Delayed or extended shifts, slips, or flares in cold weather. • Poorly performing rear AC. • Flickering interior and exterior lights. • Airbag warning lamp stays lit. • Windshield glass distortion. **2002**—Rear hatch handle broke, cutting driver's hand. • Vehicle jumped out of Park and rolled downhill. • Vehicle suddenly shuts off in traffic. • Windshield water leaks short out dash gauges. **2003**—Rear seat belts failed to release. • Weld holding the lift wheel pin is not adequate to support weight of trailer. **2004**—Engine surging, stalling. • Loss of coolant, engine overheating. • Two children's wrists were fractured after their elbows and hands were caught between the seat and handle. • Tail lights fail intermittently. • Door opens and closes on its own while vehicle is underway. • Door doesn't lock into position; slides shut and crushes objects in its path:

> We are very concerned that another child, or adult, is going to be injured in this van's automatic sliding door. We were curious just how far the 2004 Venture's door would go before it would bounce back open so we put a stuffed animal in the door and hit the auto door close button. I have to say, the stuffed animal did not fare well. We also put a large carrot and a banana in the door, in an attempt to simulate a small child's arm. The carrot was sliced right in half, and the banana was smashed and oozing out of its peel. I will never purchase a Chevrolet Venture after our experience with the van.

Secret Warranties/Internal Bulletins/Service Tips

1990–98—An oil odour coming from the engine compartment may be eliminated by changing the crankshaft rear main oil seal. **1993–2000**—GM says that a chronic driveline clunk can't be silenced and is a normal characteristic of its vehicles. • Paint delamination, peeling, or fading (see Part Two "Paint and Body Defects," pages 71–75). **1995–2000**—Dealer guidelines for brake servicing under warranty. **1996–2001**—Poor heat distribution in driver's area of vehicle (install new heat ducts). **1996–2003**—Engine intake manifold/head gasket failures (see pages 71–75):

> I just wanted to let you know that after contacting you back in January regarding our 2001 Chevy Venture head gasket problem, I have just received my judgement through the Canadian Arbitration Program.
>
> I used the sample complaint letter as well as the judgment you have posted in the Ford Canada vs. Dufour court case. This combined with an avalanche of similar Chevy Venture complaints that are posted on the Internet helped us to win a $1,700 reimbursement of the $2,200 we were looking for.

The reason for us not receiving the full amount is that the arbitrator stated that GM Canada would have only replaced one head gasket instead of replacing both as we had done, and that a dealer would have supplied us with a car free of charge and therefore did not allow us the car rental expense we incurred.

We are still extremely happy with the results and thank you for your books and website, you have a fan for life.

1997–98—A fuel tank thud or clunk noise may require new fuel tank straps and insulators. • Loose lumber noise coming from the rear of the vehicle when it passes over bumps means upgraded rear shock absorbers are required. • Poor rear windshield wiper performance may require that the fluid line be purged. • Windshield wiper blade chatter can be reduced by changing the wiper arm. • Insufficient windshield clearing in defrost mode requires the installation of new seals. **1997–99**—Upgraded front disc pads will reduce brake squeal. **1997–2000**—Front door windows that are inoperative, slow, or noisy may need the window run channel adjusted or replaced, in addition to new weather stripping. **1997–2001**—Paint blistering, bubbling, see bulletin to the left. **1997–2002**—Pssst! GM minivans may show premature hood corrosion and blistering. A dealer whistle-blower tells me that dealers have been authorized to repair the hoods free of charge (refinish and repaint) up to six years under a GM "goodwill" program. • Mildew odour; water leaks. • Wind noise at base of windshield. **1997–2004**—Defective catalytic converters that cause a rotten-egg smell in the interior may be replaced free of charge under the emissions warranty. • Second-row seat belt won't release. • Windshield wind noise. **1998**—No-start, engine miss, and rough idle may indicate that melted slush has contaminated the fuel system. **1998–99**—An inoperative sliding door may have a defective control module. **1998–2000**—Poor AC performance in humid weather may be caused by an undercharged AC system. **1999**—Diagnostic tips for an automatic transmission that slips, produces a harsh upshift and garage shifts (shifting between Reverse and Forward when parking), or causes acceleration shudders. **1999–2000**—If the engine runs hot, overheats, or loses coolant, try polishing the radiator filler neck or replacing the radiator cap before considering more expensive repairs. • Before taking on more expensive repairs to correct hard starts or no-starts, check the fuel pump. • An automatic transmission that whines in Park or Neutral or a Service Engine light that stays on may signal the need for a new drive sprocket support bearing. **1999–2002**—Transmission noise/no movement, see bulletin on next page. **1999–2003**—Incorrect fuel gauge readings caused by a contaminated fuel-tank

---

BLISTERING, BUBBLING PAINT

BULLETIN NO: 01-08-51-004   DATE: OCT. 2001

PREMATURE ALUMINUM HOOD CORROSION/BLISTERING (REFINISH)

1997–2001 Trans Sport (export only); 1997–2001 Venture; 1997–2001 Silhouette; 1997–1998 Trans Sport; 1999–2001 Pontiac Montana

Some vehicles may have the appearance of blistering or bubbling paint on the top of the hood or under the hood.

BULLETIN NO: 03-07-30-017 DATE: MAY, 2003

GRIND NOISE OR NO VEHICLE MOVEMENT WHEN SHIFTING INTO DRIVE OR REVERSE

(INSPECT TRANSAXLE, REPLACE VARIOUS TRANSAXLE COMPONENTS)

1999–2002 Century, LeSabre, Park Avenue; 2002 Rendezvous; 1999–2002 Monte Carlo, Venture; 2000–2002 Impala; 1999–2002 Intrigue, Silhouette; 1999–2002; Bonneville, Grand Prix, Montana; and 2001–2002 Aztek

IMPORTANT: If the vehicle DOES NOT exhibit a grinding condition but DOES exhibit shifting concerns, refer to Corporate Bulletin # 00-07-30-002

sensor/sender. If a fuel "cleaner" doesn't work, GM says it will adjust or replace the sensor/sender for free on a case-by-case basis (*Toronto Star*, June 13 and 14 and December 20, 2003). This failure afflicts GM's entire lineup and could cost up to $800 to repair. **2000–02**—Service Engine Soon light comes on and automatic transmission is harsh shifting. • Hard start, no-start, stall, and inoperative fuel gauge. **2000–04**—Tail light/brake light and circuit board burns out from water intrusion. Repair cost covered by a "goodwill" policy (TSB #03-08-42-007A). **2001**—Customer Satisfaction Program (secret warranty) to correct the rear HVAC control switch. **2001–02**—Poor engine and automatic transmission operation. • Slipping automatic transmission. **2003**—Shudder, chuggle (bad surge because of combustion instability), hard shifting, and transmission won't downshift. **2003–04**—Power sliding door binding. • Windshield whistle.

LUMINA, LUMINA APV, MONTANA, SILHOUETTE, TRANS SPORT, VENTURE PROFILE

	1996	1997	1998	1999	2000	2001	2002	2003	2004
Cost Price ($)									
Lumina Cargo	20,110	—	—	—	—	—	—	—	—
Passenger	22,730	—	—	—	—	—	—	—	—
Montana	—	—	—	25,130	26,625	26,755	27,870	28,520	29,380
Silhouette	—	—	29,410	29,955	30,630	31,105	33,060	35,695	36,290
Trans Sport/SE	23,475	23,690	24,650	—	—	—	—	—	—
Venture	—	23,185	24,145	24,725	24,895	25,230	25,195	25,865	26,680
Used Values ($)									
Lumina Cargo ▲	3,000	—	—	—	—	—	—	—	—
Lumina Cargo ▼	2,500	—	—	—	—	—	—	—	—
Passenger ▲	4,500	—	—	—	—	—	—	—	—
Passenger ▼	3,500	—	—	—	—	—	—	—	—
Montana ▲	—	—	—	7,000	8,500	12,000	15,000	18,000	20,000
Montana ▼	—	—	—	6,000	7,500	10,500	13,500	16,500	18,500

Silhouette ▲	—	—	8,000	9,000	12,000	16,000	20,000	21,500	22,000
Silhouette ▼	—	—	6,500	8,000	11,000	15,000	19,000	20,000	21,500
Trans Sport/SE ▲	4,500	5,500	6,500	—	—	—	—	—	—
Trans Sport/SE ▼	4,000	5,000	6000	—	—	—	—	—	—
Venture ▲	—	5,000	6,000	7,000	9,000	11,500	14,500	17,000	19,000
Venture ▼	—	4,500	5,500	6,000	7,500	10,000	13,000	15,500	17,500
Reliability	②	③	③	③	③	③	③	③	③
Crash Safety (F)	⑤	④	④	④	④	④	④	④	④
Side	—	—	—	⑤	⑤	⑤	⑤	⑤	⑤
Offset	—	❶	❶	❶	❶	❶	❶	❶	❶
Head Restraints (F)	—	❶	—	❸	—	❸	❸	❸	❸
Rear	—	—	—	❶	—	—	—	—	—
Rollover Resistance	—	—	—	—	—	❸	❸	❸	—

Honda

ODYSSEY ★★★★

RATING: Above Average (2003–04); Average (1996–2002). The upgraded 2005 model passes the Sienna in safety, performance, and convenience features. Nevertheless, there are frequent reports of safety- and performance-related failures on previous year Odysseys, hence their downgrade. Of particular concern are airbag malfunctions, automatic-sliding door failures, engine failures, transmission breakdowns and erratic shifting, and sudden brake loss. Early Odysseys get only an Average rating because of their small engines and interiors—identical shortcomings to those of Mazda's early MPV minivan. **Maintenance/Repair costs:** Average; any garage can repair these minivans. **Parts:** Moderately priced parts; availability is better than average because the Odyssey uses many generic Accord parts. **Extended warranty:** Not needed; save your money. **Best alternatives:** If you want something cheap, but still reliable, consider the 1997–2002 Quest. If you want handling and dependability, look to Toyota's early Sienna, or the revamped 2002 or later Mazda MPV. With Chrysler, it all hinges upon how much of the 7-year powertrain warranty is left. Sadly, GM's Pontiac Montana and Chevrolet Venture aren't in the running because of their self-destructing engine head gaskets and intake manifolds and malfunctioning automatic transmissions. GM's Astro, Safari, or full-sized van are much more reliable and provide additional towing muscle.

All ratings on a numbered scale where ⑤ is good and ❶ is bad. See pages 100–101 for a more detailed description.

Online help: *consumeraffairs.com/automotive/honda_van.html, www.mycarstats.com/
auto_complaints/HONDA_complaints.asp,* and *www.autosafety.org/autodefects.html.*

 Strengths and Weaknesses

When it was first launched in 1995, the Odyssey was a sales dud. Canadians and
Lemon-Aid saw through Honda's attempt to pass off an underpowered, mid-sized,
four-door station wagon with a raised roof as a minivan. In 1999 however, the
Odyssey was redesigned, and it now represents one of the better minivans on the
Canadian market.

It's easy to see what makes the Odyssey so popular: strong engine performance;
carlike ride and handling; easy entry/exit; a second driver-side door; and a quiet
interior. Most controls and displays are easy to reach and read, there's lots of passenger and cargo room and an extensive list of standard equipment, and Honda is
willing to compensate owners for production snafus.

This minivan does have its drawbacks, though. A recent decline in quality and a
high resale price make bargains rare. Owners report that front-seat passenger legroom is marginal because of the restricted seat travel; third-row seating is suitable
only for children; power sliding doors are slow to retract; there's some tire rumble,
rattles, and body drumming at highway speeds; premium fuel is required for
optimum performance; and rear-seat head restraints impede side and rear visibility.

One can sum up the strengths and weaknesses of the 1996–98 Odyssey (and the
Isuzu Oasis, its American twin through the 1998 model) in three words: performance, performance, performance. You get carlike performance and handling,
responsive steering, and a comfortable ride, offset by slow-as-molasses acceleration with a full load, a raucous engine, and limited passenger/cargo space because
of the narrow body.

Despite the above-mentioned drawbacks, the 1996–98 Odysseys have proven to be
cheaper to acquire, more reliable, and better handling than American rear-drive,
truck-inspired minivans. But their weak 2.2L 4-cylinder engine and small dimensions can't compete with GM's front-drives or with most rear-drive competitors.
The upgraded 1999 models have powerful 6-cylinder engines and a larger interior,
wiping out most of the previous model's deficiencies.

VEHICLE HISTORY: 1997—Small improvements. **1998**—A new 2.3L engine adds 10
horses (not enough!), and a restyled grille and instrument panel debut. **1999**—A
new, more powerful engine and increased size make this second-generation
Odyssey a more versatile highway performer; still, steering requires fully extended
arms and power sliding doors operate slowly. **2001**—User-friendly child safety seat
tether anchors, upgraded stereo speakers, and an intermittent rear window wiper.

2002—A slight restyling, 30 additional horses, disc brakes on all four wheels, standard side airbags, and additional support for front seats.

Reliability for all models is much better than average, but Honda still has a few problems to work out. One notable and hazardous example: failure-prone sliding doors. They open when they shouldn't, won't close when they should, catch fingers and arms, get stuck open or closed, are noisy, and frequently require expensive servicing. The Check Engine light may stay lit because of a defective fuel filler neck. There's a fuel sloshing noise when accelerating or coming to a stop, and the transmission clunks or bangs when backing uphill or when shifting into Reverse. There are also reports of rattling and chattering when the minivan is in forward gear. Owners note a loud wind noise and vibration from the left side of the front windshield, along with a constant vibration felt through the steering assembly and front wheels. Passenger doors may also require excessive force to open. And owners have complained of severe static electricity shocks when exiting. Other potential problem areas are frequent and high-cost front brake maintenance (see "Secret Warranties/Internal Bulletins/Service Tips"), and trim and accessory items that come loose, break away, or malfunction. Automatic transmission failures continue to be a major shortcoming.

Other problems include transmission breakdowns; the engine almost stalls out and produces a noise like valve clattering when shifting into Fourth gear; and transmission gear whine at 90 km/h or when in Fourth gear (the transmission can be replaced under a new "goodwill" warranty). One owner reported the following noisy annoyances with his 2000 model Odyssey:

> At 10,000 miles [16,000 km] I complained to the dealer about the torque converter rattle and was told it was not there. I have since taken it in four times to make sure it's documented and I was told last week that Honda is aware of the annoying rattle but is not willing to make any repairs at this time. As you know, Honda is experiencing other transmission "concerns" and has extended its warranty on certain transmissions….

Front-end clunking is caused by welding breaks in the front subframe; the exhaust rattles or buzzes; fuel splashes loudly in the fuel tank when coming to a stop; vehicle pulls to the right when underway; the front brakes wear prematurely; front brakes are excessively noisy; sliding side door frequently malfunctions; electrical glitches; defective remote audio controls; leather seats split, crack, or discolour; and accessory items that come loose, break away, or won't work. Plastic interior panels have rough edges and are often misaligned.

The comprehensive base warranty has lots of "wiggle room" that the service manager can use to apply "goodwill" adjustments for post-warranty problems. However, dealer servicing and after-warranty assistance have met with a great deal of criticism from *Lemon-Aid* readers. Owners complain that "goodwill" refunds aren't extended to all model years with the same defect; recall repairs take an eternity to perform; and dealers exhibit an arrogant, uncaring "take it or leave it" attitude.

 Safety Summary

All years: Passenger seatbacks collapsed when vehicle was rear-ended. • Airbag malfunctions. • Sudden, unintended acceleration when slowing for a stop sign. • Minivan was put in Drive, and AC was turned on; vehicle suddenly accelerated, brakes failed, and the minivan hit a brick wall. • Stuck accelerator. • V6 engine oil leaks. • Automatic transmission failures. • Transmission doesn't hold when stopped on a hill; gas or brakes have to be constantly applied. A class action petition has been filed against Honda in Quebec to recover recall costs incurred in re-connecting anti-theft devices, remote-controlled car starters and radios (1998–2000 Odysseys and CR-Vs, Civics, 1997–99 Accords and Preludes, and, 1997–2000 Acura CL, EL, and TL sedans.). • Power-sliding doors a constant danger. **1997–98**—Sudden acceleration upon brake application. **1999**—Fire erupted in the electrical harness. • Another fire erupted as vehicle was getting fuel. • Plastic gas tank cracks, leaks fuel. • Gasoline smell when transmission is put into Reverse. • Side window exploded while driving. • Check Engine light comes on and vehicle loses all power. • When driving, all the instrument panel lights will suddenly go out (faulty multiplex controller suspected). • When parked on a hill, vehicle may roll backward; transmission doesn't hold vehicle when stopped at a light on a hill and foot is taken off accelerator or brake. • Complete loss of power steering because of a pinhole in the power-steering return hose. • Poor power-steering performance in cold weather. • Power doors lock and unlock on their own. • Design of the gear shifter interferes with the radio controls. • Child unable to get out of seat belt because of buckle lock-up. • Faulty fuel gauge. • Inconvenient cell phone jack location. **2000**—Almost 400 safety complaints recorded by NHTSA; 100 would be normal. During fuelling, fuel tank burst into flames. • Many incidents where driver-side sliding door opened onto fuel hose while fuelling, damaging gas flap hinge and tank. • On cold days, accelerator pedal is hard to depress. • Catastrophic failure of the right-side suspension, causing wheel to buckle. • Vehicle continually pulls to the right; dealers unable to correct problem. • Excessive steering wheel vibration at 105+ km/h. • Electric doors often inoperative. • Seat belt tightened progressively around child's safety seat and fire department had to be called; other similar incidents. • Chronic automatic transmission problems: won't shift into lower gears, suddenly loses power, torque converter failure, makes a loud popping sound when put into Reverse. • Two incidents where vehicle was rear-ended because of transmission malfunction. • Power seatback moves on its own. • Dash lights don't adequately illuminate the dash panel. • Driver's seatback suddenly reclines, hitting rear passenger's legs, even though power switch is off. • Protruding bolts in the door assembly are hazardous. • Seat belt buckle fails to latch. • Driver-side mirror breaks away; mirror glass fell out because of poor design. • Easily broken sliding door handles. **2001**—While fuelling, fuel tank exploded. • In a frontal collision, van caught fire because of a cracked brake fluid reservoir. • Chronic stalling (transmission replaced). • Many reports of sudden transmission and torque converter failure. • When Reverse is engaged, car makes a popping or clunking sound. • Cracked wheel rim. • Check Engine light constantly on (suspect faulty gasoline filler neck). • Entire vehicle shakes excessively at highway speeds and van pulls to the right (dealer said some type of bar adjustment was needed). • Passenger-side door window suddenly exploded while driving on the highway. • Driver's seatback collapsed from rear-end collision. • Driver's power seat will suddenly recline on its own, squeezing rear occupant's legs and falling on child. • Rear seat belt tightened up so much that a child had to be cut free. • Too much play in rear lapbelts, which won't tighten adequately, making it difficult to install a child safety seat securely. • Inoperative driver seat belt buckle. • Faulty speedometer and tachometer. • Remote wouldn't open or lock vehicle. • Placement of the gear shift lever interferes with the radio's controls. • Unable to depress accelerator pedal on cold days. • Can hear gasoline sloshing in tank while driving. • Frequent static electricity shocks. • Many owners report that the rear head restraints seriously hamper rear and forward visibility and that it was difficult to see vehicles coming from the right side. **2002**—Over 232 complaints registered; 50 would be normal. Only 66 complaints recorded against the 2002 Toyota Sienna. • Owners say many engines have faulty timing chains. • Loose strut bolt almost caused wheel to fall off. • Axle bearing wheel failure caused driver-side wheel to fall off. • Left to right veering and excessive drivetrain vibration. • Loud popping sound heard when brakes are applied. • Many complaints that the brake pedal went to floor with no braking capability. • Sticking sliding door. • Head restraints are set too low for tall occupants. • Rear windshield shattered from area where wiper is mounted. • Rear seat belt unlatched during emergency braking. • Brake line freezes up in cold weather. • Abrupt downshift upon deceleration. • Driver-side door came off while using remote control. • Dashboard lights come on and off intermittently. • Passenger window exploded. • Airbag light comes on for no reason. **2003**—Fire ignited in the CD player. • Child injured from a side collision; second-row seat belt failed to hold her in because of gap caused by door attachment. • Rear seat belts lock for no reason. • Seat belt extenders aren't offered. • Defective speed sensor caused vehicle to suddenly lose power when merging into traffic. • Vehicle suddenly shut down in traffic. • Hard starts and engine misfiring. • Faulty steering causes wander. • Sudden brake failure. • Driver often shocked when touching door handle. • Fuel spits out when refuelling. • Inaccurate fuel gauge readings. • Sliding door closed on driver's hand.

Secret Warranties/Internal Bulletins/Service Tips

All models/years: Most of Honda's TSBs allow for special warranty consideration on a "goodwill" basis by the company's District Service Manager or Zone Office, even after the warranty has expired or the vehicle has changed hands. Referring to this euphemism will increase your chances of getting some kind of refund for repairs that are obviously factory defects. • There's an incredibly large number of sliding door problems covered by a recall, and a plethora of service bulletins that are simply too numerous to print here. Ask Honda politely for the bulletins or "goodwill" assistance. If refused, subpoena the documents through small claims court, using NHTSA's summary as your shopping list. **1999**—Poor engine performance may fall under a free service campaign whereby the company will replace, at no charge, the rear intake manifold end plate and gasket, the PCV hose, and the intake manifold cover. • Problems with the fuel tank pressure sensor are covered in TSB #99-056 and could call for the installation of an in-line orifice in the two-way valve vacuum hose. • AC knocking may require the installation of a new compressor clutch set. • Front windows that bind or are noisy. • An inaccurate fuel gauge is likely caused by a faulty sending unit. **1999–2001**—Extended warranty coverage on Odysseys with defective 4- and 5-speed automatic transmissions to 7 years/160,000 km (100,000 mi.) to fix erratic or slow shifting. **2000–01**—Third-row seat won't unlatch. • Clunk or bang when engaging Reverse. • Bulletin confirms Honda USA is currently investigating complaints of pulling or drifting (Service Bulletin Number: 99165, Bulletin Sequence Number: 802, Date of Bulletin: 09/99, NHTSA Item Number: SB608030). • Excessive front brake noise. • Dash ticking or clicking. **1999–2003**—Engine oil leaks will be corrected under a "goodwill" policy. • Deformed windshield moulding. **2002**—Hesitation when accelerating. • Diagnosing automatic transmission problems. • No-starts; hard start in cold weather. • Driver's seat heater may not work. • Thump at cold start. • Loose rear wiper arm. • AC can't be turned off while in defog setting. **2002–03**—Free replacement of the engine timing belt auto-tensioner and water pump under both a recall and "product update" campaign.

RECALL

BULLETIN NO.: 03-081   DATE: OCTOBER 27, 2003

DEFECT: On certain minivans, sedans, coupes, and sport utility vehicles equipped with V6 engines, a timing belt tensioner pulley on the water pump is misaligned and could cause the timing belt to contact a bolt on the cylinder head. Eventually the belt could be damaged and fail. If the timing belt breaks, the engine will stall, increasing the risk of a crash. **REMEDY:** Dealers will inspect the water pump, and if it is one of the defective pumps, the water pump and timing belt will be replaced.

PRODUCT UPDATE
BACKGROUND: The timing belt tensioner is filled with oil to dampen oscillation. Due to a manufacturing problem, the tensioner oil can leak. If enough oil is lost, the timing belt loosens and causes engine noise.
MODELS: 2002-03 Odyssey and 2003 Pilot
CORRECTIVE ACTION: Replace the timing belt auto-tensioner.

2002–04—Free tranny repair or replacement for insufficient lubrication that can lead to heat build-up and broken gears. Transmission noise will signal gear breakage; transmission may also lock up. • Rear brake noise.

REAR BRAKE CLUNK

BULLETIN NO: 04-019

DATE: MARCH 23, 2004

2002–04 Odyssey; 2003 Pilot; 2004 Pilot

The rear brake calipers clunk when you first apply the brakes after changing the direction of the vehicle. The outer shims on the rear brake pads do not allow the pads to slide easily when you press the brake pedal. This causes the outer pad to hit hard during a change of direction, resulting in a clunk.

CORRECTIVE ACTION: Replace the rear brake pad shims.

2003—Engine cranks, but won't start. • Troubleshooting ABS problems. • Power steering pump noise. • Warning lights blink on and off. • Exhaust rattling, buzzing. • Remote audio control troubleshooting. • Leather seat defects. • HomeLink® remote system range is too short; hard to program. • Factory security system won't arm. • Faulty charging system; electrical shorts. • Front door howls in strong cross-wind. • Squealing from rear quarter windows and window motors. • Fuel tank leak. • Front damper noise. • Steering wheel bent off-centre. • Manual sliding door is difficult to open.

ODYSSEY PROFILE

	1996	1997	1998	1999	2000	2001	2002	2003	2004
Cost Price ($)									
LX	28,796	28,995	29,800	30,600	30,600	30,800	31,900	32,200	32,400
EX	—	—	—	33,600	33,600	33,800	34,900	35,200	35,400
Used Values ($)									
LX ▲	6,000	7,500	9,000	10,500	15,000	17,000	20,000	25,000	27,500
LX ▼	5,000	6,000	8,000	9,000	13,500	16,000	18,500	23,500	26,000
EX ▲	—	—	—	11,500	16,000	18,500	21,500	26,000	29,000
EX ▼	—	—	—	10,500	14,500	17,000	20,000	24,500	27,500
Reliability	③	③	③	④	⑤	⑤	⑤	⑤	⑤
Crash Safety (F)	④	④	—	⑤	⑤	⑤	⑤	⑤	⑤
Side	—	—	—	—	⑤	⑤	⑤	⑤	⑤
Head Restraints (F)	②	②	—	②	—	②	②	②	②
Rear	—	—	—	❶	—	—	—	—	—
Offset	②	②	②	⑤	⑤	⑤	⑤	⑤	⑤
Rollover Resistance	—	—	—	—	—	④	④	④	—

All ratings on a numbered scale where ⑤ is good and ❶ is bad. See pages 100–101 for a more detailed description.

Kia

SEDONA ★★★

RATING: Average (2002–04). Sedona is a very user-friendly, roomy, versatile, and comfortable mid-sized minivan that comes with a comprehensive base warranty. **Maintenance/Repair costs:** Average. **Parts:** Likely to be back-ordered and cost more than average. **Extended warranty:** Yes, until these minivans have proved themselves on a long-term basis. **Best alternatives:** GM Astro and Safari, Honda Odyssey, 2002 or later Mazda MPV, or pre-2004 Toyota Sienna. **Online help:** *www.autosafety.org/autodefects.html, members.tripod.com/aiki_joe/i_hate_kia,* and *townhall-talk.edmunds.com.*

 Strengths and Weaknesses

Used Sedonas cost several thousand dollars less than comparable minivans. Embodying typically bland minivan styling, the front-drive, seven-passenger Sedona is 18 centimetres (7 in.) shorter than a Honda Odyssey and 11 centimetres (4.5 in.) longer than a Dodge Caravan. It comes with a good selection of standard features, including a 195-hp 3.5L V6 engine hooked to an automatic 5-speed transmission, a low step-in height, and a commanding view of the road. For convenience, there are two sliding rear side doors; folding, removable second- and third-row seats; a flip-up hatchback; standard front/rear air conditioning; and a large cargo bay. Other standard amenities are 15-inch tires, AM/FM/CD stereo, power steering, power windows, power door locks, power heated mirrors, tilt steering, rear defroster and wiper, dual airbags, and six adjustable head restraints.

On the plus side: Sedonas are reasonably priced and appointed. The transmission shifts smoothly and quietly, and the low ground clearance enhances passenger access and cargo loading. The Sedona also provides a comfortable ride, a convenient "walk-through" space between the front seats, well laid-out, user-friendly instruments and controls, lots of storage areas, good visibility, and minimal engine and road noise. Fit and finish is acceptable, though quality is uneven.

From a safety perspective, braking is efficient and predictable, with little brake fade after successive stops, and crashworthiness scores are quite impressive.

On the minus side: Engine power is drained by the Sedona's heft; it has a 10–20 percent higher fuel consumption than the V6-equipped Dodge Caravan and Toyota Sienna; handling is compromised by subpar, vague steering and a wallowing suspension; ears are assailed by excessive engine and wind noise; and the dealer network is relatively new and spread out.

Poor quality control may be too much for the base warranty to handle, making reliability the Sedona's weakest link. So far, the areas of most concern have been the engine (head gasket leaks), seat belts, fuel and electrical systems, brake pads and rotors, AC compressor, windows, and overall body construction.

 ## Safety Summary

2002—Over 100 safety-related complaints reported. • Fuel tank design could spray fuel on hot muffler in a collision. • Oil leaks onto the hot catalytic converter. • Fuel leaks from the bottom of the vehicle. • Loose fuel line to fuel pump clamp. • Fuel tank filler hose vulnerable to road debris. • Fuel spits back when refuelling. • Vehicle continues to accelerate when brakes are applied. • Intermittent stalling. • Brake failure; pedal simply sinks to the floor. • Excessive brake shudder when slowing going downhill. • ABS brake light comes on randomly. • Power steering pulley broke. • Windshield may suddenly shatter for no apparent reason. • Windshields have distortion at eye level. • Second- and third-row seats don't latch as easily as touted. • Oil leaks onto the catalytic converter. • Electrical shorts cause lights, windows, and door locks to fail. • Sliding doors won't retract if object is in their way. • Stuck rear hatch door. • Child safety seat can't be belted in securely. • Child door safety lock failure. • Inoperative back-seat seat belts. • Seat belt holding child in booster seat tightened progressively, trapping child. • Kumho tire tread separation. 2003—Under-hood fire ignited while car was underway. • Airbags failed to deploy. • Sudden, unintended acceleration. • Stuck accelerator pedal. • Brakes fail because of air in the brake lines. • Fuel odour in cabin. • Broken window regulator. • Rear seat removal instructions can throw your back out. • Tires peeled off the rim. • When reclined, passenger seatback was released upright and slammed a young child forward. • AC condenser vulnerable to puncture from road debris. • Electrical shorts cause door lock malfunctions. 2004—Excessive brake rotor wear. • Parking brake didn't hold vehicle on an incline. • Chronic stalling. • Windshield has a cloudy haze.

Secret Warranties/Internal Bulletins/Service Tips

2002—Correction for engine hesitation after cold starts. • Free replacement of seat belt buckle anchor bolts. 2002–03—Changes to improve alternator output to prevent hard starts or battery drain. 2004—Engine head gasket leak.

SEDONA PROFILE

	2002	2003	2004
Cost Price ($)			
LX	24,595	24,995	25,595
EX	27,595	28,295	28,995
Used Values ($)			
LX ▲	13,000	15,500	18,000

 All ratings on a numbered scale where ⑤ is good and ❶ is bad. See pages 100–101 for a more detailed description.

LX ▼	11,000	14,000	16,000
EX ▲	14,500	16,500	20,000
EX ▼	13,000	15,000	18,500
Reliability	③	③	③
Crash Safety (F)	⑤	⑤	⑤
Side	⑤	⑤	⑤
Head Restraints	⑤	⑤	⑤
Rear	③	③	③
Offset	③	③	③
Rollover Resistance	④	④	—

Mazda

MPV	★★★★

RATING: Above Average (2002–04); Average (2000–01); Below Average (1988–98). Mazda has accomplished an amazing turnaround in the past three years; its MPV is now smaller, sportier, and more nimble than its more space- and comfort-oriented counterparts. Early models were underpowered, lumbering, undersized, and overpriced. There was no '99 model. The redesigned 2000–01 model is still hampered by a wimpy powertrain and is just too small for most tasks. **Maintenance/Repair costs:** Average; independent garages can service these minivans more cheaply than Mazda dealers. **Parts:** Likely to be back-ordered and cost more than average, despite Mazda's best efforts to cut prices. **Extended warranty:** An extended warranty is worth having, particularly since powertrain problems plague these vehicles after the first three years of use. **Best alternatives:** The MPV is still best suited for owners who don't want the biggest family-hauler on the block, those who prefer sporty handling, and those who don't mind spending less to get less. When the MPV is compared with Honda's Odyssey, the value equation gets a little murkier. With the price reduction, the base MPV LX gains a competitive advantage over the base Odyssey. When compared with the more expensive Odysseys, there's not enough savings to make up for the MPV's smaller size and less powerful engine. And the Odyssey is already available with a DVD entertainment system. Go for a cheaper 2002 model, but make sure it's a second-series version to keep factory-induced glitches to a minimum. There are plenty of reasonably priced 2- and 3-year-old MPVs on the market that have just come off lease, but they don't measure up to the better-performing 2002–03 versions. Other models to consider: GM's Astro and Safari, a Honda Odyssey, early Nissan Quests, or a pre-2004 Toyota Sienna. **Online help:** *townhall-talk.edmunds.com/direct/view/.ee93de8, forums.mazdaworld.org/index.php?showforum=35,* and *www.autosafety.org/autodefects.html.*

Strengths and Weaknesses

Manufactured in Hiroshima, Japan, this small minivan offers a number of innovative features, such as "theatre" seating (rear passenger seat is slightly higher) and a third seat that pivots rearward to become a rear-facing bench seat—or folds into the floor for picnics or tailgate parties. Another feature unique among minivans is Mazda's Side-by-Slide removable second-row seats, which move fore and aft as well as side-to-side while a passenger is seated. Sliding door crank windows are standard on the entry model and power-assisted on the LX and ES versions.

Mazda's only minivan quickly became a bestseller when it first came on the market in 1989, but its popularity fell just as quickly when larger, more powerful competitors arrived. Mazda sales have bounced back recently as a result of price-cutting and the popularity of the automaker's small cars and pickups. This infusion of cash has allowed the company (34 percent of which is owned by Ford) to put additional money into its 2002 redesign, thus ending a sales slump that has plagued Mazda for over a decade. Early MPVs embodied many of the mistakes made by Honda's first Odyssey—its 170 horses weren't adequate for people-hauling and it was expensive for what was essentially a smaller van than buyers expected—a foot shorter than the Ford Windstar and a half foot shorter than the Toyota Sienna and the Nissan Quest.

VEHICLE HISTORY: 1992—5-speed manual transmission scrapped and the 3.0L V6 got a 5-horsepower boost. **1993**—A driver-side airbag. **1994**—A centre brake light and side-door impact beams. **1995**—Seven-passenger seating and a 155-hp 3.0L engine. **1996**—A passenger-side airbag, four-wheel ABS, and four doors. **2000**—A new model with front-drive and sliding side doors. **2002**—A 200-hp V6 and 5-speed automatic transmission, power sliding side doors, revised suspension settings, and 17-inch wheels. **2003**—More standard features (LX) that include power-sliding rear side doors, 16-inch wheels, a flip-up side table, and doormat. **2004**—Refreshed interior and exterior styling of no real consequence, except for the driver's seat additional lumbar support.

The MPV presently uses the Taurus 200-hp 3.0L Duratec V6. Some refinements produce a lower torque peak—3000 rpm versus 4400 rpm—giving the Mazda engine better pulling power at lower speeds. Making good use of that power is a smooth-shifting 5-speed automatic transmission, which should cut fuel consumption a bit. One immediate benefit: The 3.0L is able to climb hills without continuously downshifting, and Mazda's "slope control" system automatically shifts to a lower gear when the hills get very steep.

Torque is still less than the Odyssey's 3.5L or the 3.8L engine in top-of-the-line Chryslers, though comparable with lesser Chrysler products and GM's Venture and Montana. The suspension has been firmed up to decrease body roll, enhancing cornering ability and producing a sportier ride than other minivans. This firmness may be too much for some.

I've been tougher on the MPV than *Consumer Reports* and others have been because of the price-gouging, poor servicing, small size, underpowered drivetrain, and reliability problems (all too common on pre-2000 models). It now looks like most of these concerns have been addressed, although I'm still worried that the 3.0 Duratec may not hold up.

On more recent models, engine overheating and head gasket failures are commonplace with the 4-banger, and the temperature gauge warns you only when it's too late. Some cases of chronic engine knocking in cold weather with the 3.0L have been fixed by installing tighter-fitting, Teflon-coated pistons. Valve lifter problems are also common with this engine. Winter driving is compromised by the MPV's light rear end and mediocre traction, and low ground clearance means that off-road excursions shouldn't be too adventurous. The last couple of model years are much improved; nevertheless, expect some transmission glitches, ABS malfunctions, a rotten-egg exhaust, stalling and surging, and some oil leakage. Owners report that the electronic computer module (ECU), automatic transmission driveshaft, upper shock mounts, front 4×4 drive axles and lash adjusters, AC core, and radiator fail within the first three years. Cold temperatures tend to fry the automatic window motor, and the paint is easily chipped and flakes off early, especially around the hood, tailgate, and front fenders. Premature brake caliper and rotor wear and excessive vibration/pulsation are chronic problem areas (repairs are needed about every 12,000 km). Premature paint peeling commonly afflicts white MPVs.

 ## Safety Summary

1998—Rear anti-sway bar brackets snapped off from rear axle housing. • ABS brake failure. • Defective gas cap causes the false activation of the Check Engine light. 2000—Fixed seat belt anchors and buckle placement prevent the safe installation of child safety seats. • Vehicle windshield and side glass suddenly shattered while parked. • Excessive vibrations while cruising. • Rear hatch door flew open when rear-ended. 2000–01—Engine valve failure. • Cupholders will spill drink when making a sharp turn; holders were redesigned in 2002. 2000–03—Airbags failed to deploy. 2001—Engine surging. • Malfunctioning #1 spark plug causes chronic engine hesitation. • Tranny lever can be shifted out of Park without key in ignition; sometimes it won't shift out of Park when you want it to. • Brake failure. • Brake caliper bolt fell off, causing vehicle to skid. • Sliding doors don't lock in place. • Rear visibility obstructed by high seatbacks. 2002–03—Engine oil leakage, sudden stalling, shifter obscures dash and is easily knocked about. 2003—Child's neck became tangled in seat belt. • Rotten-egg exhaust smell. 2004—Engine seized when connecting rod failed. • Transmission failure because of worn shaft solenoid. • Blown tire sidewall. • Tread separation on Dunlop tires.

 Secret Warranties/Internal Bulletins/Service Tips

All models/years: TSB #006-94 looks into all the causes and remedies for excessive brake vibrations, and TSB #11-14-95 gives an excellent diagnostic flow chart for troubleshooting excessive engine noise. • Serious paint peeling and delaminating will be fully covered for up to six years under a Mazda secret warranty, say owners. • Troubleshooting tips for correcting wind noise around doors. • Tips for eliminating a musty, mildew-type AC odour. **1996–98**—Tips for correcting water leaks from the sliding sunroof. • Brake pulsation repair tips. • Front power window noise. • Wind noise around doors. • Steering wheel is a bit off-centre. **1997–98**—Front power window noise can be silenced by installing a modified window regulator. **2000–01**—Hard starts caused by inadequate fuel system pressure because of a fuel pressure regulator that's stuck open. • Front brake clunking can be silenced by replacing the eight brake guide plates under warranty (TSB #04-003/00). • Insufficient airflow at bi-level setting. • Door key difficult to insert or rotate. **2000–03**—Rotten-egg exhaust smell. • Remedy for a mildew odour. • A corroded rear heater pipe may leak coolant; Mazda will fix it for free (see TSB #07-004/03). **2001**—Rear brake popping, squealing, or clicking. • Tips for eliminating a musty, mildew-type odour from the AC. **2002**—Engine tappet noise. **2002–03**—Cargo net hooks detach. **2002–04**—Remedies for shift shock (transmission slams into gear).

MPV PROFILE

	1996	1997	1998	2000	2001	2002	2003	2004
Cost Price ($)								
Base	27,330	—	—	—	—	—	—	—
DX	—	—	—	25,505	25,095	25,975	26,090	26,600
LX	30,900	27,845	25,199	29,450	29,450	29,150	29,090	29,995
Used Values ($)								
Base ▲	4,500	—	—	—	—	—	—	—
Base ▼	4,000	—	—	—	—	—	—	—
DX ▲	—	—	—	10,500	12,500	15,500	17,000	20,000
DX ▼	—	—	—	9,000	11,000	14,000	16,000	18,500
LX ▲	4,000	5,000	7,000	12,000	14,000	17,000	20,000	22,500
LX ▼	3,500	4,000	5,500	10,500	13,000	16,000	18,500	21,000
Reliability	③	③	③	④	④	④	④	⑤
Crash Safety (F)	④	④	—	④	④	⑤	⑤	⑤
Side	②	②	②	⑤	⑤	⑤	⑤	⑤
Offset	②	②	②	③	③	③	③	③
Head Restraints (F)	②	❶	—	③	②	②	②	③
Rear	—	—	—	—	❶	❶	❶	②
Rollover Resistance	—	—	—	—	③	③	③	—

All ratings on a numbered scale where ⑤ is good and ❶ is bad. See pages 100–101 for a more detailed description.

Toyota

RATING: *Sienna:* Average (2004). There has been a resurgence of safety-related defects reported with the redesigned 2004 Sienna. Above Average (1998-2003). *Previa:* Average (1991–97). The Previa has reasonable reliability, mediocre road performance, and limited interior amenities. Nevertheless, it's far better than any of Toyota's earlier LE minivans. **Maintenance/Repair costs:** For the Sienna, like the Camry, much lower than average. The only exception is engine sludge, requiring expensive repairs. Previas aren't afflicted by the sludge problem, but their maintenance costs are still higher than average. Only Toyota dealers can repair these minivans, particularly when it comes to troubleshooting the super-charged 2.4L engine and All Trac. **Parts:** Excellent supply of reasonably priced Sienna parts taken from the Camry parts bin. Previa parts are in limited supply, but they're reasonably priced. Automatic transmission torque converters on 1998–2000 models are frequently back-ordered because of their poor reliability. **Extended warranty:** Only for the 2004 model. **Best alternatives:** Mazda mini-vans are catching up to Honda and Toyota in performance and reliability, while the less reliable and low-tech Ford and GM models are hardly in the running. Chrysler's extensive 7-year powertrain warranty, generous rebates, and innovative styling have kept its minivans on life-support for the past several years. Earlier Toyotas are outclassed by the brawnier, more innovative Odyssey. Be wary of the power sliding door. As with the Odyssey and GM minivans, these doors can injure children and pose unnecessary risks to other occupants. **Online help:** *www.auto-safety.org/autodefects.html, yotarepair.com/Sludge_Zone.html,* and *www.cartrackers. com/Forums/live/MiniVansEnthusiastDiscussionGroup/page8.html.*

Strengths and Weaknesses

The completely redesigned 2004 Sienna provides lots more interior room than previous models (accommodating up to eight passengers), handles much better, rides more comfortably, and uses a more powerful, fuel-efficient engine. Standard four-wheel disc brakes and all-wheel-drive is offered for the first time.

A new 3.3L 230-hp V6 turns in respectable acceleration times under nine seconds; almost as good as the Odyssey. Handling is completely carlike, there's less vulner-ability to wind buffeting, and there's minimal road noise.

Sienna's interior and exterior have been gently restyled. The third-row seats split and fold away, head restraints don't have to be removed when the seats are stored, and second-row bucket seats are easily converted to bench seats.

The Sienna is Toyota's Camry-based front-drive minivan. It replaced the Previa for the 1998 model year and abandoned the Previa's futuristic look in favour of a more conservative Chevrolet Venture styling. The Sienna seats seven, and offers dual power sliding doors with optional remote controls and a V6 power plant. It's built in the same Kentucky assembly plant as the Camry, and comes with lots of safety and convenience features, including side airbags, anti-lock brakes, and a low-tire-pressure warning system.

Some of the Sienna's strong points: standard ABS and side airbags (LE, XLE); a smooth-running V6 engine and transmission that's a bit more refined and capable than what the Odyssey offers; a comfortable, stable ride; a fourth door; a quiet interior; easy entry/exit; and better-than-average fit and finish and reliability. Its weak areas: V6 performance is compromised by the AC and the automatic transmission powertrain and it lacks the trailer-towing brawn of rear-drive minivans:

> Imagine our surprise when we discovered within the owner's manual a "Caution" stating that one must not exceed 72 km/hr [45 mph] while towing a trailer (full text below). This limit is not stated in the promotional literature we were provided, or on the Toyota.ca website, or in any trailer towing rating guide. This limit was also not mentioned at any time during our purchase negotiations. Alarmingly, Toyota defines a "Caution" as a "warning against anything which may cause injury to people if the warning is ignored." As it turns out, the dealer was not aware of this speed limit....

Although the rear seats fold flat to accommodate the width of a 4'×8' board, the tailgate won't close, the heavy seats are difficult to reinstall (it's a two-person job, and the centre seat barely fits through the door), and rear visibility is obstructed by the middle roof pillars and rear head restraints. There's also no traction control, less-efficient rear drum brakes, mediocre fuel economy (using premium fuel), the low-mounted radio is hard to reach, and third-row seats lack a fore/aft adjustment to increase cargo space.

Reliability is still problematic on 1997–2002 models. Although the vehicles' mechanical and body components are generally reliable, there has been a disturbing increase in factory-related defects reported by owners during the past few years. The most serious reliability problems concern self-destructing, sludge-prone engines (1997–2002 models) and defective automatic transmissions on 1998–2000 Siennas.

Toyota Canada advises owners who notice the telltale signs of engine sludge formation to take their vehicle to their local dealer to have the engine inspected. These signs may include the emission of blue smoke from the tailpipe and/or excessive oil consumption, which may cause overheating, rough running, or the Check Engine light to come on.

Other recent model problems reported by owners include automatic transmission failures; a clunk or banging in the driveline; the car jolting or creeping forward when at a stop, forcing you to keep your foot firmly on the brake; stalling when the AC engages; electrical shorts; premature brake wear and excessive brake noise (mostly screeching); a chronic rotten-egg smell; distracting windshield reflections and distorted windshields; sliding door defects; the window suddenly shattering; easily chipped paint; and various other body glitches, including a hard-to-pull-out rear seat, water leaks, and excessive creaks and rattles (seat belt, sun visor).

VEHICLE HISTORY: 1995—DX models get a supercharged engine. **1996**—Supercharged engine is the only power plant offered. **1997**—Extra soundproofing. **1998**—Introduction of the Sienna; no more Previa. **2001**—A rear defroster, some additional horsepower and torque, and a driver-side sliding door. **2004**—Completely redesigned.

Previa

The redesigned 1991 Previa's performance and reliability are so much improved over its LE predecessor that it almost seems like a different vehicle. Roomier and rendered more stable thanks to its longer wheelbase, equipped with a new 2.4L engine (supercharged as of the 1994 model year), and loaded with standard safety and convenience features, 1991–97 Previas are almost as driver-friendly as the Chrysler and Mazda competition. Still, they can't match Ford, GM, or Chrysler front-drive minivans for responsive handling and a comfortable ride, and Toyota's small engine is overworked and doesn't hesitate to tell you so. Previa owners have learned to live with engine noise, poor fuel economy, premature front brake wear, excessive brake vibration and pulsation, electrical glitches, AC malfunctions, and fit and finish blemishes. The 4×4 models with automatic transmissions steal lots of power from the 4-cylinder power plant but have fewer reliability problems than similar drivetrains found on competitors, especially those found on Chryslers.

 **Safety Summary**

Almost every model year has had serious sliding door malfunctions confirmed by owner complaints and a torrent of internal service bulletins. • Many complaints that the steering wheel locks up when making a turn, won't return to centre without extreme effort, or simply no longer responds. • Owners have also complained that the vehicle pulls sharply to one side or another when driving at moderate speeds. • Windshield distortion. • Reflection of the dashboard on the windshield impairs visibility. *Sienna:* **1998**—Sudden acceleration caused by a defective throttle cable; vehicle hit a wall. • Shape and design of the Sienna creates severe blind spots. • Headlights give poor illumination. • Rear door doesn't shut tightly. • Poor visibility because of the tinted window design. • Headrests and third-row seats are loose and vibrate. • Shoulder belts in the middle row lock up instantly when first put on and stay locked up, trapping the passenger. **1999—** Wheel lug nuts broke and allowed wheel to fall off. • Window exploded at stoplight. • Rear brake drums may overheat and warp. • Faulty fuel cap causes the Check Engine light to come on. **2000—** Sudden acceleration during rainstorm. • Check Engine light continues to come on because of a defective transmission torque converter. • Chronic transmission failure because of faulty torque converter. • Wheel lug nuts sheared off. • Driver's seat belt anchor bolt on door pillar unscrewed and fell off. • Premature tire blowouts (Dunlop and Firestone). • Right rear passenger window suddenly exploded. • Annoying dash/windshield reflection also impairs visibility (very bad with black and beige colours). **2001—** Sudden stalling when the AC is turned on. • Automatic transmission suddenly went into Neutral while on the highway. • Defective transmission torque converter causes the engine warning light to come on. • Sudden, unintended acceleration. • Vehicle rolled down a hill with shifter in Park and ignition shut off. • Rear seat belts can't be adjusted. • Centre rear seat belt doesn't tighten sufficiently when children are restrained. • Slope of the windshield makes it hard to gauge where the front end stops. • Rear window exploded as front door was closed. • Sunroof flew off when opened while Sienna was underway. **2002—** Several electrical fires in the engine compartment. • Neither front nor side airbag deployed in a collision. • Defective power steering. • Loss of steering. **2003—** Unsafe transmission Overdrive design. • Child safety seat second-row tethering is poorly designed. • Vehicle jerks to one side when accelerating or stopping. **2004—** An incredible 158 complaints (versus 35 for the 2003 Sienna). • Engine surging with minimal pedal pressure. • When proceeding from a rolling stop, acceleration is delayed for about two seconds:

> While parking, accelerating no more than 5 mph vehicle surged forward. Although I was applying the brake, the car would not stop until it ran into a tree trunk.

• Child knocked gearshift lever into Drive from Park without key in the ignition. • Difficulty shifting into a higher gear. • Sluggish transmission downshift; vehicle sometimes seems to slip out of gear when decelerating. • Skid control system lockup. • Fuel tank leakage after recall repairs; leaking fuel line. • Complete loss of brakes. • Rapid brake degradation (glazed and warped rotors). • Sliding door caught passenger's arm and child's leg; manual door doesn't latch properly (particularly when windows are open), door opens when turning, jams, or closes when vehicle is parked on an incline:

> Our 2-year-old son pulled on the sliding door handle, and the door began to open (we thought the child locks were on, but this was not the case). He was surprised and was afraid of falling out of the van, so he just held onto the handle. As the door was opening, his head then was dragged between the sliding door and the side of the van. But the van door did not stop opening. It just continued opening, exerting

even more force on our son's head. Fortunately we were able to grab the door and forcefully pull it back closed before our son was horribly injured.

• Second-row seat belt locks up; faulty seat belt bracket in rear passenger seat. • Seat belts won't retract. • Battery-saver device doesn't work, particularly if interior lights are left on (they don't turn off as advertised). • Small brake lights inadequate. • Foot gets stuck between pedals. • Rotten-egg smell. • Daytime running lights blind oncoming drivers (2004 Highlander has the same problem). • Long delay for fuel tank recall campaign parts.

Secret Warranties/Internal Bulletins/Service Tips

All models/years: Sliding door hazards, malfunctions, and noise are veritable plagues affecting all model years and generating a heap of service bulletins. • Owner feedback confirms that front brake pads and discs will be replaced under Toyota's "goodwill" policy if they wear out before 2 years/40,000 km. • Loose, poorly fitted trim panels (TSB # BO017-03 REVISED September 9, 2003). Rusting at the base of the two front doors. Will be repaired at no cost, usually with a courtesy car included. The website *www.siennaclub.org* says that to fix the problem properly, repaint the inside of doors (presumably after removing paint and rust), cover with 3M film, and replace and coat inside seals with silicone grease. **1997–2002**—Free engine overhaul or replacement because of engine sludge buildup. The program includes 1997 through 2002 Toyota and Lexus vehicles with 3.0L, V-6, or 2.2L 4-cylinder engines. There is no mileage limitation; tell Toyota to shove it if they give you a song and dance about proof of oil changes. **1998**—Upgraded brake pads and rotors should reduce brake groan and squeak noises. **1998–2000**—An 8-year/160,000 km warranty extension for automatic transmission failure. Says Toyota:

> We have recently become aware that a small number of Sienna owners have experienced a mechanical failure in the automatic transaxle, drive pinion bearing. This failure could result in slippage, noise, or a complete lack of movement.
>
> To ensure the continued satisfaction and reliability of your Sienna, Toyota has decided to implement a Special Policy Adjustment affecting certain 1998–2000 Sienna models….This Special Policy will extend the warranty coverage of the automatic transaxle to 8 years or 160,000 km, whichever occurs first, from the original warranty registration date….

• Outline of various diagnostic procedures and fixes to correct vehicle pulling to one side. • Power steering squeaks can be silenced by installing a countermeasure steering rack end under warranty. • Power steering "feel" can be improved by replacing the steering rack guide. • False activation of the security alarm can be fixed by modifying the hood latch switch. • Power window rattles can be corrected by installing a revised lower window frame mounting bracket. **1998–2003**—A

REAR BRAKE SQUEALING
BULLETIN NO: BR003-04   DATE: MARCH 16, 2004
'98–'03 Sienna
A new rear brake drum has been developed to reduce rear brake squeal noise.

new rear brake drum has been developed to reduce rear brake noise (see bulletin). • An upgraded alternator will improve charging (see TSB #EL013-03) and is also part of "goodwill" treatment. **1999–2001**—Tips on fixing power seat motor cable to prevent a loose seat or inoperative seat adjustment. • Power sliding door transmitter improvements. **2000**—Toyota has field fixes to correct washer fluid leakage from the rear washer nozzle and to eliminate moisture and odours permeating the vehicle interior. • Correction for an inoperative spare tire lift. • Speedometer or tachometer troubleshooting. **2001**—False activation of the security alarm. • Power windows rattling. • Entertainment system hum. • Faulty speedometer and tachometer. • Inoperative third-row sliding seat. • Special service campaign to inspect or replace the front subframe assembly on 2001 models. • Water leaking into the trunk area. • Troubleshooting interior moisture or odours. • Loose sun visor. • Front wheel bearing ticking. **2002**—Troubleshooting complaints that vehicle pulls to one side. **2002–03**—Steering angle sensor calibration. • Loose sun visor remedy. **2004**—New ECM calibration for a poor shifting transmission (TSB #TC007-03). • Rear disc brake groan (TSB #BR002-04). • Intermediate steering shaft noise when turning. • Front door area wind noise (TSB #NV009-03). • Power sliding door inoperative, rattles (the saga continues). • Back door shudder and water leaks. • Charging improvement at idle (TSB #RL013-03).

SIENNA, PREVIA PROFILE

	1996	1997	1998	1999	2000	2001	2002	2003	2004
Cost Price ($)									
Previa	35,908	36,998	—	—	—	—	—	—	—
Sienna Cargo 3d	—	—	24,438	24,570	24,570	—	—	—	—
Sienna CE 4d (16%)	—	—	26,808	26,940	27,770	29,535	29,335	29,060	30,000
Sienna LE 4d (17%)	—	—	29,558	29,980	30,705	31,900	32,985	31,925	35,000
Used Values ($)									
Previa ▲	4,000	4,500	—	—	—	—	—	—	—
Previa ▼	3,500	4,000	—	—	—	—	—	—	—
Sienna Cargo 3d ▲	—	—	7,500	10,000	12,000	—	—	—	—
Sienna Cargo 3d ▼	—	—	6,000	8,500	10,500	—	—	—	—
Sienna CE 4d ▲	—	—	8,500	11,000	12,000	15,500	18,500	22,000	25,000
Sienna CE 4d ▼	—	—	7,000	9,500	10,500	13,000	17,000	21,000	23,000
Sienna LE 4d ▲	—	—	10,000	12,500	14,500	17,000	20,500	24,000	27,000
Sienna LE 4d ▼	—	—	8,500	11,000	13,000	15,500	18,500	22,000	25,500

All ratings on a numbered scale where ⑤ is good and ❶ is bad. See pages 100–101 for a more detailed description.

Reliability	3	3	4	4	4	4	4	5	4
Crash Safety (F)	4	4	5	5	5	5	5	5	5
Side	—	—	—	4	4	4	4	4	5
Offset	1	1	5	5	5	5	5	5	5
Head Restraints	3	3	1	1	—	2	2	2	5
Rear	2	2	—	—	—	—	—	—	3
Rollover Resistance	—	—	—	—	—	4	4	4	5

INTERNET FACT-FINDING

You can find lots of information about used cars and minivans on the Internet, but much of it is untrue. Automobile companies have helpful—though self-serving—websites featuring detailed sections on history, research and development, and all sorts of information of interest to auto enthusiasts. Some automakers, such as Toyota, will even give you an online appraisal of your trade-in. You can easily access manufacturers through Google's search engine under the automaker's name. For extra fun and a more balanced presentation, put in the vehicle model or manufacturer's name, followed by "lemon."

Auto Safety, Costs, Servicing, and Reviews

Service bulletins unmask "lemons" like this VW Jetta.

ALLDATA Service Bulletins
(*www.alldata.com/ consumer/TSB/yr.html*)

This website gives you some free summaries of automotive recalls and technical service bulletins. Detailed summaries will cost only $25 (U.S.) for hundreds of bulletins applicable to your vehicle, dating back almost 30 years. This is a wise investment only if your car is a few years old; there are quite a few accumulated bulletins, and the base warranty has expired.

Use the service bulletins to prove that your vehicle's failure is caused by a manufacturing defect and shouldn't cost you a penny to fix, even if the expressed warranty is no longer in effect. Bulletins are highly useful as bargaining chips leading up to pre-trial mediation and small claims court hearings, especially if you threaten to present the bulletin in court and have it authenticated by the dealer's service manager or the car company's customer assistance rep.

Canadian Automobile Association *(www.caa.ca)*

A non-profit, bilingual motorists' association that spends more time denouncing high road taxes than it does fighting warranty fraud and factory-related car defects, the CAA has consumer advisors who are fairly competent but non-confrontational. CAA's "approved" garages force the association to mediate sales or repair disputes whether you are a member of the group or not. If no settlement is reached, you can make the Association jointly liable in your claim against the dealer or repair agency (see Part Two). CAA has a nice checklist for "Keeping Track of Your Own Vehicle Costs" in their "Driving Costs" pamphlet at *www.caa.ca/e/automotive/pdf/driving-costs-03.pdf.*

Canadian Driver *(www.canadiandriver.com)*

An exceptionally well-structured and current Canadian website for new- and used-vehicle reviews, MSRPs, and consumer reports. Other auto magazine websites: *Automotive News (www.autonews.com); Car and Driver (www.caranddriver.com/default.asp); Motor Trend (www.motortrend.com);* and *Road & Track (www.roadandtrack.com).*

Carfax *(www.carfax.com)*

Use Carfax (Tel: 1-888-422-7329) to see if an American- or Canadian-sold vehicle has been "scrapped," has had flood damage, is stolen, or has had its mileage turned back. There's a fee of $14.95 U.S. ($23.39 Cdn.) if the order is placed via the Internet. Be careful: The free report may tell you of several "hot" leads, and when you pay to get the specifics, that information might only be the number of times the vehicle has taken an emissions test.

Cartrackers *(www.cartrackers.com)*

Used vehicles, consumer advice, and environmental issues are all well covered in this site, which also features a terrific auto image gallery and an excellent automotive glossary.

CBC TV *Marketplace* *(www.cbc.ca/consumers/market/files/cars/index.html)*

An impressive array of auto consumer info based on investigative reports and other sources. The site features well-researched, useful, Canadian information on used vehicles and safety-related issues.

Center for Auto Safety *(www.autosafety.org)*

A Ralph Nader-founded agency that provides free online info on safety- and performance-related defects on each vehicle model. Free vehicle reports based on owner complaints and service bulletins are sometimes dated. Still, it's a good starting place for safety- and performance-related defect listings.

Consumer Guide, Edmunds, and Kelley Blue Book *(www.ConsumerGuide.com, www.edmunds.com, www.kbb.com)*

In-depth reviews and owner critiques of almost every vehicle sold in North America, plus an informative readers' forum.

Consumer Reports and Consumers Union *(www.consumerreports.org)*

It costs $4.95 a month to subscribe online, but *CR*'s database is chock full of comparison tests and in-depth stories on products and services, including a "Cars for Teens" special feature. Download info like crazy during first month of your subscription, and then wait until the need arises to buy another month's worth of info.

Crashtest.com *(www.crashtest.com/netindex.htm)*

A website where crash tests from around the world can be analyzed and compared.

DaimlerChrysler Problems Web Page *(www.wam.umd.edu/~gluckman/Chrysler)*

This is a great site for technical info and tips on getting action from DaimlerChrysler.

Ford Insider Info *(www.blueovalnews.com)*

This website is the place to go for all the latest insider info on Ford's quality problems, administrative chaos, and future models. Ford tried to shut this site down a few years ago but was rebuffed by the American courts in a precedent-setting decision.

Lemon-Aid *(www.lemonaidcars.com)*

The official website of the *Lemon-Aid* annual consumer car guides. It is frequently updated with follow-up stories and comments from regional correspondants.

Metric Conversion Online *(www.sciencemadesimple.net/conversions.html)*

A great place to instantly convert gallons to litres, miles to kilometres, etc.

National Highway Traffic Safety Administration *(www.nhtsa.dot.gov/cars/problems)*

This American site has a comprehensive free database covering owner complaints, recall campaigns, crashworthiness and rollover ratings, defect investigations, service bulletin summaries, and safety research papers. Use with ALLDATA to compare service bulletins and owner complaints.

Finally, here are a number of other websites that may be helpful:

General Auto Sites

everythingfordrivers.com/carforums.html
forum.freeadvice.com
www.all-lemons.com
www.autowarrantyreviews.org
www.baileycar.com/index.html
www.canadianwarrantycorp.com/news_tips.htm
www.carforums.com/forums
www.cartrackers.com/Forums
www.mycarsucks.com
www.straight-six.com
www.which.net and *www.60millions-mag.com/page/common.accueil*
  (British and French car ratings)
www.womanmotorist.com/index.php/welcome

Automakers

AUDI: *www.audiworld.com*

BMW: *www.bmwboard.com*
www.mwerks.com
yoy.com/auto/m3_failure_index.html (M3 engine problems)

CHRYSLER: *dodgestories.blogspot.com*
flinksnorph.com/chrysler.html
intrepidhorrorstories.blogspot.com
www.aei.ca/~gregoire/claude.html
www.angelfire.com/pa5/mspaul/autohome.html
www.daimlerchryslervehicleproblems.com
www.datatown.com/chrysler
www.dodge-sucks.com
www.donotbuydodge.ca
www.dontbuyone.org
www.mydodgesucks.org
www.ptcruiserclub.org
www.ptcruiserlinks.com
www.ptcruiserproblems.com

FORD: *www.consumeraffairs.com/automotive/ford_transmissions.htm*
www.focusfanatics.com
www.ford-trucks.com/forums
www.fordfocusbrakeproblems.com
www.v8sho.com/SHO/autoweek_online_cam_story.htm
www.v8sho.com/SHO/BlueOvalNewsCoverageofCamSprocketLawsuit.htm
www.v8sho.com/SHO/CamFailureClassActionSuitFiled.htm

GM: *www.mygmlink.com*
forums.gminsidenews.com
www.cadillacforums.com/forums/showthread
agmlemon.freeservers.com/index.html

LAND ROVER: *www.freelanderliving.com/default.asp*

LEXUS: *us.lexusownersclub.com*

MERCEDES-BENZ: *forums.mbnz.org*
www.mercedesproblems.com
www.nagele.co.uk/ml320.htm
www.troublebenz.com/my_opinion/actions/links.htm

MINI: *www.mini2.com/forum*

MITSUBISHI: *www.mitsubishisucks.com*

SAAB: *www.saabclub.co.uk/new/index.html*

TOYOTA: *www.siennaclub.org*

VW: *MyVWLemon.com*
www.tdiclub.com
www.thesamba.com/vw
www.vwvortex.com

Help for Consumers

Government and Non-Government Associations

www.consumeraffairs.com/index.html
www.epa.gov/otaq/consumer/warr95fs.txt

Insurance

www.autoinsurancetips.com
www.insurance-canada.ca/consquotes/onlineauto.php
www.insurancehotline.com

Judgments

www.ontariocourts.on.ca/decisions/2004/june/barrickC39837.htm
www.litigation-results.com
www.suv.com/indextoc.html
www.bettersuv.org
www.vehicle-injuries.com/suv-safety-news.htm
www.jjournal.net
www.cs.cornell.edu/Info/People/kreitz/Jeep/main.html
www.worktruck.com
www.dodgetrucksteeringproblems.com
www.minerich.com/dodge_ram.htm

OTHER USED CHOICES

It's true. I'm a cheapskate.

I won't pay the $31,045 average price for a new vehicle ($25,056 for a car and $37,855 for a truck) quoted by Toronto auto analyst Dennis DerRosiers. Actually, that's not all we pay. DesRosiers says taxes add another 21 to 23 percent to the suggested retail prices listed above. On top of that, fuel and insurance costs are scary, with gas prices hovering at record levels and insurance premiums soaring despite huge increases in insurance profits.

Yet millions of Canadians have no choice: They must have a vehicle that's safe, cheap to buy and run, reliable, and capable of taking them to work, school, or the shopping mall without breaking down or putting their lives in danger (two factors that are particularly important to new drivers, who usually don't have much experience with highway emergencies). Young drivers also want vehicles that they can easily repair and customize and that will still project a "cool" cachet to their peers.

So here's the good news. There are plenty of cheap, reliable used cars and minivans out there that will suit your driving needs and budget. In the 1970s, the average car was "junked" around seven years, or 160,000 km; two decades later, the average car was driven for almost eight years, or 240,000 km, before it was discarded. Industry experts now say that the 2005 models will easily last ten years, or 300,000 km, before they need to be "recycled." This means you can get good, high-mileage vehicles for less than a quarter to half of their original price and expect to drive them for five years or more.

Buyers are understandably wary of buying "someone else's troubles." Yet CAA statistics show they have little to worry about:

- Only 22 percent of owners of six- to 10-year-old vehicles got rid of them due to reliability problems.
- Less than 10 percent of owners of cars five years or younger got rid of them because of reliability problems or high maintenance costs.
- 43 percent got rid of them because their leases expired.
- 30 percent just wanted a change.
- 21 percent found that the vehicle no longer suited them.

Depreciation Quirks

Depreciation varies considerably among different vehicle types and models. For example, minivans depreciate a bit more slowly than cars, and diesel cars and trucks hold their value better than do gas-powered vehicles.

Generally, those vehicles sold with the highest rebates depreciate the fastest. Detroit spent about $4,000 per vehicle last year, European makers $2,500, Nissan $2,100, and Honda and Toyota paid out $700 and $850, respectively.

Gas-electric hybrids, which have been on the market since 1999, apparently lose their value at about the same rate as conventional cars. Undoubtedly, this is because used-car buyers are afraid of replacing the costly high-tech components (imagine paying $8,000 Cdn. for a replacement battery once the eight-year warranty has expired).

Ten Used Car "Golden Rules"

1. First, try to buy a vehicle that's presently being used by one of your family members. Although you may risk a family squabble somewhere down the road, you'll likely get a good buy for next to nothing, you will have a good idea of how it was driven and maintained, and you can use the same repair facilities that have been repairing your family's vehicles for years. Don't worry if a vehicle is almost 10 years old—that's becoming the norm for Canadian ownership, particularly the farther west you go.
2. Buy from a private seller—prices are usually much cheaper and sales scams less frequent.
3. Cut insurance and fuel costs. Use the Internet (*www.insurancehotline.com*) to compile a list of models that are the cheapest to insure. Be wary of diesel-equipped or hybrid cars that may require more expensive dealer servicing and wipe out any fuel consumption savings. Also, pay attention to the quality and performance of your fuel-efficient choice: A fuel-sipping Ford Focus will likely have higher repair bills than gas bills and a 4-cylinder minivan, though cheap to run, can make highway merging a white-knuckle affair.
4. Find out the vehicle's history through a franchised dealer, Carfax, or provincial licensing authorities, then have an independent garage (preferably CAA-affiliated) check out the body and mechanical components.
5. Look for high-mileage vehicles sold by rental agencies like Budget—a company that offers honest, money-back guarantees and reasonably priced extended warranties.
6. Refuse all preparation or "administration" fees and 50-50 warranties where the repair charges are submitted by the seller.
7. Stay away from vehicles or components known for having a high failure rate. American front-drives, for example, have more frequent failures and costlier

repairs than rear-drives. "Orphaned" American models like the Ford Contour/Mystique or Cadillac Catera are also poor choices because of poor quality components and inadequate servicing support from dealers who wish they were never made. Other sinkholes: any vehicle equipped with a turbocharger or supercharger, a CVT transmission (Audi, Ford, Honda, Mini, Nissan, Saturn, Subaru, and Toyota), multiple computers (BMW's 7 Series, for example), ABS brakes, and motorized seatbelts; minivans equipped with four-wheel-drive; Cadillacs with 4.1L engines and/or front-wheel-drive; and Chryslers with sludge-prone 2.7L engines or 4-speed automatic transmissions. If the engine has a timing chain instead of a belt, you will save a fortune. Timing chains frequently survive the lifespan of the engine, whereas timing belts must be replaced every 70,000 to 100,000 km.

8. Steer clear of European models. They are often money pits—parts and competent, reasonably-priced servicing will likely be hard to find, and quality control has declined considerably over the past decade.

9. Buy 3-year-old Hyundais, but stay away from Excels, early Sonatas, and all Kias and Daewoos. Also look for 5- to 10-year-old, one-owner Japanese models.

10. Shop for used, rear-drive, full-sized wagons or vans instead of front-drive American minivans.

BARGAIN BEATERS ($500–$3,000)

Chrysler—All rear-drive cars and vans and the Colt import
Ford—All rear-drive cars and vans; Crown Victoria, Grand Marquis, and Town Car
GM—All rear-drives; Astro and Safari, Caprice, and Roadmaster
Honda—Accord, Civic, and Odyssey
Hyundai—Accent, Elantra, and Tiburon
Mazda—929, Mazda3, Miata, MX-3 (Precidia), and MX-6
Nissan—Axxess, early Quest, Sentra, and Stanza
Toyota—Avalon, Camry, Celica, Corolla, early Sienna, and Supra

---

Alternative Used Choices

Acura—The 5-cylinder **Vigor**, a 1992–94 Honda Accord sedan spin-off, sells for $6,000–$7,000. This compact has power to spare, handles well, and has an impressive reliability/durability record. Problem areas: excessive brake noise and premature brake wear, in addition to fit and finish deficiencies. The 1992 Vigor turned in below-average crash test scores.

The **Legend** is an Above Average $3,000–$5,000 buy (1989–95); although it's Not Recommended for the 1986–88 model years. Resale value is high on all Legend models, and especially so on the coupe. Shop for a cheaper 1989 or later base Legend with the coupe's upgraded features and fewer reports of unintended, sudden acceleration.

Pre-1990 Legends were upscale, enlarged Accords that were unimpressive performers with either of the two 6-cylinder powerplants. The 3.2L V6 that appeared in 1991 is by far a better performer. Ride quality is improved, power steering is more responsive, and rear seating is more spacious. 1992 L and LS models got seat belt pretensioners and dual front airbags, but base models didn't get a passenger airbag until the 1993 model year. The '93s also got a smoother-shifting automatic transmission, while coupes were given a new 6-speed manual tranny, 30 extra horses, traction control, and high-performance tires. The '94 GS sedan was given many of the coupe's high performance features, including a 230-hp engine and 6-speed gearbox. Additionally, all Legends were restyled and given tilt/telescopic steering wheels. These improvements were the last ones made before the Legend was axed after the '95 model year.

BMW—Arriving late to the nostalgia niche dominated by the Dodge PT Cruiser, Ford T-Bird, and VW New Beetle, BMW has finally let loose with its own flashback from the past—the Mini Cooper, last marketed by Austin in 1967. The front-drive, $25,800 (S version: $30,500) Mini Cooper returns with more power (200 km/h top speed) and safety features than its predecessor.

The 2003–04 **Mini Cooper** is an Average buy. It's distinctively styled; depreciates slowly; and has been given an Above Average offset crash protection and head restraint effectiveness rating by the IIHS. On one hand, NHTSA says that the little tyke merits a four-star rating for its resistance to rollovers. On the other hand, these little urban guerillas aren't cheap, and provide a mediocre ride and handling, along with limited front visibility, glitch-prone mechanical components and body problems (example: cracked windshields caused by body panel flexing).

A 2003 base Mini is worth $20,000, or 20 percent less than what it cost new; a 2004 used model sells for about $21,000, a bargain when you consider that this second year model has fewer production glitches. Other cars you may wish to consider are the Mazda Miata and Porsche Boxster.

Although not as small as the original Austin Cooper, the Mini is still less than 4 m long, with a 239-cm wheelbase, a width of 1.9 m, and a height of only 1.4 m (smaller than a Chevy Metro). The 115-hp 1.6L 4-banger can be teamed with a 5-speed manual or auto-

The Mini's neither cheap nor fast, but it is stylish, with its uniquely hunkered-down, cute look.

matic transmission, and turns in a 0–100 km/h time of a leisurely 9.2 seconds. The Cooper S uses a 163-hp supercharged version of the same 1.6L motor (with more robust components, set on a sturdier frame) and a standard 6-speed manual transmission.

So what's not to like? How about traffic light stops? The forward-mounted windshield makes it next to impossible to see traffic lights when stopped at a corner. Take away the retro styling and you get an undersized, under-performing, and untried British import thrust into a market where many proven competitors do more for less money. When compared with the Mercedes C230, the Subaru WRX, and the VW New Beetle, the Cooper S is relatively overpriced for a car with such a small interior and cargo area. And it's built in England, which guarantees a plethora of quality bugs. Says the *Christian Science Monitor* in an early review,

> Quality is suspect in both [models]. Thrumming wheel bearings, whining steering, loose and missing interior parts marred two weeks of driving.

Finally, take all that high-speed handling praise with a huge grain of salt: Reports from professional drivers are fairly harsh. Says *Car and Driver*'s editor-in-chief:

> Turn the wheel a little bit, and as the car rolls slightly, it increases the degree of your turn by a factor of two or three times. I'm surprised no one has put this car into a ditch. Until this is fixed, the Mini is undrivable.

Most owner safety complaints concern inaccurate speedometers and jammed passenger-side seat belt shoulder retractors. Other deficiencies mostly relate to poor ergonomics, a surprising oversight for a German-engineered car. For example: Inside door handles are located too far back on the doors, getting the spare tire from under the vehicle is a chore, and shoulder belts are uncomfortable. Service bulletins target engine idle fluctuations and poor acceleration; AC whistling, sunroof squeaking, and rear hatch/door window rattling; too hot or too cold seat heaters; windshield stress cracks; and inoperative interior lights. See *www.mini.ca* or *www.mini2.com/forum* for a good overview of ownership pros and cons.

Chrysler—Dart, Valiant, Duster, Scamp, Diplomat, Caravelle, Newport, reardrive **New Yorker Fifth Avenue**, and **Gran Fury**. Problem areas: electrical system, suspension, brakes, body and frame rust, and constant stalling when humidity is high. The **Caravelle, Diplomat,** and **New Yorker Fifth Avenue** are reasonably reliable and simple-to-repair throwbacks to a time when rear-drive land yachts ruled the highways. Powered with 6- and 8-cylinder engines, they will run practically forever with minimal care. The fuel-efficient "slant 6" powerplant was too small for this type of car and was changed to a gas-guzzling but smooth and reliable V8 after 1983. Handling is vague and sloppy, though, and emergency braking is often accompanied by rear-wheel lockup. Still, what do you want for a $500–$2,000, 1984–89 "retro rocket"? Problem areas are the carburetor (don't ask what that is: Your dad knows), ignition, electrical system, brakes, and suspension (premature idler-arm wear). It's a good idea to adjust the torsion bars frequently for better suspension performance. Doors, windshield pillars, the bottoms of both front and rear fenders, and the trunk lid rust through more quickly than average.

Chrysler's 1991–93 **2000GTX** is an Above Average buy that may cost $2,000–$3,000, depending upon the model year. It's a reliable Japanese-built sedan that was discontinued in 1994. It has a competitive price, modern styling, and high-performance options that put it on par with such benchmark cars as the Honda

Accord and Toyota Camry. The major problem area is the front brakes, which need more attention than average. The car hasn't been crash-tested.

The Chrysler **Stealth** is a serious, reasonably priced sports car that's as much go as show. Although 1995 was its last model year in Canada, it was still sold in the United States as the Mitsubishi 3000GT. Prices range from $4,000 to $5,000 for the 1991–93 base or ES model. A '95 high-performance R/T will go for about $7,500—not a bad price for an "orphan" sports car, eh? Problem areas: engine, transmission, front brake, and electrical failures. The 1993 model excelled in crash tests.

Chrysler's 2004 **Crossfire** is an expensive, low-volume luxury sports coupe that gets 39 percent of its parts from the Mercedes SLK. This low-slung, sleekly styled, two-door two-passenger coupe offers a cramped interior, high window sills and low roofline that create a claustrophobic cabin. Service bulletins and owner feedback indicate only average reliability during the car's first year on the market. Depreciation has been brutal, however: A $47,745 base 2004 model is now worth only $34,000.

The Crossfire's resale price is plummeting.

bad buy The 1990–98 **Laser** and **Talon** are Not Recommended. Maintenance and repair costs are much higher than average, mainly because of a scarcity of parts and a failure-prone and complicated to repair powertrain and emissions system. Engine timing chain and head gasket failures are frequent. Although 1995 models got additional power (140–210 hp), dual airbags, and a minor restyling, they're still woefully undependable and costly to service. A 1994 Laser (its last model year) sells for $2,000 to $3,000. A 1998 Talon will cost about $5,000 and its turbocharged TSI version will fetch another $1,500. Other cars worth considering are the Ford Mustang or Probe, the GM Camaro or Firebird, the Hyundai Tiburon or Elantra, the Mazda Miata, and Toyota's Celica.

These sporty, Mitsubishi-made cars carry a competent base 1.8L engine, and the suspension is comfortable, although a bit soft. The optional 16-valve, turbocharged 2.0L comes with a firmer suspension and gives more horsepower for the dollar than most other front-drive sports coupes without much turbo lag. The 16-valve Talon and its 4×4 variant are at the top of the trim list and provide five more horses than the turbocharged TSi. The 5-speed manual is the gearbox of choice both from a performance and a reliability perspective. Torque steer makes the car appear to try to twist out of your hands when all 195 turbocharged horses are unleashed.

Beginning with the 1990–94 models, owners report glitches with the 1.8L engine and electrical system, driveline vibrations, premature brake wear and excessive noise, and poor fit and finish that includes water leakage into the interior and paint delamination. Some problems reported with 1995–98 versions were poor idling and reduced rpm when the AC is running; hard starts and stalling in cold weather; cold-weather transmission shift delays (2–3 and 3–4) that take up to two minutes; transmission defaults into Second gear (limp-in mode); frequent wheel alignments; a tendency to drift or lead to the right; speed control undershoot or overshoot; chronic electrical system, brake, and transmission failures; false theft alarm; a buzz in the centre exhaust pipe heat shield; door buzz and rattle; misadjusted door glass and poor windshield sealing, causing water leaks and wind noise; noisy clutch pedal; interior window film buildup; headliner sagging; a sticking power seat switch; stress marks on the quarter trim panel; buzz or rattle from the rear quarter trim; inoperative, noisy, and jerky sunroof operation; faulty lever latch pin; and a self-opening sunroof.

SAFETY SUMMARY: All models/years: Standard brakes often lock up or require long stopping distances. • Head restraints block rear visibility. • Airbags often fail to deploy. **All models: 1995–98**—Most of the following problems appear each year in NHTSA records: engine and fuel tank fires; fuel leakage; sudden acceleration caused by a jammed throttle; chronic transmission failures that include transfer case leakage after recall repairs (automatic and manual transaxles), causing sudden wheel lock-up; wheels fall off; engine timing belt breakage (100,000–120,000 km); loss of steering caused by going through a puddle of water or by the steering belt slipping off the pulley; collapse of suspension and steering components (front control arms and ball joints); frequent replacement of brake pads and warped rotors; electrical system failures; faulty door locks and windows; and water leakage into the interior. **1997**—Talon scored Above Average in frontal crash protection.

SERVICE BULLETIN SUMMARY: All models: 1995–97—Engine compartment popping or knocking may require an upgraded EGR valve. **1995–98**—Delayed transaxle engagement can be corrected by installing an upgraded trailing-arm bushing. • Intermittent loss of speed control can be prevented by installing new speed sensors. • Tips on reducing excessive front brake pulsation or shudder. **1997–98**—New software will prevent the transmission from shifting erratically or falling into a Second-gear limp-in mode.

 Plymouth's 1999–2002 **Prowler** is a Recommended fast sporty rear-drive coupe that handles well and is attractively styled to resemble a hot-rod roadster from the '50s. On the minus side, it has little interior room, entry and exit is a chiropractor's delight, and overall visibility is less than ideal. Its 3.5L 253-hp V6 was borrowed from Chrysler's 300M and LHS. A 1999 Prowler costs about $27,000, or half the car's original selling price; the 2002 model is worth about $42,000.

Ford—Maverick, Comet, Fairmont, Zephyr, Tracer, Mustang, Capri, Cougar, Thunderbird V6, Torino, Marquis, Grand Marquis, LTD, and **LTD Crown Victoria**. Problem areas: trunk, wheelwell, and rocker panel rusting; brakes; steering; and electrical system failures. The 1993 **Festiva** is marginally acceptable for city use as long as you check out the brakes, exhaust system, and body panels for rust. The 1990–97 **Probe** is essentially a **Mazda MX-6** sporty two-door coupe in Ford garb. It's quite reliable and gives better-than-average highway performance. Problem areas: AC, CV joints, electrical and body glitches. Good crashworthiness rating. Prices range from $2,500 to $5,000.

General Motors—Chevette and **Acadian** are inexpensive, rear-drive city runabouts. Problem areas: steering system defects, and brakes you have to stand on to stop. Rear-drive **Nova, Ventura, Skylark**, and **Phoenix**. Problem areas: undercarriage, steering system, and suspension rust-out. Front-drive **Nova, Spectrum, Camaro, Firebird, Malibu, LeMans, Century, Regal, Cutlass, Monte Carlo**, and **Grand Prix**. Problem areas: rear brake backing plate rust-out and steering failures. **Bel Air, Laurentian, Catalina, Parisienne, LeSabre, Bonneville**, and **Delta 88**. Be wary of undercarriage, suspension component, and rear brake backing plate rust-out.

GM's 1982–96 **Caprice**, **Impala SS**, and **Roadmaster** are better than average, comfortable, and easy to maintain large cars that have been off the market since the 1996 model year. Overall handling is acceptable, but expect a queasy ride from the too-soft suspension. The trunk is spacious, but gas mileage is particularly poor. Despite the many generic deficiencies inherent in these rear-drives, they still score higher than GM's front-drives for overall reliability and durability. The Impala SS is basically a Caprice with a 260-hp Corvette engine and high-performance suspension.

Good, cheap cars for first-time buyers, the 1991–93 models can be bought for $700–$1,000, while later models will cost between $1,500 and $3,000. Maintenance is inexpensive and easy to perform, and repairs can be done by any corner garage. Average parts costs can be cut further by shopping at independent suppliers, who are generally well-stocked. An extended warranty isn't necessary.

In 1993, the LTZ sedan got a 180-hp 5.7L V8; a year later, GM added a passenger-side airbag, adopted the 4.3L V8 as the base engine, and expanded the availability of the better-performing, more-reliable 5.7L (spun off of the Corvette's LT1 V8 and standard with the Impala SS). Other improvements for 1994: a redesigned dashboard, including a failure-prone digital speedometer, and an improved electronic automatic transmission.

On 1988–91 models, engine problems include crankshaft and head gasket failures, cracked cylinder heads, injection pump malfunctions, and oil leaks. Early V8s, in particular, suffer from premature camshaft wear, and the 350-cubic-inch V8s often fall prey to premature valve guide wear caused by a faulty EGR valve. Cars equipped with the 5.7L diesel V8 should be approached with caution; they aren't very durable and cost an arm and a leg to troubleshoot and repair. The 4-speed automatic transmission was troublesome until 1991, with burnt-out clutches and malfunctioning torque converters being the most common failures.

The 1991–96 models have shown the following deficiencies: AC glitches; prematurely worn brakes (lots of corrosion damage), steering, and suspension components, especially shock absorbers and rear springs; serious electrical problems; and poor-quality body and trim items.

Body assembly is not impressive, but paint quality and durability is fairly good, considering the delamination one usually finds with GM's other models. Wagons often have excessive rust around cargo-area side windows and wheelwells, and hubcaps on later models tend to fly off.

SAFETY SUMMARY: All models: Frontal crashworthiness has been above average, though head restraints have performed poorly. **1996**—Child was able to shift gear into Neutral, jumped out of car, and was run over. • Airbags failed to deploy. • Airbag light stays lit for no apparent reason. • Gas pedal sticks on initial application. • ABS brakes lock up. • Transmission torque converter/engine flywheel breakage. • Broken torque converter bolts. • Steering box loosens up despite new bolts. • Steering lock-up. • Sometimes vehicle fishtails uncontrollably while at moderate speed. • Front coil spring failure. • Premature tire wear caused by faulty suspension components that can't be fixed by repeated alignments. • Fuel pump failure caused by wiring harness short.

Internal service bulletins give the following repair advice for common problems: **1994 models**—Excessive oil consumption may be corrected by installing an upgraded intake manifold gasket kit. • GM campaign 94C15 says a misadjusted automatic transmission shift linkage could, if left alone, burn out the Low/Reverse clutch. **1994–96**—Excessive engine noise can be silenced by installing an upgraded valve stem oil seal. • A chuggle or surge condition in vehicles with a 5.7L engine will require a reflash calibration. **1995–96**—Delayed automatic transmission shift engagement may require the replacement of the pump cover assembly. **1996**—You may need to replace the transmission's reaction sun shell if you can't shift into Reverse, Second, or Fourth gear.

The **Geo Storm**, GM's Japanese-made small car, only had two model years in Canada (1992–93). Owners report serious body hardware deficiencies (not paint or rust, however), in addition to brake, exhaust, electrical, and ignition problems. Prices vary between $2,500 and $3,000, depending on the model chosen.

GM's 1984–96 rear-drive **Cadillac Brougham** and **Fleetwood** are Above Average luxury "land yacht" buys. Originally front-drives, these big sedans adopted the rear-drive stretched platform used by the Buick Roadmaster and Chevrolet Caprice in 1993. Equipped with a 185-hp V8, mated to a 4-speed automatic transmission, all models came with standard traction control and anti-lock brakes. The rear-drive configuration is easy to repair and not hard to diagnose, unlike the cars' front-drive brethren.

A smart choice for retirees who want luxury and comfort for less than $4,000 (for the 1996 model), these cars are only slightly ahead of the Ford Crown Victoria and Grand Marquis when it comes to comfort and reliability. The '94 and later models feature the most performance for your money. Repair and maintenance costs are average, and repairs aren't dealer dependent. There are plenty of reasonably priced parts sold by independent suppliers. Other cars worth considering: Cadillac's DeVille, or a fully loaded Ford Crown Victoria or Mercury Grand Marquis.

The most serious problem areas are the fuel-injection system, which frequently malfunctions and costs an arm and a leg to repair; engine head gasket failures; automatic transmissions that shift erratically; a weak suspension; computer module glitches; brakes that constantly need rotor and pad replacement; poor body assembly; and paint defects. From a reliability/durability standpoint, the rear-drives are much better made than their front-drive counterparts.

GM technical service bulletins show that these vehicles also have noisy power-steering units and cooling fans, the AC bi-level mode produces extreme temperature differences, the instrument panel squeaks and rattles, there are rear quarter-panel gaps and rusting at the rear side-door window moulding, and water leaks into the passenger side of the front compartment.

SAFETY SUMMARY: All models: 1996—Airbags failed to deploy. • Seat belts didn't restrain driver and passenger during a collision. • Chronic stalling due to fuel-sending unit failure. • Transmission pounds when shifting gears. • Water pump leakage on the serpentine belt may cause steering to lock up. • Power-steering hose and pump failure. • Brakes often lock up when applied. • Excessive brake noise caused by the premature wearout of brake rotor and drum. • AC cooling switch and high-pressure hose failures. • Instrument cluster hard to read in daylight. • Power door locks and trunk lock frequently fail to operate properly. • Loose windshield moulding. • Defective keyless entry module.

Service bulletins note the following troubles on the 1996 models: Harsh 1–2 shift. • No Reverse, Second, or Fourth gear. • 3–2 part throttle downshift flare. • Engine noise (install new valve stem oil seal). • Transmission chuggle/surge. • Transmission fluid leak from pump body (replace bushing).

Pontiac's 1991–95 **Sunbird** was GM's smallest American-built car, along with its twin, the Chevrolet Cavalier. Sunbirds were available as two-door coupes, four-door sedans, and two-door convertibles. Nearly all Sunbirds were powered by a wimpy 2.0L 96-hp 4-cylinder engine as standard equipment, mated to a clunky, performance-sapping, and fuel-wasting 3-speed automatic tranny. GT models featured a 165-hp turbocharged version of the same engine. Both engines weren't very dependable. A better-quality, optional 3.1L 140-hp V6 came on the scene in 1991. In 1992, ABS became a standard feature, increasing the complexity and cost of brake maintenance for years to come. The 2.0L engine gained 14 more horses.

Several joint ventures between GM and Suzuki from 1987 to 2001 produced four fairly reliable subcompact economy cars called the **Chevrolet** and **Geo Metro**, the **Pontiac Firefly**, the **Suzuki Sprint**, and the **Suzuki Swift**. These mini-cars are rated Above Average (1998–2001); Average (1995–97); and Below Average (1987–94). They are most reliable when bought unadorned; stay away from AC-equipped versions unless you want to invest in an AC repair facility. Look at the redesigned 1998 version for better quality, a new body style, standard dual airbags, and a peppier 4-cylinder engine. Convertibles pack plenty of fun and performance into a reasonably priced subcompact body. The Suzuki Swift carried on alone after the 2000 model year. Used prices vary, however; 1998–2001 models cost between $2,500 and $3,500. Maintenance costs are average, but powertrain parts are drying up and can be hard to find. Body components are often back-ordered several weeks. Some better cars worth considering are the the Honda Civic LX, Hyundai Accent, Suzuki Esteem, and Toyota Tercel. They all perform well and offer better quality.

Cheap to buy and run and providing better-than-average quality control and crashworthiness, these tiny 3- and 4-cylinder front-drive hatchbacks offer good performance and impressive economy for urban dwellers. In fact, these little squirts should be considered primarily city vehicles because of their small size, small tires, low ground clearance, and average high-speed handling. Interior garnishing is decent but plain, and there's plenty of room for two passengers, with four fitting in without too much discomfort. The turbocharged convertible model is an excellent choice for high-performance thrills in an easy-to-handle ragtop. The redesigned 1995s were built with more care. Additionally, they transmitted more road feel and gave a more comfortable ride. Both the 1995 and redesigned 1998 models offer the most horsepower bang for your buck. Although head restraints were rated Poor on the 1995s, frontal crashworthiness scored Average for the 1994–95 models; Above Average for the 1996–97s.

On the downside, owners will face an anemic, noisy engine that makes these cars the antithesis of "swift"; a harsh, choppy ride; lots of interior noise; a spartan interior; poorly performing original equipment tires; and inadequate braking.

Mechanically speaking, the GM/Suzuki partnership has kept factory-related defects to a tolerable level, particularly following the '95 model's redesign. Trouble spots on pre-'95 models: excessive oil consumption; automatic transmission and differential failures around 80,000 km; electrical system shorts; a faulty AC and cooling system (fogging of the side windows and windshield because of inadequate heat distribution is a common complaint); premature brake, clutch, and exhaust system wearout; and minor fuel-supply malfunctions. Body construction is subpar on these models.

Remaining problems on the 1995–2001 models have been premature front brake wear; electrical system and AC malfunctions; and subpar body assembly, highlighted by paint peeling and discoloration, early rusting, and poorly-fitted body panels, leading to rattles and air and water leaks.

 Honda's 1984–91 **CRX** is a highly Recommended and seriously quick two-seater sports car, a Honda Civic spin-off that was replaced in 1991 by the less sporty and much less popular Honda del Sol. Prized by high-performance "tuners," a well-maintained CRX is worth between $1,000 and $4,000.

Honda's 1985–2001 **Preludes** are an Above Average car buy. They are unimpressive as high-performance sports cars, and deliver, instead, a stylish exterior, legendary reliability, and excellent resale value. Preludes are nevertheless a bit over-priced and over-hyped; cheaper, well-performing makes like the Ford Mustang or Probe, GM Camaro or Firebird, Mazda Miata, and Toyota Celica should be checked out first. Prelude repair costs are average though some dealer dependent repairs to the steering assembly and transmission can be quite expensive. To avoid costly engine damage, check the engine timing belt every 2 years/40,000 km and replace it every 96,000 km ($300).

The year for big Prelude changes was 1997, while 1998–2001 models just coasted along with minor improvements (their prices vary from $7,000 to $15,000, while earlier models run about $3,00-$4,000). The '97 was restyled, re-powered, and given handling upgrades that make it a better-performing, more comfortably riding sports coupe. It got an additional five horses for the base 2.2L VTEC engine, a new Automatic Torque Transfer System (ATTS), an upgraded suspension, and standard ABS, AC, 16-inch wheels, and a CD player with six speakers. The Sequential SportShift automatic transmission (a variation of the one used in the NSX) equips the base Prelude. Overall, the car is roomier (the extended wheelbase gives added stability and provides more room in the rear seating area), has a more solid body structure, and includes a totally redesigned, user-friendly dash with analogue gauges.

There is no crashworthiness data, though head restraint protection has been given a Below Average designation. On these more recent models, owners report that the engine tends to leak oil and crank bolts often loosen (causing major engine damage). AC condensers frequently fail after a few years and often need cleaning to eliminate disagreeable odours. Most corner mechanics are poorly equipped to service these cars, and the Automatic Torque Transfer System (ATTS) won't make their job any easier. Owners also report that a poorly designed clutch disc causes harsh shifting; and clutch spring failures. Internal service bulletins confirm thet the 2000 and 2001 models are covered by an automatic transmission warranty extension up to 7 years and 160,000 km (Bulletin No.: 02-062; published May 28, 2004).

Hyundai's 1997–2004 Above Average-rated **Tiburon** is essentially a high-performance Elantra. Although dealer maintenance and repair costs can be a bit higher than average, most work can be done cheaply by any independent garage. Used prices vary from $7,000–$15,000 for 1997 through 2004 models. Better-equipped FX variants are worth an extra $1,000. This is a fun-to-drive, budget sport coupe with a good overall reliability record. On early models, the base 16-valve 1.8L 4-cylinder engine is smooth, efficient, and adequate when mated to the 5-speed manual transmission. Put in an automatic transmission and performance suffers somewhat, and engine noise increases proportionally. Overall handling is crisp and predictable. 1998 versions use a stronger 145-hp 2.0L engine and the 2003 GT is powered by a sizzling 2.7L V6.

Crashworthiness and rollover resistance as tested on the 2004 model have been outstanding. Head restraints have been judged "poor" up to 2001; "Above Average," thereafter. Standard brakes are adequate, though sometimes difficult to modu-late. As with most sporty cars, interior room is cramped for average-sized occupants. Although no serious defects have been reported, be on the lookout for body deficiencies (fit, finish, and assembly), harsh shifting, slipping with the automatic transmission, clutch failures, oil leaks, and brake glitches (premature front brake wear and excessive brake noise).

Confidential service bulletins address the following Tiburon problems: 1997–99—Poor automatic transmission performance (TSB #97-40-031). • Automatic transmission drain hole oil leak and fluid leak behind the torque converter. • Delayed engagement into Drive or Reverse (TSB #99-40-006). 1997–2001—Correction for an erratic-shifting or slipping automatic transmission that often flares or sticks in gear. 1999—Tips on dealing with a hard-to-fill fuel tank. 1999–2003—Erratic shifting remedies. 2000—Timing belt noise may be caused by the belt rubbing against the front dust cover. 2002—Malfunctioning automatic transaxle solenoid. • MIL lamp troubleshooting guide. 2003—Sunroof leaks. 2003-04—Free fuel pump and filter sub-assembly replacement for a rough-running engine (Service Campaign #T13 found in Bulletin No.: 04-01-003, published March 2004).

Jaguar's 2000–02 **S-Type** is a small rear-drive luxury sedan that shares its platform with the Lincoln LS. Its V8 engine provides plenty of power and the car handles well. Nevertheless, the S-Type is a terrible buy due to its clunky, failure-prone automatic transmission, limited cargo room, unreliable engine, electronics and fuel delivery system, and frequent brake repairs. The 3.0L V6 is derived from a Ford design, while the 4.0L V8 is Jaguar-bred. Both engines are mated to a Ford/

Jaguar 5-speed automatic transmission, which explains their overall poor performance.

 Kia's **Sephia, Spectra, Magentis**, and **Rio** are mostly low-cost, low-quality small South Korean cars that are newcomers to the Canadian market. Sephia, Kia's first entry-level model, debuted as a year 2000 model and had a two-year run until it was replaced by the Spectra. Its resale value varies between $3,500 and $4,500 for a 2000 model; a 2001 runs around $5,000 to $6,000. Sephias are powered by an 88-hp 1.6L 4-cylinder engine coupled to a 5-speed manual or a 4-speed automatic transmission. The car's good points are few: It is essentially a dirt-cheap fuel-sipper. On the minus side, owners must contend with an extraordinarily poor quality powertrain, electrical system, brake, and fuel supply components. The base radio is barely more than a crystal set, and road, wind, and body noise is omnipresent.

Mazda—Sports car thrills, minus the bills: The 1992–96 **MX-3**'s base 1.6L engine supplies plenty of power for most driving situations, and it's reasonably priced at $2,500–$4,500. When equipped with the optional 1.8L V6 powerplant (the smallest V6 on the market at the time) and high-performance options, the car transforms itself into a 130-hp pocket rocket. In fact, the MX-3 GS easily outperforms the Honda del Sol, Toyota Paseo, and Geo Storm on comfort and high-performance acumen. It does fall a bit short of the Saturn SC because of its limited low-end torque, and fuel economy is disappointing. Reverse gear is sometimes hard to engage. Brake and wheel bearing problems are commonplace. Most of the MX-3's parts are used on other Mazda cars, so their overall reliability should be outstanding. Crash safety ratings have been average. Also consider the **MX-6** (see Ford Probe review).

The keyword for the 1988–95 **929** is understatement: The engine is unobtrusive, the exterior is anonymous, and the interior is far from flashy. In spite of its lack of pizzazz and its imprecise power steering, the 929 will accelerate and handle curves as well as the best large European sedans, and it has proven to be fairly reliable. For these advantages, you can expect to pay $3,000–$5,000 for a 1988–93 model. The '94s and '95s are priced in the $8,000–$10,000 range. Owners report some problems with electronic shock absorber durability (particularly with the 1989–91 models), premature disc brake wear, electrical glitches, exhaust system rust-out, and fit and finish deficiencies. The only real safety negative is the 929's consistently poor crash test scores since the '88 model was first tested.

Selling for $3,000–$4,000 for a base 1988–91 model, the **RX-7** is an impressive performer with a ride that can be painful on bad roads, primarily because of the car's stiff suspension. The GSL and Turbo models are very well equipped and luxuriously finished. Except for some oil burning problems, apex seal failures, and leaking engine O-rings, the RX-7 has served to dispel any doubts concerning the durability of rotary engines.

Nevertheless, careful maintenance is in order, since contaminated oil or overheating will easily damage the rotary engine. Clutches wear quickly if used hard. Disc brakes need frequent attention paid to the calipers and rotors. The MacPherson struts get soft more quickly than average. Fuel, exhaust system, electrical glitches, and AC malfunctions are also common. Be wary of leaky sunroofs. Radiators have a short lifespan. Rocker panels and body seams are prone to serious rusting. The underbody on older cars should also be inspected carefully for corrosion damage. Fuel economy has never been this car's strong suit, and crash-test scores were below average.

 Mercedes-Benz—Selling for $1,000 to $2,000, 1990–1993 model **190E** was a flop from the very beginning. It was the company's smallest and cheapest sedan, powered by a 2.6L 158-hp 6-cylinder gasoline engine borrowed from the midsize 260E sedan. A 5-speed manual transmission was standard, but most models were bought with the optional 4-speed automatic. A less powerful 2.3L 130-hp 4-cylinder engine was added to the 1991 model. Standard safety features consisted of a driver-side airbag and ABS. Owners found the car to be both unreliable (automatic transmission, electrical and fuel system, and brakes) and hard to service. Now that it has been dropped, parts are almost impossible to find

Merkur's 1985–89 **XR4Ti** was a decently performing European import based on the European Ford Sierra; the Merkur **Scorpio** was a Euro Ford Granada spin-off. Either car can be bought for $1,000 to $1,500. Poor-quality components, American emissions regulations, and a poorly supported dealer network killed the car after only five model years.

The Merkur XR4ti was ahead of its time, with distinctive European styling, a sophisticated independent suspension, excellent handling, and a high-performance turbocharged engine. If properly maintained, these cars can provide many years of excellent driving pleasure. Unfortunately, they aren't very reliable and their parts have to be ordered from England. SVO Mustangs and Thunderbird turbo coupes will do for engine parts.

Nissan—The **Micra** is a $500 subcompact commuter car that was sold from 1985 to 1991. It uses generic Nissan parts that are fairly reliable and not difficult to find. Electrical shorts, premature front brake wear, and body rusting along the door rocker panels and wheelwells are the more common deficiencies.

Pulsar and **NX** models are Average small-car buys ($1,000–$2,000, depending upon the year), as long as you pick the right years and stay away from failure-prone and expensive-to-repair turbo models. The Pulsar was replaced by the 1991 NX, a similar small car that also shares Sentra components. For 1983–86 models, overall reliability is poor to very poor. As with other discontinued Nissans, the 1987–93 models showed remarkable performance improvement and better quality control. Crash test scores were below average for the 1990 and earlier models, while the 1991 and later versions scored quite well. All Pulsars built before 1991 are prone to premature wear on the front brake pads and discs and faulty air conditioners. From 1991 on, the only problems reported concern minor AC malfunctions, premature wearout of front brakes and suspension components, and exhaust systems that don't last very long (two years, tops).

The 1990–92 **Stanzas** are roomy, reasonably priced ($2,000–$2,500), four-passenger compacts that offer peppy performance, responsive steering, nimble handling, and good fuel economy. Overall reliability has been fairly good over the years. Except for some road noise, suspension thumps, starting difficulties, transmission malfunctions, and a biodegradable exhaust system, no major problems have been reported on 1988–92 Stanzas.

Owners complain of premature front brake wear and rust perforations, problems that are common for all years. Especially prone to rust perforation are wheel openings, the front edge of the hood, the rear hatch, and door bottoms. The 1990 models produced below-average crashworthiness scores, but the 1991 and 1992 models did better than average.

The 1989–96 **300ZX**, Nissan's answer to the Corvette, has everything: high-performance capability, a heavy chassis, complicated electronics, and average depreciation resulting in a price range of $5,000–$9,000. Turbocharged 1990 and later models are much faster than previous versions and better overall buys. This weighty rear-drive offers a high degree of luxury equipment along with a potent 300-hp engine. Traction is poor on slippery surfaces, though, and the rear suspension hits hard when going over speed bumps. Crashworthiness scores have been average.

The complexity of all the bells and whistles on the 300ZX translates into a lot more problems than you'd experience with either a Mustang or a Camaro—two cars that have their own reliability problems, but are far easier and less costly to repair. The best example of this is the electrical system, long a source of recurring, hard-to-diagnose shorts. Fuel-injectors are a constant problem and lead to poor engine performance. The manual transmission has been failure-prone, clutches don't last long, front and rear brakes are noisy and wear out quickly, and the aluminum wheels are easily damaged by corrosion and road hazards. The exhaust system is practically biodegradable. The weird spongy/stiff variable shock absorbers and the glitzy digital dash, with three odometers are more gimmicky than practical. Body assembly is mediocre.

Porsche's 1999–2004 **911** was redesigned in 1999, gaining additional length and width and three inches to the wheelbase. The 3.4L engine switched from air-cooling to water-cooling and produced 296 horsepower—more than the previous 3.6L powerplant. A 6-speed manual transmission, side airbags, and ABS were standard. The 2000 models got four more horses; 2001 models came with a 3.6L 415-hp twin-turbo engine; and 2002 models adopted the 320-hp 3.6L engine and upgraded the 5-speed automatic transmission. These cars are famous for high-performance acceleration and handling, impressive braking, and excellent fit and finish. You can also expect lots of engine and road noise, acrobatic entry and exit, cramped rear seating, and limited storage space. Despite these drawbacks, 911 and Boxster owner feedback has been very positive for both the car's overall performance and its dependability. A 1998 version sells for approximately $33,000, whereas a 2004 model will set you back almost $90,000.

The 1998–2004 rear-drive **Boxster** is a Recommended roadster that competes with the Mercedes-Benz SLK, the BMW Z3, and the Mazda Miata. It is powered by a 2.5L 201-hp dual-overhead-cam 6-cylinder engine, coupled to either a 5-speed manual or an optional 5-speed automatic gearbox. The car offers all of the same advantages and disadvantages as the more refined 911. A 1998 Boxster will sell for about $23,000, or only $10,000 less than the 911. A 2004 version costs about $52,000 or a bit more than half the 2004 911's price tag.

Subaru—Sold from 1988 to 1995, the $1,000–$1,500 four-wheel-drive **Justy** pairs smooth and nimble handling with precise and predictable steering. The Justy's reliability record has been below average, with pre-1991 models having the most problems. Parts and servicing are hard to find. Owners complain about poor engine idling, cold-weather stalling, manual and automatic transmission malfunctions, premature exhaust system rust-out, catalytic converter failures, and paint peeling. Servicing and troubleshooting the CVT is a mechanic's nightmare.

Not as hard to service, but only so-so performers, Subaru's 1991–94 front-drive **Loyale** models came on the scene as underpowered Japanese-built small cars that offered optional 4×4, either on-demand, or permanently engaged. The noisy 1.8L 90-hp 4-cylinder engine and 115-hp turbo variant both perform better when hooked to a manual transmission; the 3-speed automatic is harsh shifting and not very economical. Although overall reliability is about average, powertrain and emissions components are scarce. Loyale models are Below Average buys, even though many sell for less than $1,000.

Toyota (late '80s and early '90s)—All models are Above Average buys, except the **LE Van**, which has a history of chronic brake, chassis, and body rusting problems. Chassis rusting and V6 engine head gasket failures are common problems with the

1988–95 sport-utilities and pickups (Toyota has paid for the engine repairs up to eight years). **Celicas** are an especially fine buy, combining smooth engine performance and bulletproof reliability with sports car thrills.

Selling for $3,000 to $4,000, the 1987–93 **MR2** is a mid-engine, rear-drive, 4-cylinder sports car that's both reliable and fun to drive. On the downside, you have to put up with a cramped interior, quirky turbo handling, inflated insurance premiums, and undetermined crashworthiness. In order of frequency, the most common complaints on all MR2s are brake, transmission, and electrical glitches, and fit and finish deficiencies.

The **Cressida** ages well and offers an excellent combination of dependable, no-surprise, rear-drive performance, comfort, and luxury. All this comes with a price range from $3,000 to $5,000 for a 1985–92 model. There is little to fault when it comes to overall reliability, and the engine is a model of smooth power. The 1990–93 models are more crashworthy, reliable, and trouble-free than earlier versions, but they're also much more expensive. Complaints heard throughout the years: engine head gasket failures, premature front brake wear and excessive brake pulsation/vibration, AC glitches, electrical short circuits, and a quirky Panasonic sound system.

From its humble beginnings in 1979, the **Supra** became Toyota's flagship sports car by 1986 and took on its own unique personality—with the help of a powerful 3.0L DOHC V6 powerplant. Supra prices range from a low of $9,000 for a '90 model up to $26,000 for a '97. It's an attractively styled, high-performance sports car that had been quite reliable up until it caught the Corvette/Nissan 300ZX malady in 1993: Cumulative add-ons drove up the car's price and weight and drove down its reliability. The 6-cylinder engines are smooth and powerful, and handling is sure and precise—better than the Celica because of the independent rear suspension. Like most sports cars, the Supra has limited rear seating, fuel mileage is marginal around town, and insurance premiums are likely to be much higher than average. Additionally, crashworthiness has never been determined.

Early models (pre-'93) are more reasonably priced and are practically trouble-free, except for some premature front brake wear and vibrations. On later models, owners report major turbocharger problems; frequent rear differential replacements; electrical short circuits; AC malfunctions; and premature brake, suspension, and exhaust system wear. The 3.0L engine is an oil-burner at times, and cornering is often accompanied by a rear-end growl. Seat belt guides and the power antenna are failure-prone. Body deficiencies are common.

Toyota's 1991-1999 **Tercel** and **Paseo** models are Above Average buys, while the 1987-90 Tercel remains a good, Average pick. Prices vary little: a 1992-1995 Tercel will cost from $1,500 to $3,000, while the 1996-1999 versions sell for $3,500 to $5,000. Paseos will fetch about $1,000 more.

These economy cars are dirt-cheap to maintain and repair, inexpensive parts are everywhere, and repairs can be done by almost anybody. Tercels are extraordinarily reliable, and the first generation improvements provided livelier and smoother acceleration and made the interior space feel much larger than it was. Owners report these early models had hard-shifting automatic transmissions, premature brake and suspension component wearout, brake pulsation, leaking radiators, windshield whistling, and myriad squeaks and rattles. Be careful with very early models (1985–90).

Updated 1995–99 Tercels are noted for sporadic brake, electrical system, suspension, and body/accessories problems. Crashworthiness was rated Below Average on the 1992 and 1993 Tercel (Paseo scored Average); Better than Average on the 1994 through 1999 models. Head restraints were always rated "poor."

The 1996–99 Paseo is a baby Tercel. Its main advantages are a peppy 1.5L 4-cylinder engine, a smooth 5-speed manual transmission, good handling, a supple ride, great fuel economy, and above-average reliability. This light little sportster is quite vulnerable to side winds; there's lots of body lean in turns; there's plenty of engine, exhaust, and road noise; front headroom and legroom are limited; and there is very little rear seat space. Generally, safety problems and defects affecting the Tercel were also likely to affect the Paseo.

Volvo—The 1989–93 **240 Series** is an Average buy, costing $2,000–$3,000. Avoid the turbocharged 4-cylinder engine and failure-prone air conditioning systems. Diesels suffer from cooling system breakdowns and leaky cylinder head gaskets. The brakes on all model years need frequent and expensive servicing, and exhaust systems are notorious for their short lifespan.

When a '79 Volvo 240 was crash-tested, researchers concluded that both the driver and passenger would have sustained severe head trauma. The 1992–93 models, however, produced excellent NHTSA crashworthiness scores.

Selling for $3,000 to $4,000, the 1986–92 **700 Series** models are more spacious, luxurious, and complicated to service than the entry-level 240. The standard engine and transmission perform well, but aren't as refined as the 850s. The 700 Series suffers from some brake, electrical, engine cooling, air conditioning, and body deficiencies. Brakes tend to wear rapidly and can require expensive servicing. The 1988 model performed poorly in crash tests, while the 1991–92 versions did quite well.

"Beaters" You Will Hate

These cars will keep you eternally poor and healthy from your daily walks, and will quickly teach you humility—and mechanics.

American Motors—Hornet, Gremlin, Concord, Spirit, Pacer, and **Eagle 4×4**. Faulty engines, transmissions, and steering.

Aro, Dacia, Skoda, and **Yugo**—Cheap, unreliable, Eastern European imports, a step below Lada. Reliability problems affect mostly the powertrain, brakes, electrical, and fuel systems, and sloppy body construction abounds.

Audi—Fox, 4000, and **5000**. Engine, transmission, and fuel system problems; a combination of sudden acceleration and no acceleration.

British Leyland—Austin Marina, MG, MGB, and **Triumph**. Electrical system, engine, transmission, and clutch problems; chassis rusting.

Chrysler—Cricket, Omni/Horizon, and **Volaré/Aspen**. Engine, brakes, and steering problems; chassis rusting. **Charger, Cordoba**, and **Mirada**. Brakes, body, and electrical system problems. The 1985–89 **Lancer** and **LeBaron GTS** may only cost $500–$700, but they're no bargain. In fact, they suffer from many of the same problems as the Aries and Reliant K cars and their 1989 replacements, the Spirit and Acclaim. Poor reliability causes maintenance costs to mount quickly. Turbo models are especially risky buys. Head gaskets are prone to leaks on all engines. Shock absorbers, MacPherson struts, and brakes wear out quickly. Front brake rotors are prone to rusting and warping. Crash test scores are below average.

Although they don't cost much—$300–$700, depending on the year—steer clear of 1983–89 **Aries** and **Reliants**. Uncomplicated mechanical components and roomy interiors made these cars attractive buys when new, but they quickly deteriorate once in service. Both cars use dirt-cheap, low-tech components that tend to break down frequently. They have also performed poorly in crash tests. Serious corrosion generally starts along the trunk line, the edges of the rear wheelwells, and the front fenders.

Datsun/Nissan—210, 310, 510, 810, F-10, and **240Z**. Electrical system and brake problems; rusting. Not worth buying at any price.

Eagle—Medallion, Monaco, and **Premier**. These bargain-priced French imports—$500 for the Medallion and $1,000 for the Premier—had a 1988–1992 model run. Sold through Chrysler's Renault connection, they are two of the most failure-prone imports to ever hit our shores. Powertrain, fuel system, electrical system, AC, suspension, and brakes are the worst offenders.

Fiat—"Fix it, again, Tony." All Fiat models and years are known for temperamental fuel and electrical systems and biodegradable bodies. **Alfa Romeos** have similar problems.

Ford—Cortina, Pinto, Festiva, Fiesta, Bobcat, and **Mustang II**. These three-decade-old cars are disasters. Watch out for electrical system, engine, and chassis rusting; fire-prone Pintos and Bobcats are mobile Molotov cocktails.

The German import Fiesta and the Festiva, built in South Korea, are two small imports that only survived a few years in Canada. Parts are practically unobtainable for both vehicles.

The 1994–97 Korean-built **Aspire**'s size, engine, and drivetrain limitations restrict it to an urban environment, and its low quality control restricts it to the driveway. Be wary of brake, electrical, and fuel system failures. Parts are also hard to find. This said, you can pick up an Aspire dirt-cheap for less than $2,000. In its favour, the car has consistently posted higher-than-average crash-test scores.

General Motors—Vega, Astre, Monza, and **Firenza**. Engine, transmission, body, and brake problems. **Cadillac Cimarron, Allanté**, and **Catera**. All gone; all bad. Overpriced, with poor-quality components; all front-drives suffer engine, automatic transmission, electronic module, steering, and brake problems, not to mention rust/paint peeling. **Citation, Skylark, Omega**, and **Phoenix**. Engine, brake, and electronic module problems; severe rust canker.

The **Pontiac Fiero**, sold from 1984 to 1988, snares lots of unsuspecting first-time buyers with its attractive sports-car styling, high-performance pretensions, and $700–$1,000 price. However, one quickly learns to both fear and hate the Fiero as it shows off its fiery disposition (several safety recalls) and "I'll start when I want to" character.

Stay away from the **Contour** and the **Mystique** (1995–99); they are two of the most failure-prone, hazardous vehicles you can buy—industry insiders call the Mystique the "Mistake." The reason this car is an even worse buy than the Taurus and Sable is that it has been taken off the market—drying up a miniscule parts supply and driving up parts prices (try $700 for an alternator). For the latest owner reports and money-saving tips, look at the Contour website at *www.contour. org/FAQ*. Although discontinued in Canada, the Contour continued to be sold in the States through the 2001 model year. Maintenance and repair costs are higher than average because most repairs are dealer dependent. Resale values vary between $3,000 and $5,000.

The main advantages of the Contour and the Mystique are exceptional handling and a powerful V6 engine. Their drawbacks are a plethora of safety-related defects; an inadequate parts supply; cramped rear seating; a wimpy, oil-leaking, noisy 4-banger; and atrocious quality control that is highlighted by powertrain failures, electrical system shorts, poor body assembly, and ineffective brakes that are costly to maintain. Owners also report chronic steering and transmission failures, frequent computer module failures, and a long wait for parts—even those parts needed to carry out safety-related recall campaigns.

Some of the more dangerous safety failings are engine fires, fuel tank leaks, fuel and oil odours permeating the interior, and inaccurate fuel readings. Owners also complain of malfunctioning airbags that go off when they shouldn't or don't go off when they should, serious injuries caused by airbag deployment, chronic stalling, complete electrical shutdown, and brake failures (warped rotors and prematurely worn pads). Frontal crash tests are exceptionally good, earning the maximum five stars; side and offset test results, however, have been far below average.

Hyundai—**Pony** and **Stellar**. Two of the worst South Korean small cars ever imported into Canada. Their most serious problems involved electrical and fuel system failures causing fires, no-starts, stalling, and chronic engine hesitation. Stellars have irreparable suspension, steering, and brake deficiencies that make them dangerous to drive.

The **Excel** is a low-tech and low-quality economy car that was orphaned in 1995. Resale prices are low ($500 for an '88; $1,500 for a '94). Likely problem areas are defective constant velocity joints, water pumps, oil-pan gaskets, oil pressure switches, front struts, and leaking engine head gaskets.

An Excel cross-dressing as a sports car, the 1991–95 **Scoupe** (for $3,000 to $4,500) is essentially a cute coupe with an engine more suited to high gas mileage than hard driving.

Isuzu/Passport—The **I-Mark, Stylus**, and **Optima** compacts were sold from 1988 until 1992 and can be bought for $1,000–$1,500. Repair costs are higher than average because of the cars' mediocre reliability and the difficulty in finding parts at a reasonable cost. Be especially wary of transmission defects, front brake rotor warpage, and poor body construction. The 1988–89 models garnered below-average crash test scores, while the last three model years (1990–92) did quite well.

Jaguar—Chronic fuel and electrical system shutdowns. Other problems: power-train failures, lousy body construction, poor parts supply, and few mechanics who want to repair these machines. Servicing is spotty and prices are way too high. Posting half-billion dollar losses, Jaguar is one dead cat.

Renault—French for Yugo, or rather, you don't go. Fuel and electrical system failures, poor-quality CV joints and brakes, no parts, and few mechanics. The Renault **10, 12, 18**, and **Fuego** were the worst of a bad lot. The Renault **5**, the last model sold in North America, wasn't as bad as its predecessors.

Saab—900, 9000, 9-3, and **9-5** models sold from 1985 to 2003 are very poor buys. Maintenance and repair costs can be quite high and must be done by a GM or Saab dealer. 1996–2003 used prices range from $5,000–$20,000.

The 900 and 9000 series have similar deficiencies affecting the engine, cooling (biodegradable water pumps) and electrical systems, brakes, automatic transmission (clutch O-rings), and body hardware. Interestingly, the upscale 9000 series isn't as crashworthy as the cheaper 900 versions, nor is it more reliable, exhibiting similar generic deficiencies to its entry-level brother. 9-5 models have garnered a five-star crash protection rating

On more recent models, chronic stalling can make these vehicles extremely dangerous to drive. Short circuits are legion and run the gamut from minor annoyances to fire hazards. Electrical glitches in the traction control system's relay module shuts the engine down, and engine sludging affects 9-3 and 9-5 models (covered by a "goodwill" warranty).

Turbo-equipped models should be approached with caution because owner abuse or poor maintenance can make them wallet-busters. Air conditioners and exhaust-system parts have a short lifespan, and leaky seals and gaskets are common. Rust perforations tend to develop along door bottoms and the rocker panels.

Volkswagen—The original **Beetle** was cheap to own but deadly to drive. Its main deficiencies: poorly anchored, unsafe front seats; a heater that never worked (fortunately, we were young and hot-blooded enough in those days to generate our own heat); fuel tank placement that was dangerous in collisions; and poorly designed wheels and seat tracks. The **Camper** minivan was safer, but less reliable, with engine, transmission, fuel system, and heater failings. **Rabbit/Dasher** and **411/412** models are known for unreliable powertrain, electrical, cooling, and fuel systems, ineffective and poor-quality brakes, hard-to-find parts, and non-existent servicing.

VW's 1987-93 **Fox** was the company's cheapest small car, combining good fuel economy with above-average road handling. An upgraded 5-speed manual transmission was added to the 1993 model year. This Brazilian-made front-drive never caught on because of of its notoriously unreliable engine and transmission, quirky electronics, excessive road, wind, and body noise, atrocious fit and finish, and a cramped interior in the sedan. Parts are especially hard to find. Crashworthiness is way below average. Priced between $500 and $700, these cars are more skunk than fox.

VW's **Scirocco** is fun to drive but risky to own. Chronic breakdowns, parts shortages, and poor crashworthiness are just the beginning. Electrical short circuits, chronic fuel supply problems, premature front brake wear, and fragile body parts are common owner complaints. Expect to pay $1,500–$2,500.

All ratings on a numbered scale where ⑤ is good and ❶ is bad. See page XXX for a more detailed description.

Selling for $5,000 to $12,500, the 1990–95 Corrado gives good all-around performance, with the accent on smooth acceleration, a firm but not harsh ride, and excellent handling with little body roll. So why is it Not Recommended? Poor reliability, hard-to-find parts, limited servicing outlets, and undetermined crashworthiness.

LEMON-PROOFING AND CUTTING DRIVING COSTS

Now that you've chosen a vehicle that's priced right and seems to meet your needs, take some time to assess its interior, exterior, and highway performance by following the checklist below. If you're buying from a dealer, ask to take the vehicle home overnight in order to drive it over the same roads you would normally use in your daily activities. This will give you an important insight into how well the engine handles all of the convenience features, how comfortable the seats are during extended driving, whether front and rear visibility is satisfactory, and whether you have to double up like a pretzel to avoid dash glare on the windshield (particularly a problem with Volvos). Of course, if you're buying privately, it's doubtful you will get the vehicle for an overnight test—you may have to rent a similar one from a dealer or rental agency.

Safety Check

1. Is outward visibility good in all directions?
2. Are there large blind spots (such as side pillars) impeding vision?
3. Are the mirrors large enough for good side and rear views?
4. Does the rear-view mirror have a glare-reducing setting?
5. Is there a rear window washer and wiper?
6. Are all instrument displays clearly visible (not washed out in sunlight), is there daytime or nighttime dash glare on the windshield, and are the controls easily reached?
7. Are the handbrake and hood release easy to reach and use?
8. Does the front seat have sufficient rearward travel to put you a safe distance from the airbag's deployment (about a foot) and still allow you to reach the brake and accelerator pedals? Are the brake and accelerator pedals spaced far enough apart?
9. Are the head restraints adjustable or non-adjustable? (The latter is better if you often forget to set them.)
10. Are the head restraints designed to permit rear visibility? (Some are annoyingly obtrusive.)

11. Are there rear three-point shoulder belts similar to those on the front seats? Two-point belts aren't as good.
12. Is the seat belt latch plate easy to find and reach?
13. Does the seat belt fit comfortably across your chest without rubbing against your face or falling off your shoulder?
14. Do you feel too much pressure against you from the shoulder belt?
15. Does the seat belt release easily, retract smoothly, and use pretensioners for maximum effectiveness?
16. Are there user-friendly child seat anchorage locations?
17. Are there automatic door locks controlled by the driver or childproof rear door locks?
18. Do the rear windows roll only halfway down?
19. Are the airbags de-powered?
20. Are there side airbags? (Their safety value is still unproven.)

Exterior Check

Rust

Rust is a four-letter word that means trouble. Don't buy any used vehicle with extensive corrosion around the rear hatch, wheelwells, door bottoms, or rocker panels. Body work in these areas is usually only a temporary solution.

Cosmetic rusting (rear hatch, exhaust system, front hood) is acceptable and can even help push the price way down, as long as the chassis and other major structural components aren't affected. Bumps, bubbles, or ripples under the paint may be due to repairs resulting from an accident or premature corrosion. Don't dismiss this as a mere cosmetic problem; the entire vehicle will have to be stripped down, reprimed, and repainted.

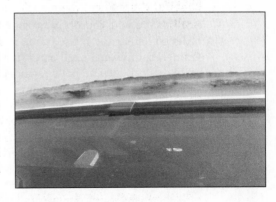

Knock gently on the front fenders, door bottoms, rear wheelwells, and rear doors—places where rust usually occurs first. Even if these areas have been repaired with plastic, lead, metal plates, or fibreglass, once rusting starts, it's difficult to stop. Use a small magnet to check which body panels have been repaired with non-metallic body fillers.

Paint overspray generally indicates a collision or repaired rust damage. It can be found beneath window seals; in the fuel tank opening; around the grille, tail lights, keyholes or door hinges; and over black adhesive tape under body side-mouldings.

Think of the practical implications of the vehicle's colour. White paint makes for a cooler interior, but highlights rust and dirt; black hides minor dents and dirt, but attracts heat and places more demand on air conditioning; red and blue are more susceptible to oxidation; and the all-popular metallic silver and light blue cost more to repaint, but add to a vehicle's resale value.

Use a flashlight to check for exhaust system and suspension component rust-out. Make sure the catalytic converter is present. In the past, many drivers removed this pollution control device in the mistaken belief that it would improve fuel economy. Police can fine you for not having the converter and force you to buy one ($300–$400) before certifying your vehicle.

Tires

Don't be concerned if the tires are worn, since retreads are inexpensive and easy to find. Look at tire wear for clues that the vehicle is out of alignment, needs suspension repairs, or has serious chassis problems. An alignment and new shocks and springs are part of routine maintenance and are relatively inexpensive in the aftermarket. However, if it's a 4×4 or the MacPherson struts have to be replaced, you're looking at a $1,000 repair bill.

Accident Damage

Accident repairs require a further inspection by an independent body shop in order to determine if the frame is aligned and the vehicle is tracking correctly. Frameless minivans need extensive and expensive work to straighten them out, and proper frame and body repairs can often cost more than the vehicle is worth. In British Columbia, all accidents involving more than $2,000 in repairs must be reported to subsequent buyers.

Here are some tips on what you can do to avoid buying a damaged vehicle. First, ask the following questions about the vehicle's accident history:

- Has it ever been in an accident?
- If so, what was the damage and who fixed it?
- Is the auto body shop that repaired the vehicle registered with the provincial government? Is there any warranty outstanding? Can you have a copy of the work order?
- Has the vehicle's certificate of title been labelled "salvage"? ("Salvage" means that an expert has determined that the cost to properly repair the vehicle is more than its value. This usually happens after the vehicle has been in a serious accident.)

If the vehicle has been in an accident, you should either walk away from the sale or have it checked by a qualified auto body expert. Remember, not all salvage vehicles are bad—properly repaired ones can be a safe and sound investment if the price is low enough.

What to Look For

1. If the vehicle has been repainted recently, check the quality of the job by inspecting the engine and trunk compartments and the inside door panels. Do it on a clear day so that you'll find any waves in the paint.
2. Check the paint—do all of the vehicle's panels match?
3. Inspect the paint for tiny bubbles. They may identify a poor priming job or premature rust.
4. Is there paint overspray or primer in the doorjambs, wheelwells, or engine compartment? These are signs that the vehicle has had body repairs.
5. Check the gaps between body panels—are they equal? Unequal gaps may indicate improper panel alignment or a bent frame.
6. Do the doors, hood, and rear hatch open and shut properly?
7. Have the bumpers been damaged or recently repaired? Check the bumper support struts for corrosion damage.
8. Test the shock absorbers by pushing hard on a corner of the vehicle. If it bounces around like a ship at sea, the shocks need replacing.
9. Look at the muffler and exhaust pipe to detect premature rust or displacement from a low-impact collision; this could channel deadly carbon monoxide into the passenger area.
10. Make sure there's a spare tire, a jack, and the tools necessary for changing a flat. Can you get at the spare easily? Also look for premature rusting in the side wheelwells and for water in the rear hatch channel.
11. Look at how the vehicle sits. If one side or end is higher than the other, it could mean that the suspension is defective.
12. Ask the seller to turn on the headlights (low and high beams), turn signals, parking lights, and emergency blinking lights, and to blow the horn. From the rear, check that the brake lights, back-up lights, turn indicators, tail lights, and licence plate light all work.
13. Check the oil dipstick to see if oil was changed regularly or if it was allowed to become tar-like and only topped up, never replenished.
14. Look for an oily residue in the radiator, or coolant overflow reservoir, which could indicate a manifold gasket leak, or engine damage. A white foamy film in the radiator cap or an oily film on the inside glass are other signs of a gasket leak.

Interior Check

The number of kilometres on the odometer isn't as important as how well the vehicle was driven and maintained. Still, high-mileage vehicles depreciate rapidly because most people consider them to be risky buys. Calculate 20,000 km per year as average and take off about $200 for each additional 10,000 km above this average. Be suspicious of the odometer reading. Confirm it by checking the vehicle's maintenance records.

The interior will often give you an idea of how the vehicle was used and maintained. For example, sagging rear seats and a front passenger seat in pristine condition indicate that your minivan may have been used as a minibus. Delivery vans will have the paint on the driver's door sill rubbed down to the metal, while the passenger door sill will look like new.

What to Look For

1. Watch for excessive wear of the seats, dash, accelerator, brake pedal, armrests, and roof lining.
2. Check the dash and roof lining for radio or cellular phone mounting holes (indicating that it was used as a police car, taxi, or delivery van). Is the radio tuned to local stations?
3. Turn the steering wheel: Listen for unusual noises and watch for excessive play (more than an inch).
4. Test the emergency brake with the vehicle parked on a hill.
5. Inspect the seat belts. Is the webbing in good condition? Do the belts retract easily?
6. Make sure that door latches and locks are in good working order. If rear doors have no handles or locks, or if they've just been installed, your minivan may have been used to transport prisoners.
7. Can the seats be moved into all the positions intended by the manufacturer? Look under them to make sure that the runners are functioning as they should.
8. Can head supports be adjusted easily?
9. Peel back the rugs and check the metal floor for signs of rust or dampness.

Road Test

1. Start the vehicle and listen for unusual noises. Shift automatics into Park and manuals into Neutral with the handbrake engaged. Open the hood to check for fluid leaks. This test should be done with the engine running and be repeated 10 minutes after the engine has been shut down following the completion of the test-drive.
2. With the motor running, check out all dashboard controls: windshield wipers, heater and defroster, and radio.
3. If the engine stalls or races at idle, a simple adjustment may fix the trouble. Loud clanks or low oil pressure could mean potentially expensive repairs.
4. Check all ventilation systems. Do the rear side windows roll down? Are there excessive air leaks around the door handles?
5. While in Neutral, push down on the accelerator abruptly. Black exhaust smoke may require only a minor engine adjustment; blue smoke may signal major engine repairs.

6. Shift an automatic into Drive with the motor still idling. The vehicle should creep forward slowly without stalling or speeding. Listen for unusual noises when the transmission is engaged. Manual transmissions should engage as soon as the clutch is released. Slipping or stalling could require a new clutch. While driving, make absolutely sure that a four-wheel drive can be engaged without unusual noises or hesitation.

7. Shift an automatic transmission into Drive. While the motor is idling, apply the emergency brake. If the motor isn't racing and the brake is in good condition, the vehicle should stop.

8. Accelerate to 50 km/h while slowly moving through all gears. Listen for transmission noises. Step lightly on the brakes; the response should be immediate and equal for all wheels.

9. In a deserted parking lot, test the vehicle's steering and suspension by driving in figure eights at low speeds.

10. Make sure the road is clear of traffic and pedestrians. Drive at 30 km/h and take both hands off the steering wheel to see whether the vehicle veers from one side to the other. If it does, the alignment or suspension could be defective, or the vehicle could have been in an accident.

11. Test the suspension by driving over some rough terrain.

12. Stop at the foot of a small hill and see if the vehicle can climb it without difficulty.

13. On an expressway, it should take no longer than 20 seconds for most cars and minivans to accelerate from a standing start to 100 km/h.

14. Drive through a tunnel with the windows open. Try to detect any unusual motor, exhaust, or suspension sounds.

15. After the test-drive, verify the performance of the automatic transmission by shifting from Drive to Neutral to Reverse. Listen for clunking sounds during transmission engagement.

Many of these tests will undoubtedly turn up some defects, which may be major or minor (even new vehicles have an average of a half-dozen major and minor defects). Ask an independent mechanic for an estimate and try to convince the seller to pay part of the repair bill if you buy the vehicle. Keep in mind that many 3- to 5-year-old vehicles with 70,000–100,000 km run the risk of an engine timing belt or chain failure that can cause several thousand dollars worth of repairs (timing chains usually last about twice as long as timing belts). If the timing belt or chain hasn't been replaced, plan to do it and deduct about $300 from the purchase price for the repair.

It's important to eliminate as many duds as possible through your own cursory check, since you'll later invest two hours and about $100 for a thorough mechanical inspection of your choice. Garages approved by the Automobile Protection Association or members of the Canadian Automobile Association usually do a good job. CAA inspections run from $100 to $150 for non-members. Oil company–affiliated diagnostic clinics are recommended only if they don't do repairs. Remember, if you get a bum steer from an independent testing agency, you can get the inspection fee refunded and hold the garage responsible for your subsequent repairs and consequential damages, like towing, missed work, or a ruined vacation. See Part Two for details.

Cutting Driving Costs

That "Cinderella" moment

There's a Cinderella moment in owning a vehicle when payments have stopped, depreciation is negligible, and repairs are all minor. As with our first love, we all want to prolong that moment for as long as possible. In most cases, we are talking about the sixth to the tenth year; after 10 years, some major repairs may be needed.

Lower insurance rates

Insurance costs can average between $700 and $2,500 per year, depending on the type of vehicle you own, your personal statistics and driving habits, and whether you can obtain coverage under your family policy. In fact, the ideal situation would be to buy a relative's car and add an insurance rider to the family policy, assuming everyone lives under the same roof. Although it seems unfair, your parents' premiums may be hiked automatically if you are a licensed driver living at home, whether you have a car or not.

The Ontario-based Consumer's Guide to Insurance (*www.insurancehotline.com*) has found that it pays to shop around for cheap auto insurance rates. In February of 2003, the group discovered that the same insurance policy could vary in cost by a whopping 400 percent. For example, a 41-year-old married female driving a 2002 Honda Accord and a 41-year-old married male driving a 1998 Dodge Caravan, both with unblemished driving records, should pay no more than $1,880, but some companies surveyed asked as much as $7,515. And that's what they might pay if they don't shop around.

The Consumer's Guide to Insurance tells consumers which companies have the lowest car insurance rates. However, there may be an $8 service charge if a selected insurer hasn't paid a fee to the hotline.

Summary of insurance discounts

A good insurance broker will offer you a variety of insurance discounts depending upon the type of car you drive, your driving record, and the number of vehicles insured. For example, some insurers will cut your rate by as much as 10 percent if a child on your policy is away at college (and not driving), or has an A or B average. Insurers also offer discounts to carpoolers and drivers who insure more than one car, have been accident-free for three years, are over 55, are longtime customers, take defensive driving courses or insure both their auto and home with the same insurer. Anti-theft system-equipped vehicles also get discounted rates.

High deductible—Take a chance only with what you are willing and able to lose. A common collision deductible is $500. Raise it to $1,000 and your premium savings could jump to 40 percent. If it's an older car, you may want to drop collision altogether.

Low-risk vehicles—The Canadian Loss Experience Automobile Rating (CLEAR) assesses lower premiums for vehicles that experience fewer and smaller losses. Set up by the non-profit Vehicle Information Centre of Canada (VICC), CLEAR publishes a free pamphlet called How Cars Measure Up. Checking a vehicle's rating in the pamphlet before you buy could mean substantial insurance premium savings. See *www.ibc.ca/vehinfo.asp* or write to VICC, 240 Duncan Mill Road, Suite 700, Don Mills, Ontario, M3B 1Z4; Tel: 416-445-1883; Fax: 416-445-2183.

Keep in mind that all sizes of minivans, vans, pickups, and SUVs can be prohibitively expensive, while small, economy cars will cost much less to insure. Also, vehicles five years or older will cost much less to insure for collision and comprehensive because they have already depreciated almost half their value.

Low mileage—Usually less than 20,000 km annually.

Driver education—While driving education can give young drivers a false sense of security and lead to an increase in deaths and injuries by allowing them on the road before their sense of judgment is fully developed, insurers continue to give this discount. It applies no matter if you take your course from a private or public agency, or whether you're a young driver or a senior citizen.

Good driver—This means no moving violations or accidents over the past three to five years.

Accident settlements

Don't settle if it's not your fault; don't settle for less than you lost; and don't settle for the loss of your deductible.

If the accident was caused by a safety-related failure of the vehicle or by other external factors beyond your control, insist that the insurance company holds the guilty party responsible. There are thousands of lawsuits each year where automakers, municipalities, and provinces pay out millions in settlements for their negligence. Send a letter to the insurer stating you deny all liability and will *not* accept a rate increase for the accident.

Don't let the repairer put in used or off-brand parts in your car. The U.S. Supreme Court has ruled that insurers must replace damaged parts with original equipment parts sold by the auto manufacturer (*Avery v. State Farm* (1999) *www.state.il.us/court/Opinions/AppellateCourt/2001/5thDistrict/April/Html/5990830.htm*). An Ontario class action is presently working its way through the courts: *Albert Hague and Terrance O'Brien v. Liberty Mutual Insurance Company*, Ontario Superior Court, Case No. 01-CV-204787CP, June 14, 2004. This class action petition, filed by attorney Harvin Pitch (*hpitch@teplitskycolson.com*), was recently certified by Justice Ian Nordheimer. The lawsuit asks for general damages plus $3 million in punitive damages. It follows two successful 1999 U.S. class action decisions (Avery and Snyder) wherein State Farm Insurance paid almost $1 billion dollars (general and punitive damages) for deceptive repair practices. State Farm admitted to repairing insured's cars with 65 percent cheaper knock-off, non-OEM (original equipment manufacturer) parts. Pitch has also filed actions against State Farm, CGU, Zurich, Wawanesa, and Royal Insurance. As of January 3, 2000, similar Quebec class actions were been filed by other law firms against Group Desjardins, ING Canada, and AXA Canada relating to their use of non-OEM parts.

Lemon-Aid readers are urged to always demand safer, more durable, and better-fitting OEM parts, and if refused, to join the Pitch class action, or use the class action Statement of Claim's extensive references in a small claims filing.

Now we'll discuss how you can get the most for your claim. If the vehicle is declared a "total loss," make sure you get its highest appraised value from either the *Canadian Red Book* or the *Black Book*. Better yet, visit a used-car lot, and ask the sales agent what a car like yours would normally fetch. Give him a few dollars to write the estimate on his business card. This gives you an expert in your pocket that most insurers won't contest. Once the appraised amount has been agreed upon, insist the insurer add the federal and provincial sales tax you would owe on the appraised amount if you were to purchase an identical vehicle to the one you just lost (restituo in integrum).

Most insurers will pay your deductible if the accident is clearly not your fault. If you are told it's your responsibility, file suit in small claims court against your insurer and the other party to recover your deductible.

Finally, when the repairs have been carried out, ask that the insurance adjuster approve the final job and ask for a copy of the work order and any warranties that may apply to the repair. If there is any failure related to the repair, don't hesitate to bring the agent back to confront the repairer as your representative. This is particularly effective if the insurer chose the garage.

Fuel savings

Buy the cheapest brand of fuel available. Sure, the oil company names and logos are different, but they mostly buy and sell the same gas from each other. So although you feel your car runs only on Shell, that last Shell fill-up may have been gas from Exxon.

Don't buy premium fuel unless it is required by the manufacturer; it can cause damages to your emissions system that will cost hundreds of dollars to rectify. On the other hand, cheapskates burning regular gas in vehicles designed to run on premium fuel can expect to trim performance by about the same percent that they save at the pump. Sometimes automakers are too optimistic in the fuel they recommend when their vehicle actually runs better with higher octane (Toyota Sienna, for example). If the engine sounds like a shaken can of marbles you accelerate, switch to higher octane before fooling with timing or emissions settings. To improve fuel efficiency on the highway, put on the cruise control or shift to overdrive to use the most fuel-efficient gearing for moderate-speed cruising.

Cheap repairs

Watch out for "service advisors." They are there to sell check-ups and repairs, and they get a commission on each sale. In most garages, just opening a work order means they must charge you $50 to meet their costs. Therefore, know which small things you can do yourself to save money, like minor rust repairs, paint touch-ups, replacing wiper blades and headlight bulbs, and changing the air filter. You'll save the labour charge and about 30 percent on the cost of parts. Just don't go overboard. No garage welcomes customers who bring in their own brake calipers, rotors and plugs.

Generally, the cheapest and most competent repairs are carried out by independent garages that specialize in a particular service and offer extensive warranties on specific parts. For example, transmission and engine repairs are best carried out by specialized garages. They will save you at least 30 percent over a dealer's charges and likely offer you a much longer warranty. And you won't have to dance the "warranty waltz" trying to get "goodwill" compensation for the repair from the dealer and manufacturer. An independent will also give you proof that the repair was caused by a factory-related failure if that is the case.

Find a mechanic you can trust

Ask friends and neighbours for recommendations and then "test-drive" the garage by taking in your car for a few small jobs, like an oil change, a tune-up, or a brake repair.

It's a good idea to frequent repair agencies approved by a national motorist group like the non-profit Automobile Protection Association, Canadian Automobile Association, or the Alberta Motorist Association. Canadian auto clubs are quite effective in steering owners to good garages. When they make a mistake, they correct it, sometimes paying the claim themselves. They have work standards and complaint procedures that affiliated garages must follow, and, they have a joint responsibility to ensure that your complaint is settled promptly and fairly.

Be a bit of a pest. Try to find a garage that doesn't bar car owners from interacting with the mechanics for so-called insurance reasons.

Trim scheduled maintenance costs

There are two ways to cut the cost of scheduled maintenance check-ups prescribed in the owners manual: Shop dealer prices (CBC TV *Marketplace* found the price varied among Mazda dealers by hundreds of dollars; or get the check-up done by an independent garage (savings of about 30–50 percent). Contrary to what dealers will suggest, warranty repairs and after-warranty "goodwill" cannot be denied simply because the vehicle was checked out or repaired by an independent repair agency. Third-party oil changes, tune-ups, and other inspections are accepted by all automakers and have nothing to do with your warranty coverage. Just keep copies of your detailed work orders.

Making your car last

Some little things you can do: Clean corroded battery terminals with a stiff brush after pouring cola on the terminals to remove built-up deposits, wash your car weekly and wax it at least twice a year, and keep it out of a heated garage in snow-belt regions with heavy highway salt use.